The Power and the Glory

Also by David Yallop

To Encourage the Others
The Day the Laughter Stopped
Beyond Reasonable Doubt
Deliver Us From Evil
In God's Name
To The Ends Of The Earth
Unholy Alliance
How They Stole The Game

The Power and the Glory
Inside the Dark Heart of
John Paul II's Vatican

David Yallop

CONSTABLE • LONDON

To the memory of my mother,
Una Norah Stanton,
And my son, Stuart Adam,
gone too soon, far too soon.

Constable & Robinson Ltd
3 The Lanchesters
162 Fulham Palace Road
London W6 9ER
www.constablerobinson.com

First published in the UK by Constable,
an imprint of Constable & Robinson Ltd 2007

A copy of the British Library Cataloguing in
Publication Data is available from the British Library

ISBN 978-1-84529-673-5

Printed and bound in the EU

Contents

List of Illustrations

The young Karol Wojtyla with his parents. Copyright © Corbis

The Solvay Quarry. Copyright © Topfoto

Poster of 'The Cavalier of the Moon' in which Karol Wojtyla performed two months before the outbreak of the Second World War. Copyright © Topfoto

Karol Wojtyla at the time of his ordination in November 1946. Copyright © Popperfoto

John Paul II on the day of his election. Copyright © Corbis

Lech Walesa and Bishop Henryk Jankowski, the Lenin shipyard, Gdansk, 29 August 1980. Copyright © Getty Images

Riots on the streets, 2 May 1982. Copyright © Corbis

Lech Walesa with Pope John Paul II. Copyright © Getty Images

Wojtyla with Cardinal Stefan Wyszynski. Copyright © Corbis

Pope John Paul II with the Reagans. Copyright © Getty Images

Preface

Within the opening pages of *In God's Name* I publicly thanked a great many people who had provided me with assistance in a variety of ways during the research for that book. In doing so I was merely repeating a lifelong habit. After naming these individuals I wrote the following:

'Among those I cannot thank publicly are the people resident within Vatican City who contacted me and initiated my investigation of the events surrounding the death of Pope John Paul I, Albino Luciani. The fact that men and women living within the heart of the Roman Catholic Church cannot speak openly and be identified is an eloquent comment on the state of affairs within the Vatican.'

The hunt by the Curial hierarchy after the book was published was not confined to anonymous informants. The Vatican also went after some of those I had publicly thanked. Precisely how many suffered I do not know but among their number was Father Bartolomeo Sorge SJ, the editor of *Civilta Cattolica*, described by Vaticanologist Peter Hebblethwaite as 'a man of impeccable orthodoxy and at the same time an influential figure on the Christian Democratic scene'. He was dispatched from Rome to Pa-

lermo. Father Romeo Panciroli had been the long-serving
Vatican Press Officer at the time of my research. Less than
six months after the initial publication of *In God's Name* he
was replaced by Navarro-Valls. Panciroli was sent to Africa. One of Navarro-Valls' first acts was to remove the vital
tessera or press card from Phillip Willan. Phillip, a freelance
journalist, had acted as one of my primary researchers and
interpreters. A journalist in Rome without Vatican accreditation is in for a very lean time. He had presumably been
found to be guilty by association. The fact that I alone was
responsible for what was written counted as nothing. He
was frozen out for the best part of two decades.

During Spring 1998, a new Vatican manual was published with Papal approval. In it there is a warning to all
Vatican staff that 'disclosing pontifical secrets is punishable
by instant dismissal'. In light of the above, I have concluded
that the overwhelming number of those who so kindly
assisted me must remain unidentified. Within the book a
number of non-Vatican sources are identified and a bibliography gives the reader an indication of written sources.

Some time in the near future, Pope John Paul II will be
beatified. Soon after that event he will be canonised. In life
much was claimed for Karol Wojtyla; in death the acclamation has reached such levels that early sainthood cannot
be far away for the Pope from 'the far country'.

What was once the fifth step towards beatification, the
nomination of a *promotor fidei* – in popular language the
'devil's advocate', an individual whose duty it was 'to point
out any flaw or weak points in the evidence adduced, and
raise all kind of objections' – has been abolished. It was
revoked by John Paul II. I have yet to hear a satisfactory
explanation that justifies the abolition. Does the biblical
injunction 'And ye shall know the truth, and the truth shall
make you free' no longer have a place within Christianity in
the twenty-first century?

When the beatification process involves a figure as controversial as the late Pope, a rigorous investigation which lays open every facet of Karol Wojtyla's entire life is paramount. Demonstrably the current rush to sainthood does not envisage exhaustive enquiry. Wojtyla's lectures and writings in the 1950s on Marxism and Communism in which he spoke and wrote very positively on both Marxism and Liberation Theology are not, as of late 2006, going to be considered. How deeply the extravagant claims that have been made for Pope John Paul II – his fight against the Nazis and subsequently against the Communist regime . . . his creation of Solidarity . . . his achievement in overthrowing European Communism – how deeply these and other acclaimed aspects of the Wojtyla Papacy will be investigated has yet to be established. Before the end of January 2006, the Vatican had received over two million letters concerning 'the life and virtues of Pope John Paul II'.

Speaking to a gathering of Catholic journalists in the Vatican in December 2002 Karol Wojtyla remarked:

'What does it mean for a Catholic to be a professional journalist? A journalist must have the courage to search for and tell the truth, even when the truth is uncomfortable or not considered politically correct . . .'

PART 1

Chapter 1

God's Will?

'WHEN ONE POPE DIES, we make another one.' So runs a popular saying in Rome. They were particularly busy in 1978. It was the year of three popes. The death of Pope Paul VI on 6 August 1978 surprised very few Vatican observers. Indeed, as his reign entered its sixteenth year, some reporters already began to write in the past tense. The reign of his successor, Albino Luciani, who took the name Pope John Paul I, was different.

One month after his election, Albino Luciani received an extensive and very detailed interim report that had been carried out at his request by Cardinal Egidio Vagnozzi of an investigation into Vatican finances. Vagnozzi had been President of the Prefecture of Economic Affairs of the Holy See, Chancellor of the Exchequer or Auditor General since late 1967. Pope John Paul I considered the report alongside additional information he had obtained from Cardinals Benelli, Felici and deputy Secretary of State, Archbishop Giuseppe Caprio. He reached a number of decisions which were certain to have a dramatic effect on the Church and the Pope advised his Secretary of State, Cardinal Villot, of these reforms on the late afternoon of 28 September. Within hours Albino Luciani was dead and the lies and the cover-up surrounding the death of the thirty-three-day Pope had begun.

*   *   *

His death stunned the cardinals. As they gathered in Rome in October to elect a new pope, many were clearly frightened. Albino Luciani – Pope John Paul I – had been murdered.[1] No Cardinal uttered that conclusion in public, of course; the party line as decreed by Secretary of State Cardinal Jean Villot held more or less steady during the three months period of *sede vacante* – the empty throne. Nonetheless, questions were raised behind General Congregation doors; the Pope's death was both sinister and politically momentous: under the Vatican constitution all of Luciani's reforms would die with him unless his successor chose to implement them. At stake were profound issues such as discipline within the Church, evangelisation, ecumenism, collegiality, world peace and a subject that now pre-occupied most of the Cardinals – Church finances.[2] The man they had elected had indeed immediately instigated just such an investigation; now he was dead.

Cardinal Bernardin Gantin voiced the fears and confusions of many when he observed, 'We are groping in the dark.' Cardinal Giovanni Benelli, a man who had been particularly close to the 'Smiling Pope', made no attempt to hide his thoughts: 'We are left frightened.' Many cardinals were shocked not only by the sudden death of a perfectly fit man in his mid-sixties but by the orchestrated lies peddled by Villot and those under him. They knew that a Vatican cover-up was under way.

In Rome, in off-the-record briefings to reporters, the Vatican machine quickly spun three stories about the late Pope. The first – alleging weak health – is fully examined within *In God's Name* as is the second exercise which attempted to demolish Luciani's remarkable talents and reduce him to a grinning simpleton. 'Really it's a blessing in disguise that he died so soon; he would have been such an embarrassment to the Church.' This attack on the late Pope was mounted particularly by members of the Roman Curia.

As with lies about his health, many of the media fell for it and stories directly inspired by this disinformation appeared throughout the world's press.

The third story was a traditional platitude. Luciani's work was done: the Lord had taken him away. Thus Cardinal Siri:

'. . . this death is not a complete mystery, nor is the event totally opaque. In thirty-three days this pontiff completed his mission . . . With his style so close to the Gospel, it can be said that Pope John Paul I opened an era. He opened it and then quietly went away.' He was echoed by Cardinal Timothy Manning, ' . . . he made his statement and then dropped off the stage.'

Other princes of the Church took another view:

'Why the lies about his health? All this nonsense about operations? Why are they lying about who found the Pope's body? Why the lies about what he was reading? What are the facts about these changes that were to have occurred the following morning? Changes within the Vatican Bank?'

Villot stonewalled on these and a host of other questions. His blanket response, that it 'was God's will', convinced very few. Cardinal Benelli's icy response was, 'I thought it was God's will that Cardinal Luciani was elected. The Lord giveth and the Lord taketh?'

Inside the Vatican village the customary intrigue, vindictiveness, rumour, counter-rumour and character assassination got under way for the election of the new pope. The Curia went ruthlessly about its task of ensuring as far as

possible that all rivals to their own man, the reactionary
Archbishop of Genoa, Cardinal Siri, were dispatched into
oblivion. But as they cut a swathe through the opposition,
the Curia was also busy organising defence strategies just in
case their man was not elected.

Before departing on the 7.30 a.m. flight to Rome from
Warsaw on 3 October Karol Wojtyla, Archbishop of Cracow, Poland, interrupted his schedule to have an ECT
examination on his heart and take the print-out with
him. It may have seemed extraordinarily prudent for a
cardinal who had attracted less than a handful of votes
in the August Conclave. But he was aware that the Vatican
was peddling *lies* about the late Pope's medical history. It
would be even easier to pump out rumours about a candidate's health, especially one such as himself, whose medical
history revealed a pattern of illnesses. Certainly, some of
Wojtyla's colleagues viewed his actions as signs that he
knew that he would not be returning to Cracow.

During the previous five days, Wojtyla had spent much of
his time with his invaluable friend and ally, Bishop Deskur,
in Rome. This friendship went back to their years together
in the secret wartime seminary in Poland. Since the war,
Deskur had guided Wojtyla through the labyrinth of Vatican politics. Never would his help be more needed. Karol
Wojtyla listened very carefully as Deskur listed the strengths
of this rival candidate, the weaknesses of another. Then he
had lunch with other countrymen including Bishop Rubin.
These meetings left Karol Wojtyla in no doubt that this time
he was a genuine candidate. Those who were pushing his
candidacy realised that if the Italians could not unify
around one of their own contenders, then the cardinals
they had been lobbying would be aware of a stunning
alternative. Karol Wojtyla was now obliged to draw on
the acting skills he had honed as a young man. Externally a
picture of detached calm, the inner self was agog at the

prospect that came more clearly focused before him. So much of his early life had been a preamble to this moment. He believed deeply in divine providence and again and again would offer divine intervention as the explanation for his good fortune. Providence, in the shape of a good contact, a patron or a protector, called with remarkable frequency on Wojtyla.

In May 1938 the Archbishop of Cracow, Adam Sapieha, came to Wadowice to give the sacrament of confirmation to those who were about to graduate. The student assigned to the task of welcoming Sapieha in the name of the college was Karol Wojtyla, speaking in Latin. When the young man had finished, there was a thoughtful expression on the face of the Archbishop. 'Will he enter the seminary?' he asked religious teacher Father Edward Zacher.

Karol responded for himself. 'I'm going to study Polish literature and philology (language).'

The Archbishop was disappointed: 'What a pity.'

Sapieha was destined to become one of Wojtyla's early protectors. There had been others before, especially his father. By the time that Karol senior died in February 1941, providence had already ensured that while many of the twenty-year-old's peer group would perish before the end of the Second World War, he would survive; his French tutor, Jadwiga Lewaj, had a quiet word with her good friend Henryk Kulakowski, the president of the Polish section of Solvay, a chemical firm with a large plant in the Cracow suburb of Borek Falecki. At the time all able-bodied Polish males were candidates for forced labour in Germany or working on border fortifications on the Eastern Front. Either route led to a brutal and usually short life. Working at Solvay carried a large range of benefits. It was in some respects a self-contained village with residential homes, containing a surgery with a resident doctor, staff canteen, a shop and a gymnasium. Apart from his wages and the perk of vodka coupons that could be traded on the black market, Karol Wojtyla also carried at all times his guarantee that he would have a good war: an *Ausweis*, or identity card, that indicated that the bearer was employed in a *kriegswichtig* industry, work that was essential to the Third Reich's war effort. The caustic soda the company created had a variety of uses, not least in the production of bombs.

It was during his wartime years at Solvay that a vocation for the priesthood first stirred within Karol Wojtyla. At this time Archbishop Sapieha had created a secret seminary and in August 1944 Karol moved with a number of other young men into the safety of his residence. Wojtyla was ordained as a priest on 1 November 1946. Two weeks later, Sapieha, newly promoted to cardinal, sent Karol Wojtyla to Rome to study for his first doctorate. The archbishop had already marked out Wojtyla for fast-track treatment. The special consideration shown to Wojtyla extended to making funds available so that during the vacations he could tour around Europe along with a fellow priest.

Wojtyla returned to Cracow in June 1948 after obtaining his doctorate with maximum marks in virtually every section. There Cardinal Sapieha continued to carefully nurture his young protégé: seven months as a village curate were followed by a post as student chaplain in the St Florian's diocese of Cracow where he rapidly developed a devoted following among the undergraduates. The position also gave him the opportunity to mix with the movers and shakers of Cracow society. Wojtyla displayed a remarkable ability at networking and during these years friendships and contacts that would last a lifetime were forged.

On 23 July 1951 Wojtyla's protector, the Prince-Cardinal Sapieha, died at the age of eighty-five. The Cardinal had seen something special about Karol Wojtyla at their first brief meeting in May 1938. Archbishop Baziak, already established in Cracow as Sapieha's successor, had discussed

Wojtyla's future at great length with the Prince-Cardinal. Seemingly, the baton had been passed. A few months later Baziak ordered Wojtyla to take a two-year leave of absence to study for another doctorate. This would qualify him to teach at a university. Wojtyla was opposed to this course of action. He wanted to stay at St Florian's where his involvement with the students was going from strength to strength, but Baziak was adamant, commanding that Wojtyla also move home from the priest's house at St Florian's and that any pastoral work he wished to undertake during the two-year sabbatical had to first be approved by Archbishop Baziak. The doctorate came first and led to a thesis, a degree and a job as a university professor.

Baziak's aim was simple: he wished to combat the tide of communist repression that was sweeping over Eastern Europe. The communists were attempting to plant assistant pastors who were members of the secret police within a great many dioceses, aiming to inevitably control the Church's infrastructure from the inside. The continuing conflict between Church and State as to who had the right to appoint bishops grew more intense. The communists came up with a radical solution: any bishops who did not meet with their approval were forcibly removed or arrested and imprisoned. In 1952 among the victims were the Bishop of Katowice, Stanislaw Adamski, and two auxiliary bishops. In November that year Wojtyla's latest mentor and protector Archbishop Baziak and his auxiliary bishop Stanislaw Rospond were arrested, an action that shook the Catholic community of Cracow to its core. Karol Wojtyla said nothing, publicly or privately, and two days after the arrests went on a skiing holiday to the Marty Mountains. Two weeks later the Primate of Poland, Archbishop Wyszynski, was advised that the Pope had named him cardinal. It was a promotion richly deserved; when the news reached Wyszynski he had just denounced the arrests of Baziak and his fellow bishop from a Warsaw pulpit. The regime's response was a refusal to grant Wyszynski an exit visa, a petty gesture that denied the Cardinal the honour of kneeling before the Pope while the red biretta was placed upon his head.

The regime's approach to the Church was that of a paranoid schizophrenic, ranging from the conciliatory to the cruel; arrests would be followed by permission to hold a great procession or pilgrimage where Wyszynski was free to make a speech on human rights. In January 1953 the situation in Poland deteriorated to a new level of barbarity when four priests and three lay workers within the Cracow archdiocese went on trial in a military court charged with collaborating with the CIA and illegally trading in foreign currency. After a five-day trial, including scathing denunciations of the late Cardinal Sapieha, Father Jozef Lelito and two of the lay workers were found guilty and sentenced to death. The sentences were subsequently commuted and all seven men were given long terms of imprisonment.

Throughout all this turmoil Karol Wojtyla continued with his pastoral duties at St Florian's. During the academic year he would give lectures to the students on ethics, he organised retreats, said Mass, heard confessions and studied diligently in preparation for his thesis. Nonetheless, he continued to remain totally uninvolved in the life-and-death struggle of his Church to secure the most basic freedoms. No amount of arrests and imprisonments could stir him into protesting.

In some ways this was a replay of his response to the Second World War when he took no part in armed resistance and urged his friends to do the same, declaring that the Polish Army had been defeated and that it was useless to fight on. During the last three months of 1939 the German invaders turned their attentions to the mentally ill and vulnerable of Poland. They began by emptying the psychiatric clinics in the north of the country. Over 1,000 Poles were transported from a number of the clinics to a wood beside the village of Piasnica Wielki and shot. A year later nearly 300 elderly people were told they were going to the town of Padernice. No such town has ever existed. The lorry conveying them stopped in a wooded area on the outskirts of Kalisz. They were gassed by the lorries' exhaust fumes and buried in the woods of Winiary. As early as October 1939, less than a month after the German occupation of Poland had begun, ghettos for the Jews were being created. Sometimes they were crammed into a section of a city that had historically been occupied by Jews, as in Warsaw where the Jews were forced to build a wall around the designated area and to pay for the wall.

During these same months Wojtyla wrote to his close friend Mieczyslaw Kotlarczyk:

'First and foremost, I must tell you that I am keeping busy. Some people are currently dying of boredom, but not I, I have surrounded myself with books, dug in with Arts and Sciences. I am working. Would you believe that I am virtually running out of time! I read, I write, I study, I think, I pray, I struggle with myself. At times I feel great oppression, depression, despair, evil. At other times, as if I were seeing the dawn, the aurora, a great light.'

His letters show an extraordinary preoccupation with his own activities. Poland was enduring the most grievous ordeal in its history and yet this exceptionally gifted graduate wrote fulsome letters which harked back to the pre-war days at university.

Now in the 1950s, confronted with communism, Karol Wojtyla had again retreated. Even when his long-time friend and teacher Father Kurowski was arrested, he re-

mained silent and within his writings or sermons he never
once directly attacked communism. This pattern of behaviour continued to flourish thoughout the 1950s. In
1953 he completed his dissertation, leading to the award
of his second doctorate; in October he began to lecture at
his former university, the Jagiellonian, on social ethics.
There were numerous excursions with his adoring students,
skiing, kayaking, and most of all, hiking. He was a prodigious walker, on one occasion walking 26 miles in a day. In
July 1958, while enjoying one of these vacations in the lake
region in Northern Poland, he received a summons to come
and see Cardinal Wyszynski. Archbishop Baziak, who had
been quietly furthering Wojtyla's career, had recommended
him to Wyszynski for the post of auxiliary Bishop to
Cracow. News had just been received by the Primate that
the Pope had accepted their recommendation. Significantly,
the Polish Communist regime had also approved of the
appointment.

Although Wojtyla obviously possessed a string of academic achievements, Baziak's recommendation ignored his
lack of any administrative experience, an essential for a
suffragan bishop. Moreover, because of the academic direction in which both Cardinal Sapieha and Baziak had
channelled him, his pastoral experience was severely limited. At thirty-eight, he was also a good ten years younger
than the norm for a new bishop. He was now the youngest
bishop in Poland. In itself it was not such a bad thing but
such early success in the backbiting world of the Catholic
priesthood can prove a handicap.

The invective within the Church hierarchy in Poland can
be gauged from the files of the *Sluzba Bezpieczenstwa* – SB –
the secret police. The regime were kept extremely well-
informed. At any given time there were well over 1,000
priests who worked as spies and informants for the Polish
Communist government. In a shocking betrayal of trust, the

confidentiality of the confessional was regularly breached. The files reveal that the most highly valued asset working for the communists was ideally placed to spy and inform on Karol Wojtyla.

The informer had been directly responsible for the arrest and imprisonment of the Bishop of Katowice, Stanislaw Adamski, and two auxiliary bishops in 1952, and in November of the same year for the arrest of Archbishop Baziak and his auxiliary Bishop Stanislaw Rospond. There were other victims of this man's treachery, yet the fact that not a hair on Karol Wojtyla's head was ever disturbed speaks most eloquently of total rejection of any involvement in the Catholic Church's struggle within Poland at this time. In 1958 the informer was in the perfect position to give a detailed report on the opposition Archbishop Baziak had faced when he had decided to promote Wojtyla.

The particular spy so prized by the secret police was Father Wladyslaw Kulczycki. During the Second World War he was active in the Polish underground, an activity that led to his arrest and imprisonment by the Nazis. After the war he returned to Cracow where for a short while he held the position of Judge at the Curia's court. He knew the Primate of Poland well and had cared for Cardinal Wyszynski's father. Well-educated, he had studied law in Strasbourg and history in Paris. The Polish secret police discovered he was engaged in a passionate love affair and blackmailed him into becoming a spy.

Wojtyla was only settling into his new role when unexpected news came from Cracow. Archbishop Eugeniusz Baziak died on 15 June 1962. His successor was not publicly announced until 19 January 1964. The eighteen-month delay was caused solely by the stubborn intransigence of two individuals. The Primate of Poland was determined that his point of view would prevail while the Communist regime's number two, Zenon Kliszko,

was equally determined to have his man running the Archdiocese of Cracow. In fact Baziak had never been recognised
by the regime and for thirteen years had officially functioned not as Archbishop but as an Apostolic Administrator, the regime's way of humiliating both the man and his
faith. Cardinal Wyszynski did not share the same universal
awe and admiration of Wojtyla as many of his peers.
Indeed, it has been suggested that Wyszynski was bounced
into the decision in 1958 to make Wojtyla a bishop by the
regime. Whatever the truth, the Primate certainly did not
want to give a further promotion to Wojtyla, whom he
regarded as little more than an ambitious man preoccupied
with networking. What particularly exercised the Primate
was the high-handed manner that Bishop Wojtyla adopted
with other members of the Cracow Archdiocese. 'Wojtyla
should not forget that he is only a *temporary* administrator
and as such should stop bossing people around,' was a
typical observation from a member of the Wyszynski circle
duly recorded by the SB. Acting on the traditional protocol,
Cardinal Wyszynski submitted three names to the Polish
Government. All three had previously been approved by the
Pope. Wojtyla's name was not on the list. Months later the
list came back to Wyszynski with all of his candidates
rejected. The files of the Polish secret police and additional
information from former Communist Party members reveal
a wonderfully ironic tale – independently confirmed by
papal biographer George Weigel.[3] A bemused Primate
retired to his study and eventually a further three names
were sent to the Vatican for papal approval, which was
forwarded to the Polish Government. After a further three
months the second list came back to Cardinal Wyszynski;
again the regime had given the thumbs down to all three
names.

  During the late autumn of 1963 Father Andrzej Bardecki,
the ecclesiastical assistant on the Catholic Church-financed

paper, *Tygodnik Powszechny*, had a visitor at his Cracow office. Professor Stanislaw Stomma headed the minority Catholic Party in the Polish Parliament. With a maximum of five members it was in reality no more than a rump yet it served many useful purposes, not least as a conduit between the Communists and the Catholic Church. The professor quietly invited Father Bardecki to join him for a stroll around part of the city. As the two men walked, Professor Stomma recounted a conversation he had recently had with Zenon Kliszko, the Communist number two. Kliszko had asked him who would be the best candidate for the vacancy in Cracow. 'I told him, firmly and categorically, that Wojtyla was the best, indeed the only choice.' Kliszko beamed and replied, 'I've vetoed seven so far. I'm waiting for Wojtyla and I'll continue vetoing names until I get him.'

Why Wojtyla? The regime considered him politically naïve and as a man who had never displayed any of the intransigence for which his Primate was internationally famous, someone who would be open to compromise. It was an opinion largely based on the stream of information they had received from the regime's prize spy planted in the very heart of the Cracow Archdiocese. An appointment such as this had considerable ramifications to the Communist Government of Gomulka. The Communists and the Catholic hierarchy were involved in a delicate balancing act and if the two failed to co-exist there was the very real possibility that Soviet tanks would appear on the streets of Warsaw and Cracow. All it might take would be a newly elected Archbishop reaching ambitiously for an international profile through confrontational tactics. Speaker Kliszko did not want a firebrand or a political agitator preaching from the pulpits of the Cracow churches. He had studied the secret police dossier, such as it was, on Wojtyla and he saw nothing worse than midnight masses in a field at Nowa Huta and a sermon commemorating the centenary of

the January Uprising against the Russians in 1863. Kliszko
was also reassured by Wojtyla's war activities, or rather
their absence; here was a man who had repeatedly refused
to join or assist the partisan army and had relied on God's
will to prevail. In Kliszko's eyes, Wojtyla was extremely
unlikely to make common cause with any Polish dissident
faction that might emerge.

The clinching element, however, had been the highly
detailed report that Kliszko had requested from the Communist Party's top agent in Cracow, Father Wladyslaw
Kulczycki. Kliszko's tactics worked a charm. When he
had received a further nomination from the Cardinal, the
list contained the name 'Wojtyla'. It is not every Communist
leader that can claim to have been instrumental in the
making of a pope, particularly a Polish pope. On 8 March
1964, Karol Wojtyla was installed as Archbishop of Cracow. He was now only two steps away from the throne of St
Peter.

When the Second Vatican Council reconvened in October
1964 Wojtyla, who had risen to speak at the first session as
a junior auxiliary bishop, now addressed the Council as an
archbishop. His promotions had given him a growing
confidence and he made influential contributions to a
number of proposed declarations, most notably during
the debate on the Declaration on Religious Freedom where
he argued that the oppressive nineteenth edict that 'error
has no rights' was in need of a modification. His views,
which were much in line with the reformers within the
Council, that tolerance and proclamation of the fundamental right to freedom of conscience were essential before there
could be any meaningful dialogue with other Christian
Churches, were reflected in the final published Declaration
on Religious Freedom – *Dignitatis Humanae*.

In May 1967 Paul VI announced the next Consistory, or
council of cardinals, and among the names of the cardinals-

elect was Karol Wojtyla. This news of yet another promotion came a few days after his forty-seventh birthday and
came as a great surprise within Poland; Wojtyla was extremely young to be so honoured. There had been no
pressure on the Pope to appoint a second cardinal and
quite a number of archbishops were older and more experienced. The man himself was heard to yet again murmur
something about Providence yet there may have been more
earthly reasons. In February that year Wojtyla had been a
key member of highly secret discussions that had taken
place at various locations in Poland. A papal delegation,
headed by the then Monsignor Agostino Casaroli and
Wojtyla's old friend Monsignor Deskur, had held meetings
with Polish officials, the Primate and Karol Wojtyla. The
main subject on the agenda was the possibility of establishing diplomatic relations between Poland and the Vatican
State. With the exception of Cuba it would have been a first
for a communist country.

Two months later, on 20 April, after yet another highly
favourable report on Wojtyla had been given to the Pope by
Casaroli, the pontiff received the man from Cracow in a
private audience. Paul was very impressed by his relatively
new archbishop; just how impressed became publicly apparent in May when the relatively new archbishop became a
completely new cardinal.

Papal biographers have written freely that by this time the
communists had long realised that they had made a dreadful
mistake in plotting to bring about Wojtyla's promotion to
bishop and that, when the news of his red hat was announced,
they were beside themselves with anger and displeasure at the
prospect of Cardinal Wojtyla. A confidential report written
by members of the Polish secret police tells a quite different
tale. The report dated 5 August 1967, just five weeks after
Wojtyla became a cardinal, is headed: 'Our Tactics Towards
Cardinals Wojtyla and Wyszynski'. It is a fascinating insight

into how the two men were perceived by at least some of the most senior members of the ruling Communist party. The authors had the benefit not only of Father Kulczycki but regular reports from a large secret service staff and spies; they also had access to evidence acquired from the full range of electronic eavesdropping equipment.

Predictably, in view of his long history of opposition, Wyszynski won few bouquets:

> 'Cardinal Wyszynski was brought up in a traditional family of Church servants. In the opinion of the clergy this is an inferior type of people, and this stigma weighs on him to this day . . . He built his "scientific career" on anti-Communist activity and anti-Communist writings which, in 1948, were decisive in his advancement to bishop . . . During the cold war his position becomes greater – he is the standard bearer of the anti-Communist front.'

There was a great deal more in similar vein. The secret police saw Wyszynski as a complete cynic:

> 'His concept of shallow, emotional and devotional Catholicism is correct and profitable from the viewpoint of the Church's immediate interests. For some years his treatment of the intellectual elite, Catholic intelligentsia and laity as "uncertain elements" has its roots in Polish realities.' For Wyszynski, according to the secret police report, the strength of the Church in Poland 'has resided for centuries not among the elites, but in the Catholic masses'.

Cardinal Wojtyla, on the other hand, was much more to the liking of the Communists. They wrote approvingly of his origins (unaware of the altar and the font of holy water in his boyhood home): 'a family of the intelligentsia – from a religious but not a devotional environment'. Inevitably they were on much firmer ground when they moved into the war years and beyond: 'He rose in the Church hierarchy not thanks to an anti-Communist stance, but thanks to intellectual values.' The Communists were impressed by Wojtyla's success as an author and noted that his book *Love and Responsibility* had been translated into many languages. In the eyes of the Communists Wojtyla had a great deal going for him.

> *'He has not, so far, engaged in open anti-state political activity. It seems that politics are his weaker suit . . . He lacks organising and leadership qualities and this is his weakness in his rivalry with Wyszynski.'* [Author's italics.]

At no time do the intelligence files on Wojtyla indicate that he represented any more than the occasional pinprick in the body politic of the country. He has been portrayed by the Vatican, by numerous journalists and countless biographers as a man who stood resolute against the Communists and fought them tooth and nail in the years leading to his papacy but the facts reveal a man who successfully survived the Polish Communists as he had survived the Second World War, namely by prudence and a complete absence of any heroics.

The recommendation was that Wojtyla be given every support even to ensuring that he should be handled very gently. 'We must risk the approach that the less he is pushed by us, the sooner a conflict (with Wyszynski) will develop.' Obversely, the Communists planned to keep maximum pressure and discomfort on Wyszynski who, they believed, would eventually erupt as he saw the young man being granted every conceivable privilege and respect. In the eyes of the Communists, 'Wyszynski had received Wojtyla's elevation to the cardinalship with explicit reluctance.' So the old man was to be humiliated and hemmed in at every turn while 'we should act positively on matters of prestige that would improve Wojtyla's self-esteem.'

Karol Wojtyla's 'self-esteem' kept pace with his irresistible rise as now, among his many other duties and activities, he began to focus on the wider world beyond Poland. During August 1969 he deputised for Cardinal Wyszynski on a three-week tour in Canada followed by two weeks in the United States. The Primate had balked at the prospect of coping with a new experience, press conferences; nor could he speak English. Wojtyla leapt at the opportunity, and accompanied by his personal chaplain, Father Stanislaw Dziwisz, and two friends, Bishop Macharski and Father Wesoly, he flew to Montreal. There and at Quebec City Wojtyla could relax into his relatively fluent French before moving on to a seven-city tour of predominately English-speaking cities. Much of the time, however, he was able to speak in his native tongue, the official purpose of the trip being to visit Polish communities. If he learned little about Canada and subsequently the United States he learned the value of cocktail parties and banquets and the networking habits of his guests; as his English improved he also began to enjoy the press conferences.

In the United States his experience was again largely confined to Polish community activities but Father Wesoly recalls that Wojtyla was advised to visit every city where a cardinal was in residence – a curious piece of advice unless the recipient was ambitious to further his career. Wojtyla did not make them all but he had a good stab at the task. In the two-week stay, apart from his many official tasks on behalf of Polish Americans, he managed to meet seven of his fellow cardinals. Then hurrying back to Rome he met quite a few more at the extraordinary session of the Synod of Bishops.

The Synod had been created by Pope Paul to ensure that the decisions that had been taken at the Vatican Council sessions were implemented. Very typically Wojtyla never missed a meeting. He had been nominated a member not by his Primate but by Pope Paul and, like other gestures by Paul, this nomination has been subsequently seen as significant. Wojtyla's biographers have contended that Pope Paul's actions were clear indications that Wojtyla was his anointed one, the man he would like to see succeed him on St Peter's throne. In fact, Paul made a very public and symbolic gesture to Albino Luciani, the man who actually did succeed him and of course Paul would not be voting in the Conclave to choose the next pope.

Without the benefit of hindsight, any contemporary observer of Cardinal Wojtyla in the 1970s would have judged him a man whose ambitions reached far beyond his current achievement. Of course, Wojtyla gave no public hint of his desire for the papacy; that would have been fatal, but as so often before, his actions spoke very eloquently for him. The international Synod of Bishops was one of a number of gatherings that saw Wojtyla at virtually every meeting. He was elected and re-elected a member of every steering committee between the Synods. At the 1974 Synod he was appointed realtor, the man who drafts the final report, on the issue of evangelisation in the modern world. When the question of evangelisation in Communist countries and Marxist-influenced societies was discussed Wojtyla was dismissive of what he considered to be the naive, ill-informed views of the delegates from Western Europe and Latin America. He considered that for them Marxism was a 'fascinating abstraction rather than an everyday reality'. Inevitably he failed to write a final report that was acceptable to the Synod. More significantly he had given a very clear indication of his ignorance that Communism had more than one face, there were varying forms of Marxism, and that the words of socialism had different effects in Europe than in Latin America or South Asia. It was a deficiency that he would never remedy and one with far-reaching and disastrous consequences.

Wojtyla's maiden journeys to Canada and the United States gave him an appetite for international travel that would never be satiated. In February 1973 he represented the Polish Church at an International Eucharistic Congress in Melbourne. During the month he managed also to travel to New Zealand, Papua New Guinea and Manila. He met Polish communities in at least seven Australian cities. None of these trips, however, could be defined as learning experiences; they fell more comfortably into the 'if it's Tuesday it must be Paris' type of travel. Travelling frequently to Rome, Wojtyla became a familiar figure not only at meetings and conferences but also within the papal apartments. Between 1973 and 1975 he was received eleven times by the Pope in private audiences, an unprecedented figure for a non-resident cardinal. In early 1976 the Pope accorded Wojtyla a singular honour when he asked the Cardinal to conduct the Curia's Lenten retreat.

Wojtyla was acutely aware of the opportunity that had been presented to him. Many of the cardinals who would at some point in the near future be choosing the successor to Paul VI would be present. To prepare himself he retired for 20 days to the mountains. There, in a convent of Ursuline sisters, he 'wrote the meditations until midday, went skiing in the afternoon, and in the evening went back to writing'. The week-long retreat was held behind closed doors in St Mathilda's Chapel within the Vatican in the presence of the Pope. Also present were the papal household and over 100 members of the very heart of the Roman Catholic Church, the Curia Romana. This was the central government of an organisation with a membership approaching one sixth of the planet. To one side of the altar, tucked discreetly out of sight sat the Pope, seventy-nine years of age and in poor health, his physical condition not helped by the penitential shirt he was wearing under his robes, a garment made of coarse horse hair and thorns that pressed into his skin.

The ranks of the all-powerful Curia sat quietly listening as the man from Cracow – speaking, at the Pope's previous suggestion, in Italian – sat at a small table with a microphone in front of him and began with a quote from the Old Testament. 'May God grant me the grace to speak as I desire and to formulate thoughts worthy of the good things given me, since he is the guide of Wisdom.'[4] Many of his listeners knew Wojtyla, but not well: only his champion Andrzej Deskur, now an Archbishop, could make that claim. He had been opening doors, arranging meetings over meals, quietly talking up the abilities of Karol Wojtyla since the earliest days of Vatican Council II. Now more than anyone else he listened in eager anticipation to his close friend.

Wojtyla had chosen as his central theme the aspirations embodied in what he considered to be the central plank of Vatican Council II: *Gaudium et Spes* – Joy And Hope – The Constitution on the Church in the Modern World. It was an impressive performance. The congregation sat listening and observing as his command of Italian grew warmer. Never had the Cardinal's previous acting experience been used for such high status. Again and again he had been able to draw on acting experiences in Wadowice. Again and again the acting technique that the Rhepsodic Theatre group had developed that relied on the voice rather than on the body, had taken Karol Wojtyla beyond the threshold that exists between actor and audience. Among the Princes of the church listening as Wojtyla developed his theme that 'it is only in the mystery of the Word made flesh that the mystery of man truly becomes clear' were: Cardinal Secretary of State, Jean Villot, the Frenchman whose icy exterior hid an icy interior; Giovanni Benelli, number two at the Secretariat of State and a pope maker in waiting; Cardinal Bernardin Gantin of Benin, young and strong; Cardinal Sergio Pignedoli, President of the Secretariat of Non-Christians and Pope Paul's 'best-loved son' and favoured by many to be the next Pope; Cardinal Sebastiano Baggio, prefect of the Congregation of Bishops, and a man who entertained no doubts about the identity of the next pope – himself.

The Cardinal made good use of other skills and talents as he expanded not least on knowledge acquired through his years of prodigious study. He quoted from a galaxy of sources, including the Old and New Testaments, Christian classics, contemporary philosophy and general literature, from St Augustine to Hans Küng. But Wojtyla also demonstrated that he was a man with a soul as well as a brain. Speaking with great power and authority, he talked of that moment when

'a man goes down on his knees in the confessional because he has sinned. At that very moment he adds to his own dignity, the very act of turning again to God is a manifestation of the special dignity of man, of his spiritual grandeur, of the personal meeting between man and God in the inner truth of conscience.'

When his Lent sermons were subsequently published, the Cracow intellectuals were impressed, more so than some of his listeners within the Vatican who regarded the abundance of sources quoted as 'reminiscent of an undergraduate's defence of his thesis'. But then some of this group of listeners would have marked down God if He had chanced to deliver a sermon. Wojtyla returned to Rome in March and April to give conferences on philosophy. In September he was back again, this time in Rome and Genoa giving more lectures, gaining more exposure.

In July 1976, Karol Wojtyla went on his second visit to the United States. The official reason was to attend the International Eucharistic Congress in Philadelphia. Yet again a passport was made available to him courtesy of the Communist Government, attempting to sow dissension between the Primate Cardinal Wyszynski and Cardinal Wojtyla. Yet this official policy of divide and rule failed completely to produce the desired results. Although theirs was far from the easiest of relationships, Wyszynski and Wojtyla had developed a mutual respect and a mutual trust over the years. It helped greatly that from the outset Wojtyla had always deferred to Wyszynski and had on a number of occasions demonstrated his loyalty to the older man. Although the Primate had a profound distrust of intellectuals he came to appreciate Wojtyla as a colleague with a variety of qualities, which included a sharp native shrewdness.

While in the United States Dr Anna-Teresa Tymieniecka, Wojtyla's co-author on the English-language version of his philosophical work *The Acting Person*, took it upon herself yet again to help his career. She had already been responsible for bringing his original book to a far wider audience. Wojtyla stated within the preface of the book that he had 'tried to face our issues concerning life, nature and the existence of Man directly as they present themselves to Man in his struggles to survive while maintaining the dignity of a human being, but who is torn apart between his all-too-limited condition and his highest aspirations to be free'. In Poland the book had largely been dismissed by Wojtyla's fellow Catholic philosophers until the appearance of the lively, vivacious Dr Anna-Teresa; through her collaboration with Wojtyla on the English-language edition she succeeded in the truly formidable task of liberating his mind so that he could articulate what he actually wished to say, something he had failed to do within the original version of the work.

When the new edition was completed Dr Anna-Teresa was determined to introduce the author to the American audience. This included arranging for him to speak at Harvard, a White House meeting with President Ford, and a mass PR campaign to the media, in which he was described as a distinguished Polish Cardinal considered by at least some European commentators to be a contender for the papacy. Wojtyla baulked at none of this though he was obliged to cancel afternoon tea with the President because of a previous commitment. He had no problem with being introduced at the Harvard gathering by Dr Tymieniecka's husband as 'the next Pope'. The *New York Times* was suitably impressed and ran an article on Wojtyla. Anna-Teresa considered Wojtyla to be 'Christ-like' and full of wisdom yet with one profound flaw: she was alarmed at his ignorance of Western democracy and his unawareness of the power of the system that stood in opposition to Communism. He had given her the clear impression during their many meetings that Communist rule in Eastern Europe could not be defeated, that it was impregnable. She found Wojtyla dismissive of the West, particularly the United States which he regarded as devoid of morality. Her alarm was shared by Professor Hendrik Houthakker of Harvard who had attempted in vain to open his eyes to the merits of capitalism and democracy. If it became public knowledge this antipathy to the United States would have destroyed any chance of the papacy for Wojtyla. Anna-Teresa worked long and hard to dissuade him from revealing his true feelings on this subject.

*　　　*　　　*

She was largely successful but not entirely. Wojtyla had weighed the United States and found it wanting. When he returned home he freely criticised American culture and what he perceived as its shallowness. In an interview with *Tygodnik Powszechny* he demonstrated not only a deep prejudice about the United States but an equally deep ignorance.

'The question of belonging to a nation of fathers and forefathers reaches deep into the conscience of man, requiring truth about himself. Not accepting this truth, man suffers a basic need and is condemned to some kind of conformism . . . This is a real problem in the structure of the American society. The extent of this problem is demonstrated today by the so-called "Black Question". I have not noticed any average American even of the WASP type express the words "American nation" with the same conviction that an average Pole in Poland speaks of the Polish nation.'

(There is no evidence that at the time these remarks were made Cardinal Wojtyla had met a single 'average' American.)

On Sunday 6 August at 9.40 p.m. Pope Paul VI died. The throne was empty. Now, after a thirty-three-day papacy and the murder of Pope John Paul I, it was again vacant.

Plots and counter-plots about who would take the vacant throne were outlined at discreet meetings. The death of John Paul sent the Church into paroxysm. The majority of the men from Latin America wanted more of the same, another Luciani; they wanted birth control, a Church of the poor and a sweeping reform of the Vatican Bank. Some of the Europeans wanted all of that plus an acceleration of the reforms that Vatican Council II had promised. Others, such as the German and the Polish Cardinals, considered that

these Council reforms were being implemented at a positively hectic pace and wanted to slow the whole process
down. Cardinal Benelli, who had worked so assiduously to
ensure the election of Albino Luciani, now worked just as
hard to bring about his own election. Other Princes of the
Church had a range of agendas: a hastily arranged meeting
in the French Seminary discussed the need to find a candidate to stop the election of the conservative Cardinal Siri.
Meanwhile, at dinner at the Felician Sisters' convent on the
Via Casaletto, others planned the promotion of Cardinal
Wojtyla's candidacy.

The Polish connection was proving a powerful gambit as
Cardinal Franz König of Vienna and Cardinal John Krol of
Philadelphia began to work the telephones. Krol was a
formidable operator with peerless political expertise. His
high-powered friends included three former American
Presidents – Johnson, Nixon, Ford – and the future President, Ronald Reagan. Krol got to work softening up his
fellow American cardinals. The first to get the treatment
was Cardinal Cody of Chicago and in this instance Krol
was pushing at an already open door as Cody had stayed
with Wojtyla in Cracow, and a Polish Pope would be
acclaimed by the large number of Polish immigrants in
Chicago. Above all, Wojtyla's victory might well save
Cody's position; the dead Pope had decided to remove
Cody, who was up to his neck in corruption. König, meanwhile, was making a pitch in a very different direction:
Stefan Wyszynski. He gently sounded him out about the
possibility of a Polish papal candidate. The primate dismissed the idea. 'It would be a great victory for the Communists to have me permanently removed to Rome.' König
gently pointed out that there were in fact two Polish
Cardinals. Wyszynski was astonished. Eventually he recovered sufficiently to dismiss the idea out of hand. 'Wojtyla is
unknown. The idea is unthinkable. The Italians will want

another Italian Pope and so they should. Wojtyla is far too young to be even a consideration.' Wojtyla, meanwhile, was discovering he had much in common with a number of cardinals he had not met before, including Cardinal Joseph Ratzinger of Germany.

The Italians were barely waiting for the Conclave: reputations were being shredded and characters assassinated, at the drop of a red biretta. They did indeed want another Italian pope but some wanted Siri, others Benelli; still others were committed to Poletti, or Ursi or Colombo. In the week prior to the Conclave, the Roman Curia mounted a major offensive on behalf of their 'favourite son', Giuseppe Siri. Those looking for a bandwagon to jump on began to move in Siri's direction. At one stage it seemed it would take a miracle to stop Siri; the miracle duly arrived. Siri had given an interview to a trusted reporter on the *Gazzetta del Populo*. A condition of the interview was that it would not be published until the cardinals were in the Conclave and uncontactable. The *Gazzetta* reporter, according to one Vatican Village rumour, contacted his good friend Cardinal Benelli and outlined to him the salient points of the interview. Whether or not on Benelli's urging, the reporter broke the embargo and, just a day before they were sealed into the Sistine Chapel, the cardinals learnt the main points of the interview. Siri had dismissed the Luciani Papacy and ridiculed the late Pope as a man who had delivered as his inaugural speech a text written for him by the Curia. He had then been equally critical of Cardinal Villot, the Secretary of State and *Camerlingo*. He had also dismissed the concept of collegiality. The interview cost him a number of votes but equally there were supporters of Siri who, convinced that the whole affair had been engineered by Siri's main rival, vowed they would vote against Benelli until hell froze over.

*　　*　　*

While news of the Siri interview flew around the Apostolic
Palace, Karol Wojtyla was preoccupied with a personal
tragedy. His friend of more than thirty years, Bishop
Deskur, had been rushed to hospital after suffering a major
stroke. Wojtyla had hurried to his bedside and the following
day, Saturday 14 October, said Mass on behalf of his
stricken friend who was lying paralysed and virtually
speechless. Wojtyla's candidacy owed more to Deskur than
to any other man and he had worked tirelessly over the
years to further Wojtyla's career. Deskur had continued to
organise events for him virtually to the eve of the Conclave:
lunch on 9 October with guests including Cardinal Nasalli
Rocca; lunch on 11 October with guests including Cardinal
Cody. Phone calls to Benelli's secretary arranged an accommodation; a meeting was held to reassure a German contact
on continuity. Now Wojtyla's fate was in the hands of
others. When the voting began on 15 October a protracted,
deeply bitter struggle opened between Benelli's supporters
and the Siri faction. These machinations were in sharp
contrast to the back room negotiations surrounding Luciani's election, which was one of the shortest debates in the
Vatican's history.

It would be logical to assume that, as John Paul I had been
the clear choice for the overwhelming majority, then little
more than two months later they would indeed be seeking
another from the same mould: a truly humble, modest
man who desired a poor Church for the poor of this earth.
When Luciani declined the pomp of a papal coronation he
said:

'We have no temporal goods to exchange, no economic interests to discuss. Our possibilities for intervention are specific and limited and of a special
character. They do not interfere with purely tempor-

al, technical and political affairs, which are matters for your governments.'

Thus in one dramatic gesture he demonstrated that the Church's timeless lust for temporal power was abolished. This presumably was the kind of man that the Princes of the Church would now be attempting to find for a second time. At the end of the first day they were still looking after four ballots. The following day after a further two ballots they were no nearer. Giovanni Benelli who, though no replica of Luciani, would most certainly have followed him down the same path of financial reform, came within nine votes of the necessary majority but it was not to be.

Lunch on the second day produced, after energetic lobbying from Franz König and John Krol, a compromise candidate, Karol Wojtyla. At the meal, after the sixth ballot, Cardinal Wojtyla affected the traditional concern and dismay at his growing support; he also began to consider what name he would use if elected. He had a particular inclination for Stanislaw in homage to St Stanislaw of Cracow, the spiritual hero of Poland, who had been martyred in 1079, but several of those who had managed his candidacy considered that at least an illusion of continuity was desirable. During the counting of the decisive eighth ballot Wojtyla picked up a pad and pencil and began to write rapidly. At the end of the ballot the throne was Wojtyla's. Asked if he accepted the nomination, Wojtyla paused for what seemed a long time. Some of the waiting cardinals feared that he was about to reject the supreme office. He was in fact composing his answer in Latin. 'Knowing the seriousness of these times, realising the responsibility of this selection, placing my faith in God, I accept.' Asked by what name he wished to be known, there was another interminable pause before he responded, 'Because of my reverence, love and devotion to John Paul and also to Paul VI, who has been my inspiration and strength, I will take the name of John Paul.'

With some reluctance he followed Luciani in rejecting the traditional opulent coronation with its waving ostrich feathers and the papal tiara encrusted with emeralds, rubies, sapphires and diamonds. Another of Albino Luciani's quiet innovations, the refusal to refer to himself using the royal 'we', was however rapidly abandoned. Small things and silence had been superseded by pomp and majesty. His election gave rise in an instant to global speculation as to what kind of pope he would be. Would Wojtyla pick up Luciani's posthumous challenge and carry out the various reforms? One fact was obvious from the very beginning of this papacy: Cardinal Bernardin Gantin expressed exactly the fear and confusions of many of his fellow cardinals when he observed, 'We are groping in the dark.' Most of the cardinals were still shocked and numbed by the sudden death of Albino Luciani. These men were ill-equipped to pick a successor to the man who less than two months earlier they had hailed as 'God's Candidate'. Cardinal Ratzinger talked of Luciani's premature death as creating conditions for 'the possibility of doing something new'. Cardinal Baum of Washington said, 'His death [Luciani's] is a message from the Lord quite out of the ordinary . . . This was an intervention from the Lord to teach us something.' These were the rationalisations of men struggling to come to terms with a disaster.

If the cardinals had potentially picked a great pope in the making, it owed almost everything to luck and very little to their collective judgement or knowledge of Karol Wojtyla. Equally, as the pre-conclave electioneering demonstrates, Wojtyla's election owed nothing to Providence. Ironies abounded everywhere: Benelli was rejected in part because he was too young at 57; Wojtyla was 58. Those who prided themselves on stopping the Siri bandwagon would discover that in many respects they had elected a Polish version of Siri. Those who wanted another Albino Luciani would come to realise that he was irreplaceable. Those who voted for Wojtyla to achieve a collegiate papacy found that they had elected an autocrat.

At 6.45 p.m. on Monday 16 October 1978, the doors leading to the second-floor balcony above St Peter's Square swung open and for the second time in seven weeks Cardinal Felici emerged to announce to the crowd below and to the far greater audience beyond Italy's shores, '*Annuncio vobis gaudium magnum: Habemus Papam!*' The crowd below roared and clapped their approval. 'We have a Pope!' Who he was at that moment was not important, what mattered was that the dreadful void had been filled. When Felici shared the name 'Cardinal Wojtyla' with the crowd, they were bemused. "Who? Is he Black? Is he Asian?"

Father Andrew Greeley, the author and noted Catholic sociologist, in the crowd below recalled the response of those around him:

'When I explained that no, he wasn't black or Asian, but a Pole, they were astonished. It was an angry sullen crowd. None of the joy of Luciani's election. There were no cheers. There were boos – but mostly total dead silence.'

Thirty minutes later Wojtyla appeared on the balcony to perform the ritual of the Papal blessing. The minor Curial officials told him to just bless the crowd and get back inside. Wojtyla ignored them. The old warrior Cardinal Wyszynski stood quietly in the background but his presence gave the younger man the moral support he needed for this crucial first meeting with the public. The actor deep within the man rose magnificently to the challenge. His words were not ad lib comments but the thoughts he had jotted down while the votes were still being counted on the final ballot. In a gesture designed to win over the crowd, he spoke in Italian. 'Praised be Jesus Christ!' Many in the crowd automatically responded. 'Now and forever.'

Wojtyla's deep, powerful voice amplified by the microphone carried to every corner of the square.

'We are still all grieved after the death of the most beloved Pope John Paul I. And now the most revered Cardinals have called a new bishop to Rome. They have called him from a distant country, distant but always so close for the Communion in the Christian faith and tradition.'

The crowd were warming to him now, calling encouragement to him as for the majority listening in the square below he continued flawlessly in their mother tongue.

'I was afraid to receive the nomination, but I did it in the spirit of obedience to our Lord and in the total confidence in His mother the most holy Madonna. Even if I cannot explain myself well in your – *our* – Italian language, if I make a mistake you will correct me.'

The deliberate little stumble was a masterstroke, and he had them in the palms of his hands.

'And so I present myself to you all to confess our common faith, our hope, our confidence in the mother of Christ and of the Church also – and also to start anew on that road, the road of history and of the Church, to start with the help of God and with the help of men.'

Wojtyla had succeeded to the papacy with his acting skills intact and well honed. All that had changed was the size of the audience. The small 'mistake' had produced good-natured laughter in the crowd, the reference to 'Madonna' had brought cheers, the reference to his coming from a 'distant' country had been received with sympathy and their more serious implications were not considered on that first autumn evening in St Peter's Square. Further afield, his election and its potential implications were being very closely considered. In virtually every capital city throughout the world Presidents, Prime Ministers and First Secretaries were issuing instructions for detailed briefing documents. Intelligence agencies, Foreign Offices and State Departments were all working late. Within the Kremlin there was dismay; inside the White House there was delight.

In Warsaw the news was greeted with stupefied disbelief. Virtually overnight the election of Karol Wojtyla transformed the attitudes and expectations of the Polish Roman Catholic faithful. The moral authority of the Church within his homeland was enormously increased, at the drop of a biretta. The response from the regime was not long in coming. Minister of Defence Wojciech Jaruzelski was uplifted. One of his countrymen sat on the throne of St Peter. Poland should share in this glorious moment. First Secretary Edward Gierek had a similar reaction; turning to his wife he remarked, 'A Pole has become Pope. It is a great event for the Polish people and a big complication for us.'

The following day a lengthy congratulatory telegram signed by Gierek, the Polish president Henryk Jablonski and Prime Minister Piotr Jaroszewicz was sent to the new Pope. With an eye towards an extremely twitchy Moscow, the signatories did not neglect to give credit for this achievement to forces other than God's Will.

'For the first time in ages, a son of the Polish nation –
which is building the greatness and prosperity in its
Socialist Motherland in the unity and collaboration of
all its citizens – sits on the Papal Throne . . . the son of
a nation known throughout the world for its special
love of peace and for its warmest attachment to the
cooperation and friendship of all peoples . . . a nation
which had made universally recognised contributions
to the human culture . . . We express our conviction
that these great causes will be served by the further
development of relations between the Polish People's
Republic and the Apostolic Capital.'

For the moment the Vatican policy of *Ostpolitik* hung in
the balance. Would Wojtyla continue his predecessors'
efforts of opening up and expanding relationships with
the Eastern bloc or would the Church revert to its position
before Vatican Council II of open hostility?

'I have accepted with special gratitude the congratu-
lations and wishes, full of courtesy and cordiality, sent
to me by the highest authorities of the Polish People's
Republic. On the occasion of the choice of a son of
Poland for the capital of St Peter, I identify with all my
heart with my beloved Poland, the Motherland of all
Poles. I earnestly hope that Poland will continue to
grow spiritually and materially, in peace and justice
and in respect for man . . .'

Thus the new Pope demonstrated to the Polish leadership
that nationalism was one of the elements that bound them
all together. For Poland at least the policy of *Ostpolitik*
would continue apace.

While the Pope was addressing the nature of the future
relationship between Rome and Warsaw, the Vatican Press

Office, aided by other Curial elements, was busily engaged in rewriting Wojtyla's past. For Cardinal Villot, a man who had already demonstrated a remarkable ability to hide the truth concerning the death of Pope John Paul I, a disinformation exercise concerning events that had occurred during the Second World War was a relatively simple matter. Few, if any, would have the necessary information to challenge either the Vatican Press Office or anonymous sources within the Curia.

While the official details of Wojtyla's life contained, for example, in *L'Osservatore Romano*, were accurate, they were a masterpiece of brevity when dealing with Karol Wojtyla's war years. Villot, already familiar with the Vatican dossiers on Wojtyla, knew better than the majority of his fellow Cardinals that in electing this man they had created a potential for both triumph or disaster. Used effectively by the Communists, the truth was capable of creating such an aura of negativity around this new papacy that it could struggle for years to overcome the damage. There was the issue of Wojtyla's non-existent wartime assistance to Jews. He had never lifted a hand to save a single life or assist any of a race marked for mass extermination. There was the issue of his wartime work for the East German Chemical Works, previously called Solvay: work that merited him the special protection of the Third Reich because it was deemed vital to the war effort. Facts such as these could easily be manipulated by the Church's enemies. Villot and those assisting him moved with remarkable alacrity. Their lies duped experienced Vatican reporters along with the naïve.

Father Andrew Greeley was one of the former, a long-standing Vatican watcher who wrote a syndicated column for over one hundred outlets and broadcast regularly from Rome. He was convinced by the biographical material passed to him from the Vatican Press Office. He was not

the only one – the Religious News Service, AP, *Time,*
Chicago Sun Times, NBC News, the San Francisco *Examiner* and *The Times* of London all concurred in the story of
Wojtyla's wartime activities. Greeley wrote:

> 'as a young man during the Second World War,
> Wojtyla was active in an underground movement
> which assisted Jews. He helped them to find shelter,
> to acquire false identification papers, and to escape
> from the country. He was blacklisted by the Nazis for
> helping Jews, and one of the reasons for his remaining
> hidden was to avoid arrest by the Nazis.
>
> After the war he defended the Jews who remained in
> Cracow from Communist anti-Semitism. He helped to
> organise the permanent care of the Cracow Jewish
> cemetery after that cemetery had been desecrated by
> secret police-inspired thugs. The Cardinal called upon
> the students of the University of Cracow to clean and
> restore the defiled tombstones. In 1964 on the Feast of
> Corpus Christi, he condemned the Communist gov-
> ernment for its anti-Semitism. In 1971 he spoke at the
> Cracow synagogue during a Friday night Sabbath
> service . . .'

Despite the fact that one of Father Greeley's sources was a
Rome-based official of the Jewish Anti-Defamation League
there is not one single word of truth in the above account.
More than twenty years into the Wojtyla papacy, the Vatican
Website was still quoting another Jewish organisation, B'nai
Brith as a source for these fantasies. Yet B'nai Brith hold no
evidence to justify any of the claims made in the quoted
passage and have also further denied to the author that they
have ever made the claims attributed to them.

Lies told often enough become the truth. What was fed to
Greeley was fed to many reporters and journalists and used.

It went around the world. Some of Wojtyla's actual wartime activities, particularly the reality of his years at the Solvay plant, were also put through the myth-making machine. The fact that he had been privileged and protected was replaced with tales of slave labour while wages, a staff canteen, a gymnasium and a company store and the other benefits did not feature in Vatican press releases. Karol Wojtyla never instigated or encouraged such fantasies but then neither did he – nor the some fifty trusted Poles who were rapidly moved into the Papal Apartments and various parts of the Roman Curia – ever correct them.

The Polish Communist regime was prepared to be largely positive about Wojtyla's election:

> 'The concordat that the First Secretary and Paul VI had been working towards will continue. There will be diplomatic relations between us and the Holy See. Better, far better, that it is Wojtyla rather than Wyszynski.'

Moscow, however, reacted with a mixture of alarm, paranoia and pessimism. Some of the Soviet Politburo saw the election as a form of coup d'état organised by a cabal that included United States National Security advisor Zbigniew Brzezinski, Cardinal Krol and the West German leadership. Brzezinski and Krol's Polish roots were seen as 'significant', a conclusion endorsed in a subsequent KGB report. The alarmists saw a call to arms from the Pope to his fellow countrymen as a likely scenario until they read the pre-election Polish secret service files on Wojtyla. The pessimists saw the potential end of the Vatican initiative of *Ostpolitik* even after studying Wojtyla's warm response to Warsaw's congratulatory cable.

When Moscow learned that the Pope was talking of visiting Poland in early 1979, the Soviet leader Leonid

Brezhnev immediately telephoned General Secretary Gierek
in Warsaw. Gierek later recalled,

> 'He said that he had heard the Church had invited the
> Pope to Poland and he wanted to know my response.
>   "We are going to receive him properly."
>   "I advise you, don't receive him because you are
> going to have a big problem with this."
>   "How can I not receive a Polish Pope, if the majority
> of my compatriots are Catholics and for them his
> election is a great holiday? Besides, do you imagine
> the reaction of the nation if I close the border to him?"
>   "The Pope is a wise man; he will understand. He can
> declare in public that he is unable to come because he
> is ill." '

The conversation became rapidly more acrimonious with
Brezhnev shouting, 'Gomulka was a better Communist;
because he did not receive Paul VI in Poland and nothing
terrible happened.' Gierek refused to back down and finally, before slamming down the phone, the leader of the
Soviet Union remarked, 'Do as you please then, provided
that you and your party won't regret it later.'

Brezhnev and the Politburo were still mulling over the
contents of the first of a number of reports on Wojtyla. The
report's author, Oleg Bogomolov, the director of the Institute for the World Socialist System, had been handpicked
for the task by Yuri Andropov, the head of the KGB.

Bogomolov saw Wojtyla as

> 'a cardinal who had always taken right-wing positions
> but one who had urged the Church to avoid frontal
> attacks on socialism. He prefers instead a gradual
> transformation of socialistic societies into pluralistic
> liberal-bourgeois systems. Initially, the new Pope will

be dependent on the Curia which, without doubt, will try to subject him to its influence. But the independent temper and energy of John Paul II suggest that he will be fairly quick to get the hang of things and break free from the guardians of orthodoxy in the Curia.'

While the world outside the Vatican was still preoccupied with the implications of the new papacy, the man at the centre of their speculation was getting acquainted with the job. Interest in Karol Wojtyla was intense; at his inauguration ceremony on 22 October, more than 200,000 pressed into St Peter's Square. The square was regularly packed with thousands for the Papal Sunday Angelus. Apart from his novelty value, he also made himself available to the media – who could not get enough of the man – but strictly on his terms. Mingling freely with the media in the Apostolic Palace and casually responding in a variety of languages, he was asked if a press conference like this one would ever be repeated. 'We'll see how you treat me,' he replied. No Pope had ever used the media like this before.

Initially he was slow to give the public indications of what kind of papacy his would be. The public signs were few and far between: there would be no relaxation of the strict rule of complete celibacy for the priesthood; he wanted to see priests, nuns and the other religious in uniform at all times. 'It reminds them of their vocation.' Privately he gave to Cardinal Villot a series of very powerful and sustained demonstrations of precisely what kind of pope he would be. The first issue was the democratic concept of power-sharing and decision-making, what the Roman Catholic Church, particularly since Vatican Council II, called collegiality. Villot, who had been reconfirmed as the Secretary of State, discussed with Wojtyla his views on the Synod of Bishops, created by Paul VI. The council did not give the bishops power but at least brought them into a consultative role. Since the Synod met only about once every three years and the subjects they discussed, usually one or two per session, were chosen for them by the Pope, it was effectively a device for the Vatican to ensure that all real power rested in papal hands.

Villot wanted to know if Wojtyla was minded to allow the bishops of the Church the freedom to set up a permanent body that would work in unison with the Pope, rather as a government or an administration, at least in theory, works in unison with a Prime Minister or a President. The Pope rejected the concept on the spot. 'The Pope will remain supreme and sole legislator, with the ecumenical council,' he declared. The ecumenical council, the grand assembly of bishops, could not of course be convened without the Pope's permission. He assured Villot that he would consult with them more frequently than Paul VI had but, 'there is no need to make this consultation obligatory.' Wojtyla had spent almost all his life under some kind of totalitarian regime. He had now signalled his intention to continue living under such a system – with himself as the autocrat. Post-Vatican Council II collegiality would remain an illusion.

On a second issue Villot discussed with Wojtyla the changes that the late Pope John Paul I had been about to implement at the time of his sudden death. There was the meeting that Albino Luciani had been particularly determined to have with the American Select Committee on Population; Luciani believed strongly that a form of artificial contraception should be available to the Roman Catholic faithful. Wojtyla told his Secretary of State not to rearrange the meeting with the Committee. It would not take place this year, next year or ever. His angry rejection of the possibility of dialogue was entirely predictable. Wojtyla and his own Cracow committee had boasted of creating at least 60 per cent of *Humanae Vitae* with its prohibition on artificial birth control. 'Rome has spoken. The case is concluded.'

Some of his other responses to his predecessor's proposed changes, reforms that had been within hours of becoming realities, were less predictable. The problem of the vacancy in Ireland was one of many that showed real differences between the two popes.

The Church's attitude to the IRA had long been a highly contentious issue. Many considered that the Catholic Church had been less than forthright in its condemnation of the continuing carnage in Northern Ireland. A few weeks before Luciani's election, Archbishop O'Fiaich had hit the headlines with his denunciation of the conditions in the Maze prison, Long Kesh. O'Fiaich had visited the prison and later talked of his 'shock at the stench and filth in some of the cells, with the remains of rotten food and human excreta scattered around the walls'.

There was much more in a similar vein. Nowhere in his very long statement, released to the news media with considerable professionalism, did the Archbishop acknowledge that the prison conditions were self-created by the prisoners.

Ireland was without a cardinal, which was a source of great pressure on Luciani. Some elements were for promoting O'Fiaich; others felt his previous promotion to the archdiocese of Armagh had already proved an unmitigated disaster.

Albino Luciani had considered the dossier on O'Fiaich and the files on Ireland. He had priests within the Vatican who were staunch Republicans including Archbishop O'Fiaich. Files showed an extraordinary picture of collusion between Irish priests and the IRA: safe houses, logistical support, providing alibis. The most shocking report concerned the assistance Father James Chesney had given to the IRA terrorist team responsible for the Claudy bombings

in 1972. Nine civilians were murdered and Father Chesney's involvement was covered up by an unholy alliance of
Cardinal William Conway, the then Primate of all Ireland,
and the then Northern Ireland Secretary, William White-
law. An Anglo-Irish example of *Realpolitik*. There were
other horrendous examples of the involvement of Catholic
priests in IRA attacks. Now Luciani was being asked to
endorse this history by promoting Archbishop O'Fiaich. He
had returned the dossiers to his Secretary of State with a
shake of his head and a one-line epitaph, 'I think Ireland
deserves better.' The search for a cardinal was extended. It
had been continuing at the time of Pope John Paul I's death.
Wojtyla read the same files and promptly gave the job to
O'Fiaich.

Then there was the notoriously corrupt Cardinal Cody
of Chicago. Cardinal Cody had improperly used Church
funds long before he had arrived in Chicago. In June
1970, whilst Treasurer of the American Church, he in-
vested $2 million illegally in Penn Central stocks. A few
days later the share price collapsed and the company went
bankrupt. He survived that scandal and set about alienating a large percentage of his 2.4 million diocese in Chicago. Priests that he considered 'problem prelates', men
who were alcoholic, senile or just unable to cope, were
dismissed with just two weeks' notice and then tossed out
onto the streets. He closed the black schools, claiming that
his diocese could not afford to run them although its
annual revenue was around $300 million. He was a
fantasist, a compulsive liar and a paranoiac. He even
showered gifts on a close woman friend, to whom he
allegedly diverted hundreds of thousands of dollars and
diverted further large sums by way of diocesan insurance
business to her son. Paul VI had shrunk from ordering him
to resign, confining himself to requesting through his
intermediaries that Cody should stand aside. The Cardinal

had refused and remained defiantly in office. Albino Luciani considered the Cody dossier.

Luciani determined that Cardinal Cody must go but he would be given the opportunity of going gracefully. He was 75 years of age and in ill health: excellent reasons for retiring. If Cody yet again refused to budge a coadjutor would be appointed. Again before that decision could be implemented, Luciani was dead. As the new Pope considered the Cody dossier, word inevitably reached Cody. He reminded the Pope of the huge amounts he had raised from his Polish constituents in Chicago, and then he upped the ante by making a new huge contribution for 'the Motherland'. He reminded all and sundry of his close friendship with Wojtyla. Ignoring the advice of every single advisor, ignoring what was in the file in black and white, Wojtyla displayed a disconcerting weakness. He offered Cody a position in Rome. Cody rejected it and the case was closed; there would be no action against Cardinal Cody.

In addition the Vatican appeared to be bulging at the seams with Masons. Freemasonry had been strictly forbidden by a succession of popes reaching back many hundreds of years. Luciani had been given a secret list of 121 alleged Masons, many working close to him in the Vatican. He had demonstrably made a start on the problem. In his meeting with Villot on 28 September, he advised his Secretary of State of various changes and transfers. Each of them involved removing a man who was on the list of Vatican Freemasons.

The changes and reforms that John Paul I had discussed with Cardinal Jean Villot on what transpired to be the last day of his life included cleaning the Augean stable of the Vatican Bank. Under the Presidency of Archbishop Paul Marcinkus the Bank had taken part in a string of corrupt and criminal transactions, Now, after an unchallenged reign since 1969, Marcinkus was going to be sent back

to where he came from, to Chicago. Also being put out to
pasture were his partners in crime Luigi Mennini, Monsignor Donato de Bonis and Pelligrino de Strobel, all senior
executives at the Bank. They were all to leave their posts
immediately. John Paul I advised Villot that Marcinkus was
to be replaced by the expert and upright Monsignor Giovanni Angelo Abbo, Secretary of the Prefecture of Economic
Affairs of the Holy See.

Within a few hours of giving his Secretary of State these
and the other instructions covering the immediate reforms,
the Pope was dead. All of the files and documents, including
the report by Cardinal Vagnozzi on the Vatican Bank, were
available to Karol Wojtyla. He was advised by his Secretary
of State Cardinal Jean Villot of the changes that Luciani had
been about to make.

Wojtyla rejected every single change and reconfirmed all
of these men within the Vatican Bank in their positions.
Marcinkus was free to continue his activities with Roberto
Calvi, most notably assisting Calvi in the continuous plundering of Banco Ambrosiano. The ultimate size of the theft
would reach $1.3 billion.

According to the terms under which the Vatican Bank
was created by Pius XII during the Second World War, the
accounts should have been very largely confined to religious
orders and religious institutes. At the time Karol Wojtyla
gave the green light to 'business as usual' only 1,047
accounts came into this category. A further 312 belonged
to parishes and a further 290 to dioceses. The remaining
9,351 were owned by diplomats, prelates and 'privileged
citizens'. Among the privileged citizens were criminals of
every hue.

The exalted personages included leading politicians of
every political persuasion, a wide variety of members of P2
(the Italian Masonic Lodge), industrialists, reporters, editors, and members of such Mafia families as the Corleones,

the Spatolas, and the Inzerillos. Also included were members of the Neapolitan crime organisation, the Camorra. All of them used the Vatican Bank for recycling the profits of their various criminal activities. Licio Gelli assisted the Corleone family with their Vatican investments and members of the Magliana gang serviced the Vatican Bank accounts of the Mafia's chief financial operator Pippo Calo.[5] The Santa Anna Gate was a very busy thoroughfare as suitcases of money representing profits from the illegal narcotics industry went in past the Swiss Guards and up the stairs to the Bank. A number of the Mafia were traditionalists. They did not trust electronic transfers.

The tellers in the Vatican Bank were always polite, always solicitous of the needs of their regular customers. After all, the bank took an additional commission for handling the accounts of the 'privileged citizens'.

It was hardly surprising that Secretary of State Villot (whose own hands were far from clean) should have been appalled with Wojtyla's complete dismissal of every single one of Luciani's proposed changes and reforms. On some of the issues, birth control for example, Villot was at one with Wojtyla but on the various Vatican reforms, the removal of Cody, the wholesale cleaning of the Vatican Bank, he knew better than anyone that Luciani's proposals were an urgent necessity. A mere seven days into this new papacy Villot spoke quietly to a friend, the French priest Antoine Wenger.

'The new Pope has a great deal of willpower and decisiveness. In the course of the first week of his pontificate he has made decisions in which listening to some careful advice would not have been out of place.'

Roberto Calvi, Licio Gelli and Umberto Ortolani, three men who benefited greatly by the sudden death of Pope

John Paul I, had gone abroad in August 1978. They stayed in South America throughout the brief reign of Albino Luciani. Calvi eventually returned home after the election of Wojtyla and only after the new Pope had reconfirmed Marcinkus as President of the Vatican Bank.

On 30 October, 1978 Calvi had a much-postponed meeting with Bank of Italy Inspector Giulio Padalino. The breathing-space gained by the sudden death of Luciani looked like being temporary. Calvi, eyes fixed on the floor of his office, yet again declined to give straight answers to a variety of questions. On 17 November the Bank of Italy inspection of Banco Ambrosiano, the 'priests' bank' as it was affectionately known by the many religious that had accounts there, was completed.

Notwithstanding the fraudulent letter from Marcinkus and his Vatican Bank colleagues concerning the ownership of Suprafin, the mysterious company that had such a voracious appetite for Banco Ambrosiano shares, despite the lies and evasions of Roberto Calvi, despite all of the help from his protector Licio Gelli, the Central Bank inspectors concluded that a great deal was rotten in Calvi's empire.

Gelli, the Puppet Master, telephoned Calvi at his private residence. Using his own special code name, he told Calvi, already wallowing in a mire of Mafia/Vatican Bank/P2 deals, that he was now very dangerously close to drowning for the second time in a few months. With Luciani in his grave and a compliant Wojtyla on the throne, Calvi, Gelli and Ortolani might have reasonably assumed that any new threat to the continuing billion-dollar theft would be minor: a bribe here and a favour performed there. That was all part of everyday life in the world of Italian banking. Within days of Inspector Giulio Padalino's handing his report to the Head of Vigilance of the Bank of Italy, Mario Sarcinelli, a copy was in Gelli's hands in Buenos Aires, not from the bank Inspectors but courtesy of Gelli's P2 network. Gelli advised Calvi that the State Bank was about to send the report to the Milan magistrates and specifically to the man that Gelli had predicted would be given the criminal enquiry back in September, Judge Emilio Alessandrini.

Calvi and his empire were again on the edge of oblivion. Alessandrini could not be bought. Talented and courageous, he represented not only to Calvi, Ortolani and Gelli but also to Marcinkus and that other great saviour of Vatican Incorporated, Michele Sindona, a very serious threat. If Alessandrini ran true to form, Calvi would be finished, Archbishop Marcinkus and the criminal activities of the Vatican Bank would be exposed, even with the powerful protection of Karol Wojtyla. Gelli and Ortolani would have lost access to the Well of Ruth that Ambrosiano represented. Sindona, currently fighting extradition from the United States, would find himself back in Milan in double-quick time.

The new Pope continued to ignore 'careful advice'. During the first week of November he made yet another decision that astonished his Secretary of State and many other insiders. This time he countermanded the orders not of John Paul I, but Paul VI. In doing so he chose to ignore an extraordinary volume of evidence compiled over four years at the direct instructions of Pope Paul. The issue was the shrine of Our Lady of Czestochowa in Jasna Gora in Poland, controlled by the Pauline Fathers. Among their other activities they administered a replica shrine in Doylestown, Philadelphia. This secondary activity had brought a Vatican investigating team on the direct orders of Pope Paul VI to the Order's American Headquarters. They established that the Superior of the Order, Father Michael M. Zembruski, and his favourites within the Order had dispensed with their vows of poverty and were living the high life with the use of credit cards, checking accounts, secret investments and huge loans. Father Michael was running a mistress as well as several Cadillacs. He had used donations to make illegal investments in two hospitals, a cemetery, a trade school, an aircraft equipment plant, a foundry and a number of other businesses. The investments were structured to obtain the greatest advantage from the Order's tax-exempt status. The Vatican investigators also established that the Order had raised $250,000 from the Catholic faithful for hearings of the Mass, a curious revival of medieval practice, except that in Philadelphia the fathers spent the money and never even bothered to say the Masses. The investigators discovered another scam involving extracting a further $400,000 of contributions towards the cost of installing bronze memorial plaques within the shrine. Again, the funds were spent. No plaques were erected. The scams were countless, the embezzlements huge. The Pauline Fathers got through a substantial part of $20 million raised in charitable donations. Father Michael obtained multi-million-dollar bank loans. His security was a letter of guarantee from Father George Tomzinski, his superior in Poland, supreme head of the worldwide Pauline Order.

The letter, in effect authority to spend the total assets of the Pauline Order valued by Father Tomzinski at $500 million, did not bear close investigation, but that did not stop the Polish Primate Cardinal Stefan Wyszynski and Karol Wojtyla rushing to intervene on behalf of a man who was a disgrace to the Pauline Fathers Order. In 1976 the Vatican investigators, with the approval of Pope Paul VI, dismissed Father Michael Zembruski from the Order. Wyszynski and Wojtyla flew to Rome and proceeded to rewrite the verdict. They successfully pressured Pope Paul and his Vatican advisors into reversing the decisions. Subsequently Cardinal Wyszynski fired every single senior member of the Order who had co-operated with the investigation. His action, however, was illegal under Church law and shortly before he died Paul had appointed a committee to re-examine the entire affair. Less than three weeks into papal office, Wojtyla dismissed the committee and issued a confidential directive upholding Wyszynski's illegal dismissal of men who were guilty of telling the truth.

The Roman Curia were dumbfounded. Senior officials within the Vatican Government saw it as a blatant misuse of papal authority in the name of Polish nationalism. Others, including a number of cardinals, saw the new Pope's actions in conjunction with his refusal to clean up the Vatican Bank as evidence of something far more disturbing. They began to consider the possibility that they had placed on Peter's throne a wilful, corrupt and potentially very dangerous man.

Those who had argued that Wojtyla's rampant nationalism was the key did not have to look far for evidence. Apart from the highly dubious support that he had given Wyszynski and a deeply corrupt Polish religious order, there was his insistence that Marcinkus should continue to run the Vatican Bank. Marcinkus had raised millions of dollars for the Polish Church, and his Lithuanian ancestry gave him a historic and deep-rooted connection with Poland. The Polish-watchers within the Curia also pointed to the snowstorm of letters and communiqués between Wojtyla and his countrymen, urgent messages to the Communist regime, to the Catholics of Cracow, to the Church of Poland. Curial eyebrows went up again when Wojtyla announced his desire to visit Poland for the feast of St Stanislaw on 8 May. This was done without any negotiations, a source of embarrassment both to Edward Gierek and his Politburo and to the Vatican machine.

Karol Wojtyla's preoccupation with Poland was evident immediately after his inaugural Mass when, instead of concerning himself with affairs of state, Wojtyla had spent much of the day talking and entertaining some of the 4,000

of his countrymen and women who had been allowed out of
Poland for the occasion. Between national songs he told
them 'the eyes of the entire world are upon the Polish
Church.' During the first week of November the Pope
met a delegation from the University of Lublin and again
wrapped the Polish flag around the Almighty. His election,
he declared, 'was a gift from the Lord to Poland'. A month
later the Vatican resounded to the traditional songs of
Poland as, along with a group of priests from his motherland, he sang in honour of the feast of St Nicholas. In the
first week of January while celebrating Mass for his fellow
Poles living in Rome he praised the ultimate sacrifice that St
Stanislaw had made as 'a source of the spiritual unity of
Poland'.

The Pope had very rapidly established a regular routine.
His bedroom on the corner of the third floor of the
Vatican's Apostolic Palace was sparse. The room contained
a single bed, two straight-backed upholstered chairs and a
desk. Apart from a small carpet near the bed, the parquet
floor was bare. On the walls were some sacred icons from
his motherland. His days began at a time when most of
Rome was still sleeping, at 5.30 a.m. By 6.15 a.m. he was in
his private chapel, praying and meditating before its altar
over which hung a large, bronze crucifix. Nearby was a
copy of Poland's most cherished icon, the Black Virgin of
Czestochowa. Sometimes John Paul would prostrate himself before the altar; at other times he would sit or kneel
with his eyes closed, forehead cradled, face contorted as if in
great pain. One Vatican insider observed: 'He makes many
decisions on his knees.'

The Pope would celebrate his own private Mass at 7 a.m.
and, having made a silent thanksgiving for about fifteen
minutes, would then greet the handful of guests who had
attended Mass, some of whom would be invited to join the
pontiff for breakfast.

Every morning before his private and general audiences, Wojtyla would devote two hours to writing and reflecting on important decisions that confronted him. And then at 11 a.m. one of the papal secretaries would remind him that it was time for the private audiences.

His relative indifference to food was a habit of a lifetime. Conversation was always more stimulating for Wojtyla than calories. As Polish journalist Marek Skwarnicki observed: 'Lunch is for bishops. Dinner is for friends.' His privacy was guarded jealously by a largely Polish retinue who, as time passed, became increasingly preoccupied with the sombre thought that, with his election, Karol Wojtyla had chosen his last home on earth.

After lunch and a solitary walk on the terrace of the Apostolic Palace, the Pope would then return to his desk to work on the various dossiers prepared for his attention by the Secretariat of State. In the early evening, he would meet with members of the inner cabal, Cardinals Sodano, Ratzinger or Battista Re.

After dinner, a second set of dossiers would arrive from the Secretariat of State and, after further work on these, Wojtyla would devote the last portion of his day to prayer and a variety of readings.

The year of the three popes had drawn to a close with Karol Wojtyla displaying his linguistic abilities from the Papal balcony. He wished the assembled throng, and the much wider audience watching him on untold millions of television sets around the world, a fulsome Christmas greeting in a multitude of languages.

He believed all that had occurred during the year was due to Providence. Others, both Princes of the Church and in the wider world, were less certain.

Chapter 2

'It Depends on Whose Liberation Theology . . .'

WOJTYLA'S PREDECESSOR POPE JOHN PAUL I, Albino Luciani, had thus declared a public sentence of death on Vatican Incorporated and ended the Roman Catholic Church's lust for temporal power.

'We have no temporal goods to exchange, no economic interests to discuss. Our possibilities for intervention are specific and limited and of a special character. They do not interfere with purely temporal, technical affairs, which are matters for your governments. In this way, our diplomatic missions to your highest civil authorities, far from being a survival from the past, are a witness to our deep-seated respect for lawful temporal power, and to our lively interest in humane causes that the temporal power is intended to advance.'

By refusing to confirm Luciani's reforms or to dismiss Marcinkus and his cronies, Wojtyla had reactivated the Church's preoccupation with the acquisition of wealth by any means, but what would he do about the Vatican's political standing in the world?

The Holy See had not been perceived as a player on the international stage since the loss of the Papal States in 1870. The last time it had been asked to serve as mediator in an international dispute had been 1885 when Germany and Spain were disputing ownership of the Caroline Islands. It took until the signing of the Lateran Treaty of 1929 for Pius XI to accept that the Papacy was now reduced to a state of 108.7 acres. Albino Luciani had therefore merely acknowledged the reality of lost temporal power, in common with the majority of Church members. But not Karol Wojtyla. Throughout his career in Poland he had largely steered clear of politics. Yet in his reign spiritual and temporal power were to become indivisible. Karol Wojtyla aspired to be the most political pope in living memory, and the greatest evangelist since the Gospel Writers.

The aspiration had a modest birth. Before Christmas 1978 the Vatican had been approached by Chile and Argentina to act as mediator on a boundary dispute in the Beagle Channel. After several weeks while the papal emissary, Cardinal Antonio Samore, talked discreetly to both sides to establish some ground rules, it was announced on 6 January 1979 that the two countries had formally requested the Vatican's mediation. Both countries had undertaken not to resort to arms during the negotiations. The talks eventually produced an agreement and a significant coup for the new Papacy.

By the middle of January 1979, while Pope John Paul II was preparing for his imminent tour of Mexico, two floors below in the Vatican Bank, Marcinkus had other preoccupations. The financial circles of Milan were yet again seething with rumours about the Knight, Roberto Calvi. Judge Alessandrini, having carefully studied a summary of the 500-page report, had ordered Lieutenant-Colonel Crestam, the commander of the Milan tax police, to pay a long-postponed visit with a full team to Banco Ambrosiano. The judge's brief sought a point-by-point check on the many criminal irregularities detailed within the report. No one outside official circles had access to the judge's brief to the Head of Financial Vigilance; no one, that is, apart from Calvi and Gelli.

On 25 January 1979, Pope John Paul II left Rome on his first visit to Latin America. His destination was a country with an uneasy relationship with the Catholic Church. Mexico was, officially, a secular state with an anti-clerical constitution. At the time of this papal visit religious orders were still banned from wearing their uniforms in public. The Holy See had no diplomatic relations with Mexico and the initial invitation to the Pope had come not from the Mexican President but the country's bishops who officially did not exist, a surreal concept in a country of nearly sixty million Catholics.

Father Marcel Maciel, the founder of a rapidly growing order, the Legionnaires of Christ, happened to know the President's confidential secretary. Wojtyla would call it Providence. Certainly Father Maciel would come to regard his intervention on behalf of the Pope as the best thing he had ever done in his life. President Jose Lopez Portillo was persuaded to issue the invitation to the Pope, although he made it clear that the Pope would not be received as a head of state and would have to have a visa like all lesser mortals.

When the Pope kissed the Mexican tarmac and got to his feet he found standing in front of him the tall figure of President Lopez Portillo. Like any astute politician, he recognised a groundswell of national enthusiasm and he welcomed Wojtyla to the country. There were no flags, bands or guards of honour to inspect but the President did invite the Pope to join him later in the day for afternoon tea. It was meant to be low-key but, unfortunately for the anti-church government, no one had told the Catholic population. At the airport a band began to play, crowds that had been held well away from the runway broke though the barriers, roses were strewn on the Pope's path and as if by magic he was wearing a sombrero, an image that went like a flash around Mexico and around the world. It took the Papal car more than two hours to travel the nine miles to Mexico City. Huge crowds estimated at over one million thronged both sides of the road, most waving flags with the Holy See's colours, a river of white and green yelling, 'Viva el papa! Viva Mexico!'

On the morning of 29 January the Pope, while talking to the impoverished Indians in Southern Mexico, railed against the many injustices that these people were suffering and called upon 'powerful classes to act to alleviate the suffering'. Simultaneously, many thousands of miles away in Milan, one of those powerful classes, the organised criminal class of Italy, was acting to protect their interest. Judge Emilio Alessandrini kissed his wife goodbye, and then drove his young son to school. Having dropped the boy off he began to drive to his office. A few seconds before 8.30a.m. he stopped at the traffic lights on Via Muratori. He was still gazing at the red light when five men approached his car and began firing. Late in the day a group of left-wing terrorists called Prima Linea claimed responsibility for the murder. The group also left a leaflet about the murder in a telephone booth in Milan Central Station. Neither the phone call nor the leaflet gave any clear reason for the murder.

The script was implausible: a left-wing group murders a judge who is renowned throughout Italy for his investigations into right-wing terrorism. In reality, groups such as Prima Linea and the Red Brigades did not merely kill for political or ideological reasons. They could be bought and frequently were. The many links between such groups in the 1960s and 1970s are a matter of record.

Marco Donat Cattin, the second man to open fire on the trapped and helpless judge, observed subsequently, 'We waited for the newspapers to come out with reports of the attack and we found in the magistrate's obituaries the motives to justify the attack.' Heaven forbid that Cattin and the others should admit to being motivated by mere money.

The murder of Pope John Paul I had bought Marcinkus, Calvi, Sindona and their P2 friends a momentary breathing-space. The election of Karol Wojtyla had resolved the problem of exposure from within the Vatican. Now the murder of Emilio Alessandrini had removed the threat of exposure by the Italian authorities. The investigation he had ordered continued – but with a marked lack of urgency.

However, in the Bank of Italy, Mario Sarcinelli and the Governor of the Bank, Paolo Baffi, were determined that the long, complex investigation which had been carried out during the previous year would not be a wasted exercise.

Roberto Calvi was again summoned for interrogation at the Central Bank. He was questioned very closely by Sarcinelli about Suprafin, about his bank's relationship with the Vatican Bank, about his own relationship with Bishop Marcinkus. With Alessandrini dead, Calvi was transformed; his eyes that had previously studied the floor during questioning were now ice-cold and unblinking, and all the old arrogance was back. He flatly refused to answer the questions of the Head of Viligance but was left in no doubt that the Central Bank had not thrown in the towel.

Not in their wildest dreams could the Vatican officials accompanying the Pope have been prepared for the Mexican reaction to this visit. There had been crowds in Rome since the inauguration, for the regular Angelus and the weekly public audiences, but St Peter's Square can only hold so many. Now for the first time the Vatican and the watching world saw the power not just of this new and unknown Pope but of the faith and the Church he represented. It would remain like this for the entire six days of the trip. The adrenalin rush that such a reaction triggers was not confined to the Pope and his retinue. Many of the news media, both Mexican and foreign, focused on the excitement and froth of the moment. Only a few reported his response to the major question he had to address on this first Papal trip: 'What about Liberation Theology?'

With his face set sternly as if confronted with an impudent pupil, Wojtyla responded, 'It depends on whose Liberation Theology. If we are talking about the Liberation Theology of Christ, not Marx, I am very much for it.'

Liberation Theology, and Marxism, meant something different in each Latin American country. One common thread was the shift in the Church's position. Before Vatican Council II the Church had traditionally sided with the rich and powerful and the right-wing regimes and military dictatorships which sustained them. After Vatican Council II declarations such as *Dignitatis Humanae* and *Gaudium et Spes* committed the Church to reject the status quo of the juntas and embrace the poor in an active struggle for freedom, peace, justice and the basic tenets contained in the United Nations' Universal Declaration of Human Rights of 1948.

Liberation Theology explored, to most people at that time, the relationship between Christian theology and political activism, particularly in areas of social justice and human rights focusing on the image of Jesus as a liberator. Emphasis was placed on those parts of the bible where the mission of Jesus was described in terms of liberation. Some of its followers within Latin America had added Marxist concepts to the theology. The father figure of the movement was Father Gustavo Gutierrez. Before setting out from Rome, the Pope had read Gutierrez's work on the subject and would have noted there was not one single reference to a relationship between Marxism and Liberation Theology. The application of the theology in the struggle for social justice and basic human rights aspired to improve the human condition of Latin America and not just for the region's three hundred million Catholics. It was an historic opportunity for the mass to escape from their subhuman conditions to break free of a situation where the Church had rights but her people did not.

In Brazil a military dictatorship had seized power in 1964. The full range of predictable repressions followed, including random murders of opponents of the regime, torture, rigid censorship, disappearances of liberals, trade unionists, intellectuals and lawyers, as well as appalling poverty for the masses. In 1979 similar dictatorships also ruled Chile, Argentina, Bolivia, Ecuador, El Salvador, Honduras, Nicaragua and Paraguay. In Mexico itself the ruling party Partido Revolucionario Institucional – PRI – had corruptly clung to power for more than fifty years.

In many countries clergy had protested against the sustained abuses of power that had been criminally seized. Many priests paid with their lives for supporting the poor. In San Salvador the week before the Pope had flown into Mexico, Father Octavio Ortiz Luna was assassinated, the fourth such murder in the past three years, the second within a month. A week later while the Pope was speaking in Puebla 600 nuns and priests and over 2,000 peasants, workers and students marched silently, their only banner proclaimed, *Basta ya* – 'Enough'. They marched through the capital of El Salvador to the Rosario Church where the previous year more than a hundred of the congregation were forced out of the church by tear gas and then massacred. During that same year another twenty-seven priests had been arrested, tortured and then expelled. Later in Puebla, Archbishop Oscar Romero of Salvador told an audience including the Pope,

'There is a lamentable cleavage among the bishops. Some think there is no persecution. They believe in the security that gives them privileges, or that renders them apparent respect. In the same way, others who enjoy a privileged position in the country don't want to lose friendships that they have, and so forth. So they don't demand the reform that is so urgent for the country.'

In the week of the Puebla Conference a report was published in São Paulo by Brazil's bishops, that detailed ten years of persecution by the Brazilian military junta including the harassment of religious and lay people working with the poor in Brazil. The study showed that thirty bishops had been harassed, nine of them arrested, while 113 religious and 273 lay people had also been arrested: thirty-four priests had been tortured and seven murdered. In the decade between the Medellin conference in 1968 and the Puebla meeting in January 1979, tens of thousands of people had been killed by the juntas of Latin America. Among that number more than 850 priests and nuns had been murdered. The minority of bishops at the 1968 meeting who supported the poor had become the majority of Puebla. After celebrating open-air Mass the Pope withdrew to talk in a closed session from which the public and the media were barred. This was one of the most important speeches he would ever make. Within this speech Wojtyla would address an issue that was crucial not only to his immediate audience and the entire Latin American continent but to every country on the planet where the United Nations' Universal Declaration of Human Rights had yet to be implemented.

Karol Wojtyla first addressed the issue in 1939. During the first week of November, writing to his friend and mentor, Mieczyslaw Kotlarczyk, the man who had first fired him with a passion for the theatre, Wojtyla talked of his growing awareness of what life in Poland had been like for the majority during his first twenty years.

'Today, after reflection, I understand with full clarity that the idea of Poland lived in us as a romantic generation, but in truth it did not exist because the peasant was killed and imprisoned for demanding just rights from the government. *The peasant was right to protest and he had law on his side, but the nation was misled and lied to.*'

He continued, 'The sons of these peasants have been chased across the world by hostile winds, like in the days of the Partisans.' In conclusion he observed, 'They have left so that they would not rot in the Motherland's prisons.'

Wojtyla returned to the issue in a stage play, *Our God's Brother*, by far the most interesting he ever wrote. Wojtyla writes with compassion and insight of what would be called several decades later 'liberation theology'. He began the play in 1945, in Archbishop Sapieha's secret seminary, and worked on it intermittently until 1950, when Poland was living under Godless Communism. The play asks: is revolutionary violence ever justified? Confronted with oppression and tyranny, with exploitation and manifest injustice how should the individual react?

The play confirmed yet again Wojtyla's chosen religious quietism to achieve the goal 'freedom'. However, the play also fully justified violent insurrection by the faithful.

During the course of the lectures Karol Wojtyla delivered at the Jagiellonian and Lublin Universities between 1953 and 1960, the man who would ultimately be seen as deeply opposed to all things Marxist demonstrated great sympathy towards both Marxism and the Communist movement. Writing in his mid-thirties[6] Wojtyla observed,

'In the contemporary Communist movement, the Church sees and acknowledges an expression of largely ethical goals . . . Pius XI has written that criticism of capitalism, and protest against human exploitation of human work, is undoubtedly "the part of the truth" which Marxism contains . . . Every person has an undeniable right to struggle to defend what rightly belongs to him . . . when an exploited class fails to receive in a peaceful way the share of the common good to which it has a right, it has to follow a different path.'

Lest there be any misunderstandings about that 'different path', the future Pope made it clear that society 'has a strict right, even a duty' to ensure justice through governance, an ability to control abuse and to acknowledge error. An absence of these crucial elements gives the people the right to passive resistance and if that fails 'active resistance against a legal but unjust power'.

Now his listeners in Puebla and much further afield awaited his Papal response to violent insurrection and the phenomenon known as Liberation Theology.

He began by exploring the role of the priest.

'As pastors, you keenly realise that your chief duty is to be teachers of the truth: not of a human rational truth but of the truth that comes from God. That truth includes the principle of authentic human liberation: "You will know the truth, and the truth will set you free." '[7]

He then developed his opening theme of 'the truth about Jesus Christ'. He continued:

'Now today we find in many places a phenomenon that is not new. We find "re-readings" of the Gospel

that are the product of theoretical speculations rather
than of authentic meditation on the word of God and a
genuine evangelical commitment. They cause confusion insofar as they depart from the central criteria
of the Church's faith, and people have the temerity to
pass them on as catechesis to Christian communities.'

Among examples of these 're-readings', the Pope said,

'People purport to depict Jesus as a political activist, as
a fighter against Roman domination and the authorities, and even as someone involved in the class
struggle. This conception of Christ as a political figure,
a revolutionary, as the subversive of Nazareth, does
not tally with the Church's catechism.'

People who saw Jesus as a political activist he suggested
were 'confusing the insidious pretext of Jesus' accusers with
the attitude of Jesus himself'. For John Paul II, Christ was
non-political and someone who 'unequivocally rejects recourse to violence'. He elaborated to the listening bishops
on 'the truth about the mission of the Church'. It was to
keep the faith that had been entrusted to them to uphold the
authority of the Church. There was to be no double
magisterium, no double hierarchy, no competing authority.
Evangelising was 'the essential mission' and this could only
be achieved by

'sincere respect of the sacred magisterium, a respect
based on the clear realisation that in submitting to it,
the People of God are not accepting the word of
human beings but the authentic word of God.'

He invoked the 'dogmatic formulas enunciated a century
ago by Vatican I' to justify universal acceptance of the

Church's authority. The most significant of those formulas had been the declaration of papal infallibility.

He then drew attention to an attitude of mistrust that was being fostered towards the 'institutional' or 'official' Church which critics saw as 'alienating' and against which a 'people's Church, one which is born of the people and fleshed out in the poor' was functioning as a rival. He desired unity of message and action. He then turned to the area where that unity was being seriously challenged by the varying responses of the bishops to the human conditions that confronted them in Latin America:

> 'Dignity is crushed underfoot when due regard is not maintained for such values as freedom, the right to profess one's religion, physical and psychic integrity, the right to life's necessities, and the right to life itself. On the social and political level it is crushed when human beings cannot exercise their right to participate, when they are subjected to unjust and illegitimate forms of coercion, when they are subjected to physical and psychic torture and so forth.
>
> 'I am not unaware of the many problems in this area that are being faced in Latin America today. As bishops you cannot fail to concern yourselves with them.'

He fully accepted that the Church should be involved in defending or promoting human dignity but there were clear parameters.

> '[the Church] does so in accordance with its mission. For even though that mission is religious in character, *and not social or political*, it cannot help but consider human persons in terms of their whole being.'

The Pope then cited the parable of the Good Samaritan as the model way of attending to all human needs. Thus when confronted with the extraordinary array of problems, imprisonment, hunger, a complete and total absence of human rights, the correct response was to extend a helping hand but always within the Christian framework. *'The Church,'* declared the Pope, *'therefore does not have need to have recourse to ideological systems in order to love, defend and collaborate in the liberation of the human being.'* [Author's italics.]

The Church would find 'inspiration' as the trustee of its Christian message

> 'for acting in favour of brotherhood, justice and peace; and against all forms of domination, slavery, discrimination, violence, attacks on religious liberty and aggression against human beings and whatever attacks life.'

The Pope did not explain precisely how any actions of the bishops would transform the wretched existence of their flocks yet referred to 'the Church's constant preoccupation with the delicate question of property ownership'. He compared the growing affluence of a few people with the growing poverty of the masses and observed, 'It is then that the Church's teaching, which says that there is a *social mortgage* on all private property, takes on an urgent character.' [Author's italics.]

Before yet again powerfully describing the 'massive increase in violations of human rights in many parts of the world', he again reminded them of the solution. 'We will reach human beings; we will reach justice through evangelisation.'

The Pope finally addressed the vexed issue of Liberation Theology. He could not bring himself to mention it by name and resorted instead to Vaticanese:

'Pastoral commitments in this field must be nurtured with a correct Christian conception of liberation. The Church . . . has the duty of proclaiming the liberation of millions of human beings . . . the duty of helping to bring about this liberation.'

He was quoting directly from Paul VI's Apostolic Exhortation, *Evangeli Nuntiandi*, and continued with Paul's warning:

'. . . but it also has the corresponding duty of proclaiming liberation in its deeper fuller sense, the sense proclaimed and realised by Jesus. That fuller liberation is "liberation" from everything that oppresses human beings, but especially liberation from sin and the evil one, in the joy of knowing God and being known by him . . .'

'There are many signs,' he continued,

'that help us to distinguish when the liberation in question is Christian and when, on the other hand, it is based on ideologies that make it inconsistent with the evangelical view of humanity, of things, and events. The content proclaimed by the would-be evangeliser was a good guide. Was it faithful to the Word of God? To the Church's living tradition? And most tellingly to its magisterium? To its ultimate Papal authority?'

From the position of an autocratic Catholic hierarchy, it was a skilful, deliberate and brilliant attack on Liberation Theology; all the more so for never naming the 'enemy'. It came from a man who believed and believed deeply that Marxism could not be defeated but it might perhaps be contained within certain already heavily infected areas such as Eastern Europe. The Pope did not understand that Marxist ideas in Latin America were not those he had lived with in Poland for so many years. He failed to acknowledge that the founder of Liberation Theology had totally rejected any linkage with Marxism. Even if he had, he would almost certainly have maintained his attack. Anything that appeared to challenge the authority of the Church, which ultimately was *his* authority, was 'the enemy'. His final words on the subject were a direct warning to his listeners against political activism.

> '*Secular duties and activities belong properly, although not exclusively, to laymen. It is necessary to avoid supplanting the laity, and to study seriously just when certain ways of substituting for them retain their* raison d'être. *Is it not the laity who are called, by virtue of their vocation in the Church, to make their contribution in the political and economic areas and to be effectively present in the safeguarding and advancement of human rights?*' [Author's italics.]

Karol Wojtyla was widely regarded throughout his Papacy as one of the twentieth century's great communicators. His output was prodigious: millions of words spoken and written, sermons, encyclicals, books, videos, records. How much of that output was clearly understood, however, is debatable. While it was eagerly anticipated, his speech at Puebla bemused and confused many within his wider world audience. It gave delight to Pinochet and the other military dictators and their death squads throughout Latin America. It thrilled the Communist regimes in Europe, particularly in his native country where First Secretary Gierek broke out the champagne as he read in his Warsaw daily,

'Pope John Paul II has underlined that the clergy's task is to work in the religious field and not to engage in politics, so the Church is not a social movement but a religious movement.'

The Communist media's collective interpretation of the speech was precisely the same as that of the majority of the secular press. In the words of the *New York Times* editorial of 30 January, the Pope had 'rejected political involvement, let alone action, by the Church . . . and spoken out flatly against the concept of "Liberation Theology".' Among the laymen who shared this take on the speech were some of the men gathering around Ronald Reagan, the governor of California. These insiders would become known as Reagan's 'kitchen cabinet', the steering committee planning his campaign for the 1980 Presidential elections. The Catholic vote was always important and, based on their interpretation of the Pope's comments at Puebla, Ronald Reagan and his advisors concluded that he was a man they could do business with.

There were two fundamental reasons for the Pope's hostility to Liberation Theology. Firstly, his knowledge of Latin America, his views, his prejudices, were entirely shaped and fashioned by his Vatican advisors, deeply conservative men who overwhelmingly desired that the status quo that existed in much of the continent should continue. The Catholic Church's accommodations with the ruling juntas, as Archbishop Romero of El Salvador had observed, suited the majority of bishops well. 'They believe in the security that gives them privileges, or that renders them apparent respect.' Secondly, these same men also suffered from a deep paranoia that extended to the higher reaches of the Vatican offices of the Secretariat of State, where there was a widely-held belief that countries such as Mexico were on the brink of 'a radical and anti-religious revolution'.

Attempting to sweeten his strictures on Liberation Theology, the very next day after his Puebla speech the Pope delivered a startlingly radical message at Oaxaca, in southern Mexico, to an audience largely composed of poor native Indian peasants and workers. Their conditions of life were typical of the overwhelming majority of the 320 million people of Latin America. Estimates of their number ranged from 25,000 to over 500,000 depending on which spin doctor was supplying the count. Their case was presented to him by a Zapotecan peasant named Esteban Fernandez who had been chosen to greet the Pope on behalf of his fellow Indians: 'We welcome you and we greet you with joy,' he began. Then, looking directly at the Pope, he continued,

'We're suffering a lot. The cattle are better off than we are. We can't express ourselves and we have to keep our suffering locked up inside our hearts. We don't have jobs, and nobody helps us. But we're putting what little strength we have at your service. Holy Father, ask the Holy Spirit for something for your poor children.'

The crowd were cordoned off behind wire netting. Many could not understand Wojtyla's Spanish, and some grew restive and began to walk away as Wojtyla talked of 'the Church's universal concern' and his admiration for their way of life. 'We love your people, your culture, your traditions. We admire your marvellous past, we encourage you in the present and we have high hopes for your future.' Expressing his desire to be the 'voice of the voiceless' he began to list the rights of Mexico's indigenous peoples. 'The right to be respected; the right not to be deprived; the rights for barriers of exploitation to be destroyed; the right to effective help.' To achieve these rights it would be 'necessary to effect bold transformations'. He now had their undivided attention. No one in a position of any significant authority had ever said to these poor wretched people that their homelands should be returned to them. 'For the Christian it is not enough to denounce injustice. He is called upon to be a witness and agent to justice.'

He called out for action, but not from the Church and not from the Mexican Indians. The action must come from those who 'are responsible for the welfare of nations, powerful classes . . . those who are most able'. Meanwhile those who were suffering must 'not harbour feelings of hate or violence, but rather gaze toward the Lord'. This call to arms was certain to be ignored by the ruling elites of Latin America. The Papal solution was fanciful but at least the Pope had accurately and publicly identified some of the dreadful problems that bedevilled the continent.

After his return to the Vatican in early February, the consensus around the Pope was that the trip had been an overwhelming success. Estimates put the total number of people who had turned out to hear or just to see the Pope at five million.

Among his listening audience at Puebla the eventual response was less than effusive. The only unqualified praise came from the bishops who were supporters of the status quo, whether the Mexican version of democracy or General Pinochet's. Among the liberal cardinals, men like Aloisio Lorscheider and Paulo Arns of Brazil who had helped get Wojtyla elected, there was dismay. How right Wojtyla had been to remark, soon after the Conclave, 'The eminent cardinals who elected me did not realise what sort of man they had elected.' They were rapidly finding out.

Karol Wojtyla had begun work on his first encyclical immediately after being elected. It was published in March 1979. *Redemptor Hominis* – The Redeemer of Man – was the summation of thirty years' work on its central subject, an analysis of the human condition or as the Pope would later describe it 'a great hymn of joy for the fact that man has been redeemed through Christ – redeemed in spirit and body'. Its inherent joy is one of the encyclical's most appealing elements but to attempt a detailed analysis of such an all-encompassing subject with a mere 24,000 words, even with the aid of a host of Vatican archivists, and several in-house ghostwriters, shows a staggering self-confidence. The result did not meet with total acclaim in the Catholic press. One reviewer's response was typical: 'The Pope is not, on the basis of this translation, a polished writer, even a cohesive thinker. The encyclical is patched together in parts . . . Hope, optimism, strength and the other personal qualities of the Pope exude from this state-ment, but it nonetheless contains enough abrupt stops, lack of continuity of thought and elements of "old fashioned" thought to give theologians, liturgists, intellectuals and commentators plenty to write about and some things to complain about. The sexist language warrants such com-plaint.'

Within the document the Pope ranged far and wide, writing of the need for human rights, freedom of religion, his own experiences in Poland, and a powerful condem-nation of the arms race. Throughout the document he pitted the Church against the secular world, the individual against the community, spirit against matter, Christian against humanist and the supernatural against the natural world. The encyclical was fundamentally an impassioned plea for Catholics to put Christ at the centre of their lives. Within it the Pope paid tribute to the man he had followed.

'I chose the same names as my beloved Predecessor John Paul I. Indeed, as soon as he announced to the Sacred College on 26 August 1978 that he wished to be called John Paul – such a double name being unprecedented in the history of the Papacy – I saw in it a clear presage of grace for the new pontificate. Since that pontificate lasted barely thirty-three days, it falls to me not only to continue it but in a certain sense to take it up again at the same starting point. This is confirmed by my choice of these two names.'

Those words stood in sharp contradiction to Wojtyla's actions. To have continuity would have required him to have implemented the changes and initiatives frustrated by Albino Luciani's murder. Every single one was rejected by the man who now claimed to be continuing the Luciani programme.

The same week that the encyclical was published Cardinal Jean Villot died. As *Camerlingo* – acting head of the Church – he had orchestrated the cover-up after the murder of John Paul I. He removed items from the Papal bedroom, the medicine by the bedside, the notes concerning the Papal transfers and appointments from the dead Pope's hands. He also removed the smoking gun – the Vagnozzi report. He had imposed a vow of silence on the Papal household on the discovery of the body and substituted an entirely fictitious account for public consumption. He had arranged for a series of 'off the record' conversations to take place. Trusted members of the Curia phoned press contacts and weaved a concoction of lies about the late Pope's health. So well was this operation performed that even today, despite the true chapter and verse on Albino Luciani's health being available, the same old lies are parroted by the duped.

In Villot's place as Secretary of State Karol Wojtyla appointed Archbishop Casaroli, the man who with Paul VI had created the Vatican's version of *Ostpolitik*, the cultivation of good working relationships with the Eastern bloc. Casaroli and the late Pope had achieved considerable success in a number of areas, not least in Poland. At the time of Paul's death the Vatican had been close to establishing diplomatic relations with Poland. Now with the man from Cracow at the helm, a question mark concerning future relations with the Eastern bloc in general had appeared.

It had become very clear within hours of Wojtyla's election that, in certain areas at least, this was going to be a hands-on papacy. Above all, Wojtyla wanted to take personal charge of foreign policy. And the key to that was, in his mind, Poland.

Old hands in the Curia had noted with interest the rising excitement among the group that had travelled to Mexico as part of the papal entourage. In late February the Papal Apartments were again buzzing with expectation. After very delicate negotiations between the Vatican, the Polish government and the Polish Church, the next overseas trip had been finalised: Poland. All parties in the negotiations were acutely aware that the Soviet Union was watching closely. Commenting on the atmosphere, one senior member of the Curia recalled,

'We rapidly realised that these preparations for the various overseas trips and indeed the immediate days after the Holy Father had returned represented excellent opportunities. If there was a difficult problem or an awkward decision to be taken, these were the best of times to get it resolved. There was such euphoria and excitement during those periods, he would sign anything and agree to the most surprising suggestions.'

The Pope had wanted to be in Poland to celebrate the feast of St Stanislaw on 8 May. It would be the 900th anniversary of his martyrdom. A Polish pope wished to stand on the soil of his homeland and pay due honour to a patron saint who had been one of the founding fathers of the Polish Church and the Polish nation, a man slaughtered for refusing to yield to a despotic ruler. The symbolism in the current context of the country was all too obvious. Brezhnev and the other members of the Soviet Politburo believed in the 'domino theory' as strongly as the Americans. They merely differed as to the identity of the dominoes. If one Communist state fell to Western democracy and 'capitalism', the others could fall in sequence. Poland had been the most likely first domino for some time and that was before a Polish pope entered the equation.

After long haggling, it was agreed that instead of coming for two days in May the Pope would come for nine days in June. Six cities would be visited instead of two. The Communists had lost the first set comprehensively. Soon after that had been agreed, Cardinal Wyszynski announced that the Polish episcopate would be extending the anniversary celebrations for St Stanislaw for a further month. They would now conclude on 10 June which by some extraordinary coincidence would be the final day of Wojtyla's visit.

The Pope wanted to visit the shrine of the Virgin Mary in Piekary, something he had done regularly while resident in Cracow. This particular shrine is in Silesia, the personal domain of First Secretary Gierek and he did not want the Pope on his patch. The Pope was also blocked from going to Nowa Huta. The regime retained bitter memories of Wojtyla's involvement with this purpose-built monstrosity of a town on the outskirts of Cracow that consisted of enormous blocks of flats that resembled filing cabinets reaching to the sky. The town lacked, very deliberately, a church. It was an omission that brought the then Bishop Wojtyla to an open field to say Holy Mass on a freezing Christmas Eve in 1959. He returned every subsequent year and continuously petitioned the regime for permission to build a church. Upon Wojtyla's promotion to Cardinal in June 1967, the regime as part of its strategy to cause dissension between Wojtyla and the Polish Primate Wyszynski promptly granted planning permission for the new church. The blissfully ignorant Wojtyla saw the permission as a personal triumph.

To allow the Pope to visit Nowa Huta and say Mass in the church was never an option. The media coverage was another subject of long and intense debate. These particular negotiations went down to the wire and were not resolved until very shortly before the papal visit began. While the Polish Church demanded television coverage and media access of a kind denied for thirty years, Gierek and his government faced pressure to ban television coverage from his neighbours, Romania, Czechoslovakia and still-Soviet Lithuania, where people could pick up Polish television. Eventually, the government reasoned that the more television coverage they gave the tour, the more chance there was of reducing the crowds. They agreed to national television coverage of the arrival and departure and certain other specified events, while other parts of the trip could be covered by regional television and radio. Crowd management throughout the trip was left entirely to the Catholic Church.

Among the regime's hardline faction there was discussion that the papal trip should be sabotaged. A variety of disruptions were considered including leaking information from the secret polices files that would cause the Vatican considerable embarrassment. It was argued that to reveal the truth of the Pope's wartime activities, of his work on behalf of the Third Reich, of just how 'good' a war he had experienced, of his failure to join the armed resistance might well put a severe spoke in the wheels of the Wojtyla bandwagon. Others recalled the scandal of the 1965 'forgiveness letter' that Wojtyla had drafted with the assistance of two other Polish bishops. The letter, addressed to all German bishops, was an invitation to attend celebrations of Poland's Christian millennium in 1966. It had caused deep offence and outrage in Poland because Wojtyla had attempted to open 'a dialogue at the level of bishops' to resolve the issue of the German territory east of the Oder and Neisse rivers that had been taken from Germany and given to Poland as compensation for the loss to the Russians of a vast tract of East Poland. Having in earlier passages of the letter detailed a number of the horrors that had been perpetrated upon Poland by Germany during the Second World War, including the murder of more than 'six million Polish citizens mainly of Jewish origin', the letter writers had in their final paragraph declared: 'We forgive and we ask for forgiveness.' The national anger within Poland at the letter was not confined to the Communists: many of the Catholic faithful were equally appalled. It was a situation that Wojtyla did nothing to alleviate. To the bitter end of a controversy that ran on for months, he angrily denounced those who had criticised him; he saw himself as a man who had been deeply wronged. In the end, however, First Secretary Gierek, having learned of what was being discussed, stamped out the suggestions of the hardliners.

In the weeks leading up to the June visit, euphoria and excitement filled the Vatican. On 8 May Wojtyla issued an apostolic letter from Rome, *Rutilans Agmen – Glowing Band* – to the entire Polish Church. Stanislaw's martyrdom was one of that glowing band of witnesses from which the Church had drawn its strength over the centuries and it was still 'at the root of the affairs, experiences, and truths' of the Polish nation. Polish nationalism was again on display eight days later when the Polish Primate, Wyszynski, arrived in Rome along with over 6,000 Polish expatriates from around the world for a solemn commemoration of the saint's anniversary. Two days later Wojtyla and Wyszynski led the thirty-fifth-anniversary commemoration of the Second World War Battle of Monte Cassino, in which Polish forces along with British troops took what was left of the ruined Benedictine monastery after a bitter five-month siege. Having avoided the political arena for most of his life, Pope Karol Wojtyla was making up for lost time and a splendid opportunity to assume a political role awaited him in his homeland.

He had left Poland as a Cardinal unknown by the wider world: he returned eight months later in June 1979 as one of the most recognisable people on the planet. John Paul II walked down the steps of the Alitalia plane and, continuing the gesture first demonstrated in Mexico and the Dominican Republic, knelt and kissed the ground. At that moment church bells began to peal throughout Poland as Wojtyla rose and joined the Polish President, Henryk Jablonski and Cardinal Wyszynski. Their statements of welcome were brief but polite. In response Wojtyla thanked both men and then stared directly at the welcoming crowd.

'Beloved brothers and sisters. My dear fellow countrymen. I greet you on this special day with the same words I used on October 16th last year to greet those present in St Peter's Square. "Praised be Jesus Christ!" '

Nine days of freedom had begun. His progress was fascinating, causing the Communist party daily newspaper *Trybuna Ludu* to observe, 'It is hard to tell where pastoral work stops and politics begin.' Nonetheless the Communist regime maintained its schizophrenic attitude to the Church throughout the visit, by turns relaxed and repressive. It ordered television crews to hold the Pope in a tight close-up shot to blank out the hundreds of thousands lining the streets of Warsaw as he drove into the city and the million-plus gathered to hear him say Mass. Against this absurdity, the regime generously provided helicopters to fly the Pope around the country, kept the security forces in the background at all times and made no attempt to prevent the huge crowds.

Hours after his arrival he stood in the rebuilt Cathedral of St John, which had been totally razed to the ground after the Warsaw Uprising in 1944. The Poles had fought for each pew, for each foot of the aisle against the German forces. Mixing nationalism with fundamental Christianity, the Pope reminded his congregation of that epic courageous battle against terrible odds, made even worse when Stalin denied the Poles help from the Red Army or the allied forces. At the papal reference to the destruction of Warsaw and 'the wait to no avail for help to come from the other side of the Vistula' (a direct reference to the Soviet Union and her forces) there was an instant reaction among the members of the Politburo watching the television transmission in Party Headquarters. Stanislaw Kania, a senior member of the Politburo, telephoned the Chairman of State Television and ordered him to fade out the microphone covering the Pope. Maciej Szczepanski refused to carry out the order. Realising there would be a political fall-out, he advised First Secretary Gierek of his refusal. Gierek, the fully committed Communist, congratulated him: 'You did very well, Maciej. Do your job as you have done so far.' It was a quintessential Polish moment.

Happily oblivious, the Pope continued his seditious path. 'To be in this rebuilt cathedral is to be reminded of what Christ once said: "Destroy this temple and in three days I will raise it up." '[8] Then he slipped in some politics:

'Salvation history is not something that happened in the past; salvation history is the dramatic context in which Poland has continued to live out its national life. Does not our tradition recall Stanislaw once saying to King Boleslaw "Destroy this Church, and Christ over centuries will rebuild it"?'

Wojtyla and his congregation all knew the modern equivalent of the historic oppressor. Later the same day he met several representatives of the oppressor at the Belvedere Palace, the official residence of the Polish President. Wojtyla and Wyszynski exchanged formal pleasantries with President Jablonski and First Secretary Gierek. The Pope moved the conversation on. He talked of the need for 'voluntary collaboration' and the need to end 'all forms of economic or cultural colonialism'. He claimed that the Church did not 'desire privileges', just the freedom to 'carry out its evangelical and moral mission'.

'Permit me to continue to consider Poland's good as my own, and to feel my sharing in it as deeply as if I still lived in this land and were a citizen of this state . . . Permit me to continue to feel, think, and to hope this and to pray for this.'

The nine days rapidly took on all the trappings of a triumphal tour. Warsaw gave way to Gniezno, a small town with a population of just 58,000 where a further million Poles were there waiting for him. Here again he mixed nationalism, politics and fundamental Christianity in his speech. Stressing the importance of religious education for children, he compared its denial to child abuse and quoted St Luke: 'It were better for him that a millstone were hanged about his neck, and he cast into the sea, than he should offend one of these little ones.'

Gniezno gave way to two days in Czestochowa and the Shrine of the Black Madonna and yet another million pilgrims. Then came four days in his 'beloved Cracow' and some of the surrounding areas including his birthplace, Wadowice. Karol Wojtyla had lived in Cracow for forty years, fourteen of them as Archbishop. He had stood at the head of a vast, rambling archdiocese which had more than one and a half million Catholics. Helping Wojtyla attend to their needs both spiritual and temporal had been 1,500 priests, a similar number of nuns and brothers and some 200 seminarians. Ranged against this force was the Communist state who, unknown to Wojtyla, was very eager to please him. And now that he was Pope, however, the regime was confronted with the reality of its own creation, moving millions of countrymen and women in a way that it would never be able to move them. It is the greatest irony of Karol Wojtyla's life story that without Communist intervention he would never have become Pope. Returning to his birthplace would also return Wojtyla to the dark heart of Poland's recent history.

Many others apart from the power players within the Church hierarchy had played a role. As the Pope moved around Cracow he met a number from his past and reminders of others no longer among the living – his French teacher, Jadwiga Lewaj, who ensured Wojtyla gained a job at Solvay and an identity card that declared the bearer was employed in work that was vital to the Third Reich's war effort. The President of the Solvay plant, Henryk Kulakowski, and his Director of the Cracow operation, Dr Karl Föhl, went out of their way to employ and protect nearly a thousand people, a considerable number of undergraduates and graduates. These individuals were seen by Kulakowski and Föhl as part of Poland's future. They reached out and offered sanctuary not only to such potential high flyers but also to a variety of waifs and strays who would otherwise have been drafted into slave labour followed by an early death. There would be no post-war recognition for two very brave and courageous men. They were accused by some of the Communists working at Solvay of being collaborators and shipped to their deaths in the Soviet Union. The fact that everyone who had worked at the Solvay plant during the war was a collaborator was ignored.

The Solvay plant was still functioning at the time of the Papal visit in 1979, its railway track still a vital element. During the war years that had been the reason that the Nazis had put such a high value on the Solvay plant: the railway line and station located at the heart of the Solvay works at the Cracow suburb of Borek Falecki. Many people would claim after the war had ended and the full horror of the Holocaust was exposed to the world that they did not know, had no idea, did not for a moment imagine that genocide was on the Third Reich's agenda. No one living in Cracow could use such excuses. The trains ran through the city. The railway line that ran through the Solvay works, the line that was considered vital to the German war effort as it carried troops, supplies and munitions to the Eastern Front, also ran through the Solvay works heading west towards Auschwitz, an equally vital requirement to ensure that another part of the Third Reich's aspirations could be fulfilled, namely the Holocaust. Professor Edward Görlich, who worked in the Solvay laboratory and became a good friend of Karol Wojtyla, is insistent that, above everything that the soda products could be used for, the reason the works had their *kriegswichtig* designation and were vital for the war effort was the existence of the railway line.

After Borek Falecki, the station for the Solvay works, there was only one stop travelling west: Auschwitz. The only way that the overwhelming majority of these wretched souls got out of Auschwitz was via the cremation chimney. When the wind blew from the west the citizens of Wadowice and Cracow rapidly came to recognise, after the Final Solution was put into action during the summer of 1941, the smell of burning human flesh.

With one exception, the entire experience for both the Pope and those who came to hear him, to pray with him, sing with him or just cheer was one of joy. The exception was his trip to Auschwitz. Huge crowds lined the road as the Pope's convoy drove to the camp. He got out and walked through the gates with their infamous exhortation *Arbeit macht frei* – Work Makes You Free. He continued down the neatly-kept gravel paths deeper into the camp until he came to Block 11 where he entered Cell 18. One of its previous occupants had been Father Maximilian Kolbe. He had volunteered to take the place of a married man, knowing that by doing so he would die.

The Pope knelt in prayer and contemplation as he had many times before in earlier years. There was not a sound at that moment in Auschwitz. He kissed the cement floor where Kolbe's life had ebbed away, then left a bouquet of flowers and an Easter candle. Outside this block was the 'Wall of Death'. Before praying at the Wall with the West German Cardinal Hermann Volk, the Pope met and embraced seventy-eight-year-old Franciszek Gajowniczek whose life had been saved by Father Kolbe's self-sacrifice. Among those who were executed by firing squad were men that Wojtyla had known – the group picked up at random from a Cracow café one afternoon, the Salesian priests at his local church, his good friend and fellow seminarian Szczesny Zachuta who was shot after being caught helping Jews obtain baptismal certificates to save them from deportation and death. Evidently no one either knew or had told Wojtyla any of this before his visit. He certainly made no reference to these events.

Continuing the journey through the ultimate nightmare, Karol Wojtyla followed the railway tracks over which 1.2 million had been transported to their deaths. Here an altar had been built. The cross on the altar had a ring of barbed wire at the top and from one of the crosspieces hung a replica of some of the striped sheeting used to make the camp uniforms. Among the congregation were elderly survivors of Auschwitz wearing their wartime prisoner clothing. The priest and bishops assisting the Pope at the altar were men who had survived wartime imprisonment in the camps. During his sermon Karol Wojtyla referred to his surroundings as this 'Golgotha of the modern world'. To those who might be surprised that he had come to this place 'built on cruelty' he explained simply:

'It was impossible for me not to come here as Pope. I kneel before all of the inscriptions that come one after another bearing memory of the victims of Oswiecim in their languages. Polish, English, Bulgarian, Romany, Czech, Danish, French, Greek, Hebrew, Yiddish, Spanish, Flemish, Serbo-Croat, German, Norwegian, Russian, Romanian, Hungarian, Italian and Dutch.

'In particular, I pause before the inscription in Hebrew. This inscription awakens the memory of the people whose sons and daughters were intended for total extermination. This people draws its origin from Abraham, our father in faith as was expressed by Paul of Tarsus. The very people that received from God the commandment, "Thou shalt not kill," itself experienced in a special measure what is meant by killing. It is not permissible for anyone to pass by this inscription with indifference.'

According to the Church's estimation, the Pope had been seen in person by more than one third of the entire national population, thirteen million Poles. Through television he had been seen by virtually the entire nation. For nine days the people had not been merely expressing their faith. Filling churches, gathering at sacred shrines, singing their traditional songs signalled a massive rejection of the regime and of Communism, and an expression of national pride in the Polish pope. After advising the bishops and priests of Latin America to stay out of politics, the Pope had delivered a very different message in Poland: stay *in* politics as long as you are fighting Communism. It was never expressed so directly but it was understood very clearly by Ronald Reagan, preparing his bid for the Presidency, and by Soviet Leader Leonid Brezhnev.

Edward Gierek and his Politburo breathed a collective sigh of relief as the papal entourage departed for Rome. They were encouraged to note in the passing days that there were no strikes, no demonstrations, no fire of counter-revolution sweeping the country. Very rapidly most visible evidence of the Pope's visit had vanished but the memories of those nine days remained burned into the very psyche of Poland. Above everything else in those nine days, Karol Wojtyla had succeeded in rekindling within the hearts and minds of many millions of Poles a personal dignity and the ability to hope.

The five-day tour of the United States by Karol Wojtyla in October 1979 resembled a rock group taking the country by storm. *Time* magazine called the Pope 'John Paul, Superstar'. Yet this was a superstar who still retained his initial deep reservations about the American way of life and the American people. He hypnotised many with his extra-ordinary charisma but the words he uttered were frequently in sharp contrast with the physical aura. The crowds were beguiled by the man, but many of those who actually listened and analysed his words were less impressed.

The American tour had got off on the wrong foot before it had even begun. In mid-September the Vatican announced that women were barred from distributing Holy Communion at a Mass to be celebrated by the Pope during his stay. The decision provoked an immediate and angry protest. There had been growing support for some years for all Church ministries to be open to women. Many nuns, expressing their ardent feminism, wanted a great deal more than acting as handmaidens during a Papal Mass. The papal critics would have been even more incensed if they could have been present when Bishop Paul Marcinkus in his role as tour stage-manager and papal minder discussed arrangements with US colleagues for the Mass. When they told him of the plan to have women assisting the Pope during the Mass, Marcinkus erupted. 'No broads. That's out.'

On 2 October, Karol Wojtyla addressed the UN General Assembly. In a powerful speech that had human rights as its central theme the Pope made constant reference to 'the fundamental document' that was the very keystone of the UN: the Universal Declaration of Human Rights. He talked of his recent trip to his homeland and, in particular, of his visit to Auschwitz, describing the death camps as 'a warning sign on the path of humanity today, in order that every kind of concentration camp anywhere on earth may once and for all be done away with'. 'The real genocide' that occurred in Auschwitz and the other death camps of the Second World War were 'the basic inspiration and cornerstone of the United Nations Organisation. The Universal Declaration was paid for by millions of our brothers and sisters.' He continued:

'. . . If the truth and principles contained in this document were to be forgotten or ignored and were thus to lose the genuine self-evidence that distinguished them at the time they were brought painfully to birth, then the noble purpose of the United Nations could be faced with the threat of a new destruction.'

Wojtyla condemned the modern continuation of

'the various kinds of torture and oppression, either physical or moral, carried out under any system, in any land; this phenomenon is all the more distressing if it

occurs under the pretext of internal security or the
need to preserve an apparent peace.'

For the papal biographer George Weigel the speech marked
the point 'at which the Catholic Church unambiguously
committed itself to the cause of human freedom and defence
of basic human rights as the primary goals of its engage-
ment with world politics'.

Shortly before his journey to Poland, Wojtyla had per-
emptorily removed all hope for a significant percentage of
the priesthood. In his Palm Sunday worldwide message to
priests he declared that celibacy was 'a special treasure' to
which the Latin Church would 'maintain fidelity'. He talked
of priests who 'do not simply have the power of forming
and governing the priestly people' but 'are expected to have
a care and commitment which are far greater and different
from those of the layperson'. In other European countries
and in the United States such views smacked to many of the
faithful as a curious form of religious elitism from a far-
gone age. For good measure, at much the same time the
Pope began wholesale rejection of requests from priests for
Laicisation – a papal dispensation releasing priests from
their sacred obligations and returning them to the lay state.

His attitudes to issues were often at odds with his calls for
universal human rights. Although he praised the various
roles of women in society and within the religious orders, he
simultaneously reiterated that the Vatican ban on the contraceptive pill and the refusal to countenance or consider
women entering the priesthood were non-negotiable issues.

He spoke often on his tours of the right to a living wage –
but did not apply it in the Vatican, where up to 4,000
workers had no trade unions and no democratic representatives. Early in 1974 a group of Vatican employees stating
they 'were in serious economic difficulties' had written to
Pope Paul VI.

These men and women had been notoriously underpaid for decades. Their letter began with the restatement of a fundamental truth.

'The figure of the Pope is the only example in the world by which the truth he preaches as head of the Church can be directly checked in his work as head of State.'

Injustice within the Vatican could, as the letter writers observed, be put right 'only by an act of sovereign justice'. Having made it clear that the Pope alone could answer their plea positively they continued:

'The principal motive in writing is the urgent necessity of solving the problem of the extremely low wages of the Vatican employees who, as always, without any right to speak are forced to ask softly in deaf ears that have no wish to hear them.'

The Vatican civil servants concluded with a reminder that the solution lay 'in a will to face these problems with – even before justice and honesty – a Christian conscience and, for this, it would be enough to recall what the Gospels say about "a just wage" which is essentially what we are asking for.'

Five years later, as John Paul II rose to begin a very long address to the United Nations on human rights, the Vatican staff were still awaiting a response.

On the final day of a tour that had appeared to have everything – except a single significant statement from women – the Pope was at the National Shrine of the Immaculate Conception in Washington. About to address a congregation very largely made up of 5,000 nuns, he was introduced by Sister Theresa Kane, in her official capacity as Administrator General of the Sisters of Mercy of the Union in the United States and President of the Leadership Conference of Women Religious News.

Sister Kane made it clear that she did not lack love or respect for the Holy Father.

> 'Our hearts leap as we welcome you . . . As women we have heard the powerful message of our Church addressing the dignity and reverence for all persons. As women we have pondered these words. Our contemplation leads us to state that the Church in its struggle to be faithful to its call for reverence and dignity for all persons must respond by providing the possibility of women as persons being included in all ministries of the Church.'

Dressed in everyday clothes, talking quietly, the diminutive figure had created an electric atmosphere. The Pope looked nonplussed and his hands, set for the customary modest acknowledgement of praise, fluttered unsurely. She drew his attention to the 'intense suffering and pain that is part of the life of many women in the United States'. 'As women,' she observed, 'we have heard the powerful message that the Church preaches about human rights.' Her pleas that these human rights should be extended to women provoked thunderous applause from the audience who clearly understood that she was not merely referring to women in religious orders or just to the issue of the ordination of women.

Her words touched many listeners both in the room and much further afield. By no means all agreed with her and in a subsequent quarter-page advertisement in the *Washington Post* many signatories apologised to the Pope for the 'public rudeness shown to him by Sister Theresa Kane' who 'was not only impertinent to the Holy Father but also offended the millions of us who love him and gladly accept his teaching'. However, an NBC poll taken on the eve of the papal visit suggested that Sister Kane did not lack for support. The poll showed that 66 per cent of American Catholics did not agree with the Church's position on birth control, 50 per cent dissented on abortion, 53 per cent on clerical celibacy, 46 per cent on the ordination of women and 41 per cent on papal infallibility.

Apart from provoking a national debate, Sister Kane had inspired a great many of the professional commentators who had covered the papal tour to assess it more realistically than they might otherwise have done. Critics considered, as the Pope had wrongly reaffirmed in *Time*, 'the thought that Christianity is a body of fixed beliefs rather than a faith that ought to be adapted to modern circumstances'. His defenders declared that Wojtyla was restating the basic truths of the Christian faith and that these could not be negotiated upon. Still others believed that Wojtyla was putting his own particular spin on the eternal truths, rewriting the Gospel according to John Paul II.

Newsweek's Religious Editor, Kenneth Woodward, writing on this occasion in the *National Catholic Reporter*, was one of many who struggled to come to terms with the Pope as his tour ended. On the positive side, he considered the speech on human rights at the UN showed the Pope at his best, though none of it would have been surprising to any who had read his encyclical published in March or were sufficiently aware of the Catholic tradition on humanism. Other positives included 'a quality which encourages other people to do deep down what they would like to do, namely throw off their pessimism, lethargy and narcissism and commit themselves to some form of service to other people'. Billy Graham's description of John Paul II as '*the* moral leader of our times' was for the *Newsweek* editor 'a comment more on the lack of quality of leadership'.

On the negative side, Woodward was devastating.

'He has set the ecumenical movement back a hundred years and that's conservative. It was evident that the man does not listen . . . It is not evident where he got his information about this country which was faulty. In New York he praised people for supporting the family structure, the opposite of what this country really does. I do not find him a warm person, particularly. I found his gestures with children stilted, the actions of an actor, not a grandfather.'

After listing other perceived failings in the Pope, Woodward concluded with an observation which many would come to share.

'What I found in the Pope's statements, and even in his manner, was a lack of empathy for Christians struggling to be good Catholics: married couples, facing the problem of birth control, or divorced people who found themselves in very difficult marriages.'

Such views were not confined to one well-informed and caring journalist; a great many observers were equally critical. Most tellingly, the Pope's critics had intuitively picked up his dismissal of America and all things American. Before the visit to the United States he had nothing but acclamation and adoration in Mexico, Poland and Ireland. Those heady experiences may have caused him in the USA to forget his lines and from time to time his performance. Like many an actor before him Wojtyla blamed his audience. Members of his personal entourage suggested on the flight home that the US tour had been the most superficial papal journey to date. Back in Rome he dismissed Sister Kane and her supporters. They were, he observed, 'irritated and embittered for nothing'. After a year in office, most observers felt that Pope John Paul II had strengthened the

Right with virtually everything he said. He was variously described as 'great box office' but also as 'a tank that crushed all opposition'.

By the middle of 1979 yet another threat to Bishop Marcinkus had emerged, this time not from Calvi but from Michele Sindona. The former 'saviour of the lira' had been fighting extradition from the United States to Italy since 1976 by every means at his disposal. These included putting out a contract for the murder of the assistant district attorney, John Kenny, the chief prosecutor in the extradition hearings. Sindona's Mafia friends attempted to explain to him that while killing a prosecutor in Milan might slow down a case, it usually had the reverse effect in New York. The $100,000 contract was tempting but there were no takers.

An additional problem for Sindona, and by association for Marcinkus and other Vatican Bank employees, was the investigation by the state liquidator of one of the Sindona Banks, Banca Privata Italiana. Giorgio Ambrosoli, like Emilio Alessandrini, was a courageous, incorruptible man. Appointed by the state in September 1974 he had by the end of May 1979 penetrated the entire criminal edifice that Sindona had so cleverly created.

The parking of shares, the buy-backs, the dazzling transfers through the myriad companies, the laundries, the illegal export of currency and, most importantly, the links that bound him to Calvi, Marcinkus and those other trusted men of the Vatican, Monsignor De Bonis, Massimo Spada, Luigi Mennini and Pelligrino de Strobel – all of these scams that Sindona had worked with the Vatican Bank had for years acted like a vast drain on the Italian lira. At any trial of Sindona in Italy Giorgio Ambrosoli would be the star witness. Before that he was destined to take on the same role when Sindona was tried in New York on ninety-nine counts of fraud, perjury and misappropriation of bank funds. The charges stemmed directly from the collapse of a Sindona bank, the Franklin First National, with losses in excess of $2 billion, at the time the biggest bank crash in American history.

On 9 June 1979, the judge who had been appointed to try the American case against Sindona had arranged for Ambrosoli to swear a deposition in Milan. On the same date William Arico, the man who had been paid to murder Ambrosoli, was also in the same city, staying at the Hotel Splendido with his five accomplices. Their weapons included an M11 machine gun fitted with a silencer and five P38 revolvers. Arico hired a Fiat car and began to trail Giorgio Ambrosoli. The first day of the deposition taking had gone very badly for Sindona's lawyers. They had hoped to demonstrate the absurdity of the charges that their client stood accused of in New York. Four years of work, over 100,000 sheets of meticulously prepared notes plus the mind of an exceptionally gifted lawyer began to reveal the appalling truth in front of a cluster of American lawyers.

Not knowing that he was being followed, Ambrosoli went on to another meeting – this time with the head of Palermo's CID, Boris Giuliano. The Sicilian police chief had recovered documents from the body of a Mafia enforcer, Giuseppe Di Cristina, a man who had worked for the families Gambino, Inzerillo and Spatola. The documents very exactly cross-referenced with a series of transactions indicating that Sindona had been recycling the proceeds from heroin sales on behalf of these Mafia families through the Vatican Bank to his Amincor Bank in Switzerland. After a lengthy discussion Ambrosoli and Giuliano agreed to a fuller meeting once Ambrosoli had finished his testifying to the US lawyers.

Later that day, Ambrosoli was still not finished with Sindona. He had a long telephone conversation with Lieutenant-Colonel Antonio Varisco, Head of the Security

Service in Rome. The subject was the matter Varisco was currently investigating, P2.

The following day as his deposition continued, Ambrosoli dropped one of a large number of bombshells. Detailing how the Banca Cattolica del Veneto had changed hands he stated that Sindona had paid a 'brokerage fee of $6.5 million to a Milanese banker and an American bishop' – Calvi and Marcinkus. By 11 July Ambrosoli had completed his deposition and it was agreed that he would return the next day to sign the record of his testimony and that the following week he would be available for questioning and clarification by the US prosecutors and Sindona's lawyers.

Shortly before midnight on the eleventh, Ambrosoli arrived outside his apartment. From the window his wife waved. They were about to have a belated dinner. As the lawyer moved towards his front door Arico and two of his aides appeared from the shadows. The question came out of the darkness.

'Giorgio Ambrosoli?'

'Si.'

Arico aimed at point blank range and at least four bullets from the P38 entered Ambrosoli's chest. He died instantly.

By 6.00 a.m. Arico was in Switzerland. One hundred thousand dollars was transferred from a Sindona account at Banca del Gottardo into an account of Arico's in the name of Robert McGovern at the Credit Suisse in Geneva. The account number was 415851–22–1.

On 13 July 1979, less than forty-eight hours after the murder of Giorgio Ambrosoli, Lieutenant-Colonel Antonio Varisco was being driven in a white BMW along the Lungotevere Arnaldo da Brescia in Rome. It was 8.30 a.m. A white Fiat 128 pulled alongside. A sawn-off shotgun appeared through its window. Four shots were fired and the Lieutenant-Colonel and his chauffeur were dead. One hour later the Red Brigades 'claimed' responsibility.

On 21 July 1979, Boris Giuliano went into the Lux Bar in Via Francesco Paolo Di Biasi in Palermo for a morning coffee. The time was 8.05 a.m. Having drunk his coffee, he moved towards the cash desk to pay. A man approached and fired six shots into Giuliano. The café was crowded at the time. Subsequent police questioning established that no one had seen anything. No one had heard anything. Boris Giuliano's position was taken by Giuseppe Impallomeni, a member of P2.

The killing, like the murder of Ambrosoli, had bought Marcinkus and his Vatican cronies more time, and this meant more money. They were left free to concentrate on the four-day meeting on the Church's cash crisis to which the Pope had summoned every cardinal in November.

Unfortunately, or perhaps fortunately, their activities in the Vatican Bank had no impact on the Church's general finances. The Vatican Bank, or IOR, is the Pope's bank and all profits derived from that source go directly to the Pope for him to use as he sees fit. No accounts covering the operation of the Vatican Bank are ever published. Any figures made public that declare yearly positions always specifically exclude the Vatican Bank.

The November meeting of all the cardinals had been called at very short notice and disrupted the plans of many people. It was not a good way to deal with a range of issues from Church finances to Curial reform needing detailed preparation. The only attendee who did not cancel previous engagements was the man who had called the meeting. The Pope absented himself for much of one of the four working days to spend time with Rome's railway workers. There was nothing unusual in this behaviour. His indifference to time, his unpunctuality and his total unawareness of the inconvenience he frequently caused others, had been well known in Cracow.

During his opening address to the cardinals the Pope very largely confined himself to generalities. 'It is obvious that the Church's possibility of offering economic contributions in relation to the many different needs in the various parts of the world is limited.' Then with an eye towards greater contributions from the wealthier countries he continued, 'Here one should also stress that this solidarity of the Church *ad extra* demands solidarity from within.' A few moments later he returned to this theme. 'In this field, the "rich and free" Church, if one may use such an expression, has enormous debts and commitments toward the "poor and constricted" Church, if one may use these expressions as well.'

Near the end of his speech the Pope again commented on the third topic to be discussed.

'Bearing in mind the different fields of the Apostolic See's activity, which had to be developed in relation with putting the council into practice and in relation with the Church's present tasks in the sphere of evangelisation and of service to people in the spirit of the Gospel, it is necessary to formulate the question of economic resources. In particular the Sacred College has the right and duty to have exact knowledge of the present state of the matter.'

The factual 'present state of the matter' would have included details of why men were being slaughtered in Milan, Rome and Palermo to protect the Vatican Bank, but this was not revealed to the cardinals. Truth and facts were in extremely short supply during the ensuing discussions on the Holy See's finances, as can be gauged by Cardinal Krol's subsequent report on the meetings to the American bishops.

'The presentation of the financial situation of the Holy See evinced beyond a shadow of doubt that the

Catholic Church is indeed the Church of the poor. The report also evinced that the age of fables and myths, as the Holy Father noted in his concluding talk, is not something of the past.'

Where the Pope led, his cardinals dutifully followed. Consequently all accounts of Vatican wealth were dismissed as 'fables'.

One specific issue for the cardinals was the plight of the Vatican employees. As Cardinal Krol put it,

'Considering the number of employees in the Vatican is over 3,000, the majority of them lay people with family obligations, the Holy See would be irresponsible if it did not address itself to this financial problem, which affects the daily life of so many people.'

Krol continued,

'It should be noted that the total budget of the Holy See is less than the total budget of all Catholic institutions of some of the large dioceses [in the United States]. In fact, there are very likely some Catholic health-care or educational institutions which have higher budgets and higher resources.'

In 1979, the real financial position of the Holy See (as opposed to fables) was scattered among a number of different institutions. There was the Administration of the Patrimony of the Holy See (APSA), with its Ordinary and Extraordinary sections. The Ordinary Section demonstrated all the wealth of the various congregations, tribunals and offices. It specifically owned a great deal of the real estate of the papacy. In Rome alone this amounted to over 5,000 rented apartments. In 1979, its gross assets were over $1 billion.

The Extraordinary Section, the Vatican's other bank, was as active in its daily stock speculations as the IOR (the Vatican Bank so-called) controlled by Marcinkus. It specialised in the currency market and worked closely with Credit Suisse and the Société de Banques Suisses. Its gross assets at the end of 1979 were over $1.2 billion.

The Vatican Bank, which Marcinkus was running, had gross assets of over $1 billion. Its annual profits by 1979 were over $120 million, of which 85 per cent went directly to the Pope to use as he saw fit. One additional figure to put the 'fables' in context: at the end of 1979 the Catholic Church in West Germany alone received $2 billion from the state as their share of the annual church tax. By the end of 1979 the Vatican civil servants who had written directly to the Pope in March were still waiting for a reply. Although the Pope and Cardinal Krol had used the plight of the Vatican staff as a device to wring more money from the wealthier dioceses around the world, there had been no pay rise.

At the end of 1979 Pope John Paul II on his return from America first demonstrated his attitude to theologians who disagreed with his views. As a newly appointed bishop at Vatican Council II, Wojtyla had admired Hans Küng, a Swiss theologian who taught at the University of Tübingen in Germany. He had a highly gifted mind and, unusually for an advanced theologian, his writings were accessible and readily understandable. This was a man who had shaped an era of thinking within the Church at a crucial time. It was inevitable that the forward-reasoning Hans Küng would rapidly come into conflict with the authoritarian traditional position of Pope John Paul II. Küng did not accept without qualification the doctrine of papal infallibility and cited numerous examples of historic errors by the Roman Catholic Church. They ranged from 'the condemnation of Galileo' through to 'the condemnation of human rights and particularly freedom of conscience and religion'. Hans Küng believed that as a matter of urgency the Church should reconsider its ban on artificial birth control and he sought a Catholic Church that believed in democracy.

As Pope, Wojtyla expected unquestioning acceptance of his authority. He had never experienced life in a democracy and he made it clear from the beginning of his Papacy that he intended to exercise power, not share it. The Holy Office, or to give it its modern name, the Congregation of the Doctrine of Faith, announced that Küng would 'no longer be considered a Catholic theologian'. It left Küng free to teach, but he was no longer a Professor of Catholic Theology. He was in the wilderness, without the weight of authority. Hans Küng was not without supporters, unlike the French Dominican Jacques Pohier who had raised questions about Christ's resurrection and as a result lost his licence to teach or give public lectures in 1978. Küng's case became a *cause célèbre*, with protests at his silencing throughout Europe. In early January 1980 there was hope that the ban might be lifted but the gap between the theologian and the Vatican remained unbridgeable.

Meanwhile, John Paul II and the Curia had to deal with a dangerous outbreak of democracy in the Dutch Church. After Vatican Council II the Dutch had led the European Catholic Churches in introducing a wide range of democratic and enlightened reforms. They had reduced the distinctions between the priest and congregation; lay people, in particular women, helped prepare the liturgy and taught scripture and catechism classes; during Mass they assisted with the communion and frequently read from the Bible. Priests and nuns were organised into democratic councils that formulated recommendations to the Bishops; they led protests against the installation of new US missiles in Europe and opposed the dictatorships of the Third World. By the beginning of 1980 it was obvious that the Dutch style of Catholicism was a huge success. It had overtaken the Protestants as the largest religious group in the country.

However, there was a conservative minority within the country both among the laity and the clergy that had remained united in its disapproval of these activities. They were supported by elements of the Curia. Until the election of Wojtyla, these elements were in a minority and consequently without power. His election shifted that balance of power overnight. The Pope summoned the Dutch bishops to a specially convened synod. The meetings over a two-week period were attended by the Pope and senior members of the Curia. The Dutch bishops had been told at the outset by the synod's secretary, Father Joseph Lescrauwaet, that they were about to be exposed to 'the ministry of authority'. When that comment reached the Pope he recognised a kindred spirit and promoted Father Lescrauwaet to auxiliary bishop.

All of the changes that the Dutch bishops had introduced were banned while the traditional authority of bishop over priest and priest over laity was reasserted. Lay members of the Church were forbidden to take part in any of the activities and there was to be no involvement in political issues nor democratic councils. The control of the Dutch Church thus passed to the Curia who would approve or reject on leading issues. The seven Dutch bishops had been kept locked up until they signed the forty-six propositions repudiating the positions they had adopted since Vatican Council II. This was done in total secrecy. Attempting to justify what had occurred, the Pope told the journalists,

'I am sure you will understand that the Church, like all families, at least on certain occasions, needs to have moments of exchange, discussion and decision which take place in intimacy and discretion, to enable the participants to be free and to respect people and situations.'

Five years later the deep and widely-felt anger was still evident when the Pope visited Holland. There were many protests at the visit and some became violent as the Dutch Catholics felt that they along with their bishops had been humiliated. Hostile posters were everywhere to be seen. 'Move over John Paul. You're hiding Jesus,' read one. If the Pope had been dismayed when he stood alongside the diminutive figure of Sister Kane during his trip to America and listened to her calm, gentle plea for change, one can only wonder at his thoughts as he listened to blunt speeches of welcome. One missionary put a question directly to him. 'How can we have credibility in the preaching of the Gospel of liberation when it is being proclaimed with a pointed finger rather than an extended hand?' The Dutch hostility and the lack of warmth affected the Pope. He told the crowds that he understood their feelings but he left them still feeling profoundly humiliated while taking with him the conviction that what he had experienced on the trip had nothing to do with him and everything to do with a range of excesses triggered by Vatican Council II.

Sitting patiently in the Vatican during this episode was another bishop waiting for the Pope's attention. Again democracy was at the heart of this man's plight, not greater democracy within his Church but the total lack of basic democracy within his country.

Archbishop Oscar Romero was an unlikely candidate for heroic martyrdom. A quiet, conservative man from Ciudad Barrios in the mountainous south-east of El Salvador near the border with Honduras, he was born on 15 August 1917, the second of seven children. At the age of thirteen he already had a vocation for the priesthood and trained at a seminary in San Miguel before studying in the capital, San

Salvador, followed by a number of years in wartime Rome. Recalled to San Miguel by his bishop in January 1944, Romero became secretary to the diocese, a position he held for the next twenty-three years. By February 1977 he had slowly and unspectacularly worked his way up to become Archbishop of San Salvador. As he had not fully embraced all of the radical liberal changes of Vatican Council II, the consensus was that here was a safe pair of hands, a quiet man who would support the status quo in a country ruled by a right-wing military junta with the help of death squads. Aiding and abetting the military were the rich landowners and the overwhelming majority of the Roman Catholic bishops who assumed that Romero was one of their own.

Within a month of his new appointment, two events radically transformed the new archbishop. A crowd of protesting farm labourers and their families were brutally attacked by soldiers in the central square of the capital, virtually on Romero's doorstep. About fifty men, women and children, all unarmed, were gunned down for complaining about the corrupt election of the latest military dictator. The police cleared the square by firing into the crowd and then hosing away the blood. Then on 12 March 1977 a radical priest who was a friend of Romero's, Father Rutilio Grande, was murdered in Aguilares. Two of his parishioners were also killed, an elderly man and his seven-year-old grandson. Father Grande's crime had been his constant defence of the peasants in their battle for fundamental rights including their aspiration to organise farm cooperatives. Grande had publicly declared that the dogs of the large landowners ate better food than the *campesino* children whose fathers worked in their fields. On the night of the murders, Oscar Romero drove out of the capital to El Paisnal to view the three bodies. The country church was packed with Father Grande's congregation. They had lost their champion and the Archbishop saw a mute question in many of the eyes staring at him. His subsequent actions gave his answer; he would be their voice for as long as he drew breath.

Within the year more than 200 of those who had silently watched as Romero had walked into their country church were dead. As the carnage continued, over 75,000 Salvadorans were killed. One million fled the country, a further million were left homeless, in a country with a population of less than five million, over ninety-nine per cent Roman Catholics. There was no official enquiry into the murder of the three men at El Paisnal. The power to authorise such enquiries was of course in the hands of the perpetrators.

Romero went on the attack from the pulpit, from the radio stations not controlled by the government, with his pen, in every avenue open to him he accused, identified and entreated. He wanted to know where the 'disappeared' of El Salvador had gone. He wanted to know who controlled the death squads that murdered again and again with impunity. He asked who gave the soldiers who wandered the country-side their orders, who had sanctioned the army to kill on a whim, to slaughter without reason. He also organised a group of young lawyers in an attempt to bring some measure of justice to victims. Anyone protesting for better wages, a better standard of living, was invariably arrested and charged with subversion. The opposition at the time of the emergence of Archbishop Romero was in the process of forming itself into the Democratic Revolutionary Front, the FDR. It was a mixture of Christian Democrats, Social Democrats and Communists. The majority of the Communists would have had the greatest difficulty in distinguishing between Karl Marx and Groucho Marx but like their colleagues in the FDR they had a very clear idea of their enemy.

Soon after the murder of Father Grande and his two parishioners, Romero announced that as a gesture of solidarity with the preachings of Grande he would refuse to appear at any public ceremonies with army or government members until the truth surrounding the triple murders was officially established and until true social change had begun. It instantly made him the hero of the people and the enemy of the military junta and the politicians. Romero's homilies on the radio became essential listening. His voice reached into the furthest corners of the country and assured his listeners that he could not promise that the atrocities would cease but that the Church of the poor, themselves, would live on.

'If some day they take away the radio station from us . . . if they don't let us speak, if they kill all the priests and the bishop too, and you are left a people without priests, each one of you must become God's microphone, each one of you must become a prophet.'

All the while the US Carter administration was continuing to pump in military aid, while it simultaneously declared its whole-hearted commitment to human rights. In 1980 Romero wrote to President Carter pleading with him to halt the military aid because 'it is being used to repress my people'.

Instead the government-controlled press continued to attack him. With one exception his fellow bishops condemned him to Rome, accusing him of being in league with Communist elements, denouncing him for actively encouraging Liberation Theology. Their right-wing friends within the Vatican ensured that the Pope was kept fully briefed not just on the facts but also the accusations that so neatly touched certain Papal nerves. Before January 1979 Wojtyla had never been to Latin America and knew nothing about its real condition, relying heavily on briefings. Having lived under a Communist regime for so long, he was especially vulnerable to the suggestion that any critic of the establishment was an agent of Communism. The Pope read the reports that had been carefully screened by various Curial departments stating that Romero had been unduly influenced by the Liberation Theology movement, that there was a grave danger of the country falling to the Communists and that Marxism would replace the faith. After the Puebla conference in January 1979 when Archbishop Romero became aware of the campaign being waged against him, not only in his own country but within the Vatican, he requested an audience with the Pope.

His treatment by the Vatican was disgraceful. He was kept waiting for four weeks by men who pulled every trick in the book to ensure that he did not meet the Pope. They hoped that Romero would tire of waiting. They did not know the man. Eventually he was received by the Pope on 7 May 1979. He brought with him seven thick files of evidence that he had painstakingly collected for the interview. Romero, like many bishops at Puebla, had hoped that the Pope would publicly condemn the murder of priests and other religious and the massacres of the poor that were occurring in Latin America. They had left the Puebla conference very disappointed.

Clutching his bundles, Romero was ushered into the Papal presence. Romero began to paint a picture of his country: two per cent of the population owned sixty per cent of the land; eight per cent of the population received fifty per cent of the national income. Nearly sixty per cent of the population earned less than $10 per month; seventy per cent of children under five were malnourished. The majority of the rural population had work for just one third of the year. Romero showed the Pope photographs of murdered priests and mutilated peasants. He told him what was blindingly obvious: 'In El Salvador the Church is being persecuted.'

The Pope responded, 'Well, now don't exaggerate it. It is important that you enter into a dialogue with the government.'

'Holy Father, how can I enter into an understanding with a government that attacks the people? That murders your priests? That rapes your nuns?'

'Well, you must find common ground with them. I know that it is difficult. I understand very clearly how difficult the political situation in your country is but I am concerned with the role of the Church. We should not only be concerned with defending social justice and love of the poor; we should also be concerned with the danger of the Communists exploiting the situation. That would be bad for the Church.'

Romero continued: 'In my country it is very difficult to speak of anti-Communism because anti-Communism is what the right wing preaches, not out of love for Christian sentiments, but out of selfish concern to promote its own interests.'

The Pope cautioned Romero against using such specifics. His advice to his archbishop was to function as he himself had done in Cracow:

'I recommend that you apply great balance and prudence, especially when denouncing specific situations. Far better to stay with general principles. With specific accusations there is a risk of making errors or mistakes.'

It was obvious to Romero that the Pope had been heavily influenced by the negative and inaccurate reports sent to him by the bishops who preferred to dine with the military junta rather than break bread with the poor. Displaying total ignorance of the realities confronting Romero in El Salvador, the Pope talked of how much harder it had been in Cracow where he had been faced with a Communist government. Wojtyla talked of the importance of unity with fellow bishops thus comparing Polish clerical bitchiness with Romero's adversaries who regularly socialised with psychopaths who came to the dinner table fresh from murdering another group of protestors. It was not the Papacy's finest hour.

At the end of January 1980 Romero had a second audience with the Pope. Yet again he valiantly attempted to enlist the Pope as an ally. An outright condemnation from the Holy Father of the atrocities of the government of El Salvador would undoubtedly have an electrifying effect on the Catholic country. It would also reverberate in the larger world. Such pressure would certainly give the rulers of El Salvador and the rich landowners pause for thought. Again Romero had to make do with platitudes. The Pope concluded this second audience with a friendly embrace and the words, 'I pray for El Salvador every day.'

The Pope was fully aware before this second meeting with Romero that, apart from praying on a daily basis for El Salvador, plans to remove the Archbishop from his homeland and his people were nearly complete. Wojtyla had been persuaded by the right-wing cabal within the Vatican, including the then Prefect of the Congregation for the Doctrine of the Faith, Cardinal Franjo Seper, to 'reassign' Romero. It was the Vatican way: remove the 'problem' to another location and the problem ceases to exist. Less than two months later, on 24 March, Archbishop Oscar Romero was shot in the chest as he celebrated Mass in the Chapel of the Divine Providence Hospital in San Salvador. He fell to the floor and, before choking to death on his own blood, forgave his killer. Shortly before he was murdered, Romero had taken a few hours away from San Salvador to walk on a beach with a fellow priest. As he sat gazing out at the waves, he asked his friend, 'Are you afraid of death?' The friend, thinking to show Christian solidarity, assured Romero that, 'No, I'm not afraid.' 'Well, I am,' said Romero. 'I really am.'

It had been a professional contract killing ordered and paid for by Major Roberto D'Aubuisson, who was never charged with the murder. He and the Death Squad he controlled went on to kill many thousands of citizens. After his death D'Aubuisson was found guilty of the murder of the Archbishop by a United Nations Truth Commission. In 1999 the newly elected President of El Salvador dedicated himself to the memory not of Romero but of Roberto D'Aubuisson. The Pope never acknowledged Romero as a martyr and continued to give credence to the 'theory' put forward by Cardinal Trujillo that Oscar Romero was murdered by left-wingers wishing to provoke a revolt.

At the time of Archbishop Romero's murder an Italian judge in a letter to *Corriere della Sera* commented that clearly the Pope liked to travel and asked,

> 'Why did this travelling Pope not immediately set off for San Salvador to pick up the chalice that had been dropped from Romero's hands and continue the Mass which the murdered archbishop had begun?'

The Vatican response to the murder was minimal. The Pope confined himself to condemning the 'sacrilegious assassination' with his 'deepest reprobation', as reported in *L'Osservatore Romano*. To represent him at the Archbishop's funeral he sent Cardinal Ernesto Corripio Ahumada of Mexico. What happened at the funeral was narrated by Father James L. Conner, President of the Jesuit Conference in Washington, in *America* magazine.

'All went peacefully through a succession of prayers, readings, hymns until the moment in his homily when Cardinal Ernesto Corripio Ahumada of Mexico, the personal delegate of Pope John Paul II, began to praise Archbishop Romero as a man of peace and a foe of violence. Suddenly a bomb exploded at the far edge of the plaza, seemingly in front of the National Palace, a government building. Next, gunshots, sharp and clear, echoed off the walls surrounding the plaza. At first the Cardinal's plea for all to remain calm seemed to have a steadying impact. But as another explosion reverberated, panic took hold and the crowd broke ranks and ran. Some headed for the side streets, but thousands more rushed up the stairs and fought their way into the cathedral.

'As one of the concelebrating priests, I had been inside the cathedral from the start. Now I watched the terrified mob push through the doors until every inch of space was filled. Looking about me, I suddenly realised that, aside from the nuns, priests and bishops, the mourners were the poor and the powerless of El Salvador. Absent were government representatives of the nation or of other countries. The ceremony had begun at 11 a.m. and it was now after noon. For the next hour and a half or two, we found ourselves tightly packed into the cathedral, some huddled under the pews, others clutching one another in fright, still others praying silently or aloud.

'The bomb explosions grew closer and more frequent until the cathedral began to shudder. Would the whole edifice collapse? Or would a machine gunner appear in a doorway to strafe the crowd? A little peasant girl of about twelve named Reina, dressed up in her brown-and-white checked Sunday dress, clung to me in desperation and cried, "*Padre, téngame!*" ("Father, hold me!") We lived through that horror of bombs, bullets and panic – now dead bodies were being carried into the cathedral from outside – for nearly two hours. At certain moments one could not help wondering if we would all be killed.'

Such evil flourishes best in a culture of indifference. While the Archbishop was rapidly forgotten within the Vatican, his enemies flourished. One was Alfonso Lopez Trujillo. As the organiser of the Puebla Conference, Trujillo had been caught red-handed plotting to rig the outcome in favour of the extreme right faction among the bishops. Four years later John Paul II promoted Trujillo and he became a cardinal. In 1990 came further elevation when he was named President of the Pontifical Council for the Family. This important position entrusted Trujillo with carrying out the Pope's 'culture of life' campaign against artificial birth control and abortion. He came to be widely regarded as a favourite of the Pope's and considered a strong candidate should the next Conclave occur 'in the near future'.

By April 1980 the Secretariat of State was deeply immersed in the final planning stages of the Pope's next overseas trip, scheduled for the following month. It was a whirlwind tour of Africa where the Pope was set to make 50 major speeches in ten days as he visited Zaire, the Congo, Kenya, Ghana, Burkina Faso and the Ivory Coast. Meanwhile, Secretary of State Cardinal Casaroli was more concerned with the Pope's travelling companions and whether they would include Bishop Paul Marcinkus.

Michele Sindona's continuing fight to stay out of prison either in the United States or Italy had by early February

1980 looked perilously close to defeat. His New York trial was about to commence. The Vatican rallied to the Sindona cause. Bishop Marcinkus and Cardinals Caprio and Guerri had agreed to assist his defence counsel by swearing depositions on video. Intrigued by what these devout men might have to say about Sindona, the state prosecution had raised no objection to what was a very unusual gambit. It is normal for witnesses to have their statements tested under oath, in a courtroom, in front of judge and jury. Trial Judge Thomas Griesa, a man whom Sindona had so far failed to have murdered, instructed the defence lawyers to fly to Rome on 1 February. On the following day shortly before the depositions were to be sworn Secretary of State Casaroli intervened. There would be no depositions.

> 'They would create a disruptive precedent. There has been so much unfortunate publicity about these depositions. We are very unhappy about the fact that the American government does not give diplomatic recognition to the Vatican.'

Casaroli's decision was not of course based upon any of the formal objections that he had raised. It was based upon his realisation of the consequences of Sindona being found guilty after three high-ranking prelates of the Roman Catholic Church had all sworn under oath that he was pure as the driven snow. The three would be branded as liars and, more disturbingly, every Italian magistrate would demand the same co-operation from the Vatican.

That in turn would lead to a direct breach of the Lateran Treaty, which granted cardinals immunity from arrest in Italy. The next step after that would be a very public examination of Vatican Incorporated. That would inevitably lead to the Pope's bank.

Casaroli had shrewdly saved the Vatican at the eleventh hour. In doing so, he had overridden a decision taken by the Pope who had happily agreed to the request that Marcinkus and the others should tell the world how highly they regarded Michele Sindona.

On 27 March 1980, Michele Sindona was found guilty on sixty-five counts, including fraud, conspiracy, perjury, false bank statements and misappropriation of bank funds. After recovering from a failed suicide attempt, Sindona was sentenced on 13 June to twenty-five years' imprisonment and fined over $200,000.

Secretary of State Casaroli was aware that Pope John Paul I had been about to remove Bishop Paul Marcinkus at the time of his sudden death. He was also aware that, notwithstanding the evidence on the Bank and its array of criminal practices that had been available to him, John Paul II had declined to replace a man he continued to hold in high regard. Casaroli very discreetly talked to a contact within SISMI, the Italian Intelligence Service. He requested the fullest available information on Marcinkus and all of his business associates. While Cardinal Casaroli grappled with the Vatican Bank teetering on the edge of a public scandal others within the Vatican village had more prosaic concerns. A second letter arrived in the papal private apartment from some very exasperated employees.

'Holy Father, do you not believe that between one journey and another you might come to earth, materially and among us, to solve, among so many problems, the ones we have and which are your exclusive competence as Head of State? In the second millennium, with so much "progress", social justice, workers' unions, and Papal encyclicals, if we want our problems solved, we are forced to write to the Pope because all other roads are barred to us.'

In Africa during an inevitable meeting with Polish missionaries in Zaire, Wojtyla directly alluded to the disgruntled within the Vatican ranks.

'Some people think that the Pope should not travel so much. He should stay in Rome, as before. I often hear such advice, or read it in newspapers. But the local people here say "Thank God you came here, for you can only learn about us by coming. How could you be our pastor without knowing us? Without knowing who we are, how we live, what is the historical moment we are going through?" This confirms me in the belief that it is time for the Bishops of Rome to become successors not only of Peter but also of St Paul, who as we know could never sit still and was constantly on the move.'

During his trip to Brazil the Pope was taken through one of the *favelas* of Rio. Confronted with the poverty of the shanty town slums that were all around him the Pope took a ring from his finger and gave it to the local diocese. It had been given to him by Pope Paul VI when he named Wojtyla a cardinal. It undoubtedly had great sentimental value to Karol Wojtyla, but as a contribution to the problems that he could see around him, it provided little more than a moment of drama and a photo opportunity for the media.

Back at Vatican base, the Pope's 'own responsibilities' were still waiting for their own less public gesture. In their latest letter the Vatican employees had talked of obtaining from the Pope a measure of 'social justice'. It was a theme that the Pope used during his Brazilian tour. At São Salvador da Bahia, a region of the country that had been denied its share of central government funds for decades, he urged the haves of Brazilian society to do something about the have-nots. He called on the country's politicians, the wealthy, the privileged, the elite to build a 'social order based on justice'.

In the short term the overwhelming majority of the papal trips had great impact, with the crowds temporarily bonding with the man from the far country. But their long-term effect on the majority was minimal. The man was loved, the message ignored. The overwhelming majority of Roman Catholics have proved very resistant to the teachings of Pope John Paul II. A significant body of evidence confirms that they have in fact rejected his teachings on a number of key issues. As for getting to know 'the local people', a one-hour walkabout in a *favela*, a brief stop in São Salvador, a speech and a wave and on to the next name on the crowded itinerary is not merely irrelevant but superficial and patronising.

Karol Wojtyla was still in Brazil on 1 July 1980. On the same day in his beloved and deeply missed motherland, the Communist regime took a routine decision which triggered a series of momentous events. It announced new price increases for meat and other basic products.

Chapter 3

A Very Polish Revolution

The command economy of a centrally planned socialist system imposed on Poland from Moscow after the Second World War was in free fall long before 1980; yet the price increases for meat and basic foods on 1 July 1980 had immense significance for Poland. Meat prices had long ceased to be a mere matter of supply and demand. The price stability of meat and other foodstuffs had become the guarantee of socio-economic stability. It was the bottom line in a compact with the working class, an implicit promise that meat prices would be held at 1970 levels, but the compact went back earlier than that.

In Poznan in June 1956, the workers at the Stalin Engineering Works (invariably referred to by non-Communists as the Cegielski Works) took to the streets to protest at an economic situation that had been deteriorating for years and had now become unbearable. The ever-growing crowd held up rough home-made banners and placards that proclaimed 'Bread and Freedom'.

Tanks were brought out against the crowd. Machine guns began to spray the streets. It was two days before the city was calm again. At least fifty-four people had been killed and hundreds injured.

At the time, Poznan was the biggest confrontation that Communism had faced since the end of the Second World

War and to Poland it was a defining moment in the country's history. Apart from the deaths and the injuries there were the inevitable arrests and imprisonments; but the Communists learnt a basic truth: you can imprison a man but not the idea he has expressed.

On 12 December 1970, in the run-up to Christmas, First Secretary Gomulka went on television and radio to broadcast news of price increases. He blandly reassured the nation that the average increase would 'only be eight per cent' but as always with a politician, particularly a Communist politician, the devil was in the detail. The price of flour was to be increased by sixteen per cent, sugar by fourteen per cent and meat by seventeen per cent. On the following Monday 3,000 workers from the Lenin shipyards at Gdansk marched on the Communist Party Committee building in the city demanding the increases be withdrawn. Their demands were dismissed and they were ordered back to work. They were not in the mood to go quietly either to the docks or anywhere else. Furious crowds of workers began to roam the streets of Gdansk; the city militia could not control the situation and the general tumult grew.

The following day the protests spread to Gdynia, Szczecin and Elblag. The army and the police, acting under specific orders from Central Government, began machine-gunning the protestors, killing forty-three shipyard workers, and over 1,000 were injured, 200 of them seriously. Polish soldiers and armed police had yet again killed Polish workers although many, such as those murdered in Gdynia, had been attempting to obey the TV appeal of Deputy Prime Minister Stanislaw Kociolek to return to work. The army had been standing on the bridge near Gdynia Stocznia railway where the workers had to pass on their way to the Paris Commune Shipyard and they were prevented by the army from going to work. More workers arrived by the minute from the railway station; those at the

The young Karol Wojtyla with his parents, devout Catholics. The father was born in the same decade that the dogma of Papal infallibility was declared. A doctrine that was instilled into the Wojtyla children at a very early age

The Solvay Quarry. Through astute networking it proved a haven for Wojtyla. It was also the scene of the birth of one of the enduring myths surrounding the future Pope's war years

Karol Wojtyla *(third row from bottom far right)* performed in 'The Cavalier of the Moon' two months before the outbreak of the Second World War. His contemporaries believed they lost a potentially great actor but the skills that he displayed at this time would be put to very effective use in later life

Karol Wojtyla *(centre)* at the time of his ordination in November 1946. With him are fellow seminarians

'I am from a far country.' John Paul II on the day of his election

August 29, 1980. The Lenin shipyard, Gdansk. Lech Walesa and Bishop Henryk Jankowski. Revolution Polish-style

Revolution Polish-style two: riots on the streets. May 2, 1982

By early January 1981 Lech Walesa had become President of Solidarity and, after initially agonising, the Pope had climbed on board

Wojtyla, the armchair general, with Cardinal Stefan Wyszynski, the guiding light behind Solidarity

The Holy Alliance that never was

Talking to Cardinal Bernardin in 1985 Karol Wojtyla observed 'I do not understand why the (American) bishops do not support your President's policies in Central America'

Men such as Nicaraguan President Daniel Ortega were anathema to the Pope. It was a dialogue with the deaf

'Why did this travelling Pope not immediately set off for San Salvador to pick up the chalice that had dropped from Romero's hands and continue the Mass which the murdered Archbishop had begun?'

back unaware of the violence began impatiently to shuffle forward. At five minutes past six in the morning the army opened up with machine gun fire. Eighteen were killed in Gdynia that day, thirteen near the shipyard and five more in the streets. The youngest was fifteen, the eldest thirty-four.

Confronted with a country on the brink of national insurrection Gomulka was rushed to hospital on December 20 'suffering from a slight stroke' and Edward Gierek replaced him as First Secretary of the regime. While visiting a sick priest in a Cracow hospital, Karol Wojtyla heard of Gomulka's removal. Father Jan Jakubczyk recounted the statement he had heard from a radio bulletin. When he had finished, Wojtyla remained silent for a long time before observing, 'Indeed God acts in mysterious ways.'

God's Church had been absent in Gdansk, Gdynia, Szczecin and Elblag. Also missing from the barricades were the intellectuals. They stayed firmly behind doors in their polytechnics and universities. This was from first to last a protest by the workers. The Christmas holidays inevitably resulted in a temporary halt in the protests. Among those who had been given an opportunity to reflect was Primate Cardinal Wyszynski. Subsequently he spoke to Karol Wojtyla to ensure they were both going to preach the same sermon from the pulpit. For Wojtyla it would be something of a maiden political speech, the first time in public that he had uttered from a pulpit criticism of the Communist regime. Wyszynski appealed for extensive reforms and listed six basic rights that every Polish citizen deserved, including 'The right to truthful information. To free expression of views and demands. The right to food. To a decent living wage'. He made the various fundamental requests calmly and at the same time urged restraint on the workers. He was acutely aware that Poland's fate was on a knife-edge.

Wojtyla in Cracow also talked of the events on the Gdansk coast. 'These were tragic events. The measure of the tragedy which played itself out in these days is that Polish blood was shed by Poles!' He too listed the six demands: 'the right to food, the right to freedom . . . an atmosphere of genuine freedom, untrammelled and not questioned or threatened in any practical sense; an atmosphere of inner freedom, the freedom from the fear of what may befall me, if I act this way or go to that place or appear somewhere.'

The torch of protest in 1956 had been wrongly thought by both regime and Catholic Church to have been extinguished. Now it had reignited spontaneously in the shipyards and factories in 1970. The consciousness of the workers had risen and this time the events would not be airbrushed out of the nation's history. One young electrician in particular, a member of the Lenin Shipyard strike committee, was deeply committed to the cause of ensuring that the dead would be remembered; his name was Lech Walesa.

In June 1976 the Communist regime in Poland demonstrated that like Gomulka before them they had forgotten what happened when central government increased food prices. As a result, across the country workers went on immediate strike, the Baltic shipyards were once again occupied. Strike committees were formed.

From the Ursus tractor factory close to Warsaw several thousand workers gave the industrial action an international flavour. They marched to the transcontinental railway lines and stood in front of the Paris to Moscow express.

In Radom, to the southwest of the capital, the workers elected to stage a more traditional form of protest. In an action reminiscent of the initial protests in Poznan during 1956 strikers marched to the Communist party headquarters and set light to it. The same evening an apprehensive Prime Minister Jaroszewicz announced that the price increases had been withdrawn. But with police and security forces there is usually a payment to be exacted, particularly when a protest is successful.

This time in Radom and Ursus the workers were forced to run the gauntlets through two lines of truncheon-wielding 'comrades'. The police with the gallows humour beloved of police officers everywhere had called the gauntlet 'the path of health'. Severe fines and prison sentences were imposed by the courts and many thousands were fired but the prices stayed down. The Alice in Wonderland economics of Poland were allowed to stagger on. Prices remained frozen at the levels of 1967. The government continued to buy off workers with wage increases paid for with huge foreign loans. It had no hope of paying back these loans from export earnings since almost no one overseas wanted Polish cars or machine tools.

Unlike the protests of 1970, the June 1976 clashes between the workers of Radom and Ursus inspired a number of Poland's intellectuals to get involved. In November a Committee for the Defence of the Workers (*Komitet Obrony Robotnikow*) – KOR – was formed. The Catholic counterpart – KIK – which had Wojtyla as its chaplain began to get actively involved in helping individuals who were being exploited by the state. Rapid-response teach-in groups whose agenda was to counter Communist propaganda with factual information began to hold seminars in some of Cracow's churches and monasteries.

Ever the pragmatic man, at the end of the year that had yet again seen wide civil unrest, Wojtyla in his New Year's Eve sermon reminded his listeners of their close proximity to Russia.

'One may not be a thoughtless Pole: our geographical position is too difficult. Thus every Pole has the obligation to act responsibly, especially at the present time. But we have to fight for the fundamental right of defining "Who is the nation? What is the State?" as we did during the first months of this year.'

Now, in 1980, the Communist regime demonstrated yet again their collective inability to learn from their own errors.

Secretary Gierek calculated that any hostile reaction to the increases could be bought off by wage increases to selected industries such as the miners, the shipyard workers and other key sections – the old successful Communist technique of divide and rule. He was wrong.

Three institutions in particular made sure that the protests of 1980 were different from the ones that came before it: the KOR, which played a crucial role during the second half of 1980; secondly, Lech Walesa – the young electrician who had been a member of the Lenin shipyard strike committee in 1970; the third human element in the extraordinary unfolding drama was the Polish Catholic Church in the shape of Primate Stefan Wyszynski and his bishops. In previous confrontations with the regime, the workers and the intellectuals had failed to unite but after the vicious clashes between the workers and the regime at Radom and Ursus in June 1976, a number of leading intellectuals had felt impelled to get involved in the struggle.

The founding members of KOR included former Communist party member Jacek Kuron, the Jewish historian Adam Michnik, and a long-time non-communist dissident, Jan Jozef Lipski. KOR began to establish direct contact with the workers and collect money to aid families where the breadwinner had been dismissed, arrested, injured or killed. KOR also raised funds to pay for defence lawyers. Money was collected not only within Poland but also in the United States and throughout Western Europe. Overseas bank accounts were established and funds were subsequently sent to KOR by a variety of means. After June 1980 other contributors to KOR, the various workers' committees and the Polish Catholic Church included the Carter administration through CIA channels and the Vatican via Roberto Calvi's access to a wide variety of money-laundering channels.

The Vatican involvement in this illicit and illegal transfer of money was not without benefit for the President of the Vatican Bank, Bishop Marcinkus. The emergence of Solidarity and its need for foreign support, legal and illegal, occurred at the same time that Cardinal Casaroli heard from his contact in SISMI, the Italian Intelligence Service for Information and Military Security, General Pietro Musumeci, head of the internal section, who revealed a great deal about Calvi, Sindona and inevitably Bishop Marcinkus. However, Musumeci had a particular problem when it came to enlightening the Vatican Secretary of State on the criminal activities of P2 members and the Head of the Vatican Bank. The General was also a member of P2.

Musumeci was far too bright to give Marcinkus a totally clean bill of health; consequently while holding back the full horror story he gave Casaroli more than enough facts and details to ensure what should have been an instant vacancy for the post of President of the Vatican Bank. Cardinal Casaroli already had the very detailed dossier prepared by Cardinal Vagnozzi, but that had not been enough for the Pope to remove Marcinkus. Now armed with additional information, Casaroli tried again. To his astonishment the Pope still refused to dismiss Paul Marcinkus. 'At this particular time, Eminence . . . With uncertainties in Poland . . . the bishop's invaluable contribution . . .' The Polish connection had served Marcinkus well in the past with Wojtyla. Yet again now it saved his neck. The Pope once more protected a man guilty on all the available evidence of a vast array of serious financial crimes. The Pope could not justify his decision on the grounds that Marcinkus was uniquely placed to funnel aid to Poland. Apart from the sources already referred to above there were plenty of alternatives. Other organisations began to emerge in the years 1976 to 1980; sometimes their agendas converged, sometimes the various groups bitterly opposed each other. KOR and 'Young Poland' shared common aspirations and by 1978 were secretly funding the underground Free Baltic Trade Union whose members included future leaders of Solidarity such as Lech Walesa and Anna Walentynowicz. The open activism of KOR was particularly effective, and the organisation attempted as far as possible to base its actions on existing rights that the regime had chosen historically to disregard. These rights were guaranteed by the Polish Constitution and by the Helsinki Agreement which all the Soviet bloc countries had signed in August 1975. KOR also relied on the fundamental labour rights again recognised by the bloc through various international agreements registered with the International Labour Organisation (ILO) in Geneva. The ILO would provide another invaluable conduit for funds and equipment to help the emergent Solidarity. These very astute tactics by KOR, to act within a range of legally recognised rights, would form the model for the Czech dissident movement, Charter 77.

Joe Hill, a legendary trade union activist, memorably proclaimed to his followers as he prepared to face a firing squad in Salt Lake City in 1915, 'Don't mourn. Organise.' KOR and the other organisations took his appeal to heart in the years leading to July 1980. Many of their members were frequently beaten up, arrested and imprisoned and denied a range of fundamental rights. Their persistence against formidable odds is testimony to their courage, commitment and sheer Polish bloody-mindedness.

Lech Walesa did not create Solidarity single-handedly, any more than he single-handedly rallied and organised workers or was sole leader of the strikers. Indeed some of his closest allies would come to regard Walesa as a Communist infiltrator. But Walesa gave the struggle at a crucial period a human face, a personality. The workers in the Gdansk shipyards could relate to and identify with him but so too could the Western media and the watching world. Today, more than a quarter of a century later, few outside Poland can recall other names, such as Anna Walentynowicz, Joanna and Andrzej Gwiazda, Alina Pienkowska, Bogdan Borusewicz, Bogdan Lis, Ewa Ossowska. There were many others who also made a valuable contribution to the ultimate victory.

When the price increases were announced on 1 July there were immediate work stoppages in protest. The protests rapidly spread; on 11 July the senior managers of various plants such as steelworks and tractor factories were flown to Warsaw. Gierek and fellow members of the government informed the managers that the tried and trusted tactics were again to be used: key industries would be given wage increases of ten per cent or more. Containers crammed with meat were to be rapidly sent to the major hot spots. It would be the old Communist divide-and-rule formula – literally beefed up.

What made these protests different was that the information network ensured the news flew across the country. The time-honoured strategy of the Communist regime – a total news blackout – was defeated by a single telephone in a Warsaw flat where KOR member Jacek Kuron, helped by a student of English from the Cracow Student Solidarity group, kept a round-the-clock strike watch and acted as a clearing house for accurate news. As the news spread, so did the work stoppages and strikes. From Kuron's apartment the information went out not only to colleagues manning other phones all over Poland but to Western correspondents and Western radio stations. Stations such as the BBC World Service and Radio Free Europe in Munich had the information on the airways in Polish within hours. By the end of the first week in August there had been 150 strikes.

Nonetheless, Edward Gierek flew off for his annual holiday in the Crimea. Confident that his philosophy of divide-and-rule would win the day, he was able to reassure one of his holiday companions, Soviet President Leonid Brezhnev, that the Polish Politburo had the situation well in hand. A week later, 14 August, workers at the Lenin shipyard in Gdansk began a sit-in strike within the yards. Their initial demands were modest: they wanted the reinstatement of one popular woman worker, Anna Walentynowicz, and a thousand-zloty compensatory pay rise to offset the price increases. These limited ambitions were to escalate to twenty-one demands that included the right to form free trade unions, the right to strike, respect for the freedom of speech, print and publication and a range of freedoms that would extinguish the Polish Communist Central Committee's control of the country.

On 15 August Primate Wyszynski had made no reference in his sermon to the events unfolding in Gdansk and other cities but chose instead to celebrate the anniversary of Marshal Pilsudski's victory over the Russians in 1920. Two days later on 17 August, aware that the Polish government was still refusing to conduct open negotiations with the strikers' committee headed by Lech Walesa, the Primate addressed the industrial reality. During a sermon at the Marian shrine in Lower Silesia he talked of the 'nation's torment and unrest' and paid tribute to 'those workers who are striving for social, moral, economic and cultural rights'. The Communist-controlled television network edited out those parts of his sermon but gratefully ran on the news another part that called for the workers to show 'calm and reason'.

On 20 August during a general audience of predominantly Polish visitors at the Vatican, the Pope spoke in his native Polish as he recited two sacred prayers entreating God to protect the motherland. He concluded:

> 'These prayers say how much we here in Rome are united with our fellow Poles and with the Church in particular, whose problems are close to the heart and for which we seek the Lord's aid.'

The same day he sent messages to Cardinal Wyszynski in Warsaw, Cardinal Macharski in Cracow and Bishop Stefan Barela in Czestochowa. In all three letters the Pope cautiously aligned the Catholic Church with the strikers.

> 'I pray that, once again, the Episcopate with the Primate at its head may be able to aid the nation in its struggle for daily bread, social justice, and the safeguarding of its inviolable right to its own way of life and achievement.'

There was a great deal more at stake by 20 August than the generalities outlined in the Pope's letters to his bishops in Poland. Though a large photograph of the Pope was tied to the gates of the Gdansk shipyard, he was, in reality, an onlooker viewing a revolution unfolding in his homeland from a distance. Three days before his message, the Strike Committee had presented the historic twenty-one demands that would change the course of Poland's history. The bishops in Poland were equally hesitant to confront the realities of what was at stake. The day that the Pope had sent his carefully worded letters, fourteen of the dissident leaders, including KOR leaders Kuron and Michnik, were arrested. By now the KOR information service had gathered a life force of its own and the arrests had little effect.

On 22 August Deputy Prime Minister Jagielski finally agreed to open negotiations. Three days earlier, the strike had been near total collapse but now the workers had achieved a significant breakthrough. Their position had gained strength when it became clear that the Warski shipyard in Szczecin rejected the Gierek gambit of a ten per cent pay rise and embraced the same demands as Gdansk. A third inter-factory strike committee had been formed in the important northern industrial city of Elblag. It represented over 10,000 workers and sent a delegation to Gdansk to declare they would be guided by decisions made within the Lenin shipyard by Walesa and his fellow negotiators. Other strikes were occurring in Warsaw, Ursus, Nowa Huta, Bydgoszcz and Torun. It was beginning to take on the appearance of a national unified movement. On 22 August, the same day that the regime had finally opened negotiations with the strike committee, a group of intellectuals arrived in Gdansk to assist and advise the workers. Among their number were Tadeusz Mazowiecki, the editor of the Catholic monthly *Wiez-Link*, and Bronislaw Geremek, an outstanding medievalist. It speaks eloquently of the shrewdness of the poorly educated Walesa that he knew the value of such men. 'We are only workers,' Walesa told them. 'These government negotiators are educated men. We need someone to help us.' It was the birth of what would become known as the 'Commission of Experts'.

The following day Bishop Kaczmarek, who had negotiated the right for a daily Mass to be performed within the Lenin shipyard, issued a public statement of support for the workers as the discussions got under way, with the strike committee on one side of the table and, sitting opposite, a government commission led by Deputy Prime Minister

Jagielski. Meanwhile, First Secretary Edward Gierek, seeking to neutralise the Catholic Church, had a four-hour meeting with Cardinal Wyszynski. He asked the Primate to help to defuse a potentially explosive situation. Everyone was acutely aware of the possibility of Soviet intervention. Gierek reassured the Primate that while he remained First Secretary there would not be any force used against the 'workers on the coast' and even though 'heavy pressure is being placed on us and on me personally I have no intention of capitulating'.

On 26 August with the negotiations delicately poised the Primate gave a sermon at Jasna Gora on the first day of Our Lady of Czestochowa. He appealed for 'calm, balance, prudence, wisdom and responsibility for the whole Polish nation'. Observing that no one involved in the dispute was without fault the Cardinal urged the strikers to return to work, warning that protracted strikes posed a profound threat to the future of the nation.

Gierek subsequently observed that the Primate 'took our side'. Much of the nation agreed. Wyszynski would later protest that his words had been twisted to convey a meaning far removed from his intention. In fact, the full speech showed a man deeply concerned that his country should learn at least some of the lessons of their own history. Referring to the heady days after the First World War, Cardinal Wyszynski had said, 'Let us remember how difficult it was to regain independence after 125 years of subjugation. And as we devoted much time to domestic arguments and disputes, so a great danger threatened us and our independence.' His explanation that his sermon was distorted by the regime was brushed to one side and the man who had done so much not just for his Church but also for his country was left damaged in the eyes of many, including at least one man who should have known better, John Paul II.

The Pope verbally flailed the Polish Primate. Relying on a garbled report of the sermon, the following day Wojtyla erupted. From the safety and comfort of his summer residence at Castel Gandolfo he dismissed Cardinal Wyszynski as an 'old man' who no longer had 'a sense of orientation' about events. The Pope did not have the faintest idea of Soviet intentions as he played the role of the brave patriot far removed from the reality of an occupied homeland complete with two resident Soviet army divisions. Instead on 27 August, he entrusted 'the great and important problems of our country' to Our Lady of Czestochowa.

Without any first-hand knowledge, he had railed against Poland's Primate. An array of newly published top secret documents from the archives of the former Soviet Union and former Warsaw Pact countries confirm the wisdom and prudence of Cardinal Wyszynski, and his acute 'sense of orientation' about events. In contrast it was the Pope who seemed to have lost touch with the reality of life in an occupied country. The same documents also confirm that Edward Gierek had been less than truthful to Wyszynski about avoiding force. Gierek had, in fact, masterminded the creation of a task force, codename Lato-80 – summer 80. Under deputy Prime Minister, General Boguslaw Stachura, a plan was created to deploy commandos in military helicopters to storm the Lenin shipyard. This would be followed by mass arrests and undoubtedly the deaths of all the ringleaders.

Stanislaw Kania and more rational government members dismissed this bloody solution as a fantasy and asked was the General 'also proposing to send his machine-gunning paratroopers into all of the areas of industrial unrest where the strikers were still holding out?' Kania and the moderates were undoubtedly influenced by the Polish Catholic Church's latest significant contribution to the crisis. A communiqué from the main Council of the

Polish Episcopate headed by Wyszynski was published on 27 August. It

> 'forcefully points out and reminds everyone that respect for the inalienable rights of the Nation is the condition of internal peace. Among these rights are: the right to God, to full civic freedom, including religious freedom and the free activity of the Church, to actual, and not only declared, tolerations of opinions.'

This late-20th-century equivalent of a Polish Declaration of Independence in a country occupied and assailed on all sides by the power of the Soviet Union identified a long list of fundamental rights. They included

> '. . . the right to truth . . . to daily bread . . . to individual property and to management of the land in farms including private farms . . . to a just remuneration for work . . . the right of association, to the independence of the workers' representative organisms and self management . . .'

The powerful document created by the Primate and his bishops gave the lie to the regime's claims that Wyszynski and the Church supported the Communist Government. It told the Primate's critics not only in Poland but within the Vatican that the Polish Politburo and the rest of the Communist world were now confronting not a minority of Poland but the vast majority.

The Agreement, as it was always described, when it was signed and counter-signed by Lech Walesa and his team and Deputy Prime Minister Jagielski and his negotiating colleagues on the last day of August, contained phrases and demands that would have been unimaginable at the beginning of the month. 'Independent self-governing trade unions . . . Guarantee of right to strike . . . Respect for the freedom of speech . . . Release of all political prisoners . . .' It was an agreement widely recognised as the most significant development in Eastern Europe since the end of the Second World War.

Many could rightfully claim some of the credit for what had been achieved but the idea that John Paul II was largely responsible is a fantasy perpetrated after the event by the Vatican and a number of papal biographers – a fantasy that the Pope himself dismissed. Tadeusz Mazowiecki, who, unlike the Pope or his biographers, was there at the very heart of the struggle as one of the team of key advisors to Lech Walesa and the other workers observed,

'. . . we meant to make sure that it did not end in bloodshed. The determination of the workers to continue their peaceful attitude to any violent provocation was decisive. The role of Cardinal Wyszynski was very significant. And a part of the KOR's role, the method that the working class used to fight, the peaceful method, was very important for avoiding bloodshed.'

As this account has demonstrated, the Pope said little publicly and not much more privately on the historic struggle throughout the entire month. Karol Wojtyla's contribution at this time was, in fact, largely symbolic. The much-abused Cardinal Wyszynski and his bishops, however, had eventually played a key part in the drama. During the night of 17 August the Soviet press agency *Tass* published allegations of subversive anti-socialist elements operating on the Polish Eastern coastal region, a propaganda ploy that might well have heralded the appearance of tanks on the streets of Gdansk. Cardinal Wyszynski sent Professor Romuald Kukolwicz to the Polish Communist

Party's Politburo as his personal representative. The Professor brought with him an offer to mediate between the Government Commission and Walesa's inter-factory strike committee. The offer was accepted and, on the morning of the 28th Kukolwicz, together with another of the Cardinal's representatives, Professor Andrzej Swiecicki, flew to Gdansk. Professor Kukolwicz had been one of Wyszynski's private advisors since 1972. He had been sent by the Primate to the Lenin shipyard as early as 21 August and from then on seldom left Walesa's side. Within three days both the Szczecin and Gdansk agreements had been signed.

If Lech Walesa and his committee had been able to hear the Polish Politburo discussion shortly before the Agreement was signed they would have realised its fragility. After rejecting the suggestion to send in commandos with orders to kill all of the strike leaders the Politburo agreed in Gierek's words to 'choose the lesser evil, sign the agreement, then find a way to get out of it'. Such duplicity met with warm approval from their Soviet masters.

A week before the Gdansk and Szczecin Agreements were made, the Soviet Politburo set up a special commission on Poland. Its first 'top secret' report illustrates the deep anxiety of the Soviet Union leadership. By the time that Brezhnev, Andropov and the other senior members of the Central Committee met in early September 1980 a third agreement had been concluded between the Polish government and the inter-factory strike committee (invariably referred to by its Polish abbreviation MKS), this time on behalf of the coal miners of the Silesian town of Jastrzebic. The secret report contained the essence of the Soviets' planned counter-attack: 'Reclaim the positions that have been lost among the working class and the people.' It also included more sinister strategies, wrapped up inside Politburo euphemisms: 'If circumstances warrant, it would be advisable to use the contemplated administrative means.'

The Soviets had already pressurised the Poles to remove Prime Minister Edward Babiuch; in September Edward Gierek was also removed from office. The new Prime Minister was Jozef Pinkowski; the new First Secretary was Stanislaw Kania. He believed it necessary to plan a large-scale nationwide counter-attack on the Solidarity movement that had quickly spread so far and wide. Within sixteen days of the Gdansk Agreement, Solidarity had acquired a membership of over three million people. By 24 September the drafting of the Statutes to enact the Agreement had been completed and they were duly submitted to the Warsaw Provincial Court for ratification. Revolutionary change was not confined to the members of Solidarity: the farmers of Poland announced that they too wanted an independent self-governing trade union; so did the students and the universities and colleges and the writers, the journalists, the doctors, the architects and the economists. Solidarity was more than a new trade union: it was now a national state of mind.

It was obvious by the end of September that the old Communist techniques of procrastination, obfuscation and obstructionism were doing all they could to neuter the Agreement. While Holy Mass had been broadcast over state radio, Solidarity were still being denied access to the media. Wage increases were either slow in happening or not occurring at all and many of the other agreed points were not being implemented. As a result Solidarity called a national strike that was uniquely Polish: just one hour for Friday 3 October between noon and one o'clock in selected factories' works departments. In certain places just one man was called out to strike for one hour, holding the national flag at the factory gate. The industrial action demonstrated that the regime and the Church had been joined by Solidarity as an organisation that commanded unswerving and national support.

In the Vatican, a hesitant Pope still needed some convincing. Tadeusz Mazowiecki, one of the council of wise men who had guided Walesa and his fellow workers through the crucial August negotiations, went to Rome in early October. It was the Pope's first conversation with someone who had actually been in the Lenin shipyard nearly three months previously and he had urgent questions concerning Solidarity. 'Will it last? Does this movement have a future?' Mazowiecki reassured the Pope. 'Yes, it will last. It has a real future.'

The Warsaw Court was still considering the ratification of the Statutes that Lech Walesa had presented when the Polish Bishops' Conference weighed in with yet another gesture of national support: on 16 October they issued a statement calling for full implementation of what had been jointly agreed at Gdansk. Primate Wyszynski followed this up a few days later by meeting with one of the other Warsaw Solidarity leaders, Zbigniew Bujak. Giving him and the union the Church's unconditional support the Primate declared, 'I am with you.' Two days later Cardinal Wyszynski flew to Rome to attend the closing sessions of the Synod on the Family and to brief the Pope.

Back in Poland, the Solidarity leaders upped the ante. Kania knew that he had the support of the Soviet leadership only to discover that, through Walesa and his committee, the private farmers were now demanding an independent trade union. Also added to the Solidarity list of demands were four other points from the summer agreements: access to the mass media, pay rises, supplies to the shops and an end to 'repressions' against union and opposition activists.

On the underlying issue that the agreement should not be altered and the Statutes should be legalised unchanged, both sides agreed to abide by the Supreme Court ruling on Solidarity's appeal. When the government negotiators reneged on some of the other points which they had agreed only an hour before, a wave of fury swept through the country. Serious fissures began to appear in the previously united front that Solidarity had presented. Western observers began for the first time to write of 'hawks' and 'doves' or 'radicals' and 'moderates'. With a membership of many millions, the fledgling movement contained all these categories and many more. Walesa and his Think Tank were opposed to any strike action until after the Supreme Court handed down its decision on 10 November. They did not prevail and preparations were put in hand for a national strike regardless of the decision on 12 November.

Denunciations of Solidarity by other Eastern bloc countries grew in volume and intensity. In East Germany and Czechoslovakia the media orchestrated by Honecker and Husak were particularly virulent. The words 'violence', 'disruption', 'provocation', 'vandalism' and 'hooliganism' were used regularly in the Czech Communist Daily *Rudé Právo* to describe Solidarity. Other Communist headlines suggested a giant conspiracy to get Karol Wojtyla elected Pope before orchestrating this counterrevolution in Poland. 'Whom does Wall Street applaud? Whom does the White House applaud? With the blessing of the Vatican. Together with the BND [West German Intelligence Service] against Poland. The CIA pays for Walesa's union.' In the United States the CIA was giving daily reports to the President on increased Soviet military activity. Since mid-October they had noted that the Soviets appeared to be gearing a number of selected divisions in the western USSR to a state of readiness. National Security Advisor Zbigniew Brzezinski (the man suspected within the Communist world to have personally orchestrated the Pope's election) was certain that the Soviets were either going to invade Poland or orchestrate an internal coup and put a hard-line regime in control.

On 10 November the Polish Supreme Court handed down its decision. The additional clauses that had so offended Walesa and his committee were removed from the Statutes but placed instead along with the first seven points of the Gdansk Agreement as an appendix. Cardinal Wyszynski threw a celebratory party for the delighted Walesa and the other Solidarity leaders at which he talked of his experiences before the Second World War when he had been a trade union chaplain. Commenting on his trip to Rome, he told them that the Pope was now the owner of a large photo album covering key moments in the Gdansk strike. Wyszynski also offered some wise advice; referring to the regime he remarked, 'Do not ask for too much too soon.' He felt that the Soviets as well as the Polish Politburo might well be provoked by this particular victory; he was right. Not only Leonid Brezhnev and his Politburo but the Communist leadership throughout Eastern Europe were infuriated that the Communist Party had been relegated to being an appendix to the Statute. Brezhnev was further enraged when he learned from his ambassador in Poland, Boris Aristov, that it had been a done deal before the Supreme Court had gone through the charade of handing down its 'independent' decision. Aristov had personally intervened in a vain attempt to get the deal thrown out before it became public, but without success.

Solidarity promptly called off its national strike and the Western media's response was summed up by the *New York Times*, which described Solidarity as 'a powerful labor movement that had forced the government to back down'. On 12 November while addressing Polish pilgrims at the end of his weekly General Audience, the Pope said he wished 'to express my joy over what had been accomplished in our motherland in recent days'. He sent 'blessings from all my heart' to the new unions. In conclusion he expressed the hope 'that the maturity that over the past months has characterised the behaviour of our compatriots, the society, as well as the authorities will continue to prevail'.

On 15 November, the Pope and his retinue left the Vatican for his next foreign trip, a four-day visit to West Germany. The visit drew a mixed response; the official line was expressed by Karol Wojtyla's old friend and editor Jerzy Turowicz reporting for Cracow's *Tygodnik Powszechny* who recorded that 'the Pope's presence wiped out worn stereotypes and changed the image of the Papacy and the Catholic Church'. His comment was true from one perspective. Ute Ranke-Heinemann, the Lutheran theologian and daughter of the former German President Gustav Heinemann, however, was one of a large number of West Germans who condemned the spending of $10 million 'for a pious spectacle' when the lives of so many starving human beings could be saved with that much money. She said, 'The rights of the poor take priority over the pious curiosity of the consumer society. The new floodlights in front of the Cologne cathedral alone cost $75,000.' Cardinal Höffner who had indeed been one of the German influences during the campaign to get Wojtyla elected, was outraged at the protests. 'How can we speak of such a mundane thing as money in connection with the spiritual pilgrimage of the Vicar of Christ to this country?' His intervention merely stoked the fires of complaint even higher. Both Catholic and Protestant critics cited the profligate costs of the outside altars in Cologne and Fulda at a combined cost of a further $500,000.

Against the background of these complaints, the Pope's comments during his sermons on unemployment and the need to share the finite resources of the world in an equitable manner were received with less than wholehearted enthusiasm. He was on stronger ground when he vowed that war would 'never again' tear Europe apart. Such sentiments uttered by a Pole on German soil carried a special poignancy, 'The frightful destruction, the indescribable sufferings of so many, the contempt for man, must never be repeated again in this generation, never again either on this continent or elsewhere.' For these observations the Pope received great applause.

A few miles away in East Germany however the leader of the Communist State and his Politburo were at that precise time urging not only their Soviet masters but also fellow Warsaw Pact members to inflict further suffering on the Polish nation.

A Soviet Invasion?

At the beginning of November, Leonid Brezhnev had written to the First Secretaries of Czechoslovakia, East Germany, Bulgaria and Hungary, demanding that they give up a percentage of the volume of oil shipments that they were expecting to receive next year from the Soviet Union. It would instead be sold on the world market to raise hard currency for Poland and keep its economy alive. Honecker of East Germany urged Brezhnev to adopt 'collective measures to assist our Polish friends in overcoming the crisis'. Observing that Brezhnev's 'timely advice' to the Polish leadership had not had the 'decisive influence which we had all been hoping for', Honecker urged an immediate Soviet invasion. He had concluded several months earlier that Poland 1980 was an identical rerun of Czechoslovakia 1968. It was a conclusion shared by the leaders of Bulgaria, Czechoslovakia and Hungary. Communism had responded to the Prague Spring with a savage brutal repression. In the collective opinion of the four heads of government, Poland demanded the same response.

As new confrontations between the Polish government authorities and the unions continued to erupt with frequent sit-in strikes the temperature was raised yet again. A two-hour strike by the railway workers on 24 November particularly exercised the minds of President Brezhnev and his

Politburo. As the Soviet Union had nearly half a million soldiers stationed in East Germany, without a functioning railway system through Poland they would be cut off from the motherland.

In the United States, the following day's Alert Memorandum, the top-secret intelligence briefing for the President and approximately 150 individuals with the appropriate security clearance, made grim reading for Jimmy Carter:

> 'The Polish regime faces the gravest challenge to its authority since the strikes on the Baltic coast ended in August . . . The demands of the Warsaw Solidarity chapter go far beyond what our intelligence analysts believe the regime can accept.'

It was precisely the situation that the wise Cardinal Wyszynski had warned Walesa and his committee to avoid. The intelligence briefing also reminded the President that although there was as yet no evidence of large-scale Soviet mobilisation, the military exercise of the previous month had left the Soviets well positioned to activate a rapid invasion force. All the relevant documents confirm that if indeed the Soviet army had entered Poland, the United States' response would have been very limited. State Department documents tell of 'the rupture of political détente . . . a reduction of East–West cooperation in Europe'.

US intelligence continued to take comfort from the lack of significant troop movements as November drew to a close. That comfort was somewhat jolted on 29 November when the commanding general of the group of Soviet Forces for East Germany announced the closure until 9 December of virtually the entire East German border with Poland. Simultaneously all East German personnel working in air defence had their leave cancelled for the same period. While the Carter administration wavered about what was the appropriate response, National Security Advisor Brzezinski was less inhibited and openly warned the media of the 'calamitous consequences of a Soviet military intervention'.

During the first days of December President Carter wrote to British Prime Minister Thatcher, West German Chancellor Schmidt and French President Giscard D'Estaing sharing his concerns over the various activities of the Soviet and East European military forces. '. . . the Polish situation has entered its most critical stage . . . preparations for possible intervention have progressed further than at any previous time.' His letter advised that the US government 'will take every opportunity to express to the Soviet leaders our deepest concern about any possible military intervention by them into Poland' and asked the Allied leaders to 'consult very closely with us on your actions to prevent Soviet intervention'. The following day CIA chief Turner wrote to Carter, 'I believe the Soviets are readying their forces for military intervention in Poland. We do not know, however, whether they have made a decision to intervene or are still attempting a political solution.' The President, despite Brzezinski's urgings, continued to approach the Polish crisis calmly. He was not assisted by leaks to the news media of 'unofficial' intelligence details on the Soviet preparations for intervention.

The pace had quickened again by 3 December with US Intelligence reporting to Carter that the Soviet forces had been alerted to a possible move within the next five days. President Carter responded with a public statement expressing 'concern at the developments in Poland' and a private letter to Brezhnev warning that relations with the US 'would be adversely affected' if force was used in Poland. But Brezhnev was not listening.

Two days later a meeting of the Warsaw Pact countries was taking place in Moscow to rubber-stamp the imminent invasion of Poland. Only two of the heads of state were opposed to Soviet intervention, the maverick Romanian leader Nicolae Ceaucescu and the Polish First Secretary Stanislaw Kania who within the forum was surrounded on all sides by seething animosity. As Honecker of East Germany, Zhivkov of Bulgaria, Husak of Czechoslovakia and Kadar of Hungary listened to Kania attempting the impossible, they saw the perfect scapegoat for all that ailed their own countries. Kania reminded his listeners of a little of the recent history of Poland, of Poznan in 1956, through to Gdansk in December 1970 and beyond to Radom and Ursus in 1976. None of those events, of course, could be laid at his door and they served to illustrate that the birth of Solidarity had followed a long period of gestation and all of it under not a Polish pope but a succession of Italians. Seeking to spike the guns of his enemies in the room, he talked of the measures currently being considered by the Polish regime, including the introduction of martial law. He revealed the operation currently being planned and implemented of arming trusted party members who would be able to function as a militia independent of the army.

'Preparations are under way to arrest the most active counter-revolutionaries . . . The situation in "Solidarnosc" is very complicated. Its leader Walesa is really only a figurehead, although many people are working at increasing his popularity. You could say he is a cunning half-stupid person who is directed by others. People who are working together with KOR are exercising influence on Solidarnosc. We want to separate Solidarnosc from KOR. We are setting ourselves this task . . . Young people have a great deal of influence on the activity of Solidarnosc. It is no longer a "Committee for the Defence of the Workers' Rights"; it is anarchy.'

Kania cleverly undermined the argument in favour of a Soviet invasion in a variety of ways and attempted to persude his peers that the Polish regime knew what needed to be done:

> 'It would be best for Poland and best for the future of all of our socialist countries if these problems are tackled internally without "assistance" from its freedom-loving neighbours.'

Many of the speakers, not least President Brezhnev, identified the role of the Polish Catholic Church as a key player. During his concluding remarks Brezhnev observed:

> 'It is clear to us that a confrontation with the Church would only worsen the situation. But with this in mind we should influence as far as possible the moderate circles within the Catholic Church in our direction and keep them from closely allying themselves with the extreme anti-socialist forces and those who desire the fall of socialism in Poland and to take over power.'

In the end Brezhnev pulled back from rolling out an invasion. Kania's commitment to introduce martial law, and the concerns of a potential massive Polish uprising, had further stayed the Soviet hand. Nonetheless, the mobilisation of Soviet troops continued to ensure that the Polish leaders were exposed to the maximum pressure.

Carter continued to misread his own intelligence and was briefing Western leaders as late as 8 December that there was a 'sufficiently high probability of Soviet armed intervention that in my view Western nations should take whatever steps they can to affect Soviet decision-making and thus try to prevent the entry of Soviet forces into Poland'. On 7 December National Security Advisor Brzezinski had telephoned the Pope and informed him that a Soviet invasion of Poland was imminent. More than a decade later, observers were still insisting that Carter's actions had stopped an invasion that had already been aborted a week earlier. It is equally claimed that the Pope's intervention was crucial. As this record of events has demonstrated, Wojtyla had made no intervention whatsoever in the run up to the 5 December meeting in Moscow. It has even been alleged that he threatened to abandon the Vatican and stand at the front of the Polish Army to confront the invading Soviet hordes. This Vatican-inspired piece of disinformation is without any foundation.

The one action John Paul II did accomplish was to write a letter to Brezhnev on December 16, more than two weeks after the Soviet Politburo had cancelled the intended invasion. He reminded the Soviet leader of the losses sustained by Poland during the Second World War and that Poland like the Soviet Union was a signatory to the Helsinki Final Act, an agreement that contained provisions on sovereignty and non-intervention. The Pope's letter, written in a combination of diplomatic language and Vaticanese, was a convoluted request that the Soviet Union abide by the principle of non-intervention. As with President Carter's letter, Brezhnev ignored it and again failed even to acknowledge receipt.

The effect on the Polish nation, once news of the 5 December summit was leaked, was instantly sobering. The same day Solidarity issued a statement to the effect that there were no strikes in Poland and that none were planned; Walesa and his committees were drawing back from the very edge of the abyss. On 10 December while discussing behind closed doors what their course of action should be in the event of an invasion – everyone to go to their workplace and practise 'passive resistance' – they issued a calm communiqué calling for a 'social alliance representing wisdom, common sense and responsibility'. It was sufficiently anodyne to soothe the most rabid Politburo mind. This was followed by a very conciliatory statement from Cardinal Wyszynski, which the grateful state-controlled media broadcast repeatedly nationwide. It applauded the 'process of renewal' but warned that the nation 'first and foremost, needs internal peace in order to stabilise social life in an atmosphere of rebuilding mutual trust'.

Restraint was also very evident at the last significant event of a year that had been so full of such events. On 16 December the dreadful conclusions of the revolts of 1956, 1970 and 1976 were fittingly remembered along with the Polish August of 1980. The guilt that had been gnawing away within Lech Walesa since his comrades had died in the Lenin shipyard in 1970 was finally still. At last those who had fallen had a proper permanent monument. For hours the crowd had continued to grow. Miners from Silesia wearing their traditional long black coats and plumed *czapka*, railway workers from Lublin, bus drivers from Pulawy formed part of a crowd of 150,000 crammed as close as they could get to the area outside the main gate of the Lenin shipyard. Towering above the crowd, three slender trunks of steel crowned by crosses that bore dark anchors rose 138 feet into the dark winter sky. The three main players in the Polish drama were there; the state was represented by President Henryk Jablonski, the church by Cardinal Franciszek Macharski of Cracow and the workers by union leader Lech Walesa.

After a minute of silence the city's church bells began to peal and in the port the ship sirens wailed. The names of those who had died at Gdansk and Gdynia in 1970 were read aloud. After every name the crowd called aloud, 'Yes, he is still among us!' Walesa lit a memorial flame, which despite the drizzling rain burned brightly. 'This monument was erected for those who were killed, as an admonition to those in power. It embodies the right of human beings to their dignity, to order and to justice.' After the Cardinal had celebrated Mass, Lech Walesa's speech was calmness personified. He knew how close they had come to a Soviet intervention. 'Our country needs internal peace,' said Walesa. 'I call on you to be prudent and reasonable.'

The next month, January 1981, Walesa, accompanied not only by an eighteen-strong Solidarity delegation but also by his wife and stepfather, made his first foreign trip to the Vatican. Although he had played no direct part in the Polish August, the Pope by the very fact of his nationality was a powerful external symbol. Any Pole as spiritual leader of one billion Roman Catholics could not fail to increase the world's awareness of Poland. That would have applied no matter who the man was but with Wojtyla's unsurpassable charisma that factor was increased.

It should have been a defining moment on Karol Wojtyla's journey through life. He had committed himself to the struggle of his people in their pursuit of their basic human rights and social justice. He had done so irrespective of their religious beliefs. Many of those involved at Gdansk and the surrounding regions were not Catholics. Indeed many of them were still committed Communists. Hundreds of thousands who subsequently joined Solidarity were Communists. Wojtyla as Pope was declaring that the Church in this particular struggle at least was no longer exclusive, no longer confining its support to Catholics but extending it to all engaged in this crucial battle.

The Papal enlightenment with regard to the struggle for basic human rights and social justice was still confined to Eastern Europe. Simultaneously, people were still dying by their thousands in Central and South America. Some, like the Poles, were Communists. Many, also like the Poles, were not. The fundamental difference between the struggle that Wojtyla embraced and the struggle he rejected was the 'enemy' in Poland. It was a Communist regime. In much of Central and South America it was right-wing dictatorships who were frequently supported by the US administration. Even the outgoing President Carter, the defender of human rights, had not been averse to sending military aid to prop up the juntas. Jimmy Carter and the incoming Reagan administration saw nothing paradoxical within these foreign policies, but they certainly saw a great many Communists, both real and imaginary.

For Lech Walesa and his delegations, these were stirring times. Apart from a number of public meetings with the Pope, there were also private discussions, not only with the Pope but also Secretary of State Casaroli and other Vatican officials. Among the subjects discussed were the needs of Solidarity. A massive national organisation which had sprung up overnight and acquired a membership in many millions needed not only finance but also the basic nuts and bolts to run the machine: communications equipment, computers, telephones, photocopying machines, fax machines, printing presses. Solidarity was already beginning to get some help through a broad spectrum of international union and labour organisations, including the TUC in Great Britain and the AFL-CIO, the American labour movement. Money was also beginning to flow via the Brussels offices of the World Confederation of Labour and the International Confederation of Free Trade Unions.

At that stage Solidarity needed the ability to communicate, to inform, to organise. Moral support was fine, whether it was religious or secular, but what Solidarity desperately needed was logistical support. None of these practical needs were directly provided for by the Pope, who only offered moral support. Tadeusz Mazowiecki, a member of the Solidarity delegation, recalled:

'The Pope was speaking about Solidarity directly to some of its founding fathers but I felt he was also speaking beyond us to the wider world. He said "Solidarity is a movement that is not only fighting against something but is also fighting for something." He made it clear that he saw Solidarity as a movement for peaceful change.'

The issue of the Pope's alleged intervention to avert a Soviet invasion surfaced again during the Solidarity visit. An unidentified French diplomat was widely quoted when he claimed that the Pope had told him, 'If the Russians invaded Poland, I would immediately go there myself.' Vatican watchers including the usually well-informed Peter Hebblethwaite speculated on a Wojtyla–Brezhnev secret pact, basing this on the far more moderate language used by Lech Walesa from mid-December onwards. As for the Papal threat: 'The Pope would never say anything like that, even if it were his intention,' said Father Pierfranco Pastore, deputy director of the Vatican press office, 'and there are no indications that he has any such intention.' But the story came from somewhere and had the knack of being repeated.

Even before Lech Walesa's party got back home from Rome, the situation in Poland had deteriorated. Strikes were breaking out for a variety of reasons ranging from an immediate demand for work-free Saturdays to a demand for an Independent Student Union. On 26 January a strike began in the province of Bielsko Biala close to the Czechoslovak border, rapidly spreading to over 120 plants. The implications of this particular action were explosive: the strikers were demanding the resignation of the provincial governor and his two deputies, accusing them of corruption, illicit financial dealings and administrative mismanagement. It was a direct challenge to the regime's chain of command. The strikes were equally damaging for Solidarity's strike committee. They had been called on local issues and without reference to or the approval of the National Co-ordinating Commission in Gdansk who were attempting to discourage local branches from taking unilateral action. As one Solidarity official observed, 'We want to stop this anti-corruption strike, otherwise the whole country would have to go on strike.'

All efforts to find a way out failed, and, again, both sides appealed to the Primate. Cardinal Wyszynski, terminally ill with stomach cancer, once more found his way through the morass and aided by several of his bishops produced a solution that was acceptable to both sides. As long as the Primate was alive there would always be, it seemed, an acceptable solution but the time left to the 79-year-old Cardinal was desperately short. Recognising this, Solidarity worked sixteen hours a day or more, desperately trying to ensure that the Polish regime was not pushed into declaring martial law.

The Polish Church became fully involved in the various negotiations; the Primate's trusted representative, Kukolwicz, led the discussions with Solidarity in Bydgoszcz while the Primate, despite his condition, took part in crisis talks with government leaders in Warsaw. It proved a formidable task, however, to bridge the demands of Solidarity and the concessions Prime Minister General Jaruzelski and Kania felt they could make without bringing down the entire edifice of government. On the eve of a four-hour strike, the Cardinal wrote in his notebook: 'The situation in the country is dangerous. There is a desperate atmosphere building up.'

On the same day, 26 March, Wyszynski and the Prime Minister had a three-and-a-half-hour meeting in which Jaruzelski laid out his bottom line. A way would be found to give official recognition to the peasant union if, in return, Solidarity ceased their demands for an investigation against those responsible for a violent attack on Solidarity members in Bydgoszcz. Jaruzelski was just as much appalled by what had occurred as Walesa and his committee, perhaps more so. The attack on the Solidarity members had been aimed to undermine the authority of the Prime Minister and First Secretary, Kania. Full investigation would almost certainly implicate the top people among the Ministry of the Interior hardliners and would ensure Soviet tanks in Warsaw before any of the ringleaders could be charged. Equally, the General advised the Primate: 'If the open-ended general strike occurs at the least it will result in martial law being declared and the Soviet tanks will be here anyway.'

During the previous December when his country was in great peril, the Pope, though fully briefed by both the Primate and US National Security Advisor, Zbigniew Brzezinski, had remained silent. His only contribution, the letter to Brezhnev, had not been written or sent until weeks *after* Brezhnev and the other Soviet Politburo members had ruled out a military intervention. At the time John Paul II seemed far more preoccupied with composing a different letter, an apostolic epistle naming two ninth-century saints, Cyril and Methodius, as co-patrons of Europe. Apparently the idea had been gestating within him for over a year. As the Polish crisis yet again bubbled up to near boiling point during the first three months of 1981 Wojtyla had not exerted himself beyond the expressions of support uttered during the Walesa visit in January. It was not until the day after Solidarity had brought the entire country to a virtual standstill for four hours on 27 March that the Pope felt motivated to write to Cardinal Wyszynski.

His letter talked of his 'deep concern for the events within my beloved country', which had become 'the centre of attention of the whole world'. Wojtyla wrote of the voices that reached him from various parts of Poland that 'emphasise the desire to work and not to go on strike', even though the approaching national strike had overwhelming support throughout the country. The Pope pleaded for 'mutual understanding, dialogue, patience and perseverance' and added with an eye on the military manoeuvres taking place on the country's border, 'Poles have the undeniable right to solve their problems by themselves, with their own efforts . . .' He finished his letter to Cardinal Wyszynski by telling him that he would be with him in spirit kneeling before the Image of Our Lady of Jasna as 'once more I entrust to her this difficult and important moment in the life of our common country'.

Cardinal Wyszynski, in the thick of the crisis, took more practical steps. He intensified his pressure on Walesa and his committee. With the country paralysed by the four-hour strike, the next round of talks between the government and Solidarity went on well into the night, only to end yet again in a deadlock.

The next round of negotiations on 28 March also ended 'without the expected settlement'. Deeply alarmed, the Primate brushed aside protests from his doctors and summoned Lech Walesa and the entire National Co-ordinating Commission of Solidarity to his Warsaw residence. Wyszynski left his audience in no doubt of the gravity of the crisis:

'The situation is becoming increasingly complicated not only internally but also externally. We talk among ourselves as Poles, citizens of this land, responsible for it not only jointly but also individually . . . If it were through negligence on my part, for whatever reason or as a result of irresponsible moves, that even one Pole should die, I would never forgive myself . . . Is it right to fulfil today's demands, however just, at the cost of endangering our freedom, our territorial integrity? Is it not better to achieve some today and for the rest say: "Gentlemen, we will return to this matter later."'

The 79-year-old Cardinal drew upon every ounce of his diminishing strength to protect his country. Having been hunted by the Nazis, imprisoned by the Communists, and frequently left isolated by various papacies, he was well qualified to give his listeners the formula for survival in a totalitarian state. He emphasised to the next generation that they should give priority to demands that would strengthen the activities and organisation of Solidarity rather than to ask for specifics such as pay rises and work-free Saturdays. 'Economic demands,' the Primate reasoned,

'should be given low priority, and administrative demands a very high one. I am not a melodramatic person but I insist the situation is dangerous. Therefore I think if we stretch our demands beyond a certain point, we could later regret the consequences that we bring on Poland.'

The Primate's words left a deep impression on Walesa. While Wyszynski and other senior members of the Polish Church were straining every nerve to defuse the situation, the hardliners in both the Polish and Soviet Politburos were throwing more fuel on the fire. The Soviet news agency *Tass* reported on Sunday 29 March from Poland in an entirely fictional story that 'subversive elements operating in the Kielce Province have set up road blocks on Motorway E-7 between Suchedniow and Laczna; all road signs in that region have been destroyed. In Warsaw and other cities anti-socialist forces tried to seize post offices. In the Polish capital, they managed to seize a television transmitter for some time.' It was fantasy but, with the Soyuz 81 manoeuvres still continuing on Polish borders, a very dangerous fantasy. Similar disinformation followed, fed to *Tass* by Vitali Paulou, the KGB station chief in Warsaw.

During the early hours of Monday 30th the mortally ill Wyszynski was aroused by a member of the Polish government. His message was succinct. 'If the general strike is not called off by midnight tonight the Council of State will proclaim martial law.' To underline the point he handed the Cardinal a copy of a poster with the proclamation printed on it.

While the entire working force of the nation made its final preparations for the general strike, Lech Walesa was planning to put the hard-won democracy of the past eight months to one side. Ensuring that a number of his more militant colleagues remained in Gdansk 'to oversee the strike preparations' he single-handedly negotiated a compromise. The general strike was 'suspended'; there would be an investigation into the Bydgoszcz beatings and those found responsible would be punished. Rural Solidarity would not be recognised immediately but the Government agreed to act as if it had been, until the formal registration process was completed. There was no mention of the other demands that Solidarity had made. Walesa declared that they had achieved 'a seventy per cent victory'. Many, including key members of his committee, bitterly disagreed. Some resigned; others were convinced that Walesa was nothing more than a KGB agent. More than twenty-five years later they remain convinced.

It is supremely ironic that after virtually excluding his entire committee from what became one-on-one negotiations with Deputy Prime Minister Mieczyslaw Rakowski, Walesa persuaded Andrzej Gwiazda to announce on television the terms of the settlement to an astonished nation. Whatever Walesa's motives, it is unquestionable that the last-minute deal saved Polish blood and lives. Only a handful of people knew how high the stakes had been.

On 2 April a delighted and greatly relieved Cardinal Wyszynski received the triumphant leaders of the now officially recognised Rural Solidarity at his Warsaw residence. He spoke at considerable length to the gathering. In less than two months he would be dead, and these were precious moments not only for the Primate but for those privileged to hear him distilling the wisdom, the values, and experiences gained over a lifetime. His comments that day offer a unique insight into the Polish Church's philosophy.

'A human being is a social person – *persona socialis*. This means that he possesses a social nature, social disposition, social competence, social expectations and social needs. This is the basis of Catholic social philosophy and social teaching. Everything arises from this. All authority must state and accept this. It is not authority's duty to confirm this since the attributes of a human being need no confirmation.'

Then in a clear allusion to the Communist regime he observed,

'There are doctrines and social systems which do not take this into account and maintain that all rights are granted by the State. This is not the case! A human being does not require the grant of rights which are his fundamental rights as a person; these rights cannot be questioned, he simply possesses them.'

That night the Cardinal was anxious that the farmers be fully aware of the significance of what they had achieved. He was also at pains to underline the vital role that the farmers played in Poland, that the soil that these men owned and worked was the true treasure of the nation.

'The Germans had only wanted our land, not us. If the soil is covered by grass even the strongest storms won't move it. When it is bare it is easy to conquer it.'

He deplored the move away from the rural areas into the cities.

'This policy is a crime. There is an urgent need to halt the process and populate the countryside. I have an instruction for you, beloved: do not allow the land to be snatched away from you.'

He talked of the importance of the entire Solidarity movement and its extraordinary achievements in so little time. 'It has authority, so we can say that besides the authority of the Party there is also social authority in Poland.' He refrained from mentioning the third power in the land, the one he represented. He was determined that his listeners should learn the lesson he had urged upon Solidarity.

'I continuously explain to Lech Walesa: "in a few months you have achieved so much more than even the most efficient political machine could have achieved . . . you must now tighten your organisation, strengthen yourself, create union administration, train people to achieve these goals, give them education in politics, social ethics, agricultural policies." '

It was a template that if adhered to could lead to ultimate victory against the Communist regime. Cardinal Wyszynski alluded to the prize.

'The time will come sooner or later when socio-economic demands will not be the only ones achieved by this massive movement of industrial Solidarity and the Solidarity of the Trade Union of Individual Farmers. These other aspirations you will certainly achieve!'

Before that golden hour there would be some very dark times.

Chapter 4

Appointment in
St Peter's Square

IN THE FIRST MONTHS of 1981, Pope John Paul II remained unconvinced that Communism could be vanquished; it appeared that he still held to the opinions that he had expressed in the mid-1970s when talking of Communist rule in Eastern Europe to his close friend and professional colleague Anna-Teresa Tymieniecka. He saw Communist rule as invincible and dismissed the United States as 'immoral, amoral perhaps'.

On 23 April the links that the Pope had begun to forge with the 'immoral, amoral' United States grew immeasurably stronger. He had a meeting in his study with William Casey, the director of the CIA. Such a meeting was far from novel. The links between US intelligence and the Vatican went as far back as the Second World War. Bill Donovan, head of the OSS (the forerunner of the CIA) was a frequent visitor to the Papal Library of Pius XII and the offices of his deputy, Secretary of State Monsignor Giovanni Battista Montini, the future Pope Paul VI.

This was not a crisis meeting. Neither was there urgent concern about the current events in Poland. At the time of this meeting more than three weeks had elapsed since the last crisis. Only the previous week on 17 April the peasants' union in Poland had finally reached full agreement with the Government Commission paving the way for the formal registration of the union on 10 May, thus honouring the promise made by General Jaruzelski. The 23 April meeting between Casey and the Pope was to discuss medium-term and long-term aims not in Poland but in other spheres of mutual interest. Inevitably top of this list was the Soviet Union and worldwide Communism. Casey's analysis of the Soviet Union was of dubious value to the Pope. Throughout his tenure as head of the CIA Casey would demonstrate an alarming naivety. The meeting in the Vatican between the head of the world's oldest intelligence agency and the head of the world's most technological advanced would be the first of a number of visits by Casey. The CIA had only one major asset within Poland, Colonel Ryszard Kuklinski, and sooner or later he would be exposed or forced to flee the country. For the Vatican, every priest, every nun – apart from those spying for the Communists – represented a potential source of information. If the Pope was prepared to co-operate, the CIA and the Reagan administration might well get into the hearts and minds of the Polish regime and also glean something of developments within the Soviet Politburo.

For such apparently disparate men they had much in common. The Jesuit-educated Casey, like Karol Wojtyla, from his student days had embraced a deep attachment to the Virgin Mary; statues of Mary and Jesus were to be found all over the Casey home on Long Island. Like Karol Wojtyla, Casey did not merely lean to the right in the fight against 'the enemy', he supported and upheld its position with every ounce of his strength. Like Wojtyla, he had supported the fascist Franco during the Spanish Civil War. The Falange might be fascists but they were Catholic fascists fighting communists. The head of the CIA had even considered the alcoholic Senator Joseph McCarthy essential in the fight against 'the enemy'. At the time of this first meeting he looked very favourably on a number of right-wing dictatorships. He and other senior members of the Reagan administration would come to learn that this was yet another position that they shared with the Holy Father. The Pope's clear and continuing hostility to Liberation Theology could cement the relationship with the Reagan administration.

The meeting did not discuss human rights, no longer the top priority of US foreign policy. For the Pope, coming from an occupied country, human rights were of paramount importance but it was unclear how strongly or consistently he would fight for them. He was whole-hearted in championing the human rights of his fellow Poles but would he show the same enthusiasm to champion the rights of the oppressed in El Salvador, Zaire, South Korea, Chile and the Philippines? Would he attempt to convince the Reagan administration, so eager to win his approval, that human rights were a vital issue?

Prior to Casey's visit, there had been ample time for the Vatican's Secretariat of State to reflect on some of the early signals that had been sent out by the new administration. The week after Secretary of State Haig's human rights dismissal of the issue, General Chun Doo Hwan, the President of South Korea, arrived at the White House as the first head of state to meet President Reagan. The previous year there had been continuous student demonstrations throughout the country against a corrupt government regime that was ruling without recourse to the national ballot box.

On 22 February 1981 the Reagan administration lifted economic sanctions against Chile and its military dictatorship and invited it to participate in inter-American naval exercises. On 3 March Reagan sent $25 million of US military supplies and personnel to El Salvador under executive authority, thereby circumventing the need to obtain approval from Congress.

On 9 March in direct contravention of a twenty-year policy forbidding any military contact with the racist regime of South Africa, UN Ambassador Jeane Kirkpatrick held meetings with South African military officers. Two days later the US voted against a UN resolution condemning human rights violations in El Salvador. On 15 March Argentina's 'President', military dictator General Roberto Viola, was invited to the US. In both Chile and Argentina there was total censorship, death squads, an ever-growing number of *Los Desaparecidos* – 'the disappeared' or 'the missing people'. On 21 March National Security Advisor Richard Allen announced that future relations with South Africa should depend on US self-interest and not on US disapproval of apartheid.

It was easy to understand why the Reagan administration sought approval for their policies from the spiritual and moral leader of nearly one fifth of the planet, but what was the exchange? What could the Pope hope to gain from the President and his cabinet?

The most glittering prize would be to affect United States policy on a range of issues. It would assist the Vatican immeasurably if Reagan could be persuaded to have full diplomatic relations with the Vatican. It would greatly increase the Pope's potential to influence and change United States policy on issues such as abortion and artificial birth control. With such diplomatic channels open the Vatican would have constant and immediate access to the State Department and through that to the Oval Office.

At the time of Casey's visit, the Pope had already publicly joined in the abortion debate, not within the United States but on his own doorstep. Italy was going to hold two referenda on 17 May, both on abortion. Three years earlier, Italy, a country with nominally 99.8% Roman Catholics, had stood the Church's teaching on abortion on its head and voted to legalise abortion for physical or psychological reasons, or because pregnancy would cause everwhelming economic, social or family problems, or if the foetus was declared deformed.

The first referendum would make obtaining a legal abortion much easier. Its supporters claimed that many women could not get the abortion that the law permitted because a significant number of doctors could use a 'conscience clause' to opt out of the state system. The second referendum, supported by the largely Catholic pro-life movement, was an attempt to make availability much more restrictive. Abortion would be allowed only if pregnancy or birth would involve grave risk to the life of the potential mother or there was clear medical evidence of serious dangers to her physical health.

Karol Wojtyla had been deeply and bitterly opposed to legalised abortion from his earliest days as a priest. His position was very powerfully reinforced when he was shown a medical film using an internal camera of a child within the womb being aborted. For Wojtyla abortion was a crime against nature and against God that could never be justified. He had confronted the issue continuously in Poland but that was among his own people. Though the issues remained the same, in Rome they required more subtle tactics. As a foreigner, the Pope needed to be aware that any involvement in a domestic issue ran the risk of being seen as interference in the internal affairs of Italy. Long before polling day the majority of the Italian political parties were accusing the Pope of just such interference. He had begun quietly enough, waiting until his Italian bishops had made their position clear in mid-March. They told their congregations that they would have preferred a referendum on the question of total abolition of abortion; they recommended that Catholics should vote for the pro-life resolution, as it was 'the lesser evil'. This advice in the words of the bishops was 'gravely binding': not advice but an order.

On the following Sunday, 22 March, his voice shaking with barely controlled emotion, the Pope read the bishops' statement in St Peter's Square. The Pope had re-entered the Italian debate on 'the killing of the unborn child'. He reverted to the interrogative form that he so favoured. He also reverted to use of the regal pronoun 'we' instead of 'I' which his predecessor Albino Luciani had abandoned.

'If we were to accept the right to take away the gift of life from those who are not yet born, how can we defend the right of man in other situations? Will we be able to halt the process of destroying the human conscience?'

On Sunday, 10 May, just a few days before the referenda, John Paul II addressed a huge rally in St Peter's Square on the coming vote: 'This is a sacred cause. Those who oppose us have sunk into a moral insensibility and a spiritual death.'

For the Pope it was not a question of reducing the categories of women who could legally obtain an abortion. Quivering with anger, he demanded a complete ban on abortion. It should never be available to any woman, not even a rape victim, not even one who was a young child or a nun. The rights of the unborn child transcended all other rights. In these and many other horrific factual cases the Pope's position was and remained until his death that no one but the unborn child has any rights. Though the issues were very different, he showed the same certitude as in the controversy over the letter asking forgiveness for Poland from the German bishops. He was right and his critics were not only wrong but grossly impertinent to challenge him. For all his learning, the Pope seemed to have missed one simple lesson taught in all Roman Catholic schools during the first half of the 20th century: 'When you are in the right you can afford to keep your temper. When you are in the wrong you cannot afford to lose it.'

Many within the Roman Curia who knew Italy and its people far better than this man 'from a far country' were deeply uneasy. If the Pope had seriously misjudged the mood of the people on the abortion issue, then by taking such a public stand he ran the danger of suffering a personal deep humiliation and, beyond that, the risk of permanent damage to the Papacy and the Roman Catholic faith.

Three days after his anti-abortion rally, at lunchtime on 13 May 1981, the Pope sat down to what should have been his last meal on earth. The menu was the usual culinary mixed blessing, part Italian part Polish. On one occasion, when asked if the cuisine in the papal household was any good, the French cardinal, the late Louis Marie Bille, replied, 'Coming from Lyon, that question is difficult for me to respond to. Let's say there are a sufficient number of calories.' Members of the household busied around the Pope and his three guests in the third-floor dining room of the Apostolic Palace.

Each Pope inevitably brings with him at least some elements of his former life. They serve as constant living reminders of times gone but still remembered. Paul VI surrounded himself with what the Roman Curia bitchily called 'the Milan Mafia'; John Paul I brought from Venice just two human mementos: Sister Vincenza, who had been his housekeeper for 20 years, and the young and inexperienced Father Diego Lorenzi, who came as a junior secretary. John Paul II was cared for by a fiercely protective retinue largely from his homeland: five nuns from the Sacred Heart of Jesus in Cracow to cook his meals and do his laundry; Sister Emilia Ehrlich who a lifetime ago had taught Wojtyla English; Father Magee, uniquely serving his third Pope; and above all 'Monsignor Stanislaw', Stanislaw Dziwisz, also from Cracow.

Dziwisz had worked alongside the Pope from the mid-1960s. Officially he was the principal private secretary, a totally inadequate job description. Yet over the years a father/son relationship had developed. The Pope trusted Dziwisz more than any other living person and in turn Dziwisz believed that his role was to ensure that the Pope's orders, instructions and wishes became reality. He did not always succeed but it was not for want of effort. No one got to the Pope without going through Dziwisz, which was another reason for the Roman Curia to display their endemic bitchiness. 'The other Pope' was one of their politer epithets for the papal gatekeeper.

In some respects this meal on 13 May was a working lunch. The principal guests were the French physician Professor Jerome Lejeune and his wife, Birthe. The highly distinguished Dr Lejeune, often described as 'The Father Of Modern Genetics', was the man who discovered the genetic cause of Down's Syndrome. Like John Paul II he was passionately opposed to abortion and to artificial birth control. It was Lejeune's film *The Silent Scream* of a foetus within the womb being aborted which had so deeply shocked the Pope. Predictably much of their lunchtime conversation focused on this issue and the appointment of Professor Lejeune as the first President of the Pontifical Institute for Studies on Marriage and the Family. The abortion referendum was but one of many serious problems that demanded the Pope's urgent attention on 13 May 1981. But it was not the only one.

By May 1981 the financial exposure of the Vatican-owned front companies that Roberto Calvi secretly controlled was in excess of $750 million. The Italian Treasury Minister, Beniamino Andreatta, had recently said in secret that the Vatican should withdraw from its various business arrangements with Calvi and Banco Ambrosiano immediately. He paid a discreet visit to the Vatican Foreign Minister Cardinal Casaroli and revealed details of the damning Bank of Italy report of 1978. Though unaware of the Vatican Bank's liability with regard to Calvi and Banco Ambrosiano he knew of some of Calvi's activities, and knew also of his ties to Licio Gelli and Umberto Ortolani.

He urged the Cardinal to break all connections with Banco Ambrosiano immediately 'before it is too late'. Casaroli delicately reminded the devout Andreatta that they were discussing the 'Pope's Bank' and the Pope had, despite the urgings of Casaroli and others, refused to remove Marcinkus and until that was done nothing could be done to end the Vatican's relationship with 'the priests' bank' in Milan.

Unknown to either man as they sat quietly talking in the offices of the Secretariat of State, their conversation was academic, for by May 1981 it had become impossible for the Vatican to sever the links. Through an array of Panamanian and Liechtenstein companies it had acquired over sixteen per cent of Banco Ambrosiano. With the rest of the shares of the bank scattered among small shareholders, that gave the Vatican – and ultimately the Pope – a controlling interest.

Even if Marcinkus had been able to disentangle the cords that bound him inextricably to Roberto Calvi, there were other attendant problems. The Vatican Bank's prime function was to offer a banking service to religious orders and to religious institutes. Officially it was virtually impossible for a layman to open an account at the Bank. As of May 1981 there were over 12,000 current accounts. A minority conformed to the statutes of the Bank; the remaining 9,351 were owned by 'privileged citizens', including members of the Gambino, Inzerillo and Spatola Mafia families who used their accounts to launder profits from their illegal narcotics activities, kidnapping and other organised crime pursuits. The 'privileged citizens' also included the Mafia family Corleone. Their bagman to the Vatican Bank was the 'Puppet Master' himself, Licio Gelli. Francesco Mannoia, the chief heroin-refining expert for the Corleone family, was one of a number of the family who learned of this arrangement from the then Godfather of Sicily, Stefano Bontate. He would later testify to this further link between the Mafia and the Vatican Bank.

This mutually convenient arrangement came to a dramatic halt in 1981 when police officers raided Gelli's palatial villa in Arezzo and his office at the Gio-Le textile factory. What they found was a Pandora's box of corruption and scandal. In Gelli's safe were the names and Masonic codes of 962 members of P2. There were also numerous dossiers and secret government reports. The list of P2 members was a veritable *Who's Who* of Italy: fifty generals and admirals, present and past Cabinet members, industrialists, and journalists, including the editor of Italy's most prestigious newspaper *Corriere Della Sera* and several of his staff. There were also thirty-six parliamentarians, pop stars, pundits and police officers and members of every single Italian Secret Service. It was a state within a state.

Many have said that Gelli was planning to take over Italy. They are wrong; he *had* taken over Italy. The only element missing at the Villa Wanda was the Grand Master of the establishment. The arrangements for the police raid had been top secret, which meant that only trusted police officers and Licio Gelli had been told. He had caught a plane to South America.

The scandal not only brought down the Italian government: it also gave considerable momentum to the Milan magistrate's investigation of Roberto Calvi. Now with a new investigating judge, Gerardo d'Ambrosio, the net yet

again began to close around Calvi and this time Gelli was
not there to valiantly corrupt all and sundry. By 13 May
1981 those prepared to stand up and publicly defend Calvi
had paid their dues. Bettino Craxi, the leader of the Socialist
Party, and Flaminio Piccoli, the president of the Christian
Democrats, got to their feet in Parliament and made plea-
sant remarks about Calvi and his bank. It was the least they
could do in view of the millions that Calvi had poured into
their parties' bank accounts.

Gelli's flight to Uruguay deprived at least one section of
the Mafia of its number one bagman, but other members of
the Cosa Nostra were still able to call on the services of an
honourable trustworthy man to ensure that their money
arrived safely at its intended destination in their account at
the Vatican Bank.

In late April 1981 the Trapani Mafia, based on the west
coast of Sicily, had a problem. Francesco Messina Denaro,
lawyer and Mafia head of nearby Campobello di Mazara,
was a fugitive from justice. At the time of his rapid disappearance he was safe-housing some ten billion lire ($6
million). The money, proceeds from drug trafficking, belonged to the Trapani family. It had to be moved to an
undetectable location before the police seeking Denaro
stumbled over it. The Trapani clan knew just the place,
one that they used frequently. Catching a plane to Rome,
three of the Mafia family plus a fourth man who was later
referred to disparagingly as 'only a corrupt man' were met
at Fiumicino airport by three limousines. Vincenzo Calacara, one of the Mafia members accompanying the money,
later testified that among the high-ranking prelates waiting
to meet the Sicilian Mafia was the man who took charge of
the money – Bishop Paul Marcinkus.

The group drove into Rome to the Via Cassia, 'to the
office of the public notary Alfano'. There Bishop Marcinkus, still clutching the six-million-dollar suitcase, and the

other priest went into the notary's office while Calacara and his colleagues returned to the international airport. The IOR might have been the 'Pope's Bank'; it was also the Mafia's.

By the time that the Pope and his guests had begun their lunch, the office of Secretary of State Cardinal Agostino Casaroli, on the second floor of the Apostolic Palace, was deserted. Casaroli was on his way to New York, a welcome break from the problems that currently preoccupied him. In particular he was greatly concerned by one issue that the Pope was studiously ignoring: the indomitable Cardinal Wyszynski was dying. From the beginning of May, his condition had worsened and he could no longer say daily Mass. He had fought this terminal illness as he had fought every battle throughout his life, with faith, extraordinary resolution and great courage, but Wyszynski was a realist and, accepting that his death was not far away, he put the day-to-day running of the affairs of the Church into the hands of Bishop Bronislaw Dabrowski in conjunction with Karol Wojtyla's successor in Cracow, Cardinal Franciszek Macharski. Who should replace Cardinal Wyszynski? The Primate, with a minimum of papal assistance, had steered Poland again and again away from the precipice. With the Soviets still baying for martial law to be declared, for a clampdown and repression, and most of all for the destruction of Solidarity, exactly what should Karol Wojtyla do to assist Wyszynski's successor? And exactly who should attempt to follow such a legend?

Another problem requiring urgent attention concerned the continuing overtures that the Vatican were getting from the Reagan administration. Just how deeply should the Holy See be sucked into a relationship with the government of one of the world's two superpowers? John Paul II's view of the world differed very sharply in a number of key areas from the Secretary of State's. That was inevitable when one compared Casaroli, the hugely experienced Foreign Minister, with Wojtyla, a man who, with the exception of his brief sojourn in Rome during the 1940s, had never lived outside Poland in his entire life. Casaroli had discovered that this Pope actually listened a great deal less than he appeared to. He believed that the Pope's entry into the political arena in Italy in such a public, confrontational manner over abortion was likely to be highly counterproductive and had attempted to protect the Pope. As for the burgeoning relationship with the United States, Casaroli was already very well acquainted with the new administration's foreign policies. Some accorded with Vatican positions but others were fraught with danger for the Roman Catholic Church. This relationship was going to be a continuing problem.

Another continuing problem demanding immediate papal attention was the Vatican City State itself. Few other communities housed such an extraordinary array of problems and forms of corruption within such a mere 108 acres. Its civil service had a deeply entrenched resistance to change; the Curia had fought a bitter rearguard action against any modernisation. In theory the Pope was the absolute ruler of the larger worldwide Church as well as his personal domain across the River Tiber. In reality, for over 500 years the Italian grip on the Church's central government had been resolute. Many within the Curia viewed the Pope as a transient figure whereas they were there for ever and a day. It was a problem that Karol Wojtyla had been determined to address but one that as of May 1981 was still awaiting his attention.

It was understandable that this most energetic of popes had prevaricated about taking on the Curia. There were so many aspects to the problem. Careerism and promotion were all-important with every seminarian determined to become a bishop. To move up the ladder required finding a protector; it also required embracing 'the five don'ts': 'Don't think. If you think, don't speak. If you speak, don't write. If you think, and if you speak, and if you write, don't sign your name. If you think, and if you speak, and if you write, and if you sign your name, don't be surprised.' Moving up the ladder with the help of a protector also frequently required participating in an active homosexual relationship. Estimates of practising homosexuals in the Vatican Village ranged from twenty to over fifty per cent. The village also housed factions including the sects of Opus Dei members, and Freemasons and fascists. The latter could be found particularly among priests, bishops and cardinals from Latin America.

One problem transcended all others in May 1981. The letters, petitions, demands and requests had begun to arrive from the African continent, from the United States, from Latin America, from Canada, from all over Europe, every country on the planet where there were significant numbers of the faithful. Many gave precise and exact details, others made allegations; others sent sworn affidavits, all of them had one underlying theme: sexual abuse.

In each case the alleged perpetrators were priests, bishops, and members of the religious communities. No child, it seemed, was too young, no woman inviolable. Complaints about bishops were eventually directed to the Secretary or the Prefect of the Congregation for Bishops, those involving priests to the Congregation of the Clergy, and those involving the various religious orders to the Congregation for Institutes of Consecrated Life and for Societies of Apostolic Life.

The Secretary assigned each letter to the appropriate member of staff. The archivist gave the letter a protocol number and noted its date, author, diocese or origin and topic. As befitted the Roman Curia with its centuries of experience, the letters were faultlessly processed into the system. Minimal action was taken. If the bishop of the diocese was unaware of the complaint, he would be made aware. At that stage the bishop would usually apply 'the secret system'. It had always been successful in the past and the bishop was answerable only to the Pope.

At five in the afternoon on 13 May St Peter's Square was crowded with pilgrims, sightseers and tourists. There was also one young man who was particularly anxious to get a good view of the Pope. He moved past the ambulance parked ready to deal with the everyday ailments of the crowd. In an open-top jeep the Pope was being driven around the square for the second time. Behind him sat Monsignor Stanislaw Dziwisz. The *papamobile* slowed as the Pope returned a young girl he had been holding to her mother. As he stood erect, pink-cheeked and exuding good health, an apparently disembodied arm jerked out of the crowd some fifteen feet from the jeep. The hand at the end of this arm was holding not a camera but a Browning 9-mm automatic pistol. Two shots were fired. One hit the Pope in the abdomen after grazing the index finger of the left hand and emerged from his back to fall at the feet of his secretary. The other hit the Pope's right elbow, searing the skin, then continued on its path, wounding a nun. There was a moment of stunned disbelief. Dziwisz saw the Pope tottering but there was no sign of blood on his white robe.

'Where?' he asked.

'In the stomach,' the Pope responded.

'Does it hurt?'

'It hurts.'

Standing behind the Pope the much smaller Dziwisz supported him so that he did not fall as the jeep made for the parked ambulance, in front of the first-aid post.

The ambulance, part of the Red Cross facilities that were ever present on such occasions, offered only brief refuge for the Pope. It lacked oxygen tanks and equipment, necessitating a second acutely painful transfer to another ambulance. On the journey to the Gemelli hospital, Karol Wojtyla drifted in and out of consciousness. His secretary heard him continuously repeating staccato short prayers. 'Mary, my mother! Mary, my mother!'

There are two primary sources for what follows: one is Father Dziwisz, the other the surgeon who operated on the Pope, Francesco Crucitti. At the hospital it quickly became apparent to the doctors that the Pope's life was ebbing away. His blood pressure had fallen dramatically, his pulse was by now weak and faltering. The last sacrament of extreme unction was administered by his surrogate son, Stanislaw Dziwisz. Externally, his injuries seemed superficial. But when Francesco Crucitti made the first incision he was shocked to find blood everywhere.

'A moment or two later and it would have been too late,'

recalled Crucitti.

'The Pope's life was literally haemorrhaging away . . .
He had lost between five and six pints of blood. Little more than a quarter of his blood was barely sustaining life. The colon had been perforated; there were five wounds to the small intestine. Twenty-two inches of intestine were removed during the five hour, twenty minute operation.'

As news of the shooting swept around the world, the power of prayer was given a severe examination. The bullet that had entered the stomach passed a few millimetres from the central aorta. If that had been hit, death would have been instantaneous. On exiting the body the bullet had missed the spine. Karol Wojtyla's lifelong and oft-repeated

belief in Providence and prayer was triumphantly vindi-
cated on that May afternoon.

Two hours after the Secretary of State's plane had landed
in New York, Casaroli boarded a return flight to Rome,
telling reporters: 'My duty is to be with the Holy Father.'
While the Pope's slow and difficult recuperation continued,
life in the world outside the Gemelli hospital went on. Four
days after the attack, with Karol Wojtyla still on the critical
list in the intensive care unit, Italy voted on the abortion
issue that the Pope had battled so passionately to overturn.
For the pro-life movement in general and for the Pope in
particular the vote was a stunning defeat. The pro-life
proposal that would have restricted abortion to cases involving danger to the life or physical health of the mother
was massively rejected by seventy per cent of voters despite
the pulpit injunctions from Italy's priests and bishops that a
'yes' vote was 'gravely binding on the Christian conscience',
despite John Paul's declaration in St Peter's Square to a pro-
life rally on the Sunday before the referendum that this was
'a sacred cause'. It was precisely the public humiliation that
the Roman Curia had privately predicted. Vatican correspondent Peter Hebblethwaite wrote: 'John Paul's immense
popularity, his crowd-pulling appeal, does not mean people
are listening to what he says, still less obeying him. They like
the singer not the song.'

The Death of Wyszynski

In Poland, the attempt on the Pope's life had initially
aroused an almost unanimous feeling of revulsion and
horror turning to general despondency. The heady early
days of the emergence of Solidarity were forgotten as the
nation confronted a future where nothing was certain
except ever-growing shortages and ever-lengthening
queues. Cardinal Wyszynski had been only too right to

advise Solidarity, 'Do not ask for more than they have to give.' The standard of living was dropping before the very eyes of a nation that had so recently believed it was entering the Promised Land. Solidarity demanded ever more and the Government ducked and dived, both sides adeptly avoiding reality. Meanwhile, the Pope, *their* Pope, lay helpless in a hospital bed. Then, as so often, there was further tragedy for Poland.

On 28 May Cardinal Stefan Wyszynski died. With his death, an extraordinary era closed. The Primate had succeeded in 1948 at a time of acute crisis both for the church and the country. Against formidable odds he had steered both through many treacherous waters. A measure of his achievements can be gauged by the response in Communist-controlled Poland when state authorities ordered a four-day national mourning period as a tribute to the cardinal. A joint statement signed by Chairman of the Council of State Henryk Jablonski, First Secretary Stanislaw Kania and Prime Minister General Wojciech Jaruzelski paid tribute to the Cardinal. They praised his patriotism and pledged the Government to persevere in its efforts to improve the relationship between Church and State. They acknowledged Wyszynski as a 'a great statesman, a man of great moral authority recognised by the nation' with a profound understanding of the 'historical process and civic responsibility', who had by his example 'created a pattern of cooperation between the Church and the socialist states'.

The Primate's funeral, attended by virtually every high-ranking Communist, was broadcast live by the state radio and television for more than five hours. The requiem Mass with a congregation of over one quarter of a million people was celebrated by the Pope's personal envoy, Secretary of State, Cardinal Casaroli. In his sermon he described Wyszynski as a 'man of an indestructible hope nourished by faith in the virtue of his people', a man who had 'only two great passions in his life – the Church and Poland'. In a special message, the Pope asked that the period of national mourning be extended to 30 days, as 'a period of special prayers, peace and reflection'.

This was a direct attempt to prevent further confrontation between Solidarity and the regime before the Communist Party Congress in July. In less than a week after the Pope's plea Solidarity's National Coordinating Commission announced a two-hour strike for 11 June. The cause hardly required such urgent action but was a signal that those responsible for a violent attack on Solidarity members at Bydgoszcz in March needed to be punished. The powerful Church influence that Wyszynski had left as a rich inheritance was being squandered by the day by his successors. There was a desperate need to fill the vacuum left by the Primate's death but the delay in appointing a successor grew ever longer.

In Rome, they were talking within the Vatican of a miraculous intervention that had saved the Pope's life. For others the reasons for the attack were more clear and present. A number of American neo-conservatives just *knew*; the attempt had happened in the fourth month of the Reagan presidency. From the very beginning a number of members of the administration attempted to link the attempt to kill the Pope with the Soviet Union. Secretary of State Haig, head of the CIA William Casey, former special advisor Zbigniew Brzezinski and a host of lesser lights were convinced that Mehmet Agca, a member of an extreme right-wing fascist group called the Grey Wolves, was in fact working for the Bulgarian secret services, themselves acting on the orders of the KGB. This scenario had a number of benefits for its supporters. The Reagan administration had made global terrorism its number one priority; if the KGB link could be made to stand up, it would make it that much easier to achieve the President's aim of a huge military build-up of resources in the USA and the placement of nuclear missiles in Western Europe. As a potential successor to the ailing Leonid Brezhnev, Yuri Andropov, head of the KGB, was an ideal target. To make him a moral leper before he had his feet under the table of the First Secretary's desk would be even better than killing him.

These accusations first appeared in print in September 1982, when Andropov had just emerged as a strong contender for the Soviet leadership, in a full-length *Reader's Digest* article by the egregious Claire Sterling, the favourite bedtime author of CIA chief William Casey and Secretary of State Alexander Haig. Although the Agency had not turned up a single piece of evidence that linked the Soviets with the Agca attack, William Casey wanted to believe Sterling's account and continually pressed his analysts to find the firm evidence; they never did. The Sterling article was followed by a cottage industry of books, TV specials, and newspaper articles who happily turned a blind eye to some very powerful evidence. In the event, they either ignored that evidence or rejected it.

If Agca had indeed been acting on behalf of the Bulgarians and the KGB, he was the most incompetent assassin ever employed by any intelligence agency. His pre-planning did not even cover the basics. He came to Rome in January to carry out a reconnaissance, staying at the Hotel Sia on Via Cicerone, a ten-minute walk from the Vatican. He attended one of the Papal audiences in the Nervi Hall and his plan for the May attack was based on the assumption that this would be where he would shoot the Pope; no one told Agca that from spring onwards the Curia transferred the audiences into St Peter's Square to accommodate the large crowds.

Arriving at St Peter's at 4.45 p.m. on 13 May, Agca was nonplussed. An open-air audience? He would have to improvise. He wandered the square, stopping at the obelisk that marked the centre of the piazza. He asked a Benedictine monk, Father Martino Siciliani, where the Pope would appear from and was directed towards the bronze gate. Shortly after 5 p.m. the Pope emerged, from the other side of the square, from the Gate of Bells. This, to say the least, does not smack of KGB planning. The location was the one place from where subsequent escape was a virtual impossibility. The idea that the Soviets would have sanctioned such a scenario and that Bulgarian agents would have accepted it is absurd.

The alleged Bulgarian connection did not emerge for seventeen months, taking Agca that long to 'decide' to reveal their existence. During those seventeen months he was visited by Italian intelligence officers on a number of occasions. Among numerous documents and photographs the intelligence officers showed him were photographs and a wide variety of details on the three Bulgarians that Agca *subsequently* named and identified as his co-conspirators. These revelations came more than three months after Agca had been tried for the attempted murder. At the outset of his trial, he strongly insisted that he had acted alone. He then announced that he would take no part in the trial and dismissed his lawyer. At the end of three days in the dock he was sentenced to life imprisonment, becoming eligible for parole in thirty years. His only way out earlier was if he could cut a deal with the Italian intelligence services. Two of the Bulgarians named by Agca had returned home; the third – Sergei Antonov, deputy head of Balkan Air – had obligingly waited from May 1981 to November 1982 in Rome until Agca denounced him, at which point the Italians arrested him.

The motive for the assassination according to Sterling *et al* was to stop the Pope carrying out his threat already contained in a 1980 letter to Brezhnev, to leave the Vatican and return to Poland and stand at the head of his people should the Soviets invade his motherland. No such letter was ever written and no such threat was ever made.

Part of the same theory also claimed that, as the creator of the Solidarity movement, John Paul II represented a continuing threat to Soviet attempts to turn back the clock to pre-August 1980 Poland and the only solution was to have him killed. As the earlier facts amply demonstrate, the Pope had nothing whatsoever to do with the creation of Solidarity and did virtually nothing to assist the movement in its early desperate struggle for survival.

A further problem for the conspiracy theorists is a letter written by Mehmet Agca after his earlier escape from a Turkish prison (where he was serving a life sentence for the murder of the editor of the newspaper *Milliyet*). He wrote to *Milliyet* about the Pope's forthcoming visit to Turkey.

> 'Fearing the creation of a new political and military power in the Middle East by Turkey along with its brother Arab states, western imperialism has . . . dispatched to Turkey in the guise of religious leader, the crusade commander John Paul. Unless this untimely and meaningless visit is postponed, I shall certainly shoot the Pope.'

The letter was published in November 1979, nine months before the Gdansk shipyard strike that led to the creation of Solidarity.

Far from being an agent of the Soviets or the Bulgarians, Mehmet Ali Agca despised their political system every bit as much as he hated the American way of life. A note found immediately after his arrest in St Peter's Square described the shooting as a political act, a protest against 'the killings of thousands of innocent peoples by dictatorships and Soviet and American imperialism'. Agca was first and foremost a right-wing Turkish nationalist who fully endorsed the fascism of his group, the Grey Wolves. The 9-mm

Browning gun with which he shot the Pope was not put in his hand by a Bulgarian or a Soviet agency but by the Grey Wolves' leader, Omer Bagci.

During the 1985 trial against the three named Bulgarian agents, the prime, indeed the sole, witness against the three Bulgarians was Agca, brought from his prison cell to confirm the string of accusations he had made over the years. The case of a Soviet/Bulgarian conspiracy went downhill from the opening day when the star witness Agca declared that he was Jesus Christ. The trial eventually ended with the prosecution recommending that the Bulgarians be acquitted for lack of evidence. They had no alternative in view of the fact that at no time during the four-year investigation had there been a single witness who could support Agca's claims. Yet still the neo-conservatives clung grimly to their discredited and fatally flawed thesis.

As of May 1981 Yuri Andropov had a great deal more on his mind than Pope John Paul II. During the preceding month he had arrived at an alarming conclusion, based on KGB analysis of the four-month-old Reagan administration. In May 1981 in a secret speech to a major KGB conference in Moscow, Andropov electrified a packed assembly as he declared that

'the American Administration was actively preparing for nuclear war and that the possibility of a first-strike nuclear attack had been created by the United States. The Soviet Politburo had concluded that the ongoing acquisition of military and strategic data and information concerning such a pre-emptive strike either by the United States or NATO would be the absolute top priority for Soviet intelligence operations.'

His audience listened in astonishment as Andropov revealed that for the first time the KGB and the GRU (Soviet Military

Intelligence) – after years of mutual suspicion and hostility and jealously guarded independence – would be collaborating in a joint intelligence operation code name 'RYAN' – *raketo-yadernoe napadenie* – nuclear missile attack. As double agent Oleg Gordievsky has revealed, although the head of the KGB had reacted with alarm to a variety of Reagan's policies, the initiative for RYAN came from the highest military command, namely Defence Minister Marshal Ustinov. Reagan's grandiose Star Wars plan served to confirm Russian fears.

Against this background the idea that the KGB or any member of the Soviet Politburo would sanction the assassination of the Pope is nonsensical.

The attempt on John Paul II may have had a minor tenuous motive concerning 'a greater Turkey' but Agca's predominant aspiration was publicity, not just for the Grey Wolves but far more importantly for himself. Agca achieved his goal. While wallowing in the worldwide media attention his imagination was boundless.

> 'I am Jesus Christ. The Vatican knows this to be a fact,' he claimed.
>
> 'The order to kill the Pope came from the Soviet embassy in Sofia. The first secretary of the Soviet embassy paid three million marks . . . I was responsible for the bombing of the US-financed radio stations in Munich in 1980.'

It is self-evident, however, that the Pope was extremely fortunate to survive; that his survival was due to divine intercession whether by the hand of God or Mary is quite another matter. The Pope never entertained any doubts as to the cause of his survival. As he observed to the French writer André Frossard, 'One hand fired and another guided the bullet.' He was convinced that he knew whose hand saved him. The attack on 13 May had occurred on the Feast

Day of Our Lady of Fatima, the anniversary of the occasion in 1917 in Fatima, Portugal, when the Mother of Jesus Christ appeared to three young children and made three secret prophecies. In May 1994, on the same Feast Day, the Pope said of his survival, 'It was a mother's hand that guided the bullet's path and in his throes the Pope halted at the threshold of death.' The bullet that had so nearly killed the Pope as it passed through his body was given to the Bishop of Leiria-Fatima who had it placed in the crown of the statue of Mary that dominates the Portuguese shrine.

Even before the death of Pope John Paul II on 1 April 2005, there were calls for him to be given the title of 'John Paul the Great', an honour that has previously only been bestowed posthumously. After his death, the collective hysteria and hagiography was boundless. 'Pope of Popes' . . . 'one of the greatest Popes in the Church's 2,000-year history' . . . 'the greatest Pope ever' . . . 'the greatest spiritual leader of the twentieth century' . . . 'without him there would have been no end of Communism' . . . 'the Pope who changed the world' . . . 'This was a man who overthrew empires' . . . 'The most significant Pontiff since St Peter' . . . 'John Paul's frame of reference was the same as the American Declaration of Independence.'

Even before his funeral, there was a clamour that he should be instantly made a saint and his former secretary obliged with details of the miraculous cure of a man terminally ill with a brain tumour. During this miraculous second life that began on 13 May 1981, what did Pope John Paul II achieve?

Soon after the actual shooting, it became evident that others shared the Pope's belief in Divine Intervention. The deputy editor of the Vatican newspaper *L'Osservatore Romano*, Father Virgilio Levi, assured his readers that Pope John Paul II was saved from death because he was 'protected by Our Lady of Fatima. This is not a product of pious imagination'. Cardinal Ugo Poletti, speaking at a meeting in St Peter's Square, talked of 'the insane act, which was directed against the God whom the Pope represents, and the humanity which he loves as a father'. Monsignor Stanislaw Dziwisz, the Pope's secretary, agreed that the Pope's survival was 'really miraculous' pointing out:

'The Holy Father saw all this [his survival] as a sign from heaven, and we – doctors included – regarded it as a miracle. Everything seemed to be guided by an invisible hand. No one spoke of a miracle, but everyone thought of one. For example, the injured finger recovered of its own accord. During the operation no one bothered about it. They thought of amputating it. An ordinary splint and the medicines intended for the patient's general health were sufficient to cure it. Yet the second joint had been broken. Now it's perfectly all right again.'

If it were so, then Pope John Paul II had been granted a second life by God. An existence that should have ended five days short of his sixty-first birthday had been miraculously extended. Such a gift if not unique is very rare; if John Paul II was correct, that gift had been given not to an unknown, impotent nonentity but to a head of state, the moral leader of a fifth of the planet, a moral leader with unfinished work. How then did the man, seen by the Roman Catholic faithful as God's representative on earth, use that second life? His numerous overseas trips – over one hundred by June 2003 – are well documented; his encyclicals, his books, his post-synodal exhortations, the Apostolic Constitutions, the Apostolic letters, and the additional letters, messages, sermons and injunctions, if not read and studied by the vast majority of Roman Catholics, have been exceedingly well publicised.

None of this mountainous quantity of material reveals how the Pope confronted and dealt with the many problems that faced him on the eve of his 'second birth'. What did he do about the financial corruption within the Vatican? The many unresolved issues in his homeland? What was his subsequent involvement with Solidarity? What action did he take about the institutionalised anti-Semitism within the Catholic Church? What of the increasing political role that he had embraced? The Church's relationship with the United States? What steps did he take to correct the many myths and fantasies that from the very beginning of his Papacy were peddled firstly by the Vatican, then subsequently by countless reporters and writers as irrefutable facts? Exactly what was his role in the collapse of the Soviet Union and European Communism? Above all else there was a truly desperate need for papal action against the global sexual abuses by priests, bishops and cardinals on children, on young teenagers, on nuns and other religious.

PART 2

Chapter 5

Vatican Incorporated I

'CORRUPTION IS HARD TO COMBAT, because it takes many different forms: when it has been suppressed in one area, it springs up in another. Courage is needed just to denounce it. To eliminate it, together with the resolute determination of the authorities, the generous support of all citizens is needed, sustained by a firm moral conscience.'

From the speech 'From the Justice
of Each Comes Peace for All'
by Pope John Paul II
1 January 1988

After the attack on the Pope, few people could have prayed more fervently for his full recovery than Roberto Calvi, Bishop Paul Marcinkus, and Licio Gelli, who knew of the arrangements between the Vatican Bank and Banco Ambrosiano. In September 1978, if the billion-dollar scam in operation for six years was to continue, it had been vital to eliminate Pope John Paul I. Karol Wojtyla was a perfect replacement for John Paul I and from October 1978 to 13 May 1981, he continued to protect and support Bishop Paul Marcinkus.

Seven days after the Pope was shot in St Peter's Square, the chairman of Banco Ambrosiano, Roberto Calvi was arrested. His arrest was the result of carelessness by his great protector Licio Gelli. The police raid had revealed documents that compromised Roberto Calvi, part of Gelli's blackmail dossiers. Desperate to deflect blame or at least have someone who would share it with the panicking banker, the Calvi family began to phone Marcinkus. Eventually Calvi's son, Carlo, got through to him. He pleaded with Marcinkus to admit his involvement publicly: 'The Vatican is its own master. It can volunteer information,' Carlo Calvi suggested to Marcinkus. He received a bleak reply: 'If the IOR accepts any responsibility it will not only be the Vatican's image that will suffer. You'll lose as well, for our problems are your problems too.'

Indeed they were; the two banks had been interlocked for years. Bishop Marcinkus was in a bind: to tell the truth would bring down on the Vatican the wrath of Italy; the alternative was to leave Calvi vulnerable in the hope that the Vatican's deep and continuing involvement would remain secret and that after Calvi's trial he could go back to business as usual. Bishop Marcinkus chose the latter course. Undoubtedly he based his decision on the fact that the charges against Calvi involved only two of his myriad illegal transactions, when Calvi had sold himself shares in Toro and Credito Varesino at vastly inflated prices. This had involved illegally exporting currency out of Italy, an offence on which the Milan magistrates were hoping to secure a conviction. Marcinkus reasoned that if everyone kept calm the game could continue. Calvi, sitting in Lodi prison, was unimpressed by the messages from his sanguine partner in the Vatican. International bankers shook their heads in disbelief as Calvi continued to run Banco Ambrosiano from inside prison.

On 7 July 1981, the Italian Government charged Michele Sindona with ordering the murder of Giorgio Ambrosoli. Calvi's reaction to the news was particularly interesting: he tried to commit suicide the following evening. He swallowed a quantity of barbiturates and slashed his wrists. He later admitted he acted in a moment '. . . of lucid desperation. Because there was not a trace of justice in all that was being done against me. And I am not talking about the trial.' If he had really wanted to end his life, he had merely to obtain the quantity of digitalis recommended by Gelli by having it smuggled into prison. His trial judges were unimpressed.

On 20 July he was sentenced to four years' imprisonment and a fine of sixteen billion lire. His lawyers immediately lodged an appeal and he was freed on bail. Within a week of his release, the board of Banco Ambrosiano unanimously reconfirmed him as chairman of the bank and gave him a standing ovation. While the international bankers continued to shake their heads in disbelief, as Marcinkus had predicted, it was indeed business as usual. The Bank of Italy also allowed Calvi to return while the Italian Government made no move to end the extraordinary spectacle of a man convicted of banking offences running one of the country's biggest banks. One banker did raise objections: Ambrosiano's general manager, Roberto Rosone, pleaded with the Bank of Italy to approve the removal of Calvi and replace him with the previous chairman, Ruggiero Mozzana. The Bank of Italy declined to intervene.

The second threat to Calvi's banking empire came from its own branches in Peru and Nicaragua. To counter it, Calvi enlisted the help of Marcinkus, who had declined to give Calvi any support, public or private, during his trial. He was now about to give him every assistance to ensure that the criminal fraud perpetuated by both men should remain secret. During the time of Calvi's trial, the Vatican announced that Pope John Paul II had appointed a commission of fifteen cardinals to study the finances of the Roman Catholic Church. The function of the commission was to recommend improvements to increase Vatican revenue. Bishop Paul Marcinkus was not included as a member of the commission but he obviously felt that as head of the Vatican Bank he could nevertheless make a powerful contribution.

He held a number of secret meetings with Calvi which resulted in the Vatican Bank officially admitting an increase in its outstanding debts of nearly $1 billion. This was the sum owed to the Calvi banks in Peru and Nicaragua on a series of enormous loans. The securities backing these huge debts were negligible. The Latin American banks, in spite of being Calvi subsidiaries, were finally displaying a little independence. They wanted greater cover. Who picked up the bill in the event of a default? Who exactly owned these mysterious Panamanian companies who had received the loans? Who had borrowed so much with so little? The Peruvians were particularly anxious, having loaned some $900 million.

In August 1981, Calvi and Marcinkus perpetrated their biggest fraud. The documents would become known as 'letters of comfort'. The letters were written on the headed paper of the *Istituto per le Opere di Religione*, Vatican City, and were dated 1 September 1981. They were addressed to Banco Ambrosiano Andino in Lima, Peru, and Ambrosiano Group Banco Comercial in Nicaragua. On the instructions of Bishop Paul Marcinkus, they were signed by Luigi Mennini and Pelligrino De Strobel. They read:

'Gentlemen:
This is to confirm that we directly or indirectly control the following entities:
Manic S.A. Luxembourg
Astolfine S.A. Panama
Nordeurop Establishment, Liechtenstein
U.T.C. United Trading Corporation, Panama

Erin S.A. Panama
Bellatrix S.A. Panama
Belrose S.A.
Starfield S.A. Panama
We also confirm our awareness of their indebtedness
towards yourselves as of 10 June 1981 as per attached
statement of accounts.'

The attached accounts showed that the 'indebtedness' to the
Lima branch alone was $907 million.

The revelations allowed the bank directors in Nicaragua
and Peru to relax. They had now clear admission that the
massive debts were the responsibility of the Vatican Bank
and the Roman Catholic Church would stand as guarantor.
No banker could wish for a better security.

There was just one small problem: the directors in Peru
and Nicaragua knew only half of the story. There was
another letter, this one from Roberto Calvi to the Vatican
Bank dated 27 August 1981. It was safely in Marcinkus's
hands before he acknowledged that the Vatican Bank was
liable for the debts of $1 billion. Calvi's letter made a formal
request for the letters of comfort in which the Vatican
would admit that it owned the Luxembourg, Liechtenstein
and Panamanian companies. This admission, Calvi assured
the Vatican, 'would entail no liabilities for the IOR'. His
letter concluded with a paragraph confirming that whatever
happened, the Vatican Bank would 'suffer no future damage or loss'. Hence the Vatican Bank was secretly absolved
from debts to which it was about to admit.

For Calvi's secret letter to Marcinkus to have any legal
validity, its existence and precise contents would have had
to be revealed to the directors in Peru and Nicaragua.
Further, the arrangement between Calvi and Marcinkus
would have had to be agreed upon by the majority of the
directors in Milan. Moreover, to constitute a legal agree-

ment, it would have been essential for the contents of both letters to have been public knowledge to all the shareholders of Banco Ambrosiano, including the many small shareholders in the Milan area. The two letters and the agreement between Calvi and Marcinkus constitute a clear case of criminal fraud by both men. On 28 September 1981, the third anniversary of Pope John Paul I's death, Marcinkus was promoted by Luciani's successor. He was appointed Pro-President of the Pontifical Commission for the State of Vatican City. This virtually made him Governor of Vatican City. He still retained his position as head of the Vatican Bank and the new post gave him automatic elevation to Archbishop.

Meanwhile Calvi had learned for the first time of Secretary of State Cardinal Casaroli's investigations into the joint activities of the Vatican Bank and Banco Ambrosiano. Casaroli's contact within Italian intelligence was after all also a member of P2. When Roberto Calvi was further advised that the Vatican investigation went back to the brief reign of Pope John Paul I he became deeply alarmed.

My previous book *In God's Name* concluded that Pope John Paul I had been murdered. Some within the Vatican observed that the evidence 'lacked a smoking gun'. In fact, the crucial evidence, the reports on the financial corruption that Albino Luciani had been studying at the time of his death, had been spirited away on Cardinal Villot's orders. Roberto Calvi discovered the existence of at least part of that smoking gun in late 1981. This was the Vagnozzi dossier, the report carried out on the orders of Pope John Paul I into the Vatican Bank and related matters. Calvi now knew that on the basis of the dossier, additional reports and Luciani's own knowledge over six years of the Marcinkus-Calvi axis, on the evening of 27 September 1978 Pope John Paul I had instructed his Secretary of State Cardinal Jean Villot to remove Marcinkus from the Vatican Bank the following morning. Just a few hours later the healthy, far from aged Pope was dead.

John Paul I had taken much of his personal knowledge with him to the grave but the Vagnozzi dossier was still in existence. It remained a powerful indictment of banking corruption but more importantly it was physical evidence of motive to murder a Pope. As soon as Calvi learnt about the dossier he became desperate to acquire it. Working through middlemen and an ex-senator, Calvi established that an expert on Vatican affairs, Giorgio Di Nunzio, had a copy that he was willing to sell. Calvi bargained his price down from $3 million to $1.2 million. Having acquired the report Roberto Calvi kept it close to him for the rest of his life.

At this point, despite the many demands upon his time and Ambrosiano's money, Roberto Calvi responded to yet another plea for help: from Pope John Paul II in person. By late 1981 the situation in Poland had deteriorated markedly. A senior member of Solidarity flew to Rome on 'union business' and in the American Embassy he briefed an Italian trade unionist, Luigi Scricciolo, and the United States Ambassador-at-large, General Vernon Walters. The main item on the agenda was the need to organise funding for the embattled Solidarity movement. Following this General Walters also had a meeting with the Pope where the two had a very wide-ranging discussion that inevitably included the Polish situation. Subsequently Bishop Paul Maria Hnilica, acting as a personal emissary of Pope John Paul II, had a meeting with Calvi. The result was the start of a black operation to funnel money into Poland. Calvi and Marcinkus activated the scheme during early 1982. Subsequently Calvi discussed this papal-inspired money-laundering exercise with his friend and business associate Flavio Carboni, who was secretly tape-recording the conversation. On tape Calvi can be clearly heard:

'Marcinkus must watch out for Casaroli, who is head of the group that opposes him. If Casaroli should meet one of those financiers in New York who are working for Marcinkus, sending money to Solidarity, the Vatican would collapse. Or even if Casaroli should find just one of those pieces of paper that I know of – goodbye Marcinkus. Goodbye Wojtyla. Goodbye Solidarity. The last operation would be enough, the one for twenty million dollars. I've also told Andreotti but it's not clear which side he is on. If things in Italy go a certain way, the Vatican will have to hire a building in Washington, behind the Pentagon. A far cry from St Peter's.'

Secret payments to the Solidarity movement were destined to become an issue of great controversy in later years. Vast amounts of money vanished somewhere between Italy and Poland. If any one man still living knows the truth about the Banco Ambrosiano millions and exactly where they went it is Licio Gelli. After the collapse of Calvi's bank Gelli succinctly observed, 'If anyone is looking for the missing millions, they should look in Poland.'

While Calvi was busy in January 1982 organising the illegal movement of millions of dollars on behalf of John Paul II, the Pope received a letter from a group of Milanese shareholders. Dated 12 January 1982, the letter was long, with a highly detailed list of appendices. The signatories were particularly distressed that the previously staid and devoutly Roman Catholic Banco Ambrosiano and the Vatican Bank had created such an unholy alliance. The letter complained:

'The IOR is not only a shareholder in the Banco Ambrosiano. It is an associate and partner of Roberto Calvi. It is revealed by a growing number of cases that

Calvi stands astride one of the main crossroads of the most degenerate Freemasonry (P2) and of Mafia circles, as a result of inheriting Sindona's mantle. This has been done once again with the involvement of people generously nurtured and cared for by the Vatican, such as Ortolani, who moves between the Vatican and powerful groups in the international underworld.

Being a partner of Calvi means being a partner of Gelli and Ortolani, given that both guide and influence him strongly. The Vatican is therefore, whether it likes it or not, through its association with Calvi also an active partner of Gelli and Ortolani.'

The letter contained an appeal to Pope John Paul II for help and guidance. Although the Pope spoke many languages, including Italian, the Milanese thoughtfully had the letter translated into Polish and also took steps to ensure that neither the Curia in general nor the Secretary of State in particular could prevent the letter from reaching the Pope. Despite their efforts, the letter was ignored. The Milanese shareholders were not even graced with a formal acknowledgement.

Although the Pope refused to make a public statement on the activities of Roberto Calvi, Marcinkus had no inhibitions. In March 1982 he granted a rare interview to the Italian magazine *Panorama*. His comments about his business associate Roberto Calvi were particularly illuminating, just eight months after Calvi had been fined $13.7 million and sentenced to four years' imprisonment and only seven months after the Vatican and Marcinkus (according to the Vatican version) had discovered to their horror that Calvi had taken over $1 billion and left the Vatican to pay the bill. 'Calvi merits our trust,' declared Marcinkus,

'I have no reason to doubt. We have no intention of ceding the Banco Ambrosiano shares in our possession: and furthermore, we have other investments in this group, for example in Banca Cattolica which are going very well.'

Although the Pope could not bring himself to give Calvi a public vote of confidence, in private he fully endorsed the continuing Vatican relationship and even envisaged giving Calvi total control over Vatican finances. Calvi's wife, Clara, has sworn on oath that around this time the Pope gave Calvi a private audience where they had discussed the problem of the Vatican's billion-dollar debt (incurred largely because of Calvi, Gelli, Ortolani, and Marcinkus) and according to Clara Calvi, the Pope made Calvi a promise: 'If you can extricate the Vatican from this debt you can have full control of rebuilding our finances.'

Notwithstanding this extraordinary Papal approval, Calvi was acutely aware that he needed shareholder confidence. His position was even more threatened by the fact that his deputy chairman, Roberto Rosone, in the Banco Ambrosiano was on the side of the would-be reformers. He therefore discussed the situation with his close friend and fellow P2 member, Flavio Carboni. The range of Carboni's 'friends' and contacts was wide. It included such men as the two rulers of Rome's underworld, Danilo Abbruciati and Ernesto Diotavelli.

On the morning of 7 April 1982, Rosone left his apartment at a few minutes before 8.00 a.m. Fortunately for Rosone he happened to live directly above a branch of Ambrosiano which like all Italian banks even in the early 1980s was protected on a twenty-four-hour basis by armed guards. As Rosone emerged into the street a man approached and began firing. Wounded in the legs, Rosone collapsed to the pavement. The armed guards retaliated.

Moments later the assailant was also laid out dead on the ground. His name was Danilo Abbruciati.

The day after the attempted murder, Flavio Carboni paid the surviving leader of the Rome underworld $530,000. Simultaneously Roberto Calvi appeared at the bedside of his wounded deputy chairman complete with the statutory bunch of flowers. 'Madonna! What a world of madmen. They want to frighten us, Roberto, so that they can get their hands on a group worth 20,000 billion lire.'

A month after the attempted murder of his deputy, the screws tightened further on Calvi. Consob, the Milan Stock Exchange Regulatory Agency, finally forced him to list his shares publicly on the stock market. Such a listing would represent the ultimate nightmare for a man whose prime talent was making money vanish from Ambrosiano's assets. At the end of May the Bank of Italy wrote to Calvi and his directors. They demanded that the board give a full account of foreign lending by the Ambrosiano Group. The board of directors, in a pitifully late show of resistance to Calvi, voted eleven to three to comply with the Central Bank's demand.

Licio Gelli, who had secretly returned from Argentina to Europe on 10 May, was also making demands on Calvi. Gelli was in the market for more Exocet missiles to help his adopted country in their Falklands war with the United Kingdom. With the bulk of Argentina's foreign assets frozen and an official arms embargo operating, Gelli was obliged to turn to the black market arms dealers, who displayed some scepticism about Gelli's ability to pay what he was offering for the deadly missiles. He was offering $4 million per missile, with a minimum order of twenty. At six times the official price there was considerable interest in the order, subject to Gelli raising the necessary money. He was well known to the arms dealers as a man who had previously purchased radar equipment, planes, guns, tanks and the original Exocets on behalf of Argentina. Now he needed at least $80 million urgently as the war in the Falklands hung in the balance.

Thus Calvi, already juggling the needs of Pope John Paul II, his Mafia clientele, his irate shareholders, the Consob watchdogs on the Milan Stock Exchange, a recalcitrant board of directors and an incompetent assassin who had succeeded in getting himself killed, yet again found Gelli with his hand out. Calvi saw only two avenues of survival. Either the Vatican had to help him fill the ever-growing hole that was appearing in the Bank's assets or Gelli, the 'Puppet Master', must yet again demonstrate that he still controlled the Italian power structure and save his P2 paymaster from ruin. Calvi discussed the options with Flavio Carboni, who continued secretly to run tape on their conversations.

It is clear from Calvi's remarks that he considered the Vatican Bank should fill the huge hole in Banco Ambrosiano if for no other reason than that they were legally obligated. Calvi observed:

"The Vatican should honour its commitments by selling part of the wealth controlled by the IOR. It is an enormous patrimony. I estimate it to be $10 billion. To help the Ambrosiano the IOR could start to sell in chunks of a billion at a time."

If any layman in the world should have known the worth of the Vatican it should have been Roberto Calvi. He was privy to virtually all of its financial secrets. For over a decade he had been *the* man to whom the Vatican had turned in financial matters. I have previously noted that at the time Albino Luciani became Pope in 1978 the wealth controlled by both sections of APSA and the Vatican Bank was conservatively estimated to be in the region of $3 billion. Now in early 1982 the highly conservative Roberto

Calvi placed the patrimony of the IOR alone at $10 billion.

Enlarging on the theme of his conversation with Flavio Carboni, Robert Calvi wrote to Pope John Paul II on 5 June: '. . . I have thought a lot, Holiness, and have concluded that you are my last hope . . .' Calvi warned the Pope of the imminent collapse of Banco Ambrosiano and predicted that in that event 'The Church will suffer the gravest damage.' He listed just a few of the financial operations he had funded on behalf of the Vatican, in the East, the West and in South America where he had 'created banks to fund the effort to halt the expansion of Marxist ideologies'. He complained bitterly that the 'authority for which I have always shown the utmost respect and obedience' – the Vatican – had now 'betrayed and abandoned me'. The letter was a desperate appeal for help. Like the devout Catholic shareholders of Milan, Calvi ensured that the letter was placed in the Pope's hands and, as with those shareholders, his letter was ignored.

In spite of the formidable range of problems confronting him at the time, Roberto Calvi was initially calm when I interviewed him by telephone during the evening of 9 June 1982. When he asked what the central subject of the book was and I told him, 'It's a book on the life of Pope John Paul I, Papa Luciani,' Calvi's manner suddenly underwent a complete change. The calmness and control vanished, to be replaced with a torrent of loud remarks. His voice became excited and very emotional. My interpreter began to translate the stream of words for me. 'Who has sent you against me? Who has told you to do this thing? Always I pay. Always I pay. How do you know Gelli? What do you want? How much do you want?' I protested that I had never met Licio Gelli. Calvi had barely stopped to listen to me before he began again. 'Whoever you are, you will not write this book. I can tell you nothing. Do not call me again. Ever.'

Eight days later the body of Roberto Calvi was found hanging under Blackfriars Bridge in the City of London. Within days a hole was discovered in Banco Ambrosiano Milan worth $1.3 billion. The coroner's jury that first considered the death of Calvi delivered a verdict of suicide. The hearing had been compressed into one day, key witnesses were missing, and several of the witnesses that did testify were obviously lying under oath. Hardly a scrap of the highly relevant background evidence was introduced. In truth, Calvi was 'suicided' by his P2 friends – yet another example of the very high risks that are attendant if one pursues a career in Italian banking.

After a number of subsequent inquests, investigations, at least two exhumations of Calvi's body and several further autopsies, in February 2003, nearly twenty-one years later, a judicial investigation in Rome concluded that Roberto Calvi had indeed been murdered. In October 2005, Calvi's good friend and business associate Flavio Carboni, the former Mafia financial director Pippo Calo and Ernesto Diotavelli were put on trial for the murder of the man whom Pope John Paul II had wished to see in total control of Vatican finances. We may soon officially learn the identity of the senior Vatican official who was present when the decision to murder Roberto Calvi was taken.

Following Calvi's death there was a much-publicised run on Banco Ambrosiano. Less publicised – in fact it occurred in total secrecy – was the run by account-holders in the Vatican Bank within the Italian Establishment who were aware of the relationship between the Pope's bank and Calvi. Many both in and out of the Italian Government knew that Calvi had had help in performing his billion-dollar vanishing trick. The names of Licio Gelli and Umberto Ortolani were placed rapidly in the frame along with others including Archbishop Paul Marcinkus but the Vatican would have none of it and they declared that Marcinkus hardly knew Calvi. The Vatican Bank were not responsible for a single cent of the missing money. The Roman Curia refused to accept judicial papers that the Italian Government attempted to serve not only on Marcinkus but a further three Vatican Bank officials.

By September 1982 Marcinkus, the man who never left the Pope's side during his visits earlier that year to Britain and Argentina, had become a virtual prisoner within the Vatican. He was replaced as organiser and advance guard on international Papal trips, yet the Pope refused to replace him at the bank. Marcinkus continued to function as the bank's head, whose own lawyers, after a great deal of prodding from the Italian Government, created a commission of enquiry.

It dragged on fitfully, yet the evidence of total complicity between the bank and Calvi's criminal schemes was overwhelming. Some of it has been recorded within these pages, a great deal more within *In God's Name*. Predictably those who benefited most from the aftermath were the lawyers. Apart from those sitting on the enquiry for the Vatican Bank, there were those assisting the Vatican City with a second enquiry, and then there were those who were helping the Italian Government with a third enquiry.

The Vatican City investigation comprised an 'objective' commission of 'four wise men'. Two of them by their very presence seriously undermined their eventual findings. One was Philippe de Weck, the former Chairman of UBS Zurich, the bank which was then holding $55 million of the stolen money on behalf of Licio Gelli, over $30 million of the stolen money on behalf of the late Roberto Calvi and Flavio Carboni and holding $2 million of the stolen money on behalf of Carboni's Austrian mistress, Manuela Kleinszig. Philippe de Weck was also at the centre of what the French called 'the sniffer planes affair', which swindled the French government out of at least $60 million during the 1980s on an aerial device which could 'smell' oil and minerals and nuclear submarines. The swindle had links to a Calvi company, Ultrafin. De Weck was also closely associated with Opus Dei, who would play a key role in subsequent events.

Another member of the Vatican commission was Hermann Abs who was head of the Deutsche Bank from 1940 to 1945. The Deutsche Bank was the Nazis' bank throughout the Second World War and was in effect Hitler's paymaster. During this period Abs was also on the board of IG Farben, the chemical and industrial conglomerate that gave such whole-hearted assistance to Hitler's war efforts. Abs had also participated at board meetings of IG Farben when members discussed the use of slave labour at a Farben rubber plant located in the Auschwitz concentration camp. The thought of Hitler's banker investigating God's bank provoked a wide protest. Letters and information poured in to President Reagan in late 1982, especially from furious Jewish communities. The Simon Wiesenthal Centre in Los Angeles produced in a 360-page report a history of Abs that overwhelmingly demonstrated his unfitness to serve, concluding:

'Hermann J Abs, a key official of the Nazi war machine, does not have the *moral credentials* to represent a *spiritual institution* such as the Vatican. Whatever expertise he might bring to banking is irrevocably nullified by his active involvement in the Third Reich, a regime universally condemned for the brutal murder and torture of millions of innocent men, women and children.' [Italics in original.]

As so often with awkward letters and reports, the Vatican ignored these demands. Vatican officials took the view that Abs, who had come heavily recommended by the German

Cardinal Höffner, had failed to stimulate any protests when for ten years he had served as an observer for the Vatican on the International Atomic Energy Commission. They claimed he was one of 'the best minds in the banking business'. A copy of the Wiesenthal dossier was given to Monsignor Jorge Mejia, the Secretary of the Holy See's Commission for Religious Relations with Judaism. Mejia discussed the controversy with the Pope and there the matter rested.

The Vatican's 'four wise men' duly concluded that the 'Vatican Bank bore no responsibility for the collapse, nor did the bank have any financial obligations towards the bankrupt Ambrosiano.' At the same time, the College of Cardinals convened in Rome for an extraordinary consistory. The purpose of such rarely called gatherings was to provide the cardinals with an opportunity to give advice to the Pontiff. Inevitably the agenda was dominated by the Banco Ambrosiano crash and the implications not just for the Vatican Bank but the entire Vatican State. The cardinals knew that the 'not guilty' verdict of the 'four wise men' was not the end of the matter but only a marker put down by the Vatican as an initial negotiating position with the Italian Government. There had been much talk that Church finances would be crippled by the crash, but again this was yet another negotiating position. In fact, its banks and investment arms were awash with money.

As in August 1978 and October 1978, so yet again in November 1982, many cardinals wanted to know why Archbishop Marcinkus was still running the bank. Their questions were stifled by others who knew that it was the Pope and the Pope alone who had constantly blocked the removal of Marcinkus. The consistory also talked of reforming the Roman Curia – an equally futile ambition while Wojtyla was in power. One Vatican resident bitterly observed of this situation, 'The Holy Father often talks of reforming the Curia. Just talks about it. No action, just words.' During his closing address the Pope referred to the many public questions being asked about the Vatican Bank and its relationship with Calvi's Ambrosiano. He said,

'The exact nature of that relationship must be approached with great prudence . . . It is a complex question which has now been weighed in all parts. The Vatican is prepared to do everything required to resolve the matter with a mind to the whole truth being revealed.'

This statement did not prevent the Pope and his principal advisors from continuing to resist every effort made by the Italian Government and its Justice Department to question the Vatican Bank's President Archbishop Paul Marcinkus, and his colleagues within the bank, Luigi Mennini and Pelligrino De Strobel. All three were wanted by the Italian judiciary to stand trial yet the Pope's advisors blocked access to them for years.

The Pope was blissfully untroubled by the scandal and the missing millions. Discussing it with close colleagues, he laughed as he observed, 'I can't wait to see how they get out of this.' The 'they' in question were certain members of the Curia. The thought that as ultimately it was his bank, and therefore the legal and moral responsibilities were his, never occurred to Wojtyla.

While the Pope talked of his desire for the whole truth to be revealed, Marcinkus was in secret returning billions of lire to the Italian banks within the Ambrosiano group. Aided by Mennini and De Strobel, his efforts to conceal the extent of the criminal activities began less than one month after the murder of Roberto Calvi. Banca Cattolica del Veneto was owed $31 million and the first tranche made its return journey to Venice on 15 July 1982. By the time

Marcinkus had finished that particular exercise the amount with interest had risen to over $35 million. When the Vatican newspaper *L'Osservatore Romano* announced on 17 October, 'The Institute for Religious Works has not received any amount of money from the Ambrosiano group nor from Roberto Calvi and thus nothing has to be returned,' Archbishop Marcinkus was returning the loot as fast as he dared. A further $47 million went back to the Ambrosiano head office in Milan. There was still the $213 million that the Vatican Bank owed to the Calvi banks of Peru and Nassau but a man can only do so much laundering at once, with so many eyes on him. The Pope meanwhile assured concerned visitors that 'I am sure that it will be all happily resolved.'

The resolution was a long time in coming. The Italian media had a field day as headlines demanded, 'Holy Father give us back our millions.' Negotiations continued throughout 1983 and into the following year far away from the public gaze. A few months before the second anniversary of Calvi's murder and the subsequent crash of his empire a deal was announced between the Vatican and the large consortium of international banks that had been taken to the cleaners by Calvi. By mid-May 1984, the details of the deal were clear. The international banks were going to get back approximately two thirds of the $600 million they had loaned Calvi's Luxembourg holding company. Of that sum $244 million would be paid by the Vatican Bank.

Cardinal Casaroli had done extremely well as chief negotiator for the Vatican. He had urged, indeed insisted, that the Vatican would have to make significant recompense. The payment was made on 30 June 1984 by the Vatican 'on the basis of non-culpability' but 'in recognition of moral involvement'. The $244 million was easily acquired. Firstly Marcinkus sold Vianni, a construction company. He had in 1980 sold two million shares in Vianni to a

Panamanian front company, Laramie, already owned by the Vatican Bank. The money to pay for the non-existent sale of the two million shares, $20 million, had come from Calvi. Now in 1984 Marcinkus sold the same shares again plus a further four million shares, thus relinquishing Vatican control over Vianni. In return he acquired $60 million.

The sale of the Banco di Roma per Svizzera in Lugano released further funds and the balance of the compensation payment to the European banks came from the Vatican's own in-house secret society: Opus Dei. Opus Dei had been negotiating with Roberto Calvi at the time of his murder. The sect was prepared to buy control of Banco Ambrosiano and cover the $1.3 billion hole.

Those who ordered Roberto Calvi's murder had not believed the Milanese banker's assurances that the money would be found and that all debts would be covered. With Calvi dead and the hole exposed, by September 1982 some of the most senior members of Opus Dei assured the Pope that when the debris was cleared away and the cost to the Vatican clarified, Opus Dei would be there with the necessary funds. In return for putting the outstanding balance on the table, Opus Dei gained something that they had craved for years. The Pope did not even wait until the financial matters were resolved. Within two months of the Opus Dei offer Pope John Paul II granted the sect recognition as a 'personal prelature'. This status ensured that this ultra-secret society was answerable to no one within the Roman Catholic Churches except the Pope and the Pope alone. No local bishop could discipline or sanction Opus Dei. Overnight Opus Dei became in effect a global movement without specific diocese. So it remains.

After the multi-million-dollar settlement in mid-1984 the word in the Vatican Village was that Archbishop Paul Marcinkus would be removed before the end of the year. A bank President who has been a partner in the criminal collapse of a string of banks and incurred for his own bank debts running into hundreds of millions of dollars could hardly expect a year-end bonus. Yet again the Pope refused to remove Marcinkus. In his defence, it has been argued that Paul Marcinkus was a 'virgin banker', a decent man gulled by criminals. But in reality, in a decade of business partnership with Calvi, Marcinkus's gambits displayed an extremely astute and devious mind. After Calvi's murder, he very secretly laundered huge sums of money back to creditors of the Banco Ambrosiano, to conceal the magnitude of his crimes.

Nor, it has to be said, was the Pope a financial innocent. Cardinal Edmund Casimir Szoka, former Archbishop of Detroit, was Head of the Prefecture of Economic Affairs of the Holy See (the Catholic Church's Treasury Secretary) when he made these comments about the Pope: 'He's very sharp, catches on quickly to the figures and accounting. He follows it closely, asks questions. Don't forget, he was a bishop of a diocese and once had similar responsibilities.' Though Wojtyla had journeyed through his religious career without benefit of a bank account or personal funds, he was very proficient in financial matters. The needs of his huge archdiocese of Cracow demanded an expertise of a very high order. Its wealth was considerable; unfortunately the diocese was asset-rich and cash-poor. A cash flow problem was a constant companion. Despite all of these difficulties and a great many others the Cracow Archdiocese under Karol Wojtyla not only survived but thrived financially. During the entire period of Wojtyla's episcopate not one programme or initiative had to be dropped for lack of funds. This was a real achievement, and it gave Karol Wojtyla a thorough training in accounting and finance before he became Pope.

Meanwhile 'the Shark', Michele Sindona, hailed by Pope Paul VI as the saviour of the Vatican, was serving out a twenty-five-year prison sentence which had begun in June 1980. He had been found guilty on sixty-five counts, including fraud, conspiracy, perjury, issuing false bank statements and misappropriation of funds in what was at that time the biggest banking disaster in United States history. By 1984 he had settled into a comfortable prison routine in New York State. He was wanted in a variety of other places for other alleged crimes, including many of which I had publicly accused him. In September 1984 the Justice Department found the evidence on these specific crimes so compelling that he was extradited to Milan for trial on charges for the fraudulent bankruptcy of his own financial empire and the contract murder of Giorgio Ambrosoli.

In the light of my central contention within *In God's Name* that Pope John Paul I had been poisoned, Sindona's first reaction upon hearing he was to be extradited back to Milan was particularly interesting.

'If I finally get there, if no one does me in first – *and I've already heard talk of giving me a poisoned cup of coffee* – I'll make my trial into a real circus. I'll tell everything.' [Author's italics.]

Back in Milan prison he was visited by other members of P2. Subsequently he had a change of mind about telling everything. He requested that his trial on the fraud charges should proceed without his presence in the courtroom. Surprisingly, this request was granted. In 1985, a Milan court found Sindona guilty of fraudulent bankruptcy and sentenced him to a term of fifteen years' imprisonment. On 18 March 1986 another Milan court found Michele Sindona guilty of ordering the murder of Giorgio Ambrosoli and he was sentenced to life imprisonment. Before he could commence either of these sentences he was due to be returned to the United States to serve the remainder of the initial twenty-five-year sentence. Confronted with the realisation that he would undoubtedly die in prison, the sixty-six-year-old man made a decision. He would break his Mafia oath of *Omerta*. He would tell all. Italian police intelligence sources advised me that he intended to barter information on a wide range of events including the circumstances surrounding the death of Albino Luciani, Pope John Paul I.

On Thursday, 20 March, after drinking his breakfast coffee he screamed, 'They have poisoned me!' He died two days later on 22 March.

The murder of Sindona is a classic example of the power of P2. Because of fears that an attempt might be made on his life, Sindona was being held in a maximum-security prison. He was subjected to constant twenty-four-hour TV surveillance, there were never less than three guards with him, and his food and drink came into the prison in sealed containers.

Luigi Mennini, the Managing Director of the Vatican Bank, was more fortunate than Calvi and Sindona. In July 1984 he was sentenced by a Milan court to seven years' imprisonment after being convicted of fraud and other charges related to *Il Crack* Sindona. Mennini – a man described by close associates as 'rabid to trade and speculate. His behaviour was that of a compulsive gambler, gambling with someone else's money' – remained under the protection of the Pope as did fellow Vatican Bank executives Marcinkus and Pelligrino De Strobel.

Double standards continued apace throughout the 1980s. While he continued to give sanctuary to the convicted and the fugitives from Italian justice, Pope John Paul II lectured the Swiss on banking ethics. In July 1984 he told them, 'The world of finance, too, is a world of human beings, our world, subject to the consciences of all of us.' While the Holy Father roundly condemned apartheid, the

Vatican Bank was secretly loaning $172 million to official agencies of the South African apartheid regime.

Although his P2 masonic network was theoretically in ruins, Licio Gelli continued to demonstrate his resilience. In August 1982 Gelli began to encounter problems with one of his secret bank accounts in Switzerland. Every time that Gelli, still in South Africa, attempted to transfer funds, the account failed to respond accordingly. The USB bank in Geneva advised him that he would have to appear personally. Using one of several false passports that the Argentinian military junta had created for him, he flew to Madrid and then Geneva on 13 September 1982. He duly presented documentation and was advised that there would be a short delay. Minutes later he was arrested. His account had been frozen at the request of the Italian Government.

The account in question had been created for Gelli by Roberto Calvi and the Milanese banker had poured over $100 million into it. At the time of his arrest Gelli had been attempting to transfer the remaining $55 million in the account to Uruguay. Extradition proceedings began but, as always when a member of P2 was involved, they took a very long time. By the summer of 1983 Gelli was still fighting extradition from Champ Dollon Swiss prison. With a general election imminent in Italy, the parliamentary investigation into P2 was suspended, allowing the Christian Democrats to field at least five P2 members at the election.

Signorina Tina Anselmi, who had chaired the parliamentary commission, was asked her views on P2 after two years' intensive study. She said,

'P2 is by no means dead. It still has power. It is working in the institutions. It is moving in society. It has money, means and instruments still at its disposal. It still has fully operative power centres in South

America. It is also still able to condition, at least in part, Italian political life.'

The evidence overwhelmingly confirmed the validity of Signorina Anselmi's statements. When news of Gelli's arrest became known in Argentina, Admiral Emilio Massera, a member of the local ruling junta, remarked, 'Signor Gelli has rendered invaluable service to Argentina. This country has much to thank him for and will forever be in his debt.' Admiral Massera, like General Carlos Suarez Mason, the First Army commander, and Jose Lope Rega, the organiser of the Argentine death squads, was a member of the Argentine section of P2. In Uruguay, P2 membership included the former Commander in Chief of the Armed Forces, General Gregorio Alvarez.

If anyone in Italy or elsewhere considered that Tina Anselmi was merely attempting to score political points before an election, they must have received a jolt on 10 August 1983. Licio Gelli escaped. The Swiss authorities, attempting to cover their deep embarrassment, laid the entire blame at the feet of one corrupt guard, Umberto Cerdana, who officially took a derisory bribe of just over £6,000 from Gelli. He was driven first to France by his son in a hired BMW, and then the pair were transported by an unwitting helicopter pilot to Monte Carlo where Gelli hoped to get emergency dental treatment. His search for a dentist took him to Uruguay, via a yacht belonging to Francesco Pazienza, a man who claimed to have been a good friend of the late Roberto Calvi. Gelli finally settled in a ranch a few miles north of Montevideo. He was wanted in many countries, accused of many crimes, but the mass of information that he had so diligently acquired over the years ensured his continued protection.

The Italian election in June 1983 resulted in Signor Bettino Craxi, one of the many beneficiaries of Calvi's largesse, becoming Prime Minister. Told of Gelli's escape he said, 'The flight of Gelli confirms that the Grand Master has a network of powerful friends.' Just how powerful has been demonstrated again and again by *l'intoccabile* – the 'untouchable'. Re-arrest would be followed by a reopening of the cell door. When he was finally put behind bars in early 1999 he applied for and was granted a change of location from a prison to his villa on the grounds of his health.

Through all this, through the murders, the imprisonments, the fines, the manhunts, the media battering, the Vatican Three continued in their posts, making money for the Pope, despite the universal condemnation of his bank and its senior staff. Wojtyla acted upon his own advice, given to Marcinkus when his banker had come complaining about the 'persecution' by his critics. 'Ignore them.'

Chapter 6

Papal Politics I:
A Holy Alliance?

F EW PAPACIES HAVE INSPIRED so many myths as the reign of Pope John Paul II. One of the most enduring concerns his role, alongside US President Ronald Reagan, in the collapse of Communism in Europe at the end of the twentieth century. Serious writers have suggested that the two men conspired to bring about the destruction of the Soviet Empire with the Pope virtually single-handedly creating Solidarity and the President secretly pouring millions of dollars into Poland to sustain Wojtyla's creation. The truth, however, is somewhat less spectacular.

Since its very beginning, the United States has been a predominantly Protestant country, ruled by Protestants, with a historic suspicion and hostility towards Roman Catholics. Even John F Kennedy, the only Roman Catholic to date to be elected President, was very careful to keep the number who shared his faith within his administration to a minimum and to keep his church at some distance from government.

Though not himself a Roman Catholic, Ronald Reagan numbered a great many who were among his close friends and acquaintances. His cabinet included a disproportionate number: Haig, Donovan, Bennett, Heckler, Clark. Among his speech-writing team and staffers in the Office of Public Liaison were Peggy Noonan, Pat Buchanan, Linda Chavez, Bob Reilly, Carl Anderson and Tony Dolan, all of them devout, practising Roman Catholics. There were also National Security Advisors Richard Allen, Director of the CIA William Casey, William Clark, Vernon Walters and Ed Rowny. William Clark, who served in turn as Secretary of the Interior and National Security Advisor, had a particularly close friendship with Ronald Reagan.

On 11 February 1981 President Reagan appointed William Wilson as his personal representative to the Holy See. Wilson, a close friend of Reagan's for many years, was one of the loyal cabal in Reagan's kitchen cabinet. Wilson's time at the Vatican was not entirely appreciated by the Vatican. Within days of his arrival he allegedly let it be known that he had a personal hit list of priests and bishops in Latin American countries whom the Reagan administration wanted removed from office. The Secretariat were unimpressed with this piece of lobbying. The story was leaked by a Vatican official to an Italian newspaper, then vehemently denied by William Wilson. Instead he began to concern himself in a wide range of activities on behalf of the Reagan administration, including lobbying for unqualified support for the Chilean military dictatorship of Pinochet and the Argentine military junta as well as US policies on numerous other South American issues, the Middle East, funding Afghan rebels, Ukrainian Church status and Poland.

Within twelve months of taking up his post, Wilson had succeeded in bewildering even himself. A memorandum from National Security Council staffer, Dennis Blair, to National Security Advisor William Clark, requesting that Clark should meet with Wilson, explains:

'The main objective of your meeting with Bill is to straighten out his chain of command. He has been confused about who he receives direction from with embarrassing diplomatic results. This has been a problem for months but it was highlighted by the incident of the President's remarks about the Pope's letter at his January 20th press conference.'

The 'embarrassing diplomatic results' were the very public demonstrations of frequent misunderstandings, confusion and total incomprehension. Some of the most spectacular of these occurred over Poland. As recorded earlier, in April 1981, the Pope had the first of a series of meetings with the head of the CIA William Casey. These meetings are very much part of the myth around the Wojtyla–Reagan relationship. There was certainly an exchange of views and opinions. The two men had much in common ranging from their deep hatred of Communism to their admiration of right-wing dictators, like Marcos of the Philippines and Pinochet of Chile, whom they considered a bulwark against godless Communism. But the exchange of intelligence information that Casey allegedly sought from the Pope and his officials at the Secretariat of State never materialised. As always the Vatican played its cards close to its collective chest.

John Paul II most certainly despised Communism but he was never enchanted with capitalism and the American way of life. He remained deeply suspicious of the United States and saw most Western countries as decadent and morally inferior to Poland. His views on such matters were well known and caused a continuing friction with his Secretary of State, Cardinal Casaroli.

At the time of Casey's first visit, John Paul II was preoccupied with the looming problem of Cardinal Wyszynski's imminent death and the appointment of his successor. The Pope attempted to exploit the memory of Wyszynski at the time of the Primate's funeral to buy some breathing space. He called for the four-day period of mourning to be extended to thirty days, which should be 'a period of special prayers, peace and reflection'. This was seen by many observers as a direct attempt by the Pope to prevent further confrontations between the regime and Solidarity before the approaching Communist Party Congress in July. The papal plea was rebuffed within days when on 4 July Solidarity's National Co-ordinating Commission called a two-hour national strike to take place in seven days' time. The situation was showing disturbing similarities to the events prior to the Soviet invasion of Czechoslovakia in June 1968.

When the Communist Party leadership in Poland turned to the Catholic Church for help, as they had done so many times during Cardinal Wyszynski's life, it had to make do with the Cardinal's former advisor, Dr Romuald Kukolwicz. The bishops gathered in Rome were contacted; they could only repeat the Pope's request for thirty days of national mourning. The Pope hesitated for six weeks and only appointed Bishop Glemp to the Polish Primacy after great pressure was exerted upon him to appoint 'somebody – anybody – but before 14th July', the date that the Polish Communist Party Congress was due to begin. Jozef Glemp was to prove to be a nobody in a somebody's chair. The Church's influence within Poland continued to diminish. Glemp's appeals for all protest actions to be halted were ignored.

Throughout the summer of 1981, life for the man in the Warsaw street or the woman in the Cracow market place became progressively grimmer. The various concessions won in the heady latter half of 1980 now seemed meaningless. The queues for the already rationed basic commodities got longer. Strikes were frequent and hunger marches a regular event. Total state censorship of the media, from which all Solidarity spokesmen were banned, tightened the screw yet further. The Soviet Union gave it a few more turns during the first week of September when they commenced a huge nine-day naval and military exercise in the Baltic. Using more than sixty ships and some twenty five thousand servicemen, the exercise included landings on the shores of Latvia and Lithuania. Simultaneously *Rudé Právo*, the Communist Party daily in Czechoslovakia, ran front-page stories declaring that Solidarity was fine-tuning its plans to seize power in Poland. The activities had been designed to coincide with the commencement of the First National Congress of Solidarity due to begin in Gdansk on 5 September.

Just how wide the gulf between the Church and Solidarity had become was demonstrated when the delegates adopted a message 'To the Working People of Eastern Europe'. It challenged the very essence of Communism as, addressing the workers of Albania, Bulgaria, Czechoslovakia, East Germany (the GDR), Romania, Hungary 'and all peoples of the Soviet Union', it offered to 'support all of you who have decided to take the difficult path and fight for free trade unions'. This political naivety won no friends within the Vatican. As for the Soviets, they told the Polish regime that the entire Solidarity congress was 'a disgusting provocation'. More significantly, the Soviets called on the Party and the Polish Government to take 'determined and radical steps'.

There was a dreadful inevitability beginning to emerge within the divided country. Crisis makes for curious alliances. The Polish Catholic Church and the Government led by General Jaruzelski and the moderate wings of both the ruling Communist Party, the PZPR (The Polish United Workers' Party) and Solidarity were urging patient negotiation. The hard-liners within both the Party and Solidarity were intent on pursuing confrontation. Shuttle diplomacy between Warsaw and Rome began to accelerate. Suggestions of power-sharing were floated by, among others, the Prime Minister: 'A grand coalition of the Communists, the Catholic Church and Solidarity' was much discussed but the Church predictably vacillated on the issue.

Pope John Paul II's biographers, including the personally approved George Weigel, are agreed that, notwithstanding the appointment of Bishop Glemp as Primate, '. . . everyone knew that, with Cardinal Wyszynski's death, the *de facto* Primate of Poland was in Rome.' That being the case, the Pope should have kept a very tight grip of a situation that continued to deteriorate.

If ever there was a moment for the Pope to seize the day, it was when Prime Minister Jaruzelski floated the idea of 'a grand coalition' of Communists, Church and Solidarity. Lech Walesa, his KOR advisors and other senior figures within Solidarity saw it as a trap to control their movement while the Polish Church looked to Rome. The Pope shrank from such political involvement either public or private. The *de facto* Primate missed an historic opportunity. Undeterred, Glemp, Jaruzelski and Walesa held an unprecedented meeting on 4 November seeking solutions to the crisis. Views were exchanged but solutions remained elusive.

In the Vatican, the Pope, talking to members of the KOR and other Polish intellectuals with ties to Solidarity, spoke of the freedom movement being irreversible, but his demeanour belied his words. Tadeusz Mazowiecki recalled,

'I remember that I told him that we had to go back quickly. We'd had worrying news from Poland. His response was, "Yes, everybody is in a hurry. Everybody is going back." He was very worried.'

What was needed at that moment was not handwringing but a political initiative, such as a papal invitation to

Walesa, Glemp and Jaruzelski to reconvene in the Vatican with Wojtyla, or his Secretary of State Casaroli, in the role of honest broker, to pull a compromise from the fire, but the man for that kind of initiative, Cardinal Wyszinski, was dead and in his grave.

On 24 November military forces were sent to 2,000 major centres throughout Poland. It was announced that the reason for this national troop movement was to co-ordinate plans for the winter. No matter how one looked at that statement it was entirely accurate. On 26 November the Polish Church issued a communiqué that indicated that both Rome and the National Church were fully aware of what was at stake. 'The country is faced with the threat of civil war and loss of all gains already achieved.'

The bishops declared that the only hope of a peaceful solution was through national unity. They condemned the authorities for hampering the process of 'bridge-building between the Government and the people . . . no under-standing or reconciliation would be possible without free-dom of expression'. There was much more in similar vein. Nonetheless in November alone there were 105 strikes of indefinite duration and another 115 strikes were planned. None of these actions, however, were addressed within the Episcopal Conference communiqué. If Poland was to be saved statesmanship was urgently required from the various leaders, particularly the '*de facto* primate' John Paul II. Lech Walesa would later admit that by the first week of December he had lost control of events. 'I took a hard position against my convictions, in order not to be isolated.' Others in the movement, including Jacek Huron and Adam Michnik, continued to oppose 'the hard position' bitterly but voices of sanity and reason were not in demand in November 1981. General Jaruzelski may well have been planning a military coup d'état since 1980. Meanwhile he and those around him were being inexorably pushed into acting in isolation against their own people by the Soviet Politburo who feared a domino effect within the Warsaw Pact countries.

The Pope, meanwhile, appeared to be greatly preoccupied in an entirely unrelated power battle with the Jesuit Order while in the Primate's residence Glemp continuously agonised over what Wyszynski would have done. In a mere six months, much of the legacy that Stefan Wyszynski had bequeathed his country had been squandered. On 27 November the Episcopate had again urged that some form of national accord was the only solution. Glemp offered himself to act as mediator. The response from the Communist Party's Central Committee was muted and on the day following Archbishop Glemp's proposal instructed their parliamentary group to introduce legislation to ban all strikes. On 3 December Solidarity's Central Committee responded. With all the hard-won agreements of 1980 now threatened, they declared that if Parliament did indeed pass such legislation they would call a twenty-four-hour general strike throughout Poland.

Glemp tried again on 5 December, meeting with Lech Walesa in an attempt to find a way out of the impasse. Walesa duly rebuffed him. The Warsaw branch of Solidarity called for co-ordinated protests throughout the country on 17 December in protest against the regime's intention to 'solve the conflicts by force'. Two days later Glemp made a further attempt. During this same period, the Pope was busily engaged with other more pressing matters, including blessing a mosaic of Mary to commemorate the 750th anniversary of the death of Saint Elizabeth of Hungary.

Little more than two years earlier the Polish Pope had been given the most extraordinary demonstration by the Polish nation during his nine-day visit of the unique place he occupied within the hearts and minds of his people. If during the autumn of 1981 he had chosen to engage

General Jaruzelski in a direct dialogue and demonstrated to the Polish Prime Minister that there was a third way and that through quiet diplomacy and mediation an acceptable compromise could be reached, an ongoing working accommodation with the Solidarity movement would have created an historic opportunity, not only for Poland but the entire Soviet European bloc. What was to occur in 1989 and 1990 could have been brought forward by six or more years. Far from bringing about the end of the Soviet Empire the Pope, by his inaction, his indecisiveness, his inability to apply the Wyszynski doctrine, prolonged it.

Archbishop Glemp had clearly seen the writing on the wall. During a meeting in November with Francis Meehan, the US Ambassador to Poland, Glemp told him that there 'was a good chance of martial law'. Meehan had duly reported this observation to Washington. In fact the concept of martial law did not exist within Poland's laws. What was declared was 'a state of war'. On 7 December, contrary to the Pope's instructions in October, Glemp waded into the choppy waters of Polish politics. He sent a letter to every deputy in the Sejm, a second to Prime Minister General Wojciech Jaruzelski, a third to Lech Walesa and a fourth to the Independent Students' Union. In different ways all four letters were seeking the same end, compromise and conciliation. Glemp's commendable effort was dismissed. On 11 December, Solidarity's National Commission met for a two-day conference in the Lenin Shipyard in Gdansk. In an act of self-delusion the Commission, after long and frequently over-heated debate and despite strong objections from their Catholic Church advisors, called for a referendum by 15 January 1982 to ask the nation to pass a vote of no confidence in the Government.

As the meeting broke up the delegates realised that none of the telephones, telexes or fax lines were working. They had been cut at three minutes to midnight, not just in the conference hall but throughout Poland, cutting off 3,439,700 private phones simultaneously.

The Government might have been having difficulty running the country but their military coup d'état was a model of efficiency. At midnight ZOMO, the anti-riot police, ransacked the Solidarity offices in Warsaw. The mass arrests had already begun and continued throughout the night. The security police had provided the militia units with the last known address of every single Polish citizen both home and abroad. Four thousand people vanished before dawn. The Solidarity National Co-ordinating Committee, who had only just finished drafting its four questions that it had planned to put to the nation by 15 January, were pulled out of their beds in a Gdansk hotel at 2.00 a.m. Lech Walesa was collected from his home and put on a plane to Warsaw. The first question of the aborted national referendum had been, 'Are you in favour of expressing a vote of no-confidence in the Government of General Wojciech Jaruzelski?'

Shortly before 1.00 a.m. the Pope was aroused to take a phone call from Emil Wojtaszek, the Polish ambassador to Italy. He told the Pope that General Jaruzelski had found it necessary to introduce 'temporary emergency measures' of a limited nature; 'temporary' being the Polish for eighteen months. The Pope was also advised that the Church would be expected to play a key role in mediation to eliminate the measures 'as soon as possible'.

At 6.00 a.m. Jaruzelski went on national television and radio. Stripped of party-speak he told the nation that there had been a military coup, the Communist party were no longer running the country, all trade union activity was banned; members of the military were appointed in Government ministries, in the provinces, the towns, the factories. To ensure the execution of orders from the Military Council there was to be a dusk-to-dawn curfew, a ban on public gatherings, a ban on wearing specific uniforms and badges, freedom of movement was to be severely restricted. Mass internment was already a reality, there was to be a strict censorship of mail and telecommunications and the closure of Poland's borders. Poland was at war with itself. The country and its peoples would suffer greatly in the years ahead not least because of the failure of will of the few who had been in a position to pull Poland back from this particular precipice.

General Jaruzelski, the Prime Minister, First Secretary and Head of the Armed Services played the role of a man who had chosen the lesser of two evils to perfection. Martial law was preferable to 'intervention' by the Soviet Union. Two days earlier on the tenth the Soviet Politburo had been in session where the first item under discussion was Poland and Jaruzelski's request for $1.5 billion in additional aid during the coming first quarter of 1982. That request was made on the assumption that the Soviets would also be shipping aid at 1981 levels. It is very clear from many Politburo documents, that since 1981 the Soviets had tied additional aid to Polish action to suppress Solidarity. In July 1981 Soviet Foreign Minister Gromyko had told Kania and Jaruzelski that 'the nature of Soviet–Polish economic, political and other relations will depend on how things shape up in Poland'. Brezhnev reiterated this formula when he spoke to Kania later the same month and again in August in a discussion with the East German leader Honecker.

Although the Soviets could ill afford such largesse they were more than happy to deliver if the Polish military and the security forces effected the coup without any external military assistance. However, up to the very eve of the martial law declaration Jaruzelski was seeking much more than a huge increase in foreign aid. During the Politburo meeting of 10 December the head of the KGB, Yuri Andropov, complained that 'Jaruzelski has been more than persistent in setting forth economic demands from us and has made the implementation of "Operation X" (the military coup) contingent on our willingness to offer economic assistance; and I would say even more than that, *he is raising the question, albeit indirectly, of receiving military assistance as well.*'

A few moments later Yuri Andropov made a truly extraordinary prophetic statement. He referred to a meeting between Jaruzelski and three senior Soviet officials on the previous day and Jaruzelski's understanding of what one of the officials, Kulikov, had said regarding Soviet military aid.

'If Comrade Kulikov actually did speak about the introduction of troops then I believe he did this incorrectly. *We can't risk such a step. We do not intend to introduce troops into Poland. That is the proper position and we must adhere to it to the end. I don't know how things will turn out in Poland, but even if Poland falls under the control of Solidarity, that's the way it will be.* And if the capitalist countries pounce on the Soviet Union, and you know they have already reached agreement on a variety of economic and political sanctions, that will be very burdensome for us. We must be concerned above all with our own country and about the strengthening of the Soviet Union.'

Andropov, the head of the KGB, knew full well the realities that were confronting the Soviet Union. He had been the principal advocate of the disastrous invasion of Afghanistan. By late 1981 it had become the Soviet Union's Vietnam. The ruinous cost of the war and a basket-case economy at home meant that Western sanctions could cripple the entire Communist bloc.

Moments later, Andrei Gromyko, the great survivor, weighed in. 'No Politburo member is coming. No troops will be sent. Economic aid will be considered later. A statement of support will be made at a time and date yet to be determined.' An anguished Jaruzelski could not hide the pain as he responded, 'You are distancing yourselves from us.' In reality there had always been that distance since the Soviets had abandoned their plans to invade Poland the previous year. The collapse of the once so powerful Soviet Union can be dated from that failure of will in December 1980.

'Be not afraid,' the Pope's first public utterance after his election, was a message that he had carried to Poland in June 1979. It had been warmly embraced by the majority of the country. On the morning of Sunday 13 December 1981 many in Poland were deeply afraid. Everywhere there were soldiers. Even the TV newscasters were dressed in uniform. The junta's control of the media was total and wild rumours blossomed to fill the vacuum along with curfew, identity cards, instant arrests. For the third time in living memory Poland was an occupied country but this time the occupiers came from within. The Polish nation turned as she had done many times in the past to her faith, to her Church. On Sunday evening Archbishop Glemp spoke in the Jesuit Church of Mary, the Patroness of Warsaw, in the old town of the city. It was a sermon that the army, who controlled TV and radio, would broadcast a number of times.

'. . . In our country the new reality is martial law . . . The authority ceases to be an authority of dialogue between citizens . . . and becomes an authority equipped with the means of summary coercion and demanding obedience. Opposition to the decisions of authority under martial law could cause violent coercion, including bloodshed because the authority has the arms at its disposal . . . The authorities consider that the exceptional nature of martial law is dictated by higher necessity, it is the choice of a lesser rather than a greater evil. Assuming the correctness of such reasoning the man in the street will subordinate himself to the new situation.'

The Church 'received with pain the severance of dialogue'. But for the Archbishop the most important thing was to avoid bloodshed. 'There is nothing of greater value than human life. I shall plead, even if I have to plead on my knees. Do not start a fight of Pole against Pole.'

Within days, other Polish bishops, appalled at the collaborating appeasement message of Glemp's sermon, had sprung into action. A stinging attack on the military junta was issued as an episcopate communiqué throughout the country. When news reached Warsaw that nine miners and four security police had been killed and thirty-seven miners injured during a ZOMO attack on men conducting a sit-in at Wujek colliery in Katowice, Archbishop Glemp, under pressure from General Jaruzelski, withdrew the communiqué.

Speaking in Polish during his traditional Sunday midday Angelus seven hours before Glemp's sermon, John Paul II was very aware that his words would be heard live in Poland via Vatican radio.

'The events of the last few hours require me to turn my attention once again to the cause of our homeland and to call for prayer. I remind you of what I said in September. Polish blood cannot be spilled because too much has already been spilled, especially during the war. Everything must be done to build the future of our homeland peacefully. I entrust Poland and all my countrymen to the Virgin Mary who has been given to us for our defence.'

A few days later during a general audience the Pope power-fully endorsed Glemp's Sunday sermon.

The resistance against the coup was widespread and varied, including sit-in strikes, street protests and a refusal to co-operate with the military. Demonstrators in the fac-tories, mines, steel works and pits were met with an excess of violence, not from the army but the members of the ZOMO who relished the opportunities of inflicting appal-ling violence without fear of any retribution. Facing them were unarmed people, ill prepared, leaderless and fre-quently very frightened who nonetheless showed astonish-ing courage. Without their Solidarity leaders, their intellectual advisors and any of the communication infra-structures necessary to mount a co-ordinated national resistance the nation experienced an internal spiritual awakening. Many of them were not particularly devout and their constant attendance at church often had less to do with Christian faith and more to do with a desire to spite the Communist regime: 'ONI' – 'THEM'.

The Polish nation was certainly going to need spiritual strength to sustain it through the darkness. The repres-sion, given such momentum on the night of 11 December 1981 produced the deaths of at least 115 and the im-prisonment of up to 25,000. Yet what was inconceivable for the Pope in early November became an imperative less than a week after martial law had been declared. A secret dialogue between the Pope and the General began as the two men exchanged regular private hand-written letters.

Apart from the periodic visits to the Vatican by the head of the CIA, William Casey, another member of the Reagan administration, General Vernon Walters, had a series of meetings with the Pope. The first occurred on 30 November 1981, just eleven days before the military coup in Poland. Walters had been appointed Ambassador at Large by

President Reagan in June 1981. His primary task, performed for a number of previous presidents, was to liaise with a wide variety of heads of state. A devout Catholic, he had been educated in several countries including France and the United Kingdom where he attended Stonyhurst College. A gifted linguist, he was fluent in French, Spanish, Portuguese, Italian, German, Dutch and Russian. He conducted negotiations with the North Vietnamese and Chinese in Paris from 1969 to 1972. As Deputy Director of the CIA from 1972 to 1976 he nursed a number of major CIA assets including King Hassan of Morocco and King Hussein of Jordan. General Pinochet of Chile had been a good friend since the two men had been majors. Ferdinand Marcos of the Philippines was another CIA asset that Walters looked after. After William Casey, the Pope must have found Walters to be the personification of refinement.

Reporting directly to Secretary of State Haig, General Walters' primary task was to persuade various heads of state to support any US position or policy under discussion. The Pope was a totally different proposition. At the time of General Walters' first audience with the Pope, Poland was on the brink of a military coup. CIA asset Colonel Kuklinski, after passing the Polish regime's plans for the takeover to Washington, had fled the country on 7 November and, long before Walters appeared in the papal apartments, was being debriefed by Langley.

On 13 November Walters' superior, Secretary of State Haig, had warned President Reagan that the crushing of Solidarity and with it the rising Polish democracy was very close. On the morning after Walters met the Pope, Haig would follow up with an even more urgent plea to the President: '. . . Our entire tradition and security interests dictate prompt action . . .' Yet it is abundantly clear from the secret cable that Walters sent to Haig immediately he left the Vatican and drove to the US Embassy in Rome, that

Poland rated only a passing reference near the end of the Pope's meeting with Walters. 'I said, Poland is the great Soviet dilemma. The Pope replied the Soviets think only in terms of military force. All their plans are based upon the threat or use of force.'

General Walters had begun the meeting by explaining the 'nature of my job as ambassador-at-large'. He then continued with details of his recent trips to South America and Africa. He briefed the Pope on his conversations in May with Chilean officials to discuss the Beagle Channel dispute between Chile and Argentina, an issue on which the Vatican was acting as mediator. Walters talked to the Pope about US activities in Central America.

'I explained our efforts to improve the human rights situation without causing counter-productive embarrassment to governments by shouting out their faults from the roof tops. Violence actually rose in the years the US used public condemnation of governments to attempt to reform their actions.'

The General's version of US involvement in Central America is remarkable in the light of realities of the region, which are examined later within this chapter. 'In El Salvador we have only fifty military security personnel; the Soviets have over 300 in Peru alone. More than the US has in all of Latin America excluding the base at Panama.' The Pope did not take issue with any of these statements. Indeed he nodded and told Walters, 'Yes, I understand that this is the situation.' In fact it was far from being the situation. The General had neglected to give the Pope the number of US forces based in Panama. It was 10,000. He neglected to mention the additional $25 million in military aid that the Reagan administration had given to the junta in El Salvador within two months of entering office. This military aid would continue to rise. In 1984 alone it reached over $500 million.

The General also neglected to mention the 17,000 US backed and financed Contras based in southern Honduras from where they waged war against the democratically elected Nicaraguan Government. There was a great deal more on US military aid to a variety of Central American regimes that the General neglected to mention. Very much the Cold War warrior, Walters talked of

'The Cuban and Soviet mischief-making in the region . . . The Nicaraguans have 152 mm guns, Soviet-built tanks and pilots trained in Bulgaria. We seek a peaceful solution that will not endanger the lives and freedom of the Latin American people.'

Walters was highly censorious of those sections of the priesthood and the various religious orders who, like a significant number of the population – in some instances the majority – were opposed to US policies and to the presence of US military advisors, security personnel and US arms being used to sustain those policies. 'The religious have posed problems for us. Unfortunately some help the guerrillas and thereby tend to undermine the credibility of many religious in the area.' Walters was particularly critical of the Jesuits. This struck a very receptive chord with the Pope who only the previous month after a long running battle with the Jesuits had placed his own nominee in charge of the Order, an act of unprecedented intervention.

Vernon Walters then took the opportunity to praise Wojtyla's papacy as he recalled being in St Peter's Square when the man from Poland had been elected. There then followed the brief interchange on Poland recorded earlier and the meeting was over.

The authors of the book *His Holiness*, Bernstein and Poletti, claim that during this first meeting between General Walters and the Pope there was a great deal of discussion on Poland, during which the Pope was shown a number of satellite photographs of huge troop movements from the Warsaw Pact countries towards the Polish border, '. . . tens of thousands of troops diverted from their barracks in the USSR, East Germany, and Czechoslovakia towards the Pope's homeland'. They recount that the Pope was told how many divisions the Soviets had moved towards Poland.

It is difficult to believe that General Walters would have been so inept, so incompetent as to have delivered this alarming and frightening scenario to the Pope. What the photographs must have shown were the Warsaw Pact troop movements and the Soviet troop movements that took place *a year earlier in December 1980*. No such activities occurred in the second half of 1981. Indeed, the absence of such activity in the weeks before the military coup, as a leading historian on the Cold War, Professor Mark Kramer, has observed: 'was one of the reasons the United States remained complacent'. Of the intelligence information from Kuklinski, Walters in fact said not a word. Of the certainty based on all available intelligence that Jaruzelski was about to declare martial law, total silence.

After his audience, General Walters at the Pope's request talked at length to the Vatican Secretary of State, Cardinal Casaroli. Sources within his department have confirmed that he learned nothing from Walters that indicated just how close Poland was on the last day of November to a seizure of power by the Polish military. In fact, Secretary of State Haig had taken a decision not to advise Solidarity of Jaruzelski's plans. He feared that to do so would lead to 'stirring up violent resistance when the US had no intention of attempting to deliver assistance'. To have advised the Pope was, in the minds of the Reagan administration, tantamount to advising Solidarity. The solution applied was to advise neither.

The lack of communication between Washington and the Vatican was to become a recurring feature over the years and the failure was not one-sided. A week after the martial law declaration on 17 December, President Reagan cabled the Pope. He, or his advisors, considered they might have come up with a way of moving the situation in Poland forward. Reagan 'strongly urged' the Pope 'to draw on the great authority that you and the Church command in Poland to urge General Jaruzelski to agree to a conference involving himself, Archbishop Glemp and Lech Walesa'. Reagan also suggested that Jaruzelski should be urged to agree to permit Walesa to have eight or ten advisors of his own choosing with him in order to assure the Polish public 'that he was acting as a free agent'. The purpose of such a meeting, the President explained, would be to search for common ground 'for eliminating martial law and restoring social peace'. President Reagan had not been advised by the Pope that he had in fact begun just such a dialogue, secretly, two days earlier.

On 29 December President Reagan announced a raft of trade and economic sanctions against the Soviet Union and Poland. The victim was to be punished along with the aggressor. The Pope received a letter from Reagan on the day of the announcement which explained the measures and asked him to urge other Western countries to join the US in imposing sanctions. On 6 January a senior member of the Curia, Achille Silvestrini, handed envoy William Wilson the Pope's response. Not content with transmitting it to the White House, Wilson could not resist putting his own and Silvestrini's off-the-record interpretation of the letter when forwarding it to Reagan. The letter had gone through a number of drafts, was very carefully worded and studiously avoided saying that the Pope approved of the action of swingeing sanctions against his own country. He expressed 'appreciation' for 'humanitarian' measures on behalf of the Polish people. Envoy Wilson advised the President that Silvestrini had told him that 'press reports that suggested the Holy See disapproved of the US actions imposing sanctions against the Soviet Union and Poland were false'.

During President Reagan's White House press conference of 20 January he declared that the Pope had written to him approving of the sanctions. Reagan did this despite the fact that since the imposition of the sanctions the Pope had endorsed a declaration by the Polish bishops opposing the US sanctions on the grounds that sanctions would penalise the people without changing the situation. On 18 January the Joint Government-Church Commission in Poland issued a communiqué that not only condemned the sanctions as being against the interest of Poland but attacked them as being counter-productive to efforts to overcome the crisis. On 21 January Casaroli authorised the release of the Pope's letter to the President to illustrate that Reagan had seriously overreached himself.

The media roof fell in on the President whose National Security Advisor William Clark was advised by White House staffer Denis Blair,

'You may wish to personally mention to the President that in the case of letters from friendly heads of state, it is safest to check with the sender before talking about the contents publicly.'

This was one of the 'embarrassing diplomatic results' concerning Envoy William Wilson's tenure in Rome. There would be more. It is one thing to have the Pope tell you during a private meeting that he fully supported the US sanctions, it is quite another matter to share that information with the general public, particularly the Polish public.

Wojtyla was inviting himself in another pressing issue of the day. Reagan was aware that in late November 1981 the Pope was in the process of writing a letter to both the US and Soviet leaders on the nuclear arms race. While advising the Pope of his country's aspirations to seek 'verifiable reductions . . . in both nuclear and conventional weapons', Reagan argued that the United States had 'to maintain a military balance in order to deter aggression . . . We are deeply concerned by the steady Soviet build-up of military power and their willingness to employ force.' It was, as the Politburo transcripts for the period establish, also a time when the Soviet Empire was financially haemorrhaging to a slow and inevitable death. If just a fraction of the $40 billion budget that the United States was lavishing on the CIA and its other fourteen intelligence agencies had shown a decent return by giving accurate information on the realities within the USSR, a decade of wanton expenditure could have been averted.

In a letter to Ambassador Wilson, Secretary of State Haig observed:

'We are pleased at the Pope's interest in the negotiations . . . It would be misleading, we believe, to imply in any way that the US and the Soviet Union are equally responsible for having created the conditions that pose a danger of nuclear war. We would hope that his Holiness would give due weight to this consideration as he determines the most appropriate means of giving expression of the Church's views.'

The letter was a heavy-handed attempt to influence not merely papal thinking but also the conclusions of the Pontifical Academy of Sciences. A delegation from that august body were due at the White House in mid-December to present the President with a statement on the consequences of the uses of nuclear weapons. Haig made it clear to William Wilson that the US Government would welcome details of the contents of their report before the meeting. What greatly concerned the Reagan administration was to keep the Catholic Church onside with the US Government's position on nuclear armaments. The majority of the US bishops were highly critical of the administration's proposals. If the Pope could be persuaded to prevail upon the bishops, then life both internally and externally would be immeasurably easier for the President.

What Reagan, Haig and the other senior members of the Government really feared was the Pontifical Academy. This was no lightweight group of idealist left wingers that could be discounted. There were professors from the Massachusetts Institute of Technology, professors of Genetics and Biochemistry and Public Health, a total of fourteen Americans. Other members of the group came from Italy, the Soviet Union, France and Brazil. Each was an acknowledged, renowned expert in his field. A month before the Vatican delegation were due to meet with the President and give him a copy of their report, one of their number, Howard Hiatt, Professor of Public Health at Harvard University, published an article in the journal of the American Medical Association entitled 'Preventing the Last Epidemic'. It gives a devastating analysis from a medical standpoint of the madness and futility of nuclear war:

'According to press reports, President Reagan was transfused with eight units of blood [following his assassination attempt]. If each Washington victim of a nuclear attack needed as much blood (a burns victim would probably need much more), the blood requirements for Washington would exceed 6.4 million units. Furthermore, it would obviously be impossible to provide the personnel and equipment to administer such a vast quantity of blood. (To put this number into context, the blood stockpile in the American Red Cross Northeast Region on one particular day last month was approximately 11,000 units. The total amount of blood obtained throughout the United States during 1979 was 14 million units.) This is simply one small illustration of the futility of suggesting that we can handle the overwhelming medical needs that would follow a nuclear attack.'

The article certainly made a deep and lasting impression on President Reagan. He specifically referred to it within one of his cables to Pope John Paul II. The statement presented to the President by the Vatican group and its description of the aftermath of a nuclear attack were a powerful indictment of the so-called 'balance of terror'. Although the Pope had a full horror of such consequences of nuclear conflict, his position on the issue was not always consistent. Reagan, a shrewd political operator under his folksy manner, continued to court the Roman Catholics of America. In April 1982 he told the National Catholic Education Association,

'I am grateful for your help in shaping American policy to reflect God's will . . . And I look forward to further guidance from His Holiness Pope John Paul II during an audience I will have with him in June.'

The two men, who had both survived assassination attempts little more than one year earlier, met in the Vatican in the first week of June 1982. Israel chose the same day to invade Lebanon, a country whose Christian-Maronite community made it a special concern to the Holy See. An additional paragraph was rapidly drafted into the speech that Reagan made in the papal library to add Lebanon to the acute 'concern' section of the President's speech along with Latin America and Poland. On Latin America, Reagan claimed that 'we want to work closely with the Church in that area to help promote peace, social justice and reform, and to prevent the spread of repression and godless tyranny'.

Another country which really was struggling against godless tyranny inevitably received special mention.

'We seek a process of reconciliation and reform that will lead to a new dawn of hope for the people of Poland, and we'll continue to call for an end of martial law, for the freeing of all political prisoners, and to resume dialogue among the Polish Government, the Church and the Solidarity movement which speaks for the vast majority of Poles. Denying financial assistance to the oppressive Polish regime, America will continue to provide the Polish people with as much food and commodity support as possible through church and private organisations . . .'

From that particular observation yet another of the myths of this papacy was born. Various papal biographers, Vaticanologists and unidentified members of the Reagan administration later claimed that among the fruits of the 'secret alliance' between the Pope and the President was a United States commitment to spend whatever it took to keep Solidarity alive. Money and equipment channelled by the CIA into Solidarity has been valued at between $50 million and $100 million. Added to that were the funds laundered by Roberto Calvi into the Polish trade union, one tranche of $50 million, other amounts totalling at least a further $50 million. That the CIA and other elements both in the United States and in Europe rallied to the cause is indisputable. The real issue is the actual size of the amount funnelled to the union and where it went.

The amounts allegedly donated via the CIA, the AFL-CIO American trade union organisation, and the National Endowment for Democracy were laundered, it is claimed, through a business bank account but both Andrzej Gwiazda, the former deputy leader of Solidarity, and Janusz Paulubicki, the former Solidarity treasurer, have denounced the claims of payments of any figure even approaching the $50–100 million. The actual figure for the entire period 1982 to 1989 was significantly less than $9 million. As for the millions that Roberto Calvi plundered from Banco Ambrosiano and insisted he had sent to Poland, Bank of Italy officials have confirmed that they hold compelling evidence that these transfers were indeed made but have declined to reveal the identity of the account holders to whom the transfers were made. Lico Gelli, who for decades through the illegal Italian masonic P2 lodge exercised more control within Italy than any Government, has always maintained, 'If you are looking for the missing millions from Banco Ambrosiano, then look in Poland.' Exactly where to look has never been established but the Polish Catholic Church would be an excellent place to begin. Such an investigation should start with questions to a certain Bishop Hnilica.

General Czeslaw Kiszcak, the Interior Minister during the years of martial law, has confirmed that Solidarity was

> 'thoroughly penetrated . . . about 90 per cent of funds arriving from the West passed through our hands. Certainly some of that money had been sourced from the CIA but if that had been known, some of our intellectuals would not have touched it. The money was always channelled under cover of some other organisation. We never seized any of it; we could have but that is an exercise you can only do once, and then the channel of information would have dried up.'

The hard currency was used mainly to print books and leaflets, to look after the families of political prisoners and to fund fugitives who were changing flats and cars to avoid detection.

In October 1982, General Vernon Walters was back at the Vatican briefing the Pope, Secretary of State Casaroli and Archbishop Silvestrini on the Middle East, Poland and the problem of nuclear disarmament. If the Pope and his colleagues had any misgivings about US foreign policy in the Middle East they remained diplomatically silent, allowing Walters to temporarily share the Pope's claim of infallibility.

On nuclear issues, Walters claimed that the US position was uniquely reasonable, while the Soviets remained aggressive and devious. He was preaching to the converted. In his cables back to the Secretary of State recounting his comments to the Pope, each paragraph ends with a recurring theme: 'He agreed completely.'

The meeting was later reported in the Vatican's own newspaper *L'Osservatore Romano* and was picked up by several members of Congress, including Patricia Schröder, who asked the President: 'Is the new political strategy by your administration to ask foreign powers to intercede in domestic political affairs?' Schröder then quoted recent news stories suggesting that 'the purpose of Walters' visit was to convince the Pope to side-track efforts by American Roman Catholic bishops challenging the morality of nuclear weapons.' She wanted to know if this was indeed the primary purpose of the meeting and went on to ask 'Will future appeals for papal intervention to squelch the peace movement be made? Does this imply that you are unable to stop the peace movement in this country?'

In their response the Department of State confirmed that the meeting took place and observed, 'They did not, however, talk about the Roman Catholic bishops' discussions of the American nuclear deterrent. In fact, neither the American bishops nor the proposed letter was a topic of conversation.' The State Department had, in fact, suppressed the truth from Schröder, namely that most of the forty minutes Walters had spent with the Pope were, in the General's own words, spent on 'the SS20 briefing and the whole nuclear question'. As to the American bishops, many deeply critical of the administration's stance on these issues, Vernon Walters was far too experienced in diplomacy to attempt a direct appeal for the Pope to help 'squelch the peace movement'. Walters was a consummate salesman, although in this instance he had a willing customer. Although Karol Wojtyla believed for much of his life that Communism could not be defeated, if the Reagan administration were prepared to take them on he would give them every encouragement. That encouragement would come to include putting pressure on the American bishops to fall into line.

These were busy times for American foreign policy makers. Of the many parts of the planet where the Reagan administration had special interests, none was more important than Central America. The Pope was scheduled to make a nine-day visit to the region in early March 1983. Inevitably, General Vernon Walters appeared in the Vatican in late February to give Cardinal Casaroli and Monsignor Carlos Romeo, the Vatican's Central American specialist, an overview of the region and a country-by-country briefing. Also present was the ubiquitous Presidential Envoy William Wilson and Archbishop Silvestrini, the Secretary to the Council for Public Affairs. Walters emphasised that

'we share common goals with the Holy See. We are opposed to dictatorships of both the left and the right. We are seeking a middle way. Pluralistic democracies, social reform, domestic tranquillity, reconciliation and the prevention of another Cuba.'

He made no attempt to address some of the glaring contradictions to that common goal that existed within the region. One was the repressive military dictatorship in Argentina responsible for the disappearance of more than 30,000 civilians. It was a regime with very close links to the Reagan administration, so close that when the US Congress severely restricted the number of military personnel that President Reagan could legally send to El Salvador, the military in Buenos Aires were delighted to make up the numbers.

In El Salvador a right-wing regime was being assisted by the Reagan administration with economic aid, military weapons and military 'trainers' as they struggled to crush a left-wing insurgency. 'The US considers it of vital importance to continue giving aid to El Salvador and to other countries in the region,' General Walters told the Vatican Secretary of State and his colleagues. 'We will not permit guerrillas to shoot their way into power in Central America.' US policy led directly to a grim alternative in which some 75,000 died in El Salvador.

In Nicaragua the Sandinistas had overthrown the US-backed dictator Anastasio Somoza in July 1979 bringing to an end over forty years of oppressive rule by his family. A State Department briefing document prepared in the 1930s for President Roosevelt commenting on the first Somoza observed, 'He may be a son-of-a-bitch, but at least he's ours.' When the revolution occurred, a hardcore of some 17,000 National Guards and Somoza's closest officials fled the country to Honduras. These were the men who had done the dictator's bidding, the killing, the raping, the suppression, the continuous disappearance of dissidents. In 1981 President Reagan ordered the covert funding of this

group who had by that time become known as the Contra
Revolutionarios – the Contras. In the President's mind he
was fighting Communism.

When the fact leaked that the United States was behind
the creation and financing of the Contras, the administration claimed that its reasons for supporting the Contras
was to stop the arms flowing from Nicaragua to the
guerrillas in El Salvador. There was no common border
between the two countries and the only arms ever 'found'
were those planted by the CIA. The serial numbers on the
M16s were traced back to US Government control stock.
Casualties among those who supported the revolution
began to mount. By the end of President Reagan's second
term nearly 40,000 people had been killed.

Nicaragua and El Salvador were on the Pope's visiting
schedule. Also on the list was Guatemala where a devout
'born-again' Christian psychopath General Efrain Rios
Montt had seized power in March 1982. His death squads
were responsible for a weekly death toll running into
hundreds. UN estimates would ultimately estimate that
Rios Montt's troops had slaughtered a minimum of
100,000 people. The guerrillas invariably described by
the Reagan administration as Marxists were very largely
Mayan Indian peasants fighting for the land they had been
promised in the early 1950s, a promise that directly led to
the toppling of the elected leader who had made it. The
coup was CIA-financed and organised on behalf of US
business interests. The new regime reneged on the promise.
After thirty years the peasants were still fighting, still land-
less and still dying. On 4 December 1982, after a meeting
with General Efrain Rios Montt, President Reagan praised
the dictator as 'totally dedicated to democracy' and added
that the Rios regime was 'getting a bum rap'. He also
ensured that they got continuous amounts of covert arms
and money.

During the Vatican briefing by General Walters in February 1983 he neglected to mention any of these US involvements in Central America. General Walters also neglected to mention an additional $50 million in US military supplies and personnel the President had sent to El Salvador by executive authority, thus circumventing the need for approval by Congress. It had also slipped from the General's memory that in March 1981 the US had voted against a UN Commission on Human Rights resolution condemning human rights abuses and violations in El Salvador. He also forgot to mention that the Reagan administration had renewed military aid to Guatemala and financial and military aid to Chile, Argentina, Paraguay and Uruguay, all under military dictatorships, all with appalling human rights records.

When Karol Wojtyla became Pope in October 1978, his knowledge of Latin America was scant. He was heavily reliant for information on Cardinal Sebastiano Baggio, the prefect of the Congregation of Bishops and President of the Pontifical Commission for Latin America. The primary role of this Commission was to monitor the activity of CELAM (the Latin American Bishops' Conference) and assist the Latin American Church with personnel and economic means. This put enormous power in the hands of Baggio, a man who had nurtured ambitions to ascend to the papal throne until his double defeats in 1978. By the time of the emergence of Karol Wojtyla, Baggio's personal experience belonged very much in the past.

Between 1938 and 1946 he had been a junior Vatican diplomat in three Latin American countries. This was followed by a two-year stint in Colombia as chargé d'affaires then between 1953 and 1969, a posting as nuncio to Chile and then later a further posting as nuncio, this time to Brazil. His politics were right-wing, his views and opinions reactionary and his influence on the Vatican's and therefore

the Pope's interpretation of Latin American affairs was
profound. He was assisted in his various tasks by a close
friend, Archbishop Alfonso Lopez Trujillo, a man even
further to the right and a vociferous critic of Liberation
Theology. From the moment he had become general secretary of CELAM, he had purged the organisation of anyone
with ties to any version of Liberation Theology. He wrote,
'Liberation Theology starts out with good intentions but
ends in terror.' In a working paper for the Puebla, the first
CELAM meeting to be attended by the Pope in 1979,
Trujillo endorsed the various military regimes of Latin
America. 'These military regimes came into existence as a
response to social and economic chaos. No society can
admit a power vacuum. Faced with tensions and disorders,
an appeal to force is inevitable.' Karol Wojtyla had much in
common with men like Baggio and Trujillo, not least when
it came to taking a position on military regimes. As early as
the 1930s the future pope had been an enthusiastic supporter of General Franco during the Spanish Civil War.

In 1990, when Trujillo was Archbishop of Medellin, two
hundred Colombian Catholic lay professionals wrote to the
Vatican demanding a canonical visit from a senior member
of the Vatican to 'clear up the anti-evangelical acts, some of
them questionable before canon law, others before criminal
courts'. They declared that they were 'scandalised' about
the 'orphaned state' of the Medellin Church and the behaviour of their pastor, Lopez Trujillo. But the Pope did not
investigate the allegations to establish if they were correct;
in his eyes Trujillo could do no wrong. In 1985 Trujillo had
given further comfort to the military dictatorships in Latin
America by masterminding the 'Andes Statement' denouncing Liberation Theology in such ringing tones that Chilean
theologian Ronaldo Munoz described it as 'a virtual incite-
ment to repression, and of a criminal nature'. Subsequently
when Pinochet's security forces arrested the Jesuit editor of

the magazine *Mensaje* because of his criticism of the government, the army cited the 'Andes Statement' in defence of the arrest, arguing that the Church itself had disavowed editor Father Renato Hevia's position.

Trujillo was not unique as a Latin American member of the Catholic hierarchy with extreme-right opinions. Archbishop Dario Castrillon Hoyos, one of Trujillo's protégés, was another Colombian prelate with a close relationship with the drug dealer Pablo Escobar. He took some of Escobar's profits from his global trade in cocaine which he gave to charity, arguing that to do so ensured that at least part of the hundreds of millions of dollars would not be spent on prostitution. He painted all liberation theologists as revolutionary terrorists, a libel that deeply angered and offended many. More importantly, Castrillon's attacks not only gave credibility to right-wing regimes throughout the region: it encouraged them to yet harsher measures and upped the continent's killing rate by an immeasurable amount.

Others who were cherished by right-wing regimes in Latin America included the Chilean cardinal Jorge Medina, the Brazilian cardinal Lucas Moreira, the Italian cardinals, Angelo Sodano and Pio Laghi, and the German cardinal, Höffner. In late 1998 when General Pinochet was arrested and temporarily held in England, the former dictator's friends were quick to rally round. They included all of the above and several like-minded high-ranking Vatican officials. Pinochet's friends and admirers within the Holy See, particularly Secretary of State Sodano, persuaded the Pope to approve a letter to the British Government urging them to release Pinochet. By interceding on behalf of Pinochet, Sodano, the other cardinals and indeed the Pope were ignoring the General's history, which included his illegal seizure of power in 1973 (with significant support from the United States) and the murder of the democratically elected president, followed by seventeen years in which at least 4,000 Chileans were murdered, over 50,000 were tortured, 5,000 were 'disappeared' and hundreds of thousands were imprisoned or exiled.

After years of protection from the Vatican cabal who regarded the General as a devout Roman Catholic and after years of affecting senility both mental and physical, doctors determined in late 2005 that Pinochet was fit to stand trial. Asked by a Chilean judge about the thousands of Chilean civilians who had been murdered during the years of the military junta, the General replied: 'I suffer for these losses, but God does the deeds; he will pardon me if I exceeded in some, which I don't think I did.'

The Vatican cabal frequently referred to by insiders as 'the fascists' looked with favour on many right-wing dictatorships during the reign of John Paul II. Even the Argentinian military dictators were not beyond the pale. When Archbishop Laghi was posted to Argentina in the 1970s the military terror was at its height. As papal nuncio he was not alone in pursuing unusual activities during his tenure in Buenos Aires. In 1976 during the early months of the military dictatorship he gave a speech to the army in which he quoted the Catholic Church's just war theory and used it to sanction the military campaign against dissent. Hardly any of the Argentinian bishops denounced the daily human rights violations. A number of priests accompanied tortured prisoners on their last journey, blessing them and giving the last rites before their handcuffed bodies were tossed out of military helicopters into the South Atlantic. At least 30,000 'enemies of the state' were killed by the junta between 1976 and 1983. This was the same junta that Pope John Paul II visited in 1982 after his trip to Great Britain to ensure that the Vatican was seen to be acting in an even-handed manner.

Appointment in St Peter's Square. This remarkable photograph was taken a heartbeat before Mehmet Ali Agca, who can be seen in the right hand corner, shot the Pope at virtually point blank range

Papal visits such as these to Argentina and the Philippines bolstered the dictatorships of Galtieri and Marcos

Last Name	First Name	Pt	Status	Notes	Source
Boston, MA Archdiocese					
Ares	Brion	5	all wip	Allegations; deadlock on indecent assault	Boston Globe 10 28 94
Balcom	Gary E.	5	all	allegations per diocesan records	Boston Globe 12 10 02
Barrett	Robert E.	2	set	settled per diocesan records	Boston Globe 12 13 02
Battista	Leo J.	5	all wip	accused of sex abuse of nun	Worc T&G 2 11 93
Beale	Robert P.	5	rem	administrative leave	Boston Arch. Dio. Website
Berthold	George	4	sued	alleged abuse of boy	Boston Globe 5.15.02
Birmingham	Joseph	5	all wip	sued; multi victims; dead	Union Leader 3.26.02
Bourgault	Richard L.	5	rem	Removed	Boston Globe website
Bolduc	Paul J.	5	Rem	Removed	Boston Globe website
Buntel	Richard A.	2	set	settled $500,000	Boston Globe 12 4 02
Burns	Robert M.	1	con	convicted molesting boy; served 6 yrs.	USA Today 11 11 02
Burns	Robert M.	2	set	settled. $2mm per diocese	Boston Globe 12 4 02
Connell	John K.	4	sued	multiple claims	Boston Herald 3 29 02
Conte	Denis A.	2	set	settled $150,000	Boston Globe 12 10 02
Cotter	John M.	2	set	settled $575,000 per diocesan records	Boston Globe 12 13 02
Coughlin	Richard T.	5	all wip	allege in Orange CA	Boston Globe 4 3.93
Cummings	William J.	5	rem	lawsuit in 1982, alleged abuse of boy	USA Today 11 11 02
Curran	Thomas A.	5	Rem	Removed	Boston Globe website
Dempsey	Thomas	1	con	convicted 1997, 200 hrs community service	Boston Herald 5 13 02
Desilets	Paul M.	2	set	settlement. Alleged abuse	Boston Herald 2 23 02
Fay	Robert D.	4	sued	civil suit, abuse of woman	Middlesex Ct 2002-02685
Ferraro	Romano	3	arr	alleged abuse	Boston Globe 4/9/02
Finegan	Paul J.	5	rem	removed by Cardinal	Boston Globe 2.4 02
Foley	James D.	5	all	alleged abuse of woman	Boston Globe 12 6 02
Forry	Thomas P.	5	rem	allegations per diocesan records	Boston Globe 12 4 02
Frey	Russ	1	con	convicted	Eagle Tribune 4/18/2002
Frost	Peter J.	5	all	allegations per diocesan records	Boston Globe 12 4 02
Gale	Robert V.	3	arr	alleged abuse	Boston Arch. Dio. Website
Geoghan	John	1	con	convicted	Boston Globe
Gilpin	Joseph	5	rem?	pending case. Removed?	Boston Globe 1 28 02
Graham	Daniel	2	set	admitted to allegation	Boston Globe 5 18 02
Guthrie	Frederick	3	arr	alleged internet solicitation, arrested 11/01	Foster's DD 2 15 02
Hanlon	John	1	con	convicted, life sentence	Boston Globe 3 20 02
Hickey	Gerald	5	rem	removed by cardinal	Boston Globe 2.8 02
Hurley	Paul	3	arr	alleged abuse; pleaded not guilty	Boston Globe 8/15/02

12/17/2002 Page 1

Lists such as this one, that in 2002 identified sexual abusing priests in New England dioceses, began to appear in many countries.
The 'secret system' had finally been exposed

Seventeen years earlier in 1985, the Reverend Tom Doyle *(pictured)* and two colleagues had created a definitive report warning the Catholic hierarchy of the scandals and the damage that lay ahead. It was dismissed by Pope John Paul II, who despite overwhelming evidence to the contrary, regarded clerical sexual abuse as 'An American problem'

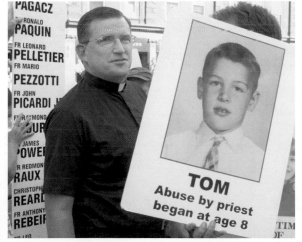

Cardinal Law of Boston had enjoyed the Pope's protection until December 2002. Law had in turn protected a considerable number of child abusing priests. Father Bob Hoatson *(pictured)*, who was the other face of the priesthood, is shown leading protestors at the installation of Law's successor, Archbishop Sean Patrick O'Malley

'Where was God at Auschwitz?'

The Pope waves to adoring crowds in Ireland.
They loved the singer but not the song

Bishop Marcinkus seen here in Nigeria in 1982. Despite the indictments, the warrants for his arrest, the repayment of $250 million to the creditors of Banco Ambrosiano, the constant urgings for his removal by papal advisors, Marcinkus continued as President of the IOR until 1990

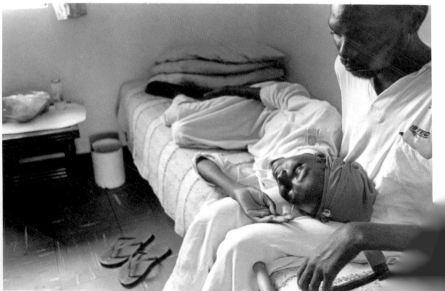

HIV and AIDS in Africa. The Church worked hard to 'help them d' dignity'. It's continuing refusal to sanction the use of condoms en' many died needlessly

Theologian Hans Küng, one of a considerable number to feel the power of the Wojtyla/Ratzinger axis

Vatican spin-doctor Navarro-Valls

'A fraud? Of course it's a fraud but the money is genuine'

Papal endorsements by the score. All in the best possible taste with a healthy percentage going into the Vatican coffers

The great communicator is finally silenced

The Pope's speeches and sermons during his visit to the country contained no direct mention of 'the disappeared ones'; neither did he have time during his trip to meet any of the human rights organisations, although he did meet the current military dictator General Galtieri.

The power and influence of this cabal within the higher reaches of the Catholic Church was not confined to hob-nobbing with murderers. In 1981 the Canadian Bishops' Conference found themselves in complete and total agreement with the other four main religious denominations. The issue that had united Canada's Roman Catholic, Protestant Anglican and Orthodox Churches had also inspired a united opposition of Catholics, Protestants and Jews in the United States. They united against the Reagan administration reactivating the supply of military aid and financial assistance to the regime in El Salvador. The Vatican response, one that was again organised by Cardinal Baggio and his like-minded friends, was a confidential letter to Canadian Government Minister for External Affairs, Mark MacGuigan. It advised the minister to ignore the Canadian Bishops' Conference decision to condemn the US intervention in El Salvador declaring that it did not represent the Holy See's position, which was one of support for the 'judgement of the US administration' on the issue. The minister, previously outspoken against the US action, dramatically changed to, 'I would certainly not condemn any decision the US takes to send offensive arms.'

Simultaneously the papal nuncio in the United States, Archbishop Pio Laghi, was having 'constant' conversations with the US bishops. These resulted in a softening of previous criticism. In El Salvador itself the regime took great encouragement from the Vatican interventions and killings continued.

In March 1980 Archbishop Romero, Primate of El Salvador, had been murdered in cold blood while performing

Holy Mass in a hospital chapel. He was shot as he raised the host before the congregation. It was a unique, horrific and profane killing, but one quickly matched by the regime.

On 2 December, four missionaries were murdered on the road to Santiago Nonualco. The four, three nuns and a social worker, were all US citizens. The perpetrators were members of the ruling regime's security forces. It transpired that all four women had been repeatedly raped by the security forces. These crimes had happened during the closing days of Carter's presidency. The US suspended all aid to El Salvador because of the suspected involvement of state security. Thirteen days later the economic aid resumed. The judge appointed to investigate the murders had himself been murdered a week after the killings. A UN-sponsored investigation concluded that the killings had been planned well in advance, that a cover-up involving the head of the National Guard, two investigating officers, members of the Salvadoran military and a number of American officials had been perpetrated.

Despite the fact that the US State Department had been given evidence that clearly implicated senior members of the Salvadoran military establishment they took no action other than to mount a smear campaign against the dead women. Reagan's UN ambassador, Jeane Kirkpatrick, observed, 'The nuns were not just nuns. They were political activists, and we should be very clear about that.'

The image of gun-toting nuns with an excess of political attitude running a roadblock did not play well within the US Press but the aid, both economic and military, kept going into El Salvador from the Reagan administration. Twenty-six years after these murders they still resonate. In death the victims have become powerful symbols of a larger truth and for many the four stand as witnesses to the many hundreds of thousands who died during these decades.

During his late February briefing to the Pope's most

senior advisors on Central America, General Walters, as befitting an Ambassador, had dressed Reagan's foreign policies for El Salvador in elegant language:

'We are seeking a middle way. Pluralistic democracies. Social reform. Domestic tranquillity. Reconciliation and the prevention of another Cuba.'

Earlier during his first term the President had put it more bluntly:

'Central America is simply too close and the strategic stakes too high, for us to ignore the dangers of governments seizing power there with ideological and military ties to the Soviet Union . . . Soviet military theorists want to destroy our capacity to re-supply Western Europe in case of an emergency. They want to tie down our attention and forces on our own southern border . . .'

Apart from releasing one and a half billion dollars worth of military and economic aid to El Salvador, creating the Contras and illegally funding them as a terrorist front against the Sandinistas of Nicaragua, Reagan's administration built up the Honduran army as a firewall against the further spread of revolution in the region, gave covert support to Guatemala's genocidal army in its war against its own people and set up secret military bases in Costa Rica to support Reagan's war effort against Nicaragua.

In 1984 the US financial commitment to the military regime in El Salvador had totalled $576.1 million. Throwing more good money after so much that had been ill spent, the apparently indestructible Henry Kissinger emerged into the light again. He had been appointed by President Reagan to investigate alternatives 'for improving the situation in

Central America'. His committee's report to absolutely no one's surprise found itself 'largely in agreement with the administration's current Latin America policy'. Kissinger recommended doubling the current 'aid' package to the region from $4 billion to $8 billion. Little of this extraordinary largesse was filtered down to the poor. The facts that Archbishop Romero had given the Pope in May 1979 were still the facts during the mid 1980s. In El Salvador two per cent of the population continued to own more than sixty per cent of the land, and eight per cent of the population continued to receive half of the national income. Meanwhile, fifty-eight per cent of the population continued to earn less than $10 a month. Two thirds of the urban population still lacked sewage services, forty-five per cent were still without regular safe drinking water, seventy per cent of children under five were malnourished and the average daily calorific intake of 1,740, about two thirds of what it takes to sustain a human being, was still the lowest consumption rate in the western hemisphere.

In early March 1983 the Pope left Rome and flew into the Central American maelstrom. The trip would demonstrate that in this area at least there was a perfect meeting of the minds. Where the President saw surrogate Soviets behind every Latin American tree, rock and bush, the Pope saw Liberation Theologists. Apparently Solidarity was desirable in Poland but not in Latin America.

In Costa Rica where his tour began, the Pope told his audience that he had come 'to share the pain' of Central America and that he hoped to provide a voice for the searing images of daily life, for 'the tears or deaths of children, of the long lines of orphans, of those many thousands of refugees, exiles or displaced persons searching for a home, of the poor with neither home nor work'. The Pope repeated his frequently stated view that it was the Church's mission to right social wrongs, but only according to Christian principles. He rejected both the ideologies of the left and the right, rejected both capitalism and communism and stressed that it was important for each nation to 'confront problems in a sincere dialogue, without foreign influence'.

In Nicaragua, the Pope's second stop, he was confronted with a country in total uproar. The ruling Sandinistas were fighting the US-backed Contras, and were constantly targeted by mercenaries trained and financed by the CIA. The Nicaraguan Catholic Church was bitterly divided between the traditional hierarchy and their followers, largely anti-Sandinista, and the 'popular' Church which blended Christianity with strands of Liberation Theology and a Latin American version of Marxism. The Archbishop of Managua, Miguel Obando y Bravo, had emerged as a symbol of the middle-class opposition to Sandinista rule.

In the Nicaraguan line-up waiting to greet him at Managua airport was at least one of the priests who was also a government minister. The Pope publicly humiliated the man, constantly wagging his finger at the figure on his knees as he admonished the priest, Minister of Culture Ernesto Cardenal Martinez, demanding, 'Regularise your position with the Church. Regularise your position with the Church.' The image went around the world and was widely interpreted as a sharp rebuke. Later the same day during a televised open-air Mass in a park, some of the most extraordinary images of this Papacy were recorded. When the Pope, reading from his prepared text, began to condemn the 'popular Church' as 'absurd and dangerous', the Sandinistas in the front rows began to take great exception. 'We want a Church allied with the poor,' they responded. That in turn provoked the loyalists. 'Long live the Pope,' they chanted. Soon everyone was joining in the impromptu debate.

Pope John Paul II was never a man to show the slightest regard for religious dissidence. Visibly angered, he shouted

at the congregation, 'Silencio!' He appeared taken aback
that his angry commands had not silenced the congregation
and again shouted, 'Silencio!' To a group chanting, 'We
want peace!' he shouted back, 'The Church is the first to
want peace.' Much of the Mass following the sermon could
not be heard through the continuing shouting and counter-
shouting. A week after he had left Nicaragua the line had
been clearly drawn. The Catholic hierarchy had begun to
display far less tolerance for the Government and for
Catholics who supported the revolution. One of the country's most progressive priests, Father Uriel Molina, recalled
an ultimatum that he and other pro-revolution priests had
been given by auxiliary bishop Bosco Vivas: 'Either you are
with me, the Archbishop and the Pope, or you can find
yourself another diocese.'

In El Salvador the Pope insisted on visiting the tomb of
Archbishop Oscar Romero and at the open-air Mass which
followed he proclaimed Romero as 'a zealous and venerated
pastor who tried to stop violence. I ask that his memory be
always respected and let no ideological interest try to distort
his sacrifice as a pastor given over to his flock.' The Pope
returned to his solution for an end to the conflicts that
convulsed the region. 'Dialogue is the answer.' Again he did
not explain how to conduct this dialogue. He adopted a
similar theme in Guatemala, telling the indigenous Indians
to 'organise associations for the defence of your rights'. This
had been precisely the 'crime' for which six 'subversives'
were executed on the eve of his visit. Under the previous
regime of Lucas Garcia, a minimum of 35,000 citizens had
been killed in four years. Since General Montt had seized
power exactly a year before the Pope's visit, between
10,000 and 15,000 – mostly native Indians – had been
killed.

Many took comfort from this papal tour but perhaps those
who derived the greatest satisfaction were the right-wing

cabals within the Vatican and the Reagan administration, particularly the State Department and the CIA. The Pope's initial reaction in 1979 against all aspects of Liberation Theology had hardened over the ensuing years. Within his first decade he had silenced a number of leading liberal theologians. He shut progressive seminaries, censored ecclesiastical texts and repeatedly promoted deeply conservative clergy to positions of great power. He had very effectively silenced the voice of those within the Catholic Church who spoke for the poor of Latin America. On the Reagan administration's activities in Central America, a number of the State Department cables sent by General Vernon Walters demonstrate that invariably the position of the Pope and his Vatican advisors was essentially identical. Confirmation of that fact came from the Pope himself. During a discussion in early 1985 with Chicago's Cardinal Bernardin, the Pope said that he did 'not understand why the US hierarchy is sending bishops to visit Cuba and Nicaragua. Neither do I understand why the bishops do not support your President's policies in Central America.'

Having admonished the clergy of Latin America to 'stay out of politics . . . regularise your position with the Church', the Pope's next trip was to the one country where he and a great many other priests and bishops were up to their necks in politics: Poland.

Martial law or to use the Polish term *stan wojenny* – a state of war – was in many respects precisely just that. The country was in the total grip of the occupying force. That it was a Polish occupying force in no way lessened the oppression. After the 'introduction' of martial law at least 13,000 people were held for varying periods within internment camps throughout Poland. The courts handed down over 30,000 prison sentences 'relating to charges of a political nature' and more than 60,000 people were fined for 'participating in various forms of protest'. Countless numbers were 'dismissed from work' or 'expelled from colleges, universities and other institutions' for 'political activities'. Every form of trade union was declared illegal. The regime, with an eye to softening Western sanctions, would occasionally make a conciliatory gesture and authorise the early release of prisoners. On 1 May 1982, 1,000 were released, but this was followed within weeks by their being re-arrested along with a further 200 people. They were all charged with 'riotous assembly', sentenced, and returned to prison.

The greatest legacy of the many creators of Solidarity was continuously demonstrated before the eyes of the nation. Though the Union's leaders were still in prison and the Union itself outlawed, the flowering of Solidarity had left a permanent mark upon the country. The clock could not be turned back; no matter how brutal their conditions, no matter how low their morale, millions carried within their minds the memories of the summer of 1980. The regime was slow to learn, but eventually Jaruzelski and the others would conclude that you cannot put ideas behind prison bars; you cannot lock memories away in internment camps.

The various top-secret CIA reports on Poland for 1982 paint a grim picture of the Catholic Church's failure to play a significant role in events.

'. . . Despite its unrivaled moral authority, however, the Church lacks the power to guide developments. Some leaders of the Church fear that the Government and party hardliners have enough momentum to threaten its access to the media and the freedom to teach catechism . . . The Church's influence probably is weakest among young people – the group most likely to engage in violent resistance . . . Archbishop Glemp seems frustrated with the intransigence of Solidarity leaders, particularly Lech Walesa . . .

Glemp adopted a middle-of-the-road position . . . He is also afraid to undercut Premier Jaruzelski, who he views as a moderate . . . The Archbishop, however, lacks the authority of the late Cardinal Wyszynski, and his tactics have been challenged by other prelates . . . The Pope is likely to endorse continuing Glemp's strategy, perhaps with some modifications. The Pontiff would be reluctant to run roughshod over his former colleagues. . .'

Before the events of December 1981 the Vatican and the Polish regime had been negotiating a return visit for the Pope in 1982. The Polish government discreetly indicated to the Church that the situation within the country lacked the necessary stability to absorb a papal visit. The Pope, acutely aware that he might provoke an uncontrollable response on Polish soil, agreed to wait until 1983. The trip and the potential gain for both sides greatly exercised many minds as the diplomatic trading proceeded behind closed doors. In Moscow on 10 November Leonid Brezhnev died. The very next day Lech Walesa was released and on 31 December 1982 General Jaruzelski announced the suspension but not the formal end of the 'state of war'. The pace of the negotiations over a papal visit quickened. The Polish Church submitted a list of sixteen towns that the Pope would like to visit.

The regime refused to consider that any part of northern Poland could feature on the itinerary. It also asked for all texts that the Pope planned to deliver to be made available in advance. The Vatican refused. The Vatican requested that a general amnesty should be declared before the visit; the regime responded with the promise that such an amnesty would be declared, but only when martial law was formally ended, and so the negotiations continued. One of the many sticking points concerned the Pope's desire to

meet Lech Walesa. 'Why does he want to meet that guy?'
and 'You mean that man with the big family?' were two of
the responses from the Polish Interior Minister, General
Kiszcak, who headed the regime's negotiating team. 'Why
would the Pope want to meet the former leader of the
former Solidarity?' was another.

The Pope was determined. He gave ground on a regime
demand and said that in return he would not only meet
General Jaruzelski but would deliver a speech and exchange
gifts. The General upped the ante; he wanted two meetings
with the Pope. In the General's mind that would give further
legitimacy to the regime. After considerable hesitation the
Holy See agreed. What was written and broadcast about the
papal visit was very tightly controlled and, unlike the 1979
trip, crowd control was totally in the hands of the state.
Karol Wojtyla was returning to a deeply troubled homeland
which, apart from the various problems already recorded,
had a deeply divided Church.

Glemp had ignored the repeated pleas from Solidarity,
now functioning as an underground movement, to act as an
intermediary between the union movement and the Church
in Rome. Solidarity believed that there was an important
role for the Church to play at this crucial time. The Primate,
now a cardinal, never responded to the letters. With other
young priests, the charismatic Father Jerzy Popieluszko
became a national hero with his mixture of a Gandhian
philosophy of non-violent resistance and Martin Luther
King-style appeals on 'Choice'. 'Which side will you take?
The side of good or the side of evil? Truth or falsehood?
Love or hatred?' While Popieluszko inspired his people, the
Primate sat in his library wondering what Cardinal Wyszynski might have done.

The Pope was also returning to a Solidarity movement
that was deeply demoralised. Their call for a national strike
in November had been an abject failure. Their printing

presses were busy. The revolutionary word was going out but at times those leaders still at liberty clearly feared that no one was listening. During his eight-day visit in mid-June the Pope had to perform a high wire act; one that was fraught with great risks requiring not the near frontal attack of a Popieluszko but something that delivered the same message with stealth and he was given early notice of the need for such tactics. On the day of his arrival he talked at St John's Cathedral in Warsaw of why he had come at this time to Poland.

> 'To stand beneath the cross of Christ . . . especially with those who are most acutely tasting the bitterness of disappointment, humiliation, suffering, of being deprived of their freedom, of being wronged, of having their dignity trampled on . . . I thank God that Cardinal Wyszynski has been spared having to witness the painful events connected with the date December 13th, 1981.'

But the censors cut the comment from all press reports.

To a crowd of more than half a million at Czestochowa, Wojtyla then preached the Gospel message complete with contemporary footnotes. 'The love of Christ is more powerful than all the experiences and disappointments that life can prepare for us.' He spoke of a 'greater freedom' that must be attained before one can look to reform the body politic. He told his audience that they must 'call good and evil by name'. He talked of the 'fundamental solidarity between human beings'. The message was exactly the same as that being constantly delivered in Warsaw by Father Popieluszko but now it was carrying the moral authority of the Pope.

On the fifth day of his trip, in a strong defence of Solidarity's record, he spoke of the events before December

1981, which were primarily concerned with 'moral order ... and not just increasing remuneration for work'. He recalled that 'these events were free of violence'. He observed that 'the duty to work corresponds to the rights of the working man' which included 'the right to a just salary, to be insured against accidents connected with work and work-free Sundays'. Then he quoted the man whom in his petulance he had dismissed as 'that old man', Cardinal Wyszynski, defending the right to create free trade union organisations.

'When the right of association of people is at stake, then it is not the right bestowed on people by some person. This is the people's own inherent right. That is why the state does not give this right to us. The state has merely the right to protect that right so that it is not breached. This right has been given to the people by the Creator who made man a social being.'

In his private meetings with the General, the Pope had no need to invoke the Almighty. He made it very plain to Jaruzelski and his colleagues. He wanted an official end to martial law and a general amnesty to be declared: and relegalisation of Solidarity. The biggest concession, which Jaruzelski had agreed before the Papal visit, was that martial law would be formally lifted within weeks of the Pope's departure but a dialogue between the regime and the 'former' Solidarity leaders was not on the current agenda.

One of his last acts on this trip was his meeting with Lech Walesa. The Polish Church and Glemp and his advisors in particular had prevailed upon the Pope to delay this meeting until the last moment, arguing that to do otherwise would be to play up the importance of a man whose fifteen minutes of fame had passed by. What really aggravated Glemp was that the Western media had very largely focused on the Wojtyla–Walesa meeting.

Revealing details of the meeting, however, were recorded in the Vatican's official newspaper *L'Osservatore Romano* by deputy editor Monsignor Virgilio Levi, a man whose sources were unimpeachable. Levi confirmed that Walesa as a significant player had been retired from the game. He was to be accorded 'great honours' but would never return to lead Solidarity. Levi confirmed that in exchange for the lifting of martial law the Pope had formally assisted in lowering the profile of the little electrician from Gdansk.

When the story broke in the Vatican newspaper and then in the world's media, the response from the papal apartments was very similar to that when Ambassador Wilson had revealed that the Pope approved of the Reagan sanctions being applied to Poland. The Pope was furious at the report, not that his actions had been misinterpreted but that the correct interpretation had become public knowledge. Within twenty-four hours *L'Osservatore Romano* was in need of a new deputy editor.

On 22 July martial law in Poland was formally ended. On 5 November Lech Walesa, written off by so many within both the regime and the Vatican, was awarded the Nobel Peace Prize. Seven years later he was elected President of Poland.

As 1983 was drawing to a close, the White House announced that it was raising US ties with the Vatican to the level of full diplomatic status. Expecting flak from critics who were already concerned at the President's appointment of William Wilson as his special representative to the Vatican in February 1981, the White House got its defence in before the attack. At the press conference announcing the appointment in December 1983, press secretary Larry Speakes in his opening statement declared, 'We did not actively promote this legislation, which passed overwhelmingly in both the House and the Senate, but we see a number of foreign policy advantages resulting from it.'

In fact the idea was born within the White House, as a memo dated 12 July 1982, from Deputy Secretary of State Elliott Abrams to National Security Advisor William Clark confirms:

'. . . There are substantial political and humanitarian benefits to be gained from giving full diplomatic recognition to the Vatican . . . If we announced our intention to so do now, it would emphasise our support of the Catholic Church as a force for freedom under the present Pope . . . It might signal that there is greater understanding between the Reagan administration and the Pope than there is with some radical Catholic bishops in the US on such issues as nuclear freeze. Needless to say there are significant political benefits as well.'

Indeed there were, not least in the message it would send to the electorate of the United States in the presidential election year 1984. The Catholic vote is always an important factor in such elections. The reference to the US bishops' nuclear stance, however, touched on a long-running and highly contentious issue. The Pope did not share the views of the majority of US bishops on the nuclear issue. His bishops wanted the United States to renounce the first use of nuclear weapons, and they were sceptical of the concept of mutual deterrence. Most importantly, the bishops were very critical of the Reagan administration's arms escalation and its support for the concept of limited nuclear wars. The administration had chosen to ignore their own scientists' advice on this last theory. They had argued that a nuclear war could never be 'limited' and that 'escalation to total war' would be inevitable. The Pope, on the other hand, believed in the concept of deterrence. He did not believe in unilateral disarmament and he held to the traditional Catholic theory of just war.

His views chimed exactly with those of the West German and French Cardinals. West German Cardinal Joseph Höffner was particularly busy promoting the Reagan line and attacking the US bishops. Privately the Pope was very sympathetic to their arguments but publicly he aspired to maintain a studied neutrality. The administration hoped that full diplomatic recognition might be the means of moving the Pope to a public and pro-USA stance on these issues.

Virtually every major religion came to protest about the Vatican upgrade. James Baker and Edward Meese listened attentively to the various arguments, responded politely to the various questions and attempted to reassure the various delegations that the new status between the Holy See and the United States would 'in no way violate the constitutional strictures on the separation of Church and State'. Having sent the delegations away, safe in the knowledge that the Catholic Church would have no input or influence at all on any aspect of US government policy, the State Department bowed to Vatican pressure and agreed to an outright ban on the use of any US aid funds by either countries or international health organisations for the promotion of birth control or abortion. They announced their policy change at the World Conference on Population in Mexico City in March 1984. Funding was withdrawn from, among others, two of the world's largest family planning organisations, the International Planned Parenthood Federation and the United Nations Fund for Population Activities. Ambassador Wilson later confirmed that 'American policy was changed as a result of the Vatican's not agreeing with our policy.'

It was but one of a number of issues where Vatican influences affected US policy but undoubtedly the most far-reaching. As the 1982 memo from Elliot Abrams makes clear, the administration was hoping for a payback, particularly on the nuclear weapons issue. The Pope, Cardinal Casaroli, and the papal delegate to the US, Pio Laghi, were fully prepared to exert pressure on recalcitrant bishops on the nuclear issue but only in private. Publicly, Cardinal Casaroli advised Ambassador Wilson in October 1983 that 'The Holy See is aware of the US position on arms reduction negotiations but our appeal to both the Soviet Union and the United States must be even-handed.' Very typically Casaroli then implied off the record that the letter which had been sent to both countries was 'principally aimed at the Soviets'.

The Reagan administration was far more successful with the President's Strategic Defence Initiative, popularly known as Star Wars. The Vatican Academy of Sciences had responded to the announcement of this surreal escalation of the arms race in March 1983 with a long, detailed study which had culminated in a highly critical report. This provoked a flurry of activity. Lobbying from, among others, Vernon Walters, Vice President George Bush, CIA Director William Casey and ultimately the President, eventually persuaded the Pope to order that the report should not be published.

On Central America, it was easy to get Vatican endorsement for administration policy, because the Pope's view of that part of the world coincided with Reagan's. The Pope saw all the insurgencies as a threat to the established order, namely the Roman Catholic Church. The President saw them as a threat to the United States. His policies met with full papal approval. However, on Poland there was a surprising fundamental difference. Initially the Pope had believed that the Reagan sanctions were a correct response to martial law. When martial law was revoked, the Pope believed that the sanctions should be lifted. His people were hurting. Reagan wanted more than the end of martial law. He wanted Solidarity and KOR leaders released simultaneously.

Communism and its multiple threats were a constant theme of General Vernon Walters in his discussion with the Pope. During his next papal briefing in December 1984, among the subjects discussed were events in Chile and the Philippines. Walters, voicing the State Department position observed,

> 'We must not allow the Communists to come to power using the genuine democratic parties, only to exclude them once in office . . . The US would welcome any initiatives that help Chile towards a smooth transition to democracy.'

The two men discussed the likely scenario that might follow the death or removal in the Philippines of the US-backed Ferdinand Marcos. The Pope asked Walters about the emergence of Corazon Aquino, the widow of the assassinated leader of the opposition, Benigno Aquino. 'I think she would be totally unacceptable as a successor to Marcos.' Again Walters was expressing not only the State Department's position but also the President's. To judge from the Pope's treatment of Cardinal Sin of the Philippines, subsequent events would appear to confirm that Wojtyla shared the General's opinion.

In March 1985 CIA chief William Casey received from an intelligence source within the Soviet Union the news that the nation's leader Konstantin Chernenko had died, but that the news was being suppressed. Casey, with all of the wealth and the facilities at his disposal, had no second source he could turn to for confirmation. Three days later he was growing increasingly disturbed that the information he had rushed to give to the President might be incorrect.

On 10 March it was announced that Chernenko had indeed died and that his successor was Mikhail Gorbachev. Casey advised the President that any difference between Gorbachev and his three predecessors, Brezhnev, Andropov and Chernenko, was only superficial. The head of the CIA predicted that the younger Gorbachev, only 54 at the time, would 'only export subversion and trouble with more zest'. It was a total misjudgement by the head of the world's most expensive intelligence agency. The same agency that ensured that its opinions, balanced or not, were invariably whispered to the Holy Father. In a conversation with Cardinal Bernadin in the summer of 1985, the Pope made it very clear that he fully supported the Reagan administration's actions throughout Central America and expected his US bishops to do the same.

During the run-up to the Reagan–Gorbachev summit in Geneva in November 1985, the administration strained every nerve to ensure that Roman Catholic opinion supported the Government position on the forthcoming arms reduction negotiations. Particular effort was made with regard to the position of various cardinals. One suggestion put to National Security Advisor, Bud McFarlane, by the State Department was to invite US Cardinals Law and O'Connor to a White House meeting with the President. '. . . Such an invitation would be viewed positively by the American Catholic community, improve our relations with the Vatican and assist in our efforts to influence the Bishops' statements on national security issues . . .' Thanking the proposer, Ty Cobb, Bud McFarlane advised him that he had recommended the idea and the presidential schedulers would try to accommodate the meeting. He continued:

'Law has been a strong advocate of our national security policies, but we are not impressed with O'Connor's stance on the MX missile. You indicated to me that these two (Law and O'Connor) and Bernadin are now the leaders of the Catholic Church in the US. What do you think that portends for our defence policies?'

One might well conclude that McFarlane and Cobb were talking about the respective merits of three US senators rather than senior members of a religious organisation.

Another Prince of the Church under the critical spotlight was Cardinal Jaime Sin of the Philippines. He alarmed the Pope, his Secretary of State Cardinal Casaroli and the papal nuncio in the Philippines, Archbishop Bruno Torpigliani, just as he disturbed the State Department. The papal nuncio was an avid supporter of the Marcos regime and a close friend of Imelda, the dictator's wife. The Archbishop worked very hard for several years attempting to undermine Cardinal Sin whose crime was his constant attempts to protect ordinary Filipinos from the worst excesses of a brutal regime. When Sin also began to support the opposition to Marcos and work for social reform within the country, the Marcos family took every opportunity to attack him. Imelda would tell the nuncio of the latest alleged provocation by the Cardinal, the nuncio would then telephone the Secretary of State complaining, whereupon Casaroli would attempt to control the activities of Cardinal Sin. This became a regular event.

The Pope's view of the Cardinal was poisoned just as his views of a great many others were poisoned over the years, and the Vatican lost no opportunity in humiliating a man who responded to a despotic regime in a manner not dissimilar to Cardinal Wyszynski's in Poland. Yet again the Pope demonstrated serious double standards. What was applauded in Poland was condemned in the Philippines.

The Pope warned Sin that he was setting a bad example by becoming too deeply involved in his country's politics.

This was after it had been powerfully demonstrated to the world that the Cardinal had the backing of his bishops and the overwhelming majority of the Philippine people. It was also after Marcos, despite having organised massive vote rigging, had been defeated at the polls and Corazon Aquino, the woman dismissed by General Vernon Walters, had become President.

President Reagan promptly switched horses, gave full diplomatic recognition to the new Government and recognised Mrs Aquino as the country's legal head. Instead of publicly acclaiming the extraordinary courage of his Cardinal, the Pope, the Secretary of State and inevitably the 'fascists' treated Cardinal Sin with contempt.

Two bishops from the Third World who were working in Rome at this time recalled certain events.

'The Secretariat of State had for a number of years been bombarded on a daily basis by Torpigliani who was at the beck and call of the Marcos family and the ruling regime . . . He turned blind eyes to torture, to death squads, to every form of repression. He regularly asked Casaroli to persuade the Holy Father to put a co-adjutor (a bishop who would for all practical purposes run the Cardinal's arch-diocese) into Manila. Casaroli backed away from that but he made sure the Holy Father was aware of the continuous complaints. They treated Cardinal Sin very badly. A lesser man would have crumpled . . .'

All this was for holding a moral position that was acclaimed around the world. When Cardinal Sin died in June 2005, Pope Benedict XVI, a man who had done nothing to support Sin in 1986, saluted the dead Cardinal for his 'unfailing commitment to the spread of the Gospel and to the promotion of the dignity, common good, and national unity of the Philippine people.' The 'fascists' were not alone in attempting to stem the irresistible tide of change that was stirring in various parts of the world. They and others within the Vatican still clung to the desire that the old order, provided it was a right-wing order, should not change. Others held with equal tenacity to opinions and positions concerning European Communism that grew daily more untenable.

By March 1986 the Soviet leader Mikhail Gorbachev had achieved considerable success in convincing the West that the 'Evil Empire' was indeed under new management. Margaret Thatcher memorably observed of Gorbachev that 'this is a man I can do business with'. But Cold Warriors die hard. President Reagan was still surrounded by men who continued to insist that virtually all the world's ills could be traced back to the Soviet Union. In a March 1986 meeting with the Pope, Walters spent the entire thirty minutes delivering an anti-Soviet lecture yet was obliged near the end to admit that 'seldom can one trace a specific act of terrorism directly to the Soviets'.

Walters did not record in his secret report to the US Secretary of State whether the Pope raised any questions or pointed out the contradiction of a Soviet State hell-bent on worldwide terrorism and simultaneously making historically unique efforts to end the Cold War. In little more than a year the Soviet leader would succeed and in doing so would initiate the collapse of the Communist dominoes all over Europe.

General Walters's meeting in March 1986 with the Pope would be the last arranged by Ambassador Wilson. Wilson had led a charmed life from the moment his close friend had accepted him to the Vatican post in February 1981. That he had survived for just over five years speaks volumes about Ronald Reagan's sense of loyalty. Some of William Wilson's embarrassments have already been recorded in this chapter. Exceptionally, Wilson had been allowed to break the normal rules of conduct for American diplomats and continue to serve as a director of the Pennzoil Corporation. He was especially valuable to them because of his continued access to Libya during a time when the US was applying stringent economic sanctions against the country. It was this link that eventually did for Wilson.

The Reagan administration never succeeded in its prime ambition in its relationship with the Vatican to persuade the Pope to commit the Church publicly to the US position on nuclear weapons, but it was not for lack of trying. When the arms reduction talks, first in Geneva and then Reykjavik, faltered solely because of US intransigence regarding the Star Wars programme – the US refusing to abandon the project, the Soviets insisting that the programme be cancelled – President Reagan yet again justified his stance in a cable to the Pope. '. . . The programme threatens no one. Such technologies offer the hope of placing deterrence of war on a safer and more stable basis. Is it not better to save lives than to avenge them?' In the Secretary of State's offices there was bemusement. How could the Americans spend trillions of dollars on a concept that could never be tested unless someone attempted to start a nuclear war?

In October 1986, a few days after the Reykjavik summit ended in deadlock, Secretary of Defense Casper Weinberger met the Pope to discuss the implications of the US position on arms reduction and to justify yet again the value of Star Wars. 'We do not seek a unilateral military advantage through SDI, but in fact we have offered to share the benefits with the Soviets.' The Pope expressed his appreciation for the briefing observing that, 'While I earnestly seek peace, I am not a unilateral pacifist.'

The Pope also took the opportunity during this meeting to raise one of his own major preoccupations, the continuing economic and commercial sanctions that the United

States had imposed against Poland. After reflection, he had concluded that the sanctions were indeed bad for Poland and attempted for years to persuade the Reagan administration to lift them. On 24 December 1986, exactly five years after the sanctions had been imposed, he tried yet again, this time while talking to the Polish community of Rome.

'I wish nobody to live any longer lacking material means and facing the everyday preoccupations of life; I wish Poland to become the "house of freedom" where everybody is subject to the same law and shares the same obligations. I wish that, with adequate efforts in this direction, Poland can again proceed on the road leading to full and fruitful co-operation and exchange of goods in every sector.'

The speech was quoted extensively in the Italian media. The new US Ambassador to the Vatican, Frank Shakespeare, cabled a copy back to the State Department. It was also discussed at length in the papal apartments on 13 January 1987 when the Pope received General Jaruzelski. Both men were optimistic that the US sanctions would be lifted in the very near future. The previous September the Communist regime had announced a general amnesty and released 229 political prisoners who represented the heart and soul of Solidarity. Now for the first time since the declaration of martial law, although Jaruzelski still deprived the movement of any legality, its essence was alive and well and active through the many underground publications, CIA-financed radio stations and the Vatican Radio.

The Pope and the General discussed Gorbachev at great length. Jaruzelski had spent many hours in conversation with the Soviet leader and was deeply impressed. He recounted his belief that through this new breed of Soviet leader 'whom we must support, there is a great chance for Europe and the World'. The Pope was also aware through the continuous reports he received from Cardinal Glemp and members of the Polish hierarchy that the General was cautiously moving Poland forward. The relaxations were not happening overnight, but they were happening. Just over one month later on 19 February President Reagan announced the lifting of the sanctions he had imposed against Poland. In giving among his reasons the claim that 'the light of liberty shines in Poland', yet again Reagan was guilty of wishful thinking.

During the first week of June 1987 the President paid his second visit to the Vatican. In his welcoming speech the Pope remarked,

> 'The Holy See has no political ambitions, but it does consider it part of its missions in the world to be vitally concerned about human rights and the dignity of all, especially the poor and suffering.'

Officially, as the Pope stated, it is an organisation devoid of political ambition; secretly, however, and sometimes not too secretly, it invariably has a political agenda. If any institution is 'vitally concerned about human rights and the dignity of all especially the poor and suffering', and then puts this concern into action, it is politically involved. Underlining the Holy See's activity, on the day of the Presidential visit a totally unpublicised meeting took place between Secretary of State Cardinal Casaroli, Secretary of the Council for Public Affairs of the Church Archbishop Achille Silvestrini, his Under-secretary Monsignor Audrys Backis and a US delegation that included National Security Council Advisor Frank Carlucci and his deputy Tyrus Cobb, Senator Howard Baker, the Senate Republican majority leader, Ambassador Frank Shakespeare and various other US officials. Among the subjects discussed were Poland, Third World debt, Latin America, Gorbachev and the Soviet Union, and Israel.

On Latin America the cardinal told his visitors that the Vatican wanted to see a 'true democracy' in every Latin American country, but that meant democracy 'in the fullest sense of the word, including socially and economically just societies'. He expressed anxieties about the future of religion in the region, particularly in the poorer countries where poverty and injustice can lead the faithful and 'even some clergy toward socialism'. The Vatican was also concerned 'about proponents of Liberation Theology' and was particularly worried about 'Mexico, where we believe a radical and anti-religious revolution is possible'. Casaroli said that 'the US has a special responsibility in Latin America as the region's "big brother". You can choose your friends, but you can't choose your brother.'

Their discussion on Gorbachev and the major obstacles facing him as he sought to bring change within the USSR elicited from Carlucci the extraordinary suggestion that Gorbachev's reforms 'resembled Khrushchev's'. This dismissal of the Soviet leader was very much in line with the opinion of the head of the CIA, William Casey, the State Department's Ambassador General Walters and many of their colleagues within the administration.

During the summer of 1987 the political involvement of the Holy See continued apace. It included a continuing secret dialogue between General Jaruzelski and the Pope with the General acting as an unofficial go-between as he assiduously worked on bringing the Pope and Mikhail Gorbachev together. It would take time but already each leader was keenly interested in learning about the other. Vatican political involvement also included Nicaragua and Haiti with the State Department pulling every conceivable lever to persuade the Pope to allow Cardinal Obando to remain in Nicaragua during October rather than attend a Synod of Bishops in Rome. The CIA, the State Department and a quiverful of ambassadors plus the President appealed to the Secretary of State Casaroli, the Vatican Foreign Minister and finally through Reagan, to the Pope. The secret cable traffic for the period shows a rampant paranoia. The administration feared that if the Cardinal who was very much their man in Managua left for Rome, the Sandinistas would block his return, and they feared without Obando's presence at the peace talks between the Sandinista Government and the Contras the US-backed Contras might not prevail. Eventually after four different approaches by the administration and Reagan's direct intervention, the Pope gave way and Cardinal Obando was back home after just one week's absence.

The State Department was less successful in attempting to get the Pope to fly into Haiti as a 'side trip while he is visiting Miami in September'. The two incidents and the tenor of the cables are very reminiscent of the language used to describe the US cardinals when the idea of having three of them at a Presidential lunch was discussed.

> 'The Pope should re-engage on this issue (unrest in Haiti) . . . It would be particularly useful if Holy Father would again become directly engaged in focusing Haitian attention on co-operation and compromise leading to elections in an environment of domestic tranquillity. A few words in Creole and French would have a positive impact.'

Treating the Pope as no more than a US roving ambassador who should be following his brief and his script is straight out of a Grahame Greene novel.

In the real world during December 1987 the United States

and the Soviet Union signed a formal treaty on arms control limitation. This was the first such agreement in the nuclear age. The Russians agreed to destroy four times as many nuclear warheads – 1,500 – as the United States – 350. Gorbachev, the man that the US administration had so easily dismissed, had delivered what no one had even dared think was possible. Because of Mikhail Gorbachev, millions of people had learned their first two words of Russian, words that Gorbachev frequently used to describe his policies: 'perestroika' – economic restructuring and 'glasnost' – openness. Now with the arms treaty the West had a practical example of both words.

The Pope, a man far better informed about the Russian leader than President Reagan, had been following the arms negotiations closely. He also studied the speech that Gorbachev made at the United Nations on the day the treaty was signed. Gorbachev had stunned his audience by announcing that apart from the arms reduction he had just agreed he was willing to make major troop and weapon reductions in Eastern Europe. These would reduce the Red Army in Europe by at least half a million soldiers and 10,000 tanks. Explaining his reasoning he observed, 'Although the Russian Revolution radically changed the course of world development, today we face a different world, for which we seek a different road to the future.' He continued, with a self-honesty never before seen in a Soviet leader, 'Closed societies are impossible, because the world economy is becoming a single organism.' On the rights of the individual Gorbachev described freedom of choice as 'mandatory'. To the listening Pope and to many others around the world, Mikhail Gorbachev was proclaiming the end of the Cold War.

The cost to both superpowers had been unimaginably high. The Soviet Union's attempts to match US spending in the arms race had resulted in an economy on its knees and infrastructure in disarray. The United States under President Reagan sustained the largest peacetime military build-up in the country's history. Then there was the development of the Strategic Defence Initiative or Star Wars programme designed to shield America from incoming missiles. The financial cost to the country was astronomical. The national debt tripled during the Reagan years, rising from $900 billion to $2,700 billion, and the trade deficit quadrupled. By the time Reagan left office, interest payments alone on the debt amounted to fourteen per cent of the Federal budget and the debt was growing by $200 billion a year. He had not only put his successors in a financial straitjacket but also, it seemed, unborn generations of Americans.

The high-cost strategy had undoubtedly accelerated the conditions within the Soviet Union that enabled Gorbachev's realism to prevail over the Soviet hard-liners. Reagan's foreign policies in other areas such as the Middle East and Latin America were also high-cost in every sense, but largely resulted in failure. The Middle East had been largely abandoned, a legacy that would come back ultimately to plague the United States. Latin America was very much a disaster area. It would take many years for the region to recover from the Reagan scorched-earth version of political settlement.

The papal briefings from US officials tailed off even before President Reagan left office in January 1989. The consultations on American policies also became a curiosity of the past. To such an extent were the Pope and his senior officials ignored that there were complaints from the Holy See during the Gulf war of 1990/91 that neither the US Secretary of State Baker nor any other senior members of the Administration considered it worthwhile to request an audience with the Pope or an appointment with the Secretary of State. Such indifference had in fact been manifesting for years.

The following letters were part of a large bundle of material, some 900 documents, obtained from the personal papers of President Ronald Reagan.

Sensitive – Handle with Discretion

6 September 1985
INTEREST IN A DISCREET DIALOGUE – POPE JOHN PAUL II TO McFARLANE

Pope John Paul II remains vitally concerned with the following issues:

- Developments in Poland.
- 'Liberation Theology' and its impact on developments in Latin America.
- African developments and how to correct the manipulation of Christian principles.
- Role of the Catholic Church in America.
- Foreign policy issues which impact on the respective interests of the Vatican and the United States.

At the moment the Pope believes his problems with the Curia – particularly with Cardinal Agostino Casaroli and Archbishop Achille Silvestrini – are such that the quality of his dialogue with the United States is less than what he would like. In an attempt to correct this, the Pope has authorized one of his personal secretaries – Emery Kabango – to undertake discreet soundings of the possibility for opening a back channel dialogue to McFarlane. This decision was taken because McFarlane impressed the Holy Father and Kabango with his sincerity and openmindedness in a previous meeting. It was also influenced by the belief that a two-tier communications system was required to enable the Pope to circumvent the restraints of Vatican political life, the

views of special interest groups, and security considerations affecting the privacy of his dialogue.

Kabango in turn has asked a trusted confidant to
assess the prospects for opening such a channel. That
is the genesis of this memorandum, for the emissary is
currently in the United States and is available for a
meeting to elaborate on this matter.

It is understood that McFarlane may find it difficult
to travel. If he were in Rome, however, a discreet one-
on-one meeting with the Pope is assured.

An expression of interest or disinterest in this Vatican probe is requested.

Sensitive – Handle with Discretion

15 October 1985
VATICAN REMAINS KEEN TO HAVE A DISCREET
DIALOGUE – POPE JOHN PAUL II TO McFARLANE
On 8 October 1985 a meeting was held at the Vatican
with Monsignor Emery Kabango, one of Pope John
Paul II's personal secretaries. The conversation took
place in a wing of the private quarters of the Holy Father
and lasted seventy-five minutes. The prime purpose of
this session was to discuss the dates and ground rules for
a magazine interview with Pope John Paul II.

After agreement was reached on the next steps to be
taken relative to the interview, Kabango adroitly
turned the focus of the discussion to themes that
obviously interested him. In this portion of the meeting, Kabango made the following points:

• A private visit at an early date by McFarlane with
  the Holy Father would be most welcome. This
  encounter would, of course, be a one-on-one session

undertaken under the most discreet circumstances. Could such a session take place before too long?

- It is recognised in the Vatican that the United States has the mission of defending peace and freedom throughout the world. Others must help America in the pursuit of this mission, but the question is how.
- The Vatican can identify with specific American foreign policy objectives. It cannot, however, sign up for a blanket policy endorsement of America's actions. As a result there must be a discussion of specific points on which cooperation can be achieved.
- The Vatican remains in close contact with its bishops. Recently conversations with 370 bishops from Brazil revealed they believe the Church should not support United States policies in an area like Latin America in total terms.

As the meeting was drawing to a close, Kabango said, 'Dr Pavoni is our very good friend. He is called upon to help us solve difficult problems. We appreciate, therefore, your assistance in attempting to find a way for Dr Pavoni to open a channel to McFarlane on our behalf.'

A few brief observations based on the 8 October meeting may help to put the above data into perspective. They are:

Sensitive – Handle With Discretion

- Dr Pavoni is on extremely good terms with Monsignor Kabango. In the discussion of all items, Dr Pavoni was a full participant and it is clear Kabango respects his advice.

- Dr Pavoni has easy access to all parts of the Vatican. He arranged the meeting with Kabango under circumstances that permitted the author to enter and leave the Vatican without being checked by any security personnel.
- It is clear a meeting with McFarlane just prior to the Geneva Summit, during the conference or just after it, would be most welcome by the Holy Father.
- While the magazine interview was the primary reason for the meeting with Kabango, the latter wanted to make certain points during this session which he hoped would be conveyed to McFarlane or his associates. All of these points have been covered in this memorandum.

Sensitive – Handle with Discretion

7 January 1986

VATICAN IS PERPLEXED AS TO WHY NO FOLLOW UP HAS TAKEN PLACE ON ITS OVERTURE FOR A DISCREET DIALOGUE

On 6 January 1986, the question was raised in a double-talk international telephone call as to why there had been no response to the Vatican's September 1985 overture for a discreet dialogue between Pope John Paul II and Mr McFarlane or his successor. The Vatican emissary said Monsignor Emery Kabango, a private secretary to Pope John Paul II, understood that Washington's top echelons had been preoccupied with the Geneva summit and other issues, such as personnel changes. On the other hand, the Holy Father was perplexed why no one had extended him the courtesy of an interim response. How was this lack of a sign of life to be interpreted?

The caller was told we had no answers to his questions, but would forward his inquiry to appropriate authorities.

Attached for easy reference are two previous mem-
oranda on this topic. They are dated 6 September and
15 October 1985.

At the time of the first two letters Bud McFarlane was
President Reagan's National Security Advisor. He was
succeeded on 4 December 1985 by Admiral John M.
Poindexter. It is inconceivable that these letters were not
drawn to the attention of both men and the fact that they
are in the late President's official papers demonstrates that
they also reached Ronald Reagan. What action the White
House subsequently took, if indeed any was taken, is
unknown. The administration's failure even to respond
demonstrates the fantasy of the 'Holy Alliance'.

The letters also demonstrate a state of affairs that had
existed within this Papacy since its inception and continued
into the 1990s. The Pope was so profoundly alienated from
his Secretary of State and his Foreign Secretary that he
attempted to open a back channel to Reagan and his
National Security Advisor. The issues of concern are
equally revealing as are the points that the Pope's Secretary
Monsignor Emery Kabango lists in the October 15th letter.
It would seem that the Pope was seeking in the mid 1980s to
establish the very relationship that has been claimed for
himself and Reagan and that his overtures were rejected.

Although the concept of a 'Holy Alliance' is a myth, the
efforts of the Reagan administration to upgrade US relations with the Holy See paid handsome dividends. US
activity throughout Latin America was not the only Reagan
agenda that escaped either public or private papal criticism.
The bottom line is by any criteria an indictment of the
Wojtyla Papacy. At no time during Reagan's two terms of
office did the Pope see fit to object, condemn or criticise the
administration. He ignored the objections of his US bishops
on the vast military build-up. He castigated the same

bishops for not supporting the carnage that the administration was wreaking in Latin America and under pressure
from the administration the Pope ordered that a highly
critical Vatican Academy of Sciences study of Reagan's Star
Wars project should be filed with the minimum of publicity.
The spiritual leader of the Catholic Church held a sincere
belief in the rightness of eight years of Reagan's foreign
policy decisions and with that belief he profoundly compromised many of the basic tenets of his faith.

Within twelve months of Reagan's stepping down from
the Presidency, the face of Europe had dramatically changed. Under Gorbachev's urging, free elections had occurred
in Poland and the country had the first government in a
Communist state in which the Communists were a minority. Again with the support of Mikhail Gorbachev, East
Germany began to move out of a forty-year darkness. When
the Soviet leader came to participate in the 'celebrations' for
the fortieth anniversary of the founding of the DDR, he
declared to the party leader Eric Honecker: 'Life itself
punishes those who delay.' Privately he advised Honecker
that he could not count on the 500,000 Soviet troops still
stationed in East Germany 'to repress the citizens of this
country'. Ten days later Honecker was gone and on 9
November the authorities made an opening in the Berlin
Wall for the first time since 1961. Within a further eleven
months, Germany was once again a united country.

Gorbachev throughout the entire period had been greatly
preoccupied in simultaneously fighting off the Soviet conservative hard-liners and encouraging Warsaw Pact countries to believe that 'the future of every East European
country was in its own hands'. By the time of German
reunification in October 1990 he had had his first highly
successful meeting with the Pope and for good measure
received the Nobel Peace Prize. The hard-liners did not yield
without a fight. In mid-1991 an attempted coup to over-

throw Gorbachev failed, but it led to the emergence of Boris Yeltsin, a man whose thirst for power far outweighed his abilities. By December 1991 Mikhail Gorbachev was forced to resign to be replaced by Yeltsin. Gorbachev's place in history was secure; the majority have already forgotten Boris Yeltsin.

While these events were unfolding in Europe, some countries in Latin America, apparently impervious to such tumultuous change, carried on their same repressive path of murders, political assassination, mass disappearances and human rights violations. Peace negotiations broke down. Peace accords were flagrantly abused and wherever there was continuing anarchy one of the inevitable elements was a core of right-wing Catholic bishops supporting the regime. The civil war in Guatemala lasted thirty-six years, finally ending in 1996. The same year, during a papal visit to El Salvador, one of the country's bishops accused Oscar Romero, the murdered Archbishop, of being responsible for the death of 70,000 Salvadorians.

The slander went unchallenged by the listening Pope. Finally in 2002 yet another peace accord was stitched together in El Salvador and – wonder of wonders – President George W. Bush flew in to attend a working lunch for the leaders of seven Central American countries, including the current Nicaraguan president, Enrique Bolanos. The region may finally be edging forward to a period of continuing peace but a quiver full of problems remain to be solved. The murder rate in El Salvador in 2000 was nearly 200 per 100,000 residents, compared with a US rate of 5.5 murders per 100,000 residents. Many of the killings are the responsibility of organised crime whose members, having begun their careers in the US, were imprisoned there and then were deported to El Salvador.

In another bizarre sign of change in late June 2004 Daniel Ortega, who led the Sandinista government in Nicaragua during the 1980s and was the declared enemy of Cardinal Miguel Obando Bravo, the man so highly regarded by the CIA and the Reagan administration, proposed that the Cardinal be nominated for the Nobel Peace Prize 'in recognition of his struggle for national reconciliation'.

Chapter 7

The Market Place

O N 11 SEPTEMBER 2003 the Alitalia jet carrying
Pope John II, his entourage, the press corps and
other unidentified personnel touched down at the
M. R. Stefanik airport outside Bratislava, the capital of
Slovakia, and the 102nd papal visit had begun. His schedule
had a minimum of public appearances and photo opportunities. Gone were the images of a strong, upright, athletic
figure hurrying down the plane steps to kiss the ground. It
took four aides twenty minutes to manoeuvre Wojtyla into
the elevator that had been especially installed to assist his
descent from the plane. The Pope remained seated as his
chair was rolled onto a platform in the reception hall of the
airport for a brief welcoming ceremony.

He read only a few lines of his prepared speech in the
Slovak language. By the end of the first paragraph he was
struggling for breath and was unable to continue. His
secretary, Bishop Stanislaw Dziwisz, quickly moved forward, took the speech from the Pope and handed it to a
young Slovak priest, who read the remainder with the
exception of the final paragraph which the Pope, struggling
and in obvious difficulty, somehow got through.

It was becoming an increasingly familiar scene on these
trips. Predictably, the Vatican spin doctor Joaquin Navarro-Valls sought to downplay what the watching reporters

had observed, reminding the press of other occasions when the Pope had been forced to rely on others to deliver his public speeches. Navarro-Valls was obliged under further questioning to concede that this was the first time it had happened during an opening speech on an apostolic trip.

The Pope's condition had not improved at the time of his second public appearance of the day, this time at the Marian shrine at Trnava in eastern Slovakia. Despite several hours of rest he was desperately frail. Many regulars in the press corps believed that the Pope might die at any moment during this four-day trip. Navarro-Valls demonstrated yet again that he saw a different reality to the majority. 'I do not see any obstacle to an eventual 103rd trip. Even if there is no concrete plan, we have already received several invitations.'

As usual, the truth was somewhat different. The large quantity of medical equipment and the doctors and nurses among the papal party had become a regular feature when the Pope travelled any distance away from the Vatican. A trip to Mongolia planned for August had been cancelled because of his worsening condition.

For years Navarro-Valls had angrily denied that the Pope was suffering from Parkinson's disease. The Pope was continually presented as the super-fit athlete of his youth long after the evidence told a different story. His health had been in serious decline well before 2003. Within the Vatican there were now open discussions of not 'if' but 'when' the Pope would hand over power. Some of those close to the Pope were terrified of that approaching moment. Unless they were able to manipulate the handover, which was a very real possibility, their own power would be in jeopardy. Meanwhile they continued to allow the 83-year-old terminally ill Pope to suffer in public. Near the end of Karol Wojtyla's ordeal in Slovakia the consensus view of the accompanying press reporters was that he 'was nearing

the limit of what medicine and willpower can do'. Within
the Vatican it was openly admitted that well before the
ordeal in Slovakia this had become 'a lame duck papacy',
and that the Pope alternated between 'periods of lucidity
and confusion'.

Apart from the human costs of shuttling a very sick man
in his eighties around the world, the papal trips always
raised other fundamental questions. Did the Roman Catholic Church actually gain from these journeys? What benefits
were derived from this unique example of evangelism which
began in January 1979 with visits to Mexico and the
Dominican Republic and then continued unabated?

'I am a pilgrim-messenger who wants to travel the world
to fulfil the mandate Christ gave to the apostles when he
sent them to evangelise all men and all nations.' Since John
Paul II uttered those words in Spain in November 1982 he
had spent 580 days and nights on the road, up in the air,
across the oceans and seas of the world. Nearly a year and a
half of the entire Wojtyla Papacy were spent on arrivals and
departures and in between preaching, praying and in every
sense of the word, pontificating.

These activities, among a number of others, provoked
extravagant praise from an unending queue of admirers.
'Man of the Century . . . Prophet of the New Millennium
. . . Conscience of the World.' The statistics of the Wojtyla
Papacy, how many trips, the number of encyclicals, the
record number of beatifications, of canonisations, of the
record crowds attending Papal Mass in the Philippines, in
Ireland, in Poland, were constantly trotted out by the
Vatican. One official statistic was never mentioned: how
much did it cost? And should the Pope have followed the
example of his predecessors and spent more time in Rome?

The question was raised within the Vatican very early in
his papacy. A senior member of the Roman Curia told me in
1981 that the Curia were extremely concerned over 'ex-

cessive and unnecessary use of human and financial resources'. If the Curia had known then just how frequently in
the future the Papal flights would take to the skies they
might have demonstrated in St Peter's Square. As recorded
earlier, the Pope raised the issue himself during his first visit
to the African continent in 1980.

'Some people think that the Pope should not travel so
much. He should stay in Rome, as before. I often hear
such advice, or read it in the newspapers. But the local
people here say,
    "Thank God you came here, for you can only learn
about us by coming. How could you be our pastor
without knowing us? Without knowledge of who we
are, how we live, what is the historical moment we are
going through?" This confirms me in the belief that it
is time for the Bishops of Rome to become successors
not only of Peter but also of Saint Paul, who as we
know could never sit still and was constantly on the
move.'

Exactly how effective was he as the messenger? Discount-
ing Vatican spin, local exaggeration and media hyperbole
the powerfully charismatic Wojtyla indisputably attracted
vast crowds when making his 'pilgrimages'. The accumu-
lative global figure for attendances at the open masses and
meetings runs into many hundreds of millions if not billions. The words he uttered amount to a similar total. The
financial cost is more difficult to evaluate. During November 1980 the Pope paid a five-day visit to the then West
Germany; the cost to the West German taxpayers was
officially put at $10 million. In 1982 the Pope made a
six-day visit to the United Kingdom; the cost was officially
put at £6 million. In 1987 the Pope made a ten-day visit to
the USA estimated at $26 million. The Vatican paid for the

first-class air fares for the twelve members of the papal party, while American taxpayers and American Catholics paid the remainder. Long after the trip, many dioceses were struggling with huge unpaid bills. The cost of other overseas trips has also been officially estimated at $2 million per day. Taking these figures as an average, the cost of the Pope's overseas trips since October 1978, *a cost that was never paid by the Vatican*, was in excess of $1.1 billion. Undoubtedly, the great majority of papal trips had an immediate effect on his audiences, with huge crowds instantly bonding to the man from the far country. However, the long-term effect was minimal. The man the audiences were prepared to love; the message they were prepared to ignore. In most countries the vast majority of Roman Catholics were to prove very resistant to the teachings of Pope John Paul II. Even in a country as historically Catholic as Ireland, where over ninety per cent of the population attended mass once a week, beliefs were changing dramatically.

Surveys, research and opinion polls carried out there in early 2001 by the American priest, author and sociologist, Father Andrew Greeley, confirmed that Ireland's attitudes towards religion were changing. This was the country where for two and a half days in 1979 the Pope took the entire nation by storm. The first Papal Mass in Phoenix Park, Dublin was attended by an estimated 1.2 million people, more than one third of the entire population. Speaking to this vast congregation the Pope urged Ireland, a country that had for centuries sent out thousands of missionaries into the world to rediscover their faith, 'be converted'.

At Drogheda, a compromise location chosen for security reasons some thirty miles from the border with Northern Ireland, John Paul pleaded for an end to the sectarian violence, an end to the murders, blasphemously perpetrated not only in the name of nationalism but also competing

versions of Christianity. He invoked the fifth commandment, 'Thou Shalt Not Kill'. He rejected the description that
a religious war was being engaged between Catholics and
Protestants. 'This is a struggle between people driven by
hate and Christianity forbids hatred.' Speaking not only to
the 300,000 gathered at Drogheda but to the entire country,
north and south, he made a powerful and very personal
plea.

> 'On my knees I beg you to turn away from the paths of
> violence and to return to the ways of peace . . .
> violence destroys the work of justice . . . further vio-
> lence in Ireland will only drag down and ruin the land
> you claim to love and the values you claim to cherish.'

Everywhere he went he was acclaimed with thunderous
applause, deafening cheers and rapturous singing. His final
mass in Limerick drew more than 250,000 people. The
Pope's plea to the men of violence had not the slightest effect
or influence upon events. The murders, the obscene bombings of civilians, the knee-capping, the intimidation and the
hatred all continued without cease. As for Irish Catholicism,
the numbers of the faithful continued to decline.

The changes in belief, behaviour and attitude that Father
Greeley's surveys recorded were certainly not the ones that
the Pope had in mind when he had exhorted 'be converted'.
'If the proper measures of Catholicism are faith and devotion, then the Irish are still Catholic,' Father Greeley
observed. His research found that ninety-four per cent of
the Irish believed in God, eighty-five per cent in heaven and
miracles and seventy-eight per cent in life after death.
However, 'If on the other hand the proper measures of
faith are acceptance of Church authority and adherence to
the Church's sexual ethic, then the Irish are no longer
Catholic,' said Greeley, adding 'but then neither are any

other people in Europe including the Italians and the Poles.'
His figures showed that only forty per cent believed that
abortion was always wrong, only thirty per cent believed
that premarital sex was always wrong and just sixty per
cent believed that same-sex relations were always wrong.
Most tellingly of all, only seven per cent of those born in the
1970s had a great deal of confidence in the Church but
seventy per cent had high confidence in their local priest.

A subsequent poll conducted in September 2003 by RTE,
Ireland's state broadcaster, confirmed Father Greeley's
findings. It showed that only fifty per cent of Catholics
in Ireland attended mass each week, seventy-five per cent
believed that celibate priesthood should be abolished, sixty
per cent believed that the priesthood should be open to
women and thirty-eight per cent rejected the concept of
papal infallibility.

A 2002 Zogby poll indicated that Father Greeley might
soon need to add the United States to those who are 'no
longer Catholic'. It found fifty-four per cent in favour of
married priests, while fifty-three per cent thought there
should be women priests, sixty-one per cent approved of
artificial birth control, a thumping eighty-three per cent
thought it was morally wrong to discriminate against
homosexuals and even on abortion nearly a third disagreed
that it was always morally wrong. In contradiction to those
figures, in the same poll no fewer than ninety per cent
thought the Pope was doing a good job worldwide in his
leadership of the Church.

The fact that so many of those polled disagreed with the
Church's position on such a wide range of key issues was a
startling illustration of the central paradox of Karol Wojtyla's papacy. They would buy his books, his CDs, his
videos, they would flock in their millions to the parks,
fields, football stadiums of this world when he was celebrating mass but in ever increasing numbers they would not

follow either his teaching or Church doctrine on a growing number of issues. His form of Christianity was becoming increasingly irrelevant and evidence was not confined to polls. In Australia, they were voting with their feet. Between 1971 and 2006, Catholic weddings in a church had declined by over 50%, from 9,784 to 4,075.

In the United States the number of priests more than doubled to 58,000 between 1930 and 1965. Since then the number has fallen to 45,000 and continues to slip away. By 2020, on present trends, there will be fewer than 31,000 and more than half of those priests will be over seventy. In 1965, one per cent of US parishes were without a priest. By 2002, 15 per cent – 3,000 parishes – lacked a priest. In that same period the number of seminarians declined by ninety per cent. The same grim picture repeated itself in the figures for Catholic nuns and members of religious orders. Almost half of the Catholic high schools have closed in the past forty years. Weekly attendance at mass hovers between thirty-one and thirty-five per cent. Annulment figures have soared from 338 to 501,000. Wherever one looks the story is the same yet the US Catholic Church still proclaimed that within the same period, 1965 to 2002, the number of Catholics within the country had risen by 20 million.

The myth of a hugely increased membership is perpetuated not only within the USA but globally. The Church's definition of a Roman Catholic – a baptised person – flies in the face of the fact that hundreds of millions of notional Catholics subsequently reject the Church's teachings on a huge range of issues and by doing so, notwithstanding what is written on their baptismal certificates, cease to be Roman Catholics. A non-practising Roman Catholic is an ex-Roman Catholic, or in Vatican-speak – a lapsed Roman Catholic.

In Britain, plans are well advanced to abolish the current oath taken before giving evidence in court. In future there will be no reference to God. In the United States in October 2003 after a long legal battle that went all the way up to the Supreme Court, a Federal Court decision banning the display of the Ten Commandments in the Alabama state judiciary building was upheld. The decision re-affirmed the separation of church and state. While the Pope created more and more saints, fewer and fewer children are being named after them. In devoutly Roman Catholic Chile, abortion morning-after pills are distributed free of charge. Vandalism, theft, drug dealing, arson, pagan rites and 'inappropriate behaviour on the high altar' have become such common occurrences in British churches that many are now kept locked outside the hours of service, with closed-circuit TV cameras on. Simultaneously Catholic churches in Scotland are recording all-time low attendances, a mere twelve per cent. Bishop Joe Devine of Motherwell observed, 'The Catholic population is diminished but not vanquished. The occult plays a part, but the main issue is that people are watching television or playing football rather than going to church.' The Pope held a bleaker view: 'Scotland is a pagan country.'

Cardinal Keith O'Brien, a man he recently promoted, agrees. 'There is a danger of Scotland declining into a bacchanalian state where everyone is just concerned with their own pleasures and to sleep with whomever they want.' In January 2003 Britain's leading Catholic clergyman, Cardinal Cormac Murphy O'Connor, dramatically spoke of a far greater crisis of faith: 'Britain has become a very pagan country.'

If there are unwanted pregnancies in Britain there are not enough of them in Italy. In *L'Osservatore Romano* in October 2001 theologian Father Gino Romano sought to find the reason for the fact that Italy, closely followed by Catholic Spain, has the lowest birth rate in Europe. He blamed 'Italian policies . . . the steady rise in divorce reflects the impact of a cyclone of secularism and consumerism.' He also called 'for new efforts to enable young couples to have more than one child'.

The Italian theologian, like the Catholic Women's League in Britain, lamented the fact that the majority of teenagers, while still believing in the value of marriage, prefer to wait until their relationships and other aspirations have matured. Choice is being exercised. Traditional marriage in mid- or late teens with three or more young children by the age of twenty is a prospect with diminishing appeal in Europe.

There has been a wholesale rejection of the Church's teaching on birth control. The majority have also rejected the Church's teaching on divorce and abortion. While renowned Catholic philosophers argued publicly with the Pope and the Jesuits on the existence of hell, the Catholic masses are more concerned with the here and now and a lifestyle profoundly at odds with the Pope's constant admonitions. They also disagree with the Church's position on married priests and women priests.

Two thirds further believe that the Catholic Church should return to the practice of priests and the congregation electing bishops within their own diocese. The Italians regard the Pope's failure to eliminate the financial corruption of the 1980s with deep cynicism. During that decade when he paid a visit to a very seriously deprived Naples, he was greeted with a huge banner that proclaimed: 'Rich Naples Welcomes Its Poor Pope'. The Italians were equally cynical about the extraordinary number of trips abroad the Pope and his entourage had made. It confirmed in the minds of many the image of a very wealthy Church squandering the people's money.

Some of the public criticism was unfair and uninformed. The visits within Italy frequently finished in profit. Vatican officials were not above requesting a facility fee if they had a request from a mayor or a factory owner for a visit from Pope John Paul. When Carol de Benedetti (wearing not his Banco Ambrosiano hat but his chief executive of Olivetti headgear) was preparing for a papal visit to his typewriter factory in Ivrea he was advised that a contribution would be required. The man from the Vatican suggested $100,000 and subsequently de Benedetti wrote out the cheque making it payable to the Pope personally and handed it to him privately during his visit.

I had been told this story some years ago and considered it apocryphal until seeing it quoted by Carl Bernstein and Marco Politi after they had interviewed De Benedetti. Subsequent research confirmed that many other Italian businessmen have been obliged to put something in the Vatican plate.

Nor did the Italian taxpayer or the Vatican pick up the $2 million daily expense of the overseas trips.

The Pope and his closest advisors never considered the possibility that the widespread collapse of Catholicism might at least in part have been due to the Vatican. For them, the answer was invariably found in the corruption of secular society rather than the corruption of those from whom secular society once sought moral guidance. As Wojtyla commented to the Belgian bishops, the decline of religious practice in their home country was 'particularly troubling' and he was in no doubt as to the reasons. It was the problem of 'a society that loses track of its traditional points of reference, promoting relativism in the name of pluralism'.

On the occasion of a visit to Rome by a group of French bishops the Pope encouraged them to confront 'the secularisation of French society, which often takes the form of rejection, in public life, of the anthropological, religious and moral principles which have profoundly marked the history and culture of the nation'. The Pope told his French bishops of his concern of the decline in priestly vocations. 'For many years now, your country has seen a grave crisis of vocations: a sort of wandering in the desert that constitutes a real trial of faith for pastors and faithful alike.' A long list of recommendations followed. The French bishops were too cowed to point out that all of them had been previously tried without success.

In December 2004 a survey of 18,000 French citizens was conducted by the Catholic daily *La Croix* and the CSA polling institute. It confirmed that in France the Catholic Church was approaching meltdown. While 64.3 per cent of French people describe themselves as Catholic, only 7.7 per cent of respondents said they attended church once a month. Of these, 28 per cent were aged over 75 years and the overwhelming majority were poorly educated, rural women. France today has 17,000 diocesan priests, half the number that existed in 1980. Parishes, too, show a 50 per cent decline.

The French might perhaps have been heartened to learn that they were not alone. The Pope delivered the same lecture to the majority of his bishops. He told the Dutch, 'Your country has experienced an intense process of secularisation for thirty years, which has spread to the Catholic Church like wildfire and unfortunately continues to mark Dutch society.' Subsequently in November 2004 Cardinal Adrianis Simonis of Utrecht offered what has become among Catholic bishops in Europe a popular explanation for the collapse of Christianity. 'Today we have discovered that we are disarmed in the face of the Islamic danger.' Pointing out that even some of the young who had been born and raised in the Netherlands had become militant Muslims the Cardinal linked the rise of Islam to 'the spectacle of extreme moral decadence and spiritual decline that we offer' to young people.

Cardinal Poupard, the president of the Pontifical Council, a Frenchman working within the Vatican, brought a broader vision to the Christian meltdown.

> 'The militant and organised atheism of the Communist era has been replaced by practical indifference, the loss of interest in the question of God, and the abandonment of religious practices, especially in the Western world.'

Among the problems that the Church must confront, he continued, were 'the globalisation of mass culture, the influence of the electronic media and the rise of new sects'. He lamented the 'absence of efficient media through which the faith can be spread'. Poupard feared that the loss of faith could 'lead to the collapse of culture with dangerous consequences for society. The era most menacing to man is not the one that denies the truth but the one that is not concerned about the truth.'

In fact the Catholic Church has highly efficient media to spread the faith. The Catholic media are a global giant with a galaxy of news agencies, newspapers, radio and television companies committed to the Roman Catholic Church's official line on all issues. All of this is based in just one city, much of it replicated in many cities around the world. Opus Dei alone has more media outlets worldwide than Rupert Murdoch. The last thing lacking in the modern Catholic Church is an absence of efficient media.

'Rome Reports', for example, is a television news agency focusing entirely on the Pope and the Church that sells programme segments in English, Spanish and Portuguese to broadcasters in Asia, Africa and Latin America. Its director Yago de la Cierva is a member of Opus Dei. Radio Maria is both a radio and TV station, broadcasting globally. *Famiglia Cristiana* is a weekly periodical published by the Fathers of St Paul. The Italian Bishops' Conference has its own newspaper *Avvenire* and a satellite television station that is rebroadcast by dozens of local Catholic stations. Telepace is yet another Catholic television station. The Catholic University of the Sacred Heart publishes the magazine *Vita e Pensiero*. *Mondo e Missione* is the monthly magazine of the Pontifical Institute for Foreign Missions. Rival Catholic monthly magazines include *Nigrizia, Missione Oggi, Il Timone* and *Inside the Vatican*. There is the Zenit news agency. There is the on-line agency Asia News, publishing in Italian, Chinese and English.

Then of course there are the Vatican's media outlets, including a press office controlled by Opus Dei numerary Joaquin Navarro-Valls; a website in six languages with daily bulletins and an extensive archive; the daily newspaper *L'Osservatore Romano*; the Vatican Television Centre; the Vatican Information Service; *Fides*, the only on-line agency of the Congregation for the Doctrine of the Faith, its seven-language service yet again including Chinese; the Liberia Editrice Vaticana which publishes all official declarations of the Holy See; and finally there are the magazines and bulletins published by the various Vatican offices.

The bishops twist and turn as they seek the enemy. Socialism has been added to Islam and Communism though in truth many from the Pope down have never been able to distinguish Socialism from Communism. His late Secretary of State Cardinal Casaroli, who really should have known better, fell into that trap when discussing the problems of Mexico. There is no doubt that when the Spanish bishops make their next *ad limina* visit to Rome the current Socialist government will be held to blame for all of the Spanish Church's problems. A late 2004 opinion poll showing sixty-one per cent support for the government's proposal to legalise homosexual marriage and a seventy-two per cent majority who thought that the state should stop the annual handout to the Spanish Church of nearly £100 million would indicate that the majority of Spaniards stand with their government and not the Catholic Church.

Further legislation being prepared in Spain is designed to give other Christian churches, Jews and Muslims some of the privileges currently exclusively enjoyed by the Roman Catholic Church. The Spanish Catholic Church has subsequently placed itself in the frontline of political opposition to the democratically elected government which cannot be held responsible for the extraordinary collapse of the Catholic faith that has occurred in Spain. In a country where ninety per cent of the population are 'declared' Roman Catholics two-thirds – sixty-six per cent – are non-practitioners. To take just one issue that was particularly close to Karol Wojtyla's heart, in predominantly Catholic Spain, polls show that forty per cent of the population believes that abortion is a fundamental right and a further twenty-four per cent believe that it should be tolerated. That was from a poll carried out *before* the Socialists came to power when the country was ruled by a right-wing government. In present-day Spain, more than fifty per cent of pregnancies occurring in girls between the ages of fifteen and seventeen are terminated.

The Pope had recognised that the challenge faces not just Catholicism but Christianity in general. In a speech to the Pontifical Academy for Culture, in March 2002, he said: 'Our contemporaries are immersed in cultural circles that are often strangers to every spiritual dimension of life . . . Christians must repair the damage caused by this rupture of the connection between faith and reason.' But his solution was a two-edged sword. 'There is a need to create an educational system dedicated to a serious anthropological study to take account of who man is and what life means.' Such studies have existed for a very long time and additional research in this field would at the very least strengthen the position of the humanist.

One of the bishops in Nicaragua had a more radical proposal. Bishop Abelardo Guevara during a Christmas Day sermon addressed the crisis in family life. He railed about the violent gangs of teenagers who had forced the diocese to cancel the traditional late-night Christmas Eve Mass. 'We urgently need to recover family unity and spiritual principles. Our society is falling apart because of lack of these virtues.' Addressing all parents within his congregation the bishop continued, 'You must be willing to do everything possible to protect values within your families. Shoot the TV set if it is necessary to keep anti-values away!'

In early December 2001 the official exorcist for the diocese of Rome, Father Gabriele Amorth, saw the threat as coming not from the small screen but the big one. His concern was the Harry Potter films and books. The priest, who is also the president of the International Association of Exorcists, believed that a great force for evil was influencing the works. 'Behind Harry Potter hides the signature of the king of darkness, the devil.' The exorcist explained that the books contain innumerable references to magic, 'the satanic art' and that they attempt to make a false distinction between black and white magic when in reality the distinction 'does not exist, because magic is always a turn to the devil'.

Wherever one looks, Christianity in all its forms appears to be in retreat. In Latin America – the Vatican's continent of hope – health officials from twenty countries gathered in Mexico at the end of 2001 in a three-day conference of more than 250 participants to help Latin American governments establish 'a free exchange of ideas' about the possible legislation of abortion. These predominately Catholic countries were concerned at the large number of secret abortions that resulted in the death of the pregnant woman. The figure was estimated as '6000 lives each year'. In March 2000 in the Pope's home country the Polish President Alexander Kwasniewski vetoed a bill that would have brought into force new tougher anti-pornography measures. The President declared that the bill 'would unfairly curb personal freedoms'. In a country where ninety per cent rate themselves practising Roman Catholics, voters were evenly divided on the President's action.

Notwithstanding all these signs of decline, the official Vatican figures rate the Wojtyla papacy and his compulsive travelling a resounding success. Global figures for baptised Catholics at the end of December 1997 were just over one billion, a figure that continues to rise. Global figures for example for the year ending 31 December 2000 show an increase in the number of Catholics of just under 12 million on the previous year. But as always the devil is in the detail. For the continent of Europe the figures show a drop of just over $1\frac{1}{2}$ million. The number of priests, brothers and sisters were all also down in Europe. Major areas of growth in most categories were recorded in all other continents except Oceania, but all the figures were based on baptism and take no account of whether the people concerned actually practise or believe in the Catholic faith.

If John Paul II's mission to evangelise the world were to succeed anywhere it should surely be within Italy. Apart from the fact that he was surrounded on all sides by the Italians, he made the most strenuous efforts to cover every *strada*, *piazza*, *villaggio*, *citta* and every sacred shrine in Italy. He made 726 pastoral visits to the various parishes within his personal diocese of Rome, a further 140 pastoral visits within Italy beyond the Rome boundaries. He preached, prayed and generally spoke to the Italian nation almost every day for twenty-five years. Every citizen, every man, woman and child was fully exposed to the views of John Paul II on an extraordinary range of subjects, particularly those having a bearing on Roman Catholic teaching.

The official figures state that Italy's population is over-whelmingly Roman Catholic. Nearly eighty per cent consider themselves Catholics. Among those who would disagree was the late Pope himself. In 1996 he called for the 'evangelisation' of Rome, which the Vatican regards as a pagan city. Volunteers went from door to door in attempts to persuade the citizens of the capital to 'return to Church'. It transpired that many had never set foot in St Peter's.

The decline in the Italian birth rate is matched by the fall in church weddings. Curial heavyweight Cardinal Julian Herranz, the President of the Pontifical Council for Legislative Texts, sees part of the reason being the high cost of a church wedding but acknowledges the more profound factor of 'the loss of a religious sense in society'. The Catholic Church in Italy suffered a national demonstration of that loss in 1984 when the Roman Catholic faith was disestablished and ceased to be the official religion of Italy.

The Pope has correctly been described as the 'most Marian Pope in history' but his infatuation with the biblical mother of Christ and his desire to awaken a genuine Marian spirituality made him alarmingly vulnerable to any exploitation of the Mary legend. It was a vulnerability formed very early in Karol Wojtyla's life. Returning home from school on 13 April 1929, the eight-year-old boy was confronted by one of his neighbours in the courtyard, who told him bluntly, 'Your mother has died.' Emilia was only forty-five years old and had suffered frequent crippling pains, caused by myocarditis and nephritis (acute inflammation of the heart and kidneys) for fifteen years.

When Wojtyla was a young man he would speak of his mother with loving affection as he recalled her invaluable, irreplaceable role in those first years of his life. Later there was a change of tone, and a bitterness replaced the love as he recalled how preoccupied his mother had been with her illness and how little time she had had to devote to him. The young boy lost the most important person in his life at an achingly young age. It was undoubtedly crucial in the formation of his paradoxical personality and the Marian obsession that dominated his view of women.

Wojtyla regularly spoke and wrote as if the only role for secular women was motherhood. His unremitting hostility to abortion even in the case of raped women, his veneration of women who had died giving birth rather than abort and save their own lives, echo the traditional Catholic teaching which prevailed at the time of his own mother's early death.

Deprived of maternal affection at a desperately early stage of his development, Wojtyla was also surrounded by a culture that deeply venerated Mary the mother of Christ. Wojtyla's childhood hero Pius IX also declared the doctrine of the Immaculate Conception of Mary, 'the Virgin Mother of Christ'. In Poland Mary has many names, many titles. Apart from the universal Virgin Mary, Wojtyla was also able to pray to The Blessed Mother, Queen of Heaven and Earth, Virgin Bride, Sorrowful Mother, Refuge of Sinners, Comforter of the Afflicted, The Black Madonna of Czestochowa and the title above all others that ensured that she was inexorably identified with Polish nationalism and the Motherland, Queen of Poland, Mary Mother of God.[9]

A lifelong friend of Wojtyla's, Halina Królikiewicz-Kwiatkowska recalls, 'We were always running to church. And in church we were praying, usually to the Virgin Mary.' Eugeniusz Mroz, one of his other childhood friends, remembers the death of Emilia.

'He impressed us with his inner peace. He believed that this loss was the will of God. Wojtyla's flat was on the second floor. His mother's room was never used after her death. Sometimes when Karol was studying, he would take a break, go into her room and pray. The

Holy Father kept a special picture that he always took with him wherever he went. He never parted with this picture, even on long pilgrimages. It shows him as a young child in his mother's arms.'

Three days after his mother's funeral, the father took his two sons on a pilgrimage to the Marian sanctuary at Kalwaria Zebrzydowska. Pointing to a famous painting of the Virgin Mary he told Karol, 'This is your mother now.' Throughout his life, Karol Wojtyla returned to this place where on the eve of the Feast of the Assumption, Poles believe the Holy Virgin dies every year and enters heaven. After an all-night vigil, hymns and prayers, they celebrate Mary's triumph over death and ascension into heaven. The eight-year-old boy may not have received all the comfort he needed at this time, for ten years later he penned these lines of poetry:

> On your white tomb
> Blossom the white flowers of life
> Oh how many years have passed
> Without you – how many years?
> On your white tomb
> Closed now for years
> Something seems to rise
> Inexplicable as death
> On your white tomb
> Mother, my lifeless love . . .

Until the latter part of the fourth century, the devotion of Mary was kept well in the background but her apparition had in fact been sighted earlier. In the third century while Gregory Thaumaturgus was wrestling with theological doctrines shortly before entering the priesthood, the Blessed Virgin appeared, accompanied by St John. She instructed St

John to disclose to Gregory the 'mystery of godliness'. John duly obliged, 'enunciated a formula well turned and completed and then vanished'. In the late fourth century Augustine felt compelled to protest against 'extravagant and ill-founded praise of Mary. This kind of idolatry . . . is far removed from the grave character of theology – that is, of heavenly wisdom.' One wonders what Augustine, who next to Paul did more than any man to shape Christianity, would make of Karol Wojtyla's lifelong 'idolatry' of Mary.

Through the centuries there have been repeated claims of sightings of Mary, conversations with her, miracles by her and statues of her shedding tears of blood, many of which have been officially recognised by the Roman Catholic Church. The manifestations, particularly at Lourdes and Fatima, have wrought dramatic changes at the locations and the surrounding areas. Whether or not miracles have occurred is a matter of continuing debate, but beyond doubt the profile of the Church has been enhanced, the faith of a great many has been strengthened and huge amounts of money have been generated.

In early June 1981 Medjugorje was a poor rural village in Bosnia-Herzegovina within what was at the time Yugoslavia. On 24 June six Croatian teenagers made varying claims to have seen 'Gospa' – the Blessed Virgin Mary. At least three of the children also claimed to have seen the Christ child in the arms of his mother. The following day they again saw the image of Mary who this time conversed with them. The apparitions and the conversations were to continue each day and they allegedly continue to the present time. Not all of the six are still privileged; by the end of 2003 only three were still on daily message.

Ten years after the first alleged apparitions at Medjugorje, the US State Department requested from their embassy in Belgrade that 'Medjugorje updates be included in the embassy's daily sitreps [situation reports]'. Successive

American administrations had become increasingly concerned about Medjugorje. This particular cable sent during October 1991 alerted the Belgrade embassy to the fact that: 'There are 30 AMCIT [American Citizens] pilgrims in Medjugorje right now with a Sister Mary from Philadelphia. Another group of 50 pilgrims led by Sister Margaret plans to travel there leaving New York. Ann is trying to head this group off. Please forgive me if I am misspelling the name of this godforsaken place. And I do mean godforsaken. Ann also hears that the Medjugorje children have left town, apparently on instructions from the Virgin Mary.'

Ten years earlier the cable traffic from the American embassies in both Rome and Belgrade was already conveying concerns about the alleged Medjugorje appearances. In September 1981 Ambassador Wilson reported back to Secretary of State General Alexander Haig with a detailed briefing on a conversation between a visiting American and Cardinal Franjo Seper, the then Prefect of the Sacred Congregation of the Faith, and the Pope's chief advisor on Yugoslavia. Cardinal Seper had expressed deep concern that the religious revival that had been sparked off in the largely Croatian village of Medjugorje and the surrounding area would lead to increased tensions between church and state and resurgence of Croatian nationalism. Events were to prove Seper's fears well founded. Cardinal Seper also told his American visitor,

'The Vatican will not comment on or investigate the reported appearances of the Virgin Mary as this is under the jurisdiction of the local bishops. I think they will be afraid of punitive reaction from the Yugoslavian Government and will therefore do nothing.'

In that at least the cardinal was wrong. Bishop Zanic of Mostar, having initially formed the view that the children

were sincere, conducted an investigation and rapidly changed his mind, condemning the whole affair as a hoax and
'hysterical hallucinations'. The bishop's unequivocal condemnation, with the full authority of the Vatican, should
have ended the affair. But as with some of the earlier alleged
sightings of Christ's mother, people with different agendas
had begun to see a huge potential.

The Franciscan Order had for many years been involved
in a series of increasingly bitter disagreements within the
diocese of Mostar. They saw many of the parishes as their
exclusive domain, while the bishop and Rome disagreed
and the Order had been forced grudgingly to yield to
Vatican authority. Now with the countryside electrified
with the stories of Mary and her daily messages to the
six children the Franciscan Order swiftly seized control of
the phenomenon.

The apparition told the children she should be known as
The Queen of Peace. Her daily messages, which only the six
could hear, had recurring themes: 'Make Peace. Pray. Fast.
Confess'. In addition a number of very specific instructions
and messages were received, but from the outset they were
excluded from general release by the Franciscans and were
transcribed by themselves. They were used by the order to
buttress their attempts to prevent further reduction of their
influence in the region. This agenda would be greatly helped
by the spiritual and commercial exploitation of the faithful,
the needy, and the just plain curious flocking to Medjugorje. The 'secret' messages were also used by the Franciscans in their attempts to end the tribal ethnic and religious
clan wars that had for centuries been a part of everyday life.

The site of the original apparitions had been on the stony
path leading to the top of Mount Podbrdo. For the benefit
of the tourists, this was rapidly renamed 'Apparition Hill'.

When the mountain was declared a no-go area by the
Communist authorities the visions continued, but this time

before evening Mass in one of the side rooms of the local church. By happy coincidence this also was close to car parking facilities and the terrain was much less of an ordeal for the elderly, the sick and the frail who were soon coming from near and far.

Within two years the authorities were taking a much more enlightened view of the Virgin Mary of Medjugorje. The mountain was re-opened, and the church grounds and a surrounding area were made available for confession and prayers. Confessions were held continuously, with extra confessors brought in to meet peak demand. What had changed the Communist regime's position? Late in the day, Belgrade had realised that there was 'tourist gold' to be made from the Queen of Peace. The Franciscans negotiated with the regime and $500,000 a year began to hit the coffers of central government. This was but a fraction of the money that was pouring in. The 'tourist gold' turned into a Balkan gold rush.

By 1990 the Franciscans were claiming that over 18 million visitors had come to Medjugorje since that early June evening in 1981. The fact that at least some of the six children had sneaked up the mountainside for an illicit cigarette had been rewritten to 'a search for lost lambs'. This deliberately echoed the young shepherd children of Fatima, which unlike Medjugorje has been recognised by the Vatican as a genuine occurrence.

There is in nearby Mostar a very small bank. In the early 1980s it was insignificant in international banking terms with a world ranking of 2,689 but Hrvatska Banka DD Mostar had some very unusual features. A bank's political and commercial standing can be gauged by the quality of its correspondents, the sister banks acting on its behalf in various countries around the world. The diminutive bank at Mostar, that held the accounts for the Franciscan Order and was also part owned by them, had the banking world's crème de la crème among its correspondents: Citibank, Deutsche, ABN-Amro, Bank Brussels, Lambert, Nat West, BCI Skand, Enskilda, CSFB, Bank of Tokyo, Cassa di Risparmio, Bayerische, Bank of America were just a few of the major league players, with Citibank acting as correspondent for New York and London. One international banking consultant found it 'very strange. Such a small bank, such a top-drawer list of correspondents.'

Ownership at the time was shared among a number of banks with illustrious names, including Unicredito Italiano Spa Genoa. One of the directors of the group of companies that controlled Unicredito, Franzo Grande Stevens, was regarded in banking circles as one of the Vatican's 'Men of Trust'. His presence on a Board of Directors is often seen as an indication that the Vatican Bank has a financial interest. Clearly the little bank in Mostar was doing something right and indeed still is. Since mid-1981 up to the present day it has acted as the financial nerve centre of the multi-million-dollar enterprise built on the alleged Medjugorje apparitions. It was taken over a few years ago by the rapidly expanding Zagrebacka banking group. The Franciscans control the Medjugorje operation from their University in Steubenville, Ohio. There are major Medjugorje centres at a number of locations in Indiana, Ohio and Alabama.

The Vatican has nonetheless repeatedly avoided openly confronting the issue of Medjugorje. No public statement on the alleged daily sightings has ever been made by a Vatican official, yet a variety of cardinals, bishops and other luminaries are on record as quoting the Pope's full approval. These include Monsignor Maurillo Kreiger. 'I told the Pope:

"I am going to Medjugorje for the fourth time." He concentrated his thoughts and said, "Medjugorje.

Medjugorje. It's the spiritual heart of the world." On the same day I spoke with other Brazilian bishops and the Pope at lunchtime and I asked him: "Your Holiness, can I tell the visionaries (the six that claim to see the Virgin Mary) that you send your blessing?" He answered, "Yes. Yes," and embraced me.' According to Father Gianni Sgreva, 'The Holy Father listened to me, drew close to me and right in my ear said to me, reminding me not to forget, "Don't you be concerned about Medjugorje, because I'm thinking about Medjugorje and I pray for its success every day." '

In private conversation with one of the seers, Mirjan Soldo, the Pope himself is supposed to have said, 'If I were not the Pope I would already be in Medjugorje confessing.' The Pope allegedly endorsed the 'apparitions' on at least twelve other occasions. On the other hand there is the unequivocal statement made by Monsignor Renato Boccardo, the Pope's Head of Protocol. During the Pope's trip to Croatia in 2003 Monsignor Boccardo was questioned closely about rumours that the Pope might comment on the alleged apparitions and might also be going to Medjugorje. He responded, 'There has never been any question that the Pope would go to Medjugorje, or make the slightest allusion to it.'

It is curious that within the initial torrent of words and messages apparently flowing from the apparition there was not a single word about the attempted assassination of the Pope or her 'intervention' in St Peter's Square on 13 May 1981. Even more inexplicable is the failure of the Virgin Mary to comment on the consecration of Russia to her by the Pope and his bishops around the world on 25 March 1984. This was an act that the Virgin Mary had allegedly specifically requested when reappearing to one of the Fatima visionaries in June 1929. She had also promised that this act would be followed by world peace and the end of atheism. The Pope chose to interpret the third message of Fatima as directly relating to the attack upon him.

As previously recorded, analysis of that third message indicates that it is far more likely to have referred to his immediate predecessor Albino Luciani, not least because it allegedly foretells a papal murder – not a papal attempted murder. Equally the words of the 'third secret' could be interpreted as foretelling the murder of Archbishop Oscar Romero in El Salvador.

Karol Wojtyla's lifelong Marian obsession may have clouded his judgement on the events of Medjugorje. Since 1981 the Vatican has defended its inaction over the alleged apparitions by saying that it awaits pronouncement from the local bishop. The opinion of Bishop Pavao Zanic of Mostar that the apparitions were 'hysterical hallucinations' was confirmed in 1982 when he established a diocesan commission to investigate further. In 1984 the Bishops' Conference of the former Yugoslavia declared that Catholic leaders, including priests and nuns, could not organise official pilgrimages to the shrine until its authenticity was established. In 1985 the Vatican concurred with that position. The tourists meanwhile kept pouring into Medjugorje. In 1987 Bishop Zanic addressed a packed congregation of parishioners and pilgrims in the local Medjugorje Church of St James. He asserted that the visions were false and then continued,

'Through all my prayers, my work and research, I have sought one goal only: the discovery of truth.

'It is said that Our Lady began appearing at Podbr-do on Mount Crnica, but when the police banned going there, she went into homes, on fences, into the fields, into vineyards and tobacco fields, she appeared in the Church, on the altar, in the sacristy, in the choir loft, on the roof, on the bell tower, on roads, on the road to Cemo, in a car, in a bus, on a carriage, in a few places in Mostar, in more places in Sarajevo, in the convents of Zagreb, in Varazdin, in Switzerland, in Italy, again at Podbrdo, on Mount Krizevac, in the parish, in the parish rectory, etc. Surely not even half the places of the so-called apparitions have been counted, and a sober person who venerates Our Lady would naturally ask himself: "Dear Mother of God, what are they doing to you?" '

On 10 April 1991 the Yugoslavian Bishops' Conference (with a single dissenting vote) supported Zanic, declaring, 'On the basis of investigation up till now it cannot be established that one is dealing with supernatural apparitions or revelations.' Bishop Zanic retired in 1993. His replacement, Bishop Ratko Peric, launched his own investigation into the apparitions. He, too, declared them a hoax and dubbed the visionaries liars. Yet still the Vatican declines to make a pronouncement. Still the spiritual, financial, and physical exploitation continues. And the money continues to pour into both Franciscan and Vatican bank accounts; as a member of the Secretariat of State explained: 'A fraud? Of course it's a fraud but the money is genuine.'

There were two wars involving Great Britain and Argentina that were fought during 1982. One is well documented and was triggered after the Argentine military dictatorship invaded the Falkland Islands and claimed them as a repossessed part of their nation. After various diplomatic initiatives failed the British, who had occupied the islands for some 200 years, were soon at war.

When the Pope visited the United Kingdom between 28 May and 2 June the fighting was at its height, but by then the other war fought very privately had been fought and won. The winners were the Pope, Cardinal Basil Hume, the Primate of England, and the British bishops. The losers were a clique of Spanish, Argentinian and Brazilian cardinals and the extreme right-wing element of the Roman Curia.

The Pope knew long before this crisis that the Curia was full of men whose philosophies were wholeheartedly fascist. They are not a new phenomenon, nor one that is confined to some of the Spanish and Argentinian residents. They can still be found among a wide cross-section of priests, bishops and cardinals from a variety of Latin American countries and from several European states. They aspired, and still aspire, to regain for the Catholic Church the degree of control that Rome exercised in the distant past; a control over every aspect of national life, in fierce reaction against socialism and democratic egalitarianism. Their predecessors created the Vatican Ratline by which thousands of Nazis, fascists and their collaborators, who should have stood trial for every conceivable crime perpetrated during the Second World War, escaped justice and found new lives in Latin America and the United States.

The fascists within the Church did not die or fade away after Mussolini was killed. They were there before him; they are still there. They rose up in 1982 and against great odds the Pope outflanked them and prevailed.

The papal trip to the United Kingdom had been some two years in the planning. The Argentine military dictatorship deliberately launched their adventure in the Falklands to coincide with it – a fact overlooked or ignored by their fervent supporters in the Vatican. Bishop Marcello Carvalheira from Brazil was one of a number who were openly critical of the planned visit to Britain.

'So long as the hostilities in the south Atlantic continue, the Pope's visit would not be a friendly gesture to the Latin American people. An original sin was committed when the British invaded the Falkland Islands.'

The Argentinian ambassador to the Holy See lobbied everyone to ensure the visit was cancelled. The Vatican Secretary of State, Agostino Casaroli, and his deputy, the Spaniard Cardinal Martinez Somalo, took every opportunity to urge the Pope to withdraw from the trip. The papal nuncio in Argentina, Archbishop Ubaldo Calabresi, a regular dinner guest of the junta, asked the Pope how he could travel to Britain while the British were spilling Argentine blood.

Throughout the years of military rule, not one of this Catholic hierarchy showed concern for the spilling of Argentinian blood by the military junta, never lifted a finger when Catholic men and women were tortured to the brink of death and then taken away in helicopters, accompanied by priests who performed the last rites as the victims were thrown into the Atlantic. Cardinal Basil Hume, with a suggestion that could have come from King Solomon, single-handedly neutered much of the opposition when he suggested that the Pope might announce plans for a visit to Argentina. The Curia, mostly hostile to the UK trip, argued that such a visit would take years to plan. The Pope ignored the protests and grabbed at Basil Hume's suggestion. He announced that that was exactly what he would do.

The joy of the Catholic faithful of the UK was nothing compared to the reaction of the executives of Papal Visit Ltd, the company created by the Catholic Church to manage the Papal tour. Equally relieved were the men at Mark McCormack's International Marketing Group – IMG – who had been hired to advise on the financial aspects.

More accustomed to marketing the potential of sports stars like Björn Borg and Jack Nicklaus, McCormack's men had been rapidly advised that it was all to be done 'in the best possible taste'. Advertisements saying 'Welcome To Coventry' in the official mass book, initial print run 1.3 million copies, were 'not felt to be consistent with the pastoral reason for the visit'. However, mail order catalogues passed the test and were sent to every parish, school and Catholic social organisation in the country. There were more than 200 items to choose from, each with the image of the Pope, including candles, brass plates, jam spoons, sweets, clocks, folding stools, cutlery, books, ornaments, medals and glassware. All items sold earned a ten per cent royalty to help defray the cost of the tour. Only much later was it revealed that twenty per cent of that royalty went into the pockets of IMG. Nothing was overlooked. Trusthouse Forte had won the contract to supply the faithful with their cups of tea and meals during the various stops. The Church again drew a royalty on every cup of tea sold, as it did on every other official amenity where charges were levied.

As with most of Wojtyla's tours, the media were overwhelmingly supportive and the tour was hailed as a great pastoral success. The pastoral impact was much reduced in Scotland, where attendances and enthusiasm were at their highest, when those attending at the open air mass in Glasgow were subjected to body searches and kept over half a mile away from the Pope.

Excluding Scotland, attendance figures told a different story. Church authorities had seriously overestimated how many people would want to listen to the Pope continually condemning the Falklands conflict with oblique references to war in general. At the time, nearly ninety per cent of the United Kingdom supported the Thatcher Government's action. Neither did the majority wish to hear condemnations of abortion and a 'contraception mentality'. The papal mass at Heaton Park, Manchester was attended by 200,000 after the Church had predicted one million. The

Church had talked of catering for 750,000 at Coventry but less than half that number actually came. This underwhelming enthusiasm was reflected in the commercial disaster that the visit produced for many traders in England and Wales. Unsold were framed portraits of the Pope, 20,000 cans of Coke and 1,000 packed lunches. Low sales resulted in heavy losses for the Roman Catholic Church in England and Wales. Years later, it was still attempting to recover some of the £6 million cost of the tour.

The 'great pastoral success' was confirmed as a media fantasy when two decades later Britain's leading Catholic clergyman described the nation as 'a pagan country'. The Pope himself passed judgement with his feet: he never returned to Britain, unlike Argentina which the Pope revisited in 1987.

Neither the British nor the Argentines took the slightest notice of the Pope's often very moving pleas that the fighting should stop. The fighting only ended when Britain had won the war. Within a few short months it was as if the Pope had never been, congregations in churches all over the country continued to get smaller and in Argentina, losing the war succeeded where papal entreaties to stop fighting had failed. The head of the military junta, General Galtieri, was promptly removed and the first steps towards free elections were taken. With the election of Raul Alfonsin in December 1983 democracy was finally restored.

Although many lay Catholics and clergy grew increasingly appalled at the marketing of the Wojtyla Papacy, Archbishop Marcinkus's view that 'You can't run the Church on Hail Marys' has prevailed.

As a senior American member of the Curia said to me, 'We are talking product. The Catholic faith is the best product in the world. Of course you have to market it. If you want to sell any product you have to market it.'

Under John Paul II, the Vatican became a modern corporation, in pursuit of the dollar, releasing comics that recount the early life of Karol Wojtyla, CDs and videos of approved music, 'prayers, homilies and chants, video singles such as Pater Noster'. The Vatican has wholeheartedly embraced the Internet, triggering a furious debate to determine who should be its patron saint. Tickets for papal masses are sold on line or through agencies, or you can sing along to the mass in traditional Latin in the comfort of your own home on the net. Going to confession via the net has currently been prohibited but it is an issue that will undoubtedly return. No need to travel to Rome any more to hear the Pope reciting the Angelus: the prayer plus the Pope's regular general audience on Wednesdays now go out into cyberspace. (The debate concerning the net's patron saint was finally resolved in favour of Saint Isidore of Seville, a sixth-century priest. His main claim to fame was the creation of a twenty-volume dictionary that had a tree-like concept similar to a primitive database. A hot rival had been San Pedro Regalado, a fifteenth-century priest who was said to have appeared in two places simultaneously, at the monasteries of La Aguilera and El Abrojo. An excellent attribute when surfing the net.)

Inevitably the Pope's best-selling book *Crossing the Threshold of Hope* went multi-media and became available on CD-ROM and, equally inevitably, the Roman Catholic Church pronounced on the sins that could be perpetrated on the net. In February 2001 it was announced, 'E-mails of a carnal nature and illicit on-line relationships are a sin.' Virtual sin was born.

As the 1990s were drawing to a close, the Catholic Church continued to demonstrate its determination to require maximum sponsorship. In Mexico during January 1999 the message was no longer the Gospel. The message was the sponsor. Many weeks before the Pope arrived for a five-day visit the posters and billboards gave a clear message that the Holy Father had taken up the Pepsi challenge: rejecting 'the real thing' he had come out as a fully paid-up member of Generation Next. 'Pepsi always faithful,' read the giant signs alongside blow-up photographs of the Pope.

To help pay for his fourth trip to Mexico the Church had done a host of sponsorship deals, all centred around the Pope's image. He was helping to sell everything from soft drinks and computers to crisps. The El Globo baking chain had presumably not paid quite enough for an 'exclusive product placement', because nearly 100 huge billboards sponsored by 'Bimbo' bread commanded the citizens to 'feed the spirit' of joy, and the cash tills of the rival bakery. Mercedes-Benz provided two Popemobiles, Hewlett-Packard supplied the computers and Electropura were giving away nearly two million litres of drinks.

Twenty-five companies sponsoring the five-day trip as 'Official Collaborator' were picking up seventy-five per cent of the trip's expenses. The Pope, not unlike San Pedro Regalado, could be found simultaneously in several places. He was on that bottle in your hand, in your packet of crisps, on the stamp that you put on the card telling those back home that you wished they were here. Local comedians had a field day. One renamed the soft drink 'Popesicola', another publicly enquired as to whether the Pope's punishing endorsement schedule would leave any time for him to pray, and in all seriousness a Church spokesman, aware that the Spanish word for both Pope and chip is 'papa', felt it necessary to reassure Mexico's 86.3 million Roman Catholics that the Holy Father 'would not celebrate Mass dressed as a potato chip'.

Notwithstanding that reassurance, many devout Mexican Catholics were deeply unhappy at such crass commercialism and dismissed the whole affair as a corporate sponsored tour.

One political activist, who had repeatedly over the years bitterly attacked the Mexican Government for its use of torture, kidnappings and organised violence to repress an increasingly desperate populace, observed of the Papal visit: 'Romans are always the same. When there is no bread they have a circus.'

Within the papal entourage and the accompanying press corps, defenders of the Pope's travels often dwell on individual moments. They recall the Ukrainian woman kneeling alone in the mud drawing comfort from the Pope's visit to her homeland; the Polish workman who asked his friend who interrupted a papal speech on the 1979 tour to 'be quiet while the Pope is talking to me'. They remember the woman dying of Aids in an Indian slum who found solace in her memory of the moment the Pope held her or the unemployed man who had walked through the night to hear the Pope during his visit to the United Kingdom. These people and countless others undeniably drew strength and comfort from such moments.

Others in the papal entourage and the Vatican pack have been disgusted at the trappings of triumphalism and pop-star superficiality that swirled around the papal tours. The World Youth Day rallies have been compared to the Nazi Nuremberg rallies, with the same 'intense fanatical devotion to a great leader'. Still others believe that the constant travelling has 'centralised authority in the Catholic Church in an unprecedented and spectacular manner'. After the deeply disturbing spectacle of the Pope's September 2003 visit to Slovakia I discussed the implications with a number of Vatican residents. One Prince of the Church assured me that the show had continued and would do so because

'the Pope wishes it to continue. The actor within the Holy Father is dying hard. He simply refuses to walk off stage. He is a man terminally drugged on the adulation of the audience.'

In a number of countries that audience has dramatically declined over the years; in others, says the managing director of one opinion poll organisation, it is 'haemorrhaging at an alarming rate'. The Church can derive little comfort from the fact that apart from the charismatic evangelicals other sections of the Christian faith have also shown a decrease both in congregations and the number of priests. Roman Catholics have suffered the highest rate of decline of any religious group within many countries. The number of practising priests within the United Kingdom has fallen from a postwar high of 7,714 in 1964 to 5,040 in 2003. By contrast, there are currently 30,000 psychotherapists practising in the United Kingdom. In Ireland only one Catholic seminary remains open. In 2004 it produced just eight new priests.

In April 2003 a poll of nearly half of the remaining priests in England and Wales revealed that sixty per cent believed that sexual intercourse with a married woman should not debar the priest from active ministry, twenty-one per cent believed that homosexuality should not be a debarment, forty-three per cent 'actively opposed' the Church's teaching on contraception. Inevitably, a spokesman for the National Conference of Priests questioned the methodology of the survey but a year later the Roman Catholic hierarchy had produced no evidence of its own to refute the earlier findings.

The current position of the Roman Catholic priests in the United Kingdom is truly wretched. A continually diminishing group confronting growing cynicism and disbelief, they struggle to survive in Third World conditions with no pension funds, no national wage, declining attendances that result in shrinking contributions from the remaining churchgoers and twenty-three dioceses each headed by an autonomous, Wojtyla-appointed bishop.

Paradoxically, the number of Roman Catholics on paper

in the same period increased from 4 million in 1963 to nearly 5 million in 2000 but as in other countries many of them are only nominal Catholics who rarely if ever enter a church. During the same period the number of Roman Catholics in Great Britain attending mass declined from 2.63 million in 1963 to less than 1 million in 2000. A European values poll undertaken in mid-2003 shows just how deep and widespread is this curious doublethink throughout Europe. Asked two simple questions, 1. 'Do you belong to a religious denomination?' and 2. 'Do you attend services once a month or more?' not one single European country produced anything approaching a matching set of figures. In Italy the figures were 82.2–53.7 per cent. In the Pope's home country of Poland 95.7–78.3 per cent. In Great Britain the disparity between nominal and practising religious people was an enormous 83.4 – to 18.9 percent. Christianity can still claim to be Europe's main religion even if the figures hide a very large percentage of notional Christians. But since 1978, when Karol Wojtyla became Pope, no matter how the figures are shuffled and cut, the number of practising Roman Catholics in Europe has fallen by more than a third.

In the United States *Time* magazine carried out a poll in 1994 to coincide with their award to the Pope of 'Man of the Year'. It revealed that 89 per cent of American Catholics believe that it is possible to disagree with the Pope on doctrinal issues and still be a good Catholic (a position that he would have vigorously disputed). It also showed that three quarters of American Roman Catholics wanted to make up their own minds on the birth control issue. With regard to attending mass, the American faithful showed the same elasticity as the self-serving Europeans. Only forty-one per cent of those who considered themselves Roman Catholics in the United States claimed to attend weekly mass. In Canada, recent surveys suggest that less than twenty per cent of nominal Roman Catholics actually go to Church each week, and the figure drops to twelve per cent of those aged fifteen to twenty-four years. To find good news for the Holy See one has to look to the Third World.

The Vatican for several years had anticipated the Millennium Holy Year as a potential bonanza, notwithstanding the Pope's declaration, as he formally ended the Holy Year by closing the Holy Door of St Peter's, 'It is important that such an important religious event be completely disassociated from any semblance of financial gain.'

In fact the 'financial gain' made during the year had been so great that the Pope announced that after *all* expenses had been paid, the balance would be donated to charity. The Vatican marketing machine had come a long way since the Pope's face adorned bags of Mexican chips. Reproductions of celestial charts by Ptolemy hand-painted with 22-carat gold leaf could be purchased at $1,400 from the Vatican Library Collection (and are still available online) – or, for that expected and happy event, ceremonial baby clothes starting at $105 for a minute white polyester matt satin tuxedo.

The Jubilee sponsors were also a far remove from the total tackiness of former years. Telecom Italia, in exchange for exclusive rights and a Jubilee logo, provided more than $80 million worth of telephone and Internet services including the installation of a secure Internet link between the Holy See and its 120 embassies around the world.

The pilgrims could take their pick of a range that included $17,500 platinum watches to the parchment papal blessings, a bargain at $48, or the $125 Ferragom services. The ultimate market pitch for the Jubilee was inevitably made by the Pope. To stimulate tourists or pilgrims he announced that God would be honouring indulgences earned by making 'pious pilgrimages' to 'Rome, Jerusalem and other designated places'. With this offer the Pope had turned the clock back nearly 500 years to Martin Luther and the Pre-Reformation. With the Holy Year at an end, the Vatican, having duly donated a profit they refused to disclose to a charity that remained unidentified, had opportunity to consider the future.

With its more than four hundred million Catholics, Latin America is, without doubt, the 'Catholic Continent' in the early years of the new millennium. More than one member of the Curia has described it to me as 'the Continent of Hope'. Representing about forty-two per cent of all Catholics, both nominal and practising, in the world it is frequently seen as the new power base for the faith as Europe slips ever deeper into 'godlessness'. That being so one would expect the Pope and those around him to lavish great care and attention upon the region. In fact, in Catholic terms, Latin America lags behind the rest of the world. In North America with 68 million Catholics there is one priest for every 1,072 Catholics. In South America with its 400 million faithful there is one priest for every 7,200 Catholics. Even Africa does better than that with one priest for every 4,393 Catholics.

Within weeks of becoming Pope, Wojtyla had identified Liberation Theology as one of the greatest threats to the Roman Catholic Church. The fact that much of that theology is strikingly similar to early Christianity speaks eloquently on the current state of affairs within the Church. In 1987 the then Secretary of State, Cardinal Agostino Casaroli, during the course of a confidential meeting with members of the second Reagan administration elaborated on the Church's position on Latin America.

'The Vatican wants to see a true democracy in every Latin American country. But this means democracy in the fullest sense of the word, including socially and economically just societies.'

Casaroli then shared his concerns about the future of religion in the poorer countries,

'where poverty and injustice can lead the faithful and even some of the clergy towards socialism. Certainly the Vatican is concerned about proponents of Liberation Theology. But we are even more concerned about the concrete conditions of economic and social injustice. We are particularly worried about Mexico where we believe a radical and anti-religious revolution is possible.'

By the late 1990s the identified threat, and a very real one, was the corresponding rise of religious sects and capitalism as the Catholics of Latin America began to embrace alternative religions and simultaneously the message of the shopping mall. In October 2002 the Brazilian bishops were making their *ad limina* visits to Rome. Representing a country in which at least nominally over eighty per cent were Roman Catholics should have ensured that their audience with the Pope would be a far happier experience than that endured by their European colleagues. Unfortunately for the Brazilians, the Pope, if not his Curia, was well able to distinguish between nominal and practising. 'Brazil must rediscover her Christian heritage . . .' Calling for leadership in the world's most populous Catholic country, the Pope urged his bishops to 'combat the difficulties that threaten to obscure the message of the Church'.

Notwithstanding the strictures of the Pope and his Secretary of State on Liberation Theology, the missionaries in the field, confronted with everyday realities, whether in Latin America, the far reaches of Africa or the vast highlands of South East Asia, frequently operate on a mixture of socialism and Liberation Theology among the oppressed, the downtrodden and despised societies. They often pay the ultimate price. In 2001, thirty-three Catholic missionaries were murdered. Other Catholics were killed in riots in Nigeria, a massacre in Pakistan and during attacks by Islamic extremists on the Moluccas Islands of Indonesia. Increasingly the missionary is confronted by institutionalised hostility and laws that forbid religious conversion, India being the latest to impose such restrictions. In the Indian Federal Supreme Court in September 2003 it was ruled that there is 'no fundamental right to convert'. In China anyone caught bringing a Bible into the country faces imprisonment. The Islamic faith under sharia law calls for the death penalty for those who convert to other faiths. Though it is a law that is not widely implemented in the majority of Muslim-dominated countries it certainly keeps conversion figures down. The battle lines between the two Abrahamic faiths grow more clearly delineated with every passing year and Judaism is hardly more tolerant towards the competition in the market place. Proselytising children in Israel is a criminal offence. In December 2001 when an Israeli sixth-grade student brought a Bible to school that he had been given by a missionary, one of the teachers publicly burnt the Bible in front of the entire class.

Confronted with this range of hostility, the Pope and his central government in Rome appeared to be much more concerned with retreating further into the past by creating ever more saints and demanding that Christianity and its contribution to Europe should be fully recognised within the written constitution of the European Union. The Pope never failed to lobby on this issue when given the opportunity. He bitterly complained of 'the marginalization of religion' in the European Union.

As 2003 drew to a close the issue of Christian recognition within the constitution had begun to obsess the Pope. He constantly complained of the omission and marshalled his forces. The Jesuit Journal *Civilta Cattolica* weighed in with an attack declaring that the omission was 'a clear ideological deformation'. The Jesuits were profoundly dissatisfied with a preamble that makes a 'generic allusion to religious heritage without any clear recognition of the historical fact that the Judeo-Christian heritage was a major factor in the development of a common European culture'. The omission is 'a silence that speaks in a significant way, and will always speak that way'.

The Vatican redoubled its efforts with strenuous lobbying of predominantly Catholic Spain, Portugal and Poland. The Pope passionately declared that the answer to Europe's problems lies 'in a return to its Christian roots that are the sources of its original strength. These offer an indispensable contribution to progress and peace'. Critics recall that this same Europe has over the past 2,000 years also spawned not only the Holocaust but also a seemingly endless list of wars and suggest that Christianity has much to answer for. In June 2004 the Pope lost the argument, the European Parliament having concluded that Europe was a largely secular continent, a view that has received support from some surprising quarters.

The Catholic Church believes that it was divinely founded and that it is divinely guided. The greatest irony of the reign of the late Pope John Paul II is that, during his watch as God's representative on many parts of the planet, both Communism and its deadliest adversary Christianity have been largely reduced to insignificance. Cardinal Cormac Murphy O'Connor, the current leader of the Roman Catholic Church in England and Wales, described Britain as a country where 'tacit atheism prevails'. His opinion was shared by the then head of the Anglican Church, Archbishop George Carey.

The former Cardinal Joseph Ratzinger, close friend and confidant of the late Pope, head of the Vatican's Congregation for the Doctrine of the Faith, a latter-day version of the Inquisition, one of the most powerful and influential men not only in the Vatican but within the entire Roman Catholic Church even before his papal election, recently remarked of his mother country: 'Christianity must start anew in Germany.' In France Cardinal Jean-Marie Lustiger presided over what he described as 'a remnant Church'. One of the Italian Church's most brilliant theologians, Bishop Alessandro Maggiolini, has recently published a book entitled *The End of Our Christianity*. He believes that the forces that are weakening the Church come not from outside but that they were born and are flourishing within the Church. Many in the higher reaches of the Vatican have a range of explanations for what they see as the greatest calamity in the Church's history. They include 'watching too much television . . . consumerism . . . New Age practices . . . modernity . . . the "transient" pleasures of alcohol, drugs and recreation sex . . . the permissive Sixties . . . rock and roll . . .'

The pernicious and continuing saga of the sexual abuse of children, young adolescents and women by priests is in the Pope's words the fault 'of your modern society which is corrupting my priests'. The blame for the various financial crimes perpetrated by the Vatican Bank 'has nothing to do with Holy See; the bank is not part of the Holy See', according to Cardinal Szoka. In fact the Pope owns the bank. Cardinal Castillo sees the Vatican as the victim of a conspiracy.

'Here in Italy there is a big Masonic influence in some banks and in some newspapers and they attack the Holy See and the IOR (The Vatican Bank) in everything.'

Cardinal Martini widened the attack to exonerate the Vatican City State, the Holy See and the Roman Catholic Church and asserted, 'We should blame society as a whole.'

The collective humiliation within the Catholic hierarchy after the rejection by the European Parliament coupled with the further European rejection of one of the Pope's close friends, Rocco Butiglione, because of his opinions on homosexuality and abortion, has provoked a very un-Christian response. Italian journalist Vittorio Messori has denounced what he sees as 'anti-Catholicism' as

> 'a substitute for anti-Semitism . . . before blacks, wo-men, Jews and homosexuals were the object of sar-casm and criticism . . . now fortunately these groups cannot be attacked but I don't see why other groups have to be harmed.'

Cardinal Ratzinger returned to the fray to declare that the European Parliament action 'tends to reinforce Islamic perceptions of Europe as a decadent society. What offends Islam is the lack of reference to God, the arrogance of reason, which provokes fundamentalism.'

Archbishop Domingo Castagna of Argentina sounded a warning that 'in some traditionally Catholic countries such as Spain and Mexico an open merciless campaign of de-christianisation exists'.

The president of the Pontifical Council for Justice and Peace agreed. 'Opposition to the Catholic Church is domi-nated by the new holy inquisitions full of money and arrogance.' These influential lobbies in the Cardinal's mind 'try to ensure that the voices of the Pope and the Catholic Church are not often heard especially in the environment of the rich and comfortable countries'.

Vatican insiders give many reasons for the spectacular collapse of Christianity and the Roman Catholic faith in particular, but they never remotely consider that it has any connection with the papacy of the late Pope John Paul II or the Church's particular position on a number of issues. The current global figure of some 1.1 billion Roman Catholics, based on all available data, would be less than half that figure if one extracted the merely nominal Roman Catholics, the 'pick 'n' mix' Catholics who practise their faith – in the words of Pope Benedict XVI – 'on a do-it-yourself basis'.

As 2004 neared its end, Karol Wojtyla was continuing to defy the reporters who for two or three years had been preparing to flash the news of his death around the world. His resilience continued to astonish many within the Vatican. The day-to-day running of the Catholic Church was in the hands of others and the papal input to many decisions came through his secretary, now *Archbishop* Dziwisz. This had convinced many of the cynics that 'the other Pope' had become the power in front of the throne, but only when dealing with the minutiae of state affairs. All major policy decisions were on permanent hold as the Roman Catholic Church continued to drift.

Chapter 8

The Jewish Question

F OR KAROL WOJTYLA it had been a considerable
journey, for the papacy a much longer one. On 13
April 1986 Pope John Paul II crossed the Tiber and
was driven to the nearby Great Roman synagogue. It was
more than seventeen years since Wojtyla had entered the
synagogue in the Kazimierz section of Cracow and stood
quietly throughout the service. No Pope had ever entered
this building or any other synagogue in the nearly two
thousand years of Roman Catholicism. Only John XXIII
during the 1960s had come close, for while driving he
ordered his car to stop outside the Temple, got out and
blessed a bemused congregation of Jews leaving the Sabbath
service.

Wojtyla's passage to this historic moment in 1986 had
been far from tranquil. Immediately following the end of the
First World War the virus of anti-Semitism erupted again in
Eastern Europe. There had been numerous pogroms
throughout the region. Poland was no different. In 1919,
eighty were killed in Vilna, a further seventy in Lvov and
within the province where the future Pope was born 500
were slaughtered. Nineteen twenty, the year of Wojtyla's
birth in Wadowice, was not only marked by fine parades for
Marshal Pilsudski in Warsaw.

The peasant and tenant farmers of Wadowice were no

different from other Poles: they were unremittingly hostile
to Jews, influenced by local priests who were no more
enlightened than their parishioners. The contention, nearly
2,000 years old, that the Jews were directly responsible for
the death of Jesus Christ, was central to this hatred. Added
to that came envy, for although the majority of Jews were
poor, even those obliged to live in the *shtetls* – Jewish
villages – enjoyed a higher standard of living than the
Catholic peasants. At the time of Karol Wojtyla's childhood
many Polish peasants still believed that Jews stole and
murdered Christian children to mix their blood with matzo
meal for the Passover ritual meal. Although Jews represented a small minority, around nine per cent, of the Polish
population this did nothing to ease the prejudice.

Barred from owning land, they found many other outlets
for their natural talents and abilities. They managed the
great estates for the Polish nobility, thus ensuring the
peasants regarded them as natural enemies. They also
became lawyers, merchants, artisans, and members of the
professional class. In Wadowice during Wojtyla's childhood they acquired forty per cent of the shops through
talent and hard work yet were only twenty per cent of the
population: this created more envy and anti-Semitism.
Many Catholic families had Jewish landlords, yet another
frequent running sore.

The third-floor apartment rented by the Wojtyla family
was in a building owned by a Jewish family and the
apartment next door was occupied by the Beer family, also
Jewish. Regina 'Ginka' Beer became a close friend of
Karol's and his first stage appearance as a budding actor
was as her leading man. Yet, contrary to the mythmakers of
the Vatican Press Office, Wojtyla's childhood in Wadowice
was indeed exposed to institutionalised anti-Semitism.
Close friendships with Jewish families like the Beers did
not blind Karol Wojtyla to the realities of Jewish life but

until the day he stood before his overwhelmingly Jewish audience he had never confronted or condemned anti-Semitism.

The feast of the Assumption is celebrated in mid August at Kalwaria Zebrzydowska and Wojtyla's surviving contemporaries are happy to talk about it. They are less forthcoming, indeed they are silent, on some of the events that occurred at Kalwaria during Holy Week, events that Wojtyla also attended regularly throughout his pre-papal life. Easter at Kalwaria was a time of acute danger for any Jew living in the surrounding areas. Jews learned through bitter and violent experiences to ensure, if they could afford it, that they had food and other necessities to last for several weeks. To go out, particularly alone, was extremely dangerous at this time. There would be anti-Jewish riots, their homes and their businesses would be wrecked or set to the torch and all too frequently Jews would be severely beaten and killed. This had been going on long before Hitler and it was destined to continue long after the end of the Third Reich.

For many devout Polish Catholics the Jew became the perfect scapegoat and the Catholic rituals of Easter served to justify the unjustifiable. There was the Good Friday prayer 'The Act of Reparation', the prayer for the conversion of all that did not follow 'the true faith', which described the Jews as 'that pernicious race'.

Another prayer, also recited on Good Friday, rewrote the New Testament and had not the Romans but Jews piercing Christ with a spear and subsequently offering him vinegar to drink.

What really whipped up the anti-Semitism in the crowds who flocked to Kalwaria was the Passion Play, a crude, dramatised ritual in which the role of the villain was taken by Judas, and the theatre invariably focused not just on Judas but his entire race. All of this was played at Kalwaria with a large range of buildings and locations designed to transfigure the Polish town into a vision of Jerusalem at the time of Christ. Many a young peasant already in a mentally disturbed condition by the end of the drama would then queue to file past a seventeenth-century painting in the Bernardine monastery. It is designed to stoke up the sight-seer's anti-Semitism even higher. It shows Jesus Christ falling under the weight of his cross as a horde of crazed semi-human Jews tear at him. It catches the message of the Passion Play very exactly and freezes an image in the mind. After that it took nothing else for many a young man on his way back to his village to pause awhile and indulge in some 'retribution' on behalf of Christ.

The Wojtyla family's attendance at the Easter perfor-mances at Kalwaria was something of a tradition. Both his paternal grandfather and great-grandfather served as guides for the pilgrims. In later life Karol Wojtyla indicated that he preferred the feast of the Assumption to the Easter Pageant. Certainly the former had powerfully influenced him. Woj-tyla returned again and again to Kalwaria as a place to think and reflect yet he apparently never connected the events of Kalwaria and anti-Semitism. To him it was a sacred place. Unlike Wojtyla, Adolf Hitler did make the connection. After attending the world famous Passion Plays in Oberammergau during the 1930s he enthusiastically observed, 'Never has the menace of Jewry been so convin-cingly portrayed.'

In Wadowice, while Orthodox Jews generally kept them-selves to themselves, the liberal Jews were more outgoing. Karol junior played in goal for the local Jewish team when their regular goalkeeper was unavailable. Karol senior, along with his son, would on occasions go to the local synagogue just as in turn Jurek Kluger, a particularly close Jewish school friend, would seek out Wojtyla in the local church where Karol was an altar boy. These attitudes and experiences were very unusual in Poland at the time. This is shown by a pastoral letter, 'On The Principles Of Catholic Morality', from the then head of the Polish Church, Cardinal August Hlond, on 29 February 1936.

'There will be a Jewish problem as long as Jews remain in Poland . . . It is a fact that the Jews are fighting against the Catholic Church, persisting in free thinking, and are the vanguard of Godlessness, Bolshevism and subversion . . . It is a fact that the Jews deceive, levy interest and are pimps. It is a fact that the religious and ethical influence of the Jewish young people on Polish people is a negative one.'

Such views were very widely held among the Roman Catholic hierarchy in the interim years between the two world wars. The same year as Cardinal Hlond's public letter a Polish Jesuit periodical asserted, 'It is necessary to provide separate schools for Jews, so that our children will not be infected by their lower morality.' Maximilian Kolbe, a Franciscan monk later canonised by Pope John Paul II for sacrificing his life in Auschwitz in order to save the life of a fellow prisoner, was during the inter-war years the editor-in-chief of a Catholic weekly, *The Knight of the Immaculate*. Rabidly anti-Semitic, it was very popular in Poland not least because it was seen as a Franciscan-financed paper that promoted the official position and contributed significantly to poisoning public opinion against the Jews.

Once in power Hitler banned Jews from marrying non-Jews. He then deprived them of German citizenship and banned them from public life. They were excluded from employment in public services, stripped of their pension rights and barred from working as teachers, journalists, lawyers or doctors. During the summer holidays of 1938, Wojtyla was often visited by next-door neighbour and frequent acting companion Ginka Beer. Her father, a bank manager, was taking the family to live in Palestine as Poland was no longer safe for Jews. The anti-Semitism had become bolder and louder, and there were demonstrations in the streets. Agitators were demanding a boycott of Jewish shops and, in a foretaste of *Kristallnacht*, their business windows were being smashed to emphasise the mob's feelings. The courtly elder Wojtyla was very distressed. 'Not all Poles are anti-Semites. I'm not. You know that.'

Four decades later Ginka Beer, at 64, vividly recalled saying goodbye in the Wojtylas' apartment.

> 'He was very upset. Lolek [Karol] was even more distressed. He did not say a word but his face went very red. I said farewell to him as kindly as I could but he was so moved that he could not find a single word to say in reply. So I just shook his father's hand and left.'

Later Lolek attempted to persuade Ginka to stay but without success. Within weeks Hitler's army would be in Czechoslovakia while his ally Generalissimo Franco, favoured by the young Karol Wojtyla, tightened his grip on Spain. Ginka's parents never made it to Palestine. Her father was killed in the Soviet Union; her mother died in Auschwitz.

The same month that Ginka began her journey, the Wojtylas moved to Cracow to prepare for Karol's first term at the Jagiellonian University. Father and son moved into a small basement apartment in a part of the city known as Debniki, near the Vistula River. In late 1938 and throughout the first nine months of 1939, while Wojtyla remained immersed in university life and its many attractions, war grew ever more inevitable. Not even the basic military training for the undergraduates impinged on the surreal world of the campus. The Polish philology students continued to dream, breathe and live their poetry. Through his close friend, Kydrynski, the villa of the Szkockis was opened to Wojtyla and this became *the* meeting place in Cracow for writers, poets, artists and musicians; there they would recite and discuss their latest works and the musicians would regale the assembled creative spirits with their latest compositions.

Wojtyla was introduced to Jadwiga Lewaj, a teacher of French and literature (an introduction that would prove very fortuitous to the young man), and while he would recite long passages of 'Bogumil' by Norwid, while he allowed the extreme right-wing element that controlled student housing to elect him their president, while he and his new-found friends discussed the relative merits of romanticism, lyricism and messianism, reality was edging ever closer.

At the end of 1938, even after it had become obvious that the international Baltic port of Danzig was to Hitler a prized target for acquisition, life continued as before at the Jagiellonian University. Karol Wojtyla was able to write to one of his friends, 'For us life consisted of evenings on Dluga Street, with refined conversation until midnight and beyond.' By the end of August 1939 posters had gone up in every village, town and city in Poland ordering all reservists and retired troops, and all men up to the age of forty years with call-up papers, to report to barracks. At the University, Wojtyla and his friends were anxiously studying not call-up papers but the syllabus for the autumn term. Earlier the same day Wojtyla had handed back the army uniform he had worn at the summer military camp. As an undergraduate he was temporarily exempted from military service.

On Friday, 1 September Cracow experienced its first air raid. German divisions were already pushing into Poland from the south and the north and the west. War had come to Poland. Confronting a Wehrmacht force of 1.25 million men that included six armoured divisions and eight motorised divisions supported by Göring's Luftwaffe, the Polish cavalry and the other elements of the Army fought with enormous courage against overwhelming odds. By the time that Warsaw surrendered and all resistance had been crushed, over 60,000 Poles had been killed, 200,000 had been wounded and 700,000 had been taken prisoner. The Government had fled to Romania; Poland had ceased to exist.

Once again Poland found itself being carved up and annexed by its neighbours. The Soviets took 76,000 square miles of the eastern region with its population of some 12.8 million. Germany took the west, including Warsaw. A large central region that acted as a buffer zone became a Nazi 'protectorate' and was controlled by 'The General Government'. Within this area were Cracow and Wojtyla and his son.

Catholic Poles quickly discovered that Hitler had plans for them as well as the Jews. Before the end of October 1939 forced labour was imposed on the entire Polish population between the ages of eighteen and sixty. The only exceptions were those occupied in 'permanent useful social labour', which of course was defined by the Nazis. Before the end of the year twelve forced labour camps had been created to 'house' male Jews. Jews, including children over twelve, would be directed to whatever work was decreed for them and disobedience was punishable by fines of unlimited amounts, prison, torture and confiscation of all assets.

Wojtyla's fellow undergraduates were beginning to come to terms with living in an occupied country. It should have concentrated the mind of even the most self-obsessed student to witness food shortages, coal suddenly scarce in a country with a vast surplus, and long queues forming instantly on a whisper that something edible was being sold.

As early as October 1939, less than a month after the German occupation of Poland had begun, ghettos for the

Jews were being created. Sometimes they were crammed into a section of a city that had historically been occupied by Jews, as in Warsaw where the Jews were forced to build a wall around the designated area and to pay for the wall.

Karol Wojtyla refused to become involved in any partisan actions. Indeed, he actively attempted to persuade others to abandon violent resistance and to trust in the power of prayer. At the end of December 1939 writing to his friend and mentor, Mieczyslaw Kotlarczyk, the man who had first fired him with a passion for the theatre, Karol Wojtyla demonstrated that the world he lived in was somewhat detached from the general experiences in war-torn Poland.

> 'First and foremost, I must tell you that I am keeping busy. Some people are currently dying of boredom, but not I, I have surrounded myself with books, dug in with Arts and Sciences. I am working. Would you believe that I am virtually running out of time! I read, I write, I study, I think, I pray, I struggle with myself. At times I feel great oppression, depression, despair, evil. At other times, as if I were seeing the dawn, the aurora, a great light.'

Wojtyla's literary output of the period shows scant acknowledgment that hell had become a reality in Poland. He composed a great many poems during this period. He also wrote three dramatic plays and translated Sophocles' *Oedipus Rex* from the original Greek into Polish in a language that 'even women cooks can listen to with full understanding'. The three dramatic plays all had biblical themes: David, Job and Jeremiah. Writing to his mentor in Wadowice yet again, he observed of Job: 'The play's central message is that suffering is not always about punishment' and that Christ's crucifixion shows the 'meaning of suffering'.

His letters show an extraordinary degree of self absorption on the part of the exceptionally gifted undergraduate. They harked back to the pre-war days at the Jagiellonian University. Although he had repeatedly refused to join the *Armia Krajowa*, the Home Army known as the AK, Karol Wojtyla had in fact become active in another clandestine movement, UNIA. This was a Catholic underground cultural resistance movement committed to keeping the country's culture, language and traditions alive. It regarded the heritage of the motherland's religion, poetry, drama, music and learning as sacrosanct. Just as the Nazis had publicly declared war on Polish heritage, UNIA was dedicated to its survival. Karol Wojtyla took the UNIA oath at around the time of his father's death in February 1941.

The dramas that he and others performed secretly, his activities on behalf of the Rhapsodic Theatre, could have resulted in his arrest, if not the short train ride to Auschwitz, which after its creation in May 1940 soon became one of the principal concentration camps for members of the Polish intelligentsia. Thus, both the rehearsals and the performances always took place in the home of one of the group, never in a full-scale theatrical production. Everything was conducted in great secrecy.

At no time did Karol Wojtyla veer from his belief that prayer and a belief in a Divine Providence were preferable to an armed struggle to overcome the Third Reich. When his close friend Juliusz Kydrynski was arrested and sent to Auschwitz, Wojtyla consoled Kydrynski's mother and prayed. Kydrynski was released after three months. Other friends and former classmates were less fortunate. Jozef Wasik was publicly executed in Cracow for his underground activities. Tadeusz Galuska was killed in action. Others just went missing, somewhere in Auschwitz.

Wojtyla had retreated into a world of secret acting and religious quietism; he also made no effort to help even a few of wartime Poland's Jewish population. After Wojtyla's election as Pope, the Vatican addressed this problem by pumping out disinformation that was accepted unquestioningly by the news media. The media were rapidly followed by the first wave of biographers, who recycled the original disinformation and gave it fresh life. According to the Vatican website, 'B'nai B'rith and other authorities have testified that he (Karol Wojtyla) helped Jews find refuge from the Nazis.' His Vatican biography says:

> '. . . He (Karol Wojtyla) lived in danger daily of losing his life. He would move about the occupied cities talking to Jewish families out of the ghettos, finding them new identities and hiding places. He saved the lives of many families threatened with execution.'

Jerzy Zubrzycki, a high school classmate of Karol Wojtyla, was quoted in *Time* magazine in October 1978: 'All around him Karol saw suffering and misery. Despite the fact that his life was in constant danger, he moved about the occupied areas taking Jewish families to safety and finding them new identities.'

In *The Pope In Britain*, Peter Jennings wrote,

> 'The most effective thing the Cardinal (at the time, Archbishop Sapieha) did was to authorise the issue of baptism certificates for some Jews who would otherwise have perished in the massacre. The young seminarian Wojtyla naturally took part in the various forms of assistance given to those who were persecuted.'

This last claim has been made by other biographers. There is compelling evidence that the late Pope did not in fact do anything at any time to save any of the Jews.

In 1985 the filmmaker Marek Halter, himself a Polish Jew, came to the Vatican to interview Pope John Paul II for a documentary about gentiles who had helped Jews during the war.

'I didn't ask him if it was true that he saved Jews, that he helped Jews, what he did at that time of the war really. I had testimonies. People of Stanislaw Gibisch. Other people, his Jewish friends, the son of the lawyer, Kluger, but I never asked the Pope. So when I arrived the Pope said:

"Ah you are here. You came from Paris?"

"You had a lot of Jewish friends," I asked, "before the war?"

He said, "Yes."

I said to him, "And all of them were killed?"

And his face changed. He said, "Yes. It's horrible. Right. They were killed."

And I told him, "But some of them survived. They were saved."

He said, "*Gott sei Dank!*"

Then I asked him the real question. "And you, Holy Father, you did something for them?"

And then his face changed and he said, "I don't believe I – no. No," he said.

And I was so surprised because in my mind I believed that he was going to tell me a story. A story that during the war he was busy preparing the false papers, passports for the Jews, because I'd heard that, because people told me about that and he told me "No" so I was stopped. I didn't know what to ask him next and my interview – that too was stopped, was finished. Except for this gesture. He took me in his arms like a brother with a very bad, guilty feeling and I was very frustrated. Very frustrated.'[10]

B'nai B'rith – Sons of the Covenant – is the oldest and largest Jewish service organisation within the United States. It has a wide range of activities embracing an extensive cross-section of American Jewry. Possibly the most widely known is the Anti-Defamation League, a civil rights organisation. During the course of researching this book I drew their attention to the claims that had been made in their name with regard to the wartime activities of Karol Wojtyla. After extensive research, they confirmed that they had never made the claims attributed to them and that they held no evidence to justify such statements.

I contacted Professor Jerzy Zubrzycki in Australia. He claimed that the interview published by *Time* magazine never took place and the remarks attributed to him were never made. The Simon Wiesenthal Organisation advised me that they had no information regarding the various claims that had been made on behalf of the Pope. I contacted Yad Vashem in Israel, an organisation founded to commemorate and perpetuate the memory of the six million Jewish victims of the Holocaust. Dr Mordecai Paldiel, the current Head of the Righteous Department advised me, 'We have no record of Wojtyla's rescue of Jews during the war years . . . We have received no testimonies or documentation on this matter.'

The claims made over many years about Wojtyla's wartime actions on behalf of Jews are a fantasy without any foundation. He had every opportunity. UNIA apart from having a cultural underground element also had a very active resistance arm with over 20,000 guerrillas. It provided false papers to more than 50,000 Jews and hid nearly 3,000 Jewish children during the war years. This secret organisation was named Zegota. Wojtyla was very well acquainted with a number of its members, men like the writer Zofia Kossak-Szczuka who was very active in Zegota. Wojtyla never took an active role in either Zegota or any other group involved in helping the Jews.

Many people would claim after the war had ended and the full horror of the Holocaust was exposed to the world that they did not know. No one living in Cracow could use such excuses. The railway line that ran through the Solvay works, the line that was considered vital to the German war effort as it carried troops, supplies and munitions to the Eastern Front also ran through the Solvay works heading west, to Auschwitz, an equally vital requirement to ensure that another part of the Third Reich's aspirations could be fulfilled. Professor Edward Görlich is insistent that above everything that the plant's soda products could be used for, the reason the works had their *kriegswichtig* designation and were vital for the war effort was the existence of the railway line. In addition, after 1941 one other factor would have denied the claim of ignorance. When the wind blew from the west the citizens of Wadowice and Cracow rapidly came to recognise the smell of burning human flesh.

In August 1987, nearly nine years after becoming Pope, Karol Wojtyla wrote to Archbishop John L May.

'It is precisely by reason of this terrible experience that the nation of Israel, her sufferings and her Holocaust are today before the eyes of the Church, of all peoples and of all nations, as a warning, a witness and a silent cry. Before the vivid memory of the extermination, as recounted to us by the survivors and by all Jews now living, and as it is continually offered for our meditation within the narrative of the Pesah Haggadah, as Jewish families are accustomed to do today, *it is not permissible for anyone to pass by with indifference.* Reflection upon the Holocaust shows us to what terrible consequences the lack of faith in God and contempt for man created in his image can lead . . .'

Unlike the Good Samaritan that Wojtyla alludes to in his letter, throughout the Second World War Karol Wojtyla had indeed passed by with indifference.

In the wartime Vatican, Pope Pius XII, notwithstanding his detailed specific briefings, continued to ignore the fact that the Nazis had transformed Poland, even when those briefings detailed the numbers of priests and religious who perished in the camps. He continued to vacillate. Several of the detailed reports on the Nazi atrocities in Poland that were carried to Pius XII by trusted messengers came directly from Archbishop Sapieha in Cracow. He told the Pope that the prisoners within the camps

'were deprived of human rights, handed over to the cruelty of men who have no feeling of humanity. We live in terror, continually in danger of losing everything if we attempt to escape, thrown into camps from which few emerge alive.'

Discussing the fate of the Jews, Sapieha told a Knights of Malta chaplain, en route to Rome and who had personally witnessed the deportation of a large number of Jews from the Cracow ghetto to Auschwitz, 'We are living through the tragedy of these unfortunate people and none of us is in a position to help them any more. There is now no difference between Jews and Poles.' Not everyone either in Cracow or the rest of Poland shared the Archbishop's uncharacteristic pessimism. Jews were even saved and hidden by devout Catholics who were also anti-Semitic. They would upbraid the Jews as they shared their meagre rations with them: 'Christ killers. Christ killers.'

When Eduardo Senatro, a journalist working on the Vatican's daily newspaper, *L'Osservatore Romano*, suggested to Pius XII that a critical article should be written about the Nazis' atrocities the Pope replied, 'You must not forget, my dear friend, that there are millions of Catholics in the German army. Would you like to place them in a crisis of conscience?' Yet in May 1940 the Pope observed to Italian diplomat Dino Alfieri, 'Terrible things are happening in Poland. We should say words of fire against such things.'

The Pope was a firm believer in the doctrine of 'impartiality', a policy that he himself had helped to draft at the time of the First World War. In essence the Vatican believed that because there were Catholics fighting on both sides the Church should support neither. Pius XII never did utter 'Words of Fire' on the Holocaust. However, he was active in other ways against the Nazis, including an attempt to get Britain's wartime government to back a plan conceived by senior German officers to overthrow Hitler. In hoping the plot succeeded and urging the Allies to help, the Pope moved some distance from the doctrine of 'impartiality'.

In October 1943 Adolf Eichmann initiated a round-up of all Jews within Rome before deporting them to certain death. His recently revealed diaries establish that papal intervention saved the vast majority of them. Pius made three immediate and forceful protests. These were not public condemnations but via three different emissaries, Cardinal Maglione, Father Pancrazio Pfeiffer and Bishop Alois Hudal. These separate protests on behalf of the Pope were made directly to the German army commander in Rome, Rainer Stahel. These vital interventions were also recorded by Monsignor John Carroll-Abing who was directly involved with Father Pfeiffer's efforts on behalf of the Jews. In January 1944 the Pope opened the gates of his summer residence at Castel Gandolfo, giving asylum to some 12,000 refugees. Pius XII, according to the author Pinchas Lapide, 'was instrumental in saving at least 700,000, but probably as many as 860,000 Jews from certain death at Nazi hands'. Undoubtedly Pius XII could have done more on behalf of the Jews. But based upon all the available evidence, he could also have done less. To have saved the lives of 860,000 people is a formidable achievement.

In the summer of 1941 Himmler briefed the Auschwitz commandant Rudolf Höss about 'The Final Solution'. A few weeks later Soviet prisoners of war were used in trials of the poison gas Zyklon-B. They were gassed in underground cells in Auschwitz block eleven. Subsequently a gas chamber was built just outside the main camp.

The same month, June 1941, that Himmler was briefing the Auschwitz commandant, the citizens of Jedwabne, a town in eastern Poland, decided to celebrate their recent liberation from Soviet occupation by the German army, by killing every Jew in the village – 1,607 people. Some of the Jews had allegedly collaborated with the Soviet army. They were attacked with heavy wooden clubs studded with nails. Some were ordered to dig a pit and were then axed and clubbed and their bodies thrown into the pit. Some were stoned to death. Children were battered with the wooden clubs, men had their eyes gouged out and their tongues cut out. The Germans watched and took photographs as women were raped before being beheaded. The overwhelming majority were whipped and prodded into Farmer Slezynski's barn which was doused with kerosene and set alight. The attackers played musical instruments to drown out the screams. Sixteen hundred died. The seven survivors had been hidden by Antonia Wyrzkowska who later was severely beaten by her neighbours.

During that same summer life improved for Karol Wojtyla. He was transferred from the quarry to the main plant in Borek Falecki. He continued to be allocated the extra rations and the monthly vodka coupons, which he was able to exchange on the black market for meat, eggs or other rare provisions. Wojtyla preferred the night shifts because they presented him with a great deal of time to pray and to study for his degree. He performed his various work duties quietly and efficiently. He listened a good deal more than he talked, a sensible habit for a man planning to survive the Second World War.

The war in Europe would continue until April 1945, but in Cracow it officially finished in the minds of Wojtyla and his fellow seminarians when two Soviet majors appeared at the gate to the Archbishop's palace seeking not Nazis but a bottle of vodka. On 8 May 1945 the Allied Forces accepted the unconditional surrender of Germany. Since the invasion of Poland in 1939 more than eleven million Polish civilians had been murdered in cold blood. Among that eleven million, a minimum of six million Jews were killed. Of these, 1.1 million had been exterminated at Auschwitz. The Nazis had also gassed many thousands of gypsies, homosexuals, Jehovah's Witnesses, prisoners of war, freemasons, priests, nuns and handicapped people. Theodore Adorno memorably questioned whether after Auschwitz it was still possible to write poetry or philosophy.

'For the world to which Auschwitz belongs is a world without soul, and the spiritual activities which remain serve to furnish it with an appearance of legitimacy which flagrantly contradicts its reality.'

It is hard to understand that just thirty miles from Auschwitz a future Pope drew continuous strength and comfort from his certain knowledge that God was constantly intervening, incessantly protecting him, an obscure young Pole, as he went about his labour, work that was deemed vital to the Third Reich's war effort. Such a devout young man might have learnt a profound humility and compassion from the fact of surviving when so many like him were exterminated.

The killings in Poland did not stop when the war ended. The identity of the killers changed but not the category of victims. The virus of anti-Semitism within Roman Catholic Poland continued as if there had never been a world war, or places such as Auschwitz, Treblinka or Belzec. Returning Jews who had survived the Holocaust found that the Germans had indeed gone but the Jew-hating Poles had not.

In October 1943 Leon Feldhendler and Alexander Pechersky had led a planned break-out from the Sobibor death camp of more than 600 Jews. Some 200 were shot while escaping; 400 escaped, of whom 100 were recaptured and killed. The majority of the others either died of typhus or were killed by hostile Polish gangs. Only thirty survived the war including the original two leaders of the revolt. By 19 March 1946 the war in Europe had been over for ten months yet on that day Leon Feldhendler was murdered in his home town of Lublin by fellow Poles. Chaim Hirschmann, one of only two survivors of the Belzec death camp, was also murdered on that day.

Some of these postwar murders occurred because the returning Jews came back to claim homes illegally seized by Catholic Poles; the majority were murdered because they were Jews. Over 1,000 were murdered between 1945 and mid-1947. In Karol Wojtyla's birthplace of Wadowice, the town so lovingly described by the Vatican Information Service and numerous papal biographers as being free of anti-Semitism during the inter-war years, Polish Catholics were admitting, in the privacy of the confessional, crimes ranging from theft of Jewish property to the murder of returning Jews.

Having run away in the face of the German advance in 1939, Cardinal Hlond had returned and was once again head of the Catholic Church in Poland. After a vicious pogrom in Kielce in 1946 during which forty-nine Jews were murdered, the pre-war anti-Semitic Primate gave a

clear indication that nothing had changed. He knew who
was to blame for the pogrom. It was the returning Jews. He
declared: 'Yet again they are holding important positions.
Yet again they wish to impose a regime alien to the Polish
nation.' The Jews rapidly got the message. During the same
period of time over 100,000 Jews fled the country, many
heading for Palestine. This was also the same period that
many in Poland laboured under the delusion that they were
a free country.

In 1965 one of the key declarations of the Council of
Vatican II was *Nostra Aetate* – In Our Time – that dealt
with the relationship of the Catholic Church to non-Christian religions, including Muslims and Jews. Its passage
through the Council was fraught with difficulties that
continued up to the vote in favour of the declaration.
The very root of Christianity's institutionalised anti-Semitism that began at the moment of Christ's crucifixion was re-
examined, re-evaluated and finally overwhelmingly rejected. This vital and ultra-sensitive issue is the source of
many dramatic but totally unfounded claims about the role
of Karol Wojtyla.

The supporters of a change in the Church's position
sought to include within the declaration a statement that
acknowledged that, notwithstanding the Jewish authorities
pressing for the death of Christ,

'What happened in His passion cannot be charged
against all Jews, without distinction, then alive, nor
against the Jews of today. Although the Church is the
new people of God, the Jews should not be presented
as rejected or accursed by God, as if this followed from
the Holy Scriptures. . . . Furthermore, in her rejection
of every persecution against any man, the Church,
mindful of the patrimony she shares with the Jews and
moved not by political reasons, but by the Gospel's

spiritual love, *decries hatred, persecutions, displays of anti-Semitism, directed against Jews at any time and by anyone.*' [Author's italics.]

Many bishops at the Vatican Council II were deeply opposed to the inclusion of these statements. They fought a bitter rearguard action.

Cardinal Augustin Bea had been charged by Pope John XXIII to prepare the draft document for debate by the Council. He later observed, 'If I had known all the difficulties before, I do not know whether I would have had the courage to take this way.' Cardinal Walter Kasper, recalling the controversy in November 2002, remembered,

'There was vehement opposition from both outside and within. From inside the old well-known patterns of traditional anti-Judaism emerged, from outside there was a storm of protest especially from Muslims with serious threats against the Christians living there as a minority faith.'

There was also a threat to blow up the entire basilica along with the 2,100 bishops debating the issue. Pope Paul VI had added to an already highly charged atmosphere when in a Passion Sunday sermon on 4 April 1965 he said,

'That people (the Jews), predestined to receive the Messiah, who had been awaiting him for thousands of years . . . not only do not recognise him, but oppose him, slander him and finally kill him.'

During the making of the television documentary 'The Millennial Pope' for PBS in the United States, among the many people interviewed by the producers was a former priest, James Carroll. He talked of a friend (unidentified but

demonstrably a bishop) who had been at Vatican Council
II. The friend had recounted the fierce debate on the issue of
whether or not the Jews were guilty of Christ's murder.

'All of a sudden down at the end of the table, a man
began to speak, a voice that he had not heard in any
debate. In many debates, on many questions, he had
never heard this voice.'

Carroll, recalling his conversation with his informant continued: 'He knew it was a different voice because of the
heavy accent. And the man spoke of the Church's responsibility to change its relation to the Jews . . . I lifted up my
head. I thought, who is this prophet? I looked down and it
was this young bishop from Poland. And no one even knew
his name. And it was the first intervention Wojtyla made at
the Council. And it was very important. That's the beginning of the large public impact he would have on this
question.'

Papal biographers and others have written that Wojtyla
was highly active during this debate. The following extract
from the *Encyclopaedia Britannica* is very typical of the
writings on this aspect of the Pope's life:

'He was invited to Vatican II, where he argued force-
fully for Pope John XXIII's redefinition of the
Church's relationship to the Jews. Wojtyla supported
the assertion not only that the Jews were not guilty of
killing Christ, but also that Judaism had its own
ongoing integrity, that it had not been replaced by
Christianity in God's eyes.'

Claims have also been made that he was the leading
author of the final declaration. In just fifteen lengthy
sentences, *Nostra Aetate* was a groundbreaking document

launching a movement to reverse 2,000 years of hatred, oppression, vilification and annihilation of Jews by Catholics in the name of God. But it owes nothing to Karol Wojtyla for its existence. Just as the stories of Wojtyla's wartime dramatic interventions to save Jewish lives are fantasies piled on myths so the claims that have been made on behalf of Wojtyla regarding his input and influence on the creation of this historic declaration are without foundation.

The credit for this historic document should be given in particular to two men, the Jesuit Cardinal Bea and Father Malachi Martin who had doctorates in Semitic languages, archaeology and Oriental history and was destined to become a highly controversial author. Working closely with Cardinal Bea, Martin drafted the document, which exonerated the Jews from culpability in the execution of Jesus Christ. Father Martin received overwhelming if not unanimous approval from the Vatican Council and many accolades from around the world. With regard to the recollections of the anonymous friend of James Carroll and his references to the hitherto 'silent bishop' from Cracow, Karol Wojtyla made at least seven spoken interventions and at least four written interventions during the Council sessions. *But none of them dealt with anti-Semitism, an issue on which he was mute.*

That so many false claims should have been made regarding the Pope's historic relationship and involvement with the Jewish people is highly disturbing. Equally troubling is the fact that neither Pope John Paul II nor any member of the Vatican, including his spin doctor, Dr Joaquin Navarro-Valls, ever tried to correct a false record that paints him in an undeserved heroic light.

There is one brief notable exception, which, as previously recorded, occurred when the Pope was about to be interviewed by Marek Halter.

The year of revolutions was 1968 when Europe caught fire and student-led protests erupted spontaneously but with mutual support across many countries. In Poland it began with a play, a theatrical performance of Adam Mickiewicz's patriotic and anti-Russian play *The Forefather's Eve*. It was hardly hot from the press; the author had been dead for 113 years but his writings had maintained their relevance and an energy and passion for Polish independence sprang from the page and in 1968, from the mouths of dramatic actors, they sounded like a call to arms. The playwright's references to Russian oppressors and the Russian occupation of the homeland in the mid-nineteenth century were loudly cheered by the audience who happened to include the Soviet ambassador. The Soviet embassy would subsequently deny any involvement but the play was promptly banned. Warsaw erupted as students took to the street to protest the ban.

The protest spread through the country. Interior Minister General Moczar sent in the ORMO (Volunteer Reserve of the Citizens' Militia). Just as in Paris, London, West Berlin and a dozen other capitals, the violence of government reaction to the protests and the brutality of militia and the police were planned and calculated. For the majority of the security forces it 'made the job worthwhile'. When criticisms of his orders and his methods began to swell, the General picked on the scapegoat used so many times before to justify the unjustifiable. He cited a 'massive Zionist conspiracy to overthrow the Government' and gave out that the student organisers (or as the General preferred 'ringleaders') were Jews.

General Moczar's main target was not the Jews but the Communist Party's First Secretary, Wladyslaw Gomulka. A year earlier, Gomulka, confronted by growing criticism, had sought to deflect it by blaming a Zionist fifth column at work. Now the General, who lusted after Gomulka's position, sought to be acclaimed as the nation's saviour by

singing the same hymn, only louder. First Secretary Gomulka had reasserted the power of the censor's office and
when serious food shortages and higher prices began to
really hurt in 1967 leading to the inevitable protests, he had
blamed the Jews. Now as the streets filled with protesting
students whose preoccupations moved rapidly from a
banned play to a concern about the events in neighbouring
Czechoslovakia, Gomulka again blamed the Jews. The
regime began to purge the universities and colleges of Jews,
and liberals and reformers. Anyone on the streets who
looked Jewish was beaten up.

The Prague Spring of democracy under new leader Alexander Dubček was flowering at an increasing pace throughout Czechoslovakia. It was of course in Moscow's eyes
another Zionist conspiracy. Taking full note of events
across the border, Gomulka raised the pressure on Poland's
Jewry. The regime let it be known that any Jew who wanted
to leave the country could apply to the Dutch embassy in
Warsaw and begin the process to apply for entry into Israel.
No other country, just Israel.

Applicants had to make a written request for permission
to renounce their Polish citizenship. Supporting documents
had to be acquired from employer, housing association and
anyone else that officialdom could add to the list. The
application took three months to be considered. During
that time applicants had no idea if they were still Polish or
had moved into a bureaucratic anonymity. They were
deemed to be without a nationality, without a Polish address or job, without any of the basic data that reinforces a
person's identity.

If after three months the applicants had successfully
cleared every hurdle that had been put in their way they
were handed a piece of paper, which declared: 'The holder
of this document is not a Polish citizen.' It was valid for two
weeks. In those two weeks people had to pack their lives

into a couple of suitcases and say goodbye to their homeland. Of the approximately 37,000 Jews then in Poland at
least 34,000 left.

Tadeusz Mazowiecki, one of Poland's leading intellectuals, was also a lifelong friend of Pope John Paul II. Deeply
disturbed at this latest example of the darkness within the
Polish psyche, he went to Cracow to raise the issue with
Wojtyla.

'I had a conversation with Cardinal Wojtyla about the
anti-Semitic issue and asked him to make a stand. He
agreed that it was a matter that needed to be reflected
upon, that the Church should indeed make a stand.'

'But neither he nor Cardinal Wyszynski, nor indeed
any member of the Polish episcopacy, spoke out
against what was being done to the Jews?'

'That is correct.'

What contemporary observers described as a 'bloodless
pogrom' was allowed to run its course. Both Wojtyla and
Wyszynski also remained silent throughout the year on
what was occurring in neighbouring Czechoslovakia. Gomulka was far less reticent and watched with increasing
concern as the newly elected Dubček abolished literary and
press censorship and began to rehabilitate victims of Sta-
linist terror trials. Next it was announced that freedom of
minority opinion was guaranteed. Then travel restrictions
were lifted. Then on 15 April 1968, this remarkable man
and his progressive Communist regime published a 27,000-
word Action Programme. That confirmed Moscow's worst
fears. Three weeks later Gomulka and a number of other
Warsaw Pact leaders took part in a top-secret meeting with
the Soviet Politburo. Within hours Soviet troops stationed
in Poland began moving towards the Czechoslovak border
south of Cracow.

Gomulka did not merely identify with Soviet policies on the Prague Spring, he pushed a hesitant Russian leadership towards a total invasion of Czechoslovakia. On 3 August 1968 in Bratislava, Gomulka and the other Warsaw Pact leaders signed a solemn 'declaration of intent', which was also signed by Brezhnev and Dubček. It gave the Czech leader and his colleagues everything that they had sought: freedom to continue their internal reforms, freedom to continue their process of democratisation. Eighteen days later, during the night, the tanks rolled into Czechoslovakia. The Prague Spring of democracy had become a Moscow winter of suppression. All of the Dubček reforms were abolished. Full censorship returned. All meetings that 'endanger socialism' were banned. In October it was announced that the Warsaw Pact troops would stay in the country 'indefinitely'. The following April saw Dubček removed from power and replaced by Gustav Husak. He would do what Moscow told him to do. Among the troops who entered and violated a sovereign state were Polish forces. Not a voice was raised in protest by anyone within the ruling Polish Politburo or the Polish Catholic Church.

Karol Wojtyla's first, tentative, step towards any form of political involvement occurred the year after the Prague Spring and the Polish bloodless pogrom. On 28 February 1969 during a visit to the parish of Corpus Christi he visited the Jewish Community and then the synagogue in the Kazimierz section of Cracow. This was an act of significance not merely for the small community of surviving Jews in Cracow but for Wojtyla himself. He was greeted by Maciej Jakubowicz, the leader of the community; then with his head covered he entered the synagogue and remained standing at the back throughout the service.

The visit was an isolated act and a mute one. He went because the rabbi had invited him. He made no condemnation or mention of the Government-led attack in the previous year on Polish Jewry. Many years later he was asked again by the then Prime Minister, Tadeusz Mazowiecki, why he had not spoken out in 1968. The Prime Minister recalled: 'The Pope made no answer with words. He shook his head then put his face in his hands.' It was virtually identical to the reaction witnessed by film-maker Marek Halter over the same issue of his inability to save Jewish lives during the Second World War. There would come a time when the Pope would indeed have a great deal to say on anti-Semitism but only when he no longer lived in Poland.

His complete detachment, not only during the war but for decades afterwards, from issue after issue engulfing his fellow man, stands in stark contrast to his outspoken defence of the Catholic faith. Part of Wojtyla appears to have remained a timid youth seeking monastic sanctuary well into his middle years. A multitude of fears and weaknesses can so easily hide behind the philosophy that 'our liberation (from the Third Reich) lies at the door of Christ', and a belief that 'prayer is the only weapon that works'.

As a bishop and a cardinal, Wojtyla had visited Auschwitz-Birkenau many times. Like his visit to the Cracow synagogue in February 1969, these visits had been low-key, discreet and unreported. It was as if he feared to draw attention to his acts when as a man who abhorred anti-Semitism he could have set such a powerful positive example by speaking out. This inexplicable contradiction and the failure to connect were constant and recurring themes in Karol Wojtyla's responses to anti-Semitism. Only as Pope, during his first trip back to Poland in 1979, did he make a high-profile visit to Auschwitz-Birkenau – and he went to Kalwaria first.

Now in 1986 in the Rome synagogue, the Pope quoted from the historic Vatican Council II decree *Nostra Aetate*, the foundation of the Roman Catholic Church's revised position on the Jews. He reminded his Jewish listeners, needlessly, of their own past:

'Nevertheless, a consideration of centuries-long cultural conditioning could not prevent us from recognising that the acts of discrimination, unjustified limitation of religious freedom, oppression on the level of civil freedom in regard to the Jews were from an objective point of view, gravely deplorable manifestations. Yes, once again through myself, the Church, in the words of the well-known Declaration *Nostra Aetate* (No 4) "deplores the hatred, persecutions and displays of anti-Semitism directed against the Jews at any time and by anyone". I repeat "by anyone".'

The Pope's use of the words 'well-known Declaration' was ironic. In 1970, while Cardinal of Cracow, Wojtyla wrote a book, *Sources of Renewal*, to serve as a guide to the Vatican Council II texts. It has enjoyed great success in many languages. In none of the editions will the reader find the 'well-known Declaration' that is the very essence of *Nostra Aetate*. Only Karol Wojtyla knows why he censored the following clear-cut condemnation of anti-Semitism:

'. . . although the Church is the new people of God, the Jews should not be presented as rejected or accursed by God, as if this followed from the Holy Scriptures. All should see to it, then, that in catechetical work or in the preaching of the word of God they do not teach anything that does not conform to the truth of the Gospel and the spirit of Christ. Furthermore, in her rejection of every persecution against any man, the Church, mindful of the patrimony she shares with the Jews and moved not by political reasons but by the Gospel's spiritual love, decries hatred, persecutions, displays of anti-Semitism, directed against Jews at any time and by anyone.'

Between constant references to *Nostra Aetate* the Pope also talked of the visit he had made to Auschwitz in June 1979 and of how he had paused in prayer at the memorial stone in Hebrew: 'Before this inscription it is not permissible for anyone to pass by with indifference.'

However, at that precise moment at Auschwitz a group of Carmelite nuns were displaying, with the Pope's support, not only indifference but exceptional insensitivity. In August 1984 they had taken over a building adjacent to the camp. Known as 'the old theatre' it had been the storehouse for the Zyklon B poison used in the Nazi gas chambers. The nuns had been granted a ninety-nine-year lease by the local authorities and within a month high-ranking members of the Polish Church had voiced approval for the creation of a convent at Auschwitz. It was later claimed that this was the Pope's idea, originally expressed during his tenure in Cracow.

In fact Wojtyla wanted much more than a convent in Auschwitz. During a broadcast on Vatican Radio on 20 October 1971 he said,

'The Church of Poland sees the necessity of a place of sacrifice, an altar and a sanctuary, previously in Auschwitz. This is even more necessary after the beatification of Father Maximilian. We are all convinced that in this place of his heroic immolation, a church should be erected, in the same way that since the first centuries of Christianity, churches were built on the tombs of martyrs, beatified people and saints.'

The idea of a Catholic convent at a site where over one million Jews had been murdered was deeply offensive to Jews in many countries. The Pope did nothing to end the controversy and when the nuns added a huge cross seven metres high by the camp gates with the active encouragement of Polish Primate, Cardinal Glemp, the Pope's conciliatory words in the Rome synagogue began to take on a very hollow ring. The controversy at Auschwitz rumbled on, accompanied by a silence from Karol Wojtyla. More than 300 small crosses followed the large one. For many Jews the cross is second only to the swastika as a symbol of anti-Semitism.

It became very obvious that for many Poles who took up this issue, piety was merely a cloak for anti-Semitism. The controversy also demonstrated Roman Catholic ignorance, or perhaps indifference, towards a different faith with a different tradition. Roman Catholics venerate and make sacred any site of martyrdom, but Jewish tradition believes that such a place should be left desolate. In May 1985 a Belgian branch of an organisation calling itself 'Aid to the Church in Need' issued a bulletin asking for funds to help the Carmelite nuns camping in the Auschwitz convent to modernise the building. The bulletin, issued shortly before the Pope paid a visit to Belgium, described the funding as 'a gift for the Pope'. It made no reference to the annihilation of over one million Jews at a site that was described as 'a spiritual fortress'.

It was to become a running sore in Catholic–Jewish relations, one that could have been rapidly healed if the Pope had interceded. Unfortunately, it proved to be another example of Wojtyla's timidity. He repeatedly refused to get involved. He made fine speeches, urging Catholics to 'fathom the depths of the extermination of many millions of Jews during World War II and the wounds thereby inflicted on the consciousness of the Jewish people', reminding the world that 'freedom of religion for everyone and for all people must be respected by everyone, everywhere'. There was a flow of conciliatory documents from the

Vatican Commission for Religious Relations with the Jews that included 'Notes on the Correct Way to Present the Jews and Judaism in Preaching and Catechesism in the Roman Catholic Church'.

The Pope continued to offend many Jews, with the canonisation in 1982 of the Franciscan martyr, Father Maximilian Kolbe. In 1922 Kolbe had founded and edited a monthly review, *Knight of The Immaculate*. In 1935 Kolbe and his fellow Franciscans were running Poland's main Catholic publishers, printing eleven periodicals and a daily newspaper *The Little Daily*, among whose readers was Karol Wojtyla. Within them Kolbe published over thirty anti-Semitic articles in his own name and others by different authors. Kolbe appealed to his readers to pray for

'the straying children of Israel, to lead them to the knowledge of the truth and the achievement of true peace and happiness, since Jesus died for everyone, and therefore for every Jew also'.

He accepted without question the notorious anti-Semitic forgery *The Protocols of The Elders Of Zion*, describing its alleged authors as 'a cruel and crafty little known Jewish clique . . . a small handful of Jews who have let themselves be seduced by Satan'. Elsewhere he referred to 'judaised organisations and judaised political parties which had subverted people's faith and robbed the young of shame' and, repeating the Roman Catholic Church's historic accusation, he wrote, 'Since Jewry's most horrible crime against God, the crucifixion of the Lord Jesus . . . Jewry had fallen even lower'. Echoing Hitler's propaganda in Germany he said that 'Jews are interlopers in our country and can never become truly Polish without converting to Catholicism'.

Beatification in the Roman Catholic Church involves a critical examination and a minute investigation of the candidate. It must be assumed that this element of Kolbe's past was fully examined, then ignored. The Catholic Church has always been silent on this facet of Maximilian Kolbe's life, understandably preferring to dwell on his compassion for others and his singular courage when he begged the Auschwitz camp commandant to let him take the place of a married man with children who had been selected to die. His wish was granted and after being thrown into a starvation bunker with nine other men he prayed with them as one by one they died. After two weeks he was the last man alive and the Nazis injected phenol into his veins. He died in agony.

It is also a matter of record that in late 1939 after the Polish armies had been defeated and the country was occupied by the Germans, Kolbe and his fellow Franciscan monks gave shelter to some 3,000 Polish refugees, including 2,000 Jews. They housed, fed and clothed them. Before being arrested in February 1941 he was able to publish a final edition of *The Knight of The Immaculate*. He wrote, 'No one in the world can change Truth. What we can do and should do is to seek truth and to serve it when we have found it.'

Kolbe's intermittent bigotry before the Second World War does not diminish, rather it enhances, his subsequent journey that ended on the floor of an Auschwitz cell. But by failing to acknowledge it at the time of his beatification, the Pope and his advisors made a propaganda gift to opponents of rapprochement between Roman Catholics and Jews.

Kurt Waldheim had served in the German army during the war. According to his own account, he was conscripted and served on the Russian front until he was wounded in December 1941. His story that he then returned to Vienna and spent the remainder of the war years studying law was not challenged until he ran for President in the Austrian elections of 1986. During a bitterly fought campaign information began to emerge that told a different story of the war years that had been concealed by Soviet and Yugoslav intelligence, and by the Vatican. The Soviet silence had been prompted by the prospect of gaining benefits during Waldheim's two terms as Secretary-General of the United Nations from 1972 to 1981. The Vatican's continuing silence may have been based on old-fashioned prudence. Vatican wartime policy in the Balkans, one of the areas where Waldheim subsequently served with the Wehrmacht, included tacit approval of genocide in Croatia and the active protection both during and after the war of men who should have been tried as war criminals.

After he had recovered from his injury Waldheim resumed his career in the Wehrmacht in April 1942. Subsequently he was the liaison officer with the General Bader Combat Group while it perpetrated mass murder and deportations in the region of Eastern Bosnia. His unit was also responsible in July 1944 for the deportation to Auschwitz of the Jewish population, nearly 2,000, of Salonika in Greece. In 1944 he also approved a quantity of anti-Semitic propaganda that was dropped behind Russian lines. One pamphlet read 'Enough of the War! Kill the Jews. Come Over!'

The Secretariat of State's office was fully aware of his wartime activities when they arranged for Waldheim an audience with Pope John Paul II. The fact that Waldheim had served in the Wehrmacht was enough to trigger a global condemnation of the Pope. It was a replay of the protests after the Vatican's decision in 1982 to appoint Hermann Abs, former paymaster to Adolf Hitler and the Third Reich, one of the 'four wise men' in the wake of the Ambrosiano scandal. The Reagan administration took the greatest interest in the Waldheim protests. Confidential documents from the National Security Council and the State Department reveal its deep concern.

The State Department analysed reaction in 16 different newspapers published between 22 June and 5 July 1987:

'. . . with the exception of one paper, all were highly critical of the Pope. Thirteen papers criticised him for granting the audience; ten said that having done so, the Pope should have chastised Waldheim for his World War II activities.'

There was a similar media reaction in many countries. The fact that the Pope was scheduled to hold a meeting with American Jewish leaders during a September visit to the United States also attracted considerable press comment. An editorial in the *Miami Herald* was typical:

'. . . if he still hopes for a positive September meeting, Pope John Paul II should mend his ecumenical fences with a conciliatory gesture to the freedom-loving citizens whom he offended by his blunder in an affair of State.'

Far from being contrite, the Pope dismissed the uproar as an irrelevance. The Vatican's hardline response can be clearly gauged by comments to the then American ambassador to the Vatican, Frank Shakespeare. Cardinal Casaroli, who happened to be in New York when the storm broke, changed his schedule to have a meeting with a number of the Jewish leaders who were due to meet the Pope in September to discuss various proposals to further Jewish–Catholic relations. The Jewish leaders requested an urgent additional meeting with the Pope to express their views on Waldheim's papal audience. In the event they had to settle for an invitation from Cardinal Willebrands of Holland in his capacity as a member of the Holy See's Commission on Catholic–Jewish relations.

Ambassador Shakespeare discussed this meeting with Monsignor Audrys Backis, the Under Secretary of State of the Vatican's Foreign Ministry, and Father Pierre Du-prey, Vice President of the Commission. They told Shake-speare:

> 'The Pope did not invite the group to Rome. They asked to come . . . There will be no question of discussing the Waldheim audience . . . There will be no discussion of the Holy See's actions during World War II. If the Jewish delegation publishes a list of subjects to be discussed, the proposed September meeting in Miami will be cancelled . . . It is a complete lie for the *New York Times* to state that the Pope and four senior aides will meet with five Jewish representatives for sixty to ninety minutes.'

The Monsignor and the priest went relentlessly on. The Jews were behaving 'in a framework of excitement'. It was made abundantly clear that the Jewish leaders could come to Rome and discuss 'substantive questions relating to the religious dialogue between Christians and Jews' which would be followed by a private audience with the Pope during which 'there will be no mention of Kurt Waldheim or the Second World War'.

Apart from salvaging the scheduled Miami meeting of the Pope with Jewish leaders, the Pope and his advisors from the Secretariat of State and the Commission for Catholic–Jewish relations undertook to create, after reflection, a Vatican position document on the Shoah (the Holocaust) and its relationship to anti-Semitism. Another positive outcome from the débâcle was a valuable dialogue on the relationship between the Holy See and Israel, a subject that had preoccupied not only Jewish leaders but also the Reagan administration from 1980 onwards.

The American administration regarded Israel as a client state and took every opportunity to pressure the Vatican to enter full diplomatic relations with Israel. Cardinal Casaroli and his staff found themselves frequently explaining the Vatican position to American official visitors. The Vatican

'was very sympathetic to Israel: our officials and theirs consult often. A variety of Israeli leaders, Meir, Eban, Shamir, Peres had been received by a variety of Popes . . . we feel as friends. There is no question that the Vatican recognises Israel and as soon as possible, we will have formal relations. For the present we must continue without them.'

Casaroli enumerated a few of the problems to his American listeners:

'If we formalised our relations with Israel now (1987), it would prevent the Holy See from playing any role in bringing peace to the Middle East, because all of the Arab States except Egypt would break relations and stop talking to the Vatican if we exchange Ambassadors with Israel . . . There would also be a real danger to the Christian populations of Arab and other Islamic States. The status of Jerusalem is another grave issue. For a number of reasons we believe that the City should be internationalised . . . We also have a deep and continuing concern for the Palestinian people and their fate particularly their lack of a definitive homeland.'

The following year the Pope made a state visit to Austria. On the plane, a member of the travelling press corps asked him why he had received Kurt Waldheim when he stood accused of war crimes. He snapped at the reporter, 'He was elected democratically in a democratic country.' Virtually every other head of state in the world applied a different set of moral values and refused to invite Waldheim or accept his invitations. The United States went further and banned the former Secretary General of the United Nations from their country. The Pope continued to inflame the controversy, and demonstrate his own self-righteous stubbornness, when he arrived in Austria. He made a point of receiving Kurt Waldheim.

An extraordinary postscript to the Waldheim affair occurred seven years later. In 1994, when the full truth of Waldheim's wartime activities was public knowledge, Pope John Paul II granted him a knighthood. Among those that the Pope discussed the honouring of Waldheim with was Cardinal Ratzinger, possibly on this occasion not the most appropriate of papal advisors. As a former member of the Hitler youth movement and the Wehrmacht, the Cardinal's opinion might well have been open to misinterpretation. During a ceremony in Vienna on 6 July Waldheim was inducted into the *Ordine Piano* of Pius IX. Papal Nuncio Donato Squicciarini praised Waldheim for 'fighting for human rights on the fateful dividing line between West and East'.

Earlier that same year, this fraught relationship had been further strained by the beatification of Edith Stein. Born into the Jewish faith in 1891 this multi-talented modern-minded woman converted to Roman Catholicism at the age of 31 and entered the Carmelite order in the 1930s. She was arrested in the Netherlands along with other Jewish converts to Catholicism on 2 August 1942 and transported to Auschwitz-Birkenau where she was executed a week later. Jewish scholars argued that the sole reason she had been executed was because she was a Jew. They saw her beatification as an attempt to 'convert' the Holocaust to Christianity.

It was palpable nonsense, as the Pope demonstrated in his sermon during the beatification mass in Cologne on 1 May 1987. Speaking with great eloquence and a wonderful sensitivity, he confronted the issue head on:

'For Edith Stein, baptism as a Christian was by no means a break with her Jewish heritage. Quite on the contrary she said: "I had given up my practice of the Jewish religion as a girl of 14. My return to God made me feel Jewish again." She was always mindful of the fact that she was related to Christ "not only in a spiritual sense, but also in blood terms".'

He continued, 'In the extermination camp she died as a daughter of Israel "for the glory of the most Holy Name" and, at the same time, as Sister Teresa Benedicta of the Cross, literally "blessed by the Cross".'

With surviving members of Edith Stein's family among the congregation he concluded,

'Dear brothers and sisters, we bow today with the entire Church before this great woman whom from now on we may call one of the blessed in God's glory, before this great daughter of Israel, who found the fulfilment of her faith and her vocation for the people of God in Christ the saviour . . . She saw the inexorable approach of the cross. She did not flee . . . Hers was a synthesis of a history full of deep wounds, wounds that still hurt, and for the healing of which responsible men and women have continued to work up to the present day. At the same time it was a synthesis of the full truth (about) man, in a heart that remained restless and unsatisfied "until it finally found peace in God" . . . Blessed be Edith Stein, Sister Teresa Benedicta a Cruce, a true worshipper of God – in spirit and in truth. She is among the blessed. Amen.'

For a man who constantly proclaimed his commitment to that rapprochement, the Pope was capable of making remarkable blunders. During his 1991 visit to Poland he enraged the small surviving Jewish community, when he equated the Holocaust with the abortion issue, 'the great cemeteries of the unborn, cemeteries of the defenceless, whose faces even their own mothers never knew'.

When from time to time the Secretary of State Cardinal Casaroli was called upon to explain why the Holy See had yet to have full diplomatic relations with Israel there were two potent reasons that he never mentioned. For all the efforts of Karol Wojtyla and a great many others there was still within the Roman Curia a deeply imbedded suspicion of Israel born of an apparently indestructible anti-Semitism that refused to accept Pope John XXIII's courageous initiative that had led to *Nostra Aetate*. Although such attitudes flew in the face of all John Paul II's efforts to close the gap between the two faiths, this mattered little to the hard-core faction within the Curia who operated with stealth.

On Israel, the Roman Catholic Church had legitimate concerns which were openly expressed: Israel's refusal to negotiate on the Vatican's pursuit of international status for Jerusalem; the threat of restricted access to many sacred locations; the treatment of the Palestinians. Nonetheless, many within the Church were eager to claim the credit for the signing on 30 December 1993 of a 'Fundamental Agreement' between the Holy See and the State of Israel that led directly to the establishment of full diplomatic relations for which the Pope was particularly responsible.

The start of diplomatic relations with Israel did not mean the end of the historic controversies between the Roman

Catholic Church and the Jews. Eleven years after promising to create a Vatican position document on the Holocaust or the Shoah, *We Remember: A Reflection on The Shoah* was finally published in 1998. The Pope and his Commission for Religious Relations with the Jews rightly saw this latest statement as a continuation of previous significant initiatives, commencing with *Nostra Aetate* in 1965. He had hoped that this latest document 'will help to heal the wounds of past misunderstandings and injustices'. It received mixed reactions. Meir Lau, a Holocaust survivor and the Ashkenazi Chief Rabbi of Israel to the United States, described it as 'too little, too late'. At the other extreme, a fellow American Rabbi, Rabbi Jack Bemporad, saw it more positively and called it 'a spectacular document'.

Inevitably people skimmed the fourteen-page document and used the parts which propped up their own unchanging views. In the Pope's letter accompanying the document, he described the Shoah as 'an indelible stain on the history of a century that is coming to a close' and referred to its 'unspeakable iniquity'. The document itself was even more explicit.

> 'This century has witnessed an unspeakable tragedy, which can never be forgotten: the attempt by the Nazi regime to exterminate the Jewish people, with the consequent killing of millions of Jews. Women and men, old and young, children and infants for the sole reason of their Jewish origin, were persecuted and deported . . . Some were killed immediately, while others were degraded, ill treated, tortured and utterly robbed of their human dignity, and then murdered. Very few of those who entered the camps survived and those who did remained scarred for life. This was the Shoah. It is a major fact of the history of this century, a fact which still concerns us today.'

The document nonetheless caused great concern in its reading of history, when it appeared to overlook the Christian, and indeed papal, contribution to the attitudes which led to the Holocaust. It suggested that

'by the end of the seventeenth century and the beginning of the nineteenth century, Jews generally had achieved an equal standing with either citizens in most states and a certain number of them held influential positions in society.'

The document then identified the causes of anti-Semitism or (in its term) anti-Judaism in the nineteenth and twentieth centuries as

'a false and exacerbated nationalism . . . essentially more sociological than religious . . . In the twentieth century, National Socialism in Germany used these ideas (an affirmation of an original diversity of races) as a pseudo-scientific basis for a distinction between so called Nordic-Aryan races and supposedly inferior races.'

It was a breathtaking attempt to rewrite history. It made no mention of the sordid anti-Semitism of Pius IX (1846–78), who confined Jews to the Rome ghetto and called them 'dogs of whom there are too many present in Rome, howling and disturbing us everywhere'. On his orders a young Jewish boy, Edgardo Mirtara, was kidnapped by the Papal guard and brought up in the 'true faith' as the Pope's adopted 'son'. It also airbrushed his successor Leo XIII (1878–1903) and his reign that depicted Jews simultaneously as 'rich greedy capitalists' and 'dangerous socialists'. With Leo's approval in 1880 *La Civilta Cattolica* described the Jews as 'obstinate, dirty, thieves, liars, ignoramuses, pests . . . a barbarian invasion by an enemy race'. It also failed to mention the blood libel, which persisted among Roman Catholics well into the twentieth century, that Jews murdered Christians and drained their blood for Passover rites. It said nothing of the Catholic clergy in Poland who proclaimed anti-Semitism as frequently as they quoted the New Testament, including men like Jozef Kruszynski who wrote in 1920, the year of Karol Wojtyla's birth, 'If the world is to be rid of the Jewish scourge, it will be necessary to exterminate them, down to the last one.'

Several times within this reflection on the Shoah, however, regret and sorrow was expressed: 'for the failures of her (the Catholic Church's) sons and daughters in every age'. But nowhere did the Church acknowledge institutional failure. The document was especially provocative in extolling the virtues of the highly equivocal wartime Pope Pius XII, without honestly confronting his failings.

The Jubilee Year 2000 also saw an event with more lasting significance, a public apology by the Pope for the past errors of the Church. It was a stunning break from a tradition of never admitting wrong, which alarmed Roman Catholics in many countries. The Vatican panel of theologians admitted that 'there was no Biblical basis for Papal repentance' and that 'in no previous Holy Year since 1300' had there been 'any awareness of the faults in the Church's past or in the need to ask God's pardon'. The apology was expressed in a document *Memory And Reconciliation: The Church and The Faults of The Past*, based on three years' work by more than thirty scholars. In its fifty-one pages it did not attempt to enumerate all the wrongs perpetrated by the Church over the past 2,000 years.

The 'Church' was defined not merely as

'the historical institution alone or solely the spiritual communion of those whose hearts are illuminated by faith. The Church is understood as the community of the baptised, inseparably visible and operating in history under the direction of her pastors, united as a profound mystery by the action of the life-giving spirit.'

After a long, highly-detailed, historical and theological examination of the concept of forgiveness and various key elements of the Church and its place in history, the scholars turned to specific areas where events indicated the need to ask for forgiveness. These included the Catholic Church's role in the historic divisions that had occurred within Christianity and the use of force in the service of Truth. It went on to ask whether the Nazi persecution of the Jews

'was not made easier by the anti-Jewish prejudices embedded in some Christian minds and hearts . . . Did Christians give every possible assistance to those being persecuted and in particular to the persecuted Jews?'

The remarkable document showed a rare virtue under Wojtyla's papacy – humility. It led to an act by John Paul II that was also without precedent, when he declared 12 March 2000 a 'Day of Pardon'. He celebrated the Eucharist with a number of cardinals in the Vatican Basilica, and in his sermon stated that 'the Church can sing both the *Magnificat* for what God has accomplished within her and the *Miserere* for the sins of the Christians, for which she stands in need of purification, penance and renewal'.

'Given the number of sins committed in the course of twenty centuries,' said the Pope, any recital and request for pardon 'must necessarily be rather a summary.' He made it clear that this confession of sins was not addressed to anyone other than God 'who alone can forgive sins, but it is also made before men, from whom the responsibilities of Christians cannot be hidden'. During the service, the sins and errors quoted above from the *Memory and Reconciliation* document were proclaimed by members of the Curia. Many others were also confessed, including *Sins Committed in Actions Against Love, Peace, The Rights of Peoples*, and *Respect for Cultures and Religions; Sins against the Dignity of Women* and the *Unity of the Human Race*; and *Sins in Relation to the Fundamental Rights of the Person.*

Within hours of this act of self-abasement before a global audience of hundreds of millions, the Chief Rabbi of Israel, Israel Meir Lau, welcomed the papal plea for forgiveness but declared himself 'a little bit disappointed' that the Pope had made no mention of the Nazi Holocaust or the wartime role of Pius XII. A member of the Secretariat of State was still incandescent when I discussed the Chief Rabbi's response with him more than a year after the event.

> 'No matter what the Holy Father said it was never going to be enough. Sometimes they remind me of traders in the market place. The haggling. The hand-wringing. We've conceded so much to this small group of people.'
>
> 'Small group?' I questioned.
>
> 'Do you know how many Jews there are in this world?'
>
> 'Not the precise figure . . . fifteen million?'
>
> The member of the Curia moved his hands to a palm upwards position and raised his shoulders slightly as he nodded and smiled.

Less than two weeks later the Pope again expressed his grief at the Holocaust and 'the hatred, acts of persecution and displays of anti-Semitism directed against the Jews by

Christians at any time and in any place'. This time he was speaking at the Yad Vashem Holocaust Memorial in Israel. During this long-desired journey he visited Bethlehem and other historic locations. He also spent time in the Palestinian refugee camp of Dheisheh telling the thousands of refugees

'not to lose heart . . . the Church will continue to be at your side and will continue to plead your cause to the world . . . I call on the political leaders to implement agreements already in place.'

Historic controversies between Catholics and Jews are still very much alive in the twenty-first century. For example, a year-long study by a commission of three Catholics and three Jewish scholars of the Vatican's wartime policies and the role of Pius XII concluded that there were many hundreds of documents that had yet to be made available from Vatican archives. Critics of these investigations have argued that enough is enough and that the apologies given by the Pope should suffice. There is a growing belief that to apologise for the inaction of a generation long dead is meaningless and that further 'the drive to affix blame often ignores the actions by many Catholics – lay, priests and bishops – that saved thousands of Jews from genocide.' Critics have also suggested that the demands by the World Jewish Congress for further apologies have actually fed the growing anti-Semitism it fears.

Nostra Aetate demonstrated a Roman Catholic Church determined to unshackle itself from a specific historical position, one that it had held for nearly 2,000 years. Pope John Paul II had also travelled far from the Second World War and the subsequent three decades when he was one of the silent ones who did indeed 'pass by with indifference' but the myths of his 'involvement' to save and protect Jews in Poland still abound. On the twenty-fifth anniversary of his papacy, the Anti-Defamation League congratulated Pope John Paul II and proclaimed 'he has defended the Jewish people at all times, as a priest in his native Poland . . .' Not so: there was no Wojtyla defence of the Jews at that time. He asked God many times for forgiveness. His penance was to push forward, through numerous obstacles, towards the present time when the Roman Catholic Church has acquired a greater understanding and appreciation of Judaism. There is still much to be done, on both sides.

December 2003 was the tenth anniversary of the signing of the 'Fundamental Accord' that led to the establishment of full diplomatic relations between Israel and the Holy See in June 1994. The ensuing years have presented those within the Vatican who fought against the Accord with considerable ammunition and those who battled on behalf of the agreement with precious little to show for their efforts.

Israel has failed to enact the legislation that the agreement called for; failed to honour the agreements on Church properties within the Holy Land; consistently broken off talks without offering any explanation; failed to renew visas for Catholic missionaries working in the Holy Land; failed to agree terms on the promised economic accord; consistently failed to address Vatican concerns regarding Israel's so-called 'security wall' which has dispossessed Catholic communities from their lands and restricted access to churches and shrines in total violation of the Fundamental Accord; and in further violation of the Accord threatened to seize funds from Church-related institutions such as the Saint Louis Hospital which cares for the terminally ill. Despite every effort from Vatican diplomats and sharp prodding from the Bush administration, promises to address these issues have been followed by a refusal to resolve them. The Pope's initiatives, bravely taken in the face of considerable hostility, have over the past nineteen years been continuously trampled upon by successive Israeli governments. As of January 2007, Israel had still failed to implement any of the above.

Anti-Semitism is on the rise again throughout Europe, in the United Kingdom, France, Belgium, Germany, the Netherlands and the Pope's motherland. In Poland, a nationalistic radio station, Radio Maryja (Mary) controlled by Catholic priests, pumps out the old poison of 'Jewish conspiracies' and condemns 'American Jews' while the Polish Catholic hierarchy remains silent. Although the European Jewish Congress strenuously denies any linkage, the continuing Israel–Palestinian conflict is undoubtedly a primary cause of rising anti-Semitism.

At the end of March 2004 a movie loomed large over the relationship between the Holy See and worldwide Jewry: *The Passion of the Christ*, made by Mel Gibson, a man committed to a singular branch of Catholicism and a set of secular myths.

Gibson defended himself from charges that his film was anti-Semitic and said that he was 'well aware of the evil of anti-Semitism and I oppose it'. He added that 'as an Irish-Catholic-Australian I know more than a bit about religious and social prejudice and relate to Jews as fellow sufferers.'

That the film does not confine itself to the Gospel sources, that there are totally fictional scenes and elements in the Gibson version of Christ's last twelve hours is self-evident. That is of course any filmmaker's right but it undermines the claim of authenticity. The source for the additional material is Anne Catherine Emmerich, an Augustinian nun born in Germany in 1774. An alleged stigmatic and ecstatic, her 'visions' were written down by Clemens Brentano and subsequently published. They include grotesque anti-Semitic characterisations of Jews, an aspect that Gibson has clearly seized upon and used within his film. Mel Gibson's father believes that Vatican Council II was 'a

Masonic plot backed by the Jews' and is also on record as denying the full size and magnitude of the Holocaust. His son does not embrace such views but shares with his father the belief that the papal throne has remained vacant since the death of Pius XII and that the election of John XXIII was fraudulent, which would also void all subsequent elections. It is curious that the film-maker should have sought papal approval of his film from a man that he considers to be a 'false Pope'.

Both Opus Dei and the Legionnaires of Christ have played key roles as active supporters of Mel Gibson and his movie. Members of the Legionnaires arranged a number of private screenings to very carefully selected invited audiences of influential people. Opus Dei arranged two particular private screenings for the Pope in his private apartments within the Vatican. The Pope usually refrained from expressing public opinions on artistic works. Privately he is alleged to have said, 'It is as it was.' The only other person in the room was his personal secretary and friend for forty years, Archbishop Stanislaw Dziwisz. To the general embarrassment of the Vatican the alleged remark was given global publicity as a papal endorsement of a film, already being attacked by many as being rabidly anti-Semitic. Dziwisz denied that the Pope had ever expressed an opinion, which came as a surprise to one of its producers, Steve McEveety, who had heard it directly from Dziwisz.

The papal spokesman and Opus Dei member Navarro-Valls privately e-mailed McEveety on the alleged comment: 'Nobody can deny it. So keep mentioning it as the authorised point of reference. I would try to make the words, "It is as it was" the leitmotif in any discussion on the film.' The e-mail concluded: 'Repeat the words again and again and again.'

The private screenings, courtesy of the Legionnaires of Christ, were also paying rich dividends with a series of powerful endorsements from Curial heavyweights and theologians. Opinion was manipulated long before public release of the movie. These events powerfully underline the current level of control exercised within the Vatican by Opus Dei, the Legionnaires of Christ and other extreme reactionary forces. With that kind of endorsement, global success was guaranteed and it duly followed. The film has been both acclaimed and denounced. Some have described it as powerfully conveying the core of Christianity; others regard it as virulently anti-Semitic. By the end of 2004 Gibson was £200 million richer and the Pope had beatified Emmerich.

Its long-term influence remains to be seen, but one must wonder whether the late Pope's succinct reaction came not from his knowledge of the Gospels but from his experiences as a child and young man watching the Passion Plays at Kalwaria.

In July 2006 after being arrested in Malibu, California, on suspicion of driving under the influence of alcohol, Gibson launched into a tirade that included anti-Semitic statements, 'Fucking Jews. The Jews are responsible for all the wars in the world . . .' The following day a contrite Gibson issued a statement that talked of his shame and admitted that he has 'battled with the disease of alcoholism for all of my adult life and profoundly regret my horrific relapse'.

Chapter 9

Beyond Belief

ACCORDING TO JOHN PAUL II and many of his bishops, 'modern society' is to blame for the epidemic of sexual abuse by priests, monks, brothers and nuns of victims ranging from young boys and girls to handicapped adolescents, religious and lay women. But 'modern society' is a catch-all phrase which means everything and nothing. In fact, the problem of priestly sexual abuse goes back to the second century. When Karol Wojtyla was elected Pope in October 1978, alongside the financial corruption of the Vatican Bank was the equally rampant moral corruption of sexual abuse within the priesthood. Over the previous 1,800 years the 'secret system' had evolved that had not eliminated the problem of sexual abuse but covered it up. Its efficiency can be gauged from the fact that before the Gauthe case in 1985/86 (see below) public allegations of sexual abuse by priests were very rare. The exposure of a priest either in criminal or civil proceedings was simply unheard of.

The Roman Catholic Church looked after its own, and offending clerics could not be brought before civil courts unless special permission was obtained to do so. The system was one that clearly had the full approval of Pope John Paul II. In 1983, after twenty-four years' deliberation, the current Code of Canon Law was published and among the many changes from the previous 1917 Code, Law 119 covering the need for special permission was removed. It was a decision that many of the Catholic hierarchy have since bitterly regretted. In less than two years, the floodgates had been opened. Within a decade the cost of sexual abuse to the Roman Catholic Church at every level was devastating. In the United States alone, since 1984 the financial cost in legal fees and awards to the sexually abused is in excess of $1 billion. The cost to the image and reputation of the Catholic hierarchy is inestimable.

It is very unlikely that the Pope was unaware of the scale of the problem at his election, and of the traditional response of the secret system. Up until 1981, he had ignored every request for help from victims of clerical abuse to himself and to various Vatican congregations. The origins of the 'Secret System', like the crimes it kept hidden, go back a very long way in history. Prior to 1869 when the description 'homosexual' was first coined by Karl Maria Benkert, the term used to describe sexual acts between two or more of the same gender was 'sodomy'. Sodomy was used to describe not only sexual acts between adult males but also sexual intercourse with animals and sexual abuse of a child or youth. This latter act was also frequently described as 'pederasty'. The term 'paedophile' was first used by the physiologist Havelock Ellis in 1906. Current scientific usage defines the sexual abuser of a pre-pubescent as a paedophile and the sexual abuser of an adolescent as an ephebophile.

As early as AD 177, Bishop Athenagoras characterised adulterers and pederasts as enemies of Christianity and subjected them to excommunication, then the harshest penalty the Church could inflict. The Council of Elvira in 305 enlarged on this earlier condemnation as did the Council of Ancrya in 314.

An invaluable source of information on the subject is the body of penitential literature dating from the seventh century. The penitential books were handbooks compiled by priests and used by them in hearing the individual confessions of members of the Church. A number of them refer to sexual crimes committed by clerics against young boys and girls. The Penitential of Bede, dating from England in the eighth century, advises that clerics who commit sodomy with children be given increasingly severe penances commensurate with their rank. Laymen who committed such crimes were excommunicated and made to fast for three years; clerics not in holy orders had the fasting period extended to five years; deacons and priests seven and ten years respectively and bishops who sexually abused children were given twelve years of penance.

The Catholic Church during the first millennium clearly took a more severe position on sexual abuse by clerics than it has taken in more recent times. The first millennium writings make no special pleadings on the basis of ignorance, nor do they ignore the fact that paedophiles do not confine themselves to one single act of sexually abusing a child. They do not blame the lay public's lack of morals, or accuse the faithful of deliberately tempting the priests. However, there is evidence to suggest that paedophile priests were quietly moved to another diocese. Most significantly the supreme head of the Church took notice when his attention was drawn to widespread sexual abuse by his priests and bishops, but then failed to act upon many of the recommendations that had been made.

Probably the most important piece of evidence that has survived from the early Church is *Liber Gomorrhianus – the Book of Gomorrah* – composed by St Peter Damian around AD 1051. The work denounces the widespread extent of active sodomy then being indulged in by the clergy of the day and demands that the Pope should take decisive action. Damian was a priest at the time he wrote the book.

He was highly regarded by a succession of Popes and became a bishop and then a cardinal.

The book is written with great clarity. Damian was a would-be Church reformer of a wide range of practices. One of his particular preoccupations was the sexual immorality of the clergy and the tolerance of Church superiors who were either equally culpable or declined to act against the abusers. The sexual activities of priests with young boys particularly appalled him.

He called for the exclusion of sodomites from ordination and, if already ordained, that they should be dismissed from Holy Orders. He was contemptuous of priests who 'defile men or boys who have come to them for confessions'. He castigated 'clerics who administer the sacrament of penance through confession to those they have just sodomised'. Damian assessed the damage being done to the Church by the abusers and his final chapter was an appeal to Pope Leo IX to take immediate action. Leo praised the author and independently confirmed the truth of his findings; however, his actions have a curiously contemporary ring about them.

Damian's recommendations concerning the range of punishments were largely modified. The Pope decided to remove only those prelates who had repeatedly abused over a long period of time. Although Damian had addressed at length the damage caused by the priests upon their victims, the Pope made no mention of this and instead focused only on the sinfulness of the clerics and their need to repent. Leo's response matches that of John Paul II over the period October 1978 to April 2002. On 25 April 2002, he finally defined child abuse as a 'crime'. Previously it had merely been a 'sin'. The former can be dealt with in the secular courts; the latter is the exclusive domain of the Church.

Nearly 100 years after the publication of Damian's book, *The Decree of Gratian*, published in 1140, confirmed that clerical paedophilia was still a flourishing activity. Gratian included specific references to the violation of boys and argued that clerics found guilty of pederasty should suffer the same penalties as laymen, including the death penalty. Gratian's book, widely considered the primary source of canon-law history, also recommended that if the death penalty were considered too harsh, those found guilty of sexual crimes against children should be excommunicated. At the time this was a particularly severe punishment since it meant that the individual was shunned by society for the rest of his life. But no matter how severe the punishment, the crime continued unremittingly.

In his *Divine Comedy: Inferno* – written in the early fourteenth century – Dante wandering through hell encounters a wide variety of sodomites including a group of priests and a former bishop of Florence, Andrea de Mozzi, recently descended from Earth.

Sixteenth-century canon laws urged bishops to admonish and punish priests whose lives were 'depraved and scandalous'; punishments included cutting them off from all financial support. A papal decree entitled *Horrendum* dated 30 August 1568, declared, 'Priests who abuse are deprived of all offices, benefices, degraded and turned over to secular courts for additional punishment'.

The secret system that protects the clerical sex abuser was functioning effectively as far back at least as the early part of the seventeenth century when the founder of the Piarist Order, Father Joseph Calasanz, suppressed the sexual abuse of children by his priests from becoming public knowledge. One such paedophile, Father Stefano Cherubini, the member of a well-connected Vatican family, was so successful at covering up his crimes he even succeeded in becoming head of the Order. It took fifteen years of complaints against him and other senior members of the Order before action was taken by Pope Innocent X and the Order was temporarily closed down. As historian Karen Liebreich, in *Fallen Order* shows, the seventeenth-century secret system had a very modern ring, including 'promotion for avoidance' – elevate the abuser away from his victims.

Until the 1980s, John Paul II and many of his cardinals and bishops, including Cardinal Ratzinger, chose to ignore centuries of sexual abuse by priests. There is undeniably a direct unbroken line which stretches back over centuries from the present scandals of paedophile priests to the first millennium. Wherever one looks in the present furore, there are powerful echoes of the dim past.

Recently yet another secret Vatican document concerning the crime of solicitation has surfaced. The document, *Instructions on the Manner of Proceeding in Cases of Solicitation*, deals with the crime of a priest attempting to procure sexual favours from an individual whose confession he is hearing. It was published by the Prefect of the Holy Office, Cardinal Alfredo Ottaviani, with the approval of the then Pope, John XXIII, in March 1962. The document has never been made available to the general public. The distribution list was confined to 'Patriarchs, Archbishops, Bishops and Other Diocesan Ordinaries'. Among those receiving a copy would have been the newly promoted Bishop of Cracow, Karol Wojtyla.

It deals with the secret trial arrangements of any cleric charged with the offence. The document has recently been described by lawyers as 'a blueprint for deception and concealment' while apologists have argued that as the Sacrament of Penance is protected by a shroud of absolute secrecy, the procedures for dealing with this 'ecclesiastical' crime also invoke secrecy, putting the offender above the criminal law of the land. This was precisely the position that the Vatican has taken for many centuries on all acts of clerical paedophilia perpetrated in or out of the confessional box.

The 1962 Holy Office instructions for 'addressing this unspeakable crime' go to remarkable lengths to ensure total secrecy. The victim must lodge a complaint within 'thirty days' of the crime. Failure to do so will mean the victim's automatic excommunication. As the victim was often a young child, that particular directive beggars belief. The alleged perpetrator was able to 'be transferred to another assignment unless the Ordinary of the place has forbidden it'. Both the perpetrator and the victim are ordered to observe 'perpetual silence', under pain of excommunication. Again an element of the secret system has come into play. 'The oath of keeping the secret must be given in these cases also by the accusers or those denouncing the priest and the witnesses.' Chapter Five of the document, entitled 'The Worst Crime', states 'by the name of the worst crime is understood at this point evidence of any obscene, external deed, gravely sinful act, perpetrated by a cleric or attempted with a person of his own sex or attempted by him with youths of either sex or with brute animals (bestiality)'.

The 1962 document powerfully illustrates a twentieth-century Church still struggling with the same crimes that St Peter Damian addressed over one thousand years earlier. But unlike Damian the modern approach aspired to ensure that not only the crime of solicitation but all sexual crimes committed by members of religious orders were covered up as far as possible. In addition, the document implicitly acknowledged that error, vice, depravity, immorality and vile, vicious, worthless behaviour are found only among the flock and never among the shepherds.

In 1984 the first 'clergy malpractice' lawsuit in the United States by an adult woman was instigated by a Los Angeles lawyer on behalf of Rita Milla. More than two decades of stunning revelations of sexual abuse were ushered in by one of the forgotten victims. Like so many victims, Rita Milla was first abused by her priest while taking her confession.

Father Santiago Tamayo reached through the flimsy screen within the confessional and caressed the breasts of Rita Milla, who was sixteen and planning to become a nun. Over the next two years he systematically set about seducing Rita. On that first occasion he told her in the confessional that he had a secret and as she leaned forward he opened the screen and kissed her. By the time she was eighteen in 1979, after being repeatedly advised by the priest that 'God wants you to do all you can to keep his priests happy . . . it is your duty', Rita and her confessor were having regular sexual intercourse. Father Santiago then began to put pressure on the young woman to make his fellow priests at St Philomena Church in Los Angeles happy too. First one, then a second, then a third. Eventually Rita was making seven priests 'happy'. None of them took any precautions and in 1980 she became pregnant.

Father Tamayo persuaded her to go to the Philippines to hide her pregnancy. Her parents remained unaware and were told she was going abroad to 'study medicine'. The group of priests gave her $450 to last seven months and told her to leave the baby in Manila. Rita was critically ill during childbirth and nearly died of eclampsia, convulsions occurring at the end of pregnancy as a result of blood poisoning. Her family discovered the truth and brought both Rita and her baby daughter back to Los Angeles. This happened after Bishop Abaya in the Philippines had undertaken to give her financial assistance, not merely to cover her travelling expenses but towards the upkeep and education of the baby. When that aid failed to materialise, Rita went to Bishop Ward in her Californian diocese, who also was unable to help. It was only then that Rita and her mother filed the landmark clergy malpractice suit. They sought to establish paternity, sue the priest and the Church for civil conspiracy, for breach of fiduciary duty, fraud, deceit and 'to protect other young women from the pain and suffering caused by priests who abused their position of trust'.

The case was dismissed by the courts who cited a one-year statutory time limitation. When attorney Gloria Allred called a press conference in 1984 to draw attention to the case it transpired that all seven priests had vanished. Far from following the precise steps ordered by the Vatican in such cases, the Los Angeles archdiocese had ordered all of them to leave the country and to stay abroad until further notice. It would be 1991 before the role of the archdiocese was made public by a guilt-stricken and remorseful Father Tamayo. Letters also confirmed that the archdiocese had regularly sent money not to Rita but to her abusers hiding in the Philippines.

In August 2003 Rita's baby, now the twenty-year-old Jacqueline Milla, finally learned that her father was Valentine Tugade, one of the seven priests who had had sex with her mother. This was confirmed by a court-ordered paternity test. Tamayo, the man who had manipulated the sixteen-year-old Rita, publicly apologised to her in 1991 and admitted his role in the affair. Nonetheless, the only financial compensation that Rita has ever received was a $20,000 trust fund set up by the Los Angeles Church in 1988 for her daughter and this was done only after Rita had finally agreed to drop a slander action against a bishop. The Church lawyer insisted that the fund was not an admission of liability but 'an act of benevolence for the child'.

The initial cover-up by the Catholic Church had been orchestrated by Cardinal Timothy Manning. When he was succeeded as Archbishop of Los Angeles by Bishop Roger Mahony the cover-up and the payments to the fugitive priests from the archdiocese continued. No action was ever taken against Cardinal Manning by Cardinal Ratzinger's Congregation for the Doctrine of the Faith, the CDF, the department responsible for canonical discipline, or against any of his subordinates or against Mahony and his staff. Roger Mahony was subsequently made a cardinal by John Paul II. Father Tamayo was eventually stripped of his priesthood by Mahony, not for the repeated sexual abuse of Rita Milla, but for getting married to another woman. After it had been established by the Los Angeles court that Father Tugade was the father of the child, Cardinal Mahony declined all requests for an interview, but the same week during a visit to Rome he told a local reporter, 'I have a zero-tolerance policy towards abusive priests.'

Before the recent appearance of the stillborn policy of zero tolerance, sex abuse cases, not just in California but throughout the world, were effectively contained by using the 'secret system' which had been perfected over a very long time. When the abuse of a child became known to the parents their first instinct was not to call in the police but to go seeking help from the local bishop. Depending on the evidence, the bishop would usually follow a well-trodden path. If the bishop felt that the evidence justified the priest's removal he would be transferred to another diocese. If he was an established repeat offender he might be sent to one of a number of rehabilitation centres. In the United States these included a number run by Servants of the Paraclete. They also have a centre in Gloucestershire in the United Kingdom. There are rehabilitation centres in many countries. These offer counselling and support to alcoholic, homosexual and paedophile clergy.

The more usual practice until very recently was to move the offending priest to a new location or parish without alerting anyone of the potential risk. In cases where the parents showed a strong inclination to sue, they would be persuaded to accept an out-of-court settlement on the basis of strict non-disclosure. The insurance companies preferred it that way too. A case that went before court and jury would very likely produce a far greater sum of damages than a quiet deal with the parents pressurised by their Church. Publicity was to be avoided. Apart from the damage to the Church's image and reputation, a public hearing would alert other victims. In some cases the Church would pay medical bills for psychological counselling, but not always.

Until 1985 that was how the secret system worked (and in many countries, including Italy, Spain, Germany and Poland, still functions). The case that Rita Milla had attempted to bring went nowhere. It would take a great deal more than that to shake the system and it was not long in surfacing.

In January 1985 in Boise, Idaho, Father Mel Baltazar was sentenced to seven years' imprisonment after pleading guilty to a reduced charge of lewd behaviour with a minor. Baltazar's plea-bargaining was a shrewd move as diocesan records showed a history of continuous sexual abuse by the priest over a twenty-year period. The victims were invariably young boys. He abused a critically ill boy on a kidney dialysis machine in a hospital in California. He abused another young boy in double leg traction in a Medical Centre in Boise. Baltazar had previously been dismissed from his post as chaplain in the US Navy for homosexual behaviour. Subsequently he had been transferred from three dioceses for sexually abusive behaviour. His superiors, with full knowledge of his record, took no action when confronted by distraught parents other than to transfer him to a new diocese.

Among those unimpressed with the Catholic Church's approach to the problem was the trial judge Alan Schwartzman. When passing sentence he paused to stare unblinkingly at the priest standing before him, then observed: 'I think the Church has its own atonement to make as well. They helped create you and hopefully will help rehabilitate you.'

The pace of clerical exposure was beginning to quicken. In February 1985 a priest in Wisconsin was accused of sexually abusing a number of minors. In March a Milwaukee priest resigned his licence as a psychologist after admitting sexually abusing a patient. In April Father William O'Donnell of Bristol, Rhode Island, was indicted on twenty-two counts of sexual abuse. He was subsequently sentenced to one year's imprisonment. The same month in San Diego another priest paid to settle a pending action accusing him of sexually abusing an altar boy.

The abuse of altar boys was also a trait of Father Gilbert Gauthe, who at the time of his initial exposure in June 1983 was a parish priest in the parish of Henry, in Vermilion, Louisiana. The revelations began with a pathetic simplicity. A distressed nine-year-old boy confessed to his mother that God did not love him because he had done 'bad things'. The child slowly and painfully elaborated and talked of the secrets that he and Father Gauthe shared. First his mother then his father listened as the boy began to reveal some shocking truths. The priest had been sexually abusing him for at least two years. Gauthe had also been abusing his two elder brothers. Before the story was all told, it would be estimated that Father Gauthe had molested more than 100 boys in four parishes, some of them many hundreds of times. Learning the truth as far back as the early 1970s the Church had responded in the usual manner: they moved him to another parish. An early report on Gauthe described his problem as 'a case of misguided affection'.

Confronted with the initial allegations Gauthe made no attempt to deny them. He began to cry. He asked to be sent way for treatment and said he needed help. He made no mention of the urgent help that his many victims also needed. Told he was being immediately suspended from all duties for an indefinite period of time, he raised no objection and meekly signed his acknowledgement of the

written declaration of suspension. His superior ordered
Gauthe to get out of the village of Henry. Gauthe's initial
remorse was short-lived. When he returned to the village ten
days later to collect his personal belongings he found time
to contact his eldest current victim, a fifteen-year-old boy.
Before leaving the parish he had sex with him.

The secret system was very much in evidence in the
Vermilion Parish from June 1983 right through to the
summer of 1984. Gauthe's bemused congregation were
told initially that his abrupt departure was due to 'health
reasons'. Moral pressure was brought by the diocese to bear
on the Catholic lawyer, Paul Herbert, retained by a number
of victims' families. Monsignor Richard Mouton had urged
the lawyer to be 'a good ol' Catholic boy'. Bishop Frey
tightened the screw, counselling 'caution' upon a number of
parents, advising that they avoid civil proceedings to 'avoid
scandal and harm to the Church, but primarily to avoid
further injury or trauma to the young victims, their families
and other innocent parties'.

The families of nine of the victims were prevailed upon to
drop their civil legal action that would inevitably trigger
wide publicity when it moved to a public hearing. They
were told that Father Gauthe would be sent to the House of
Affirmation, a rehabilitation centre for the clergy in Massachusetts. The majority of the families bowed to the intense
pressure from their spiritual leaders and eventually agreed
that a secret settlement was in the best interests of everyone.
By June 1984 after six months' haggling the two sides had
agreed on a $4.2 million settlement to be spread between six
families with nine victims. Out of that sum the lawyers took
about $1.3 million, the various medical experts another
portion.

Although many details of Gauthe's sexual abuse were
known, nothing had been published at the time of the
settlement in June 1984. It might well have remained a

secret scandal except for one brave family and their courageous son. The only way that some of the families discovered that one or more of their children had been violated by Gauthe was when a neighbour whose own child admitted that he had been abused went on to name other victims. Within the close-knit community, a list of names began to escalate. It was in this manner that Glenn and Faye Gastal discovered that their nine-year-old son had been abused.

The Catholic Church in Louisiana, from Archbishop Phillip Hannan down, strained every sinew to ensure that the Gauthe scandal remained a private matter. They sought to stop the issue coming to trial, for as long as none of the victims testified before a Grand Jury, no indictment could be handed down. The strategy of out-of-court settlements appeared to be working but neither the local Church, the papal nuncio's office in Washington nor the Vatican had bargained for the Gastal family. The parents deeply resented the secret suppression of the truth, as in their mind this treated them as criminals. They would neither be silenced nor cut a deal and were determined that their son would testify before a Grand Jury. Encouraged by the collective bravery of the Gastals, other families rallied to their cause. In August 1984 Glenn and Faye Gastal gave their first hesitant television interview. They were unlikely heroes but the impact and the effects of their stand are still reverberating not only around the United States of America but also much of the rest of the world.

The Secretariat of State within the Vatican were deeply shocked by the Gastals' defiance and began to exert more pressure, both on Archbishop Pio Laghi, the Vatican nuncio to the USA and on Archbishop Hannan down in New Orleans. Reports were coming in from many dioceses throughout the United States of other actions being filed. Encouraged by the Gastals, other victims were emerging from the twilight existence imposed on them by their own clergy. At no time did Pope John Paul II, Cardinal Ratzinger, Cardinal Casaroli or any of the other senior Vatican luminaries consider the alternative course of action: candid confession, humble contrition and public commitment to attack this particular cancer and eradicate it.

In October 1984 a Grand Jury viewed videotapes containing the testimony of eleven boys ranging in age from nine to seventeen and returned a thirty-four-count indictment against Father Gilbert Gauthe. Eleven counts were for aggravated crimes against nature, another eleven for committing sexually immoral acts, another eleven for taking pornographic photographs of juveniles and a single count of aggravated rape – sodomising a child under twelve years of age. The final count carried a mandatory life sentence. The trial was set for 11 October and as that date approached the Vatican increased pressure on Father Gauthe's defence counsel, Ray Mouton, to find a compromise that would enable a plea-bargaining deal. When Mouton, whose first interest was his client, insisted on negotiating with the District Attorney and the prosecuting counsel in his own manner rather than the Vatican way, the New Orleans archdiocese attempted to fire him. Nonetheless, Ray Mouton outflanked him and carried on negotiating.

Hannan then changed tack, after concluding that working with the defence counsel the Church had hired might be more productive than working against him and a deal was finally cut. Gauthe would plead guilty on all counts and would be sentenced to twenty years' imprisonment without parole. It was sold to the judge, who sought reassurance before the hearing that the victims who were nerving themselves to testify and their families would be content with the proposed sentence. The prosecuting counsel assured the families that come what may and wherever he served sentence, Gauthe would be locked up for twenty years.

Despite everything, most of those listening to the proposition were still devout Roman Catholics. When prosecuting counsel murmured about the need to protect the Church it was a done deal. On Tuesday 14 October, accompanied by Ray Mouton, Father Gauthe entered the Louisiana courtroom and faced Judge Brunson. He pleaded guilty to all thirty-four counts and was duly sentenced to the agreed twenty years. With the sentences went these words from the judge:

> 'Your crimes against your child victims have laid a terrible burden on those children, their families and society, indeed, your God and your Church as well. It may be that God in his infinite mercy may find forgiveness for your crimes, but the imperative of justice, and the inescapable need of society to protect its most defenceless and vulnerable members, the children, cannot.'

The victims had been spared the searing ordeal of giving evidence in a public arena. The Church had been spared the long-term damage from such public testimony and, through the dubious arrangement of a plea bargain, justice of a sort had been achieved.

Between the end of the court hearing and sentencing of Gauthe and the civil case that the Gastal family had brought, great pressure was again exerted by the Catholic Church on Glenn and Faye Gastal to settle the case out of court and consequently out of the public's gaze. The Gastals believed that the harm that had been done to their family and, in particular, to their young son merited a larger settlement than that accepted by the other families but more than that, they wanted the facts of what Gauthe had done to their son laid out before the court and the wider world. Many ostracised them as a result and treated them like criminals, and there was talk that the lawsuit was a costly unnecessary expense. The Church had offered to settle out of court; it was just those damn stubborn Gastals that were preventing the whole wretched affair from being forgotten. And that for the Gastal family was precisely the point of putting their son through this emotional trial of obliging him to publicly recount every sordid detail.

During the hearing, attended by a variety of Catholic clerics including Bishop Frey and Monsignor Mouton, Faye Gastal was asked by her lawyer, 'When you look at Bishop Frey here, what goes through your mind?' Faye Gastal was a devout Catholic who had earlier testified that 'getting absolution is the only way to get to heaven'. Now she stared for a moment across the courtroom. 'When I look at Monsignor Mouton and Bishop Frey, I think of Gauthe sticking his penis in my child's mouth, ejaculating in his mouth, putting his penis in his rectum. That's what I think about.'

The worst nightmares of the Catholic Church hierarchy were unfolding in front of them. The Church was doing all it could to suppress the truth, including phoning organisations and companies that advertised regularly in the *Times* of Acadiana, a local paper that had withstood Church pressure to censor its coverage of the Gauthe affair. The advertisers were urged to boycott the paper.

'We were a close, loving family, still are,' said Glenn Gastal, 'except when it comes to the relationship which I can't have with my son as a young child. He is unable to tolerate physical displays of affection . . .' In the witness box the father broke down, then struggling to gain control he continued, 'He kissed me only if I demanded it before he went to bed.'

The judge cleared the courtroom before the son testified but the presence of the press, including Jason Berry, the source of the quoted court testimony, would ensure that the words of the child would be a matter of public record.

In the State of Louisiana a jury is not allowed to award punitive damages. The award must be 'fair and reasonable' for the damages sustained. This jury did not stay out for a long time, just one hour forty-five minutes and awarded $1 million for the Gastals' son and $250,000 for the parents. The Gastals' greatest victory lay not in the wholly inadequate monetary awards but in breaching an enormous dam. When the verdict had been announced, the lawyer acting for the Catholic Church declared that his client would appeal the settlement. They had no intention of doing so – it would have undoubtedly resulted in yet more adverse publicity – but the Gastals were vulnerable to such apparent obduracy and, as a result, the Church were able to haggle the settlement figure down. Of the eventual figure of $1,000,020 the Gastals' lawyer took one third plus his expenses.

The plea-bargaining deal cut behind closed doors called for Gauthe to serve the full twenty years. In 1998 a sympathetic judge looked favourably upon Father Gauthe's parole application and released him after less than twelve years. A few months later he was arrested for sexually molesting an underage boy and placed on probation.

Ten months before the criminal trial of Father Gauthe and more than a year before the civil proceedings brought by the Gastal family, three men from diverse walks of life were brought together by the Gauthe case and its implications. One was Ray Mouton, the lawyer hired by the archdiocese of Louisiana to defend Father Gilbert Gauthe. If one wanted a lawyer with a street-fighting mentality who would go the extra mile for his client, a man of courage as well as integrity, then Ray Mouton was the man. At times hard-drinking, at times filling the air with colourful expletives, he cared deeply about the concept of justice. To take the Gauthe case needed no little courage, particularly when some of the facts became public knowledge. Mouton believed that everyone was entitled to the best possible defence. Ray Mouton's occasional profanities masked the soul of a God-fearing Roman Catholic.

The second was Father Michael Peterson, a psychiatrist in charge of a rehabilitation programme for priests at St Luke Institute in Suitland, Maryland. Peterson, the founder of the Institute, had a boundless compassion for others, all the more remarkable because for many years he was confronted with case histories of patients without virtue or humanity. As a man with an acknowledged expertise in sexual pathologies he was repeatedly called upon by dioceses throughout the country to deal with priests who had transgressed.

Ray Mouton was in Washington to meet Peterson and explore the possibilities of his client going to the St Luke Institute for evaluation and treatment. He had been put in contact with Peterson by the third member of this triumvirate, Father Thomas Doyle, secretary-canonist of the Apostolic Delegation in Washington DC. As canonist at the Vatican embassy, Doyle had been given the task by papal nuncio Archbishop Laghi of monitoring the correspondence on the Gauthe case and keeping a close watching brief on every development. Father Thomas Doyle was clearly destined for great things. Promotion to bishop was considered by many who knew him as a certainty, a cardinal's hat a strong possibility. An expert in canon law, with other doctorates in Political Science, Philosophy and Theology, also a prolific writer, Doyle could boast a daunting list of achievements.

The two priests were friends and collaborators but Ray Mouton was unknown to them until the Gauthe case. As Father Peterson discussed the various treatment options that were available at St Luke's, the lawyer talked not only of his own client but other priests in Louisiana who were paedophiles, men whose crimes had been covered up by the diocese, men who still held positions of trust among their unknowing communities. As always with Mouton, his primary concern was not to alert Catholic officialdom but to protect his client. If it became public knowledge that the Gauthe case was not unique, the District Attorney Nathan Stansbury would be unlikely to take a soft approach on Gauthe in any plea-bargaining scenario. Any chance of Father Gauthe being merely hospitalised or confined in a secure facility where he could receive treatment would fly out of the window. Because of his professional work, Father Peterson was already aware that there were other paedophiles within the ranks of the clergy and not just in Louisiana. He phoned Father Doyle, telling him that the three of them urgently needed to hold a meeting.

As Doyle listened to the two men detailing other paedophilic activity in Lafayette and much further afield, he was shocked. As the eyes and ears of the Vatican on the Gauthe case, he had assumed that this was an isolated case. As Peterson talked of the information he had received from 'confidential sources' of priests 'all over the USA who have sexually abused children' the three men rapidly realised that a bishop with a legal background should be sent to manage the Gauthe crisis and that urgent action was needed to address the problem at a national level.

After briefing Archbishop Laghi and senior officials within the Vatican it was agreed to send Bishop Quinn of Cleveland to Lafayette. With the Gauthe civil case looming, it was apparent to all three men that the Catholic Church in the United States was about to confront an unimaginable disaster and that the sooner they were aware of that fact and prepared to meet it, the better. Tom Doyle recalled,

'Within a short time we had decided to collect information and put together a manual or a book that would be set up in a question and answer format. The full edition would also contain copies of several medical articles about paedophilia. Most of these were taken from medical journals and several were authored by Dr Fred Berlin of the Johns Hopkins University Hospital Sexual Disorders Clinic.'

The 100-page document was a detailed guide to damage limitation for the American Church hierarchy. It was also an attempt to make those who controlled the Church face reality. The authors believed that the days of the cover-up, of reliance on Catholic judges and attorneys and favourably disposed newspaper, television and radio proprietors were numbered. The manual dealt with every conceivable aspect of the problems confronting a bishop when allegations of sexual child abuse were made against one of his priests or a member of one of the religious orders. Without specifically identifying the Gauthe case, the writers drew on the fiscal implications of that 'catastrophe' the cost of which 'exceeds $5 million and the projected cost of the civil cases in that diocese alone is in excess of $10 million'.

The authors, three men whose motivation in creating this document was to protect the Catholic Church, did not pull their punches:

'It is not hyperbolic to state that the dramatic description of the actual case [the Gauthe case] referred to above is indicative that a real, present danger exists. That other cases exist and are arising with increased frequency is evidenced by reports of same. If one could accurately predict, with actuarial soundness, that our exposure to similar claims, namely one offender and fifteen or so claimants, over the next ten years could be restricted and limited to the occurrence of one hundred such cases against the Church then an estimate of the total projected losses for the decade could be established of one billion dollars.'

The authors subsequently described that figure as 'a conservative cost projection'. History was to prove them correct. One section entitled 'Clergy Malpractice' predicted that as lawyers began to exhaust medical malpractice as a source of income they would see the Roman Catholic Church in the USA as a 'potential deep pocket'. Over the ensuing years, many a lawyer in the United States has grown rich from the litigation they have undertaken on behalf of the sexually abused. A number of victims living in Boston have alleged to me that their respective lawyers not only took a substantial part of the settlement figure as their fee, plus more for their expenses, but that they also received from the archdiocese a 'commission' for persuading their client to settle at a specified amount. As one victim put it: 'As a boy I was screwed by my priest. As a man I was screwed by my lawyer.' Independent evidence that substantiates these allegations has proved elusive.

The authors predicted a monstrous explosion of problems for the Church: hundreds of people going public with accusations of appalling crimes, bishops ineptly handling the response and a bill of over $1 billion. In making such a warning the two priests had done no favours to their careers.[11] They had therefore attempted to take out some insurance of their own. As previously recorded, Doyle and Peterson had the Pope's personal representative, Archbishop Laghi, on side and Bishop Quinn was already attempting a damage-limitation exercise in Louisiana. Quinn had been selected by senior members of the Vatican. It would be some time before Father Doyle learned that Quinn's brief was exclusively directed towards ensuring that the Catholic Church should evade its moral and legal responsibilities. At a subsequent convention in Ohio, Quinn recommended that every diocese in the United States should send their files on 'problem' priests to the Vatican Embassy in Washington, thereby putting the evidence beyond legal reach. In May 1985, shortly before the report was completed, Father Peterson had a private meeting with Cardinal Krol of Philadelphia, the most powerful man in the US Catholic Church. More than any other Prince of the Church, Krol was responsible for the election of Karol Wojtyla to the papacy. The two men were in constant and intimate contact, and through Krol, the Pope was kept fully briefed on the unfolding scandal. Krol was impressed with the Manual and praised it fulsomely. He saw it as an invaluable contribution – as indeed did a number of bishops, and Cardinal Krol personally handed the Pope a copy of the report in the spring of 1985. Another who saw great value in the work was Cardinal Law of Boston.

The Vatican response both to the Manual and its implications was to apply the Polish solution. Pope John Paul II always believed that the Church should deal with its problems in 'a special room' behind closed doors. Now he urged Krol and his fellow American cardinals and bishops to deal with this 'essentially American problem' discreetly; the secret system would be maintained.

The Manual had little to do with justice: for the victims and their families that was dealt with in less than half a page. Though concise it was, however, highly pertinent. It talked of the 'sexual abuse of children by adults' having

'long-lasting effects that go well into adulthood, not only physiological effects but also the spiritual effects since the perpetrators of the abuse are priests and clerics. This will no doubt have a profound effect on the faith life of the victims, their families and others in the community.'

The authors also talked of the need for direct approaches to be made to the families in question saying, 'There should be some form of healing if possible between the priest and the family . . .'

Cardinal Law told the authors that he would get the Manual taken up by the National Conference of Catholic Bishops – NCCB – by creating a special ad hoc committee of his own. Archbishop Levada, Secretary to the Committee, soon indicated that they were making progress yet rapidly Church politics and bitchiness intervened. Levada told Father Doyle that the project was being shut down because another committee 'was going to deal with the issue and a duplication of effort would not make the other committee look good'. In fact a member of the NCCB executive had taken an intense dislike to Father Doyle and this lay behind the deliberate killing of the one chance for the US Church to conduct a decent salvage operation.

Announcements, a mere PR exercise, were made at a press conference that a committee had been established to study the issue of sexual abuse by clerics. There was no such committee and at no time did anyone within the NCCB make contact with any of the authors. Meanwhile melt-down was already occurring. Four years later, with the country awash with the scandal of child-abusing priests, the executive member was still grossly misrepresenting both the document and its authors' intentions.

The collective response of the bishops of the United States was of men in denial and yet the authors of the Manual had been told by several bishops that clerical child-abuse was an inevitable topic of conversation whenever bishops met. Most bishops remained so in thrall with the secret system that they could imagine no alternative.

Pope John Paul's observation that clerical sexual abuse was 'exclusively an American problem' was rapidly contradicted by exposures in country after country. In 1988 in

Newfoundland, Canada, a scandal which began with allegations of sexual abuse by two parish priests grew until ten
per cent of the clergy were implicated. The following year
the Mount Cashel boys' home in St John's, Newfoundland,
was the focus of a sexual abuse scandal that implicated the
Christian Brothers Congregation, the Church hierarchy and
the province in a cover-up that had continued for many
years. The abuses of the children had been perpetuated
systematically since before the Second World War. Subsequently the Christian Brothers would be exposed as a
brutal congregation, many of whose members were simultaneously sexually abusing and savagely punishing the
children in their 'care' in Ireland, Canada and Australia.

Just as in Louisiana, in Canada one case led to another
then another. There were criminal trials, civil actions, and
an internal investigation by the Catholic Church and ultimately a Royal Commission by the Government. The
official transcripts of the Royal Commission and the Law
Commission of Canada make for some of the grimmest
reading imaginable. It transpired that Mount Cashel was
not an isolated example of the physical and sexual abuse of
the most vulnerable section of Canada's society. Over thirty
institutions stood condemned. In its introduction, the report
observed that the institutions examined in the inventory are
the 'tip of the iceberg'. It continued: 'The problem is
pervasive; abuse is prevalent in all different types of facilities
and it extends to government-operated and/or funded institutions throughout the country.' What follows is a selection of verbatim extracts from that 'tip of the iceberg'.

'*Mount Cashel Orphanage.*

Perpetrators of the Abuse: The Christian Brothers.
Both priests and the Superintendent of the orphanage
committed abusive acts on many students. In the
Royal Commission Report, Justice Hughes stated that

the offensive acts, caused by "cruelty" and "lust" tended "to corrupt their childhood and destroy its happiness". Some of the acts committed by the Christian Brothers included forced mutual fellatio, buggery, forced mutual masturbation, fondling of the students' genitalia, "inappropriate" kissing, and insertion of fingers in rectum. The sexual abuse often began with kindness and demonstration of affection.

Excessive corporal punishment was suffered by many students, some as young as five years old, at the orphanage. The acts were often sadistic and the discipline was frequently arbitrary. For example, Brother Burke "mercilessly" beat a nine-year-old child on his back and his buttocks for losing a library card. Strapping was often violent and insensate with bruising and blistering of hands and arms up to the elbow joint, and frequently laid on, not systematically but with furious anger. Beating was in the main hitting the bare buttocks with a strap or stick but went as far as punching, kicking and banging heads against the wall.'

There had been previous attempts to investigate Mount Cashel. In 1975, the Federal Government was finally obliged to act via its Department of Health and Welfare to investigate the institute. Evidence was laid before the Department that a regime of sustained physical brutality and sexual abuse operated at Mount Cashel, but the liaison official Robert Bradley ignored the allegations. Later the same year he received another report repeating the allegations. Bradley reported to his government superior that he was perplexed as he had been *instructed not to interfere with the affairs of Mount Cashel*. [Author's italics.]

Before the end of 1975 police detectives visited the school and apart from interviewing boys who were extremely fearful managed to establish a prima facie case that the range of offences described above had been perpetrated. The two detectives sought permission from their police superiors to arrest the two Brothers, who later confessed their crimes, and charge them. The then Chief of Police of the Royal Newfoundland Constabulary, John Lawlor, ordered the senior police officer Detective Hillier to *excise all references to sexual abuse* from his reports, despite the fact that the investigation was incomplete and that more than twenty-five boys had made complaints to the police of physical and sexual abuse. The police were ordered to stop the investigation. The abuse was allowed to continue without hindrance for more than a further thirteen years.

There are similar details covering the other twenty-nine institutions. The number of victims runs into many hundreds and these are merely the ones that the Federal Government was able to identify. It is officially accepted that a great many more victims of these institutions will never be known. Paedophile 'clans' of Catholic priests in Canada are not confined to state-run institutions. A clan involving at least twelve men, three of them priests, a further two Roman Catholic lawyers, another who was a Brother teaching at a Catholic school and a Catholic physician was only uncovered in 1996 after functioning for the best part of a decade in the Diocese of Alexandria Cornwell in Ontario. Its final exposure owed much to one incorruptible police officer, Constable Perry Dunlop. With great courage he established a corrupt conspiracy between his own police force and the paedophiles. Eventually twelve men were finally charged with offences involving indecent assault and gross indecency.

In 1988 time was finally called on Mount Cashel but Louisiana was offering yet a further example of the cancer within the Catholic priesthood. When, by accident, a huge collection of commercially produced child pornography was discovered in his room at a Parish Church in New

Orleans, Father Dino Cinel was already on his way to Italy for a Christmas holiday. Also found were some 160 hours of homemade videotapes. If possession of the first stack was a criminal offence with a mandated prison sentence, the second hoard should have ensured Cinel's removal from society for many years.

The videocassettes showed Father Cinel engaged in a number of sexual acts with a variety of male partners including at least seven underage boys. After the Gauthe affair one would have expected the local hierarchy to act with alacrity. It took three months for the archdiocese to turn the material over to the District Attorney's office. During that time the Archbishop and his staff suppressed the fact that there was an active paedophile in one of the parishes. District Attorney Harry Connick Senior sat on the file for more than two years. He later admitted during a television interview that he had not filed charges against Cinel because he did not want 'to embarrass Holy Mother the Church'.

Despite orchestrated cover-ups by the Catholic Church, the deliberate suppression by elements of the media who were vulnerable to pressure from the Church hierarchy, devout District Attorneys, judges and police officers seeking to protect 'the good name of the Church', the truth was getting out and not only in North America. The abuse was not confined to one continent. To even confront a fragment of the evidence that I have acquired over the past five years is to journey to the heart of darkness. Priests and, in some instances, bishops and cardinals have been disgraced in country after country. Egardo Storni, the Archbishop of Santa Fe in Argentina, resigned after being accused of abusing at least forty-seven seminarians. He said his resignation did not signify guilt. Bishop Franziskus Eisenbach of Mainz, Germany, resigned after being accused of sexually assaulting a female university professor during an exorcism. Yet he denied the allegation. In Ireland, Bishop Brendan Comiskey resigned after his use of 'the secret system' came to light. In Poland a close friend of the Pope's, Archbishop Juliusz Paetz of Poznan, resigned after allegations that he had made sexual advances to young clerics became public knowledge. Paetz denied the allegations, declaring he was resigning 'for the good of the Church'. In Wales, Archbishop John Aloysius Ward was forced by the Pope to resign after continuing public criticism that he had ignored warnings about two priests later convicted of child abuse.

In Scotland, among a plethora of cases that shocked the most hardened, a brilliant crusade by Marion Scott of the *Sunday Mail* and a three-year police enquiry exposed abuse at one of the schools run by the De La Salle Brothers. Subsequent evidence made it clear that abuse at St Ninian's school at Gartmore in Stirlingshire was typical of schools run by the Order in many countries. What occurred at St Ninian's took place between the late 1950s and 1982. In Australia, the De La Salle Brothers were involved in similar activities as far back as 1911.

In St Ninian's the monks varied the regular beatings, rapes and the gamut of sexual abuses of the boys with their own version of torture and brutality. An electric generator was set up in the boot room where boys were forced to hold onto the bare wires leading from the machine and receive a series of electric shocks. The children were also subjected to whippings with a riding crop with the ends tied to cause greater pain. Christopher Fearns, a social worker, recalled,

'I was beaten with the riding crop two or three times a week for four years. They told us they'd whip the Devil out of us. I was battered so many times on my head and ears I cannot hear a thing on my left side, and I've undergone extensive surgery because of it.'

To date just three people have been brought to trial; all were found guilty. Among the ten charges that were proved against Brother Benedict were assault, forcing children to eat their own vomit and breaking a boy's arm. The three men were given token sentences of two years' imprisonment. Brother Benedict appealed and was granted bail. More than a year later his appeal has yet to be heard and he walks freely among his fellow citizens.

Jimmy Boyle, formerly the most feared man in Scotland, recalled his years in another De La Salle school, St John's in Springboig:

> 'Even today I can still hear the sounds of breaking bones as a monk deliberately smashed a child's leg to smithereens. Or footsteps in the night that heralded yet another horrific rape of a terrified, crying child.'

In 1999 the Sisters of Mercy faced over 100 charges of abuse in the High Court of Dublin. At exactly the same time in England, Father David Crowley was being sentenced to nine years' imprisonment after pleading guilty to fifteen charges of sexual abuse on a child under ten years old and a number of boys under sixteen years of age. Many of his victims were altar boys. His offences occurred at parishes in West Yorkshire, Northern England and Devon between July 1981 and August 1992. On at least two separate occasions complaints were made by the parents of victims. Crowley was sent for counselling. He was then allowed to continue working on condition he *restricted his access to young people*. [Author's italics.] On one occasion Crowley watched as he encouraged a nine-year-old boy to perform an indecent act upon a thirteen-year-old boy.

Prosecuting Counsel Peter Benson told the court,

'The abuse was systematically contrived and the Crown say the accused cleverly exploited his position of trust and authority as a Catholic priest to seduce impressionable young boys. He would set about winning their trust by allowing them to smoke and plying them with alcohol as a prelude to seducing them. He would often target the emotionally vulnerable young men who he came into contact with as suitable candidates for his attentions.'

At much the same time that Father Crowley was using these techniques in various parts of England, Father Gerard Stock, also in the United Kingdom, was doing precisely the same and targeting the same group of potential victims – altar boys. He too was eventually caught and pleaded guilty to thirty-four counts of gross indecency involving sixteen young boys over a twenty-two-year period spanning 1959 to 1981.

Father Adrian McLeish, as parish priest in Gilesgate, Durham, was an avid user of the Internet. When the police raided St Joseph's presbytery they discovered that the priest had built up one of the world's largest collections of Internet pornography. He was also regularly abusing at least four young boys. After police had taken the computers away, Father McLeish, fully aware that he would be going to prison, took a final opportunity to abuse one of his victims. The boy's mother subsequently said, 'It was as if he was having a last fling.' It was further established that McLeish had been using parish funds to pay for his computer pornography. He was sentenced to six years' imprisonment.

Yet another who used his authority to seduce the young was Father Michael Hill. Among the victims of twenty to thirty offences of sexual abuse were two handicapped boys of fourteen and ten. One was confined to a wheelchair and the other had cerebral palsy. They were two of a number of victims who would have been spared their ordeal if the man who is now the Catholic Primate of England, Cardinal Cormac Murphy O'Connor, had been alert on his watch as Bishop of Arundel and Brighton. Less than a year after Murphy O'Connor's promotion to the diocese in 1977, Father Michael Hill came under his control. Hill had been an active paedophile since 1959. One of the features of Hill's later career is the number of times he was shuffled around the diocese. Murphy O'Connor has subsequently gone on record asserting that Hill's removal from Godalming to Heathfield was 'wholly unconnected with any question of child abuse' but was due to 'disagreement and unrest in the parish'. He has yet to specify the causes of the unrest but in late 1980 a number of parishioners from Godalming came to complain to Bishop Murphy O'Connor of the unnaturally close interest Hill was taking in their sons. As one mother recalled, 'I told him what was going on. He said he would deal with it.'

In a classic demonstration of how the secret system operates, Hill was moved to the Parish of Heathfield and sent to a rehabilitation centre run by the Servants of the Paraclete in Gloucestershire. Among other conditions, the centre specialises in treating paedophilia. Cardinal Murphy O'Connor's subsequent comments regarding his confrontation of Father Hill in 1981 confirmed the truth of the allegations made by the citizens of Godalming. When Hill came to the diocese, his reports carried a health warning that he remained a potential danger to children. Notwithstanding that information, O'Connor allowed him to return to Heathfield parish. By 1983 at least one mother had strongly complained to O'Connor that Father Hill's behaviour towards her two sons was unacceptable and a cause of great concern. Hill received further counselling and this time O'Connor's response to the professional advice that the priest should not be allowed access to children was followed and Father Hill's licence to work in a parish was withdrawn. Then in 1985 the bishop again softened his stance towards Hill. Part of the advice he had received from the medical experts in 1983 was that Hill might be allowed at some point to work in some restricted pastoral role outside the parish.

The Bishop then made an inexcusable decision. He appointed Father Hill as chaplain to Gatwick Airport, which by the time in question, 1985, was known as 'the Leicester Square of Sussex' and 'a magnet for homeless youngsters'. Father Hill took full advantage of his new appointment and committed further sexual attacks upon young boys. When Murphy O'Connor's decision on Father Hill became public knowledge in November 2002, *The Times* newspaper commented that 'the scale of Cardinal Murphy O'Connor's moral blindness is potentially devastating'. Hill was subsequently arrested and found guilty of a number of sexual attacks between 1969 and 1987 including molesting a cerebral palsy sufferer on his way to Lourdes. Father Hill was sentenced to five years' imprisonment.

The Primate of All England has sought to justify his actions with regard to Father Hill on the grounds of a 'genuine ignorance that there was (in the mid to late 1980s) not only among bishops and priests, but also in society at large, including the medical profession, about the compulsive nature of child abuse'. It is a defence without a shred of credibility. In November 2002 Father Hill pleaded guilty to a further string of sexual assaults committed between 1969 and 1987 and was sentenced to a further five years' imprisonment.

The Primate apologised for the 'grave mistake' but his contrition did not extend to resigning his position, despite the many demands from the faithful and from the media that he should leave the national stage. The credibility gap between the Cardinal and his bishops and the ever-shrinking Catholic congregation in England continues to widen. According to the

Cardinal's spokesman, the secret deals with victims that have involved the payment of 'hush money' were nothing to do with the Church. 'It does not go near the Church. It is done between solicitor and solicitor.' The spokesman did not say who instructs the solicitor to pay up.

By 1999, as the Catholic Church in England and Wales maintained a silence over the growing convictions of priests for sexual abuse, it had become obvious that paedophilia within the United Kingdom would not be defeated by denying that there was a problem. Twenty-one priests had been convicted in a four-year period. At this crisis point Cardinal Cormac Murphy O'Connor fully acknowledged his mistaken handling of Father Hill. Soon afterwards, a full review was established under the chairmanship of Lord Nolan (a former Law Lord and Chairman of the Committee on Standards in Public Life). In April 2001 his report was published, with more than fifty recommendations to protect the potential victims.

It was a positive step and one of its recommendations that was swiftly implemented called for an annual report. Despite numerous instances of clerical sexual abuse over many decades, the Catholic Church of Scotland has not been inclined to follow the example set south of the border. The most important recommendation of the Nolan Report was also rapidly introduced; the creation of a national child protection unit within the Church to 'root out child abusers by vetting clergy, its lay staff and volunteers before they take up new posts'.

The report observed within its executive summary:

'Child abuse is a great evil. It can leave deep scars on the victims and their families. It is particularly abhorrent when a child or young person is abused by someone in a position of trust and responsibility. It is most abhorrent when that position of trust is held by

a member of the clergy or a lay Catholic worker. The
care of children is at the forefront of the teachings of
Christ and is, therefore, one of the primary responsibilities of all members of the Church led by their
priests and bishops.'

Further, within the summary Lord Nolan and his committee
observed a self-evident truth. 'The fact is that should every
parish throughout England and Wales follow our recommendations the problem of child abuse would not therefore
be eradicated.' It was commendably honest and their final
aspiration should have touched a chord within every Roman Catholic within the country:

'Our hope is that this report will help to bring about a
culture of vigilance where every single adult member
of the Church consciously and pro-actively takes responsibility for creating a safe environment for children and young people. Our recommendations are not
a substitute for this but we hope they will be an
impetus towards such an achievement.'

The Church's commitment to openness certainly struck a
chord with the hitherto silent victims. Within the first
eighteen months of the new guidelines going into operation,
the Church had received nearly 150 further complaints of
sex abuse. Another 100 complaints followed in 2004.
Archbishop Vincent Nichols of Birmingham welcomed
the abuse claims as a clear indication that progress was
being made in addressing an historic backlog of abuse.

The Archbishop may have been less enthusiastic when his
own archdiocese was obliged to pay out £330,000 to a
former altar boy who had been sexually abused by a priest
over an eight-year period. The settlement reached in January 2004 was at the time the largest known payout in the

United Kingdom. The payout, made days before the case was due to come to the High Court, is a further indication that in England and Wales the times are finally changing, but only in some areas.

In late June 2005, the Birmingham archdiocese was obliged to set the compensation bar twice as high after being ordered by the court to pay over £600,000 (over $1.5 million) to a victim who, as a young boy, had been repeatedly abused by Father Christopher Conlan who had fled the country to Australia where he had died in 1998.

One of the most extraordinary aspects of this scandal had been the dogmatic refusal by the Vatican to accept and acknowledge, until very late in the day, that such abuse was anything more than a local difficulty confined to the United States. As these pages illustrate, the sexual abuse by Catholic priests and religious of children, youths, adolescents and adults knew no frontiers. Pope John Paul II was aware from very early in his reign that this was an issue that he had to address and act on. He failed to address it.

In Austria, a close friend of the Pope's, Cardinal Hans Hermann Groer, was forced after a protracted struggle to resign following allegations of repeatedly abusing students at an all-male Catholic school. Groer rejected the allegations. In Switzerland, Bishop Hansjörg Vogel of Basel resigned after admitting he had impregnated a woman following his promotion to the hierarchy in the previous year. Standing behind every bishop referred to above is the same pattern of institutional abuse, the same range of paedophiliac sexual abuses by priests. Appalling abuse by the Christian Brothers has been matched by cruelty from the Poor Sisters of Nazareth or the Daughters of Charity of St Vincent de Paul or the Sisters of Mercy. For more than 100 years there were Nazareth homes all over the United Kingdom, Australia, South Africa, the United States and Ireland.

From the mid-nineteenth century to recent times 'Nazareth homes' cared for the young and the old. The orphanages were run by nuns from the order of the Sisters of Mercy. Violent degradation and thrashings were a daily event. The children woke up to the screams of other children and to the familiar sound of the strap. In 1965 Helen Cusiter was eight years of age when her mother disappeared and she was taken, along with her five brothers, to the Nazareth House in Aberdeen. In 2004 at the age of forty-seven, after a chance meeting with one of her childhood tormentors, Helen became one of over five hundred former residents to bring an action against the Sisters. Her recall of what she had endured was corroborated by other former inmates who had not met for a lifetime. It included a particular incident with Sister Alphonso who had come looking for her while Helen had been playing on the swings.

'She took me off by the hair, twisted me round and threw me against the church wall. She broke all my front teeth, my face was a mashed mess, the other kids were all screaming.' Helen Howie, one of those screaming children, remembers the blood pouring from Helen's face: 'Sister Alphonso didn't use leather straps, she used her fists, she had such strength.' When the dentist queried the extensive bruising on the eight year old's face he was told, 'She fell.'

Sister Aphonso was convicted on four charges of cruel and unnatural treatment. Because of her age she was merely admonished rather than imprisoned. There are all too many similar testimonies from hundreds of damaged people. Many sought not compensation but just the opportunity of being heard, of having the pain they still felt acknowledged.

The Poor Sisters are no longer poor. They have approaching £200 million in their bank and have eventually dropped the 'Poor' from their title. There is now an international campaign to bring the Order to the bar of justice. It will be an uphill struggle with the insurance companies combining with a number of the bishops to ward off the attack.

Many bishops are still in denial about the enormity and extent of clerical sexual abuse over the past forty to fifty years. They still consider it as a 'problem' that should be dealt with in-house – without publicity or criminal charges. In January 2003 the Irish commission created to enquire into child abuse publicly complained that 'the Government and most religious orders are obstructing our work'. The Commission was investigating Church-run institutions to which the Irish Government sent 'problem' children and orphans. As in Canada, in Ireland much had been covered up. There were fifty-two 'industrial schools' in the mid-twentieth century where physical and sexual abuse were rife. An industrial school functioned as an early type of reform centre or Borstal. They were devised as 'Means for Decreasing Juvenile Crime'. Often the only 'crime' was that the child had been orphaned or abandoned. In theory, apart from teaching the ordinary elementary subjects, the children also were taught a trade. The varying circumstances made no difference to the treatment meted out. Whether those entrusted with the children were Christian Brothers, Daughters of Charity or Poor Sisters of Nazareth the viciousness of the various religious orders had a disturbing uniformity. Since 1985 more than 4,000 survivors of a *child slave labour regime* have sought compensation from the Irish Catholic Church. One who is beyond winning any compensation is Willie Delaney.

In 1966 at the age of nine, Willie was the oldest of ten children, living in a caravan without sanitation or running water. It was his responsibility to help to feed the family. His father, a tinsmith confronting a shrinking market with the advent of long-life kitchen utensils, needed all the help he could get. Willie was caught stealing piglets and sentenced to six years in Letterfrack, an industrial school in the west of Ireland, described by survivors as 'a hell on earth'. Inmates suffered physical, mental and sexual abuse. Willie was treated brutally. In 1970, by now thirteen, a few days before he was due home for a precious two-week holiday, Willie was continously beaten about the head. Survivors have recently testified that one of the Christian Brothers was continuously beating Willie's head with a bunch of keys; others remember him using a pole. At home Willie complained of severe headaches, then he suffered a fit, went into a coma and died. Doctors at St Luke's Hospital in Kilkenny said he had died of meningitis. His father was certain his death was linked with the treatment he had suffered from the Christian Brothers.

In April 2001 Willie's body was exhumed and subjected to a post-mortem. It was determined that he had died from natural causes but Willie's death and its aftermath had given a further thirty former inmates the courage to come forward and lay complaints against Christian Brothers and lay staff. The eventual number of complaints rose to 140. Twenty-nine Christian Brothers and lay staff were identified as alleged abusers. Forty-eight priests and Christian brothers had already been convicted of abusing, physically and sexually, children in their care.

In an unrelated case in Ireland a few months before the exhumation of Willie Delaney, a former Franciscan Brother, Robert Keoghan, pleaded guilty to eight charges of indecently assaulting eight boys aged between nine and sixteen on various dates between 1969 and 1972. Before sentencing Keoghan, who was already serving an eighteen-month prison sentence for two similar crimes, the court heard that when Keoghan had gone to confess these offences he had been sexually abused by his confessor, a Franciscan priest. Keoghan was sentenced to a further two years' imprisonment.

As the dam was breached worldwide, it was striking how frequently the activities of the paedophiliac priests could be traced back twenty, thirty or even forty years earlier. It is inconceivable that just one particular generation of priests who took Holy Orders in the late 1950s and the 1960s should be any more or less inclined to paedophilia than the generation before or the generation after. Traditionalists have blamed the rise in abuse on the reforms of Vatican Council II, but they have yet to reveal the cause of the clerical paedophilia that predates the mid-1960s. One is left with the nightmare possibility that but for the case of Father Gauthe, the secret system would still be functioning efficiently, with just as many new victims being abused. Yet even after 1985, there were attempts to keep the old order. In the early years of the new century, Hong Kong police were investigating clerical crimes. They discovered that the secret system was still alive and fully operational in May 2002. Police Superintendent Shirley Chu, who was investigating eight abuse cases, publicly complained that the Catholic Church was refusing to hand over written confessions by a number of priests made during an internal Church investigation. Chu's response echoed that of judges, police officers and district attorneys around the world: 'It seems that the Church has been protecting its reputation and priests rather than the victims.'

The Catholic hierarchy in the Philippines were also forced to apologise to victims. In September 2000, thirty-four priests and a number of bishops were suspended as the full extent of clerical sex abuse began to be known publicly. Unlike in many other countries, the majority of cases involved the sexual abuse of women. It was subsequently revealed that in New Zealand in early 1991 six Roman Catholic dioceses had confirmed thirty-eight cases of sexual abuse by priests and brothers, within two years of a complaints procedure being set up: a great many more were in the pipeline including complaints of abuse that reached back fifty years to the 1940s. For most of that period the Catholic population of New Zealand was less than 500,000, with only around 500 priests: the confirmed cases indicated a historic average of some seven per cent of priests being sex abusers.

Commenting on the figures, Lyndsay Freer, the National Director of Catholic Communications, displayed the national gift for understatement: 'There was a tendency in the past to protect the institution or the profession.' Then, singing from the same hymn sheet as the rest of the Catholic Church, Freer attempted to defend the indefensible.

'The recidivist nature of psychosexual dysfunction or paedophilia was not understood, and it was thought that if a person admitted guilt, confessed it, and was given absolution in the sacrament in Confession . . . rehabilitation and forgiveness was possible.'

In Australia, Cardinal Pell was obliged to admit that the Church had not relied on mere Christian forgiveness on the part of the victim. Many thousands of dollars of hush money had been paid to those who had suffered sexual abuse. Less than two weeks later the Roman Catholic Order the St John of God Brothers revealed that they had reached an out-of-court settlement with lawyers representing twenty-four mentally handicapped men who had been sexually abused by up to twenty Brothers while in their care. The amount to be paid was 2.1 million US dollars and is believed to be the largest such settlement in Australian history. Finding courage in the example set by the mentally handicapped victims, a further 157 alleged victims came forward. Meanwhile the head of the Church in South Africa admitted that about a dozen priests had been accused of sexually abusing children 'many years ago'.

Demonstrably, the secret system had worked well in all of these countries.

In Brazil, the world's largest predominantly Roman Catholic country, Church officials admitted there was a paedophilia problem among the clergy. Bishop Angelico Sandalo Bernardino in an extraordinary attempt at justification observed, 'The problem of sexual appetite is one that afflicts every human being.'

In Holland, the pragmatic Dutch Church attempted an unusual and highly dubious strategy in secret negotiations with its insurers. They demanded that an additional clause covering sexual abuse compensation be inserted in their policies. They further demanded that it be applied *retrospectively* to cover the past decades. Both demands were rejected.

A similar contretemps occurred in Ireland. It transpired that the insurance cover for the Irish Church that included the aspect of sexual abuse had first been taken out by the Irish Bishops' Conference between 1987 and 1990, a period when the bishops were still using the secret system and busily moving offending priests from parish to parish. In the words of the bishops' spokesman, Father Martin Clarke, the cover 'offered only modest coverage at low premiums'. Once a wave of child abuse scandals began engulfing the Irish Church in 1994, the insurance policies proved 'ambiguous and uncertain', a discovery with regard to insurance policies that is not unique to the Catholic Church. Insurance companies all over the world pushed the panic button overnight; premiums rose to anything between thirty per cent and 130 per cent for far less coverage.

Following the example set by the Church in England and Wales, the Irish Bishops' Conference commissioned an independent study of child abuse by the Catholic clergy in Ireland. It was carried out by the Royal College of Surgeons in Ireland and a press release, but not the report itself, was made public in December 2003 on behalf of the Irish Bishops. Having noted that 'over half' of the report's recommendations were already being followed, Bishop John McAreavey then pointed to the report's 'acknowledgement that when dealing with abusers in the past, bishops followed, in good faith, the best psychiatric advice available at the time'. This acknowledgement flies in the face of decades of lies, cover-ups, evasions and wilful disregard of the victims. He continued: 'Clearly in relation to clerical sexual abuse we failed many young people over too long a period.'

One of the authors of the report, Professor Hannah McGee, saw her own conclusions rather differently. 'The occurrence, and more importantly the mismanagement, of clerical child abuse, represents a loss throughout Irish society rather than an isolated problem for an unfortunate few.'

Bishop McAreavey did have the good grace to apologise publicly for the wrongs of the past and to make a commitment to improve 'upon our existing policies'. The undertaking would have carried greater conviction if the bishops had not sought to shift the burden of blame onto the shoulders of consultant psychiatrists.

At the time of the Royal College of Surgeons' report, another enquiry, this time into alleged sexual abuse of children in the diocese of Ferns in Ireland, was already one year into what would eventually become a three-year investigation. The Commission identified over 100 allegations of sexual abuse by twenty-one priests between 1962 and 2002. Their report, published in October 2005, confirmed that sexual abuse was widespread over many years in Ferns. Ten of the accused priests were dead, two were convicted and the remainder were 'not in active ministry'. Quite why that gave them immunity from prosecution has yet to be explained.

The Catholic Church in Ireland insists that under Canon Law sexually abusing clerics are immune from criminal prosecution unless that immunity is lifted by either the bishop or by Rome. Far too many of the hierarchy in Ireland still cling to a Supreme Court judgement of 1925 when the highest court in Ireland accepted the right of the Bishop of Kerry to remove a parish priest from West Cork against the priest's wishes. That judgement is now being used by Irish bishops to thwart natural justice as the Church clings to a fantasy that abusing a child is not a criminal offence but a moral issue.

In April 2003, twenty-five years after the Gauthe case, Vatican officials sat with psychologists and therapists behind locked doors while they held a conference on the sexual abuse of children. Still the desire not to 'embarrass Holy Mother Church' persisted – although the image of the Church already lay in shreds.

In France, the secret system was preserved until the twenty-first century. In January 2000 Abbot Jean-Lucien Maurel was sentenced to ten years' imprisonment for raping and sexually abusing three boys aged between ten and thirteen. Maurel was seventy-one at the time of his trial and sixty-seven at the time of the attacks. The boys were pupils at the school where the Abbot was headmaster. Between fifteen and twenty other French Catholic clergy were also under investigation for alleged sex abuses.

A year later in 2001, a French bishop, Pierre Pican of Bayeux-Lisieux, was convicted of covering up the sexual abuses of one of his priests. He said, 'It is unfortunate that this verdict has limited the Catholic priest's right to keep professional secrets.' In truth it had nothing to do with the sanctity of the confessional and everything to do with what is still a very widely held view within the Catholic Church that her priests and bishops are above the law. The abuser in question, Father René Bissey, is now serving an eighteen-

year prison sentence; his bishop got a three-month suspended prison sentence.

The attitude of Bishop Pican is not unique: in fact it is the
norm. In 2002 the Chairman of the German Bishops'
Conference, Cardinal Lehmann, was asked by *Der Spiegel*,

'When cases are suspected, are the judicial authorities
called in?' He responded, 'This is not our task. The
authorities involve themselves . . . in clear-cut cases –
we ourselves are often in the dark – we motivate the
culprit to self-denunciation. That is better for everybody. In addition, we undertake our own preliminary
investigations; that is dictated by Canon Law. If there
is enough evidence the relevant person is suspended
from office. But that is a matter for individual dioceses.
The Bishops' Conference is not responsible for such
matters.'

Pressed on the need for 'binding rules' that would apply to
all dioceses with regard to their dealings with paedophile
priests, Cardinal Lehmann disagreed:

'We have large dioceses where over decades they have
accumulated their own experience as to how to handle
these offences and they do not just want to hand the
matter over to a higher authority.'

That accumulated experience represents the ability to cover
and conceal the great majority of paedophile cases that
threaten to come to light in Germany. Diligent application
of the secret system ensures that exposure of paedophile
priests on the scale of the United States scandal will not
happen in Germany or other European countries.

The Catholic psychotherapist Wunibald Müller, a man
with decades of experience in the treatment of priests with

psychological and psychiatric problems, has estimated that there is a minimum of two per cent of all priests in Germany with a predisposition to paedophilia, giving a national figure of between 250 and 300. Paedophiles are invariably serial offenders and therefore the number of children at very real risk in Germany today, even by the most conservative of estimates, is somewhere between 5,000 and 10,000. The actual figure is undoubtedly much higher. Müller's estimate was based on the evidence that has been made available to him through clinical study of the general German population. But the extraordinary efficiency of the German application of the secret system has for decades dramatically suppressed the abnormal incidence of sexual abuse among the clerical population. Consequently Müller's estimates are only around half of comparable estimates for other countries, notably the USA. His figure is disturbingly low.

In the United States during the fifteen years after the Gauthe case of 1985/86, over 1,200 paedophile priests were exposed. In view of the fact that there have continued to be weekly if not daily exposures, new civil claims and continuous fresh allegations, the actual total continues to move in the United States inexorably towards 3,000 paedophiles or five per cent of the Roman Catholic priesthood. Even those estimates may prove to be far too low when more exhaustive research has been completed. If the evidence from the Indiana diocese of Lafayette was to be replicated across the United States, all of the previous estimates would have to be rewritten. In a diocese of just seventy-five active priests, by early 1997 it had been established that at least sixteen per cent were guilty of a wide range of sexual abuses.

It should be remembered that these figures were not reached against a background of an open, transparent Church but one which used every delaying tactic that it could dream up with the help of its lawyers and insurers, a

Church where paedophile bishops protected paedophile priests with a bodyguard of deceit. One example was Bishop J. Keith Symons of Palm Beach, who compiled the 'professional psychiatric evaluations that at the time clearly demonstrated the fitness of Rev. Rocco D'Angelo to serve as a priest'.

At the time of these evaluations both the bishop and the priest were sexually abusing young boys. After complaints from the parents of the victims were made to the archdiocese of Miami in the 1960s the parents had been promised that D'Angelo would be kept from children. The secret system was applied and D'Angelo was transferred to the Tampa area where he worked for more than two decades while continuing to molest young boys, one of them in 1987, more than twenty-five years after the Church had given an undertaking that it had never intended to honour.

Father D'Angelo took early retirement in 1993 after his sexual activities became public knowledge. Bishop Symons followed him into early retirement in June 1997 after admitting that he had sexually molested five boys more than three decades earlier. His 'new broom' replacement was Bishop Anthony O'Connell. Four years later there was need of another new broom, as Bishop O'Connell was forced to resign in March 2002 after revelations about his sexual activities with young men who had been under his supervision as rector of a Missouri seminary.

In Boston, an archdiocese that serves a Catholic population of over two million, the Church has been brought to its knees financially. The faith of many has been shattered by an endless stream of clerical sex abuse scandals. In 1992 Cardinal Bernard F. Law of Boston called down 'the power of God' on the news media after their coverage of the activities of the Rev. James R. Porter. A quick résumé of Porter's life leaves one marvelling that the Cardinal went to the barricades for him.

In 1953, aged eighteen, Porter molested a thirteen-year-old boy in a playground in his hometown of Revere, Massachusetts. In the later 1950s Porter, then a seminarian, worked during the summers at the Cathedral Camp in East Freetown, Massachusetts. He molested children at virtually every opportunity and was reported by a victim to another worker-priest. No action was taken and back in Revere, Porter sexually molested numerous local children. In 1960 Porter received his first assignment as a priest – at a kindergarten to eighth grade school, St Mary's Church and Elementary in North Attleborough. During a two-year period Father Porter sexually assaulted scores of children aged between six and fourteen.

Decades later, 68 of these victims recounted their experiences to psychologist James Daignault. 'The first time I remember was when I was eleven,' said Ms Burns. 'I heard someone crying in the school bathroom.' When she went in to see who it was she found Father Porter raping a six-year-old girl. 'I tried to stop him, but he grabbed me and sodomised me. He was absolutely violent. He told me that he was stronger than me and that he had the power of God.'

Stephen Johnson also told his experiences to Daignault:

'When I would scream, he would put his hand over my mouth so no one would hear me. James Porter sexually assaulted me countless times, and each time he would chastise me by saying that what I had done was very bad and that God would punish me if I told anyone.'

Stephen, who was an altar boy at Porter's North Attleborough Church, expressed a sentiment that accurately describes not only his own trauma but that of countless victims of paedophile priests.

'Shame and guilt became the foundation of my being.'

In 1962 when a group of parents and relatives of some of the victims went as a deputation to see pastor Father Booth and Father Annunziato of St Mary's Church to complain and demand action, Father Booth responded, 'He is already receiving treatment. What are you trying to do? Crucify him?' Diocesan records released in 1992 revealed that as of 1962 Bishop Connolly's office had details of over thirty boys who had been abused by Father Porter to whom the secret system was applied again and again. He was transferred to Fall River, some twenty-five miles away from North Attleborough. He continued to abuse children, and after more complaints he was transferred to New Bedford, fifteen miles from Fall River. The priests were told by the Diocesan Office to 'watch Father Porter' because he has 'a problem with little boys'. The watching was inadequate, and more sexual abuse of children by Father Porter was followed by a complaint to the New Hampshire police, who simply escorted Father Porter over the state line and then released him.

In 1967 after yet more attacks on children, the Diocesan Office at Fall River sent Porter for treatment to the rehabilitation centre run by the Servants of the Paraclete at Jemez Springs, New Mexico. After a period of treatment he was allowed to go out on a trial basis to say mass at churches in New Mexico and Texas and also work as chaplain at a children's hospital, where he sexually abused a patient confined in a full body cast. The rehabilitation centre records for the period noted that Father Porter was once again indulging in 'his old failings'. Uncured, Porter was given a letter of recommendation by the Paraclete Centre to the parish of Bemidji in Minnesota. Between 1969 and 1970 while at the parish Father Porter sexually abused a further twenty to thirty children. Again he was caught.

Eventually in 1973 Porter made a written application to Pope Paul VI to be allowed to leave the priesthood. In his letter he told the Pope that he had molested a large number of children in five different states. His papal dispensation was granted on 5 January 1974. Two years later Porter married and subsequently fathered several children. Despite this external normality, he was still an active paedophile and sexually molested a number of local boys in the area of Minnesota where he was then living. In 1984 he molested a teenage female babysitter caring for his four children. In 1987 he molested her fifteen-year-old sister. In 1989 Porter was questioned in connection with the disappearance of an eleven-year-old boy, Jacob Wetterling. During interrogation by FBI officers he admitted that while a Catholic priest he had sexually abused and molested at least thirty to forty children. The FBI took no action.

In 1992 what had begun as a one-man crusade by Frank Fitzpatrick, a former child victim of Father Porter, culminated in a TV programme in which eight victims told of the abuses he had perpetrated upon them many years earlier. The programme inspired yet more victims to come forward, which in turn triggered yet more publicity. It was this exposure that so angered Cardinal Law that he called down 'the power of God' on the news media.

Notwithstanding the Cardinal's efforts to suppress the truth, Porter was indicted the same year in Massachusetts for molesting twenty-eight children, offences that were still within the statute of limitations. The same day he was also indicted in Minnesota for the molestation of his babysitter. Subsequently he was found guilty of the latter offence and sentenced to six months' imprisonment. In 1993, confronted with forty-one counts of indecent assault, unnatural acts and sodomy involving twenty-eight of his victims, the former priest made a plea-bargained deal and was sentenced to eighteen to twenty years' imprisonment. By that time, ninety-nine of his victims had come forward from the three parishes. The number is now approaching 150 and continues to increase. The Catholic Church has paid out between $5 million and $10 million in various settlements to Porter's victims.

Around this time an Italian Cardinal described the child abuse scandal to me as a 'curious American hysteria that would soon wither and die away'. His attitude was common in the Vatican. Yet it was exploded by further scandalous revelations as the 1990s progressed. In July 1997 a Texas jury awarded eleven former altar boys $119.6 million. It was the largest known settlement in a clergy sexual molestation case in the United States. Only ten of the plaintiffs were still able to derive any benefit from the award: the other, Jay Lemberger, shot himself at the age of twenty-one. The jury found that the Dallas Catholic Diocese and the sexual abuse by the defendant Father Rudolph Kos were the 'proximate cause' of his suicide. Kos had sexually abused around fifty boys between 1981 and 1992. One of the victims testified that the priest abused him over a four-year period beginning when he was ten. Another told the jury he was sexually abused by Kos over 350 times.

The size of the award stunned the Catholic Church. It brought nearer the billion-dollar estimate of potential financial loss made twelve years earlier by Father Doyle and his colleagues, once dismissed as wildly fanciful. The diocesan lawyers and the lawyers representing two insurance companies, Lloyds of London and Interstate Fire and Casualty went to war. After a range of tactics that included endless stalling and countless negotiations they eventually succeeded in pushing the settlement down to $30 million dollars but alarm bells were ringing in many an archbishop's residence, nowhere more loudly than in Boston.

The man ringing the bell of Cardinal Law's residence was John Geoghan, ordained a priest in 1962 and defrocked with the Pope's authority by Cardinal Law in 1998. Over thirty-one years Geoghan had served in six parishes in the Boston area leaving human wreckage behind him in every one. Successive bishops had operated the secret system and moved the compulsive paedophile around, spreading his damage far and wide. By the time he had been stripped of his priesthood, the archdiocese had settled twelve civil lawsuits against Geoghan, paying at least fifty victims a total of around $10 million. But fifty victims in thirty years was far from the final tally for Father Geoghan and those who had knowingly protected him.

Cardinal Law was the last in a long line to accord Geoghan facilities that enabled him to continue his paedophilia activities. Law was not, unfortunately, unique. The much beloved Cardinal of Chicago, Joseph Bernadin, and the majority of cardinals, archbishops and bishops functioning in the United States over the entire second half of the twentieth century also operated the secret system. It took until January 2002 before the state succeeded in bringing criminal proceedings against the man whose protectors reached back far beyond Cardinal Cody. As Geoghan's career as a serial sex abuser flowered so did the careers of those who had assisted him. Cardinal Humberto Medeiros had protected Father Porter as a Monsignor. As a Cardinal, controlling the entire archdiocese, he protected Geoghan. Bishops Daily, Banks, McCormack and Murphy had also in the past protected Father Geoghan in a growing number of dioceses before they moved on with promotions. Archbishop Alfred Hughes of New Orleans was another who looked out for Geoghan in earlier times.

In January 2002 the former priest was found guilty of sexually molesting a ten-year-old boy and sentenced to eight to ten years of imprisonment. Additional criminal charges were scheduled to be heard at later dates. An additional eighty-six victims were now free to bring civil cases against Geoghan and the archdiocese of Boston. They sought damages against Cardinal Bernard Law. The case concentrated the cardinal's mind wonderfully. By May, Law had agreed a settlement with the eighty-six victims of $30 million. The cardinal's finance council were acutely aware that many other victims of paedophile priests were watching developments with their lawyers. They baulked at the settlement figure and the cardinal's lawyers were sent back to the negotiating table.

The Geoghan trial had triggered an extraordinary new wave of claims across the United States. By April 2002, 177 priests had been removed in twenty-eight states. By June more than 300 civil law suits alleging clerical sexual abuse had been filed in sixteen states. Lawyers confirmed that a further 250 cases were being informally mediated between dioceses and accusers. Attorneys estimated that it would take two to three years to resolve the cases already filed and new cases were emerging virtually every day. By June the number of priests who had either been dismissed or resigned since January had risen to 250. Every prediction that Father Doyle, Father Peterson and Ray Mouton had made within their advisory Manual in 1985 had come to pass.

By mid-April 2002 many observers considered that Cardinal Law's position as head of the Boston archdiocese was untenable. The Geoghan scandal had still to be resolved and further shocking revelations were imminent, including the identities of other paedophile priests protected by the cardinal and his bishops. The Boston judges were beginning to exercise their power and demand that the archdiocese hand over the files on two of these, Fathers Mahan and Shanley. Mahan's activities allegedly covered a period from 1962 to his removal from the priesthood in 1998. Shanley was accused of crimes that ranged from paedophilia and public advocacy of sexual intercourse between men and boys to teaching youngsters how to shoot up with heroin.

Cardinal Law's officials dug in and were applying a range of delaying tactics to avoid handing over the incriminating files but the clock was showing 'time' everywhere but within the Vatican. In mid-April 2002 Cardinal Law secretly travelled to Rome. For a man accustomed to arrivals and departures with the full pomp and ceremony that befitted a Prince of the Roman Catholic Church, it was a sobering experience to be smuggled out of his own residence and hustled through Logan airport like a fugitive from justice.

The Cardinal and the Pope were close friends but there was a gulf of perception between them during the meeting. Bernard Law's exposure to the media coverage, the rising tide of protests, not only from the Catholic in the street but from people within the Boston hierarchy, could not be ignored. The calls for his resignation had been growing by the day. Law had refused for more than two months to talk to the news media; he did not consider himself accountable either to the public at large or to his Catholic flock. He was answerable to the Pope and none other. Technically the Cardinal's position was correct but neither the news media nor ordinary Catholics pay much attention to Canon Law. In the preceding months the Cardinal had attempted to win the day by hiring public relations consultants and addressing the scandal from his pulpit. As for responsibility, the Cardinal had confined himself to apologising twice and simultaneously blaming 'inadequate medical advice', 'inadequate record keeping of erring priests' and 'an excessive media focus on clergy sexual abuse'.

Throughout the entire seventeen years since the Gauthe case, neither the Pope nor his senior advisors had confronted the cancer of paedophilia within the Catholic Church. It was an extraordinary omission and a devastating

failure with far-reaching consequences. At his meetings
Cardinal Law attempted to bring the Vatican up to date
with developments within the Boston archdiocese. When
Archbishop Marcinkus had come complaining about the
drubbing he was getting over his mismanagement of the
Vatican Bank, the Pope had airily dismissed the matter as
being something to be ignored. For many of the preceding
seventeen years he had adopted much the same attitude to
the sexual abuses being perpetrated by his priests, bishops
and religious. Even now with the Boston Cardinal sitting in
front of him recounting the Goeghan case, the Shanley case,
the Porter case and others, the Pope was inclined to blame
influences outside the clergy. When the Cardinal offered to
resign the Pope waved the offer away. 'Your place is at the
head of the Archdiocese.' And sent him back to Boston.

The Pope had been convinced for a long time that 'this
problem' was unique to the United States and that it would
burn itself out. He had chosen to ignore a global reality and
his continuing inaction had ensured a constantly deteriorating situation that no amount of media messaging could
solve. Perhaps inevitably, the Church decided on a press
relations exercise. The Boston cardinal's deep aversion to
the media, which he largely blamed for the crisis, ensured
that he would continue to treat them with contempt. No
one had been advised he was going to Rome and no one was
going to get to interview him now he was back in Boston.
He elected to make a press statement. Having in the past
week offered his resignation to the papal nuncio in
Washington and to the Pope in Rome and having been
told to ignore his critics, he said, 'I return home encouraged
in my efforts to provide the strongest possible leadership in
ensuring, as far as is humanly possible, that no child is ever
abused again by a priest of this archdiocese.'

It was an admirable statement but it was obvious that,
rather than reach out to his flock of over two million souls

through every available news outlet, the cardinal with the Pope's approval had chosen an esoteric form of communication.

'It is my intent to address at length the record of the archdiocese's handling of these cases by reviewing the past in as systematic and comprehensive a way as possible, so that the legitimate questions which have been raised might be answered. The facilities of Boston Catholic Television and *The Pilot* will assist in making this record available.'

He deemed only a minority channel and the parish magazine competent to carry the information on a story with national and international ramifications. As an example of how to lose friends and alienate people it was definitive.

The *Boston Globe and Mail* carried Cardinal Law's statement as well as the results of its most recent poll on the scandal. This showed that sixty-five per cent thought Law should leave his job, seventy-one per cent thought the cardinal had done a poor job handling the various instances of sexual abuse of children by priests and fifty-three per cent said they had now lost confidence in the Catholic Church as an institution because of the scandal. The survey polled 800 Catholic adults. Meanwhile, lawyers redoubled their efforts to obtain archdiocesan records on Father Shanley and other paedophiles and judges were insisting that Cardinal Law make a formal deposition and provide the archdiocesan files on Father Goeghan.

The Vatican then announced that the Pope had summoned every American Cardinal to Rome. Many observers in the United States saw this as a positive step, a sign that Pope John Paul II was finally going to get a grip on the most serious crisis to confront his papacy since the Banco Ambrosiano crash. The cynics within the City State nodded and smiled. They fully agreed with the comments of Cardinal Dario Castrillon Hoyos, Head of the Vatican Congregation of the Clergy, who only three weeks earlier dismissed the media preoccupation in the United States scandal. Hoyos believed that the Holy Father's agenda allowed no time for concerns over the abuse of children. He airily declared, 'The Pope is worried about peace in the world.'

From 1978 until April 2002 the Pope had deliberately and studiously avoided any public references to the global epidemic of sexual abuse by his priests and members of Catholic orders, apart from a few oblique comments. He had talked in March 2002 of 'a dark shadow of suspicion' that had been cast over priests 'by some of our brothers who have betrayed the grace of ordination' and have succumbed to the 'most grievous forms of the mystery of evil at work in the world'. He could not quite bring himself to utter the word paedophilia.

Equally silent was the Prefect of the Congregation for the Doctrine of the Faith – the CDF – Cardinal Ratzinger. What made his failure to go public on the worldwide scandal of clerical sexual abuse inexplicable was the fact that at least since June 1988 by direct command of Pope John Paul II the CDF was duly authorised to investigate and sit in judgement on a range of clerical sexual abuse including 'violation against the sixth commandment of the Decalogue committed by a cleric with a minor below the age of eighteen years'.

The one significant exception to the papal silence was a curious paragraph hidden away in a 120-page document that summed up the themes of a Synod of Bishops of Oceania in the Vatican in 1998.

'Sexual abuse by some clergy and religious has caused great suffering and spiritual harm to the victims. It has been very damaging in the life of the Church and has become an obstacle to the proclamation of the Gospel. The Synod fathers condemned all sexual abuse and forms of abuse of power both within the Church and in society as a whole.'

Although the speech dates from 1998 no one within the Vatican saw fit to make it available to the public until it was put on the Internet on 22 November 2001. The comments were widely understood within the Vatican as referring not to child abuse but to another aspect of clerical and religious sexual abuse, one that is examined later within this chapter.

Just three days before the US cardinals were due to arrive at the Vatican, the Pope delivered a strong reaffirmation of the importance of priestly celibacy. His remarks were seen as cutting the ground away from under the feet of some of the US cardinals who had gone on record a week earlier declaring that the entire issue of celibacy should be re-examined. Many believed that the imposition of celibacy was directly linked to a significant proportion of the clerical sexual abuse cases. The Pope was not prepared even to discuss this idea. His eulogy on priestly celibacy was given in the presence of the visiting Nigerian bishops, who interpreted the comments to refer to the fact that in Africa many priests were indulging in regular sexual relationships with women.

The image of the Pope seated on a slightly raised dais with twelve American cardinals ranged out in a long horse-shoe before him and two senior members of the Curia standing behind him stays in the memory. The cameras had been allowed in briefly to record part of the Pope's welcoming speech and concluding remarks. This was intended as the first stage in the Vatican's press relations exercise. The speech did indeed contain a number of head-line-grabbing phrases:

'The abuse which has caused this crisis is by every standard wrong and rightly considered a crime by society; it is also an appalling sin in the eyes of God. To the victims and their families, wherever they may be, I express my profound sense of solidarity and concern . . . People need to know that there is no place in the priesthood and religious life for those who would harm the young . . .'

'. . . Because of the great harm done by some priests and religious, the Church herself is viewed with distrust, and many are offended at the way the Church leaders are perceived to have acted in this matter . . . The abuse of the young is a grave symptom of a crisis affecting not only the Church but society as a whole.'

Defending the Catholic Church in America, the Pope talked of how it had always promoted human and Christian values with 'great vigour and generosity, in a way that has helped to consolidate all that is noble in the American people'. That was a highly debatable proposition, as was his image of the Church in the United States and in the wider world: 'A great work of art may be blemished, but its beauty remains; and this is a truth which any intellectually honest critic will recognise.'

While the cardinals sat within the Vatican discussing the child abuse scandal, back in Philadelphia the District Attorney announced a grand jury investigation into sexual abuse claims against thirty-five local priests. The alleged abuse ranged over the previous fifty years. Opinion polls in the *Washington Post* and ABC News indicated that seventy-five per cent of Americans believed the Church's image to be deeply tarnished.

The meeting concluded with the Pope and his American cardinals at one on the need to weed out paedophile priests with a policy of zero tolerance. The cardinals were given the express task of creating guidelines to deal with the crisis that would be presented to the US Conference of Catholic Bishops in June in Dallas. The American cardinals then gave a press conference and responded to questions from the huge crowd of reporters. The main item on the agenda for the news media was whether or not Cardinal Law had resigned. The smart money was betting that Law's time as head of the Boston archdiocese was over. Not for the first time the smart money was wrong.

Of the twelve cardinals only three attended the press conference: the missing nine included Cardinal Law who had not resigned. Though the majority of his colleagues had wanted him to fall on his sword, the Pope had declined to let him. In considerable disarray, the cardinals and their camp followers returned to the USA.

The cardinals' evident divisions were nothing compared with the Pope's advisors. Many of them still believed that this was an American problem. They were also deeply divided about the Pope's apparent commitment to zero tolerance. The Pope's forthright denunciation of clerical and religious sexual abuse in April 2002 had been preceded by an almost complete denial of the scandal. Firm action taken early in his papacy would not have wiped out the obscenities perpetrated before October 1978 but through transparency and honest confrontation, and a rapid abolition of the secret system, John Paul II would have saved the Church much grief and, more importantly, he would have prevented untold suffering and pain for the victims yet to come. By also reaching out with counselling, compensation and compassion to those already abused, the Church could have begun their healing nearly thirty years earlier. For some it can now never begin.

Celebrating World Youth Day in Denver, Colorado, in 1993 the Pope had alluded to the scandal which had already convulsed America for nearly ten years. He told a packed audience that he shared the concerns of US bishops for the 'pain and suffering caused by some priests' sins'. He did not mention the pain and suffering caused by the bishops through the operation of the secret system, nor did he endorse any specific punishments for the offenders. The suffering of the victims would be eased 'by prayer'. The cause of the abuse scandals in the USA was a 'widespread false morality . . . America needs much prayer lest it loses its soul'. The issues of birth control and abortion 'have caused strains between US Catholics and the Vatican . . . polarisation and destructive criticism have no place within the Church'. A few weeks later the Vatican released a statement repeating their claim that clergy sexual abuse was an American and Canadian problem.

Among those listening to the Pope in Denver were a number of the victims of this 'North American' problem. One was Tom Economus, a former altar boy who had been raped and regularly abused by family friend and mentor Father Don Murray. During my research for this chapter I interviewed Tom Economus and he recounted in detail how Murray had manipulated and used him. He also recounted how when he subsequently sought counselling, the priest he turned to for help attempted to rape him.

Father Murray had been an 'out-of-control alcoholic', the counsellor 'was just out of any control'. Economus became a member of the breakaway Independent Catholic Church and was ordained a priest. Because of his experiences Economus became a powerful advocate for the victims of clergy abuse. He led efforts to expose perpetrators and demanded accountability from religious leaders. He also became President of Linkup, a support group for clergy abuse victims of all faiths.

I asked him about his attendance in Denver. He replied,

'It was obvious to me by the early 1990s that neither the Vatican nor the Pope were going anywhere with the issue of clergy sexual abuse. World Youth Day in Denver, when the Pope was going to pray with more than 150,000 young people, seemed a good place to make a point. We were demonstrating on behalf of the victims. I'd got together getting on for 3,000 letters from victims and their families. I presented them to the Vatican security staff to be given to the Pope. They refused to take them. Threw them on the ground. I brought them back to this office and sent them to the Vatican. I never had a response.'

Father Economus observed, 'About two months later the Mount Cashel scandal erupted in Newfoundland. Within the year twenty-eight countries were engulfed in the "North American" problem.' In March 2002 Tom Economus, aged 46, died of cancer at his Chicago home. Father Economus is one of a long line of victims ignored by the Vatican and the Pope.

Press relations exercises for the Pope have ranged from talking to Bono, the lead singer of U2, to photo opportunities with Fidel Castro, but the victims of clerical sexual abuse are not seen as good PR. John Paul II made numerous speeches castigating 'particular offensive forms of injustice'. He singled out 'violence against women and against children of both sexes . . . forced prostitution and child pornography, and the exploitation of children in the workplace in conditions of veritable slavery'. But he never referred to the exploitation of children and their veritable sex slavery by thousands of his priests. Though many of the victims tried to meet him, there is not a single known instance of such a meeting.

The Pope's silence was deliberate. He brought with him from Poland to the Vatican practices that he had embraced throughout his life as a priest. They included an intense pathological hatred of any revelation that indicated the

Catholic Church was not a perfect institution. All dissent must be kept behind closed doors, whether of Church politics, scandalous behaviour or criminal activity.

During the Pope's third visit to Austria in June 1998, he gave an illustration of his belief that child abuse and other such matters should not be discussed publicly. The Pope had strained to protect his close friend cardinal Hans Hermann Groer against the demands of hundreds of thousands of Austrians for his resignation following compelling evidence that the Cardinal had sexually abused young boys. The Pope dismissed the evidence even though it demonstrated that the cardinal had been a persistent paedophile over many years. Far more important to the Pope was that Cardinal Groer shared his Marian obsession. Eventually he and his advisors were forced to acknowledge that the controversy would not abate and a month before his 1998 visit the Pope had sadly been forced to agree to the nationwide demand for Groer to leave his post. As he arrived in Austria he was looking for scapegoats. In a private meeting with the Austrian bishops he castigated them roundly for failing to suppress the public outrage, which had culminated in a petition by over 500,000 Austrians demanding a wide range of reforms. He was particularly incensed at the open debate on clerical sexual abuse: 'like every house that has special rooms that are not open to guests, the Church also needs rooms for talks that require privacy.'

The insistence on such secrecy when it came to the washing of the Church's dirty linen was a lifelong obsession of Wojtyla. As a bishop in Cracow no public dissension, no exposure of the Church's faults was the eleventh commandment. In 1980, the locking of the Dutch bishops in a Vatican room until they repudiated the positions they had held since Vatican Council II indicates how rigidly the late Pope applied such tactics. To the Austrian bishops, Wojtyla made it very clear that Cardinal Groer's crimes of repeated sexual abuse of the young were as nothing compared to the crime of publicising that abuse.

Three years later the papal preoccupation with secrecy and cover-up was again demonstrated in a letter sent to every bishop in the world. It came from Cardinal Joseph Ratzinger in his capacity as head of the Congregation of the Faith, but a subsequent apostolic letter from the Pope made it clear that the 'initiative' was his. Ratzinger advised the bishops of a new set of norms covering juridical control of cases of sexual abuse by priests. The rules, which gave control of any proceedings to Ratzinger's Congregation, imposed 'pontifical secret' on all such cases, which would be heard by an all-clerical jury. Priests judging the word of a victim against the word of a fellow priest was not a scenario to inspire confidence. A Vatican-based bishop observed somewhat ruefully,

'these rules are going to give the appearance of a "cover-up". That's because they are a cover-up. As for what some are saying in this place that the secrecy is necessary to protect both the accuser and the accused – they have clearly to catch on to what in here would be a truly radical idea. That justice should not only be done. It should be seen to be done.'

Among the many victims of sexual abuse who would wholeheartedly endorse that sentiment are nine of the survivors of at least thirty who have alleged in sworn depositions that they were continually sexually abused by one particular priest over three decades from the 1940s into the 1960s. The priest in question is Father Marciel Maciel Degollado, the founder and superior general of the Legionaries of Christ. The nine men, now in their late 50s and mid-

60s had, as young boys, all been founder members of the Legionaries.

Juan J. Vaca was recruited by the Reverend Maciel Degollado at the age of ten while living with his parents in Mexico. Maciel told them that he 'saw something special in Juan' and offered the boy the chance of a good education at a seminary he was creating. Flattered, the parents accepted and when two years later Maciel told them that he would like to take Juan along with a number of other boys 'to my seminary in northern Spain for special training with the order', Juan recalled that there were 'tears from my mother but like my father she saw this as a wonderful opportunity'.

As Vaca recalled:

'we were isolated from the outside world by Maciel, all contacts were controlled by him and my mail was censored. After a short while in Spain he began to sexually abuse me. The first time this happened, when he had finished, I went to leave his room and he asked me where I was going. "To confession. I want absolution for what just happened." He told me that he would give me absolution, which he did.'

It was the beginning of years of sexual abuse in which the victim continually felt guilt but the perpetrator never appeared to. Maciel had explained that he regularly suffered from stomach pains and pain in his genitals, which could only be relieved by frequent masturbation. 'Soon,' Juan recalled, 'I became aware that he was abusing many of the other twenty-three children who were my school-mates.' For Juan the abuse continued for almost ten years during which he experienced 'an intense ethical and spiritual confusion, fear, shame and anxiety. I endured countless days of severe stress, and nights of debilitating sleeplessness'.

It was twelve years before Juan was permitted to see his

parents again. The handsome young boy of ten was now a very disturbed twenty-two-year-old. Subsequently, while in the Legionaries residence in Rome, Juan summoned up the courage to confront Maciel and denounce him, but the young man's attempt to exorcise the demon he was confronting ended in the older man turning the tables and, after humiliating Juan, exiling him back to northern Spain as punishment. He was to remain there for six years.

Assuming that he had broken Juan's spirit, Maciel persuaded him to enter the priesthood. Juan, now a priest, was made Vice-Rector and Spiritual Director of the seminary in northern Spain. Subsequently four adolescent students came to him to denounce the Rector for sexually abusing them. Juan recalls the irony of that situation. 'I knew that the Rector, like me, was one of Maciel's original victims when we were all pre-adolescents. We now had second-generation abuse.'

Juan advised Maciel what had occurred.

'He gave me instructions that all traces of the abuse should be covered up. The perpetrator was fired from his post and immediately transferred secretly to a mission in the Yucatan peninsula of Mexico. For my "good work" in covering up the mess, the founder rewarded me with the appointment of superior and president of the Legion of Christ in the United States. In 1976 after five years in that post, I resigned the post and confronted Maciel and denounced him and three months later in October 1976 I formally denounced Maciel to the Vatican, through the proper channels of my bishop, the Reverend John R. McGann, and the Vatican embassy in Washington.'

Juan has since made an impressive success of his life. When I interviewed him in late 2004, I was aware that he had been a Professor of Psychology and Sociology at the Manhattan Campus of Mercy College for the past five years. All of the other surviving victims have also achieved considerable success in their respective lives. With regard to the sexual abuses they suffered from the Reverend Marcial Maciel Degollado, they do not seek financial compensation. They first wrote to Pope John Paul II soon after his election in 1978 and again in 1989 simply seeking official recognition that they had been sexually abused by a man he held in the highest regard. Monsignor John A. Alesandro, a canon lawyer in the Rockville Centre diocese, has confirmed that in both instances the correspondence seeking an investigation into Maciel had been forwarded to the Pope.

Over the years there have been several investigations of Father Maciel by the Vatican. These included a two-year period between 1956 and 1958 when he was suspended from his duties as superior General of the Legion after allegations of drug taking, misuse of funds and 'other improprieties'. Close study of Father Maciel's life indicates that either he has led a charmed existence or he has some very powerful protectors.

For the very first of his numerous pastoral pilgrimages, Pope John Paul II went to Mexico. Although a largely Catholic country, because of its history during the first half of the twentieth century, Mexico was constitutionally anti-clerical. Officially the Church did not exist. The Mexican bishops, not the government, had invited the Pope to a country which did not have diplomatic relations with the Vatican. The family of President Lopez Portillo were all devout Catholics and Father Maciel was a confidant of the President's mother and particularly the sister who was the President's confidential secretary. As a result Portillo listened to them and overrode the objections from his government ministers. Nonetheless the Pope was invited not as a head of state but as a visitor needing a visa.

During his visit to Mexico, the Pope and his secretary Father Dziwisz expressed their gratitude to Father Maciel for his timely intervention. They were both deeply impressed by the man who had created the beginnings of his 'spiritual army' while still a mere theology student of twenty. Before being inspired to do this in 1941, he had already been expelled from two seminaries for what his official history describes as 'misunderstandings' and had suffered a two-year suspension from his duties while a range of accusations had been investigated. Although in 1979 the Pope had only recently received extremely detailed allegations of continual sexual abuse by Maciel from nine of his victims, it did not give him or his secretary pause for thought. Maciel was never far from their side during the remainder of the trip.

The Legionaries of Christ blossomed through the ensuing years. They shared many characteristics with Opus Dei, and still do. Both are highly secretive, impose a regime of unquestioning total obedience, recruit aggressively, are wealthy and, most important, both have had the ear of the Pope and the most powerful papal secretary for seventy years. When Opus Dei and the Legionaries of Christ wanted to establish ecclesiastical universities in Rome (on the basis that only they could teach true orthodox principles) they were opposed by every current ecclesiastical university and the Congregation of Education. Discreet conversations were held with Dziwisz and after an appropriate time a papal decree announced the formation of two new universities.

The complaints by the nine former members of the Legionaries of Christ in 1989 were given further impetus when a tenth complaint from the terminally ill Juan Amenabar was sent to the Vatican in 1995. Amenabar was a former priest in Maciel's order, and as he lay dying, he dictated a damning indictment of the Rector. He had been moved to do so by a statement by the Pope a few months before, describing Maciel as 'an efficacious guide to youth'. In 1998, encouraged by the papal nuncio in Mexico City, the survivors brought a case against Maciel under canon law. They had never sought compensation, or even apologies; they sought only accountability by the Church for Maciel's sexual misconduct. Three years later in December 2001 the Vatican halted the canon law investigation, 'for the time being', without giving reasons or details.

In December 2004 the victims were told that a Vatican prosecutor from the Congregation of the Doctrine of Faith would be holding a formal inquiry. Juan J. Vaca remains sceptical. 'I have absolutely no confidence in the bureaucracy of the Vatican. Even now they are trying to cover up the fact that the Pope is dying.' Juan Vaca's misgivings were well founded. Cardinal Ratzinger secretly ordered the enquiry to stop 'to spare the Holy Father any embarrassment'.

The Vatican had less control over events in the United States. When Cardinal Law returned from the April 2002 meeting in the Vatican he tried to pick up exactly where he had left off. The Church resumed its delaying tactics to prevent courts and victims' lawyers getting access to files. As a result, the cardinal was ordered by judges to depose evidence in the case of Father Shanley in the ongoing cases against the defrocked John Geoghan. The spectacle was humiliating not merely for the cardinal but for every Roman Catholic in the United States. It would have been avoidable if Cardinal Law and his advisors had accepted that in a democracy no one is above the judicial process.

Father Shanley was charged with sexually abusing a six-year-old boy and continually raping him over many years. In February 2005 he was found guilty as charged and was sentenced to serve a term of twelve to fifteen years' imprisonment. The files showed that as late as 1997 Cardinal Law was still judging Shanley worthy of a warm glowing letter of introduction. It was as if the 1,600 pages in Shanley's file in the Boston chancery had never existed. Law claimed that he had transferred Shanley around the archdiocese 'without referring to the files'.

In September the initial claim by eighty-six victims of John Geoghan was settled at the reduced figure of $10 million. This left the way clear for the next claim by additional victims of the same former priest, whose number had risen to over 200.

While similar scenarios were being played out across the country, the bishops had also been addressing the task that they had brought back from the April meeting with the Pope. A month after they had departed from the Vatican in May 2002, the Pope was obliged yet again to address the sex-abuse scandal – this time in private conversation with President George Bush. Confronted with the sight of large parts of the United States in tumult, the President (a born-again Christian) was anxious that his wide-ranging faith-based initiatives should not be damaged by the fall-out. The Pope assured him that Catholics in the US would overcome the current scandal and 'continue to play an important role in building American society'. This was of course the same American society that the Pope had declared was largely responsible for the crisis.

Wojtyla continued to avoid any close-up contact with the scandal and in July 2002 embarked on a twelve-day trip to Canada, Mexico and Guatemala. His failure to make even a symbolic stopover in the United States was seen by many American Catholics as a deliberate snub and yet further evidence of how much he was out of touch. Within the Vatican that reaction was seen as further evidence that the American response to the scandal was 'exaggerated, even hysterical'.

When Canadian victims of clerical sexual abuse requested a meeting with the Pope during the World Youth

Day celebrations in Toronto they got a response similar to that given to the late Father Tom Economus: 'the Pope is far too busy to give time to such a meeting'. He was also too busy to address the subject of clergy sexual abuse at any point of his tour.

At much the same time the American bishops gathered in Dallas to find the solution to the problem. The buzzwords of the day were 'zero tolerance, one strike and you're out'. During the two-day conference Bishop Wilton Gregory made the most clear-cut statement of contrition by any senior figure of the Church since the crisis had begun. At the end of the conference he declared, 'From this day forward no one known to have sexually abused a child will work in the Catholic Church in the United States.' Nonetheless, the meeting struggled to define sexual abuse, and it struggled to provide safeguards for priests who might be unjustly accused. They failed to give a guarantee that the norms they were seeking to establish would be applied fairly. They neglected to affirm that the bishops themselves would be subject to the proposed discipline. Above all other omissions, one in particular was startling: they failed to address the root causes of clerical sexual abuse.

The lines of communication between Dallas and the Vatican began to get seriously busy. The Vatican was 'concerned that some of the proposals may well conflict with canon law'. The Vatican believed 'that some of your number are being unduly pressurised by both pressure groups (victim support groups) and the media'. The Vatican chose to ignore a current opinion poll that showed eighty-seven per cent of US Catholics in favour of a zero-tolerance policy.

The Dallas document did not in fact call for an automatic defrocking or a total ban on priestly activities. A priest found guilty would be banned from public ministry and working with parishioners, but not automatically defrocked. Depending on the particular circumstances the priest would have the chance to function 'in a controlled environment' such as a 'monastery'. Though publicly the bishops approved the document by 239 to 13 votes, many were unhappy with the rulings, which would be binding, while others felt the directives and the new policy did not go far enough.

While the US bishops had been holding their meeting, Cardinal Oscar Rodriguez Maradiaga of Honduras, considered by many to be a leading contender as a Third World successor to Pope John Paul II, went public with views that a majority within the Vatican endorsed – but usually only in private. For Cardinal Maradiaga the reason that the United States was enraged about clerical sexual abuse was the gross exaggeration 'by the media', which were intent on 'persecuting the Church' because of its firm stand on abortion, euthanasia, contraception and the death penalty. As for Cardinal Law, he was being victimised as if he were 'a defendant in a show trial staged by Nero or Stalin'. The Cardinal declared that Ted Turner, the founder of CNN news network, was 'openly anti-Catholic. Not to mention newspapers like the *New York Times*, the *Washington Post* and the *Boston Globe* which were protagonists of what I define as persecution against the Church.' He was also at pains to tell the world what a fine man Cardinal Law was.

Cardinal Maradiaga made his remarks during an interview with the Italian magazine *Thirty Days*. No sooner had he left the building than his Mexican colleague Cardinal Norberto Rivera entered and virtually repeated Maradiaga's denunciation. A few months later, a third Central American Cardinal, Miguel Obando y Bravo from Managua, Nicaragua, granted the same magazine an interview (nothing orchestrated, of course) and said, 'Anyone who attacks Cardinal Law today must not recognise the strength of his involvement, the weight of his ministry and the

coherence of his life.' He felt sure that the faithful Catholics
of Boston would recognise the 'golden nugget' in Cardinal
Law's personality, which 'continues to shine'. The remainder of his interview was largely confined to yet another
vilification of the American media.

As early as May yet another Latin American Cardinal,
Eugenio Araujo Sales of Brazil, had led the attack on the
allegations, describing them as 'over-exposed – many are
old accusations – they account for less than a half of one per
cent of 46,000 priests'. Disturbingly, this princely defence
of Cardinal Law met with full Vatican approval. It showed
up the gulf between the hierarchy and the victims and the
overwhelming majority of rank-and-file Roman Catholics.

This gulf was again exposed in September 2002 when
lawyers representing 250 plaintiffs who were suing the
Boston archdiocese released personnel records on five
priests showing that several bishops had known about
the abuse allegations against the five for years, but left
them in positions where they could abuse more children.
One of the five had only been removed in March 2002,
eight years after he was accused of abuse.

In November yet another judge, Constance Sweeney,
delivered a handwritten note to the Boston archdiocese
ordering the release of further thousands of documents
covering the personnel files of priests accused of sexual
misconduct. She complained bitterly that the archdiocese
had engaged in a pattern of conduct designed to stall the
implementation of prior court decisions. 'The court simply
will not be toyed with,' she wrote.

In a separate order the judge strongly suggested that
officials of the Boston archdiocese had conveyed an inaccurate picture of Church policies during their testimony on
various sex-abuse cases. 'The available records raise significant questions of whether the archdiocese was really
exercising the care they claimed to use in assigning offend-

ing priests.' She referred the case of Father Bernard Lane to the Attorney General of Massachusetts for possible perjury charges. What was unfolding in the Boston archdiocese had its counterpart in many another archdiocese and many another country.

While the events in Boston continued to move to an inevitable climax, the issue of establishing a national policy in the United States Church to respond to clerical sex abuse was back with the US bishops. The Vatican response to the Dallas proposal was to reject it. The Pope's zero-tolerance agenda of April 2002 was no longer his position in September. Though the US bishops had baulked at throwing sex abusers out of the priesthood, they had gone too far for the Pope and Ratzinger and their Vatican advisors, who favoured the opinions of the four Latin American Cardinals.

In the Pope's view, the Dallas accord could not be reconciled with the canon law, the rules that governed the Catholic Church. The Pope and his Heads of Congregations were primarily concerned with protecting the rights of the accused priest, and they were also unhappy with the American definition of sexual abuse. A fudge was in the making, which is best described as 'one strike and after every conceivable avenue of defence has been offered to you, if found guilty, you might be defrocked or you might be forced to wear civilian clothes and be confined to barracks'. Nowhere were the needs of the victim addressed or even recognised. Nowhere was there any mention of the legal necessity to inform civil authorities.

By early December 2002 the Pope's refusal to accept Cardinal Law's resignation in April had ensured months of constant humiliation for the Cardinal and continuous assault on the faith of over two million Catholics in Boston. During the first week of December the public release of yet more documents showed that the cover-up through the secret system had been even more extensive than previously realised. Confronted with lawsuits that could run into further compensation payouts of $100 million, the Cardinal obtained permission for his finance council to file for bankruptcy protection.

Boston priests soon began organising petitions calling for the resignation of Law. Many hundreds of angry Catholics gathered outside Boston's Holy Cross Cathedral to confront him. When they were told he had gone to Rome, they continued with their demonstration, demanding his removal. Three days later a furious Massachusetts Attorney General complained that the Boston archdiocese is 'using every tool and manoeuvre' to 'obstruct' an inquiry into sexual abuse by 'clergy'. Thomas Reilly told the *Boston Globe* that the archdiocese has been engaged in 'an elaborate and decades-long effort to cover up clerical misbehaviour'. On Friday 13 December the Boston Cardinal met with his protector and again offered his resignation. This time the Pope accepted it.

Bishop Richard Lennon was appointed apostolic administrator while the Vatican considered its options. Lennon announced that he hoped the archdiocese could avoid filing for bankruptcy. In the event they did but the price was high. Nine days after Cardinal Law's successor Archbishop Sean Patrick O'Malley was installed, at the beginning of August 2003, the archdiocese offered $55 million to settle some 500 outstanding clergy sex abuse lawsuits. The settlement would resolve claims from many hundreds of victims who had been abused as children by some 140 clergy within the Boston archdiocese. The offer was rejected.

While both sides considered their options, news broke that the former priest John Geoghan had been murdered in prison. A man who had caused so much pain, damage and heartache and destroyed countless lives had experienced prison's version of zero tolerance. A number of the plaintiffs who had just rejected the $55 million were men who had identified Goeghan as their abuser. Some of them began to feel the heat as legal advisors urged them to reconsider the rejected settlement. Some were in desperate need of a settlement, any settlement. In the event several busloads of lawyers sat down with Archbishop O'Malley and a new improved offer of $85 million was put on the table which was picked up.

When previous payments are included, the minimum figure paid out as compensation to the victims of clerical sexual abuse in the Boston archdiocese over a ten-year period is $116 million. The archdiocese was forced to put up its cathedral and seminary as collateral against loans it was forced to take out. Archbishop O'Malley has also decided to sell the Archbishop's residence and other church property worth many millions to help fund the compensation payout.

Archbishop O'Malley and men like him are clearly determined upon a new approach, which fully and honestly recognises the Catholic Church's culpability in this still-continuing scandal. At the present time such men are unfortunately in a minority within the higher reaches of the Church. Far too many still cling to a bizarre range of explanations either for the abuse or the Church's long-standing response.

The Latin American cardinals who saw a media conspiracy were not alone. US cardinals were largely at one with their brothers south of the border. Cardinal Theodore E. McCarrick of Washington spoke for many when he told the *Washington Post*, 'Elements in our society who are very opposed to the Church's stand on life, the Church's stand on family and the Church's stand on education . . . see this as an opportunity to destroy the credibility of the Church. And they are really working on it – and somewhat successfully.' Of course the *Washington Post* was regularly accused of being one of the leading media conspirators.

Others within the Roman Catholic hierarchy adopted a different line of attack. The Prefect of the Vatican's Congregation for the Clergy, Cardinal Dario Castrillon Hoyos, insisted that the problem of abusive priests was 'statistically minor . . . less than 0.3 per cent of priests are paedophiles'. Other clerics took a similar view without necessarily quoting the extraordinary figure of 0.3 per cent, plucked from the Roman or the Brazilian air. A document presented to Australia's bishops in late 1999 saw sexual abuse by clergy as part of the product of

> 'an all-male atmosphere within the seminaries that reflected male values and did not deal adequately with sexuality in general or with feminine issues in particular. As long as the culture of the Church does not put men and women on a basis of true equality, then women and children will remain vulnerable to abuse.'

Archbishop Rembert G. Weakland had an alternative explanation. 'Sometimes not all adolescent victims are so "innocent"; some can be sexually very active and aggressive and often quite streetwise.' The Archbishop, evidently speaking from personal experience, was subsequently forced to resign when it was revealed that he had paid a male lover nearly $500,000 to buy his silence. The money had allegedly come from diocesan funds.

Others blamed not streetwise adolescents but trial lawyers greedy for the Church's money. Maurice Healy, Director of Communications for the archdiocese of San Francisco, told the *New York Times* in early December 2002, 'There is a gold rush to get into the priest litigation business.' The next edition of the archdiocesan newspaper mailed to Catholics through Northern California headlined one article: 'Lawyers Aggressively Seek Sex Abuse Business', without mention of the initial aggression perpetrated on successive generations of young children. Healy's claim of a Church with 'limited resources' was made at precisely the same time that the new cathedral was opened in the south of California. Our Lady of Angels had been built at a cost of $200 million. At the time of the opening ceremony the Los Angeles diocese had seventy-two current or former priests under criminal investigation and was assailed with a large number of claims by victims of clerical abuse. Two weeks after the opening ceremonies, the archdiocese announced a deficit of $4.3 million and a range of cuts and closures in its counselling services.

Other reasons for the cause of the scandal put forward by elements of the Roman Catholic Church included:

'Paedophilia is spread by Satan . . . Catholic-bashing is fashionable. In fact the Protestants and the Baptists have even more paedophiles . . . the cover-ups were more out of frustration and ignorance . . . the seminaries were infiltrated thirty to forty years ago by homosexuals and dissidents . . . Pope John XXIII and his Vatican Council are solely responsible.'

Those who blamed the Second Council managed to condemn its rulings openly but simultaneously cited 'dissent' as the greatest reason for the sex abuse scandals. They meant dissent on issues of sexual morality that covered birth control, celibacy, homosexuality, abortion and divorce. Those who had identified widespread dissent from the Church's teaching on these subjects blamed not society in general but the bishops, whom they accused of failing to define doctrine firmly or to impose it, and declining to investigate credible evidence of violations. In early 2003 while priests as far apart as Pennsylvania and Hong Kong were pleading guilty to sexually abusing young boys, Bishop John McCormack of Manchester, New Hampshire, was attempting to justify his failure to inform the authorities of sexual abuse by priests. His deposition revealed that in the 1980s while working as an assistant to Cardinal Law he suppressed evidence concerning the sexual activities of a number of priests in Boston because he 'was acting as a priest and not as a social worker'. As the information had not come to him in a confessional setting, he was, in fact, obliged to pass it to the authorities. Bishop McCormack had also avoided asking the paedophile priests 'direct questions or making written notes'. He was aware that his records would be 'discoverable' if a victim filed suit against the archdiocese.

In March 2003 the Attorney General's office in New Hampshire issued a 154-page report accompanied by over 9,000 pages of documents which the Attorney General described as establishing that the Church leaders of the diocese of Manchester had been 'wilfully blind in dealing with clergy sex abuse and the related danger to children'.

In mid-2003 powerful independent evidence emerged that confirmed that at least part of the cause pointed to the bishops. One of the most positive initiatives to emerge from the Dallas conference of mid-2002 had been the creation of a lay panel whose brief was to investigate the sex abuse scandal. This national review board had the full power to question any cleric in the United States. The man appointed to chair the panel was former Oklahoma Governor Frank Keating. It was a highly popular appointment. Keating, a devout Catholic and a man of integrity, was viewed as honest and independent. Many of the bishops he interviewed gave the panel full co-operation; others did not. Keating compared the recalcitrants with Mafia leaders who pleaded the Fifth Amendment and refused to answer questions.

One of those who refused to cooperate was Cardinal Roger Mahony of Los Angeles. His personal skeletons dated back a long way and included a continuation of the cover-up of the seven priests who had repeatedly sexually abused Rita Milla. In 2001 it had been revealed that Cardinal Mahony had written to President Clinton during his second term requesting that the fifteen-year prison sentence passed on Los Angeles cocaine dealer Carlos Vignali be commuted. Clinton controversially obliged on his last day in the office.

In late May 2002, just a few months before the national review board headed by Keating was created, a lawsuit was filed against Cardinal Mahony. Brought under the American federal racketeering laws designed to counter organised crime, the lawsuit was filed on behalf of four men who declared that they had been sexually molested as boys by Father Michael Baker. The men accused Mahony of conspiring to commit fraud and obstruct justice by covering up the activities of Baker. The plaintiffs also alleged that the cardinal paid off two of the victims in a $1.3 million settlement that required them to remain silent about the sexual abuse. A week before the lawsuit had been served, the Cardinal had admitted keeping secret for fourteen years a case of child abuse by Father Baker. Confronted by the lawsuit, Mahony dismissed the various allegations as 'groundless' but a short while later, when Frank Keating and his national review board came into town, Mahony was hostile.

The cardinal objected to being compared with the Mafia and forced Keating's resignation, thus confirming to many that some bishops were simply refusing to be accountable for their actions. Frank Keating's letter of resignation acknowledged what had been achieved during the year, including the appointment of a law enforcement professional to underline the message: 'Sex abuse is not just a moral lapse. It is a crime that should be fully prosecuted.' It continued:

'As I have recently said, and have repeated on several occasions, our Church is a faith institution. A home to Christ's people. It is not a criminal enterprise. It does not condone and cover up criminal activity. It does not follow a code of silence. My remarks, which some bishops found offensive, were deadly accurate. I make no apology. To resist grand jury subpoenas, to suppress the names of offending clerics, to deny, to obfuscate, to explain away, this is the model of a criminal organisation, not my Church. The humiliation, the horrors of the sex scandal, must be a poisonous aberration, a black page in our history that cannot ever recur. It has been disastrous to the Church in America.'

And not only to the American Church. The global reach of the scandal was revealed by a report from Sister Maura O'Donohue. Many believed that it inspired the unusually explicit reference to sexual abuse in the Pope's address to the Church of Oceania in 1998. Sister Maura's report was submitted confidentially to Cardinal Eduardo Martinez, prefect of the Vatican Congregation for Religious Life, in February 1994. Sister Maura, a physician in the Order of Medical Missionaries of Mary, had over forty years of pastoral and medical experience. Her report was headed 'Urgent Concerns for the Church in the Context of HIV/ AIDS'.

Her investigations established that priests and religious were dying from AIDS-related illnesses. In many of the countries where Sister Maura worked, prostitution was widely accepted. However, with the increased awareness that prostitutes formed a high-risk group, many men looked for an alternative. One group considered 'safe' targets for sexual activity were religious sisters. Sisters began to report sexual abuse from their professors and their teachers and sexual harassment from men within the general population. The other group that targeted women within religious orders were priests. In one country, a Superior of a community of sisters was approached by priests requesting that sisters be made available for sexual favours. When the Superior refused, the priests explained that if she did not cooperate they would be obliged to 'go to the village and find women and risk getting AIDS'.

Sister Maura's report irrefutably established a shocking catalogue of sexual abuse. She observed,

'It does not apply to any single country or even continent, nor indeed to any one group or all members of society. In fact the following examples derive from experience over a six-year period and relate to incidents in some twenty-three countries in five continents: Botswana, Brazil, Colombia, Ghana, India, Ireland, Italy, Kenya, Lesotho, Malawi, Nigeria, Papua New Guinea, Philippines, South Africa, Sierra Leone, Uganda, Tanzania, Tonga, United States of America, Zambia, Zaire, Zimbabwe.'

It was her devout hope that the report would 'motivate appropriate action especially on the part of those in positions of Church leadership and those responsible for formation'. The report detailed priests and bishops abusing and exploiting their powers to indulge in sexual relations. Potential candidates to religious life were coerced into granting sexual favours to ensure they obtained the required certificates and/or recommendations. Sisters who became pregnant were forced to leave their congregation, but the priests responsible continued in their ministry.

The report also contained many positive recommendations to overcome the abuse of women within the

Church. A year after she submitted the report to Cardinal Martinez, no one in the Vatican had taken any action other than to invite Sister Maura and her colleagues to a meeting with Martinez and three members of his staff. As she dryly observed in a subsequent memorandum, 'It was clear that there was no prearranged agenda.'

Subsequently other concerned senior women from religious orders created similar reports. Still there was no action either from Cardinal Martinez or any other senior Vatican figure. The Pope's brief comments quoted earlier had still not been made public when in great frustration some of the authors of the reports contacted the *National Catholic Reporter* in early 2001. As a result, the newspaper ran a cover story on 16 March 2001. *La Repubblica*, Italy's largest daily, followed up four days later with a long report on the issue.

The Vatican was forced to respond. Its statement came not from the Pope or Cardinal Martinez but from the ubiquitous Navarro-Valls. 'The problem is known, and is restricted to a geographically limited area.' That comment should be compared with the list of countries given earlier, a list that is by no means complete. The statement continued,

> 'The Holy See is dealing with the question in collaboration with the bishops, with the Union of Superiors General (USG) and with the International Union of Superiors General (USIG). The work has two sides, the formation of persons and the solution of single cases.'

Setting up committees does not constitute a solution. No positive action had been taken by the Holy See over the seven years since they had first been made fully aware of this additional dimension of sexual abuse by Sister Maura O'Donohue and other experts. Far from seeking a 'solution of single cases', the Holy See needed a root and branch purge within the ranks of the clergy. The Vatican spokes-man concluded, 'Certain negative situations cannot cause to be forgotten the frequently heroic fidelity of the great majority of male religious, female religious and male priests.'

Navarro-Valls' claim for the 'heroic fidelity of the great majority' flies in the face of powerful research evidence. Researchers at the Saint Louis University carried out a national survey in the United States. It was completed in 1996 but intentionally never publicised. It estimated that a minimum of 34,000 Catholic nuns, about forty per cent of all nuns within the United States, had suffered some form of sexual trauma.

Largely financed by a number of Catholic religious orders, the researchers dealt with three areas of sexual victimization: childhood sexual abuse where the victim is younger than eighteen years, sexual exploitation/coercion by those in a position of power over the nun and, thirdly, sexual harassment at work and within the community of sisters. At the time of the survey there were approximately 89,000 Catholic sisters in the United States and about 85,000 (ninety-five per cent) were members of active religious institutes or communities. The fifteen-page survey was sent to 2,500 names randomly selected from the 25,000 made available to the University team. Every American state was represented plus additional names working in a number of foreign countries.

The responses showed that 18.6 per cent had been sexually abused as children. Most of the abusers were male with brothers, uncles, male strangers, male family friends, fathers and male cousins topping the list in that order. Clergymen and nuns accounted for nearly 10 per cent of the child abusers. In the second stage 12.5 per cent had been sexually exploited and in the third stage 9.3 per cent had been sexually harassed during their work as a religious. The results also suggested that taking their entire life from childhood to the present time 40 per cent had suffered some form of sexual trauma and nearly 22 per cent had been abused during their religious life. As the research team observed, 'The interpretations and implications of these events for the individual woman and religious life in general are compelling.'

Catholic priests and nuns formed the largest group of abusers of women religious, frequently when acting as a spiritual advisor to the victim. Other roles that were identified for the sexually abusing priests included pastor, retreat director, counsellor and mentor. The most frequent roles for nuns guilty of sexual abuse were mentor, formation director, religious superior and teacher.

In July 2001, representatives of 146 religious, women's rights and human rights groups launched an international campaign aimed at pressurising the Vatican to end the Catholic clergy's sexual abuse and sexual violence against nuns and lay women. Earlier the same year the European Parliament passed an emergency motion censuring the Vatican and requesting 'that the Vatican seriously examine every indication of sexual abuse committed in the heart of its organisation'. It also demanded that the Vatican 're-establish women in their posts in the religious hierarchy, who were removed from their responsibilities because they called the attention of their superiors to these abuses'. The Holy See was also asked to cooperate with any judicial enquiry. As of early 2005 it had yet to respond.

While the petitioners to the Vatican waited, clerical sexual abuse continued to be exposed. In May 2004 Margaret Kennedy, a Catholic who founded Christian Survivors of Sexual Abuse, revealed to me some of the details of a study yet to be published. She had previously compiled details of 120 cases of alleged sexual abuse of women by clergy but her latest report deals with a further sixty cases.

Just as sexual abuse of children and adults is not confined to Roman Catholic clerics, the same applies to the sexual abuse of women. All faiths have ministers who are sexual predators. Among the new sixty cases were twenty-five that involved clerics from the Church of England, twenty-five from the Roman Catholic Church and the remainder spread among Methodists, Baptists and Presbyterians.

The report noted

'Approximately fifty per cent of the clergy involved in these particular cases are married men, which rather demolishes the proposition that celibacy is at the heart of the problem of clerical sexual abuse. It's not about celibacy, it is about abuse of power.'

Margaret Kennedy believes that most of the clergy involved should be treated as sex offenders:

'The priest in his capacity as a professional must accept that when a woman comes to him seeking help, spiritual direction, counselling and advice that there are boundaries. The woman is a client and should be regarded at all times as such. We are not talking about a social meeting on a golf course. I actually believe that the client should be able to walk into a meeting with her priest stark naked and that the priest should still be able to hold a boundary between himself and his client.' Many of Margaret Kennedy's case studies dealt with the priest or the minister within a pastoral relationship moving inexorably to sexual abuse. 'The same rules that apply to doctors, physiotherapists and psychologists should apply to clergy.'

The testimony against the men included in Kennedy's report had a very familiar ring: 'He would tell me this was our

secret and I shouldn't say anything to anyone. This was
what God wanted – God would be pleased with me.' Or,
'He told me it was God's will to have sex with me and when
I turned him down that I wasn't being obedient to God . . .
He started off trying to kiss me and fondle my breasts.'
Father Tamayo and his fellow priests were saying exactly
the same things to Rita Milla during the 1970s. Father
Gauthe repeatedly told his altar boys that what he was
doing to them was God's will. Virtually every clerical sexual
abuser that has been exposed over the years has brought
God into the equation and created a blasphemous and
sacrilegious ménage à trois.

The exact nature of the coercion varies from abuser to
abuser. Father Kamal Bathish did not invoke the Almighty
directly but used a very effective technique of making his
victim dependent on himself as her spiritual mentor. In
1983 Pauline Cunningham had just finished a three-year
commission as a nurse in the British Army when she saw
an advertisement for volunteer nurses in Jerusalem. At the
time she had been considering a future in nursing in
California. 'Working there as a nurse, meeting a great
American, getting married, having three children, that was
my dream.' Instead she found herself working in St
Joseph's, a small Christian hospital in East Jerusalem,
where her childhood Catholic faith was reawakened.
She began to attend Mass again: 'Well, something just
touched me. I'd always worked as a nurse and worked
towards physically helping people to heal but frequently
thought there was something missing.'

In April 1985 she entered a Carmelite Convent in Bethlehem as a novitiate. Pauline assumed that within a Carmelite Order all was peace, harmony and tranquillity but
she was very rapidly disabused. Nothing had prepared her
for the bitchiness, the warring factions and the frequent
disappearance of Christianity:

'The legitimate Superior was rather weak. The sister who had previously been Prioress for a long time was very into power games . . . I was totally shocked. I have been brought up very strictly in the Catholic faith and never for one moment had I thought that nuns and priests could bitch and gossip, be so uncharitable and behave as if they were living in a secular world rather than a Carmelite Order.'

Pauline, or Sister Marie Paul as she had become, and another novitiate complained to the Latin Patriarch's office who had overall responsibility and authority over the Order:

'They came and saw us a couple of times but their response was, "Just accept the suffering. This is Jerusalem. You will have to accept the unfairness and all that occurs within the Order. It is part of your particular suffering towards your personal purification."'
This advice had come from the Patriarch's secretary, Father Kamal Bathish.

Pauline attempted to follow the advice but by September 1986 the Mother Superior was constantly seeking *her* guidance and support; the novitiate was completely out of her depth and decided to leave the convent. Two years later in 1988, still seeking a form of life with a religious base, she returned to Jerusalem. Out of courtesy she advised the Patriarch's office of her return. At this time she discussed her future with Father Bathish and her plans to resume nursing. Bathish urged her to become a 'consecrated person,' an individual who while living and working in the secular world offers his or her life in the service of the Church. In essence it was a lay vocation, with a life of poverty, chastity and obedience. Such a commitment appealed to Pauline who saw it as 'an appropriate way of being of service'. Bathish suggested a fellow priest, Father Grech, as her spiritual director. The kindly and thoughtful Bathish also said he would 'always be available for any future problems you might have'.

Pauline recalls that Bathish became 'a good listener, particularly after I had made a complaint to him concerning another priest who had attempted to sexually assault me.' The incident had occurred just a month after her return in March 1988. It left Pauline even more dependent on Father Bathish for support and counselling. The secret system was applied to Father Peter Madros, the priest who had allegedly assaulted Pauline, and he was moved to another location, Biet Sahour. Soon the Patriarch's office received another complaint after Madros had harassed a married woman. Yet again he was quietly moved.

Pauline found it difficult to relate to Father Grech. He would never discuss the events that had occurred at the Convent, events that Pauline was still attempting to come to terms with. Bathish was different and by early August 1988 the thirty-one-year-old nurse and the forty-six-year-old priest had established a mutually trusting relationship. She turned to him increasingly for support and guidance:

'Then one evening, he kissed me. I was totally and utterly astonished. Oh my God! I just didn't say anything. You know when you are out with someone and they suddenly kiss you. You don't push them away or make a scene or say anything. You just go really quiet and back away so that you don't embarrass the other person. I thought, well I'm not going to say anything, maybe it was just a one-off. I valued his support and his understanding of my situation and of the background I had come from and I valued that far far more. So I just kept on seeing him and talking to him. But the more I saw him the more insistent he became sexually. Sometimes when I cried, he would kiss me or touch me and become more comforting. I had a very strong spiritual dependence on him. Not physical, not at all, but I did whatever he told me to do. I had misgivings, I felt guilt, I felt shame.'

Over the ensuing nine months this curious relationship continued to develop, with Pauline deriving spiritual comfort and Father Bathish obtaining physical satisfaction. The kissing became fondling, and then the priest persuaded her to relieve his frustration by masturbating him, then oral sex. Father Bathish belongs to the same sexual school of ethics as former President Bill Clinton: anything short of sexual penetration was not sexual intercourse, not even for a priest who has taken a vow of chastity. Pauline continued to display an almost reverential attitude to Father Bathish:

'He used to fondle me and put his hands up my skirt, things like that and I used to push his hands away but I never actually verbally said the word "no" because I thought that to do that would embarrass him or humiliate him and I had no wish to do either . . . I thought that if I did that he would be angry and then I'd lose that support, the moral support, the comfort – not so much the comfort but the understanding and care that he gave me that I needed at the time very much.'

I questioned her closely about the obvious paradox of suffering humiliation rather than the risk of causing it, of showing such consideration for his feelings while he demonstrably had shown none for hers. During her time in the convent she had strenuously objected to behaviour from others that was mild in comparison to this priest's behaviour. While a novitiate she had taken strong exception to any invasion of her privacy yet here she was accepting a much more profound invasion. Why accept such behaviour? She replied, 'Because it was somebody that I knew could understand me and understand where I was coming from, somebody that you could share things with. That you could trust.'

A year later in July 1989 Pauline was offered the opportunity of running a guest house that was owned by the Patriarchate, the Knight's Palace. She had made a number of attempts to end the sexual element of her relationship with Father Bathish while rather unrealistically maintaining the spiritual aspect. Now she tried again but without success. The priest still represented someone to turn to when there was a problem. By the summer of 1992 their relationship was an open secret within the religious community. There was no question in the minds of the various priests when it came to apportioning blame. The fault was Pauline's and hers alone. The injustice was compounded when Pauline was dismissed. From that date Pauline Cunningham, the woman who went to Jerusalem seeking a religious life, began fighting for justice. Both elements were to prove elusive.

Eventually, after a criminal trial that started in March 1997 alleging sexual exploitation and 'constructive rape', the patriarchate of Jerusalem was found guilty and Pauline was awarded 240,000 shekels, about £25,000. The trial ended in 2003. Subsequently she was also awarded 5,000 shekels after the Jerusalem hierarchy had tried to prevent publication of the initial ruling.

Father Tom Doyle is familiar with the case, and has sworn an affidavit in support of Pauline's struggle to establish the truth. For him, this is

'a classic case of reverential fear. This fear is induced in a person by reason of the force of the other person's stature, position, rank or special relationship with the victim . . . The victim has such an emotional and psychological respect for or fear for the one imposing the force that he or she cannot act in any other way than the way the person wishes. In Catholic culture it is common for lay people, children, or others to be induced by this force when in the presence of clerics. Catholics are indoctrinated from their childhood that priests take the place of Jesus Christ and are to be obeyed at all costs and never questioned or criticised. This exalted position is even more firmly rooted in a Catholic's mind and emotions if the person is a high-ranking cleric or holds an exalted title such as "monsignor" or is a bishop.'

During Pauline's relationship with Father Bathish, he became first a monsignor and then a bishop. Father Doyle observed,

'The trauma bond that comes into existence in a cleric–lay relationship, especially a sexual relationship, is a pathological or sick bond that becomes firmer and sicker the longer the relationship goes on. A common example of such a bond is that which exists between a battered spouse and her battering husband as she continues to go back to him in spite of the violence.'

The Latin Patriarch, Michel Sabbah, consistently refused over many years to meet Pauline Cunningham, despite the fact that there were at least four other women who had suffered sexual abuse from Bishop Bathish, and that the bishop has admitted the truth of Pauline's allegations. He made this confession to a commission of enquiry set up by the Patriarch. The Patriarch is directly answerable to the

Pope, yet the Vatican's position is that the case is a matter for the Patriarch.

The closed-doors Vatican seminar on clerical sexual abuse conducted in April 2003 had ended with the content of the discussions, the agenda and the conclusions all a closely guarded secret. It was a further ten months before the Vatican deigned to share a little of what had transpired. Typically out of touch, the Vatican airily declared that the proceedings of the seminar 'might be available in late March or might remain a private document available only to bishops and to consulting professionals working with the bishops' approval'.

The seminar had heard from a dozen or so eminent doctors and psychiatrists. The experts were all of one mind: they were all apparently horrified that the Dallas meeting of US bishops should have advocated zero tolerance on abuse. At a brief press conference held at the Vatican in late February 2004, Bishop Elio Sgreccia, the President of the Pontifical Academy for Life, summed up the most disastrous conclusion reached during the previous year's Vatican seminar. He said that the specialists assembled by the Vatican had concluded

'It is possible and necessary to find an approach even for priests who are guilty of sexual abuse, to pursue treatment and rehabilitation and not to abandon them or consider them useless to the Church.'

During the seminar, a number of the experts including the American psychiatrist Martin Kafka spoke of the 'excessively punitive' policies adopted by American hierarchy. Kafka and his colleagues were sure they knew the way forward. Their approach was based on professional self-delusion and threatened to subvert the course of justice. The most telling indictment of the conclusions of the seminar is in the selection criteria for those invited. Bishop Sgreccia explained that 'The institutions they represent are *de facto* used by bishops' conferences for the treatment of priests and religious.' It was akin to inviting the makers of the SS *Titanic* to build an icebreaker. Despite an almost unbroken record of failure in treating clerical sexual abusers, the chosen experts expressed themselves dogmatically. The Canadian psychologist William Marshall told the Vatican officials that zero tolerance for sex abusers is

'a disaster. If I kick this fellow out of the Church and he loses his job, his income, his health benefits and all of his friends . . . with no other skills to get a job, that's not the conditions to ensure a former priest won't commit more abuse.' He claimed that a number of American bishops and clergy came up to him at the first break and said, 'That's exactly what the bishops in the US need to hear.'

Apart from turning bishops into welfare officers for clerical sex abusers, the approach of the seminar sought to keep abusers away from judicial investigation or trial. This is the ultimate irony: after turning themselves into secular priests, psychiatrists, psychologists and doctors set themselves up as judge and jury over priests who sin. From Pope John Paul II down to the most recently appointed bishop, in any aspect of the sexual abuse scandal, the first line of defence for the Church has been:

'We did not know. We did not understand. We relied on our own judgements when confronted with clerical sexual abuse. There were no data, no information, no studies. There was nothing available on this and associated behavioural problems.'

The falsity of that defence was demonstrated by Monsignor Charles Scicluna, an official of Cardinal Ratzinger's Congregation for the Doctrine of the Faith, during the secret Vatican seminar. The experts who had been invited were all non-Catholics and Monsignor Scicluna gave them a much needed history lesson on how the Church had dealt with clerical sex abusers in earlier times. He quoted among others Pope Alexander II, at the Third Lateran Council in 1179 on sexual abusers. 'If they are clerics, they will be dismissed from the clerical state or else will be confined to monasteries to do penance.' Scicluna also quoted Pope Pius V declaring in 1568 that sexual abusers 'must be handed over to the secular authorities for punishment and if he is a cleric will be demoted from everything'.

My informant gave no clue as to the response of Messrs Kafka and Marshall to the history lesson. For good measure Monsignor Scicluna also drew attention to the early twentieth-century Church position quoting from the 1917 Code of Canon Law: 'Priests who engage in sexual misconduct with children will be suspended, they will be declared unworthy, they will be deprived of any office, benefice, dignity, or responsibility they may have.' However, he does not appear to have quoted from the 1984 revised Code of Canon Law, whose language on the offence of sexual abuse of a minor (meaning under the age of sixteen) was much softer. It said that the abuser 'is to be punished with just penalties, not excluding dismissal from the clerical state if the case so warrants'. For much of its existence and until six years *after* Karol Wojtyla was elected Pope, the Church applied a policy of zero tolerance without exception or excuse. How did it manage to forget its history?

Having quoted copiously from the history of how the Roman Catholic Church had dealt with sexual abuse over the centuries Monsignor Scicluna unfortunately failed to examine the other side of the coin. What *contemporary* information was available to the Church's bishops and cardinals? In case after case, the cover-up, the lies, the deceit, the careful use of the 'secret system' gives the lie to the repeated suggestion that 'there was so little known at the time and the cardinal or the bishop were guilty only of ignorance'. If those who protected the sexually abusing priest genuinely believed, as they have claimed, that all could be cured by the power of prayer, then why go to such elaborate lengths to hide the crime? Why not have an open day of prayer for the offending priest at his local church? Is it possible to believe that the bishops and cardinals were unaware of the necessity of removing paedophiles from any possible contact with children?

As of the mid-1980s, the time of the Father Gauthe case, the Church had access to abundant studies of the origins and effects of clerical sexual abuse. One was *The Catholic Priest in the United States: Psychological Investigations* by Father Eugene C. Kennedy and Victor Heckler. This ground-breaking work paid particular attention to the emotional and developmental problems of priests. The authors concluded that seven per cent of priests were emotionally developed, eighteen per cent developing, sixty-six per cent underdeveloped and eight percent mal-developed. The extraordinarily high percentages indicating emotional immaturity are illuminating. The personal profile of the immature reminds me vividly of the description of psychopaths by Sir David Henderson to the Royal Commission on Capital Punishment in the early 1950s:

'They are dangerous when frustrated. They are devoid of affection, are cold, heartless, callous, cynical and show a lack of judgement and forethought, which is almost beyond belief. They may be adult in years, but emotionally they remain as dangerous children whose conduct may revert to a primitive, sub-human level.'

Father Kennedy's study had been commissioned by the National Conference of Catholic Bishops in the late 1960s. It was delivered to them in 1971. It would have been an invaluable aid towards understanding the mind of the sexually abusing priest, particularly those priests who abused young children and adolescents. However, the bishops did not even discuss the questions raised within the report, let alone implement its suggestions. They simply ignored their own report.

The Church could also have consulted the centres for the care of 'problematic priests' run by the Servants of the Paraclete, the first of which was opened in Jemez Spring in New Mexico in 1949. It also included the records of the Seton Psychiatric Institute, a Catholic-owned and Catholic-operated hospital in Baltimore, Maryland, established in 1844. Richard Sipe worked at Seton from 1967 to 1970. He was professed a Benedictine monk in 1953 and ordained a Roman Catholic priest in 1959. He is also a qualified psychotherapist and psychiatrist. He recalled,

> 'Shortly after I was ordained in 1959 I was assigned as a teacher and counsellor in a parish high school. This was my first introduction to parish life and the secret world of sexual activity on the part of Catholic priests and religious with both minors and adults. I also became aware of the "secret system".'

It was this revelation that prompted Sipe's interest in counselling Catholic priests and religious. It was to become a life's work. He revealed to me that Seton had kept records all the way back to 1917, many of which include priestly sexual abuse cases:

> '[Case of clerical sexual abuse] was frequently masked by fellow priests working in the clinic . . . deep de-

pression, or "his activities have led to heavy drinking" but sexual abuse was the fundamental problem. By the time I came to work there in the late sixties virtually all referrals to Seton were for priests and religious for sexual contact involving minors. The referral was a device used by the Church to avoid public exposure or a court action.'

Sipe then continued to confine the extent of the problem and his response to such cases:

'I collaborated with colleagues from many countries who were working in the same field. The Netherlands, Ireland, England, Australia, India and Africa. . . . Canada, Spain, much of the Third World. It's global.'

He also put paid to the lie that the bishops could not have known the extent of clerical abuse. Not only was data, the information, the records on clerical sexual abuse at the various other clinics and hospitals available to any bishop who wished to be informed on paedophilia, Sipe also stated that the bishops 'were fully acquainted anyway'.

There was certainly no reason for the Church to be shocked or ignorant about clerical sexual abuse when the Gauthe case erupted in 1985. Apart from the sources already mentioned, the Church could have read legal articles on clergy malpractice, or consulted reference books such as the *Diagnostic and Statistical Manual Of Mental Disorders* which defined paedophilia as follows:

A The act or fantasy of engaging in sexual activity with prepubertal children as a *repeatedly* preferred or exclusive method of achieving sexual excitement.

B If the individual is an adult, the prepubertal children
   are at least ten years younger than the individual. If
   the individual is a late adolescent, no precise age
   difference is required, and clinical judgement must
   take into account the age difference as well as the
   sexual maturity of the child.

In the United Kingdom Bishop Murphy O'Connor could
have referred to *Child Abuse and Neglect. A study of
prevalence in Great Britain* or at least twelve other studies
that were all in print at the time he was ignoring advice and
protecting a paedophile. Better still, he could have contacted the Servants of the Paraclete in Gloucestershire, an
organisation with over thirty years' experience in the treatment of paedophiles – where he himself had sent the serial
paedophile Father Hill. Instead the wretched Hill was given
carte blanche by the man who sits today at the head of the
Roman Catholic Church in England.

The Vatican was fully aware of many of these studies. In
1971 for example, it invited Doctor Conrad Baars and Dr
Anna Terruwe to present their paper dealing with 'the causes,
treatment and prevention of emotional immaturity and illness in priests' to a meeting sponsored by the Synod of
Bishops. Among those listening in the audience was Cardinal
Wojtyla, who was elected to the Synod Council at the end of
that Synod. Dr Baars' report was based on the medical
records and files of 1,500 priests treated for mental problems.
A Dutch-born Catholic psychiatrist, Baars concluded that
less than fifteen per cent of priests in Western Europe and
North America were emotionally fully developed. Twenty to
twenty-five per cent had serious psychiatric difficulties that
often resulted in alcoholism and sixty to seventy per cent
suffered from lesser degrees of emotional immaturity. The
report made ten recommendations, including a more effective vetting of potential priests. None were implemented.

While an overwhelming majority of Catholics polled around the world continue to condemn the Church's response to clerical sexual abuse, the Vatican maintains its traditional long view of history. Although eighty per cent of American Catholics polled by Zogby believe that the legal system and not the Church should process allegations, the Vatican listens only to its hand-picked experts, congregations and bishops who continue to believe in keeping the problem within the Church. In Dublin's recent Royal College of Surgeons survey, seventy-five per cent of those polled consider the Church's response to be 'inadequate', fifty per cent believe the damage done to the Church in Ireland to be 'irreparable' and ninety-two per cent do not think that a priest who has abused children should return to ministry. While the rank and file made abundantly clear what they believed should happen within their Church, the Vatican continued with the old way and ignored the congregation. Instead, it heeds the words of psychologists who wish to show the sex abuser every conceivable consideration.

On more than one occasion, Pope John Paul II declared that secular politicians must adjust civil law to God's. However, in regard to financial and sexual crime he practised a third way – protecting clergy who reject both the civil law and God's. Some of his defenders with no sense of irony berated reporters and journalists for what they call 'media abuse' yet they ignored the frequent acknowledgements of law enforcement officials who applauded the media's efforts to get to the truth. For example, District Attorney Martha Coakley of Massachusetts publicly thanked the press after the arrest of Father Paul Shanley. She acknowledged that her office had no resources for manhunts and thanked the media for tracking Shanley down. She also acknowledged the court's debt to the writers who devoted time, energy and money to researching and profiling the 'predator priests like Shanley'.

This is clearly another aspect of the scandal that has angered the Vatican. Not only are they opposed to the due legal process in spirit, they also object to it in practice. The Arizona District Attorney, Rick Romley, wrote to Vatican Secretary of State Cardinal Angelo Sodano requesting that the Vatican instruct priests that had been indicted in Arizona in child abuse cases to return to the State. His letter came back unopened with a covering note: 'The item here enclosed is returned to sender because it has been refused by the rightful addressee.' Romley was pursuing a number of fugitive priests, including one hiding in Rome and others in Mexico and Ireland.

If the Catholic Church in Massachusetts has finally faced up to its responsibilities, in many another part of the United States the Church is fighting a bitter rearguard action reminiscent of Cardinal Law's years of lies, prevarication and deceit. In Rhode Island, for example, thirty-eight victims of sexual abuse have waited so long for their lawsuits to be resolved that four of the eleven accused priests have died. The Diocese of Providence has succeeded in delaying the legal process for more than ten years by every conceivable device.

In July 2003, to the undisguised glee of the reactionary element within the Church and certain insurance companies, the United States Supreme Court ruled by five to four as unconstitutional a California law removing the statute of limitation on past crimes, thus allowing prosecution for sexual abuse crimes. In a dissenting opinion, Justice Anthony Kennedy wrote: 'The court . . . disregards the interests of those victims of child abuse who have found the courage to face their accusers and bring them to justice.' Many bishops worldwide would like to see similar statutory limitations introduced. Off the record, they will admit that their view is heavily coloured by their financial advisors, their insurance companies and their lawyers. To avoid going into financial bankruptcy many a bishop is rapidly exhausting his moral capital.

In England and Wales, the Church shows a similar ingrained reluctance to face up to its legal responsibilities. It continues to hide behind the curious argument that it is not responsible for its individual priests. It claims that as priests are 'office-holders', they are neither employed nor self-employed. The spokesman of the Catholic Primate of England and Wales attempted to justify the secrecy clauses in agreements made with the victims by claiming, 'These are not gagging orders; these are agreements drawn up by solicitors. The Church does not draw up these agreements.' Of course, the Church gives no instructions to its solicitors. It meekly signs agreements then hands over the compensation payments (which the Vatican has always condemned).

In late November 2003 Archbishop Daniel Pilarczyk of Cincinnati walked into court after a bitter eighteen-month battle during which the archdiocese had used every legal device possible to block prosecution access to its Church records on paedophile priests. He publicly admitted that on at least five separate occasions between 1979 and 1982 archdiocese officials were told of allegations concerning sexual abuse of children by priests and 'knowingly failed' to report them. It was an historic admission, the first time that an archdiocese had been convicted for its role in clerical sexual abuse cases.

Pilarczyk had been one of the bishops who had failed to act upon the recommendations within the 1985 report written by Father Doyle, Father Peterson and lawyer Ray Mouton. In 1992 Archbishop Pilarczyk in response to a letter from Tom Doyle revealed why the report had been ignored. 'The fact remains that your report presented no new issue (of which the NCCB was unaware) or information that required some materially different response.' Perhaps if the Archbishop had studied the report more closely he would not have found himself in court. Having accepted the guilty plea judge Richard Niehaus fined the archdiocese the nominal sum of $10,000. He then revealed that he was a Catholic as he looked directly at the Archbishop and continued, 'I believe that a religious organisation not only should follow the civil law but also the moral law.'

Two months later in January 2004, with the Church hierarchy in the United States and Rome deeply split over the correct response to clerical sexual abuse, yet another scandal began to unfold. The Archdiocese of Washington (DC) was informed by a law firm that it represented at least ten alleged victims of a sex abuse ring in a suburban Maryland parish. Between the 1960s and the 1980s 'dozens' of boys aged between eight and sixteen years had been treated as 'sexual servants' by a ring of priests based in the parish. By the end of 2003 the archdiocese had announced that twenty-six priests had 'been credibly accused of sex abuse over the past 56 years'. In January 2004 that total rose to over thirty.

In February 2004, a week after the Vatican had released a minimum of information on the evidence and conclusions of the closed-doors seminar of 2003, the American Bishops' National Review Board released a detailed report covering a year-long investigation into sexual abuse by clergy in the US Catholic Church. Many had hoped that this independent review would finally produce unassailable facts and figures. The Review Board had been greatly assisted by the John Jay College of Criminal Justice who had been commissioned by the Board to develop empirical data on the nature and scope of 'the problem that precipitated the crisis'.

Neither the Board nor the John Jay College were met with open doors in every diocese. They nonetheless created a report with much invaluable information, which reflects great credit on the Board and its Chairman, Governor

Keating, and on the tenacious questioning of the John Jay team. According to the report, Church records indicate that between 1950 and 2002 4,392 priests were accused of engaging in sexual abuse with a minor. This figure represented four per cent of the 109,694 priests in active ministry during that period. There were approximately 10,667 reported child victims of clergy sexual abuse during this time and the Church expended more than $500 million in dealing with the problem.

As the report notes, 'In very few cases, however, did the diocese or religious order report the allegation to the civil authorities.' As a consequence 'more than 100 priests or former priests served time in prison for conduct involving sexual abuse of a minor'. Put another way – less than 200 out of a total of 4,392 priests were imprisoned.

Victim survivor groups have denounced the report as 'a whitewash' and claim that the real figures for clerical sexual abusers during the period are far higher. The report's comment that fifty-six per cent of the accused priests had only one reported allegation levied against them provoked much criticism from experts. As Father Tom Doyle observed, 'This statement defies the data provided by mental health professionals concerning the average number of victims of sexual abusers, both paedophiles and ephebophiles (abusers of adolescents).' Tom Doyle speaks with a wealth of personal knowledge on the subject – mainly acquired since he was forced out of the Vatican diplomatic service by a faction within the American bishops. During the intervening twenty years Doyle has been involved in over 700 cases of clerical sexual abuse, either advising or testifying on behalf of the victims.

The figure of $500 million that is given for the cost of the scandal to date is widely seen as a serious underestimate. For example, it does not include the $85 million paid out by the Boston Archdiocese. The amount generally accepted is

$1 billion. Even this can be comfortably absorbed by the US Catholic Church. Its annual revenue is in excess of $8 billion, and it owns real estate with an estimated value between $10 and $15 billion.

As many as twenty per cent of the allegations were not subjected to any investigation by the dioceses in question because 'the priest was deceased or inactive at the time of the allegation'. A further ten per cent were characterised as 'unsubstantiated', which as the authors of the report note 'does not mean that the allegation was false; it means only that the diocese or religious order could not determine whether the alleged abuse actually took place'. Consequently there is a potential rogue thirty per cent floating through the various statistics.

The Review Board are on much firmer ground when they share the fruits of their interviews, including those conducted with many of the hierarchy of the US Catholic Church. They record how prior to 2002

'the Vatican had refrained from assuming a significant role with respect to the response of the bishops in the United States to allegations of sexual abuse of minors by members of the clergy. The Vatican did not recognise the scope or the gravity of the problem facing the Church in the United States despite numerous warning signs; and it rebuffed earlier attempts to reform procedures for removing predator priests.'

The report then gives a detailed account of how 'a number of influential bishops in the United States' beginning in the late 1980s asked the Vatican to create a fast-track process for removing sexually abusing priests because the process under Canon Law was a long-drawn-out affair which at every turn was designed to protect the accused priest even after he had been found guilty. The process also required 'the participation of the victim. A number of bishops, concerned in part that victims would find it traumatising to address their abuser in a formal proceeding, were reluctant to ask for their assistance.' In this way, concern for the victim protected the abuser. There were repeated and continuous requests by the bishops for a fast-track process 'throughout the 1990s but again to no avail'.

Eventually even the arch-procrastinator John Paul II had accepted that he had to take some form of action. In 1993 he set up a committee to study how best Canon Law could be applied to 'the particular situation in the United States', for till his dying day he still believed that the sexual abuse by Catholic clergy is 'a uniquely American problem'.

The Heads of the various Vatican Congregations; close friends and colleagues like Cardinal Ratzinger; the numerous papal nuncios around the world: any or all of them could have told the Pope the truth. He could have had the various religious orders investigated – the Salesians or the Franciscans, for example. Both have been operating a global version of the secret system for decades. They move sexually abusing priests from Latin America to Europe, from Asia to Africa.

He could have recalled the United States bishops to the Vatican and demanded to know why so many of their number were determined to stop the National Review Board from doing the very job that the bishops created it to do, namely ensure that every bishop in the United States is subjected to a yearly national audit to ensure the dioceses are complying with the official policies on clerical sexual abuse. He might have asked his bishops just what it is they are so frightened of the Review Board uncovering.

With the first round of reports in, the noted critic Father Andrew Greeley observed in March 2004, 'The Catholic Left would have us believe that the most serious problem the Church faces is clerical celibacy. The Catholic Right, on the other hand, wants to blame everything on homosexuals.' Father Greeley backs neither. For him

> 'the guilty people are the bishops – insensitive, cowardly, ignorant, clericalist – who reassigned such priests [i.e. sexual abusers]. Equally guilty are their staffs – vicars general, vicars for the clergy, civil and canon lawyers, psychiatrists, chiefs of Catholic mental institutions.'

It is a long list but as the National Review report powerfully illustrates there are quite a number of the 'guilty' missing.

The Review Board had concluded that ninety per cent of the nearly 200 Catholic dioceses within the United States were 'in compliance with the pledge that the Bishops had made in mid 2002 to better protect children and punish offenders'. But victim support groups dismissed the report as biased. One such group, SNAP (Survivors Network of those Abused by Priests) revealed that only two of its nearly five thousand members were invited to speak to the investigators. Far more significantly the bishops had recommended to the investigators whom they should interview. As for those archdioceses which had failed to comply, New York and Omaha were two. 'There is no mechanism to sanction church officials who do not comply . . .'

A similar Alice-in-Wonderland situation still prevails within the Roman Catholic Church in England and Wales. For all the fine words of the original Nolan reports, in July 2004 the latest annual report revealed that during 2003 there had been sixty complaints of sexual, physical and emotional abuse and that as of mid-2004 not one of the alleged abusers had been prosecuted. The continued use of the secret system was demonstrated to parishioners in Kentish Town, North London, when they learned in late 2004 that for the past two years a paedophile priest, Father

William Hofton, had been ministering to their spiritual needs. The truth only came to light when Hofton was charged with sexually abusing a further two young boys. He pleaded guilty and was sentenced to four years' imprisonment.

Back in the United States, fall-out from the scandal continued to emerge. In May 2004 it was announced that the Boston archdiocese would be closing at least one sixth of its parishes, churches and schools. Cardinal O'Malley was insistent that the closures were not linked to the huge payout of over $100 million to sexual abuse victims. In fiscal terms perhaps he was right but the scandal has stripped the Catholic Church in the United States of much of its prestige and trust and that has been reflected with empty pews.

In July the Archdiocese of Portland became the first Catholic diocese to file for bankruptcy. The diocese having already paid out more than $50 million was faced with further claims totalling over $150 million dollars. The bankruptcy hearing under 'Chapter 11' protects essential assets and temporarily halts any ongoing litigation.

During the summer of 2004, Austria was rocked with a second clerical sex scandal involving a good friend of the Pope's. Bishop Kurt Krenn, a leading supporter of the paedophile Cardinal Groer, was accused of condoning a wide range of sexual activities that were occurring within a seminary that was under his control. The offences included possession of child pornography, downloading vast quantities of obscene material from a Polish web site, sexual abuse of seminarians by priests and overwhelming evidence of the existence of a homosexual network. Bishop Krenn refused to resign and dismissed the various activities as 'childish pranks'. With Austria yet again plunged into an uproar because of clerical sexual abuse, the Vatican prevaricated. Eventually an Apostolic Visitator-Investigator was sent from Rome and after yet more closed-door discussions, Bishop Krenn reluctantly resigned.

In 2002 the American bishops had also been promised a visit from an Apostolic Visitor. As of early 2005 he had still to put in an appearance, yet the scandals in the US continued to emerge. In September the former bishop of Springfield, Massachusetts, Thomas Dupre, was charged on two counts with child rape. Subsequently the county district attorney said that although he was satisfied the offences had been commited he would not prosecute because the charges fell outside the statute of limitations. The same month, across the country in California, fresh indictments were filed in court. The papers detail thirty-one priests who are alleged to have sexually abused sixty-three children in Santa Barbara County. The victims include three girls who were repeatedly assaulted inside the San Roque confessional on Saturday afternoons between 1979 and 1981. The entire litany of alleged offences covers a period from the 1930s to the 1990s.

In Kentucky a class action with some 200 alleged victims is currently in mediation. In Tucson, Arizona, in the face of nineteen civil lawsuits alleging sexual abuse by 126 of the diocesan priests, the local bishop, Gerald Kicanas, is preparing to declare the diocese bankrupt. The legal actions have been brought on behalf of over 100 people. The bishop has already overseen the paying out of nearly $20 million. In mid-2004 Pope John Paul II defrocked two of the Tucson priests, Teta and Robert Trupia. The latter was described by Bishop Kicanas as a 'notorious and serially sexual' predator. Teta had been suspended by the diocese in 2002 after being the subject of 'credible accusations of child abuse'. In December 2004 the diocese of Orange County, California, agreed a settlement of $100 million to be paid to eighty-seven victims. Next up is Los Angeles, the nation's largest diocese, facing over 500 claims. During the same month, the

Archdiocese of Louisville agreed to pay out $27.7 million and the Archdiocese of Chicago agreed to pay out $12 million. In the pipeline is a major suit naming the Vatican as the first defendant.

I asked Father Doyle to estimate just how many cases are currently working their way through the legal process within the United States.

'I would say probably close to 2,000 and there are still more coming up. You know, what you also have are the orphanages and schools where the kid victims are coming forward. It is a never-ending process. And I along with others who are deeply involved believe we are nowhere near the end of it. Nowhere near cleaning up the garbage and the depth and breadth of the abuse.'

Hard on the heels of Father Doyle's grim predictions came confirmation. In February 2005 a criminal investigation was opened in Dallas by the district attorney. Three years after the Dallas diocese had claimed that all allegations of clerical abuse had been reported, new revelations indicated the diocese had suppressed information on additional cases. The same week, Archbishop Daniel Pilarczyk of Cincinnati was exposed for the second time as protecting a serial sexual abuser. Father David Kelley abused dozens of boys and was able to continue his assaults over many years because of the effectiveness of the secret system that operated in Cincinnati. Pilarczyk, it will be remembered, was one of the bishops who had been so dismissive of the 1985 report written by Father Doyle, Father Peterson and lawyer Ray Mouton. He was also the bishop who in November 2003 had been obliged to admit in open court that his archdiocese had 'knowingly failed' to report to the relevant authorities a string of clerical sexual abuse cases.

Within a few days of this latest scandal in Cincinnati, the results of the second yearly audit of sex-abuse prevention policies in American dioceses were published. It revealed that 1,092 new claims were filed against clergy in 2004 and that more than $840 million had been paid out in legal settlements since 1950. Again it must be emphasised that the compensation figure is dismissed by many as being a serious under-estimate. By early June after the announcement that the diocese of Covington, Kentucky, was to pay out $120 million, the official figure of compensation paid stood at $1.06 billion. In Southern California alone, lawyers acting for abuse victims have insisted that, when their various cases have been resolved, additional payments will add a futher $1 billion. The spiralling cost of the compensation claims is a crisis that is not confined to the United States. It exists in many countries. In late March 2005, for example, the Catholic Church in Ireland was facing further claims over the next five years that one estimate put at £35 million.

In August 2005, the Portland litigation took several more bizarre directions. Every one of the nearly 400,000 Roman Catholics in the west coast state of Oregon were advised that they were defendants in the case and the man who had succeeded Cardinal Ratzinger as Head of the Congregation for the Doctrine of the Faith, Archbishop Levada, was named as a defendant. He had previously been Archbishop of Portland. Levada, having waived diplomatic immunity, agreed to be examined under oath in January 2006. The naming of Levada as a defendant was not without an ironic aspect. The Archbishop had early access to the detailed report of Fathers Doyle and Peterson and Ray Mouton in 1985 and after initial enthusiasm for the recommendations it contained had been one of those who allowed the report to wither on the vine. By 2005 abuse victims in Portland had already had judgement against the diocese amounting to over $150 million. Dozens of other plaintiffs are seeking $400 million in pending lawsuits.

During the last week of September 2005, the Apostolic Visitation, an official inspection of every one of the 229 Catholic seminaries in the United States agreed upon in April 2002, finally began. That it took over three years to commence is an eloquent comment on Vatican priorities.

In October, the Ferns Report was published in Ireland, revealing for the first time the extent of clerical sexual abuse over many decades. It was also the story of physical cruelty, neglect and incompetence, compounded by criminal conspiracy, corruption and arrogance by men unfit to be priests. There was Bishop Donal Herlihy, for twenty years in charge of Ferns, a man who refused to treat the issue of sexual abuse as a criminal matter, regarding it as a moral issue. Then there was his successor, Bishop Brendan Comiskey, who consistently failed to remove clerical abusers because he considered that to do so would be 'unjust', since the allegations of abuse were not substantiated.

The Ferns scandal opened the floodgates in Ireland. Not a day went by it seemed without further revelations up and down the country, from Cork and Ross in the south to Derry and Down and Connor in Northern Ireland. It was revealed that over the past forty years, 241 priests had been accused of sexual abuse. Twenty-two had been convicted but many had died before trial. In November, the Irish Government announced an in-depth probe in the Dublin diocese in response to allegations of sexual abuse against sixty-seven Dublin priests. Subsequently Justice Minister McDowell announced that an independent investigation would take place within every diocese in the country.

A week after the Dublin revelations, police in North Yorkshire revealed that they had concluded a fifteen-month investigation into years of sexual abuse by English clerics. The location stunned not only devout Catholics but also much of the nation. Ampleforth College, England's most celebrated Catholic public school, has as its mission the 'spiritual, moral and intellectual' education of children who will 'become inspired by high ideals and capable of leadership'. For at least three decades, between 1966 and 1995, pupils were also at high risk of sexual abuse by some of the monks who taught there. The assaults ranged from minor abuse to rape. There were at least thirty to forty victims but the ultimate number of victims during that period has been estimated by former pupils to be 'in three figures'. Some of the victims at the prep school were under ten years of age. During those years, Cardinal Basil Hume was Abbot of Ampleforth and the Archbishop of Westminster, the Primate of England. Three of the paedophile priests have been before the courts; three others died before their abuses of the children became known. Cardinal Hume covered up the activities of Father Piers Grant-Ferris. These included sexually abusing fifteen boys over a nine-year period. The cardinal also offered a woman who had been molested by another priest an unsolicited £1,500 'donation' towards counselling while urging her not to contact the police. There is no doubt that the Primate would have been forced to resign his office if these facts had become public knowledge before his death in 1997. Cardinal Hume's motive has a familiar ring: 'For the good of mother church.'

In the United States, a federal judge in Kentucky has recently ruled that the Holy See is a foreign state that enjoys certain immunity protections. In the judge's opinion these included protection for the Vatican against any claims arising from sexual abuse litigation: immunity from not only criminal prosecution but any form of legal action with regard to the clerical abuse of children. In December 2005 another federal judge, this time in Texas, ruled that Pope Benedict XVI enjoys immunity as a Head of State and removed him from a civil lawsuit accusing him of conspiracy to cover up sexual abuse of minors by a seminarian.

If 2005 had finished on a positive note for the Pope and his colleagues within the Vatican, they would have taken little comfort from the news coming out of Boston during the first weeks of the New Year. It was revealed that in the past two years alone the Archdiocese of Boston had received more than $215 million from insurance and land sales, enough to pay alleged victims of clergy abuse twenty-eight times the compensation that the Archdiocese has offered. Simultaneously it was revealed that 200 new claims have been made by alleged victims against the Archdiocese. By March 2006 the official 'audit' for US dioceses for the previous year reinforced the belief that clerical sexual abuse continued to be the biggest problem confronting the Church. There had been 783 credible new accusations of sexual abuse against American clerics lodged that year, eighty-one per cent involving male victims. The American dioceses paid out in compensation nearly half a billion dollars, $466.9 million. This represents an increase of nearly three hundred per cent over the 2004 figure of $157.8 million. The Church paid out a further $13 million to support offending priests.

Also in March 2006 the results of an investigation by Archbishop Martin into clerical paedophiles within the Dublin diocese were revealed. Over one hundred priests had been accused over a period reaching back to 1940. The Archbishop observed, 'It's hard for me to see that in some of these cases, so many children were abused. It's very hard to weigh that up against anything.' The diocese has already paid out some $10 million dollars and like so many of its American counterparts faced selling property to meet further compensation claims.

The global backlog of cases is now so great that any bishop writing to the CDF seeking a decision on an errant priest faces an eighteen-month delay before he will get a response. On top of this case load the now Cardinal Levada has continuing problems of his own. Among the unresolved issues in Levada's former diocese of Portland are allegations that he applied the secret system personally, including secret payments to victims and allowing a self-confessed paedophile to continue working in a number of parishes.

In May 2006, some two months after this book was published in Italy, the allegations contained within this chapter regarding Father Marcial Maciel, the founder of the Legionaries of Christ, reached a resolution. The enquiry that the then Cardinal Ratzinger had ordered and then suspended 'to spare the Holy Father any embarrassment' had been reactivated. Cardinal Levada and Pope Benedict XVI had concluded that at least some of the allegations were well-founded. Why it had taken decades to reach this conclusion was not explained. A group of men who had been systematically abused over many years, and vilified when they sought Vatican recognition of what they had suffered, had finally achieved a small measure of the justice they so richly deserved. The late Pope John Paul II, who was fully aware of the detailed evidence against Maciel, had responded with words of praise for the paedophile and honoured the man. His successor, who refused to act during Wojtyla's lifetime, has finally approved Levada's decision to remove Maciel from priestly ministry and to order him to spend the remaining days of his life in 'penitence and prayer'. He was to be spared a canonical trial because of 'his advanced age and delicate health'.

The Vatican that for centuries has told people on pain of eternal damnation how they should lead their sexual lives now demands that the clerical sexual abuses that have been revealed over the last thirty years should be forgiven and forgotten. Pope John Paul II, Cardinal Ratzinger and a great many other like-minded Princes of the Church are on public record claiming that it is the abusers who are the victims. To quote Cardinal Ratzinger:

'It has to do with the reflection of our highly sexualized society. Priests are also affected by the general situation. They may be especially vulnerable, or susceptible, although the percentage of abuse cases is no higher than in other occupations. One would naturally expect it to be lower . . .'

For Cardinal Norberto Carrera of Mexico, the villains of the story were not the sex-abusing clergy, but the *New York Times*, the *Boston Globe*, the *Washington Post* and any other media outlets that sought out the truth about Cardinal Law of Boston. Their activities resembled for Carrera 'what happened in the past century with persecutions in Mexico, in Spain, in Nazi Germany and in communist countries'. Prelates in many countries have expressed similar sentiments. Those who expose the sex abusers are denounced as 'enemies of the Church'. Demonstrably, the Catholic Church's concept of zero tolerance is to apply it to its critics while offering maximum tolerance and understanding to the criminals within its ranks.

By the failure not only of Pope John Paul II and his successor but also of virtually the entire Catholic hierarchy to confront the issue of sexual abuse within the clergy, the Catholic Church has abdicated any historic rights it has previously claimed to speak to her laity on the issues of faith and morals. To abuse a child, to violate an innocent, is for the vast majority an act beyond belief. For a member of the priesthood or a religious order to abuse a child, an adolescent or adult is the ultimate betrayal of trust. The damage may be eventually sublimated, but it is permanent. Clerical sex abuse is a total attack on the body, mind and soul of the victim. It combines physical pain, mental anguish, and emotional and spiritual rape.

As of now, many people across the world would not allow an unaccompanied child to enter a Roman Catholic Church. The Catholic Church in England and Wales and in other countries feels obliged to ban priests from being alone with a child. The late Pope John Paul II and his advisors instructed priests throughout the world to avoid getting into 'risky situations with the opposite sex' and to 'use caution' when dealing with women parishioners because of 'sexual temptations'. Many of the sexually abusing priests are treated with injections of Depo-Provera, a drug frequently prescribed as a female contraceptive.

Recently a Rome-based prelate observed to me, 'There will not be, either in the short or medium term, a policy of zero tolerance with regard to the sex abusers. If such a policy existed and was applied across the board, irrespective of position, there are many bishops who would be forced to resign . . . many cardinals who would have to take early retirement . . . As for zero tolerance towards homosexuals, we already have that. It just happens to be confined to the laity. If it were applied to the priesthood, the infrastructure would collapse.'

All of these things have come to pass within 'the one true Church' under the leadership of the late Pope John Paul II, closely assisted by Joseph Ratzinger who has now become the last absolute monarch on earth.

'At the same time came the disciples unto Jesus, saying, Who is the greatest in the kingdom of heaven?

2 And Jesus called a little child unto him, and set him in the midst of them,

3 And said, Verily I say unto you, Except ye be converted, and become as little children, ye shall not enter into the kingdom of heaven.

4 Whosoever therefore shall humble himself as this little child, the same is greatest in the kingdom of heaven.

5 And whoso shall receive one such little child in my name receiveth me.

6 But whoso shall offend one of these little ones which believe in me, it were better for him that a millstone were hanged about his neck, and that he were drowned in the depth of the sea.'

St Matthew 18: 1–6

Chapter 10

Papal Politics II:
After the Cold War

Y UGOSLAVIA HAD BEEN held together by Marshal
Tito from the end of the Second World War until
his death in 1980. Less than ten years later it was
heading in the opposite direction to Germany. Now unified
for the first time since the end of that same war, Germany
was about to play a key role in the disintegration of
Yugoslavia, aided and abetted by Pope John Paul II and
his Secretariat of State. Tito, a Croatian Communist, had
presided over a federation of republics with disparate
religions and cultures with consummate skill. He rotated
the presidency so that a Croatian followed a Serb or a
Slovenian or a member of one of the other federal units in
what was a one-party state. No discussion of the solely
artificial boundaries that had been created was permitted
and Tito observed that the frontiers between the various
republics were only 'administrative'.

After Tito's death the collective presidency, despite the
emergence of nationalistic aspirations, held together until
the federal elections in 1990. In May of that year Dr Franjo
Tudjman was elected President of Croatia and in neighbouring Slovenia a new government also emerged headed
by President Kucan. Even before the elections in their

respective countries there was an open telephone between the two republics enabling them to coordinate plans to bring about the break-up of the Yugoslavian Federation. They were greatly assisted in this by the Croatian, Stjepan Mesic, who took over the revolving national presidency in May 1990.

'When prevailed upon by European and other international mediators, I accepted the presidency to use this top position as a way to get in touch with the most influential leaders, utilising Yugoslav diplomatic channels to convince them of the pointlessness of Yugoslavia's survival.'

At the time the overwhelming majority of the EU member states believed that Yugoslavia had a future as a single entity. The sole exception was West Germany, just months away from its own historic unification with East Germany. Chancellor Kohl's government was very receptive to the persuasive Mesic. No matter that as President of the Federation it was his duty to preserve it, to Mesic this was a lost cause:

'At that time not one single institution of the Federation functioned because everything was blocked, so the Presidency was blocked and the federal assembly was blocked and could not function and the same was true of the supreme and constitutional court. So practically Yugoslavia ceased to exist and simply melted away.'

In conversation with me, Stjepan Mesic called Yugoslavia a 'dead corpse'. If so, it was a body not unlike Caesar's with many an assassin's handiwork upon it. There are the usual suspects: Milosevic of Serbia, Tudjman of Croatia, Izetbegovic of Bosnia-Herzegovina to name but three. Others are rarely if ever mentioned: former Chancellor Helmut Kohl and his foreign minister Hans-Dietrich Genscher and Pope John Paul II are three of a considerable number who should be added to the list for their respective roles in consigning Yugoslavia to a premature grave. The French General Pierre Gallois observed:

'Since 1991 and probably before, Germany was providing arms for Croatia through Italy, Hungary and Czechoslovakia; so, more than a thousand vehicles carried light weapons but also anti-aircraft and anti-tank weaponry, ammunitions and replacement equipment.'

The Former US Ambassador to Yugoslavia Warren Zimmerman wrote:

'We discovered later that Genscher, the German foreign minister, was in daily contact with the Croatian foreign minister. He was encouraging Croatia to leave the Federation and to declare independence.'

Other intelligence sources in the West have asserted that the arms from Germany were flowing into Croatia as early as 1989. Slovenia and Croatia simultaneously declared their independence on 25 June 1991. They were assured of the support of both Germany and the Vatican. Speaking in the Hungarian city of Pecs in August 1991, the Pope urged the world to 'help to legitimise the aspirations of Croatia'. The Pope chose to ignore the fact that the Vatican had been one of the principal supporters of the unilateral acts of secession, acts that were illegal under Yugoslav and international law. Archbishop Jean Louis Tauran, a senior member of the Secretariat of State, was particularly active on behalf of

Croatia and Slovenia during the latter half of 1991 when, using Vatican diplomatic channels, he worked hard to drum up support for the two countries.

On 26 June, less than twenty-four hours after the joint declaration, the Yugoslav army moved to secure airports and frontier posts between Slovenia and Serbia and met fierce resistance. Fighting also occurred between Yugoslavian troops and Croatian forces. Dubrovnik was under siege from early June. Vukovar was reduced to rubble between August and November. Tudjman had already activated a policy of ethnic cleansing aimed at eliminating many hundreds of thousands of Serbs, Muslims and Jews from Croatia and Bosnia as early as June 1991. The European Community rapidly dispatched a peace mission in an attempt to mediate an end to the fighting. On 7 July under the auspices of the EC, the Brioni Declaration maintaining Yugoslavia as a single entity was adopted. Under the agreement both Croatia and Slovenia agreed to suspend their decisions to declare sovereignty and independence for three months. Two months later on 7 September 1991 the EC Peace Conference on Yugoslavia opened at The Hague. While some genuinely strained to find a peaceful solution others were busy stoking the flames.

With one exception, the European Community of twelve still believed that the way forward for Yugoslavia was as a unified country. Their view was shared by many beyond Europe, including the United States. The major obstacles at this stage were not Slovenia and Croatia but the German Government and the Vatican, who were determined that their joint position would prevail. One factor for Chancellor Kohl and his government were the half million Croats resident in Germany that ensured that anti-Serbian sentiment was a constant. After the joint declaration of independence the demand that their adopted country recognise their motherland was expressed with increasing urgency.

These were heady times. The Berlin Wall was down, Germany was unified and apparently united and Kohl had long entertained fantasies of being acclaimed as a latter-day Bismarck.

For Kohl, assisting Croatia and Slovenia to a full and lasting independence would be another jewel in his crown and an extra half a million voters at the next election would pile triumph on triumph. Helping Kohl and Genscher every step of the way was the Catholic Church.

In October the Bishop of Limburg, Monsignor Kamphaus, was dispatched to Croatia by the President of the German Episcopal Conference. Upon his return he criticised the EC commitment to a unified Yugoslavia and demanded the 'rapid' recognition of Croatia. He declared that if the twelve countries of the EC maintained their position then Germany should make a unilateral declaration of recognition. Another German bishop, Monsignor Stimphle, organised street demonstrations demanding 'military aid for Croatia, bastion of the liberal democratic order'. Presumably no one had told the Monsignor that shipments of arms from Austria and Germany were already being sent to both Croatia and Bosnia. Later evidence would emerge of Vatican bearer bonds worth $40 million being provided by the Holy See to the Croatian government for the purchase of weapons.

In November 1991 foreign minister Genscher speaking in the Bundestag declared that Germany demanded from its EU partners the immediate recognition of Slovenia and Croatia and sanctions against the Serbs, 'otherwise, the Community will face a serious crisis'. To people of a certain age with long memories and to students of Second World War history, his words and his overwhelming desire to be Croatia's 'protector' stirred deep unease. Hans-Dietrich Genscher like any good foreign minister was a man who was singularly adept playing both ends against the middle.

In Cabinet he appeared to be the one voice of sanity who for a long time had resisted the clamour to assist in the break-up of Yugoslavia. In his secret meetings with Tudjman of Croatia and Kucan of Slovenia well before the joint declarations of independence he assured them that Germany would give full recognition before the end of 1991.

During another series of secret meetings with Stjepan Mesic, who had been smuggled into Bonn, Genscher told his Croatian guest that he was fully committed not only to full independence for the two countries but the subsequent inevitable break-up of the other parts of Yugoslavia. Dr Bozo Dimnik who had arranged the meeting recalled, 'Genscher said, "I will help you but as Foreign Minister of Germany and because of the things that happened during the Second World War, I cannot openly support your cause." ' He was referring to the historic relationship between Croatia and Nazi Germany. He suggested that Mesic should talk to both Italian Prime Minister Andreotti and the Pope: 'Genscher wanted to hide behind the Pope's robes.'

Within a month the doors both to Prime Minister Andreotti and the Vatican Secretary of State Cardinal Angelo Sodano had been opened. In the late summer of 2004 Stjepan Mesic, now President of Croatia, talking of that Vatican meeting on 6 December 1991 told me: 'Sodano told me that the Pope had been fully informed of the various Croatian demands and that he fully supported them. He also told me that the Holy Father agreed to maintain Croatian independence.'

In late 1991 EC heads of state, foreign ministers and senior politicians were gathered at Maastricht. Their collective struggle to agree a treaty that would signpost the way forward for the future development of the community was hampered at the eleventh hour by a deadlock occurring during an increasingly acrimonious debate about European security. The German delegation had introduced the Yugoslavia issue. Specifically they demanded that Croatia and Slovenia be given diplomatic recognition of their independence by the European Twelve. In the run-up to the conference, there had been a clear eleven to one majority opposed to the proposition. The general view was that the way forward was for Yugoslavia to stay unified as a federation. Vatican shuttle diplomacy between July and late autumn had reduced the majority to eight to four. At 10.00 p.m. German Foreign Minister Genscher announced that he would not leave the table until all twelve EC members voted unanimously in favour of the resolution. Genscher was apparently prepared to torpedo the entire Maastricht Treaty unless the other eleven submitted to the German point of view. By four in the morning Genscher, Kohl and the Pope and his Secretariat of State had prevailed.

That extraordinary turnaround came despite the profound misgivings of the French President François Mitterand, the British Prime Minister John Major and his Foreign Secretary Douglas Hurd and a host of other senior players both at the table and further afield, including the United Nations Secretary General, the US President George Bush and his Secretary of State James Baker who had predicted in June that

'If there are unilateral declarations of independence followed by use of force that forecloses possibilities for peaceful break and peaceful negotiations, as required by the Helsinki Accord, it will kick off the damndest civil war that this region has ever seen.'

The joint declarations and the use of force to seize the border posts by Slovenia and Croatia had been the trigger that Baker had feared. The violence that ensued between June and December 1991 should have been cause enough for urgent peace negotiations. The failure of negotiations during that period to secure peace should have ensured that nothing further was done to inflame the situation – such as acknowledging and recognising two illegal acts of independence. Germany and the Vatican had a different agenda. Chancellor Helmut Kohl described the vote as 'a great victory for German foreign policy'.

To salve the consciences of those countries at the table who had handed the Germans their 'great victory' a fig leaf had been created. The European Community would recognise the two republics as of 15 January but only if Slovenia and Croatia pledged to respect human and minority rights, demonstrated a willingness to settle border questions and other disputes peacefully and guaranteed a democratic government. The Germans promptly undermined that caveat by declaring that they intended to recognise the two countries immediately. They were not prepared to wait while the rest of the membership determined whether or not the conditions had been met.

The fact that the most fervent advocates of the recognition were Germany, Italy, Austria and the Vatican did nothing to allay widespread apprehension. Yet again it seemed the Croatia card was in play in the European theatre of war. In demanding a pledge of respect for human and minority rights, the majority of the European Community demonstrated its well-founded fears concerning the fate of any non-Catholics in Croatia. By the end of 1991 the evidence of the previous six months furnished ample proof that Croatian history was repeating itself.

Fifty years earlier, on 10 April 1941 the German 14th Panzer division had entered the Croatian capital of Zagreb to a flower-strewn enthusiastic welcome from the Croatians. Within hours, a German envoy announced the formation of the Independent State of Croatia, the ISC, under the 'Poglavnik' (Führer) Ante Pavelic, Croatian leader of the fascist *Ustashi* terrorist movement. Within a week, the Axis forces of Germany and Italy controlled all Yugoslavia. The highly regarded Pavelic was given not only Croatia but also Bosnia, Herzegovina, the Serb areas of Slovenia and Srem and part of Dalmatia.

On taking office Ante Pavelic stated:

'It is the duty of the *Ustashi* movement to ensure that the Independent State of Croatia is ruled always and everywhere only by Croatians, so that they are the sole master of all the real and spiritual good in their own land. Within Croatia there can be no compromise between the Croatian people and others who are not pure Croats; *Ustashi* must extinguish all trace of such people.'

The campaign of ethnic cleansing was already operating when Pope Pius XII received in audience Pavelic and the state delegation of the ISC on 18 May 1941. Secretary of State Montini, later Pope Paul VI, and a number of other Vatican luminaries maintained throughout the war the closest of relationships with Pavelic's regime. As for the Jews, as in every act of genocide, the numbers game has been played extensively. The exact number slaughtered by the *Ustashi* between 1941 and April 1945 will never be known but it is possible to arrive at minimum figures. Jasenovac, before the Second World War, was a large and prosperous town with a predominantly Serb population. On 26 December 1945 a Government Committee of the Federal People's Republic of Yugoslavia stated in a report that was accompanied by documentary evidence that 'By the end of 1943 at least 600,000 people were killed in this camp . . . The victims were mostly Serbs, then Jews, Gypsies and even Croats.' To that total must be added at least 350,000 non-Catholics butchered in their homes, churches, valleys, woods and various other locations across the entire area ruled and controlled by Ante Pavelic. Another 250,000 were forcibly converted to Catholicism although many of them were then murdered, and a further 300,000 or so were driven out of Croatia into the remote mountain regions of Serbia.

In carrying out these acts, the *Ustashi* were from the very beginning assisted by the Roman Catholic Church both in Rome and within Croatia. Within days of Pavelic's installation, Archbishop Alojzije Stepinac of Zagreb strongly recommended to the papal nuncio in Belgrade that the Holy See should immediately recognise the *Ustashi* regime, as the legal government of the annexed country. Stepinac was already very aware of the *Ustashi* doctrine defined by its Minister of Education and Culture, Mile Budak.

'The basis for the *Ustashi* movement is religion. For minorities such as the Serbs, Jews and Gypsies, we have three million bullets. We will kill a part of the Serbs. Others we will deport and the rest we will force to accept the Roman Catholic Religion. Thus the new Croatia will be rid of all Serbs in its midst in order to be 100 per cent Catholic within ten years.'

The Franciscan clergy were particularly rabid. Friar Dionizije was appointed head of the regime's Religious Department.

'In those regions yonder, I arranged for everything to be cleared away, everything from a chicken to an old man, and should that be necessary, I shall do so here too, since it is not sinful nowadays to kill even a seven-year-old child, if it is standing in the way of our *Ustashi* order . . . Pay no heed to my religious vestments, for you should know that when the necessity arises, I take into my hands a machinegun and ex-

terminate everybody down to the cradle, everybody
who is opposed to the *Ustashi* State and Government.'

Friar Dr Srecko Peric from Livno observed in one of his
sermons in July 1941: 'My Croat brethren! Go and slay all
Serbs! First of all my sister who is married to a Serb. After
that, come to me, and I shall take on my soul all of your
sins.'

Pope Pius XII appointed Archbishop Stepinac as senior
military chaplain. A Catholic priest was subsequently appointed to serve with every *Ustashi* military unit. There is
no record that Stepinac ever attempted to restrain the
priests and friars who were answerable to him. Even when
a member of the Franciscan order, Friar Miroslav Filipovic,
was appointed commander of the Jasenovac camp for four
months, the Archbishop did nothing to stop the mass killings that ensued. Filipovic is believed to have overseen the
killing of between 20,000 and 30,000 inmates. Having
previously organised massacres in a number of villages,
the friar was particularly adept at killing, as he noted of his
time at the concentration camp: 'I personally killed about
100 from Jasenovac and Stara Gradiska.' A large number of
the killings by the *Ustashi* were carried out with hammers
and knives. Gouging out the eyes of victims became a
regular occurrence. The evil would undoubtedly have continued until the *Ustashi* had run out of victims but for the
defeat of the Axis powers. In late April 1945 during the
closing days of the war in Europe the leaders of the *Ustashi*,
having ensured that a substantial amount but by no means
all of the evidence of their sub-human reign of terror had
been destroyed, fled the country. Ante Pavelic went to
Austria. With him and some of his inner circle went the
entire contents of the Croatian State Bank and Treasury.
During the war Pavelic had not only orchestrated genocide.
He had also had all the private property of his victims

seized, including their homes and businesses, bank deposits, share certificates – everything and anything of value. A great deal of loot also accompanied Croatia's Führer as he slipped under cover of darkness into the British-controlled sector of Austria. Pavelic had also sent twelve cases of gold and jewels to Austria prior to his own escape, which were hidden near Salzburg. Other assets, including 1,338 kilos of gold and twenty-five tons of silver coins, were shipped out of Croatia in 1944 to the Swiss National Bank. Both British and US intelligence were fully aware of these movements of looted assets. For good measure Pavelic had also seized the entire assets of the Croatian State Mint and all tangible assets of the Croatian Army. Pavelic lived in Austria until the spring of 1946. This man who was wanted as a war criminal on a whole range of charges, who had been sentenced to death *in absentia* for his involvement in the 1934 assassination of King Alexander of Yugoslavia and the French Foreign Minister Louis Barthou, enjoyed the protection of the British Eighth Army in Austria. US Army Intelligence reports of the period refer to an ongoing investigation. When Pavelic moved to Italy in the spring of 1946 the plunder accompanied him in a military truck convoy supervised by 'British officers, or by Croatians wearing British Army uniforms'.

Pavelic was returning to the country where Mussolini had been his patron and protector both before and during the war. His other great champion had been the Holy See, who in 1946 yet again accorded the 'Butcher of the Balkans' every hospitality. Along with the most senior members of his *Ustashi* regime Pavelic enjoyed the protection of the Vatican until July 1947. That protection reached up at the very least to the higher reaches of the Secretariat of State and to Monsignor Giovanni Battista Montini, who sixteen years later would be elected Pope and become Paul VI.

During the immediate postwar years the Vatican provided safe houses for thousands of *Ustashi* war criminals. The centre for the organising and financing of this activity was the Pontifical Croatian College of St Jerome (S. Girolamo) on Via Tomacelli in the centre of Rome, and the key figure was Monsignor Krunislav Draganovic, a Vatican official who functioned as the Apostolic Visitator for Pontifical Assistance for Croatians. In this role Draganovic answered directly to the Secretary of State, Montini. Draganovic was a man of many parts. US Intelligence reports describe him as

> 'The ideological leader of the *Ustashi* movement in Italy, priest and professor of theology, who should represent at the Vatican the interest of Croatian emigration . . . but has put himself to represent only the *Ustashi* and their interests.'

In mid-1947 the versatile Draganovic, ably assisted by Bishop Alois Hudal, produced his greatest contribution to ensure the fascist *Ustashi* would live to help create a bloody sequel to their four-year reign of terror in the Balkans. He negotiated a secret contract with the US Army for the delivery of war criminals by the Counter-Intelligence Corps to Draganovic for their export to South America. Captain Paul Lyon of the 430th CIC based at headquarters in Salzburg negotiated the deal, which called for a set fee, plus expenses to be paid for each war criminal. The notorious 'ratline' had been born. Down it would go some of Europe's greatest mass murderers and a great deal of Nazi gold, including a substantial part of the looted assets of Croatia – all courtesy of a Vatican official. Among those smuggled out of Europe with the full knowledge not only of Pope Pius XII and his Secretary of State Cardinal Montini, but also British and US high command, were Klaus Barbie,

Ante Pavelic, Adolf Eichmann, Heinrich Müller and Franz Stangl. The total number of war criminals who escaped to new lives through the Vatican's ratline was in excess of 30,000.

In September 1946 Archbishop Stepinac was arrested by Tito's Communist regime that now controlled Yugoslavia and was accused of 'collaboration with the enemy and of conspiracy against the Federal People's Republic of Yugoslavia'. He was put on trial along with fifteen others similarly charged and on 11 October having been found guilty he was sentenced to sixteen years' imprisonment with forced labour. From 1946 to 1951 he was confined in a former Pauline monastery in Lepoglava. His ill health in 1951 resulted in his transfer to a parish residence in Krasic where he was held under house arrest. Pope Pius XII made him a cardinal in January 1953. He remained at Krasic until his death in February 1960.

At the time of his trial his attempts to defend his actions were at best half-hearted. In part it echoed Eichmann's 'I was only obeying orders.' He said,

'You accuse me as an enemy of the State and the people's authority. I acknowledge your authority. What was my authority? I repeat again you have been my authority since May 8th, 1945 but not before that. Where is it possible in the world to obey two authorities: you in the woods; they (the *Ustashi*) in Zagreb?'

One might expect an archbishop to have regarded as his ultimate authority neither the partisans in the woods or the fascists in Zagreb but the pope. The evidence that Stepinac actively and freely collaborated with the *Ustashi* was overwhelming.

When the trial of Stepinac finished in October 1946 the Vatican announced that the court officials who were Croatians and Roman Catholics were all excommunicated as were 'all persons who had taken part in or were responsible for the prosecution of the Archbishop, on the grounds that no member of Catholic clergy could be prosecuted without the consent of the Holy See'.

At the time of that mass excommunication Ante Pavelic and a large number of the men who along with him bore direct responsibility for the deaths of between 600,000 and 1 million people were living under the protection of Pope Pius XII in the Vatican and surrounding church property in Rome. The slaughter in wartime Croatia and indeed throughout Yugoslavia should have made both Germany and the Vatican during 1989 and later move with the greatest caution when confronted with Croatian and Slovenian politicians seeking support for the declarations of independence.

In 1991, echoing Pavelic, the new President Tudjman of Croatia introduced a 'new' constitution that defined Croatia as a national state of Croatian people 'and others', immediately relegating the Serbs, Muslims, Slovenes, Czechs, Italians, Jews and Hungarians and other Croatian-born nationals to a second-class status. On the orders of President Tudjman all the remaining buildings and structures of the Jasenovac concentration camp with many of the artefacts and records inside were destroyed 'to make way', Tudjman explained, 'for a rare bird sanctuary'. On 20 January 1991, a mere week after Croatia and Slovenia had been recognised by Germany, the Vatican and then the other members of the EC as independent states, Tudjman addressing a huge rally declared,

'We are in a war against the JNA (the Yugoslav Army). Should anything happen, kill them all in the streets, in their homes, throw hand grenades, fire pistols in their bellies, women, children . . . We will deal with Knin (a Croatian Serbian area) by butchering.'

In the event, butchering was perpetrated on all sides and by all sections of the country that had been Yugoslavia. Between 1992 and 1995 more than 200,000 were killed and more than two million made homeless.

In death the late Cardinal Stepinac has remained as controversial as he was in life. Claims and counterclaims have been made about the man, some hailing him as a modern saint and others insisting that he was evil personified. In October 1998 Pope John Paul II entered the fray. Declaring that Stepinac was 'one of the outstanding figures of the Catholic Church', he proclaimed the beatification of Alojzije Stepinac. During the previous month, deeply alarmed at this prospect, the Simon Wiesenthal Centre wrote to Vatican spokesman Navarro-Valls asking that the Pope 'postpone this beatification until after the completion of an exhaustive study of Stepinac's wartime record based on full access to Vatican archives'.

The Centre, internationally recognised for many decades as the pre-eminent hunter of war criminals, specifically those who were complicit in the Holocaust, pointed out to the Vatican that the beatification was proceeding 'despite public expressions of indignation' and asked that the ceremony be postponed 'in view of the bitter memories and current religious sensitivities in the structure of the ex-Yugoslavia, and also his Holiness' oft-repeated hope for reconciliation with the Jews'.

The Vatican ignored the plea and the beatification of Stepinac took place in Croatia on 3 October 1998. Almost exactly one year later, the Croatian President Franjo Tudjman visited the Vatican. He had previously 'requested' that the then Secretary of State should personally administer Holy Communion to the Presidential party in the crypt beneath St Peter's. That Tudjman should 'order' a Mass, specify who should say it and also select the location carried his self-importance to new heights. The Vatican acceded to the request from the man who in a fit of rage had grabbed Prime Minister Mesic by the throat and screamed, 'All I want is Bosnia. Give me that and I will demand no more.'

Croatia and Slovenia, like any aspiring nation-state, had the right to seek independence, but that does not excuse either Helmut Kohl or Pope John Paul II for pursuing their conspiracy with such reckless disregard for the consequences. They and their defenders have argued, with Slovenia in the EU and Croatia on the way, that time has proved them to be visionaries. The 250,000 who died and the two million made homeless in the Balkans after January 1992 might have a different view.

In 1999 the Vatican had cause to reflect on its historic relationship with the *Ustashi*. A lawsuit was filed in the San Francisco Federal Court by Serb, Jewish and Ukrainian survivors of the Holocaust. They sought $18 million damages from the Vatican Bank, the Franciscan Order and the Croatian Liberation Movement and 'the return of Nazi loot stolen from wartime Yugoslavia by Croatian Nazis, called the *Ustashi*'. The three defendants were accused of concealing up to an estimated $200 million looted from Yugoslavia during the Second World War and using it in the early postwar period 'to fund the infamous Vatican ratline'. The Vatican has claimed immunity on the grounds that it is an independent state. As of mid-2006 the case was still pending.

The influence that Pope John Paul II and his Secretariat of State exercised in the Balkans will be felt in the region for decades. Other foreign policy initiatives were without a single medium or long-term effect. The Papal trip to Castro's Cuba in January 1998 eloquently demonstrates Wojtyla's impotency in the face of Communism.

One year earlier than his trip to Mexico the Pope had been visiting Castro's Cuba. Yet again he had been accompanied by some eighty journalists whose news outlets had as usual paid many thousands of dollars for the privilege of travelling with the man described by his spin doctors as the most powerful pope in history.

This journey was no exception, as Cardinal Ricardo Carles from Barcelona proved more amenable to answering questions from international reporters than from the Naples magistrates. 'The Papacy has never before had such moral force.' The all-powerful Pope was about to meet the man who had defied a world superpower for nearly forty years, in its own backyard.

This meeting between John Paul II and Fidel Castro had raised great expectations within the Catholic world. It was thought that profound democratic change would follow, that human rights would flourish.

The Pope was equally optimistic when addressing 100,000 Cubans in a baseball stadium, declaring, 'No ideology can replace Christ's infinite wisdom and power.' He urged the audience to reclaim their role as 'primary educators' of their young. Catholic schools had been shut after the 1959 revolution, leaving no alternative to an education steeped in Communist doctrine.

Nearly two years after the visit, in late 1999, a detailed and extensive assessment paper was compiled by Douglas Payne, an expert and independent consultant on human rights in Latin America and the Caribbean. The report was one of a series compiled to assist United States Asylum and Immigration Officers.

The report acknowledged that the visit had indeed opened a window, albeit a small one, but observed that Castro 'did not heed the Pope's call for democratic change' and that since the visit Castro had disregarded similar pleas from Canada, the European Union and the Organisation of American States. He was still running a one-party Communist state under 'totalitarian control'. Critics within the country had continued to be subjected to 'harassment, surveillance and intimidation. Cuba used short-term, arbitrary detentions together with official warnings of future prosecution to urge activists to leave Cuba . . . As 1998 drew to a close, Cuba stepped up prosecutions and harassments . . . refused to grant amnesty to hundreds of political prisoners or reform its criminal code, it marked a disheartening return to heavy-handed repression.'

The Pope had appealed for the release of some 270 prisoners on a list submitted by the Vatican. Some weeks after the papal visit, Castro released several dozen prisoners, a large number by Castro's standards, but as the Payne report observes, it was part of 'a historical pattern as a way to gain favour with visiting foreign dignitaries'.

Pope John Paul II had had much higher expectations. Just three days after returning from Cuba, during his regular Wednesday audience in the Vatican he drew a parallel between Cuba and Poland 'where he visited in 1979 and helped stimulate that country's eventual democratic transition'. The US report then quoted the Pope as saying, 'I expressed my hope to my brothers and sisters on that beautiful island that the fruits of this pilgrimage will be similar to the fruits of that pilgrimage.'

As has already been recorded, the Pope was rewriting reality in Poland: he had been little more than a benevolent onlooker of the efforts of Wyszynski, Walesa, and the men and women of Solidarity and KOR. The fruits of the Pope's Cuban pilgrimage were some temporary relaxations and the eventual release of some 200 prisoners, of whom some eighty had been on the Vatican list.

Before the end of the year a comparable number had been rearrested and imprisoned to join the estimated 100,000 prisoners held in a series of gulags that stretched right over the country. Five years after the Pope's visit, Cardinal Jaime

Ortega y Alamino of Havana declared that prospects for religious freedom 'are foundering in Cuba . . . in place of hope, despair is settling in'. The hopes of the faithful that had been raised by Wojtyla's visit had been shattered. The cardinal confirmed that shortly after the visit 'the government inaugurated a powerful ideological campaign, completed with the sort of propaganda that marked the 1960s.' The papal visit had resulted not in an improvement but deterioration.

In early 2003 Cardinal Ortega observed, 'Relations with the Cuban government remain essentially the same. There is no substantial change . . . the social-political space is always very limited and it appears often that the Church is ignored.' Commenting on the fact that the Church was still banned from operating schools and also denied access to the media, the cardinal continued: 'The government does not recognise the Church as a public entity that should have access to the communications media. There is a silence in terms of information about the Church.'

Within the Vatican at much the same time the Secretariat of State's office gave its blessing to a series of articles that subsequently appeared in the Pope's newspaper, *L'Osservatore Romano*. The occasion was the inauguration of a convent given by Fidel Castro to the Brigittine order. The seven-page spread appeared over four days. It sang the praises of Castro and told of his warm friendship with the Brigittines' Abbess Sister Tekla and the man from the Secretariat, Cardinal Crescenzio Sepe.

Notably absent from the festivities was the Archbishop of Havana, Cardinal Jaime Lucas Ortega y Alamino. He appears to have been the only senior member of the Vatican who was aware that Castro was about to have eighty-three opponents of his regime arrested, the overwhelming majority being Roman Catholics.

Four days after the photo calls had finished, the arrests duly took place and in April 2003, after what passes for a trial in Cuba had taken place, eighty of the dissidents were sentenced in total to more than 1,500 years in prison. The other three were executed. This particular piece of repression caused Cardinal Ortega to make his public comment on the absence of religious freedom and the growth of despair. The Vatican Secretary of State, Cardinal Angelo Sodano (considered by many Vatican insiders to be by far the most inept holder in history of the position that is second only to the Pope) moved quickly – not to condemn Castro but to placate him. On 31 April 2003 he stated that neither he nor the Pope 'have at all repented from placing trust in Castro' and that they continued to hope that 'he leads his people towards new democratic goals'.

The Cuban reality in the aftermath of the Pope's visit is not unique. The killings, the repressions, the intimidations, the suppression of basic human rights enshrined in the Universal Declaration of 1948 continued or even erupted in many places after the papal flight had returned to Rome. Whether in Marcos's Philippines or the Middle East or Pinochet's Chile, the Pope's recurring pleas for peace and respect for humanity were constantly ignored, in country after country.

In September 1990 the Pope flew to the Ivory Coast and, in an act that provoked deep unease within Roman Catholic communities in many countries, consecrated the basilica church Our Lady of Peace in the capital city of Yamoussoukro. No expense had been spared in this impoverished African country. At 525 feet it is the world's tallest church. The cost of the building was between $150 million and $180 million. The Pope described the building as a 'visible sign' of God's presence on earth. On the tenth anniversary of the consecration, the President of the Ivory Coast was in

Rome and about to have an audience with the Pope when he was forced to cancel and hurry home to a civil war that a multi-million-dollar church and papal injunctions had failed to prevent.

The Pope's condemnations of the blood bath in Bosnia-Herzegovina in 1995 and his fifteen public appeals for peace were all ignored. The previous year, Rwanda, a country 90 per cent Christian and two thirds Roman Catholic, ignored the Pope's entreaties as it collapsed into genocide and over 800,000 people were murdered. Bishops, priests and even nuns were among the perpetrators of atrocities, and the Rwandan Catholic Church was deeply compromised by its links to the ruling Hutu government. Within a year of the slaughter the Pope, speaking on behalf of the Roman Catholic Church, denied any responsibility.

Three days after the Rwanda killings commenced, the Pope publicly pleaded for the slaughter to stop. Many, if not the majority, of those responsible were Roman Catholic. They along with the Rwandan clergy and religious ignored the Pope. The murders continued for one hundred days. Four hundred thousand of the victims were children; a further 95,000 children were left orphaned. Two years later in a response to the allegations that many members of the Catholic clergy were among the killers, the Pope declared, 'All members of the Church who sinned during the genocide must have the courage to face the consequences of the acts which they have committed against God and their neighbour.' The response was not overwhelming. The Church made no effort to ensure otherwise. Instead, in February 1997 through the papal nuncio in Rwanda, it was made clear that the accused would continue to enjoy the support of the Church.

Among the number enjoying the protection of his superiors was Father Athanase Seromba. He was discovered in 1999 working under a false name in a parish in Florence.

He is accused of paying to have over 2,000 people crushed to death with caterpillar tractors and of having personally supervised the massacre. In 2002, faced with extradition hearings and international publicity, Father Seromba 'volunteered' to return to Rwanda. As well as using a false name Seromba had also travelled to Italy on a false passport. His trial began in September 2004. He was subsequently found guilty of genocide and crimes against humanity and sentenced to 15 years' imprisonment.

In the savage conflicts of the late twentieth century, it would be absurd to expect the entreaties of one man, even the spiritual leader of a 'billion' people, to quell man's inhumanity to man. Stalin had a point in his cynical question: how many divisions has the Pope? It is equally absurd for Vatican propagandists to insist that the Pope's words have prevailed against tyranny and war.

The myth of the Pope as peacemaker reached new heights during 2003 when a Vatican-orchestrated pressure group lobbied strenuously for him to be awarded the Nobel Peace Prize. Vatican officials let it be known that the Pope would accept the award and would travel to Oslo for the award ceremony. The Nobel committee thought otherwise. Having carefully investigated his claims, they passed him over and awarded the prize to a woman, which merely served to add to the chagrin inside the Vatican.

The woman, the Iranian lawyer and human rights activist Shirin Ebadi, has been imprisoned by the theocratic authorities and threatened by the hardline ideologues. Iran's first woman judge, she was told by the conservative clerics after the 1979 revolution that women could not sit as judges. Displaying that same level of extraordinary courage as Aung San Suu Kyi of Burma she has stood as a rallying point for all who seek to improve human rights in the Muslim world. The Pope's supporters considered he should have been given the award among other reasons 'because he spoke out against the 2003 war in Iraq'. Others talked of his 'ceaseless journey spreading the word of God'.

Papal politics was a constant, indeed incessant feature of Karol Wojtyla's reign. As with many other issues, his attack on abortion was never confined to the pulpit or the pastoral letter but was expressed repeatedly and openly in the political arena. When French President Valéry Giscard d'Estaing was granted a papal audience in 1981 the Pope berated him for 'allowing abortion' in a largely Catholic country.

The Pope believed that the Catholic Church's view on abortion should indeed be imposed upon every person in every country. He may have understood how democracy works, but he had very little sympathy for the concept as he observed more than once during his papacy. In September 1987 while visiting the United States he ignored a request from American bishops to affirm his belief in freedom of speech, choosing instead to observe: 'The Roman Catholic Church is not a democracy. Dissent from the Magisterium is incompatible with being a Catholic.'

In 2004 many American bishops tried hard to make the Catholic laity obey this precept. In January of that year Bishop Raymond Burke, a rising star in the US hierarchy, excited the media's attention when he stated in his diocese of Lacrosse, Wisconsin, that any Catholic politician that he considered to have shown 'support' for abortion or the legalisation of euthanasia would not be granted Holy Communion within his diocese. The pronouncement, deliberately timed to coincide with the early Democratic primaries, was seen as a direct attack on Senator John Kerry, one of the contenders for the Democratic nomination. Promoted to the archdiocese of St Louis, Burke upped the ante by declaring that John Kerry, now the Democratic presidential candidate, would be refused communion and that any individual Catholic voters who voted for him in the coming election should also be excluded from communion until such time as they had repented their 'sin' in voting for such 'a pro-choice politician'. Bishop Michael Sheridan of Colorado Springs got in on the act by warning that Catholics voting for Kerry would 'jeopardise their salvation'.

The papal encyclical *Evangelium Vitae*, 'On the Value and Inviolability of Human Life', was frequently quoted by such bishops. The news media, both Catholic and non-Catholic, gave increasing coverage to a totalitarian undemocratic Catholic Church on a collision course with John Kerry, a devout Catholic churchgoer seeking the highest democratic office in the world. His 'sin' in the eyes of his critics was not to be pro-abortion, but to be pro-choice. In May 2004, some time before he was even the official Democratic candidate, a Zogby poll of nearly 1,500 Catholic voters gave clear indication of what lay ahead for Kerry. The right-wing Catholic World News agency trumpeted 'Low Catholic support for Kerry on Church issues'. Only 23 per cent approved of Kerry's position on stem cell research, which he supports. He was given the same approval rating on the same-sex unions issue: Kerry supported unions but opposed homosexual marriages. The attack on Kerry had now broadened to embrace a spectrum of moral issues.

The editor of *Catholic World News*, Phillip Lawler, one-time official of the extreme conservative Heritage Foundation, the first of the New Right think tanks, ensured that the attacks on Kerry received prominent coverage throughout the summer of 2004. Lawler had also headed the American Catholic Committee, a group of right-wing Catholics opposed to the US bishops' position on nuclear control, had been at the heart of the campaign against the liberal Archbishop Hunthausen and was a long-time Republican who had worked on the presidential campaigns of Ronald Reagan in 1980 and 1984. In 2000 he announced his intention to run against Senator Edward Kennedy. For Lawler 'the key issue has always been abortion' but he also wanted to see the abolition of income tax, the Department of Education and the National Endowment for Humanities and Arts. He also wished to see the power of the Supreme Court restricted and was opposed to any form of gun control. To run on that kind of platform in Massachusetts against Kennedy required not blind courage but profound stupidity. It also required funding and substantial support even to get on the ballot. In the event Lawler attracted neither. He and other similarly minded people saw John Kerry as the natural enemy.

Among that number were Pope John Paul II, Cardinal Joseph Ratzinger, as then was, and the overwhelming majority of the Catholic hierarchy. In June after conferring with the Pope, Ratzinger wrote an official letter to the US Bishops declaring that 'public figures who openly dissent from Church teachings should not receive Communion'. The bishops had by this time demonstrated that they were divided on the issue.

The Republican Party seized on the implications. Constant public references by Republicans reminded the electorate that President Bush was opposed to abortion, same-sex marriages and stem cell research. The President, while in conversation with Vatican Secretary of State Cardinal Sodano, complained about the division within the ranks of the bishops: 'Some of the American bishops are not with me on the issues of abortion and stem-cell research.' By August the Kerry campaign was being assailed on a wide variety of fronts. Lawler's *Catholic World News* gleefully reported an interview by Cardinal Theodore McCarrick with the Italian daily *Avvenire* that stated 'No "ideal" US presidential candidate Cardinal McCarrick says' for the headline. The US bishops – whatever their various views – were united on at least one thing.

A ten-page 'Voter's Guide for Serious Catholics' was created by *Catholic Answers*, a lay apostolate based in San Diego, California. They identified five issues as 'non-negotiable'. They were abortion, euthanasia, foetal stem-cell research, human cloning and homosexual unions. Any candidate supporting any of these policies was in the opinion of the guide 'automatically disqualified as a viable option for a faithful Catholic voter'. In August alone, a million copies were distributed and a further four million went out before election day. Full-page advertisements for the booklet in *USA Today* served as a counterpoint to President Bush's constant reminders to the electorate of his own born-again Christian virtues. When someone at a Republican rally shouted at Bush, 'I am glad to see that God is in the White House', the President did not demur. In his third and final TV debate with John Kerry, Bush said:

'Prayer and religion sustain me. I receive calmness in the storms of the presidency. I love the fact that people pray for me and my family all around the country. Somebody asked me one time, how do you know? I said I just feel it. Religion is an important part. I never want to impose my religion on anybody else. But when I make decisions I stand on principle. And the principles are derived from who I am . . . I believe that God wants everybody to be free. That's what I believe. And that's one part of my foreign policy. In Afghanistan I believe that the freedom there is a gift from the Almighty. And I can't tell you how encouraged I am to see freedom on the march. And so my principles that I make decision on are part of me. And religion is part of me.'

By now the separation between Church and State that is enshrined by the Founding Fathers within the American

Constitution had been suspended until further notice. Official Republican fliers were sent out in Arkansas and West Virginia claiming that if elected John Kerry would ban the Bible. The Democratic candidate was not a born-again Christian: he had always been one. It is not within the nature of such men, particularly Roman Catholics, to go about endlessly and loudly proclaiming their faith. This natural reticence placed Kerry at a distinct disadvantage as polling day got closer.

The ubiquitous Archbishop Burke was never far from the headlines. In early October he sent a pastoral letter to over half a million Catholics in his diocese, with copies to all media outlets. He declared that voting for a candidate who endorsed any of the five issues that the voters' Guide had identified 'cannot be justified'. All were 'intrinsically evil', although war and capital punishment were not. It was an unusual way of endorsing George W. Bush. The news media quoted significant numbers of the electorate who shared the views of John Strange of Plymouth, Pennsylvania:

> 'I support the President not because I am a Republican, but because he is a Christian. I believe that a growing number are supporting Bush because of the values he has, the pro-life message and the fact that he supports traditional marriage. These values transcend party lines.'

When Phillip Lawler ran a story entitled 'Kerry Said To Be Excommunicated', it did not matter that it was a piece of fluff based on the response that the under-secretary of a Vatican Congregation had conveyed to an obsessive canon lawyer in Los Angeles who had previously initiated an action in an ecclesiastical court charging John Kerry with heresy. Within twenty-four hours it was front-page news throughout the United States. The witch hunt was in vogue again. Kerry had been demonised by his political opponents, by some of the American bishops and by the Vatican. If the electorate had read John Paul II's 1995 encyclical *Evangelium Vitae*, and understood his position that the democratic process must obey Catholic teaching, John Kerry would have been defeated by a much larger margin.

There was one overriding issue that swept Bush back into the White House. It was not Iraq, terrorism, or the economy. It was 'moral values'. At exit polls twenty-two per cent of the electorate identified that as the most important issue. Within the Vatican during the closing weeks of 2004 a quiet satisfaction at 'a job well done' was clearly discernible. The reactionary wing of the Catholic Church in the United States had not only succeeded in alienating John Kerry from nearly fifty per cent of the Catholic vote, traditionally a Democratic stronghold, but they had also made it much easier for the Republican party to capture many millions of evangelical Christian votes. They had helped to spread the false belief that John Kerry was pro-abortion: he was not and never has been. He is pro-choice as are the majority of Americans. A five-point swing in the Catholic vote for Bush gave him the states of Ohio and Florida and with them the White House.

In November 2005, the Hitler Syndrome – tell a lie long enough and loud enough and it becomes the truth – was again in evidence among the Catholic hierarchy in the United States. Archbishop José Gomez of San Antonio, Texas, declared that

'most Catholic politicians in the United States have fallen into a distorted understanding of what their faith is. Seventy per cent of politicians, who claim to be Catholic in Congress and the Senate, support abortion, and that figure reaches almost ninety per cent in traditional states such as Massachusetts or New York.'

Gomez talked of Senators who, while professing to be Catholic, 'voted 100 out of 100 times in support of abortion, euthanasia, homosexual unions and experimentation with embryonic stem cells'. The archbishop cited as an example John Kerry: 'Kerry claimed to be Catholic, yet openly supported abortion.' It is difficult to believe that the archbishop did not know when he uttered those words that Kerry did not, and does not, support abortion. John Kerry is on record many times on this. What he does support, like many of his Catholic colleagues in both Congress and the Senate, is *the right of women to exercise their own choice*. To the archbishop, the solution was simple: deny Holy Communion to the erring politicians until they recant.

The delight of the Pope and his advisors at the result of the United States presidential elections was counterbalanced by their anger at the rejection as an EU Commissioner of the Italian politician, Rocco Buttiglione, a close friend of the Pope and one of his earliest biographers. Buttiglione was in line for the job of Justice Commissioner until he expressed the opinion that homosexual acts were sinful. On another occasion he compared the relationship of the United States with Europe to that of children of a single mother, saying, 'Children who have no father are not children of a very good mother.' A majority within the European Parliament found such views incompatible with being a Justice Commissioner. After a political impasse of several weeks, Italian Prime Minister Silvio Berlusconi prevailed upon Buttiglione to withdraw his nomination and he was replaced by a candidate who was discreet enough to keep his views on homosexuals and single mothers to himself.

The affair came on top of the European Union's refusal to bow to the intense and at times rabid lobbying from the Vatican on the written constitution. From the Pope down, it seemed that every member of the Roman Catholic hierarchy demanded that the constitution should acknowledge in its preamble Europe's 'Christian' origins. By making such a high-profile, high-powered campaign on the issue, Pope John Paul II risked a public humiliation if the campaign failed, as it duly did. Archbishop Giovanni Lajolo, the Secretary for Relations with the States, saw the absence of any reference to Christianity in the European constitution as 'more than anti-Christian prejudice . . . It's the cultural myopia that astonishes us.' Cardinal Christoph Schönborn of Vienna expressed the belief that 'powerful anti-Christian forces are in evidence on the European scene today'. Buttiglione weighed in with the opinion that his own experiences showed the existence of 'an anti-Christian inquisition' and alleged that he had been subjected to a 'campaign of hate that twisted and distorted my public statements' but it was the Princes of the Roman Catholic Church that caught the ear.

Not one of them acknowledged that any failing by the body politic of the Church was to blame for such widespread alienation. What was beyond doubt was that if Christianity, albeit evangelical Christianity, was flourishing in the United States, Christianity in all of its many persuasions was on its knees throughout Europe, and not in prayer.

Chapter 11

Thou Shalt Not . . .

'IN THE PRESENT PERIOD, the corruption of morals has increased, and one of the most serious indications of this corruption is the unbridled exaltation of sex. Moreover, through the means of social communication and through public entertainment, this corruption has reached the point of invading the field of education and of infecting the general mentality.'

Cardinal Seper, the then Head of the Sacred Congregation for the Doctrine of the Faith, made this observation in a document, 'Certain Questions Concerning Sexual Ethics', published in December 1975. But the essence of the document has been declared many times by leading members of the Catholic Church. Among the first was St Ambrose, Bishop of Milan from 373 to 397. Ambrose did not approve of sex and he was not overly keen on marriage: 'Even a good marriage is slavery. What, then, must a bad one be like?' he asked and added, 'Every man is persecuted by some woman or another.' For Ambrose the best course for a woman was virginity, to redeem the sin of her parents in conceiving her.

Ambrose's teaching had much in common with that of Karol Wojtyla. As Pope, he extended Ambrose's approach and pronounced on more aspects of sex than any of his predecessors. These include birth control, abortion, sex before marriage, sex during marriage, sex after marriage, sex for the physically handicapped, sex for the infertile, sex after divorce and remarriage, divorce, married priests, women priests, homosexual sex, masturbation and sex in popular music, sex in books, movies and the media, and that list is far from complete. The late Pope's line has been propagated by his then lieutenant, Cardinal Joseph Ratzinger, Prefect of the Congregation for the Doctine of the Faith, and a host of other elderly celibate men.

This preoccupation with an activity that is forbidden to priests may in part explain why in the first world so few Roman Catholics go to confession. On sexual matters, the gap between the Catholic laity and the Vatican is unbridgeable. The laity is occupied with sex: the Vatican merely preoccupied. No member of the Church can plead ignorance on any aspect of sexuality. Central to many of its attitudes to sex and sexuality is the Roman Catholic Church's treatment of women.

Aristotle has much to answer for. He taught that women were inherently inferior in mind, body and moral will. His grasp of human reproduction left much to be desired. He believed that only the 'superior' man possessed the ability to procreate and that the only contribution from the 'inferior' woman was the raw material that was then fashioned by the male seed within the woman's womb, the potter working with unformed clay. For Aristotle, if the result was a male, then the potter had achieved perfection; but if the child was a female then something within the creation was flawed. He naturally concluded that such flawed humans cannot govern either themselves or others and must be ruled and controlled by men.

Aristotle was one in a long line of men to expound such views. The thirteenth-century Thomas Aquinas incorporated Aristotelian elements into his own theology, together with many of St Augustine's third- and fourth-century writings. These included *Marriage And Concupiscence*, a book that continually influenced the thinking of Karol Wojtyla, as priest, bishop and pope. It includes the following passage:

> 'It is one thing not to lie except with the sole will of generating: this has no fault. It is another to seek the pleasure of the flesh in lying, although within the limits of marriage: this has venial fault. I am supposing then that, although you are not lying for the sake of procreating offspring, you are not for the sake of lust obstructing their procreation by an evil prayer or an evil deed. Those who do this, although they are called husband and wife, are not; nor do they retain any reality of marriage, but with a respectable name cover a shame . . . sometimes this lustful cruelty or cruel lust, comes to this, that they even procure poisons of sterility, and, if those do not work, extinguish and destroy the foetus in some way in the womb, preferring that their offspring die before it lives, or if it was already alive in the womb to kill it before it was born.'

This position, as elaborated by Aquinas, and endorsed by Luther, Calvin and other theologians, remained orthodox teaching in all Christian Churches until after the First World War and, in the case of the Catholic Church, until 1951. It was then that Pius XII tore up the hitherto accepted dogma by declaring to a group of Italian Catholic midwives that the use of the so-called 'safe period' as a method of birth control was lawful. Augustinian teaching specifically denounced use of the safe period in his *The Morals Of The Manichees*: the 1951 concession also destroyed Augustine's whole doctrine of marriage.

Notwithstanding a wave of changes including female suffrage, equal rights legislation and the Universal Declaration on Human Rights, the Vatican Council II's Declaration on Religious Freedom and the irresistible rise of feminism, current thinking at the highest levels of the Roman Catholic Church on a wide range of sexual ethics is still an amalgam of Aristotle, St Augustine and St Thomas Aquinas. The three profoundly influenced Karol Wojtyla from his earliest years and those closest to him, such as Cardinal Ratzinger, Archbishop Dziwisz and the other members of the papal cabal were completely at one with his position on these issues.

On women and women's issues the Pope yet again presented a paradox. He consistently proclaimed his deep respect, admiration and appreciation for women and simultaneously enraged them across the world. The Pope had explored the significance of the 'feminine genius' within the Apostolic Letter, *Mulieris Dignitatem – On the Dignity of Women*, in 1986. The Pope's chosen biographer, George Weigel, described this work as 'John Paul's most developed effort to address the claim from some feminists that Christianity in general, and Catholicism specifically, is inherently misogynist'. For many of its critics it reads like an attempt to justify via judicious selection from the Bible, from Genesis through to Revelations, the historic chauvinism of the Catholic Church.

At the time of the Fourth World Conference on Women in Beijing in September 1995, the Pope wrote an open letter to 'women throughout the world'. This was part of his 'attempt to promote the *cause* of women in the Church and in today's world'. Constantly italicising to underline the importance he attached to certain thoughts, he thanked 'women who are *mothers*! You have sheltered *human beings* within yourselves in a unique experience of joy and travail'. He praised 'women who are *wives*! You irrevocably join your future to that of your husbands, in a relationship of mutual giving . . .'

He worked his way through women who are *daughters*, women who are *sisters*, women who *work, consecrated* women, until he got to 'thank you, every woman, for the simple fact of being women'. He fulsomely acknowledged the contribution of women throughout history and how so little recognition had been given to their collective achievements, often against formidable odds. Without any sense of irony he extolled the virtues of '*common priesthood* based on baptism'. He also ignored the fact that his own bank, the IOR, operated a discriminatory policy towards female employees. Women are obliged to sign an undertaking when taking up employment within the Vatican Bank that they will not get married or have children. If they wish to marry, they are compelled to leave the Bank's employment.

His letter continued with reference to the 'genius of women' and inevitably linked that with Christ's mother, Mary, 'the highest expression of the feminine genius'. There was a great deal more on Mary and her example for all women in accepting her vocation as 'wife and mother in the family of Nazareth. Putting herself at God's service, she also put herself at the service of others: a *service of love*.'

Much of the papacy of Pope John Paul II can be better understood by considering his early environment. Born in 1920, the same year that the victorious Polish Marshal Jozef Pilsudski returned to Warsaw with an army that had won a spectacular victory over Lenin's Soviet republic, Karol's birth coincided with the only period of Polish democracy that would occur until 1989. After six years, the 'liberator of Poland' overthrew the government. The military coup d'état resulted in a dictatorship until Pilsudski's death in 1935. This was followed until the German invasion in 1939 by a military junta posturing under the label of parliamentary democracy. Wojtyla's father, also named Karol, by the

time of Karol junior's birth had risen in the newly formed
Polish Army to the rank of first lieutenant.

Emilia, the convent-educated mother, was deeply devout.
The household reflected that devotion. At the door to the
apartment there was a font containing holy water for
crossing oneself on the way in or out. On the walls hung
holy images and copies of icons. There was a small altar in
the parlour where morning prayers were recited. Every
evening the Bible was read aloud by one or other of the
parents. There were prayers at meal times and at bedtimes.
Feast days and fasting days were observed rigorously. This
preoccupation with the Roman Catholic faith was not
confined to Emilia. The future Pope remembered Karol,
his father, as a 'very religious man'.

Karol senior was born in 1879, the same decade that Pius
IX, after years in which he had agitated to be recognised as
infallible, finally succeeded in realising his ambition. His
critics saw him as a 'theological monster' who had become
'a Papal Louis XIV' but they were in a minority. The
overwhelming majority of the faithful accepted the doctrine
of infallibility without question. A few years earlier they
had equally accepted the same Pope's 'Syllabus of Errors',
an attack on the entire modern world. Among the various
views and opinions that the Pope declared 'no good Catholic should hold' was a belief in an unrestricted liberty of
speech, freedom of the press, equal status for all religions
and democratic forms of government. The Holy Father
preferred absolute monarchies and condemned pantheism,
naturalism, absolute rationalism, socialism, Communism,
Bible societies and liberal clerical groups. The final item Pius
IX had condemned had been the proposition that 'the
Roman pontiff can and should reconcile and harmonise
himself with progress, with liberalism and with recent
civilisation'. Just how deeply and lastingly these values
would influence the young Wojtyla can be gauged from

the fact that in September 2000 John Paul II beatified Pius IX. The act caused very deep offence throughout world Jewry (Pius IX was a rabid anti-Semite) and simultaneously shocked and appalled many devout Catholics.

The lieutenant devoted the last twelve years of his life to his son Karol, from the time of his wife's death and his own simultaneous retirement in 1929 to his own death in 1941. Although in later life the Pope was given to bitterness when he talked of his mother's illness and early death, he also expressed joy and gratitude for the crucial dedication he had enjoyed from his father. The lieutenant had filled the long hours of tedium as a clerical officer by voracious reading and an unquenchable hunger for knowledge. Self-taught, he developed a cultured mind and demeanour. Like his late wife he was deeply religious but he added to his faith an interest in literature, athletics and a concern for the destiny of his country. In the eyes of many in the town of Wadowice he seemed to be an eccentric man who shunned people and made few friends. In truth he enjoyed his own company and the space that solitude brought, but as a man without racial or religious prejudice he was able to draw friends and acquaintances from both sides of the racial line and religious divide – something that only a minority in the town could lay claim to. Perhaps, as Zbigniew Silkowski, the Pope's friend from that time has recalled: 'The Wojtyla household was a community of two people.' But it was for these two a very rewarding time. The father revelled in the opportunity to pass on the knowledge that through his reading he had acquired. Polish history was something they discussed long and often. The lieutenant compiled a Polish-German dictionary and taught his son to speak German. When the son demonstrated to his teachers and to his classmates that he could read Kant's *Critique of Pure Reason* in the original German they were astonished.

Karol Senior paid particular attention to his son's religious education. Poland had long been regarded as the *antemurale christianitatis*, the 'rampart of Christendom'. Immediately after the declaration of papal infallibility in 1870, the Italian crown seized the Papal States and incorporated them into the newly created Italian state. Pius IX refused to accept this situation and declared himself 'prisoner in the Vatican'. Successive popes took the same unrealistic line, refusing to recognise the Italian regime, its government and parliament. The Papacy had dug in for the long haul and the siege mentality extended far beyond Rome. The crisis remained unresolved until the Vatican and Mussolini's fascist government signed a treaty in 1929. Against that background the Catholic Church had need of every rampart it could muster. Poland was not the only one. Spain and Ireland were also countries where the village priest's word was law and all Popes, good, bad and indifferent, were nationally revered. Questioning the local priest was not on the agenda. Disagreeing with any papal utterance, not just an edict on faith or morals, but anything, was unthinkable. This was the Roman Catholicism that the Wojtyla family accepted unhesitatingly.

The Virgin Mary had a constant vital influence upon the Pope from his childhood and the premature death of his mother. His encyclicals, his apostolic letters, his books, his sermons reveal an obsession with the Biblical image of Christ's mother. Conspicuously absent from the *Apostolic Letter* are any references to the positive roles played by women such as Mary Magdalene, Junia, Hagar, Rahab, Deborah, Jael, Judith and a great many other women of influence within the Bible. Throughout his career the Pope consistently suggested that the ideal woman is a virgin and a member of a religious order. Failing that, he sought a world where there is no birth control, no abortion, no divorce, no women priests, no married priests, no masturbation, no sexual intercourse outside heterosexual marriage and no homosexuality. It was a world that Karol Wojtyla had been seeking for much of his life.

In 1960, Wojtyla's play *The Jeweller's Shop* was published in a Catholic monthly. The author was identified as 'A. Jawien'. Among those who knew who was hiding behind the pseudonym were certain members of Wojtyla's extended family. The play tells the intimate personal story of three marriages. Much of it is not a work of fiction but is lifted verbatim from real life actual incidents and dialogue that came directly from the mouths of some of the members of the group of students who were particularly close to him whom he regarded as his 'family'. Wojtyla later recalled, perhaps as an attempt to justify what he had done, 'Only those who had been present at the original time would have recognised themselves.'

It is not unusual for writers to 'borrow' from real life, but the writer walks on thinner ice when he is the priest and confessor of his characters. Even more so when he is also a man who lectures on ethics. During the same year of 1960 some further fruits of all those vacations with his 'family' were laid before the Polish public. Karol Wojtyla published his personal guidebook on family life and sexual morality, *Love and Responsibility*. Wojtyla's book was a driving manual written by a lifelong non-driver, and aimed at a very limited readership. It offered nothing to non-Catholics, co-habiting couples, users of artificial birth control, homosexuals, bisexuals, or anyone who took pleasure from any form of sex which was not directed at the procreation of children within a Catholic marriage.

Karol Wojtyla's very close friend and collaborator, Anna-Teresa Tymieniecka, knew Wojtyla more deeply and completely than any other layperson in the world. Highly intelligent with a string of qualifications, her particular speciality was philosophy. She played a very important role in the creation of the English-language edition of his philosophic work *The Acting Person*, of which she was co-author. Her opinion of her fellow author's earlier solo effort is less fulsome.

'To have written (as he has) about love and sex is to know very little about it. I was truly astounded when I read *Love and Responsibility*. I thought he obviously does not know what he is talking about. How can he write such things?'[12]

If Wojtyla exploited just six members of his 'family' for his play *The Jeweller's Shop*, he cast his net much wider for *Love and Responsibility*. Not only did he freely use many of his one-to-one private conversations, he also mined the group discussions and then handed around draft copies of the manuscript for reaction and comment from the young students. All of this was topped up with information Wojtyla had acquired from within the sacred confines of the confessional. Anticipating a particular reaction, Karol Wojtyla acknowledged in his introduction to the book that what followed was indeed based on 'second-hand information'. This in his mind did not matter because as a priest he was exposed to a very much wider range of second-hand information than the average person. This might be a valid proposition coming from a priest who had spent a lifetime involved in pastoral work. On this occasion it came from a man who had spent eight months in a rural parish and two and a half years at St Florian's, the University parish in Cracow. From there on his pastoral work was limited to his contact with his extended family, only a few of whom had been married at the time of initial publication.

Wojtyla's declared intention was to make moral sense of human sexuality through the conversations he had had with the men and women who had invited him into their lives as 'their pastor and their confidant'. In attempting to make that 'moral sense' and of course simultaneously breach those confidences, Wojtyla ranged from the banal ('If a woman does not obtain natural gratification from the sexual act there is a danger that her experience of it will be qualitatively inferior, it will not involve her fully as a person.') to the bizarre ('Love in its physical aspect is naturally inseparable from shame, but within the relationship between the man and the woman concerned, a characteristic phenomenon occurs which we shall call here "the absorption of shame by love". Shame is, as it were, swallowed up by love, dissolved in it, so that the man and the woman are no longer ashamed to be sharing their experience of sexual values.'). Later Wojtyla defined this love that occurs at the advent of sexual intercourse. 'In marital intercourse both shame and the normal process of its absorption by love are connected with the conscious acceptance of the possibility of parenthood. "I may become a father", "I may become a mother". If there is a positive decision to preclude this eventuality sexual intercourse becomes shameless.'

Thus, according to Wojtyla, artificial contraception degraded both partners. He later described homosexuality as a 'perversion' and 'a deviation'. He asserted that 'pain is an evil to be shunned'. It would be interesting to know if he ever told that to the Roman Catholic Church's own secret society, Opus Dei, with which he was intimately involved for over fifty years who go in for self-inflicted pain with a variety of instruments. These include self-flagellation on the bare back and wearing tightly bound strips of studded metal bands pressed into the upper thigh. Wojtyla evidently excused, perhaps even approved, such activities provided that they were being performed for the greater glory of God and not to create sexual arousal.

In mid-2004 the Pope and Cardinal Ratzinger took to the arena of 'women's rights and duties' again. In a 'Letter to the Bishops of the Catholic Church on the Collaboration of Men and Women in the Church and in the World' published with full Papal approval by Cardinal Ratzinger, they sought to counter the claims of feminism and to emphasise the Christian understanding of 'women's dignity'. The letter left a great many women very indignant. Ratzinger got off to an unfortunate start within his introduction when he described the Catholic Church as 'expert in humanity'. In the eyes of many of his readers from there on it was all downhill. Talking of new approaches to women's issues in recent years he observed,

> 'women in order to be themselves, must make themselves the adversaries of men. Faced with the abuse of power, the answer for women is to seek power. This process leads to opposition between men and women in which the identity and role of one are emphasised to the disadvantage of the other, leading to harmful confusion regarding the human person, which has its most immediate and lethal effects in the structure of the family.'

Ratzinger then identifies a second strand of feminist ideology. 'In order to avoid the domination of one sex or the other, their differences tend to be denied . . .' This 'calls into question the family, in its natural two-parent structure of mother and father and makes homosexuality and heterosexuality virtually equivalent, in a new model of polymorphous sexuality.' The solution for the Pope and Cardinal to this situation was for all men and women to seek a deeper understanding of the Scriptures. To assist them the Cardinal then quotes copiously from a large array of sources, including the Bible, commencing with the first three chapters of Genesis leading ultimately and inevitably to the Virgin Mary. All women whether serving within the Church or living secular lives 'are called to follow her example'.

To judge from the global reaction from women, Dr Mary Condren's response was kinder than many. Dr Condren lectures in gender and women's studies at Trinity College, Dublin.

'Presented by a first-year undergraduate, this essay would barely merit a pass. So why bother to respond? The continued assault on lesbian and homosexual relationships fuels homophobia. Faulty logic, backed by the veto power of the Vatican and aligned with right-wing fundamentalisms will, at forthcoming UN meetings, have serious consequences for non-western women struggling for self-determination. If Jesus were here today he would be crying out, "Not in my name." '

In 1968 as the Prague Spring promised liberation for the country's fourteen million inhabitants, there were also hopes that a Papal encyclical on birth control offered potential liberation for a fifth of the planet, nearly one billion people, by ending an untenable and oppressive Church ruling on birth control. It turned instead into a Vatican winter. Without the need for a single tank, precious freedoms and the right of choice would be denied. Wojtyla played an important role in this result. He helped to shape the document known as *Humanae Vitae*, 'On Human Life'. The views of the author of *Love and Responsibility*, who believed that sex was shameful unless it admitted the possibility of procreation within marriage, carried particular weight with Pope Paul VI as he very characteristically agonised over the problem of whether or not to approve for Roman Catholics the use of artificial birth control.

In 1966 Wojtyla had created within Cracow his own

commission to study the issues that were being examined by a Papal Commission in Rome appointed by not one Pope but two, John and his successor Paul. Those issues were of course the problems of Family, Population and the Birth Rate. Quite why Wojtyla thought he should appoint his own commission is not known. It is clear that Wojtyla went to great lengths not only to get into this debate but to control it and stay well ahead of the other players. His local group, largely if not totally comprised of celibate men, also gained access to two drafts of the proposed encyclical. These were leaked to the Poles by priests on the commission who were hostile to any change in the Church's position. The men in Cracow considered one draft that had been prepared by the Holy Office, the Vatican's doctrinal experts, to be 'stupid conservatism'. The other reflected the Majority Report of the Commission which argued that there should be a change of the Church's position and declared that to ban artificial birth control would mean the Church losing all credibility with married couples and with the modern world.

The men of Cracow considered this to be seriously flawed in its approach to moral theology. They further contended that this very large group of learned people who had been studying the subject for several years had misread what God had written into the nature of human sexuality. The Poles had the answer to all this. What was needed was to tear a large chunk out of *Love and Responsibility*, dress it up slightly, and post it to the Pope. Thus for the Cracow commission artificial birth control was rejected in favour of 'living in marital chastity'. They acknowledged that this would involve a 'great ascetic effort and mastery of self'.

When *Humanae Vitae* was published, forbidding Roman Catholics the use of artificial contraception, the men of Cracow were delighted and thrilled. One of their number, papal theologian Father Bardecki, is on record as boasting,

'About sixty per cent of our draft is contained in the encyclical.' Whatever the actual percentage of the Cracow input to *Humanae Vitae*, Wojtyla was praising the document from the pulpit within days. 'If it poses great demands on a person in the moral realm these demands must be met.'

Wojtyla put great store on the element of continuity with regard to the teachings of the Church. He had argued very forcibly for the ban on artificial birth control on the grounds that to do otherwise would 'contradict and invalidate all previous Papal pronouncements'. The previous statement on the issue had been made by Pius XII in 1951 during a speech to a gathering of midwives and not as an encyclical for which infallibility was claimed. Since it had been made before the oral contraception pill had been invented, it can hardly be claimed to be definitive. Significantly the *Humanae Vitae* encyclical is also free of imprimatur. Pope Paul made no claim of infallibility for his document. It is undoubtedly an issue that will be revisited when the current Papacy ends and a new man sits on Peter's throne.

However, Wojtyla saw *Humanae Vitae* as 'the expression of the unchanging truth, always proclaimed by the Church'. Only a few years earlier during Vatican Council II he had helped to secure a profound change of the Roman Catholic position on a range of issues. Presumably some truths remain more 'unchanging' than others. He founded '*Humanae Vitae* Marriage Groups', an institution with severe rules. Their purpose was to ensure that married couples made the commitment to obey all of the requirements of the encyclical, particularly the ruling on artificial contraception. Only then, according to Wojtyla, could the 'shame' of sexual intercourse be overcome. His rules left the couple the freedom to choose between unprotected sex or joining their Cardinal in a completely celibate life.

Wojtyla had from his earliest years believed that the role of conscience lay at the very heart of Christian ethics and decision making by Christians in their everyday lives. However, there was an unspoken catch. The informed Christian conscience must base all of those decisions upon Christian 'Natural Law' which within the Church is defined ultimately by the Pope. Freedom of choice is therefore for the Catholic faithful an illusion. For non-Catholics the moral rulings of the Pope and the Catholic Church are matters for the Church alone. However, this particular papacy did not confine itself to regulating Catholics. It sought, often with great success, to undermine the democratic process of government. It intervened repeatedly in the affairs of nations and without any mandate from the people it brought about profound changes, not just for the Catholics of a country but for every citizen. Evaluating the papacy of Pope John Paul II very much depends on where the individual stands on a wide range of moral issues. It also depends critically on whether the individual is a man or a woman.

On the issue of abortion, Karol Wojtyla throughout his life held to the Church's historic position. For him, it was the greatest crime and he was adamant that there are no exceptions, no justifications. As for the frequently raised argument that if there were fewer unwanted pregnancies there would be fewer abortions Wojtyla wrote nearly fifty years ago in *Love And Responsibility*, 'There are no grounds for discussing abortion in conjunction with birth control. To do so would be quite improper.' In a document entitled 'The Problem of Threats to Human Life', a report to the Consistory of Cardinals in April 1991, the head of the Sacred Congregation for the Doctrine of the Faith, Cardinal Ratzinger, developed the line of defence for the Church's position on both abortion and birth control:

'it is precisely by developing an anthropology which presents man in his personal and relational wholeness that we can respond to the widespread argument that the best way to fight abortion would be to promote contraception. Each of us has already heard this rebuke levelled against the Church: It is absurd that you want to prevent both contraception and abortion. Blocking access to the former means making the latter inevitable. Such an assertion, which at first sight seems totally plausible, is, however, contradicted by experience: the fact is that generally an increase in the rate of contraception is paralleled by an increase in the rate of abortion.'

Ratzinger offered no sources or statistics for that remarkable statement. In May 2003 the Pope had a meeting with 500 Italian pro-life activists to 'commemorate' the twenty-fifth anniversary of the legalisation of abortion in Italy. He commended the group for 'never ceasing to work in defence of human life'. Then he recalled the warning of Mother Teresa of Calcutta, the woman whom in October 2003 he beatified in St Peter's Square: 'Abortion endangers the peace of the world.'

Cardinals in a variety of Latin American countries have reminded their congregations that the penalty of excommunication *Latae Sententiae* – automatically imposed – still applies to all those involved in an abortion 'including the assistant doctors, the nurse, whoever provides the money . . . etc, etc.'

The Pope's frequent stern injunctions to his bishops and priests to stay out of politics do not apply to abortion, birth control or homosexuality. The American bishops had been into politics long before Karol Wojtyla became Pope, and he knew it. But so long as their views coincided with his there was no attempt to silence them. In 1974 an American report ordered by President Nixon was presented to his immediate successor Gerald Ford. Nixon had specifically commissioned a study of the 'implications of worldwide population growth for US security and overseas interests'. The report – National Security Study Memorandum 200 – addressed a range of problems directly arising from the predicted increase in world population in the foreseeable future. Underpinning many of the report's recommendations was the implicit need for urgent action to improve family planning worldwide. What occurred subsequently has been the subject of exhaustive documentation by Doctor Stephen Mumford in a series of works listed within the bibliography. They are required reading for anyone with concerns on world population growth. They detail a constant and unremitting battle by the Vatican, in particular, to outlaw abortion and artificial birth control methods globally.

One of many successes of the Papacy in changing legislation enacted by a duly elected government occurred in the Reagan years. At the time Reagan took office in January 1981, the United States foreign aid funding included programmes that promoted both birth control and greater availability to procure a legal abortion. In the United States two historic Supreme Court rulings in 1973, Roe vs Wade and Doe vs Bolton, had established respectively that there was a constitutional right to abortion and that abortions were permissible through the entire term of pregnancy. Within twenty-four hours of the Roe vs Wade decision, a consensus of America's Catholic bishops had begun to plan a sustained campaign to overturn the Supreme Court decisions by forcing government to introduce a constitutional amendment prohibiting abortion. They did not seek to limit abortion to certain categories or situations; they wanted a total ban.

On 20 November 1975 the Roman Catholic bishops of America issued their Pastoral Plan For Pro-Life Activities. Dr Mumford has described this detailed blueprint as 'the bishops' strategy for infiltrating and manipulating the

American democratic process at the national, state and local levels'. Timothy A. Byrnes, Professor of Political Science at the City College of New York, saw it is as 'the most focused and aggressive political leadership' ever exerted by the American bishops.

The plan included a brilliantly conceived campaign with an attention to detail worthy of a major political party. It also sought to justify the campaign by utilising the classic Vatican technique of doublethink:

'We do not seek to impose our moral teaching on American society, but as citizens of this nation we find it entirely appropriate to ask that the government and the law be faithful to its own principle that the right to life is an inalienable right given to everyone by the Creator.'

The Pastoral Plan has had a long list of successes since its inception. Although it has yet to achieve the total abolition of abortion within the United States it has chalked up an impressive array of victories in the continuing fight. One of the most stunning achievements directly attributable to the Catholic lobby was to persuade the Reagan administration to alter the foreign aid programmes so that they accorded with the Roman Catholic Church's position on both birth control and abortion. In 1984 at the world conference on population in Mexico City, the United States withdrew funding from two of the world's largest family planning organisations, the International Planned Parenthood Federation and the United Nations Fund for Population Activities.

The first US Ambassador to the Vatican, William Wilson, has confirmed that

'American policy was changed as a result of the Vatican not agreeing with our policy. American aid programmes around the world did not meet the criteria the Vatican had for family planning. AID (the Agency for International Development) sent various people from the Department of State to Rome and I'd accompany them to meet the president of the Pontifical Council for the Family, and in long discussions they (the Reagan administration) finally got the message. But it was a struggle. They finally selected different programmes and abandoned others as a result of this intervention.'

In Spain, Chile, the Philippines and Poland, as well as a raft of countries where the Catholic vote can significantly affect the outcome of a general election, the Catholic Church has infiltrated into the democratic process. At world conferences, in the United Nations, in the Council of Europe, at Strasbourg, the Church has fought a no-holds-barred campaign in its efforts to have abortion and artificial birth control banned globally.

In the United Kingdom during the last week of March 2004, Prime Minister Tony Blair announced a series of faith-based initiatives with the release of a document entitled 'Working Together: Cooperation between Government and Faith Communities'. 'Faith-based initiatives' is an idea 'borrowed' from the Bush administration. It has provided back-door access to the democratic process whereby unelected pressure groups such as the Roman Catholic Church can influence the administration on many issues, headed predictably by abortion, birth control and homosexuality. President George W. Bush was highly susceptible to the Catholic position on these issues.

In the United States, Catholic bishops have regularly acted against Catholic candidates running for political office who believe it wrong to impose their moral position on others. Governor Tom Ridge of Pennsylvania and Texan candidates Tony Sanchez and John Sharp were banned from speaking at any Church-controlled event. In 2004 Presidential candidate John Kerry was hounded, slandered and repeatedly subjected to character assassination. Their collective experiences give the lie to the Roman Catholic Church's assurance in 1974 that it did not want to impose its moral teachings on American society.

Ironically the Pope complained that many 'religious believers are excluded from public discussions'. He then claimed to 'recognise the legitimate demand for a distinction between religious and political affairs' but 'distinction does not mean ignorance'. He called for 'a healthy dialogue between the State and the Churches, which are not competitors but partners'. He concluded these comments in mid-December 2003 to all the ambassadors accredited to the Holy See by yet again returning to his frequently repeated request for recognition that religion should continue to play an important influencing role within the European Union. He said that 'Europe is having difficulty in accepting religion in the public square.'

Both the late Pope and the majority of his bishops never accepted the separation of church and state, whatever they said to the contrary and whatever Concordats they signed. In the United States the Conference of Catholic Bishops have frequently represented themselves to be acting on behalf of the entire community of the Catholic Church in the United States. They have created over the decades policies and procedures that aspired to impact not only on Catholics but upon every American. Examples of their attempts to manipulate the democratic process include policy on nuclear deterrence, policy relating to immigration and illegal aliens, health care issues and practices in both Catholic-funded and non-Catholic hospitals, the Right to Life Movement and legislation related to abortion, the Hispanic and Black Ministry Movements, the Family Life ministry, the Youth ministry and legislation involving education, minorities, immigrants and rights of children.

In September 1994 the UN population conference convened in Cairo. Attending were representatives from 185 nations and the Holy See. The agenda was a 113-page plan calling on governments to commit $17 billion annually by the year 2000 to curb population growth. Some ninety per cent of the plan had been approved in advance, but the Pope was determined to destroy some of the remainder. He was convinced that one proposal in particular was aimed at controlling global population through abortion. The offending clause owed its inclusion at least in part to a Clinton administration directive to all US embassies that had been sent on 16 March 1994: 'the United States believes access to safe, legal and voluntary abortion is a fundamental right of all women.'

President Clinton and his administration had been adamant that the Cairo conference should endorse this policy. The Pope was equally adamant that they should not. For nine days, various Vatican delegations gave a powerful demonstration of how to wreck an international conference. Under the Pope's personal long-range direction they lobbied, filibustered and formed unholy alliances with Islamic nations who were traditionally opposed to abortion. They kept a vice-like grip on their Latin American bloc. The Pope prevailed over the governments of 185 nations. A statement was inserted: 'In no case should abortion be promoted as a method of family planning.' In return the Vatican gave 'partial consent' to the document. The Pope received a largely hostile press. One Spanish critic observed that he had 'become a travelling salesman of demographic irrationality'.

Anti-abortion pressure groups have gone to extraordinary lengths to impose their point of view. In December 1988 Nancy Klein was the victim of a near-fatal car accident on

Long Island, New York. Badly injured, she lay in a coma as doctors in the North Shore University Hospital fought to save her life. They advised her husband and her family that there was little hope and that if she should survive she would be in a vegetative condition. There was a complication: the thirty-two-year-old woman was ten weeks pregnant. Doctors concluded that an abortion might well save her life. When her husband Martin applied for court permission for the abortion to be carried out on his unconscious wife, a group of anti-abortion activists entered legal submissions. They wanted the court to grant them control over Nancy by appointing them guardians of her unborn foetus. This would give them the power to force her to continue her pregnancy. Although the unconscious Nancy would almost certainly die long before her body could carry the child to full term, this was a minor consideration for the 'pro-life' activists.

As the case began to proceed through three State courts on its way to the US Supreme Court, other anti-abortionists appeared and threatened to chain themselves to Nancy's hospital bed. Three months after the accident the Supreme Court described the anti-abortion activists who had brought the case to court as 'absolute strangers' to Nancy who as such had no right to determine her fate. The Court ordered that the abortion could take place. Shortly after the abortion Nancy regained consciousness. The enforced three extra months of pregnancy plus the injuries sustained at the time of the accident caused severe neurological damage; she can no longer use her limbs properly or speak with total fluency but her brain is 'as sharp as ever'. So sharp, in fact, that she subsequently lectured and spoke in favour of abortion rights and stem cell research.

The separation of church and state and the Pope's blurred 'distinction' between them were a significant election issue in the 2004 presidential race. A controversy, instigated by the Vatican and fuelled by the US bishops and Roman Catholic pressure groups, built up a good head of steam during the Democratic primaries, centred on the party's standard-bearer, Senator John Kerry. As shown above the Roman Catholic Senator was targeted by the anti-abortionists from the outset of the race. A group called the American Life League (ALL) published in early January a list of its 'Deadly Dozen'. All were Roman Catholic Democrat politicians who believed that it was a woman's right to choose whether or not she has an abortion. ALL is a front organisation for the Vatican. Its President, Judie Brown, is a member of the Vatican's Pontifical Academy for Life. She was described by the *Daily Catholic* as one of the top 100 Catholics of the twentieth century. Another board member of ALL is Dr Philippe Schepens, also a member of the Pontifical Academy for Life. A number of leading Republican politicians are also pro-choice, but have yet to be targeted by ALL.

The pressure group claims to have 375,000 members. Part of its campaign to put the greatest possible pressure on Catholic politicians to bring 'the moral teachings of the Church to their decision-making while in public office' is to encourage bishops to take disciplinary action against dissenting politicians. They did not have to wait too long. In April the Vatican had adopted as policy a global ban on giving the Eucharist to any politician who held a pro-abortion position. A number of the American bishops did not want to limit the issue to abortion. They sought to confront Senator Kerry and other politicians for their supposed failure to carry out their religious duties on the death penalty, the role of marriage and family, war and peace, the rights of parents, the priority for the poor, the correct way to respond to immigrants, and many other issues.

The Catholic activists are determined to rewrite history. As recorded earlier, while campaigning for the Presidency in

September 1960, John F. Kennedy had sought to settle for ever the issue of the relationship between a Catholic politician and his faith. In the Vatican, some applaud the American Church's new activism, but most regard it as a high-risk strategy. Others are more cynical. A senior member of the Curia remarked, 'If it distracts attention from the child abuse scandal it will have served a useful purpose.' He then made an alarming prediction. 'There's a lobby in the Vatican that wants the Holy Father to go public and instruct the Catholic Americans to either vote Bush or Nader or abstain.' In the event the Vatican obtained the result it desired without resorting to that tactic.

Even if one agrees with the Pope's description of abortion as 'the culture of death', one may still disagree with his declaration that a woman who uses the contraceptive pill is 'already on the road to abortion'. To any rational person, one motive for a woman to use a contraceptive device is precisely to avoid the risk of an abortion – and the risk of death.

Abortion can certainly be wrong, even obscene, in certain settings. In Russia, for example, sixty per cent of pregnancies now end in abortion and one in ten of these abortions involve girls under eighteen. In the United States girls as young as fourteen use abortion as a method of contraception because they reportedly 'don't believe in birth control pills because they mess up your body and condoms, diaphragms and other methods make you feel like you are planning sex. It isn't the romantic way.' In women's athletics, pregnancy followed by abortion is used deliberately to boost performance. The Roman Catholic Church is right to condemn such contempt for life just as it is wrong for the Church to dogmatically insist that abortion is always morally wrong.

Every year more than half a million women die from complications during pregnancy, under the World Health

Organisation (WHO) definition of 'maternal mortality' – the death of a woman during pregnancy or within forty-two days after pregnancy. WHO has established that every minute, somewhere in the world

> 'a woman dies as a consequence of complications of pregnancy. One hundred women suffer from pregnancy-related complications. Three hundred women conceive an unwanted or unplanned child. Two hundred women acquire a sexually transmitted disease.'

Clearly if a full range of family planning methods was freely and readily available to all men and women throughout the world that appalling toll would be dramatically reduced. If even a limited, stringently-controlled abortion service was available, many of these deaths that are directly caused by women resorting to illegal and dubiously induced abortions would be prevented, but the real key is contraception, a key denied to all women by the Roman Catholic Church.

In the first months of 1993 thousands of women were raped in Bosnia by Serb forces. UN relief workers distributed what is frequently called a 'morning after pill' that acts as an abortifacient. The Vatican promptly denounced this action and Pope John Paul II sent a message to the raped victims urging them to 'transform an act of violence into an act of love and welcome' by 'accepting' the enemy into them and making him 'flesh of their own flesh' by carrying their pregnancies to term.

During April 1999 it was revealed that an increasing number of Albanian women were being separated from refugee columns and removed to a Serb camp near the Albanian border where they were repeatedly raped. Many of the raped victims were in their early teens. When it became known that the UN Population Fund was providing 350,000 emergency reproductive health kits to be distributed to the Kosovo refugees, and that the kits contained 'morning after' contraceptives, the Vatican was again quick to condemn that action. Calling the pill an 'abortion technique', Monsignor Elio Sgreccia, Vice-President of the Pontifical Academy for Life, said it was important to distinguish between 'the act of violence and the reality of new human beings who have begun their life'.

In 2003 an even younger victim, a nine-year-old girl, Rosa, became the unwitting centre of controversy in Nicaragua. While on holiday with her parents in late 2002 in Costa Rica, she was raped by a twenty-year-old man, and there was also a suspicion that her uncle had sexually assaulted her. Back in Nicaragua when it became apparent that Rosa was pregnant, her parents attempted to obtain an abortion for the child. In Nicaragua abortion is allowed only when the health of the 'woman' is at risk. A Government board concluded that Rosa faced the same health risk whether she carried the pregnancy to term or had an abortion. The Nicaraguan Family Ministry stated that it would prosecute anyone who helped the girl obtain an abortion. A key figure in this story is Cardinal Miguel Obando y Bravo. Having succeeded in preventing an abortion, the Catholic Church as an inducement to Rosa's parents to abandon their search for a doctor who would terminate the pregnancy offered Rosa food and shelter in an orphanage where they proposed the nine-year-old girl would be able to have her baby and then raise the child.

The case was by now attracting attention far beyond the shores of Rosa's homeland. When a medical team carried out the abortion, the Cardinal publicly announced that the child, her parents, the medical team, doctors, consultants, nurses and any individual who had helped in any way were all excommunicated. The Cardinal's action merely succeeded in throwing petrol on the bonfire. Women's groups in a number of countries erupted. A petition signed by

25,000 in Spain was delivered to the Vatican, with the promise that a million-signature petition would soon follow. The signatories, predominantly women, demanded that they too should be excommunicated. With churches rapidly emptying in a number of countries, the Vatican reversed the Cardinal's decision on the excommunications.

In January 2005 yet another nine-year-old girl was the centre of an abortion controversy. The country on this occasion was Chile. The girl had been raped and by the time the case had become a national issue, she was seven months pregnant. Consequently, the demands from the pro-abortion groups were denied by Health Minister Pedro Garcia who called on Chileans to denounce the sexual assault of young children. The controversy demonstrated that the Church does not have a monopoly on irrationality when it comes to the issue of abortion.

In the Pope's home country, relentless Church pressure over a number of years brought about in 1993 an end to abortion virtually on demand. Now with very few considered eligible under the latest stringent legislation, the wealthy resort to a private abortion, the poor resign themselves to a greater poverty. An estimated 200,000 illegal abortions are carried out each year at the cost on average of £125, the equivalent of one month's salary. Prime Minister Leszek's Democratic Left Alliance, SLD, has pledged to legalise abortion on the pre-1993 basis. It has further incensed the Catholic Church in Poland with plans to grant legal recognition to homosexual relationships.

In Ireland, a country split down the middle on the abortion issue where access to termination is as difficult as in Poland, thousands of women every year cross the Irish Sea to have abortions in private clinics in England. In Northern Ireland the situation has for decades bordered on the surreal. The six counties are part of the United Kingdom in every respect other than the abortion law.

Abortions are strictly limited to criteria that do not apply in mainland England. The anomaly is maintained through a group of Catholic bishops resisting the will of Parliament.

Catholic Church officialdom is capable of going to extraordinary lengths to enforce absurd or cruel sexual rulings. In 1982 a Munich priest's actions were upheld and defended by his archbishop after he refused to marry a young couple because he claimed that the bridegroom, crippled by muscular dystrophy, would be unable to consummate the union. The archbishop's office declared, 'Sexual impotence is a natural barrier to the contract of marriage.' The priest told the young man who was confined to a wheelchair that he would have to prove the marriage could be consummated by subjecting himself to a medical examination. He refused. A local Protestant Church agreed 'without hesitation' to marry the couple.

On 19 May 1991, in a letter on combating abortion and euthanasia to all bishops throughout the world, the Pope wrote,

'All of us, as pastors of the Lord's flock, have a grave responsibility to promote respect for human life in our dioceses. In addition to making public declarations at every opportunity, we must exercise particular vigilance with regard to the teaching being given in our seminaries and in Catholic schools and universities. As pastors we must be watchful in ensuring that practices followed in Catholic hospitals are fully consonant with the nature of such institutions.'

In August 1994 Cardinal Ratzinger's Vatican Congregation declared that any woman whose damaged uterus could pose a threat to her health in a future pregnancy is not permitted to have a hysterectomy or a tubal ligation. They had been asked for a ruling by American bishops on behalf of

Catholic hospitals throughout the United States and had declared that surgical intervention was not 'morally acceptable'. Previously in March 1987 the Church ruled that in vitro fertilisation (IVF) was also morally unacceptable even for a woman suffering from endometriosis who was therefore unable to conceive naturally. The issue of contraception and the Church's teaching of the past fifty years that approved 'the rhythm method' descended into a black farce with the announcement in July 2003 that the method does not work for all women. Canadian scientists have established that some women can ovulate up to three times a month. Since any of these eggs can be fertilised, 'natural family planning is pointless'.

The Church has made it very clear that its teaching puts an absolute ban on abortion, to the extent of allowing a woman to die rather than sacrifice the life of the unborn child. To underline that particular teaching, in May 2004 the canonisation of an Italian laywoman, Gianna Beretta Molla, took place in St Peter's Square. Gianna, thirty-nine years of age at the time of her death in 1962, is the first married saint for centuries. Present at the ceremony were her ninety-two-year-old widower, Pietro, and her four children. Gianna was a far remove from the usual candidate for canonisation. Happily married, devoted to her young children, an active woman who enjoyed skiing and going to La Scala, nothing was exceptional in her life except the manner of its ending.

Gianna was carrying her fourth child when she was diagnosed with a tumour in her womb. The options were limited. She would have to have a hysterectomy so that the surgeons could remove the tumour. The only alternative was to terminate the pregnancy. Gianna elected for a third course of action; she would carry the baby the full term and then undergo delicate surgery to remove the tumour. She was fully aware that there was a high probability of severe

possibly fatal complications at the time of the birth. 'If you
have to choose between me and the baby, save it, I insist,'
she told her husband as the birth date approached. In April
1962 a healthy baby girl was born; a week later Gianna died
from septic peritonitis. The Vatican objects to descriptions
of Gianna as 'the first anti-abortion saint' but that in the
opinion of many is precisely what the Pope had created.

In March 2004 the Catholic Church brought US-style
politics into the impending United Kingdom general election. Cardinal Cormac Murphy O'Connor and his bishops
set about disrupting the Labour Party's bid for a third
successive term of office. Prompted by comments from
the then Conservative leader, Michael Howard, that he
favoured a reduction in the abortion time-limit from the
present twenty-four weeks to twenty weeks, the English
Primate took to the hustings. He praised the Tory leader
and declared that abortion was 'a very key issue in the
election'. In fact, there had not been one single mention of
abortion until that moment. Warming to the attack, the
cardinal cast out on the traditional view that the Catholics
of the United Kingdom were largely Labour voters. The
cardinal's own constituency consists of a notional four
million Catholics of which only 20 per cent are practising.
The week after the cardinal's entry into the election, he
returned again to the fray, this time to raise the issues of
stem-cell research and euthanasia.

The Roman Catholic Church moves regularly into the
political arena in her efforts to obtain a global ban on stem-
cell research and to severely limit the use of in vitro
fertilisation (IVF) to married heterosexual couples, and
then to the creation of no more than three embryos. Italy
has some of the most restrictive laws concerning IVF. In
June 2005, a referendum on the issue offered the Italians an
opportunity to vote for more liberal laws. The Church
swung into action and, from Pope Benedict XVI down,

Italy was urged to ignore the referendum. The population obliged and the turnout was less than twenty per cent, thus ensuring the laws remained unchanged.

In Spain the conflict between the Church and the Socialist government elected in March 2004 has been at crisis level since the new government came to power. Legislation passed since the election that has liberalised divorce rules, ended mandatory religious education in public schools, promoted stem-cell research, allowed same-sex marriage, and future legislation that will ease legal access to abortion has resulted in a Spanish Church in a constant state of apoplexy.

In October the Synod of Bishops meeting in Rome passed a number of propositions that include the reiteration of certain current Church doctrines. These included a continuing ban on married priests, a continuing ban on divorcees who have remarried 'being admitted to Holy Communion'. The Synod also 'exhorted' such couples to refrain from sexual intercourse. The Synod declared a continuing ban on non-Catholics taking Communion and told all Roman Catholic politicians throughout the world that they should not receive Communion 'if they support policies that are contrary to justice and natural law', i.e. Catholic doctrine.

The battle to hold the Catholic line on these various issues is global. The fact that the Spanish government had an election mandate to make reforms was regarded by the Church as an irritating irrelevance. In the United Kingdom, the United States, Australia and a great many other countries, the late Pope's contempt for democracy still deeply influences the minds of the bishops and cardinals that Karol Wojtyla created. The Vatican's latest assault on Italy's abortion laws is to join forces with politicians from the right and the left who are anxiously courting the Catholic vote for the general election due in April 2006. The Catholic Church is backing a proposal that women should be paid not to have abortions. Under the scheme, women in straitened economic circumstances would get between 250 and 350 euros a month for up to six months before the birth of the child. Quite how the child would be kept after birth has not been addressed.

The scourge of HIV-AIDS is yet another area where Catholic teaching and treatment are in direct conflict with the practices of non-Catholic health care. More than 26.7 per cent of HIV-AIDS treatment centres throughout the world are Roman Catholic facilities. The range of treatment available at these centres does not include the distribution of condoms and instructions on 'safe sex' practices. The Catholic alternative, one they share with the Bush administration, is to advocate total abstinence from sex. Neither does the Church approve of HIV-AIDS prevention campaigns that feature the use of condoms. In the words of Archbishop Javier Lozano Barragan, the Holy See's top official on health-care issues, it sees such campaigns as 'contributing to the spread of the culture of sexual licence'. Since many priests and nuns are known to break their vows of celibacy, one wonders how lay people are expected to keep such vows without the benefit of a vocational calling and the constant support and supervision of the Church. It would be instructive to compare the success of the condom-free clinics against the non-Catholic centres, but, predictably, no accurate figures are available.

In repeated pronouncements, the hierarchy of the Catholic Church have demonstrated total ignorance on the value of condoms in preventing unwanted pregnancies and checking the spread of AIDS. For example, the then Cardinal Ratzinger declared

'to seek a solution to the problem of infection by promoting the use of prophylactics would be to embark on a way not only *insufficiently reliable from the technical point of view*, but also and above all, unacceptable from the moral aspect. Such a proposal for *"safe"* or at least *"safer"* sex – as they say – ignores the real cause of the problem, namely the permissiveness which in the area of sex as well as that related to other abuses, corrodes the moral fibre of the people.'

Cardinal Alfonso Lopez Trujillo has said, 'The AIDS virus is roughly 450 times smaller than the spermatozoon. The spermatozoon can easily pass through the "net" that is formed by the condom.' Writing in the British-based *Guardian* newspaper, columnist Polly Toynbee responded specifically to Cardinal Trujillo.

'No one can compute how many people have died of AIDS as a result of Wojtyla's power, how many women have died in childbirth needlessly, how many children starve in families too large and poor to feed them. But it is reasonable to suppose the silent, unseen, uncounted deaths at his hand would match that of any tyrant or dictator. It may be through delusion rather than wickedness, but it hardly matters to the dead.'

In September 2004, Ann Smith, HIV corporate strategist for Cafod, the development agency for the Catholic bishops of England and Wales, revealed that the agency, contrary to the Vatican line, distributes condoms as part of its three-layered approach to fighting the HIV virus. Writing in the *Tablet* she said:

'The data is clear that condoms, when used correctly and consistently, reduce but do not remove the risk of HIV infection. This fact cannot be excluded from or misrepresented in any information on risk reduction strategies, regardless of the political or moral position of those promoting them.'

This enlightened approach has incensed the recently formed Catholic Action Group (CAG) who in early 2005 mounted a City of London-backed campaign calling for a financial boycott of Cafod.

HIV-AIDS was first indentified in 1981. Over the ensuing twenty-five years nearly sixty-five million people were infected with HIV and an estimated twenty-five million have died of AIDS-related illnesses. It is estimated that close to forty million live with HIV. The vast majority of that number are unaware of their health status. During 2005 an estimated 2.8 million AIDS victims died.

That the late Pope John Paul II, his successor Pope Benedict XVI and men such as Cardinal Trujillo should have remained so obdurate regarding the use of condoms is particularly ironic when one considers the report created by Sister Maura O'Donohue which was mentioned earlier. I refer to the report again as it is of great importance.

Sister Maura's report was submitted confidentially in February 1994 to Cardinal Eduardo Martinez, prefect of the Vatican Congregation for Religious Life and her ultimate superior. A source within the Congregation kindly made a copy available to me. Sister Maura, a physician in the Order of Medical Missionaries of Mary, had entitled her report 'Urgent Concerns for the Church in the Context of HIV/AIDS'.

During the previous six years she had travelled extensively through Africa, Asia, the Americas and Europe. The visits were part of her work as AIDS Coordinator for the Catholic Fund for Overseas Development (CAFOD) that serves as lead agency for HIV/AIDS programmes for

Caritas Internationalists (CI). The main purpose of her work was to raise awareness about HIV/AIDS among Church personnel.

Sister Maura's report began by laying out the reality of the AIDS pandemic. Her data showed one particular country with an infection rate of thirteen per cent among the diocesan clergy, and in another sixteen members of one religious order who had already died of AIDS. Sister Maura recorded that as the disease spread, there was a culture of secrecy among the Church hierarchy.

Many of the bishops and religious superiors began to institute compulsory HIV tests for all candidates for seminaries and religious life, but failed to address those serving priests or religious who were already infected or who might contract HIV in the future.

As noted earlier, Sister Maura's report established a shocking catalogue of sexual abuse. Such abuse was not restricted to any single country or even continent. It spread throughout the globe. Sister Maura discovered examples of sexual abuse over a six-year period in some twenty-two countries in five continents: Botswana, Brazil, Colombia, Ghana, India, Ireland, Italy, Kenya, Lesotho, Malawi, Nigeria, Papua New Guinea, Philippines, Sierra Leone, South Africa, Tanzania, Tonga, Uganda, United States of America, Zambia, Zaire, Zimbabwe.

Sister Maura had hoped that the report would motivate the appropriate action, particularly by those in positions of authority in the Church.

However, a year after she had submitted the report, the only action to have been taken was an invitation for her and her colleagues to meet with Martinez and three members of his staff. That meeting did not result in action either. As she wrote in a later memorandum, 'It was clear that there was no prearranged agenda.'

Other reports from similarly concerned senior women in religious orders were also issued. Again, no action was taken either by Cardinal Martinez or any other senior Vatican figure.

Frustrated by the lack of any progress whatsoever, some of the authors of the reports contacted the *National Catholic Reporter* in early 2001. This resulted in the newspaper running a cover story on 16 March 2001. Four days later *La Repubblica*, Italy's largest daily newspaper, published a long article on the subject.

The newspaper coverage forced the Vatican to respond. However, it was not the Pope or Cardinal Martinez who made a statement to the press. It was Navarro-Valls, who simply stated, 'The problem is known, and is restricted to a geographically limited area.'

His statement continued and affirmed that the Holy See was dealing with 'the question in collaboration with the bishops, with the Union of Superiors General (USG) and with the International Union of Superiors General (USIG).'

In reality, however, no positive action was taken by the Church throughout the seven years since the Vatican had first been made fully aware of the problems with sexual abuse and HIV-AIDS by Sister Maura O'Donohue and the other experts.

During the past twenty-five years it must have frequently seemed to the Catholic faithful that no matter which way they turned there was the man from Poland saying 'no', particularly when it came to matters that involved sex or the female gender. It was not as if Karol Wojtyla frequently created additional activities to add to the existing list that were banned. It was the constant repetition of what was already proscribed, the total absence of compassion, the obvious relish in the Niagara of angry abominations that cascaded unceasingly from the Pope or his soulmate Cardinal Ratzinger.

Vatican Council II was invariably put to one side and forgotten as the Pope mentally moved back through the nineteenth century, only pausing to pick up the worst legacy of Vatican Council I, the declaration of Papal infallibility. He also embraced Pius IX's Syllabus Of Errors and the accompanying encyclical *Quanta Cura*.

John Paul II had much in common with Pius IX, a man who showed an intense dislike for democratic government and a preference for absolute monarchies. Pius also denounced 'the proponents of freedom of conscience and freedom of religion' as well as 'all of those who assert that the Church may not use force'. Spiritually, Wojtyla seemed to have been living some time after the onset of the sixteenth-century Counter Reformation and before the Papal States were finally lost in the mid-nineteenth century.

Apart from Mother Teresa and the Virgin Mary, his understanding of women was severely limited. The issue of women priests is a further example, not of a failure of communication so much as an inability to comprehend.

Sister Kane's courageous confrontation of the Pope in October 1979 on the issue of women priests has been recorded within an earlier chapter, as has his comment back in Rome when he dismissed the nun and her supporters as women who were 'irritated and embittered for nothing'.

The Pope's inflexibility was not confined to doctrinal matters. His bigotry was equally set in concrete. He brooked no argument, no discussion and no exchange of views. On the issue of women priests, the Pope declared: 'It will never happen and it is not to be discussed.'

With the Church suffering a continually growing shortage of priests during the late Pope's entire papacy, with devout, highly intelligent, multi-talented women begging for the opportunity to join the priesthood, every available opinion poll suggests that the solution of women priests would be welcome throughout the entire Catholic world – except for the Holy See.

There are no scriptural objections that the Pope, Ratzinger and the rest of the reactionaries could produce; instead they were reduced to declaring that Christ did not choose any women for Apostles. He did not choose any Gentiles either.

When the Anglican Church began to ordain women priests in 1982, apoplectic reaction was not confined to the ranks of the Protestant traditionalists. It was very evident within the congregation buildings in Rome.

Prior to that, notwithstanding all the fanciful talk of reconciliation, it would have taken a number of miracles before Rome and Canterbury might close the gap.

Full reconciliation between the two main branches of Christianity is at least three Popes away. By that time there will be a minority of university-educated women left in the Church.

It is invariably the mother rather than the father who ensures the faith continues down the line. Alienate the mother and you will alienate the family. The Vatican with its normal long view of history believes firstly that feminism is 'something' confined to the United States and, secondly, 'It is a passing fashion.' Every day that view is maintained is another day of damage for a Church that has been haemorrhaging its lifeblood since artificial birth control was banned in 1968.

The Pope's lack of practical compassion was further demonstrated in his response to requests from priests who had asked to be released from their vows in order to return to a lay status. Paul VI had granted nearly 33,000 such requests. Soon after his election, John Paul II stopped the automatic granting of what he described as 'decrees of laicisation'. For him priesthood was a vocation for life. He could not accept that vocations may be lost. Direct pressure alone made him change course. According to one Vatican source,

'It was only when the Pope was preparing for his first trip to Brazil in 1980 that he moved on the question on laicisation. The Brazilian bishops told him that if he had not officially indicated before the trip that steps were in hand to create legislation that would enable men to leave the priesthood he would be facing public demonstrations during his Brazilian tour from large numbers of priests. That got it moving and the new deal was made public in the autumn.'

To judge from what the Vatican source told me, the new deal that Pope John Paul II created brought great anguish over the ensuing years. A man can leave the priesthood only if one of three conditions applies.

First, a long period has passed since he had lived as a priest and his current situation was not one he could walk away from, the unspoken assumption being that he had a wife and family.

Second, the applicant had been partly or totally coerced into the priesthood.

Third, his superiors had failed to notice early enough that he was not suited for the celibate life.

Thus two of the three criteria have a sexual orientation.

The idea that a priest, like a nurse, a teacher, a doctor or a member of dozens of vocational professions could lose his vocation for a myriad of reasons ranging from disenchantment or loneliness to spiritual burnout apparently never occurred to the Pope and his advisors. Without papal dispensation many are condemned to live in a half world, neither priest nor layman.

So we have a Church where women cannot enter the priesthood and men find it nearly impossible to leave.

Chief among Karol Wojtyla's many advisors was the man who in December 1981 was appointed Prefect of the Congregation for the Doctrine of the Faith, formerly the Holy Office. Cardinal Joseph Ratzinger has earned over the years a number of other titles including Vatican Enforcer. The neutering of the German theologian Hans Küng was orchestrated by Ratzinger even before he ascended to such high Vatican office. The list of some of the Catholic Church's finest scholars and thinkers silenced by Ratzinger over the past 24 years is lengthy.

Small surprise then that according to Clifford Longley, editorial consultant for the *Tablet* and long time internationally respected religious affairs author and journalist, Cardinal Ratzinger is 'disliked and feared throughout the Catholic world'.

And not only the Catholic world. In 1986 the cardinal, with the full support of the Pope, issued his letter to the bishops of the Catholic Church on the Pastoral Care of Homosexual Persons. It began by reminding the reader of the contents of the document quoted at the start of this chapter, the 1975 document on sexual ethics issued by one of Ratzinger's predecessors, Cardinal Seper, which had talked of the current period of moral corruption as 'the unbridled exaltation of sex'.

Cardinal Ratzinger was concerned that after the 1975 document

'an overly benign interpretation was given to the homosexual condition itself, some going so far as to call it neutral or even good. Although the particular inclination of the homosexual person is not a sin, it is a more or less strong tendency ordered

toward an intrinsic moral evil; and thus the inclination itself must be seen as an objective disorder.
Therefore special concern and pastoral attention
should be directed towards those who have this
condition, lest they be led to believe that the living
out of this orientation in homosexual activity is a
morally acceptable option. It is not.'

Ratzinger has condemned homosexual activity because
'It is not a complementary union, able to transmit life; and
so thwarts the call to life of that form of self-giving which
the Gospel says is the essence of Christian living.' But this is
precisely the same situation which every celibate priest and
virgin religious vows to uphold. Ratzinger has asserted that
in denying either passive or active homosexuals their freedom of thought and action the Church 'does not limit but
rather defends personal freedom and dignity realistically
and authentically understood'. He regards the abandon-
ment of homosexual activity as a 'conversion from evil'. For
a letter that claims to be concerned with the pastoral care of
the homosexual, its tone is one of singular hostility not least
in the final injunction,

'All support should be withdrawn from any organisations which seek to undermine the teaching of the
Church, which are ambiguous about it, or which
neglect it entirely. Special attention should be given
to the practice of scheduling religious services and to
the use of Church buildings by these groups, including
the facilities of Catholic schools and colleges.'

The Pope not only wholeheartedly approved of this
position during his regular Friday meetings with Cardinal
Ratzinger, but greatly assisted in the creation of such
documents. Another example occurred when the Vatican's

Enforcer issued a further proclamation in 1992, entitled 'Considerations Regarding Proposals to Give Legal Recognition to Unions between Homosexual Persons'. It was one part of the Vatican's attempt to mobilise Roman Catholic opinion against equal rights legislation for homosexual men and women currently imminent to a number of countries. After restating many of the views and directives contained in his 1986 letter, Cardinal Ratzinger defined who should and who should not be granted the right to be protected from discrimination. 'Sexual orientation does not constitute a quality comparable to race, ethnic background etc. in respect to non-discrimination. Unlike these, homosexual orientation is an objective disorder and evokes moral concern.' After a series of attempted justifications for this position the Cardinal observed,

> 'In addition, there is a danger that legislation which would make homosexuality a basis for entitlements could actually encourage a person with a homosexual orientation to declare his homosexuality or even to seek a partner in order to exploit the provisions of the law.'

Ratzinger did not confine himself to specific areas such as the potential of adoption or foster care by a homosexual couple: he clearly wished to keep homosexuals confined as second-class citizens because in his mind they were obviously second-class human beings. During the summer of 2003 the Pope and Ratzinger grew increasingly concerned, in the light of actual or prospective legislation in many countries, that they were losing the argument. They took to the barricades once more and yet another document emerged from Ratzinger's congregation that showed a nut-like resistance to a rising wave of tolerance and understanding of homosexuals across many societies.

'Those who would move from tolerance to the legit-
imisation of specific rights for cohabiting homosexual
persons need to be reminded that the approval of
legalisation of evil is something far different from
the toleration of evil.'

Ratzinger then told the reader:

'In those situations where homosexual unions have
been legally recognised or have been given the legal
status and rights belonging to marriage, clear and
emphatic opposition is a duty . . . One must refrain
from any kind of formal co-operation in the enactment
or application of such gravely unjust laws and, as far
as possible, from material cooperation on the level of
their application. In this area everyone can exercise the
right to conscientious objection.'

One can only wonder precisely how many international
criminal lawyers Ratzinger had consulted and taken opinion
from before issuing such a foolish and dangerous doctrine. In
Ratzinger's view no law was valid that granted any legal
rights 'analogous to those granted to marriage, to unions
between person of the same sex'. Writing on homosexual
marriage, Ratzinger in 2003 used the same argument:

'Homosexual unions are totally lacking in the bio-
logical and anthropological elements of marriage and
family which would be the basis, on the level of reason,
for granting them legal recognition. Such unions are
not able to contribute in a proper way to the procreation and survival of the human race.'

Like much of Cardinal Ratzinger's work, the sting was
reserved for his closing thoughts. These dealt with the

position of the Catholic politician when confronted with proposed legislation to recognise homosexual unions. Ratzinger instructed that the Catholic politician had 'a moral duty to express his opposition clearly and publicly and to vote against it. To vote in favour of a law so harmful to the common good is gravely immoral.' If such a law had already been passed, Ratzinger advised the politician that 'he should oppose, try to repeal it and do everything he could to limit its harm'. The reader will notice that in Ratzinger's world all politicians are male.

If at the beginning of Pope John Paul II's papacy the issue of clerical sexual abuse had been addressed with a fraction of the vigour that the Church has expended on its persecution of homosexuals, the scandal would have been resolved nearly twenty years ago. What the Pope and his cardinal were attempting through this line of attack on homosexuals was not merely to undermine the historic separation between church and state but in doing so to pre-empt the democratic process. Unelected men sitting in the Vatican were demanding that their views and opinions should not merely prevail for the Roman Catholic faithful but for all non-Catholics as well.

The Catholic faith is not the only branch of Christianity currently struggling with the issue of homosexuality. The Anglican Church is on the verge of schism over precisely the same controversy, yet even as it perches on the edge of the precipice its leader Dr Rowan Williams still manages to maintain a calm, reasoned, conciliatory position to both the pro and anti groups within his flock. Instead, when the Pope met the Archbishop of Canterbury in October 2003, he lectured the Archbishop and then attacked him for 'undermining Christ's teaching' and accused him of caving in to secularist pressure. The fact that the Vatican is awash with homosexuals was ignored by the Pope, and the Archbishop diplomatically neglected to point it out to him.

As Christianity and its leaders were confronted in many parts of the world with an increasingly secular society, the Pope and his advisors within the Church chose to revert to a pre-Vatican Council II position. We are back to the reign of the papacy that gave the world the Syllabus Of Errors and the accompanying encyclical *Quanta Cura*. In these, Pius IX denounced unrestricted liberty of speech and the freedom of press comment. The concept of equal status for all religions was totally rejected. To Pius IX 'Error has no rights', a view demonstrably shared by both Pope John Paul II and Cardinal Ratzinger.

The combination of Karol Wojtyla and his enforcer Ratzinger most certainly spread considerable apprehension among a fair percentage of Catholic theologians. Among those silenced was the Brazilian theologian Father Leonardo Boff, one of many who suffered because of his support of liberation theology. He was ordered to refrain from speaking, teaching and publishing his views and was eventually driven out of the priesthood in the early 1990s. Another theologian who suffered from what critics described as 'Ratzinger's excessive zeal' was Father Jacques Dupuis, a professor at the Gregorian University in Rome who dared to see value in non-Christian religions. In view of the fact that the then Cardinal Ratzinger extends his contempt beyond non-Christians to include non-Roman Catholic branches of Christianity, finding them 'in a gravely deficient situation', a hard time from Ratzinger and his underlings was inevitable. It duly arrived. Dupuis, a seriously ill man at the time of his inquisition by Ratzinger in 2000, died in 2004.

The list of those theologians who were either silenced, driven out or damaged by the Prefect of the Congregation for the Doctrine of the Faith is impressive and inevitably includes the father of Liberation Theology, Father Gustavo Gutièrrez, subjected to a witch hunt by the Peruvian bishops on Ratzinger's orders. It is probably cold comfort to the Catholic laity who have suffered and continue to suffer from a variety of edicts that flowed from the late Pope and his executioner but they certainly have some very illustrious companions.

Today within the higher reaches of the Vatican, the railing at the modern world on occasions reaches the surreal. Ratzinger, who enjoys playing the music of Beethoven for relaxation, has described rock music as

'an expression of base passions, which, in large musical gatherings, assumes cult characteristics or even becomes a counter cult opposed to Christianity. Rock music seeks to falsely liberate man though a phenomenon of mass, underpinned by rhythm, noise and lighting effects.'

He further believed that pop music is 'an industrially produced . . . cult of banality' and concluded opera had 'eaten away at the sacred' in the last century.

For both the late John Paul II and his successor, followers of any religion other than Roman Catholicism are in 'a gravely deficient situation' – so much for ecumenical and inter-religious advancement. With the release of the document *Dominus Iesus* in December 2000, the Vatican reaffirmed its doctrine that the Catholic Church is the only 'true' Church. Ratzinger has also written, 'Catholics don't want to impose Christ on the Jews, but they are waiting for the moment when Israel says yes to Christ.'

During the first week of November 2003, John Paul II declared himself 'satisfied' with the ecumenical efforts undertaken during his pontificate. He remarked that 'the ecumenical progress of the past twenty-five years has been substantial'.

Given the Pope's comments to the leader of the Anglican Church, the publication of a document that has asserted the followers of all other Churches and faiths are gravely deficient, and the virtual state of war that exists between the Vatican and the Russian Orthodox Church, the Pope's satisfaction remains a mystery.

The Vatican gave a powerful demonstration on 29 November 2005 that Karol Wojtyla lives on, not only in spirit but in the earthly form of his successor, when it released an Instruction on homosexuals and seminaries. The document, the product of more than a decade of deliberation, was prepared at the request of the late Pope and is the first Instruction to be issued during the pontificate of Benedict XVI. It bans homosexual men from the seminaries. Would-be priests who experience a 'transitory problem' could still be ordained, provided they had lived a chaste life for a period of three years. As for the many thousands of active homosexual priests around the world and the active homosexual bishops and cardinals, the Instruction was silent.

The Catholic Church hardly ever recognises a divorce or a second marriage while the original spouse is still alive. The solution for those wishing to remarry and remain good Catholics is to seek an annulment, in which the Church after due process rules that a perfectly valid marriage never existed in the first place. Such an arrangement is inevitably open to abuse. In Italy on 3 July 1974 Claudio Cesareo and Marina Volpato contracted a marriage at a religious ceremony held in the parish Church of Santa Maria in Trastevere. Near the end of 1980 Claudio left the marital home to continue an adulterous affair. He continued sleeping with his wife and ten months later he returned to Marina shortly before she gave birth to their first child. In 1984 a second child was born. Both children were christened and the father arranged for their first communion and subsequently his elder daughter's confirmation.

A devout man, Cesareo had attended a pre-marriage course with Marina during which the couple became fully conversant with the various religious obligations they were about to acquire. He also attended a wide variety of religious services including the celebration of various wedding anniversaries and religious funeral services. He also insisted that he and his wife should go to the shrine of Medjugorje in Yugoslavia and kneel in prayer before the Holy Virgin. In 1993 Claudio again left the marital home, this time permanently. He set up home with a Danish girl and this relationship produced a son. Marina, eventually accepting that the marriage was at an end and anxious that her two young daughters should at least be materially provided for by their father, sued for a civil divorce during which she had every expectation that the court would make adequate provision for the children.

In an attempt to avoid alimony payments, Claudio turned to the Vicariate of Vatican City seeking an annulment. Initially his grounds were that though he had gone through a religious ceremony he did not and never had believed in God. Advised by the court officials that in the light of his attention to a wide variety of religious activities the contention that he was an atheist was going to be rather difficult to establish, Claudio changed his position. He 'acquired' a witness who stated that before the wedding Cesareo had told him that he did not believe in the indissolubility of the Wedding Sacrament. Cases such as this are helped considerably if money is placed in the right places; Marina's father Sergio would insist that this case was no different. The Vatican Tribunal found in favour of Claudio and magically his marriage was annulled. Notwithstanding the physical evidence of a wife and two children, his marriage had never existed and as such no alimony was due. The court also ruled that, if she wanted, Marina was free to get married but Claudio was forbidden to 'remarry without previously consulting the local ordinary'.

A few years before this sad tale reached its conclusion, Cardinal Ratzinger in yet another edict from his office to bishops throughout the world stated that divorced Catholics in unsanctioned second marriages cannot receive Communion unless they renounce sex. Demonstrably, any estranged couple wishing to avoid a life of celibacy should abandon divorce plans, 'acquire' a couple of persuasive witnesses and head for the Vatican courts. In January 2002 while addressing members of the Roman Rota the Pope suggested to the lawyers gathered before him that they might invoke their rights of conscience to avoid becoming involved in divorce cases. One eminent Italian lawyer was heard to mutter, 'What – and lose two thirds of my income?'

By March 2004 only three countries still maintained a complete ban on divorce and one of them, Chile, the only country in the Americas where the total ban applied, had initiated legislation to legalise divorce. It had been a long and bitter fight with a resistance headed by the Catholic Church. Before the end of the year, divorce was legalised, dealing a stunning and humiliating defeat to the Church. Only Malta and the Philippines remain as divorce-free zones.

Chapter 12

Vatican Incorporated II

T HROUGHOUT THE DECADE of the 1980s Archbishop Marcinkus and his cohorts within the Instituto per le Opere di Religione (IOR), or as it was universally referred to the Vatican Bank, continued to make money for the Church as they followed Pope John Paul II's advice and ignored their critics. It was more difficult to ignore the Holy See's continuing budget deficit. Year in year out, its finances were in the red. This had happened since 1970 and would continue until the early 1990s. Catholic congregations across the world were told that theirs was a Church of the poor, and asked for ever bigger donations. But the real reason for the deficit was Vatican accounting. The rare figures that the Vatican made public were only a partial declaration. Excluded were the annual accounts and profits of the Vatican Bank, and the annual accounts and profits for the Vatican City State budget. The consolidated financial statements of the Holy See listed stocks and shares at purchase price – not market value. The Holy See's vast real estate investments were deliberately undervalued. This pick-and-mix approach ensured that the Holy See always appeared to be in deficit. In 1985, it was apparently in the red by just under $40 million and in 1990 by over $86 million.

The Vatican's explanation was invariably the same: '. . . the main causes of the projected increases in the deficit are the recent salary increases for the lay employees . . . International market conditions . . . Unforeseen circumstances.' Nothing had changed since Pope Paul VI had instructed Cardinal Vagnozzi to establish and produce an exact summary of the Vatican's financial position. Vatican crisis meetings on finance were a regular feature. In 1985 the College of Cardinals met yet again, as the Vatican projected a shortfall for the year of just over $50 million. After the German, American and Italian Cardinals had been subjected to the customary squeeze, this figure had over $10 million shaved from it.

The process was repeated in 1986, reducing the shortfall to $22 million. Still the Vatican three, Marcinkus, Monsignors Pelligrino De Strobel and Luigi Mennini, were ignoring all demands from investigating Italian magistrates to present themselves for questioning. Archbishop Marcinkus declared: 'Why should I answer their questions? They're all Communists.' He continued to divide his time between the Palace in his capacity as Deputy Governor and the Bank. Out of working hours he kept a lower profile than in former days.

In November 1986, Cardinal Joseph Höffner of Cologne demanded that Marcinkus be replaced by a non-clerical President. Cardinal John Krol of Philadelphia raised publicly a proposal for the Vatican Bank to be subjected to an annual audit by a company of international stature. The majority of the other cardinals, even the Vatican Governor Cardinal Sebastiano Baggio, complained about having a Bank president who was so mired in scandal and the constant threat of arrest that he was of little use. Most of the fifteen cardinals on the Vatican Financial Commission created in 1981 concurred with Höffner and Krol yet still nothing could be done without the Pope's approval and that was not forthcoming.

On 11 February 1987, in a charming little ceremony Archbishop Marcinkus handed the Pope a gold medal to celebrate the centenary of the Vatican Bank and in a not too subtle nudge the Pope also received a cheque for $150 million, representing eighty per cent of his bank's profits for the past year.

Part of those profits had been derived from administering the huge sums in dollars and gold deposited in the Vatican Bank by the Philippine dictator, Ferdinand Marcos. Handwritten notes by Marcos, made while swearing a deposition in Hawaii, confirm the details and reveal that the Holy See and specifically Pope John Paul II were trustees for the Marcos estate. They did not explain why the Pope or his bank regarded the estate, looted over decades from the people of the Philippines, as a religious foundation.

By early 1987 Marcinkus had taken up permanent residence within the Vatican, after being tipped off by Italian Minister for Foreign affairs Giulio Andreotti that an arrest warrant for the Vatican three was about to be issued by the Milan Public Prosecutor's Office. Andreotti, a devout Roman Catholic, had no intention of watching the public arrest of the Archbishop bring further shame on the Church. When the police made a dawn raid on the Marcinkus home at Villa Stritch, the Archbishop had already taken up lodgings across the Tiber. The arrest warrants charged the three men with complicity in a fraudulent bankruptcy and accused the trio of acting for personal gain. This enabled the Pope and his advisors to declare that the accused had acted without the knowledge of those in authority above them. The Secretary of State Casaroli saw the warrants as an attempt to breach the Lateran Treaty that governed the relationship between the two states.

During the following month, March 1987, the Vatican's representative in the United States, the Pro-Nuncio Archbishop Pio Laghi, held a meeting with his opposite number in Rome, Ambassador Frank Shakespeare. It had been less than a year since the Ambassador had replaced William Wilson who had been obliged to resign after several scandalous episodes. According to a confidential cable from the American Embassy in Rome on 16 March 1987 Laghi and Shakespeare identified five major issues that should feature in President Reagan's forthcoming meeting with the Pope.

'First, and most important, was the question: What is Gorbachev? Second: Central America, especially Nicaragua. Third: the Middle East and the constellation of problems in that area. Fourth: the Philippines, and finally Poland.' An additional subject, 'Vatican Finances', appears to have occupied their meeting for the majority of the time available.

According to the Archbishop: "Two thirds of the Vatican is self-supporting . . . Both St Peter's itself and the State of Vatican City operate in the black . . . The other third which maintains the Curia, *L'Osservatore Romano* and Radio Vatican is deeply in deficit.' But Archbishop Laghi noted that 'even here it is *L'Osservatore* and Radio Vatican that account for most of the red ink.' It transpired that Laghi then recommended that the Vatican make most of its budget publicly known, 'like any other government . . . This would improve the Vatican's chances for additional funding from the Churches around the world, while protecting the rights of the bank's depositors.' The Archbishop did not mention that those depositors included five Mafia families still laundering their profits from illegal narcotics trade, extortion, protection, racketeering, prostitution; every Italian political party, still using secret accounts as slush funds; and members of organised crime organisations from the United States, Canada, the United Kingdom, Colombia and Venezuela.

At much the same time, Vatican finances were the subject

of an acrimonious luncheon in the papal apartments with the 15 Cardinals appointed to the Church's financial commission. Cardinal Gerald Carter of Toronto told Karol Wojtyla that it was morally indefensible to buy computers and pay Vatican salaries by diverting Peter's Pence, which is given by the faithful to help the poor. 'Using that money which is yours to use as you see fit, Holy Father, to prop up Vatican finances is wrong. No way to run a budget.' Cardinal Krol, a man particularly close to the Pope, weighed in: 'APSA (Administration of the Patrimony of the Holy See) is under-performing. An income of $15 million or so on investments of $200 million does not stack up.' Krol and Cardinal O'Conner of New York and some others thought the solution lay in persuading an elite group of wealthy Catholics to fund a foundation that would send its yearly profits as a further additional income for the Pope. Carter and another group were opposed to the plan. 'It will buy patronage and give too much power to a small group of people.'

The more the Pope listened the more impatient he became. He saw himself as a universal pastor not as Chairman of the Board. In reality he was both. The cardinals complained of the battle against Vatican secrecy and deplored the fact that it had taken more than five years to get even the beginning of more open accounting. They expressed bitterness of the fact that even they, the duly appointed Financial Commission, were denied even a fragment of information from the Vatican Bank. They could not ascertain how much of the bank's annual profits were going each year from Archbishop Paul Marcinkus to the Pope.

Throughout the Vatican's finances there were curious, inexplicable practices. The Vatican Workers' Union believed that the Vatican was investing wisely for their retirement pensions. It would be 1993 before a properly administered pension fund was created. Over $500 million in gold assets sat in the Federal Reserve Bank of New York instead of being put to work in investment portfolios with an annual return. Vatican property worth billions of dollars had a book valuation of $100 million. The Vatican's many embassies and residences scattered around the world were not included as assets.

In 1987 Cardinal Casaroli was supervising the rewriting of rules to limit the Vatican Bank's financial activities with secular banks across the Tiber. But this would do nothing to remedy the Vatican's paranoid financial secrecy or its grossly inefficient business strategies. Not only the Vatican Bank but the entire Vatican financial government needed radical overhaul. 'I may be a lousy banker but at least I'm not in prison,' Marcinkus would boast to callers' enquiries. Being a fugitive from arrest appeared to sit easily on his conscience. On 17 July 1987, the Italian Court of Cassation decided that the Italian Courts' criminal process under the existing Lateran Treaty had no jurisdiction over Vatican citizens. The Milan prosecuting magistrates immediately appealed the decision and for a further twelve months the Vatican three remained firmly as guests of the Pope. Finally, on 6 June 1988, the Supreme Court in Rome confirmed that, guilty or not, Italy could not compel citizens of the Vatican to face the Italian judicial process. Three principal actors in the theft of $1.3 billion now had official confirmation that they had got away with it.

With the threat of arrests and further disgrace for Vatican residents removed, Cardinal Casaroli could finally speed up his protracted negotiations with the Italian government over the revised Lateran Treaty. The Secretary of State was at long last finally handed the means to prise Marcinkus out of the Vatican Bank. He contacted five laymen whom he regarded as *uomini di fiducia* – men of trust – an Italian, a Swiss, an American, a German and a Spaniard, with decades of experience in international banking. The

Italian, Professor Angelo Caloia, was elected President of the IOR to replace Archbishop Marcinkus. The five had previously advised Casaroli they would not come in until Marcinkus had been removed.

The Pope appointed five cardinals as a Commission to ensure that the lay experts did not breach any of the new statutes concerning governance of the bank. Acting as liaison between the bankers and the cardinals was a relic from the Marcinkus days, the IOR Secretary, Monsignor Donato de Bonis who had survived against formidable odds: Pope John Paul I had wanted him out of the Bank in September 1978; the Milan magistrates had withdrawn his passport along with Mennini's and De Strobel's, yet he avoided arrest and astonishingly slipped through the reforming purge unscathed, although without any power or authority.

This brave new world of IOR banking got off to a less than glorious start. The new board had its inaugural meeting in June 1989, yet Marcinkus had not yet left. Part of the delay was caused because the Pope wanted to promote Marcinkus from his post as Deputy Governor of Vatican City to Governor. For Marcinkus the promotion would carry with it a Cardinal's hat and immunity from arrest. The transition would be rocky. Secretary of State Casaroli, amongst a group who had never accepted Marcinkus for no other reason than that he was an overbearing American, marshalled his allies. This final chance to put the knife into Marcinkus was too good an opportunity to pass. In December 1990 Marcinkus officially resigned as acting Governor and announced that he would not be returning to his roots in Chicago but would instead seek the warmer climes of Phoenix, Arizona. 'After forty years in Rome, your blood thins out.'

There was a second reason for the difficulty within the Commission. Since their injection of millions to bail out the bank after the Ambrosiano débâcle, Opus Dei kept an ever-closer watch on events within the Vatican Bank. Of the five banking experts at least three were described as 'close to' Opus Dei: Angelo Caloia, the new Vatican Bank President, the Spanish-banker Sanchez Asiains and the Swiss banker Philippe de Weck. Among the five supervising cardinals, Opus Dei was represented by his Eminence Eduardo Martinez Somalo.

Under the statutes of the bank, which have never been made public, the account holders must be members of religious organisations recognised as such by the Vatican. There are also ethical criteria regarding share dealing, which is confined to State bonds and the bonds of major industrial companies. Investments are to be made only in triple-A companies. The Bank at this time also retained a 2.1 per cent share of the capital of the successor of Banco Ambrosiano, the Ambrovento.

In 1990 in one of Italy's weddings of the year, Carlo Sama, managing director of the chemical giant Montedison, married one of the owners, Alessandra Ferruzzi. Young, beautiful and very determined, Alessandra was the daughter of Serafino Ferruzzi, the patriarch who built a multi-billion-dollar business in the grain and cereal industry. After Serafino's death in an aeroplane crash in 1979 the business was controlled by his son-in-law Raul Gardini, Alessandra, her brother and two sisters. By the time of the 1990 wedding, the Ferruzzi business group were second only to the Agnelli dynasty of Fiat in the list of the hyper-rich clans. Sales of grain and sugar and starch-based produce were estimated at $12 billion per year.

Three years earlier in 1987 the group had stunned the Italian business community by seizing control of Montedison, the chemical and pharmaceutical conglomerate. The takeover, which had involved a $2 billion buyout, had been far from friendly, with the Montedison management publicly hostile and critically questioning how the two giants could possibly create synergy. Gardini's plans included an imaginative use of Ferruzzi's starch, grain and seeds as the biodegradable feedstocks for Montedison's paper, pharmaceuticals and plastics. One of his schemes called for a $1 billion investment to produce ethanol, a natural petrol additive, from grain.

The Italian politicians of the day were equally sceptical and hostile to the takeover and they were able to put very serious obstacles in the way. Thanks to bribes, slush funds, kickbacks and sweeteners, the opposition melted away and the takeover proceeded. Then in 1988 Raul Gardini masterminded an even more spectacular coup, a merger with ENI, the Italian state energy and chemicals giant. Gardini and the Ferruzzis used the merger to create ENIMONT, a global company. Again there was resistance to the partnership. Again huge kickbacks and bribes were handed out.

Between 1988 and 1993 Montedison was simultaneously concealing losses and hiding bribes. The losses were at least $398 million, bribes at least a further $300 million. Serafino the patriarch had once memorably observed, 'Someone should make a monument in honour of debt.' The company that he had created was to become precisely that. By the end of 1990 Raul Gardini and his colleagues at Montedison were in desperate need of a money laundry. The relationship with ENI had gone very sour but Gardini and ENI chief executive Gabriel Cagliari had nonetheless agreed that ENI should buy the forty per cent of ENIMONT owned by Montedison. The two men loathed each other but they now co-operated in a deal which involved paying out bribes in excess of $100 million. It would become known in Italy as 'the mother of all bribes'.

It was agreed that Cagliari would buy back the forty per cent holding for $2.5 billion, a sum vastly in excess of its real value. To ensure a safe passage and a satisfactory conclusion to the deal bribes were made to at least two former Prime Ministers, every major political party, bankers, civil servants, financiers, executives, lawyers, upper men, middle men, lower men and as always a kickback to the laundry.

Carlo Sama had friends and contacts in a wide variety of places. One of them, Luigi Bisignani, was responsible for ensuring that the 1990 wedding had been officiated by Monsignor Donato De Bonis, the only Vatican Bank senior employee to survive the Marcinkus era. Bisignani was a man of many parts: thriller writer, editor-in-chief at the news agency ANSA, friend and confidant of Giulio Andreotti and his wing of the Christian Democrats, a good friend of the recently departed Marcinkus and many other senior members of the Vatican. Bisignani also found time to exploit his old membership of P2 and his continuing close relationships with Licio Gelli and Umberto Ortolani and to launder millions of dollars through the Vatican Bank on behalf of some of his friends. When Sama indicated that he would appreciate an account at the Vatican Bank, Bisignani yet again obliged. The method involved converting the money into Italian Government Treasury Bonds that were washed through his various accounts within the IOR. One such transaction in the supposedly corruption-free post-Marcinkus era occurred on 13 December 1990 for $2.5 million in Italian Treasury Bonds, part of the kickback being paid to Domenico Bonifaci, a property developer, to ease the ENIMONT deal.

In 1991 Carlo Sama along with his wife Alessandra and a financier, Sergio Cusani, went to the Vatican Bank where waiting for them was the man who had married Carlo and Alessandra, Monsignor Donato de Bonis. Luigi Bisignani was also on hand to ensure that all of his mutual friends were at ease. The couple that the Monsignor had wed now wanted to open a deposit account on behalf of a religious foundation. Its name, in honour of the founder of the Ferruzzi empire, was to be St Serafino. Between 1991 and mid-1992 over $100 million was banked in this account. None of it found its way to the followers of the nineteenth-century Russian saint. It went instead to three foreign accounts, two in Switzerland and one in Luxembourg, where the money was converted into Italian Treasury Bonds. The ever-busy Luigi Bisignani became an even more frequent visitor to the Bank as he hurried in with the numbers of the foreign accounts. He was well rewarded for his work as postman with some four billion lire ($2.3 million) in Treasury Bonds.

When the storm eventually broke, at the first attempt Bisignani avoided arrest because the warrant was deemed to be 'legally flawed' by the Court of Cassation. By the time that this had been remedied the 'postman' had taken holiday leave abroad 'for health reasons'. Carlo Sama had also been handsomely remunerated by two to three billion lire – $1.7 million. The leaders of all wings of the Christian Democrats, the Socialist Party including former Prime Minister Craxi, the Banco Commerciale President, Enrico Braggiotti, politicians of every hue, industrialists, journalists, bankers, brokers were implicated. Before the Milan trial had commenced Braggiotti left for Monaco where he has remained a Monegasque national.

The only religious organisation to derive direct financial benefit was the Vatican Bank. There were 'conversion charges' and there were the 'agreed percentages' which are 'withheld by the institution (the bank) for "charity works"'. Cardinal Rosario Castillo Lara, head of the Commission, considered that the Vatican had been 'used for an instrumental operation, the purpose of which we were unaware of'. He denied that the bank asked the devout three who had created the San Serafino account for thirteen per cent commission as was widely believed to be the case.

That commission would have amounted to some ten billion lire, approximately $7 million.

Refuting that allegation, the cardinal said, 'It would be absurd that in order to exchange stock (government bonds) a commission of thirteen per cent was paid. They could have made that exchange anywhere else, without that kind of cost.' Which is true if they had not needed to launder over one hundred million dollars offshore in an independent country, on the other side of the Tiber.

Public exposure of the mother of all bribes came in the midst of the 'clean hands' campaign by a group of very courageous investigating magistrates led by Antonio Di Pietro. The scams and the corruption ranged far and wide. Every walk of life, every form of Italian business had, it seemed, been contaminated by the culture of bribes. The ENIMONT scandal was but one of a large number but it rapidly became apparent that it was special both in its size and the range of people who had profited. Eventually 127 people were charged but the man who had been called 'Monsignor Montedison' on both sides of the Tiber, Donato De Bonis, continued to work in the Vatican Bank until 25 March 1992. By that date the Italian media had become as cynical about the protests of innocence from the Vatican officials as they had been during the Banco Ambrosiano scandal. The only one to walk free from the trial absolved of all charges was Alessandra. Her husband, Carlo, was sentenced to four and a half years. His good friend, Luigi Bisignani, was sentenced to five years' imprisonment.

In March 1992 De Bonis was quietly removed. He reappeared on Sunday, 24 April the following year in the Church of Santa Maria della Fiducia as a newly ordained bishop, to receive what several Vatican sources have described as 'his just reward for accepting the role of scapegoat in the ENIMONT scandal'. De Bonis's sermon drew from the bishops and cardinals present sustained applause for Giulio Andreotti who was in the congregation. De Bonis praised Andreotti for saving the Vatican Bank from total disaster 'in the dark days that had followed the Ambrosiano-Calvi scandal'. No one mentioned the role played by De Bonis in that scandal or in the mother of all bribes.

However, the aftermath of the mother of all bribes brought a refreshing change in the Vatican Bank. Its first lay President, Angelo Caloia, and his colleagues agreed to co-operate with the Italian investigating magistrates. But Caloia also decreed the line on the San Serafino affair which the cardinals dutifully followed: the Vatican Bank had been the innocent dupe in 'a technical operation'. Di Pietro and his fellow judges, relieved to get any co-operation from the Vatican, refrained from asking the new expert directors why the Bank had failed to carry out even the most basic checks on the San Serafino foundation.

The Vatican never returned any of the $7 million 'donation' it received from the foundation. Indeed only a tiny percentage of the $100 million it laundered was ever recovered. The rest remained with a wide variety of corrupt Italian citizens. Sergio Cusani, one of the three devout account holders, served four years in prison. The two men who had put together the corrupt ENIMONT deal both killed themselves. Cagliari suffocated himself with a plastic bag and three days later Gardini shot himself. The note that was found near his body had one word on it: 'Grazie'. The principal actors in the 'wedding of the year', Alessandra and Carlo Sama, surface from time to time in the society pages sinking the occasional yacht or hosting yet another lavish party.

Although the Vatican Bank was doing well from money laundering and black money, Cardinal Edmund Casimir Szoka of Detroit, the new President of the Prefecture for the Economic Affairs of the Holy See, found a more traditional and legal solution to the eternal problem of acquiring more money for the Roman Catholic Church. He invoked Canon Law 1271 from the code of laws governing the Roman Catholic Church first published in 1983, 'Bishops are to join together to produce those means which the Apostolic See may from time to time need to exercise properly its service to the universal Church.' To make sure that his audience of Cardinals got the message Szoka also quoted Canon Law 1260: 'The Church has the inherent right to acquire from the faithful whatever is necessary for its proper objectives.'

He also revealed that the anticipated deficit for 1991 was $90 million. It was to be the last year in that decade that the Vatican books would finish so deeply in the red. Szoka brought in computers and other essential technology and cut administration expenses wherever he could, but his greatest single contribution to Vatican finances were increased donations from dioceses. Between 1990 and 2000 this source of income more than tripled to $22 million per year. Added to that was Vatican access to the extraordinary annual income of the German Church from the state and (after 1993) that of the Italian Church.

The scale of overseas annual donations to the Holy See is not widely appreciated by local Roman Catholics. Peter's Pence, the annual collection that goes directly to the Pope, and plebeian items such as sales of Vatican stamps are no secret but the Holy See remains reluctant to reveal exactly how much it receives from its foreign cash cows.

An ingenious renegotiation by Cardinal Casaroli of the Lateran Treaty in the 1980s was particularly beneficial. Instead of the Italian Finance Ministry paying direct contributions to maintain the Italian dioceses, a system was introduced to allow Italian taxpayers to elect on their tax returns which religion/charity should receive eight lire for every 1,000 lire of tax that they were paying. During the next three years while the Italian Government carefully monitored returns, the annual payments were held at the

1989 figure of 406 billion lire (approximately $320 million or £246 million). Then the jackpot began to roll in from Italian taxpayers. *For the year 2000, the Roman Catholic Church in Italy received 1,500 billion lire, approximately $750 million or nearly £500 million.* In the same year, the money that went to the German Roman Catholic Church from the German taxpayers' similar system was 9.1 billion Deutschmarks or $4.5 billion dollars or £3 billion.

In January 1992 the Vatican began to sell off some of the gold it had hoarded since before the Second World War; gold acquired by the creator of Vatican Incorporated, Bernardino Nogara. Unfortunately, Cardinal Szoka demonstrated that, while his grasp of Canon Law was excellent, he had something to learn about gold markets. He sold when the market was low and held stock when the market was high.

It was such ineptitude which provoked the laymen running the Vatican Bank to organise a Vatican conference on business techniques and ethics in 1992. The Vatican wise man from Spain, José Sanchez Asiains gained great kudos by persuading the current star of Spanish banking Mario Conde, president of Banco Español de Credito (Banesto) to come and lecture. He received a standing ovation. The following year his reception in Madrid was somewhat less effusive when he was arrested after a deficit of over £3.5 billion (approximately $5.1 billion) was discovered at his Banesto Bank. As *El Pais* observed at the time, 'Mario Conde has beaten many records, two of them very difficult to better in the future. He was the youngest man to become President of a Spanish bank and he has been the youngest to leave it.' Conde was sentenced to ten years' imprisonment.

However, Conde's lecture was not the only link between the Vatican and the Banesto crash. The common thread between them, and the Ferruzzi and Montedison débâcles, also joins the Vatican to a much greater disaster – the fall of

BCCI. In an attempt to salvage the international reputation of the Vatican Bank, Philippe De Weck and his fellow expert directors appointed outside auditors. They claimed that this would be the first step towards complete banking transparency. De Weck was insistent that the company chosen should be non-Italian and have a faultless reputation. The company chosen was Revisuisse of Zurich, part of Price Waterhouse. For two years, in De Weck's words,

> 'they controlled everything, as we wanted to obtain the certification given to the main banks world-wide, based on international standards. The balance sheets in 1995 and 1996 were certified by Price Waterhouse, in accordance with the hallowed expression, "fair and true-international standards". That was a gigantic task. Now the IOR can see its profits progressing from year to year and from now on it is a certified bank.'

By any criteria the choice of Price Waterhouse as auditors was bizarre. During the 1980s Price Waterhouse was one of the then Big Eight accountancy firms in the world. One of their most lucrative contracts was with the Bank of Credit and Commerce International (BCCI). Price Waterhouse did the accounts for the Grand Cayman division of BCCI from its inception in 1975, and in 1986 they assumed responsibility for the audit of the entire BCCI international infrastructure. They continued to sign off the annual accounts based upon seriously inadequate records as being 'true and fair'. A United States Senate Committee on Foreign Relations investigation into the BCCI concluded: 'BCCI's accountants failed to protect BCCI's innocent depositors and creditors from the consequences of poor practices at the Bank of which the auditors were aware for years.'

The Senate Committee also established that

'BCCI's criminality included fraud by BCCI and BCCI customers involving billions of dollars; money laundering in Europe, Africa, Asia and the Americas; BCCI's bribery of officials in most of those locations; support of terrorism, arms trafficking, and the sale of nuclear technologies; management of prostitution; the commission and facilitation of income tax evasion, smuggling, and illegal immigration; illicit purchases of banks and real estate; and a panoply of financial crimes limited only by the imagination of its officers and customers.'

Price Waterhouse had deliberately failed to protect innocent depositors and creditors, but suppressing the knowledge they had of 'gross irregularities' allowed BCCI's criminality to continue. The crash, when it came in 1991, revealed the biggest bank fraud in world history. $13 billion had vanished. Creditors subsequently brought an action against both Price Waterhouse and Ernst and Young who had audited part of BCCI until 1987. The sum claimed was $11 billion. The accountancy firms eventually settled out of court.

At exactly the time that the auditors of Price Waterhouse were being ushered into the Vatican they were also being sued by Montedison for negligence and failure to provide adequate controls over the company's accounts during a ten-year period from 1983 to 1992. Two months after that action began Ferruzzi also launched a similar suit against Price Waterhouse. Their joint action outlined a catalogue of accounting malpractices that included an irrecoverable credit of $261 million to a company in the British Virgin Islands, recognition of revenues of $146 million on non-existent sales and huge undocumented payments to offshore companies, supposedly for consulting work. The combined claims for over $1 billion were eventually settled by Price Waterhouse in 1996 when they paid out $33.68 million.

The accountants acting for the Banesto Bank in Spain at the time of discovery of a £3.5 billion/$5.1 billion hole were Price Waterhouse. The Banesto affair like the other cases involving Price Waterhouse raised at the highest level the most serious questions about their performance as auditors, and about the ability of any auditors to detect major financial crime. Only four months before the discovery of not so much a hole as a chasm, Banesto had successfully completed the first two parts of the biggest share issue in Spanish banking history for 130,000 million pesetas. The issue had been made with the approval of the Central Bank of Spain and with a share document and recent annual accounts sanctioned by Price Waterhouse. In essence the auditors approved accounts which were not an accurate reflection of the net worth of the bank. Less than six months after these unqualified accounts had influenced millions of small investors to buy Banesto shares, the discovery of the multi-million-dollar hole demonstrated an over-valuation of the assets of astronomical proportions.

In early 1994 Price Waterhouse found itself yet again being sued for negligence, this time by the association that had been created to protect the small shareholders. A Spanish Parliamentary Commission unanimously concluded that Price Waterhouse's audit report on Banesto's 1992 accounts masked the bank's underlying position.

It remains a mystery why the cardinals and the wise laymen on the Vatican Bank Commission appointed auditors with this track record. Meanwhile, under the noses of Price Waterhouse, the Mafia continued to launder its profits from the illegal narcotics industry through the Vatican Bank and rich and powerful members of Italian society continued to use it for tax evasion and hiding illegal profits.

While Price Waterhouse got down to controlling the entire Vatican Bank operation, Cardinal Szoka and his colleagues pressed on with their attempts to increase both income and donations. While the dioceses were being asked for more and more donations each year, the Pope also looked closer to home. He created an Italian equivalent of the American Papal Foundation, an organisation of rich and successful Catholics who had been persuaded to contribute to the economic needs of the Holy See. In its first year, 1993, the Italian foundation brought in five billion lire ($3 million).

Yet some within the Church were uneasy. Many bishops agreed with the chairman of the German Bishops' Conference, Bishop Karl Lehmann, when he urged the need for complete transparency and for independent controls not just on the Vatican Bank but the entire Holy See spending programmes. He suspected that the lack of budgetary transparency hid black money, particularly among those congregations whose financial status remained a closely guarded secret.

Thanks largely to the generosity of the global Catholic population, the Vatican went into the black in 1993. After twenty-three years of deficits, the Vatican balance sheet in summer 1994 showed a modest working surplus of £1 million or $1.5 million. Cardinal Szoka described the document as 'the first consolidated balance sheet in the history of the financial institution of the Papal State, including all the Vatican organisations and companies'.

It fell a long way short of that, but in view of the fact that the Vatican had never published any accounts at all until 1985 it represented a step towards the much talked-about 'total transparency'. Missing from the figures were the total for 'Peter's Pence' or any revenues from the Vatican City State, including income from the Vatican Museum and stamp sales. The so-called 'consolidated balance sheet' contained not one single reference to the IOR – the Vatican Bank.

The Vatican stayed in the black for the rest of the decade, mainly because of the new annual income from the Italian state. After being frozen for three years at the 1989 figure of 406 billion lire, it all but quadrupled to 1,500 billion lire in 2000, close to half a billion pounds sterling or in excess of three quarters of a billion US dollars. The new income was not accompanied by any greater accountability to the Italian taxpayers who provided it. The Vatican continued to withhold the profits and assets of the IOR and even the Statutes which defined the criteria for permitted investment and account holders. They maintained that the religious nature of both the holders and their intended use of their money must be 'paramount'.

The President of the Board of Directors was obliged to oversee the documentation personally and vet every prospective new client. In turn his Supervisory Commission was overseen by a five-man Council of Cardinals and the auditors Price Waterhouse. In theory it was a watertight structure that ensured a total elimination of even one dubious account. However, it did not prevent the bogus San Serafino foundation, nor the money laundering activities of Luigi Bisignani. Neither did criminal activity cease with the arrival of the men and women from Price Waterhouse in 1993/94.

In 1994 Antonio Di Luca disappeared from his hotel room in San Diego. No trace of Di Luca has ever been found. In his hotel room he had left a number of documents relating to a real estate transaction worth $342 million. Among the documents were records that established the money had been deposited in the Vatican Bank. Among Di Luca's papers was a note with the names of five men: four were either Mafiosi or men linked to organised crime activities; the fifth name was Alfonso Gagliano.

The Sicilian-born Gagliano has been for decades a powerful figure in the ruling Canadian Liberal Party. As Minister of Works in the years 1997 to 2002 there were constant allegations from opposition MPs and the media that Gagliano had behaved corruptly in the granting of lucrative government contracts.

Prime Minister Jean Chrétien moved Gagliano from his ministerial post at precisely the time when he was due to face hostile questioning on the various allegations from opposition MPs. Gagliano was posted to Denmark as Canadian Ambassador. Outraged MPs protested. Apart from allegations of political graft and corruption there had also been accusations that Gagliano had strong Mafia links which Gagliano has always denied. In mid-2003 the Canadian Prime Minister was obliged to cancel his plans to send Gagliano to Italy as Canada's Ambassador to the Vatican as the Vatican had objected to the posting.

A Vatican Bank 'religious foundation' was used in 1995 for laundering $100 million. It featured in what became known as 'the cheque to cheque' investigation. In November 1995 Italian prosecutors asked Spain for permission to interrogate Cardinal Carles, an Opus Dei favourite and close friend of the Pope's who was frequently tipped as his successor. They wanted to investigate whether the account was in Carles's name or controlled by him and whether he had guaranteed the recycling of $100 million through the Bank. The money was destined for a Swiss businessman, as part of the proceeds from illicit trading of arms, precious stones and radioactive material. Arrest warrants were issued for thirty-six people and a further thirty-one were advised they were under investigation.

Cardinal Carles refused to respond to the Italian summons and to all subsequent requests to make himself available for questioning. Carles, politically to the far right, uttered what could be called the Sindona defence, that it was all a plot by the enemies of Liberty against the Church: 'These attacks have in the past been levelled at particular

Cardinals and have been subsequently found to be false. Now it's my turn.' Fellow Opus Dei member, the Vatican's spokesman Navarro-Valls, issued a statement declaring that '. . . no relations exist between the Cardinal, the IOR and the people mentioned in the Naples investigation.' The Spanish Justice Department also weighed in on behalf of the Cardinal, dismissing the allegations.

In June 1996 what had appeared to be a closed investigation erupted. In Italy twenty people were arrested and a further ten were sought on international warrants. The investigating magistrate yet again declared his belief that the Archbishop of Barcelona had assisted in the laundering of at least $100 million through the Vatican Bank. Karol Wojtyla, concerned that a close friend and Opus Dei favourite for the Papal succession was on the brink of disaster, summoned Cardinal Carles to Rome and had a private meeting of nearly one hour with him. Subsequently Wojtyla promoted Carles to the governing board of the Holy See's Prefecture for Economic Affairs headed by Cardinal Szoka. Under the terms of the Lateran Treaty between the Vatican and Italy, cardinals are immune from arrest. Eventually prosecutor Ormanni was forced to abandon this part of his investigation.

Martin Frankel was a serial fantasist who developed an early obsession with Wall Street. His first job was at the Toledo, Ohio, branch of the New York brokerage firm, Dominick and Dominick. He was fired in 1987 by head of the branch, John Schulte, for 'failing to produce', but not before he entered a long-term relationship with Sonia Schulte, his boss's wife. Frankel left Toledo, hired a bodyguard/security man, David Rosse, and began to invest increasingly in security equipment. Then in the late 1980s he ran a money management firm, boasting of exotic clients such as the former King of Yugoslavia and a former queen of Romania. Some of his real clients noticed significant shrinkage in their investments and brought a series of legal actions against the 'Frankel Fund'. The Securities and Exchange Commission froze the company's assets and imposed a lifetime ban on Frankel dealing in securities.

Undeterred, Frankel moved on to greener pastures and greener people. He took to saying that his name was Eric Stevens and went into business with Tennessee bank executive John Hackney. Frankel began to target struggling insurance companies, which were state-regulated and not policed by the SEC. Their funds were therefore vulnerable to embezzlement. Hackney acquired the insurance companies on behalf of 'Stevens' and was paid a salary for managing them. They created a company called Thunor Trust and their first acquisition was the Tennessee company, Franklin American Corp. Frankel's name does not appear on the acquisition documents but among those that do is Sonia Schulte. Within one month of acquisition of Franklin, he had wired the entire assets of the associated insurance company, the Franklin American Life Insurance Company, some $17.5 million, via a series of money transfers to his account at Banque SCS Alliance in Switzerland.

Between 1993 and 1999 Frankel through Thunor, his front company, acquired eight further insurance companies, including some based in Mississippi, Oklahoma, Arkansas and Missouri, and stole all their assets. With false statements and false declarations Frankel, Hackney and an increasing number of friends and associates duped the state regulatory bodies and stole over $200 million. Some of the funds went to acquire yet more insurance companies; some went to set up Frankel's increasingly bizarre life-style; more went as kickbacks to those who were in on the scam. On paper all of the insurance companies were thriving.

Soon after he got his hands on that first $17.5 million, Frankel bought a large mansion in Greenwich, Connecticut.

He converted much of it into a replica of a Wall Street trading floor complete with 80 computers, countless satellite dishes and direct links to the New York Stock Exchange. He bought several other houses in the area, to house a collection of pornography, sadomasochistic accessories and bought-in mistresses. He continued to demonstrate acute paranoia about his personal safety, using armed guards, six-feet-high metal fences, security cameras and floodlights. His neighbours were periodically disturbed by continuous screaming and on one occasion the body of twenty-two-year-old Frances Burge was found lying on the ground outside a house bought by Frankel under a new alias of Michael King. The police concluded that Frances had committed suicide and ignored the testimony from neighbours about the repeated screaming they had heard before the discovery of the body.

In spring 1998 Frankel decided to operate on a far greater scale. He would need to create a new and far more credible front to conceal his intended acquisition of up to $150 billion in additional insurance holdings. At much the same time he met Thomas Corbally, who was then employed by the internationally known private detective agency, Kroll Associates. Corbally had an impressive and extensive range of contacts – business, personal, religious, political – not merely in the United States but globally.

Shortly afterwards, Frankel (now using the name of his head of security, David Rosse) decided that the perfect front would be the Vatican. While the ever-obliging Corbally provided high-level contacts, Frankel procured through an Italian businessman an introduction to Father Christopher Zielinski, a well-connected priest who was the director of The Genesis Centre in Florence. The Jewish-born Frankel was simultaneously doing a crash course on the Roman Catholic faith. His library in the Greenwich home soon had Catholic literature by the yard, histories of the saints, and

Papal encyclicals. Alongside his porn videos there was now a copy of *Brother Sun and Sister Moon*, Franco Zeffirelli's film on the life of St Francis.

The Italian businessman told Father Zielinski that 'a wealthy investor wanted to donate $50 million to the Centre'. Subsequently the Centre's lawyer met the ever-helpful Thomas Corbally who outlined the proposition. Frankel would not actually 'donate' the $50 million to the Centre, but would maintain control of the money using it to purchase United States insurance companies. When these insurance companies went into profit the Genesis Centre would receive donations from these profits. The Centre's suspicions that it was being asked to participate in a money laundering operation were not assuaged when the Italian businessman, aptly named Fausto Fausti, turned up for a meeting with Father Christopher Zielinski accompanied by one of Frankel's former girlfriends and co-conspirators, Kaethe Schuchter, who was wearing just a brief pair of hot pants and a bikini top. Father Christopher and the Centre's attorney, by now convinced they had been targeted as a laundry by the elusive David Rosse, turned down the offer.

Frankel merely raised his sights. Through Corbally he met Thomas A. Bolan, a New York lawyer with excellent links within the Roman Catholic Church. Before the introduction, Corbally had explained to Bolan that he was friendly with a man who was making millions a day through his trading on Wall Street, who wanted to help the poor and thought he should do it through the Roman Catholic Church. Through Bolan, Frankel was introduced to Father Peter Jacobs, a Roman Catholic priest with ties to the Vatican, who in turn contacted his friend Monsignor Emilio Colagiovanni.

With Colagiovanni, Frankel had struck gold. The elderly Monsignor was President of the Monitor Ecclesiasticus

Foundation, which publishes a journal on Canon Law, and had served as a judge on the august Church Tribunal, the Roman Rota. The Foundation that he controlled had bank accounts both at the IOR and the Vatican's other bank, the APSA. The Monsignor also had personal bank accounts at both. He was a highly respected man who could open virtually any door within the Vatican.

At Frankel's invitation the Monsignor, accompanied by Father Jacobs, flew from Rome to the United States and together with lawyer Bolan met with 'David Rosse' at his home in Greenwich, Connecticut. Rosse impressed all of his guests with his knowledge of St Francis of Assisi and talked of his desire to emulate the saint and help the poor and what better way than through the Church that had inspired St Francis? Looking Monsignor Colagiovanni directly in the eyes he exclaimed, 'If I cannot trust the Catholic Church, who can I trust?' The Monsignor shook his head vigorously in agreement. Confident that he had landed his fish Frankel elaborated:

'I plan to set up a charitable foundation. It will be formed in the Vatican, under Vatican law. I will not be named or identified on any documents and I do not wish any outsider to know that I, David Rosse, am the true source of the funds. I seek no public acknowledgment or honour for this. Like St Francis I want no credit for any good I am able to achieve. This work is for the greater glory of God.'

Frankel proposed to control the foundation secretly through 'my ability to elect a majority on the Board of Trustees who share my vision'. He added,

'I am prepared to transfer $55 million to this Vatican foundation. The Vatican will be permitted to keep $5 million of that amount to do with as they see fit. I will retain control of the balance, which will be used to assist in the acquisitions in the insurance industry.'

Frankel told the Monsignor that subsequent profits from the acquisitions would also be donated to the foundation. His guests were entirely taken with the proposal and over a meal prepared by Frankel's two chefs they eagerly discussed how to spend the promised $5 million.

Subsequently Frankel confirmed in a letter to the lawyer Bolan a key element of the concept.

> 'Our agreement will include the Vatican's promise that the Vatican will aid me in my effort to acquire insurance companies by allowing Father Jacobs or another Vatican official to certify to the authorities, if necessary, that the source of the funds for the foundation is the Vatican.'

While the shy Frankel divided his time between his dealing floor and his extracurricular activities within his mansion, Thomas Bolan and Monsignor Colagiovanni flew to the Vatican to propose the plan to Bishop Francesco Salerno. Bishop Salerno was then the highly placed Secretary of the Prefecture for the Economic Affairs of the Holy See. He was also, by one of those happy coincidences with which this tale abounds, on the board of Monsignor Colagiovanni's Foundation, Monitor Ecclesiasticus. The Frankel proposal was discussed in great detail, specifically the aspect where 'Rosse' would retain control over the $50 million even after it was 'donated' to the Vatican foundation.

On 18 August 1998, Salerno approved the plan declaring it to be 'a good idea'. He instructed Bolan to draw up the protocols of the foundation. He did so, including a clause

allowing Frankel to appoint two of the proposed foundation's three trustees with the third to be appointed by the
Vatican. Salerno subsequently contacted the Cardinal of
New York, John O'Conner, seeking a recommendation for
the third position on the board of trustees.

Father Jacobs then, however, received a telephone call
from Bishop Salerno, saying that the Secretariat of State had
expressed some misgivings about the plan. The Secretary of
State, Cardinal Angelo Sodano (who had replaced the
tough-minded Cardinal Casaroli in 1990) had commented
that Frankel/Rosse 'could not control a Vatican foundation
as we should not create the perception that we are running
insurance companies'. Frankel's increasingly well-paid lawyer Bolan and Father Jacobs were again despatched to the
Vatican where they held a meeting in the Secretariat of
State's offices with two of the Secretariat staff, Monsignor
Gianfranco Piovano and Father Brian Farrell. As they
explored the problem, the accommodating Monsignor Piovano declared that 'some other way will have to be found to
make the donation'.

The ever-inventive Frankel had the answer. He would
form a new foundation that would be created outside the
Vatican, the St Francis of Assisi Foundation to Serve and
Help the Poor and Alleviate Suffering, not exactly the most
memorable of names. A Vatican-related charity would be
the settlor for the foundation and this charity would be able
to state that it was funded by the Vatican, so that Frankel
would be able to claim that its funding originated from
Vatican sources. In reality St Francis would be entirely
funded by looted funds held in Frankel's Swiss bank account. Monsignor Colagiovanni then agreed to allow his
own foundation, Monitor Ecclesiasticus, to be identified as
the 'settlor' for St Francis.

If this scheme could be sold to the Vatican executives
Frankel was up and running. No one would be wary of

doing business with a foundation which had the Vatican as the lender of last resort. What better guarantor could a company wish for? Monsignor Colagiovanni spoke to Bishop Salerno of the Prefecture of Economic Affairs and Monsignor Piovano at the Secretariat of State. Both gave the scheme their blessing and Colagiovanni then faxed a letter to Bolan on Rota letter-headed paper informing him that his foundation, the Monitor Ecclesiasticus Foundation (MEF) 'had been authorised' to receive Frankel's $55 million. Others within the Vatican were made fully aware of what was being done. These included Monsignor Giovanni Battista Re, head of the First Section of the Vatican Secretariat of State and at the time the third highest-ranking Vatican official.

Father Jacobs discussed Frankel's plan with Cardinal Pio Laghi, former Vatican Nuncio (ambassador) to the United States. At the time of this discussion Laghi was the head of the Congregation for Catholic Education. When Frankel was still trying to win approval for his scheme Laghi intervened on Frankel's behalf within the Vatican. In return he received in August 1998 a 'donation' of $100,000 for a hospital. When Cardinal Laghi responded with a gracious thank you letter it was returned to him via Father Jacobs with the request that he should refrain from thanking 'Rosse' personally for the payment. A new letter was sent thanking Frankel's foundation for the funds.

Others who were fully conversant and approving of the scheme included Father Giovanni D'Ercole, a leading official in the first section of the Secretariat of State and Archbishop Alberto Tricarico from the Second Section of the Secretariat, who oversaw the Holy See's relations with the former countries of the Soviet Union. So taken was he by the scheme he considered flying to Connecticut to meet 'Rosse' in person. The Archbishop was anxious to persuade him to 'donate' funds to Kazakhstan. The Vatican Bank was also touched by the Frankel charm and impressed by his apparent endless wealth. Frankel frequently wired some of his stolen funds to Colagiovanni and Jacobs for their IOR accounts. He requested from Monsignor Colagiovanni a letter from the IOR declaring that the Monitor Ecclesiasticus Foundation (MEF) was in good standing. Before they issued such a letter the Vatican Bank requested full information on the 'Rosse' plan.

Surely with all of those top international bankers and Price Waterhouse at the helm, to say nothing of the Commission of Cardinals keeping a close watch on the Bank the game would now be up for Frankel and his co-conspirators? Once the experts took even the most cursory of glances at the details surely it would be obvious that what was being created was a money laundry. In fact once the IOR had satisfied itself that Frankel did indeed have funds to the value of $55 million in his Swiss account they were entirely content. The Vatican Directors, Dr Lelio Scaletti and Dr Anthony Chiminello, were happy to sign a letter that confirmed the long 'uninterrupted relationship' between the Vatican Bank and Monsignor Colagiovanni's Monitor Ecclesiasticus Foundation. The letter along with the letter of thanks from Cardinal Pio Laghi and other documents all served to bolster the credibility of St Francis with insurance regulators and lawyers.

The documents registering St Francis as a British Virgin Islands trust were backdated to 10 August 1998 to accommodate Frankel's belief that it was an astrologically favourable date for him. In the Deed of Settlement, the MEF was identified as the settlor and suggested that it had contributed $90 million to St Francis.

Emboldened by the ease with which he and his co-conspirators had conned so many within the Vatican, Frankel's associates began to make more and more outlandish claims. While negotiating to buy the Western United Life Assurance

Company of Spokane, Washington, the men from St Francis revealed that 'Rosse' did bond trading for the Vatican and that the source of the funds for the Western Union deal was the Vatican. They claimed that the purchase was part of a strategy to bring about substantial growth of Vatican assets and the Pope himself had authorised the funds to go through the MEF, which had then contributed them to St Francis.

The Vatican were aware of these dramatic claims. They were informed on several occasions that individuals representing St Francis were demonstrably misrepresenting their relationship with the Vatican and the source of their funds. In January 1999 C. Paul Sandifur, the President of Western United's parent company, wrote directly to the Secretary of State, Cardinal Sodano, asking for confirmation of three statements. Was St Francis an agent of the Holy See? Was the MEF a Vatican foundation? Had the Holy See given $190 million to the MEF and St Francis as had been represented? Monsignor Giovanni Re replied on behalf of the Vatican. He stated that with respect to St Francis 'no such foundation has the approval of the Holy See or exists in the Vatican'. The Cardinal did not deny that the Vatican had donated $190 million to the MEF or that the MEF had donated $190 million to St Francis. Nor did he deny that the MEF was a Vatican foundation. The careful cryptic response was in sharp contrast to the Vatican's reaction when the scam became an international scandal.

Neither Re, the number three in the Vatican, nor anyone else took any steps to correct a situation where they knew that false statements and misrepresentations about the Vatican's relationship with Frankel and his accomplices were being made to insurance companies in the United States. Indeed by giving only a fragmented response to very specific questions Cardinal Re had boosted confidence in the statements that he had failed to address. Monsignor

Colagiovanni helpfully explained to the insurance companies that it was Vatican policy that failure to address certain facts in a response of this nature indicated that those facts were indeed true. Ever eager to serve Frankel, the Monsignor then faxed Western United to advise them that as President of the MEF he had contributed $1 billion to St Francis. These funds had come from 'various Roman Catholic tribunals and Roman Catholic charitable and cultural institutions'.

To allay any remaining unease within the minds of the men from Western United, Frankel and Monsignor Colagiovanni arranged for two executives from the parent company to travel to Rome, meet Vatican representatives and clarify whether or not the various representations that had been made were in fact true. It was a bold move but their insurance company had huge assets and Frankel wished to buy control.

On their trip, the Western United executives Sandifur and his Chief Financial Officer William Snider shrewdly brought with them Father Eugene Tracey, a former insurance executive now serving as a Catholic priest in Spokane. The three met Colagiovanni, who confirmed that the funds from the MEF had been provided to St Francis *and* that they included secret Vatican funds that officially did not exist.

Colagiovanni gave Frankel excellent value. On an appropriate cue, the trio met Bishop Salerno, who posed for a photograph with the visitors. Colagiovanni then took them on a tour of the Vatican which included a number of areas that the general public never see. The Spokane executives were reassured. The MEF and St Francis were indeed known within the Vatican. Colagiovanni was who he claimed to be and the MEF and St Francis were indeed recipients of Vatican money. Colagiovanni also arranged a meeting with Alan Kershaw, an American lawyer who frequently argued cases before Vatican tribunals and from time to time represented the Vatican interest in legal proceedings. Kershaw assured the insurance executives that a group of 'northern Italian laypeople' who wanted to obtain the tax benefits available by a donation to the Vatican had secretly given large sums of money to the MEF, and confirmed that the MEF received funds from the Vatican. Kershaw also told the executives that in fact the Vatican exercised supervisory power over St Francis and that St Francis funds and money management would go through the IOR.

Yet the initial letter that Monsignor Re had written had rankled with Frankel, attorney Bolan and the irrepressible Monsignor Colagiovanni. His minimal response to the Western United questions had put the conspirators to considerable trouble and they wished to avoid a repetition. In March 1999 the Monsignor arranged for Bolan to meet with Re. In the event he met Cardinal Agostino Cacciavillan, the President of the Administration of the Patrimony of the Holy See, APSA, the supreme government official in charge of the Holy See's investments. The Sandifur letter and Cardinal Re's response were discussed at length.

Cacciavillan was informed that a private individual (Rosse) and not the MEF or the Vatican was the source of St Francis funds. He was aware that the MEF would be used as a vehicle through which this private individual would make 'donations' to St Francis. Armed with this knowledge it is astonishing that the cardinal did not on the spot demand that Bolan, Colagiovanni and their colleagues stop claiming that the funds originated with either the MEF or the Vatican. He confined himself to one request, that St Francis should not be described as being a Vatican foundation. He expressed not the slightest concern about the other false accounts of the relationship between St Francis and the MEF and the Vatican. It was agreed by all three that if the Vatican received any future enquiries about the St

Francis purchase of United States insurance companies they would be referred to Colagiovanni or to someone else who understood the MEF/St Francis plan.

Notwithstanding the great success achieved within the Vatican by Bolan and Colagiovanni, the end was near for the latterday St Francis. Frankel had been stupid. He and his colleagues had gone to extraordinary lengths to sell the concept that either the St Francis Foundation was Vatican-owned or had Vatican money flowing into it and that it was underwritten by the Monitor Ecclesiasticus Foundation based in Rome.

However, foreign ownership of insurance companies is specifically forbidden in a number of American states, including Colorado and Washington.

Therefore the attempted purchase of Capital Life Insurance in Denver and Western United in Spokane by Frankel's Thunor Trust was impossible once Frankel had arranged for St Francis to acquire Thunor Trust. By early May 1999 Martin Frankel was on the run and a $200 million hole had been discovered in the insurance companies that he had bought and plundered.

In the light of all of the above, the following statement by Vatican spokesman Joaquin Navarro-Valls is as slippery as the 1982 Vatican denial of any involvement in the Banco Ambrosiano crash and its 1974 self-exonerations after *Il Crack* Sindona.

'I wish to make it clear that the "Monitor Ecclesias-ticus" and "St Francis of Assisi" Foundations do not have Vatican juridical character and are not in-scribed in the registers of Vatican juridical person-alities. I wish to add that the Holy See does not have any relationship with Father Peter Jacobs and had neither furnished nor received funds from either the Monitor Ecclesiasticus Foundation or the St Francis of Assisi Foundation. Contrary to what has been affirmed, the St Francis of Assisi Foundation does not have an account in the Institute for Works of Religion (IOR) and indeed is not recognised by this Institution. Monsignor Emilio Colagiovanni is president of the Monitor Ecclesiasticus Foundation, established by the archdiocese of Naples in 1967. This foundation has always acted totally outside of any Vatican context, and does not have any relationship with it whatsoever.'

Like many Vatican statements, that of Navarro-Valls begged more questions than it answered. Why did it take until 30 June 1999 for the Vatican to issue such a denial, when the Frankel scam and the plundering of insurance companies' funds had been international front-page news for two months? During the previous twelve months the Vatican had been presented with mounting evidence of the scam, but it did nothing to warn anyone that Frankel's scheme was bogus and illegal. Instead, the Vatican had effectively encouraged insurance companies to trust Frankel and his associates. By the time that Navarro-Valls made his statement Frankel and his millions were long gone.

By April 1999 Frankel had obviously realised the game was up. During that month the bulk of the missing funds had been moved to the Swiss bank account. On 15 May firemen were called to the $3 million Frankel mansion. They found blazing documents falling out of some of the fireplaces and a filing cabinet on fire in the kitchen. With the fires doused, one of the surviving items caught their attention. It was a 'To-do' list. Number one on the list read 'Launder money'. They also found evidence of Frankel's obsession with astrology: he had asked his stars for answers to pressing questions that included 'Will I go to prison?' and 'Should I leave?' Meanwhile account number

70026 at Banque SCS Alliance in Switzerland was extremely active.

Frankel was eventually arrested after a four-month man-
hunt. He spent the last eight weeks of freedom at one of
Germany's best hotels, the Prem Hotel in Hamburg. Along
with Frankel in his room was yet another long-time girl-
friend, Cynthia Allison, and $2 million in diamonds and
cash. Subsequently Frankel was charged by the Hamburg
authorities with smuggling diamonds and possessing false
passports. He was sentenced to three years' imprisonment.
He was extradited to the United States after serving eighteen
months. In his absence he had been indicted by a Connecticut Grand Jury on thirty-six counts of wire fraud and
money laundering. He was also wanted on a great many
other charges in different states.

On 5 May 2002, Frankel pleaded guilty in a Connecticut
court on twenty-four charges involving racketeering, wire
and securities fraud, and conspiracy. Sentencing was suspended until Tennessee and Mississippi court hearings
could take place and then further delayed while Frankel
assisted the various prosecutors in their attempts to recoup
the stolen millions. Eventually in late 2004, Martin Frankel
was sentenced to sixteen years' imprisonment.

On 9 September 2002, Monsignor Emilio Colagiovanni
pleaded guilty to criminal fraud and conspiracy. The Monsignor was another who eagerly offered his full cooperation
to the insurance commissioners.

After Martin Frankel had pleaded guilty, Joaquin Navarro-Valls popped up again to assure all and sundry that
the Vatican had no involvement in Frankel's schemes. As
for Monsignor Emilio Colagiovanni and the foundation he
controlled, Navarro-Valls declared, 'Colagiovanni was already retired at the time of his dealings with Frankel, and
the Monitor Ecclesiasticus Foundation, incorporated in
Naples, is in no way a Vatican foundation.' Colagiovanni

'acted purely as a private Italian citizen and the Vatican received no funds from Frankel's enterprises'.

The insurance commissioners of Mississippi, Tennessee, Missouri, Oklahoma and Arkansas filed a Federal lawsuit against the Vatican. They claimed more than $200 million. As Mississippi commissioner Lee Harrell explained,

> 'The fact that the Vatican never benefited from the $200 million is not relevant. Under the Racketeer Influenced and Corrupt Organisations (RICO) Statute, a party involved in the conspiracy is responsible for the entire amount stolen.'

Despite his role Monsignor Re was promoted by Karol Wojtyla. He was elevated to cardinal on 21 February 2001. The implications of the RICO statute had demonstrably not been conveyed to Pope John Paul II when he discussed the affair with Cardinal Re. His advice to the cardinal when he complained of some of the media coverage of the affair was precisely the same that he had offered after the Banco Ambrosiano crash to Bishop Paul Marcinkus. 'Ignore them. We haven't lost any money, have we?'

'No, Holy Father.'

'Then ignore them. It will pass.'

By 2002 the amount that the US insurance commissioners were seeking from the Vatican Bank had risen to $600 million.

One group that still considers itself to be good God-fearing Catholics is the Mafia. They regard themselves as 'Cristiani che corrono' – Christians on the run. The Mafia have maintained close links with the Catholic faith and its hierarchy from the mid-nineteenth century. The Church's historic silence on the activities of Cosa Nostra has resonated down the years more powerfully than her occasional criticism of an organisation that regards murder as a legitimate business strategy.

In 1993 while in Sicily the Pope broke his own long silence on the Mafia with a powerful denunciation when he referred to the assassinations of Judges Giovanni Falcone and Pablo Borsellino and defined the Mafia as the 'devil' and those who had been murdered as 'martyrs'. The Mafia with its 'culture of death' was 'profoundly inhuman, anti-evangelical' and, calling for it to repent, he reminded it that 'One day the judgement of God will come!'

The Mafia got their judgement in first. They had been at a state of war with the Italian government and the judiciary for some time. In July 1993 a car bomb at Via Ruggero in Rome had as its target the journalist Maurizio Costanzo. His crime had been to write critically of the Mafia. Twenty-one other people who happened to be in the area were also injured. On 27 July 1993 a massive explosion in the centre of Florence destroyed a large section of the Georgofili Academy killing the caretaker, his wife and their two young daughters. Thirty-six people were injured and a huge collection of irreplaceable works of art were either destroyed or seriously damaged.

On the same day as the Florence atrocity two further Fiat car bombs were exploded in Rome. This time their target was the Catholic Church in response to the Pope's May condemnation. The first bomb exploded in the Piazza San Giovanni in Laterano and the other attacked the church of San Giorgio al Velabro. Because of the timing of these two attacks, the former occurring at two minutes to midnight, the latter four minutes later, there were no casualties.

There were a number of other bomb attacks on the Italian mainland at this time but the two on the Rome churches were seen by Italian investigators not as part of the Mafia's war on the Italian state but as its direct response to the Pope and to the growing number of anti-Mafia priests who, with great courage, were attempting to loosen the grip of the Cosa Nostra on Italian and Sicilian society. The Mafia leaders considered that their mother church had betrayed them. In September 1993 the most outspoken of the anti-Mafia priests, Father Puglisi, was murdered by four men on the orders of Giuseppe Graviano who controlled the Brancaccio district to the east of Palermo.

From then on Pope John Paul II remained silent on the Mafia and the Catholic Church's long relationship with it continued to flourish.

In October 2000 police in Palermo, Sicily, arrested twenty-one members of a criminal group, including some with direct links to the Mafia. The gang had succeeded in cloning a replica of the computer system used at a branch of Banco de Sicilia. Preparations to divert $500 million were well advanced and included telephonic negotiations with members of staff at the Vatican Bank where the money would have been transferred onward to banks in Portugal and Belgium.

Doubtless the Mafia in Sicily knew that the Vatican Bank regularly features in official global top ten money laundries. A 2001 report placed the Vatican at number eight, and estimated the *annual* amount laundered through the Vatican Bank at $50 billion. This almost certainly explains the absence of the Holy See among the list of members of the Financial Action Task Force on Money Laundering and its absence among the list of international bodies and organisations that have observer status with the Task Force.

The Vatican hierarchy ignored these facts and continued to lecture the financial world. Cardinal Tettamanzi in November 2003 proclaimed,

'Man is not made for the financial world; the financial world is made for man . . . Profit is not the only

criterion for the proper functioning of a business . . .
One should consider the effects of the pursuit of profit
upon the individual.'

In January 2004 the President of the Italian Bishops'
Conference, Cardinal Camillo Ruini, told his fellow
bishops that they should draw the correct lessons from
Italy's latest financial scandal, the collapse of Parmalat. 'It
could help Italian business leader to rediscover the value of
ethics . . .'
Vatican Incorporated meanwhile was more concerned at
rediscovering greater profitability. The annual budget for
the financial year 2003 showed a 'deficit' of nearly $12
million, the third consecutive budget deficit for the Holy
See. The latest figures for 2004 showed the budget had crept
back into the black by $3.71 million. Fifteen million euros
had been unnecessarily lost by the failure to hedge against
the Holy See's dollar exposure. The positive trend was
maintained in 2005 with another small surplus but the
'accounts' continue to be inadequate, the financial operations of the IOR are not disclosed, and investments
continue to be recorded at cost rather than at market value,
a practice that is widely considered by auditors to be
unacceptable. There are lessons to be learned about the
'value of ethics' on both sides of the Tiber. As of mid-2006
the action against the Vatican to recover the $600 million
lost in the Frankel Affair was unresolved.

By the same period the trial of Flavio Cerbini and three
other defendants for the murder of Roberto Calvi was
heading towards its second anniversary. One key witness,
Archbishop Marcinkus, eluded all attempts to compel his
appearance. His death in February 2006 left unresolved the
allegation to the author from a Mafia source: namely, that
Marcinkus was present when the decision to murder Calvi
was taken.

'A *culture of respect for the rule of law is urgently required*.

Nor can we pass over in silence the evil of corruption which is undermining the social and political development of so many peoples. It is a growing phenomenon insidiously infiltrating many sections of society, mocking the law and ignoring the rules of justice and truth. Corruption is hard to combat, because it takes many different forms: when it has been suppressed in one area, it springs up in another. Courage is needed just to denounce it. To eliminate it, together with the resolute determination of the Authorities, the generous support of all citizens is needed, sustained by a firm moral conscience.'

From the speech 'From the Justice
of Each Comes Peace for All'
by Pope John Paul II, 1 January 1988

Chapter 13

The Village

MANY VILLAGES ARE much bigger. Many villages have far more people. This village is 108.7 acres and has fewer than 600 inhabitants, but it is the most powerful village on earth. Officially known as the Vatican City State, for all its grandeur and its importance as the nerve centre of Roman Catholic faith, it is still a village, inward-looking, self-absorbed, with all the concentrated virtues and vices of small community life. But with a village headman regarded worldwide as God's representative on earth, those virtues and vices have an added edge. In theory, the people working at the heart of Catholic Christendom should derive the greatest benefit from its teachings; in practice that does not always happen. Apart from the residents there is a further mixture of priests, religious and lay employees, mainly Italians who 'commute' from Rome and the suburbs each day to their workplaces within the Vatican. Like any other state, it has its own laws and its own civic infrastructure complete with police force, postal service, refuse collection, pharmacy, stores and petrol station and, instead of an army, 100 members of the Swiss Guard.

Vatican residents and employees alike can avail themselves of many duty-free products. As of 1 July 2002 they could continue to buy their cigarettes at the previous low price but no longer smoke them anywhere in public while on Vatican territory, the first country in the world to introduce such a ban. Unlike the largely ceremonial Swiss Guard, the Vatican police force is kept extremely busy. More crimes are committed per inhabitant than in any other country in the world. The vast majority (98 per cent) are robberies perpetrated on tourists visiting the Sistine Chapel, the museums or the Vatican's sole supermarket. Pickpockets and bag snatchers are rife.

The Vatican comprises two separate administrations, the Vatican City State and the Holy See. The City State is the last remnant of former glories, its 108.7 acres all that is left of the once powerful Papal States. Its government provides the municipal services mentioned above for the world's smallest sovereign state. The Holy See rules the worldwide Church, organises the papal trips, controls the nearly 120 diplomatic missions, the radio station, the newspaper, and ensures that papal policy is implemented through forty commissions, nine congregations and a range of secretariats, councils and services. Most of the City State's 1,300 employees are lay workers but the majority of the Holy See's staff of 2,300 are clergy. The term Roman Curia refers to the 2,300 who assist the Pope in the governance of the Universal Church, and like civil servants everywhere they are frequently bloody-minded and immovable, particularly when 'Papal Reform of the Curia' is mentioned.

However, both clergy and lay workers have welcomed one aspect of curial reform: their pay. As recorded earlier, in 1979 and again in 1980 the lay workers had written directly to the Pope. Having then suffered ten years without any wage increases, they were seeking not only substantial awards but also the right to form their own version of a trade union. A threatened protest march by the workers' association was only averted at the last moment when the Pope agreed to meet a delegation. He reminisced about his wartime work at Solvay, said that the members could form an association, delegated instructions and returned to making speeches supporting Solidarity. By May 1982 the association had grown weary of waiting for the papal promises to be honoured and held a silent protest march, the first in the history of Vatican City.

The association also threatened to call a strike on 14 June, the day prior to the Pope's departure to Geneva where he was due to address the International Labour Organisation. The Pope, who regularly donned a hard hat and proclaimed his solidarity with workers all over the world, almost faced the embarrassment of being picketed by his own chauffeur and being unable to get to Rome airport. The issues were eventually resolved and a range of improvements implemented.

If the pay has been historically poor until recent years, the Vatican workers have one of the finest work locations in the world. In their lunch break staff can stroll in the Sistine Chapel and through the museums to stand and stare at one of the world's finest art collections, admire the Caravaggios, the Raphael tapestries, and the paintings of Leonardo da Vinci. The offices might be too cold or too hot, the lifts few, the air-conditioning largely non-existent, but there are compensations.

History is omnipresent and visible throughout the Vatican. Less obvious is the way in which that history inexorably influences those who work within the Vatican, particularly the Curia Romana, the Church's civil service. Every Pope since the early twentieth century has entered office determined to make great changes within the Curia, and each has failed in that ambition. Around the world many bishops see the Vatican as a dumping ground, somewhere to send the diocesan failures and misfits; others with an excess of ambition know that it is the best place to be talent-spotted. Quite a number from the Third World aspire to a position in the Curia simply because it offers a higher standard of living than their home country. Finally, there are those who come because they wish to serve the Faith in any way they can. This latter category is not necessarily in the majority. This curious mix of humanity frequently makes for very unchristian behaviour. The intrigues, the plotting, the struggles for greater privileges or power often have a Borgian quality.

By mid-October 2003 even the public loyalty towards those around the Holy Father was showing signs of considerable strain. Since earlier that year, the Pope could function only as a token Head of State. A cabal was formed that included the Pope's secretary, newly promoted to Archbishop, Stanislaw Dziwisz, Vatican press officer Joaquin Navarro-Valls and the Head of the College of Cardinals and *Camerlingo* Cardinal Eduardo Martinez Somalo. As *Camerlingo* or acting Pope, Somalo would have absolute control of the arrangements for the funeral of Pope John Paul II and the election of his successor. Apart from their close friendship over many years, all three men also share an allegiance to Opus Dei, as do the other members of an unelected group who by the latter months of 2003 were in effect running the Roman Catholic Church. These included Secretary of State Cardinal Sodano, Cardinal Ratzinger, the all-powerful Prefect of the Congregation for the Doctrine of the Faith, and Archbishop Leonardo Sandri, Deputy Secretary of State. A gerontocracy was in power.

On Monday, 13 October 2003 the cabal were in some disorder. The Vatican denied that the Pope's condition had deteriorated and also denied published reports that the Holy Father needed dialysis to purge his body of the highly toxic drugs being used to relieve Parkinson's disease. Within hours these assurances from Navarro-Valls were shown to be yet another of the Press Officer's fantasies. The Pope had the greatest difficulty in speaking during a meeting with the Uruguayan President Jorge Batlle Ibanez and later during a meeting with the entire Uruguay delegation, including a number of reporters. The Pope 'struggled in great pain as he attempted and failed to talk, remaining silent throughout'. Three days later came another ordeal for Karol Wojtyla – the October anniversary Mass to celebrate a papacy that had lasted a full 25 years. It was only the third time that the Church has celebrated a Pope's silver jubilee.

A further three days and, with an increasingly ailing Pope unable to read even a line of his homily, the beatification of Mother Teresa of Calcutta took place. Another two days and yet again his homily was read for him, this time by one of the trusted members of the cabal, Archbishop Leonardo Sandri, during a consistory that added a further thirty-one new members to the College of Cardinals. Some of the older members of the College, visibly shocked by the deterioration in the Pope's health, blurted out their concerns as they wondered aloud if, in the words of Cardinal Napier of Durban, South Africa, '. . . we might soon face the awesome responsibility of choosing a Pope.' Others argued the pros and cons of papal resignation. The Curia were particularly exercised by this aspect. Cardinals José Martins and Mario Pompedda declared that 'even if the Pope loses his ability to speak, he could still signal his wishes in writing, and thus could continue as head of the Church'. Interviewed by the Argentine daily *La Nacion*, the Vatican Librarian, Cardinal Jorge Mejia, disagreed. 'If the Pope can't speak then he can't say Mass, which raises the questions about his capacity to provide spiritual leadership.'

When he heard this, the leader of the cabal, Archbishop Dziwisz, declaimed, 'John Paul II will be Pope as long as God shall wish.' The cabal was determined to prolong the illusion of a fully functioning Head of State for as long as possible. An American member of the Curia provided me with some of the background:

'I think it was only in 1996 that they were forced to finally admit, off the record of course, that the Holy Father was suffering from Parkinson's disease. By that time everyone in the world knew what his illness was but here the press office in particular had been flatly denying the truth for years. "The other Pope" and his friends have been running the show for much of this year but in many ways they have been in charge much longer.'

'The other Pope' was the name given by many to the Pope's senior secretary and close companion since the mid-1960s, Stanislaw Dziwisz, who was ordained by the then Bishop Wojtyla in 1963 and became his second secretary in 1966. The relationship was for many years that of a father and son. In the latter years, particularly since Parkinson's disease began to tighten its grip on a once strong, vigorous, athletic body, the roles had been inexorably reversed. The route to the Pope had for a long time been via Dziwisz:

'When the Holy Father promoted Dziwisz to Bishop in 1998, something unheard of for a secretary, it merely confirmed an already established fact. A special request? The need for a "difficult" decision? Then don't go through usual channels. Chances are you would never make first base. Dziwisz is the man. How do you think Opus Dei got that personal prelature or got Escriva beatified? How do you think the Legionnaires of Christ got such fast-track recognition? Come to that: who do you think got Degollado[13] off the hook? It's very useful if what you represent is reactionary or way out to the right. If it is then the other Pope is your man – even more so since his latest promotion.'

As my American companion began to recount the Vatican reaction to the subsequent career of the Pope's secretary, his cool laconic demeanour for once became greatly animated:

> 'We thought making him a Bishop was nepotism running wild, then the Holy Father really upped the ante. Archbishop? There were some, particularly among those working for Ratzinger, who were convinced this was all part of a plan ensuring that "the other Pope" became the next Pope, that when the Holy Father felt his time was drawing to a close he would give Dziwisz the red hat . . . Late sixties – perfect age for a Pope and what better way to ensure that there is a total and absolute continuity? And with all that certain backing from Opus Dei . . . Thank God it did not come to that.'

Apart from Dziwisz, the 'little Polish family' around the Pope over the years significantly reduced his continuing homesickness. The one notable exception was the charming Monsignor Vincent Tran Ngocthu, a Vietnamese priest who served as a private secretary to the Pope from 1988 to 1996. The Polish nuns cooked and cleaned for Wojtyla, his confessor was Monsignor Stanislaw Michalsky until his death in September 2003. There was also Cardinal Andrzej Deskur who did as much as any man to ensure Karol Wojtyla's election in 1978.

The American's views on Archbishop Stanislaw Dziwisz were echoed by a number of the nameless. All papal personal secretaries, certainly in recent times, have wielded considerable power. Paul VI's personal secretary Pasquale Macchi 'controlled' the Pope during his final years, telling him whom he should see, what he should eat, even what time he should go to bed, but Macchi's power was nothing compared with Dziwisz's. When this secretary said, as he did with increasing frequency, 'the Holy Father wishes . . .'

or 'what the Holy Father says . . .' very few would challenge the instruction.

With regard to the rise and rise of Opus Dei, Archbishop Dziwisz had been merely pushing at an open door. Opus Dei is a Roman Catholic sect of international dimensions. Although its actual membership is relatively small, its influence is pervasive. It is a secret society, something that is strictly forbidden by the Church. Opus Dei denies that it is a secret organisation but refuses to make its membership list available. It was founded by a Spanish priest, Monsignor Josemaria Escriva, in 1928.

As befits an organisation that flourished greatly in a Fascist culture it is to the extreme right wing of the Catholic Church, a political fact that has ensured that the organisation has attracted enemies as well as members. Its members are composed of a small percentage of priests, about five per cent, and lay persons of either sex. Although people from many walks of life can be found among its members, it seeks to attract those from the upper reaches of the professional classes, including students and graduates who are aspiring to executive status. Dr John Roche, an Oxford University lecturer, and former member of Opus Dei, describes it as 'sinister, secretive and Orwellian'. It may be that its members' preoccupation with self-mortification is the cause for much of the news media hostility that has been directed towards the sect. Certainly the idea of flogging yourself on your bare back and wearing strips of metal with inward-pointing prongs around the thigh for the greater glory of God might prove difficult for the majority of people in the early part of the twenty-first century to accept. No one, however, should doubt the total sincerity of the Opus Dei membership.

Under Pope John Paul II, Opus Dei flourished. If the Pope was not a member of Opus Dei, he was to its adherents everything they could wish a Pope to be. One of his first acts after his election was to go to the tomb of the founder of Opus Dei and pray.

This organisation has, according to its own claims, members working in over 600 newspapers, reviews and scientific publications, scattered around the world. It has members in over fifty radio and television stations. During the nearly three decades of the Wojtyla papacy Opus Dei – the work of God – succeeded beyond the worst nightmares of its critics and opponents.

Its late founder, Escriva, courtesy of an Opus Dei investment of some $750,000 placed by senior members where it would do the greatest good in oiling the wheels (as my American source wryly observed), achieved beatification in 1992 and canonisation in October 2002. Pope John Paul II, who created more saints than the entire number originated by all of his predecessors, handsomely repaid that multi-million-dollar 'contribution'. In doing so he may well have ultimately demythologized not only the entire process of canonisation but the papacy itself.

The granting of the personal prelature by Wojtyla in 1982 is an act that will eventually come back to haunt the Church. Since 1982 Opus Dei has not been under the jurisdiction of the worldwide infrastructure of the bishopric. It can do as it wishes regardless of any objections in any diocese and is answerable only to its leader, currently the Madrid-born Xavier Echevarria, and through him to the Pope. When a number of Irish bishops in recent years objected to Opus Dei activities within their dioceses and indicated that they wished them to leave, they were ignored. In September 1994 when the popular Portuguese magazine *VISAO* carried a critical article on Opus Dei, the magazine was subsequently deluged with an unending torrent of hostile and threatening correspondence. A short while later the offices of *VISAO* mysteriously went up in flames. Since then *VISAO* appears to be disinclined to criticise Opus Dei.

On university campuses or in the nearby cities around the world, Opus Dei has established residences that serve as recruitment centres. The methods used by some Opus Dei priests are again very reminiscent of the tactics of more recognised sects. Their favourite targets are young adolescents away from home for the first time. Disenchanted former members and the embittered parents of 'lost' children talk of 'mind control' – an echo of Escriva's writings:

> 'This holy coercion is necessary; *compelle intrare* – compel them to come in . . . We do not have any aim other than the corporate one: proselytism, winning vocations . . . When a person does not have zeal to win others, he is dead . . . I bury cadavers.'

A sustained charm offensive or 'love-bombing' is used upon any potential member and when he or she joins they are gradually, almost imperceptibly, alienated from family or friends. It is, for example, a strict rule that all correspondence is first read by a senior member who may or may not decide that it can be read by the intended recipient.

On university campuses across the United States the activities of Opus Dei have recently caused deep concern among non-Opus Dei Catholic clergy. Donald R. McCrabb, executive director of the Catholic Campus Ministry Association, an organisation with over 1,000 Catholic chaplains across the country, observed,

> 'I have heard through campus ministers that an Opus Dei spiritual "director" is assigned to the candidate. The director has to approve every action taken by that person, including reading mail, what classes they take or don't take, what books they read or don't read.'

Staff at Stanford and Princeton Universities are on record detailing the excessive pressure that first-year students have been put under by Opus Dei priests, including continuous questions about their sexual activities, constant coercion to go to confession, instructions on which courses to take and which professors to avoid.

The Opus Dei 'friends' who attach themselves to the target have a disturbing close-of-sale routine, including a staged 'vocation crisis' during which two existing members working in tandem on the target build to an emotional climax. As former member Tammy DiNocala recalled: 'Basically it's a one-shot deal. If you don't take it, you're not going to have God's grace for the remainder of your life.' In the USA, Opus Dei operate not only on university campuses but also at a number of high schools with pupils as young as thirteen. In England, after complaints and an official investigation, the then Primate, the late Cardinal Basil Hume, banned Opus Dei from proselytising anyone under the age of eighteen.

From its very inception Opus Dei regarded women as inferior, and assigns them mainly domestic work. They are at all times subordinate to their 'superiors'; the sexes are strictly segregated and the women are disenfranchised. Although some women members achieve doctorates, their talents are frequently ignored. Escriva wrote: 'Women needn't be scholars – it's enough for them to be prudent.' Much stress is placed upon 'modesty'. The late founder would have had mixed feelings about the meteoric rise in England of Opus Dei member, Ruth Kelly, promoted in January 2005 to the post of Education Minister within the Blair government.

Since May 2006 when Kelly was moved in a Cabinet reshuffle she has been in direct conflict with Catholic teaching on a number of issues, particularly homosexuality. As Secretary of State for Communities part of her brief is to implement the Equality Act which became law in early 2006. The Act makes it illegal to discriminate against an individual on a wide number of grounds including sexual orientation. Asked about the edicts handed down by both Pope John Paul II and his successor Benedict XVI that condemn homosexuality and call upon Roman Catholic politicians to express their opposition 'clearly and publicly and to vote against legislation that recognises homosexual unions' Ruth Kelly observed, 'I don't think it's right for politicians to start making moral judgements about people.' Which is precisely what the Pope has instructed her to do.

During the canonisation ceremony the Pope quoted from Escriva's *The Way*, a collection of spiritual maxims. One that did not make the ceremony was in praise of Escriva's habit of whipping himself until the walls of the room were splattered with his blood. 'Let us bless pain. Love pain. Sanctify pain . . . Glorify pain!' (Number 208.) Unsurprisingly, many of Escriva's philosophical gems, coming from a man who for many years was close to Spanish dictator General Franco, are demonstrably fascistic, as indeed were many of his spoken statements. These include the following attributed to him by Father Vladimir Felzmann, a former Opus Dei priest who devoted twenty-two years of his life to the sect. Escriva once remarked to his fellow priest that Hitler had been 'badly treated' by world opinion because 'he could never have killed six million Jews. It could only have been a million at the most.'

Josemaria Escriva had strong views on books. Unlike the Führer, he did not burn them but used an alternative method of censorship. 'Books: don't buy them without advice from a Christian who is learned and prudent. It is easy to buy something useless or harmful. How often a man thinks he is carrying a book under his arm, and it turns out to be a load of rubbish.' (Number 339.) Escriva also taught that we are not all equal in the eyes of God. 'Next to the prayer of priests and of dedicated virgins, the prayer most pleasing to God is the prayer of children and that of the sick.' (Number 98.)

The sect also tries to keep its members on message with advice on which newspapers to read, radio stations to listen to and TV channels to watch. Because of the secrecy, the precise number of media outlets either owned or controlled by Opus Dei is difficult to establish. One Opus Dei insider estimated that the media empire 'was at least as large and far reaching as News Corp', Rupert Murdoch's multi-media organisation. Apart from pushing a strong pro-Opus Dei line, this media control also ensures a powerful degree of censorship that effectively prevents any critical coverage. It was brought fully to bear on the issue of Escriva's beatification in 1992. A number of former members of Opus Dei felt 'morally obligated' to testify before the tribunal in Rome who were considering the matter. Opus Dei influence was brought to bear to ensure that with one exception only testimony favourable to Escriva was called.

One of the fifteen whose evidence was never presented and who was not called to testify was Maria Carmen del Tapia. An Opus Dei member of nearly twenty years, she had for six years been Escriva's personal secretary and a Major Superior in the Opus Dei Women's Branch Central Government. She had been the first director of the press at Opus Dei headquarters in Rome, a vitally important area within the infrastructure. In 1956 she had been sent to Venezuela as Director of the national Women's Branch. She remained there for nearly ten years until being suddenly summoned by Monsignor Escriva to Rome. Maria, who had been told by Escriva that she had 'saved the day for Opus Dei' was told the reason for the visit was 'to give you a few days' rest'.

Nearly a month later Maria became aware that within the hothouse atmosphere that passes for normality within Opus Dei she had been secretly accused of various breaches of discipline, most notably allowing the women under her supervision to choose which priest they went to for spiritual guidance and confession. Although allowed, exercising such a choice rather than meekly accepting an instruction is considered 'bad spirit'. From that day on, she was under the Opus Dei version of house-arrest and deprived of all contact with the outside world. The imprisonment lasted for five months. The mind games, the interrogations, the continuous mental cruelty, particularly the insults and constant repetition of how worthless a person she was, all of this is recounted with a calmness and a quiet clarity in her book, *Beyond the Threshold: A Life in Opus Dei*.

During 1991 Maria was astonished when the Vatican announced details of the beatification process for Escriva. It was unthinkable for her that he should be venerated. She wrote to Pope John Paul II at considerable length to justify her assertion that 'the life of Monsignor José Maria Escriva de Balaguer, which I witnessed for many years, was not admirable and much less was it worthy of imitation'. She sent her letters via Cardinal Angelo Sodano, the Secretary of State. Whether he delivered them into the hands of the Pope or his Opus Dei secretary Bishop Stanislaw Dziwisz is not known. Cardinal Ratzinger acknowledged receipt of both letters but from the Pope she heard nothing. Shortly after Escriva had been declared 'blessed', the distinguished religious editor of *Newsweek*, Kenneth Woodward, asserted in an article, 'Opus Dei had sufficient influence on the tribunal to prevent critics of Escriva testifying . . . It seemed as if the whole thing was rigged. Escriva's supporters were given priority and the whole thing was rushed through.'

In the run-up to the beatification process, articles very favourable to Escriva appeared all over the world. It was far from obvious that they were written by journalists who were Opus Dei members and invariably appeared in Opus Dei-controlled media.

Opus Dei's membership is still not vast, about 90,000, but its very high quality is a tribute to the sect's ability to handpick undergraduates at elite institutions. Within the Vatican Village, Opus Dei probably has some two hundred members but the quality of their access and control within the Vatican would be very difficult to better. Further afield in the US, Spain, Latin America and the UK and many other countries, they pop up again and again in positions of power and influence and in areas where they have access to the ultimate wealth of the world, information and knowledge. These people do not leave their Opus Dei commitment at home when they go to work; very few openly admit their membership. When challenged on this secrecy they have two responses. 'It is not secret, it is private' or 'Of course we cannot publish a list of members; that is contrary to the Data Protection Act and a part of the members' private life would be revealed if such a list were published.' In the United States Escriva's followers can be found in both the CIA and the FBI. The recent head of the FBI, Louis Freeh, is a member.

Attending the same Church as Freeh was one of his agents, Bob Hanssen. He and his wife Bonnie were considered to be the perfect couple; devout, spiritual, they epitomised many greatly cherished American values. Hanssen worked in counter-intelligence, an excellent position from which to create a second profession – treason.

From October 1985 until his arrest in February 2002 he passed top-secret information to the intelligence services of the Soviet Union (later Russia). According to Louis Freeh, the damage he did to his country's security was 'exceptionally grave' and his betrayal constituted 'the most traitorous actions imaginable'. In return he was paid by the KGB some $600,000 in cash plus three diamonds and had been told that a further $800,000 was sitting in a Moscow bank account in his name. He was directly responsible for the deaths of several US agents. In the words of another FBI executive, 'He sold the farm.' The entire United States intelligence programme for Eastern Europe had been compromised.

Part of the money Hanssen received from the Russians was used to finance the education of his six children at private Opus Dei schools. Another part of the payments went on lavish entertainments he shared with a stripper from Ohio. When unmasked, Hanssen insisted that the stripper and he had a non-sexual relationship. 'I was trying to save her,' he claimed, an unlikely scenario for a man who also secretly filmed himself having sex with his wife so that a friend could watch the performance. Part of the software that he sold to the Russians found its way into the hands of the Al-Qaeda network. After the attacks on September 11 the FBI reassured Bonnie that they would not be putting any of the blame for the carnage in New York on her husband's traitorous activities: given their ineptitude in the run-up it is hard to see how they could be so certain.

Ever the devout Catholic while working for godless Soviet intelligence, Hanssen continued to attend Mass regularly and also make his confession of sins. In the confessional box he admitted that he was betraying his country and went into considerable detail. At least one Opus Dei priest initially urged Hanssen to go to the authorities, then rapidly changed his mind and told him that for his penance he 'should pay $20,000 to Mother Teresa's charity'. The penitent Hanssen duly sent the money, part of his Soviet pay. As he was rotating his confessions several different Opus Dei priests were fully aware that this pillar of the Church was also delivering top-secret intelligence information to the enemy (eventually his total reached over 6,000 pages).

Apart from donating $20,000 to the Sisters of Mercy in Calcutta, Hanssen as a deeply committed member gave

Opus Dei at least ten per cent of the money he received for betraying his country. It is not known whether any attempt has been made to recover it, as proceeds of a serious felony, or whether Opus Dei returned it voluntarily. Hanssen's contribution from his Soviet income was in addition to the tithe which as an Opus Dei member he was obliged to contribute from his regular American salary. Tithing is one of the many sources of Opus Dei revenue: since it is generally tax-deductible Opus Dei is benefiting from many of the world's finance ministries, and less-privileged tax-payers.

Many members of Opus Dei continue to deny that the full membership list is a carefully guarded secret. They are either lying or ignorant of the rules of their own written constitution drawn up in 1950. In recent years some members have claimed that the original constitution has been superseded, yet the 1950 rules include the declaration, 'These constitutions are the foundation of our Institute. For this reason they must be considered holy, inviolable and perpetual.' The Spanish author Jesús Ynfante fully explores this issue within his highly revealing book, *La Prodigiosa Aventura del Opus Dei* where he quotes the entire constitution including the following:

Article 189 states that

'To attain its goals in the most effective manner, the Institute (Opus Dei) as such must live an occult existence.'

Article 190 adds,

'Because of (our) collective humility, which is proper to our Institute, whatever is undertaken by members must not be attributed to it, but to God only. Consequently even the fact of being a member of the Institute should not be disclosed externally; the number of members should remain secret; and more expressly, our members must not discuss these matters with anyone outside the Institute.'

Article 191 follows:

'Numerary and supernumerary members must always observe a prudent silence regarding the names of other members; and never reveal to anyone the fact that they belong to Opus Dei . . . unless expressly authorised to do so by their local director.'

With a potent mix of the super-rich and the flower of highly talented university graduates, Opus Dei has created a global business empire that is frequently described as 'Octopus Dei'. Like the IOR, the Vatican Bank it now largely controls, the sect never publishes annual accounts. In true IOR tradition, Opus Dei hides behind offshore outlets, shell companies and nominees. If there is indeed a life after death Roberto Calvi and Michele Sindona must be viewing in silent awe an organisation that had for many years as its principal protector and Chairman of the Board, Pope John Paul II.

Opus Dei's headquarters in the United States is appropriately located in mid-Manhattan not far from Wall Street. The seventeen-storey building costing some $50 million is mute testimony to a global wealth built on a great deal more than the tithes of its 90,000 or so members. From an obscure humble beginning in October 1928 in Madrid the 'Work of God' now has assets that Swiss banking sources have valued as 'one billion US dollars and rising'.

As early as 1974 Escriva was already in a position to offer to provide in perpetuity thirty per cent of the Vatican's annual expenditure. But the donation came with a price.

Escriva was prepared to take on most of the loss, so desperate was he to have Opus Dei granted the privilege of personal prelature. Despite much that has been written, Pope Paul VI by that time had deep reservations about Opus Dei and Escriva, and politely declined the offer.

Long before the mid-1970s, Opus Dei had pushed out far from Spain. Italy, Germany, France and the United Kingdom all had well established Opus Dei centres by the early 1960s as did virtually every Latin American country from Mexico to Chile. Infiltration of the United States and the Far East rapidly followed. The highly focused members targeted potential recruits with the zeal of a powerfully motivated sales force determined come what may to achieve its monthly target figures. The current billion-dollar rating from the Swiss is due in no small measure to the very high success level of those targeted recruits in their secular lives. The global power and success of Opus Dei owes more to Mammon's work than it does to God's. In politics, banking, investment consultancy, the legal professions, education, publishing, Escriva's followers have their hands on a wide range of the levers of power and influence. Spain, the country where it all began, serves as an enlightening example.

Successive Spanish Governments since the 1950s have invariably contained either Opus Dei members or men who happily 'co-operated' with the sect. In October 1969 General Franco decided the country needed a new government. Ten of the new cabinet were Opus Dei members, a further five had very close links with the organisation, a further three frequently collaborated with it and the Prime Minister Luis Carrero Blanco's commitment to Opus Dei was total. This fact was confirmed to me several years before Admiral Carrero Blanco was assassinated by ETA in December 1973. More recently Opus Dei members in Spain have included a President of Banco Popular, an Attorney General, Jesus Cardenal, a Head of Police, Juan Cotino, literally hundreds of senior academics, journalists and some twenty members of the Spanish Royal Family. Inevitably Opus Dei is also very well represented in the Spanish Church, at every level from priest to cardinal.

The children of the recently deposed Prime Minister José Maria Aznar were Opus Dei educated. Within the Aznar government, the judicial system, the universities, the schools, Opus Dei flourished at the highest levels. With the exception of the newly elected Socialist government, all previously acquired strongholds remain intact. Like it or not, the Spanish taxpayer is subsidising the teaching of an ideology throughout the country that has been rejected at every polling survey by the majority of Roman Catholics. Opus Dei's ideology does not recognise freedom of conscience and does not respect the principle of equality.

In Italy during the 1960s and 1970s it was frequently said that 'if you want to succeed in this life you must join the Masonic lodge P2'. In modern Spain and many other countries there is a new version of P2, just as secret, just as pernicious as Licio Gelli's Lodge. The same is true in Rome. The President of the Pontifical Council for the Family, Cardinal Alfonso Trujillo, probably did more than any other man to persuade the late Pope that liberation theology was a major threat to the Church, a position that was directly responsible for an escalation of the carnage in many parts of Latin America during the late 1970s and throughout the following decade. Cardinal Trujillo is very close to Opus Dei. The late Professor Jerome Lejeune, who was the lunchtime guest of the Pope hours before the Agca attack in St Peter's Square, deeply influenced Karol Wojtyla on a range of issues, particularly birth control and abortion. Lejeune's family are France's premier Opus Dei dynasty. The beatification process for the Professor has already begun, with the late Pope John Paul II's full approval.

My American Vatican source was one of several within the Curia who were fully prepared to discuss the ever-tightening grip of Opus Dei at the very heart of the Roman Catholic Church. I was told,

'They control the Bank, the information services, the Council of this, the Congregation of that . . . Look, every time there's a Synod or a gathering secret meetings take place. It's been happening since 1991–1992 in the Via Aurelia, in particular colleges – the Europeans (cardinals) even held one in Paris . . . Apart from the known cardinals, apart from the fifty or so Opus Dei members in place in the congregations and on pontifical boards, there are their "friends" outside. Across the Tiber those are the "friends" who in 1986 were able to block a parliamentary and juridical enquiry into Opus Dei that the Government Finance Department had asked for.'

Opus Dei's friends within Italy number many thousands. Their actual members within the country are only some 4,000 but, as always with Opus Dei, they put quality before quantity. On one side of the Tiber they can call on the current Vatican Secretary of State; on the other side, they can access leading industrialists, editors, bank governors including the current Governor of the Bank of Italy, and an array of leading politicians. Asked in 1993 whether the Vatican had entrusted a special task to Opus Dei, the organisation's Rome spokesman Giuseppe Corigliano's response was a masterpiece of brevity: 'Europe.'

Opus Dei does not have a monopoly on Vatican intrigue, however. There are the Masons, notwithstanding 500 years of papal anathema, as indestructible as the very walls the medieval masons built. There are the Bologna

Mafia, the Venice axis, the clans from Romana and Piacenza. There is the Emiliana Mafia. Even various colleges have spawned their own Vatican 'lodges'. There is even evidence that Satanism is alive and well within the Vatican. Every new entrant to the Curia is delicately lobbied by various emissaries. He would do well to hesitate. Any choice he makes on entry has no opt-out clause. It is for life.

Paul Maria Hnilica is one of many village residents that any writer of fiction would shrink from creating. He was born in what was then Czechoslovakia in 1921 in the Archdiocese of Travni. According to Hnilica, his mother was a devout Catholic who prayed as a little girl that she would one day become the proud mother of a priest. Her prayers were answered.

At the time the Communists seized control of the country after the Second World War, Hnilica was training for the priesthood. He was later to tell how he and many others were seized by the Communist regime and taken to a prison camp. His ordination as priest took place in a section of the quarantine unit of a hospital. He has yet to explain how he got out of the prison camp and to the hospital at Roznava but he has explained why his entry to the priesthood took place in such bizarre surroundings:

'All the bishops had been arrested. There was no one free to ordain me but one particular bishop was receiving regular medical treatment at the hospital. On this occasion his doctor, a Catholic, told the three security guards that the bishop was to be treated within the unit for contagious diseases. The police, afraid of being infected, waited outside. I was waiting in the unit and was ordained. It was 29 September, the feast day of the Archangel Michael.'

In possibly the fastest religious promotion in modern times, three months later Father Hnilica became Bishop Hnilica.

'It was in a basement. I fought against it. But my provincial ordered me to accept this ordination under obedience, so I agreed. As you know every bishop receives a diocese when he is ordained. I was told: "Your diocese covers Peking-Moscow-Berlin." This was meant symbolically not geographically but I did not understand that at the time.'

Within months Hnilica was hard at work as a clandestine bishop. His activities became known to the police and an arrest warrant was issued in July 1951. On 24 August Hnilica was in Bratislava, with the police in pursuit. He ordained Jan Korec as a clandestine bishop; then, evading the police, jumped in the nearby river Danube and swam to a new life in the West. Now a bishop without a country or a diocese, he made his way to Our Lady of Fatima. He journeyed several times to the Fatima shrine in Portugal meeting Sister Lucia, the remaining survivor of the three children who had claimed in 1917 to have seen the Virgin Mary. It has been alleged that during these years he was also trained as an agent of the KGB or the CIA or both.

In May 1964 the newly elected Pope Paul VI appointed Hnilica titular Bishop of Rusado, a diocese that has long ago ceased to exist. It is a custom of the Church to assign a new bishop a defunct diocese as a reminder of times past. The appointment carries no jurisdiction or authority but is normally accompanied with the assignment of a regular diocese. That did not occur in Hnilica's case, he was left free to make a reality of the symbolic appointment he had received in Czechoslovakia – the entire Communist-controlled empire. His range of contacts and friends grew rapidly, ranging from Popes Paul VI and John Paul II, to the future Secretary of State, Cardinal Casaroli and Flavio Carboni, a man who in the summer of 2005 was put on trial for the murder of yet another of Hnilica's good friends, the former chairman of Banco Ambrosiano, Roberto Calvi.

In 1968 when Czechoslovakia was invaded by the Soviets there was no thought of returning to the motherland he had swum away from in 1951, but when Pope Paul VI returned from a visit to Colombia to be greeted by Prime Minister Giovanni Leone, a dozen cardinals and the entire diplomatic corps, he was also welcomed by Paul Hnilica. He had rounded up about one hundred of his countrymen temporarily trapped in Rome and he led the Pope over to them for a highly emotional meeting. It was clear that His Holiness held Hnilica in high regard. Earlier that year Pope Paul had given his approval for the creation by Hnilica of Pro Fratribus, a charitable organisation with the aim of helping the Catholic Churches of Eastern Europe.

Pro Fratribus was destined by various means to acquire huge amounts of money. Exactly where it all went has yet to be established. Some undoubtedly went into Russia and was used to create religious institutes. The Family of Mary Co-Redemptrix has centres for male religious in Ufa, and the village of Alekseevka and for women at Shumanovka and Talmenka in the Altai *krai* (administrative territory). All of these are wholly owned and controlled by Hnilica and his associates. There may be others in the former Warsaw Pact group of countries. No accounts have ever been published and no annual reports ever made; a remarkable omission for an organisation that claims to be a charity.

John Paul II never entertained any doubts about the man and his work. The two men enjoyed a close friendship for many years. Hnilica was even accorded the rare privilege of concelebrating Mass with the Holy Father in the Papal

Chapel. He recounted afterwards how they breakfasted together.

> 'I said to him. "Holy Father, only you have a bigger diocese. It comprises the whole world. Mine comes right after that size. Peking-Moscow-Berlin." The Pope said, 'Paul, this is your mission field. Find yourself the best Christians as missionaries!"'

Hnilica has also recounted how after the attempt on the Pope's life, during his recovery in the Gemelli hospital, the Pope asked him to bring all of the documents held by the Vatican on Fatima to the hospital. The two men, both with a deep obsession about the mother of Christ, rapidly concluded that the Virgin Mary had interceded and saved the Pope's life. When the Pope was discharged from the Gemelli, Hnilica brought him a statue of Our Lady of Fatima, 'the most beautiful statue I have even seen', at which point the Pope told him,

> 'Paul, in these three months I have come to understand that the only solution to all the problems of the world, the deliverance from war, the deliverance from atheism, and from the defection from God, is the conversion of Russia. The conversion of Russia is the content and meaning of the message of Fatima. Not until then will the triumph of Mary come.'

The following year Bishop Hnilica accompanied the Pope to Fatima, where the two men again talked to Sister Lucia and then prayed in front of a life-size statue of the Virgin Mary in whose own crown had been placed the bullet that had been intended by Mehmet Agca to kill the Pope.

These were busy times for Hnilica. Apart from his considerable time with the Pope, he was also fully occupied with Roberto Calvi in organising the transfer of huge quantities of money to Poland and more particularly to the empty coffers of Solidarity. That at least is what Calvi was told. The reality is that Solidarity never saw or had use of a single cent of this money, a sum approaching $100 million. Bishop Hnilica's final destination for this money and what has subsequently happened to it remains a carefully kept secret known only to him and his business associates. Calvi was 'suicided' under Blackfriars Bridge, London, in June 1982 but even in death the bishop saw business opportunities, particularly when it became known that the black attaché case that had been bulging with documents when Calvi fled from Milan was empty when opened by the police after his death.

Before that episode the bishop without a diocese began to take a great interest in Medjugorje. He was a frequent visitor to the Medjugorje gold rush during the 1980s. The Franciscans in Medjugorje were recycling 'donations' on a regular basis. Throughout the decade, hundreds of millions of dollars were transferred to the United States. Hnilica was allegedly laundering money both into and out of Medjugorje during the same period, an activity that ceased only with the disintegration of the former Yugoslavia and the outbreak of a Balkans war which in no small way was initiated by the Vatican.

In early 1984 Hnilica was working with another of his good friends, Mother Teresa in Calcutta. In February, he learned that the Pope had called bishops throughout the world to join with him on 25 March in consecrating Russia on behalf of the Virgin Mary, the first step in the Pope's mind to the conversion of the country and 'the solution to all the problems of the world'. Hnilica decided to join in the ceremony, not in a church in India, but in Communist Russia. He then gave an excellent example of his powers of persuasion. He first persuaded the Russian Embassy in

India to grant him a visa, then charmed his way past the customs and security police at Moscow and finally beguiled the security guards on duty at St Michael's Church to let him enter with his bag which should have stayed at security. Inside the church, which had been converted by the regime into a museum, he took out an edition of *Pravda* and from its inner pages a copy of the text that the Pope and bishops around the world were reciting and proceeded to say the various prayers. For good measure, he then went to the Marian Church of the Assumption of Our Lady, repeated the consecration ritual and then celebrated Mass.

When next in Rome he recounted in great detail to the Pope what he had done. When he described how once people in the Soviet Union learned that he was a Catholic they begged him to send them Bibles, the Pope was moved to tears.

The mystery of Calvi's black attaché case or rather the missing contents of the case remained. These included the Vagnozzi report referred to earlier, a large number of documents that incriminated people in both Italy and the Vatican, and finally the keys to a fortune locked away in various deposit boxes and the numbers of secret bank accounts in Switzerland and other countries. In 1985 this particular mystery took another bizarre turn.

Flavio Carboni, one of the last people to have seen Roberto Calvi alive, quietly advised Bishop Hnilica that he 'might be able to put his hands on the various documents, at a price'. Among those that Hnilica turned to were the Pope and the Secretary of State, Cardinal Casaroli. They authorised the bishop to negotiate. The agreed price was £1 million, approximately $1.5 million. Hnilica demanded some evidence that would demonstrate that Carboni was indeed holding the genuine documents. Among the items that the bishop was given was a letter written by Calvi thirteen days before his death. It was to the Pope.

There were ample documents within the Vatican Bank bearing Calvi's signature. The letter, written when life was closing in on Calvi from all sides, sought help at this desperate hour from the Pope. He wrote, 'It was I who disposed of large sums of money in favour of many Eastern and Western countries and political-religious organisations.' The banker continued with a description of his activities on behalf of the Roman Catholic Church. He had 'co-ordinated all over Central and South America the creation of numerous banking operations for the purpose of halting, above all, the penetration and expansion of Marxist and related ideologies'.

While asking for help from the Vatican, the organisation that above all others he blamed for the crisis confronting him, Calvi was at pains to point out to the Pope the potential embarrassment he could cause the Church.

'I have been offered help by many people on condition that I talk about my activities for the Church. Very many people would like to know if I supplied arms and other means to some South American regimes to help them combat our common enemies. I will never reveal it.'

Those within the Vatican who studied the letter were in no doubt that it was genuine and Hnilica was instructed to close the deal. He wrote out a number of cheques to Giulio Lena, a criminal well known to the Italian police. Two of the cheques were for £300,000 each. Owing to the Vatican's failure to place Hnilica's Vatican accounts in sufficient funds, the cheques bounced and the deal was never concluded but the parties concerned had left an incriminating paper trail and there were also tape recordings of Carboni talking to Hnilica about the deal. Then in a scene that could have come directly from the film 'The Gang That Couldn't

Shoot Straight', while on trial for a totally different matter Giulio Lena blurted out details of the criminal conspiracy concerning the Calvi documents. The Italian financial police raided his home and what they found there led inexorably to Carboni and Bishop Hnilica and Lena being indicted.

In Italy the judicial process can halt for years. Granted bail, the bishop got on with his busy life. There was his global diocese, his creation of a chain of religious centres in Russia, his activities in Medjugorje and his continuing conversations with the Pope. A year had gone by since the worldwide ceremonial consecration of Russia by the bishops. World peace had yet to break out but there was a new man at the helm in Moscow. Mikhail Gorbachev would give the world a great deal including the words *perestroika* (restructuring) and *glasnost* (openness). Bishop Hnilica would later claim that both he and the Pope attributed all of the dramatic changes that would occur to the Virgin Mary. However, the late Pope acknowledged very publicly the crucial role played by Gorbachev.

The bishop's main task after the outbreak of war in former Yugoslavia in 1990 was to find an alternative source of revenue to replace Medjugorje, which was no longer the number one must-see shrine on the pilgrims' list. He went to the United States in 1992, preceded by one of his secretaries, Father Luciano Alimandi. The secretary's brief was to identify a visionary, one who was ideally in contact with the Virgin Mary at The Franciscan University in Stubenville, Ohio. Father Luciano happily found one studying theology with other members of Hnilica's *Pro Fratribus* organisation. She was a self-proclaimed mystic, Christine Mugridge. Alimandi clearly had a talent for spotting visionaries. He rapidly had four to choose from. Apart from Christine he found Veronica Garcia, Sylvia Gregor and Theresa Lopez.

Alimandi selected Theresa Lopez. It is said that the casting couch featured heavily in his choice. Lopez admits to four marriages, but her former husband Jeff believes it could be five and he has also revealed that she has six children. Mental arithmetic was not one of Theresa's assets, for she has had at least twenty-five different credit collection and debt recovery notices and pleaded guilty in 1990 to a second degree forgery/cheque fraud charge. Bishop Hnilica arrived in Denver in May 1992 to take control of Theresa Lopez. Before his arrival the ever-versatile secretary Father Alimandi had arranged a meeting for Hnilica with the National Conference of Catholic Bishops. The NCCB fell for Hnilica's persuasive patter and gave him full permission to fund-raise in the United States for the 'Catholic Evangelisation Mission for Russia'.

Shortly after the bishop had met Theresa Lopez, a huge publicity campaign was mounted to publicise 'this amazing seer' who 'regularly has visions and communicates with the Virgin Mary'. Hnilica and Theresa became regulars on the Medjugorje tour circuit as it made increasing inroads into Catholic communities. Unofficial estimates placed the value of these tours at $50 million per annum.

In December 1993 the then Archbishop of Denver, Francis Stafford, concluded a three-year investigation of Theresa by declaring that her 'visions' had no supernatural origin. Entirely unabashed Hnilica carried on with the tour, which included targeting carefully researched potential donors. In November 1993 at a retreat for a group of devout and wealthy Catholics in Snow Mountain Ranch, Colorado, Theresa Lopez approached Mrs Ardath Kronzer and proclaimed that the Virgin Mary had a special message for her. During a subsequent conference in May 1994 held at the Notre Dame University Mr and Mrs Kronzer were again in the front row when the guest speaker was Bishop Hnilica. Subsequently he asked Mrs Kronzer to make an $80,000 cash donation. Within a few short years, Phillip Kronzer had lost his wife and a very lucrative business. His legal actions against the Medjugorje Mir Centre, Colafrancesco's Caritas and over 100 defendants have been on going for some years and remained unresolved as of May 2006.

In between his appearances with his seer in the United States the bishop was obliged to make a number of other appearances, in a Milan Court. In 1993 the trial began of Hnilica, Carboni and Giulio Lena, the latter *in absentia*, having unsportingly jumped bail and fled abroad. One of the high points occurred when the bishop was questioned about some cheques he had made out to Flavio Carboni. The records revealed that over the years he had made out a great many of these. He certainly acted confused very well.

'Is that your signature on the cheque?'

'Yes, I signed it.'

'How much is the cheque made out for?'

The bishop spent a considerable time peering at the cheque through his spectacles.

'It's either ten million lire [approximately $10,000] or ten billion lire [about $10 million], I don't know which.'

The bishop later observed, 'These external things don't mean very much to me.'

In March 1993 both men were found guilty. Flavio Carboni was sentenced to five years' imprisonment and the bishop to three years. As mentioned earlier, while waiting for his appeal to be heard the bishop continued his normal everyday life. There were his regular meetings and long conversations with the Pope, and the fund-raising activities both in Medjugorje, war permitting, and in the United States with his visionary Theresa Lopez. The Appeal Court annulled the sentences on a technicality: a legal document had been one day out of time. A second trial, this time with the previously elusive Giulio Lena, took place in March 2000. This time Carboni was again found guilty and sentenced to four years. Lena was found guilty and sentenced to two years and the bishop was acquitted.

The court found that the Vatican had reneged on the deal and failed to put up the money and that Hnilica had not taken possession of Roberto Calvi's documents even though he, Cardinal Casaroli and the Pope had all conspired that he should. He was therefore, in the opinion of the court, technically not guilty. From the way that he was received within the Vatican by Pope John Paul II, Cardinal Ratzinger or any other member of the hierarchy, Bishop Paul Hnilica's life and his values are clearly considered acceptable. But such standards are normal in the Vatican Village.

For a village where the overwhelming majority have sworn a vow of celibacy there is an unusual preoccupation with sexual matters. Homosexuality, if not rife within the Vatican, is constantly evident, and is a frequent factor in career advancement. Young, attractive priests, invariably referred to as *Madonni*, use their charms to accelerate their promotion. Certain bishops have found the need to work late in a locked room with only a *Madonno* to assist them. Satanic masses have happened regularly with hooded semi-naked participants and porn videos have been shown to very carefully selected audiences. I was introduced through one source to an elegant Roman whose main source of income was arranging 'safe apartments' for Vatican assignations both heterosexual and homosexual. His clientele includes two homosexual cardinals, a German priest who has frequent assignations with his 'wife' and until recently an American bishop who had conducted an affair with a former beauty queen over many years. He also supplies child pornography videos to 'a number' of Vatican residents.

Paedophile and adolescent pornography videos are a multi-million-dollar business in Italy. A large part of this particular industry is Russian-controlled. The films range from children running about in bathing costumes or naked, which sell at about £50, to films showing the torture and murder of children that sell for approximately £1,500. In October 2000 when magistrate Alfredo Ormanni brought charges against 831 Italian nationals and 660 foreigners for either selling or downloading child pornography from the Web there was uproar, not least from the 'paedophile lobby' of politicians that the magistrate claimed were obstructing his investigation. There was also considerable anxiety within the Vatican. Aware that computers leave a record of the viewing history of the machine a significant number were replaced. Two independent sources assured me that a number of the original machines went into the Tiber.

One particular scandal symptomatic of the sickness within this Vatican Village occurred in spring 1998. On the evening of 4 May Alois Estermann had every reason for feeling satisfied with his life. Only a few hours earlier he had heard the official announcement to confirm what he had been told unofficially over the previous weekend: he was to be promoted to Commander of the Vatican Swiss Guard. He had worked hard and lobbied even harder for the post; now it was his. Enjoying the triumph with him was his Venezuelan-born wife, Gladys Meza Romero. Just after 8.45 p.m. there was a phone call from a family friend who had heard the news and wanted to convey his pleasure.

The friend chatted to Gladys for a few minutes and then Estermann came on the line. Their everyday conversation concerned the caller's desire to attend the annual swearing-in ceremony for the latest batch of recruits, due to take place in two days' time. It was interrupted by an unusual sound, as if Estermann had cupped a hand over the mouthpiece or placed it upon his chest. The caller could hear voices coming, it seemed, from some distance away. He was able to distinguish Gladys but not the words. There was a curious humming sound followed by two 'sharp blows', then more noise from a distance. Assuming that Estermann had dropped the phone upon the arrival of a guest, the caller hung up, planning to call back later.

Precisely who had called and exactly what then took place in the Estermanns' apartment is still a matter of speculation and conjecture within the Village. Beyond all doubt is that their neighbour Sister Anna-Lina, disturbed by the unusual sounds, walked in on a scene of carnage. Just inside the front door Gladys was lying in a heap on the floor, blood still pouring from gunshot wounds. The petrified nun stood for a moment in shock, and then raised the alarm. Lance-Corporal Marcel Riedi of the Swiss Guard was the first to arrive. He established that Gladys Meza Romero was dead and moved through the entrance area and into the sitting room. To his left Estermann was stretched out on the floor, still bleeding, and the handset of the phone was still swinging slowly from a nearby table. Close by was a third body that despite the gunshot wounds to the head and the blood was instantly recognisable to Riedi. There was no mistaking the good-looking Cédric Tornay, a fellow lance-corporal in the Swiss Guard. There was nothing that Riedi could do for any of them except carry news of their shocking deaths to his superiors.

In the secular world, certain basic police procedures are automatically triggered upon such a discovery: 'Secure the scene. Access to be limited to essential personnel: photographer, fingerprint expert, pathologist, officer in charge and his subordinates.' In the Village they have their own way of life and death. Within minutes of the discovery of the triple killing the apartment and the surrounding areas were a bedlam. Some had come to help, others to gawp, some to take control, a function that included tampering with vital evidence.

According to one well-placed source Alois Estermann was in fact still alive when the bodies were discovered. If so, no one thought to summon medical help. One of the first on the scene was the Vatican spokesman, Joaquin Navarro-Valls. Monsignor Giovanni Battista Re, the Deputy Secretary of State, appeared almost simultaneously. Others who came and crowded into the apartment for all the world as if they were late arrivals at a party included yet another Secretariat of State official, Monsignor Pedro Lopez Quintana, three officials of the Corpo di Vigilanza Vaticana, forensic experts Pietro Fuci and Giovanni Arcudi and the man who by happy coincidence would be appointed to head the enquiry into the triple deaths, Gianluigi Marrone, a qualified lawyer who had never practised. Marrone, an Italian civil servant, also had a part-time job as an occasional Vatican Judge. Monsignor Re either came bearing chocolates or went off for them and returning offered them to the onlookers.

More than two hours later, the area was still awash with people. Some witnesses recall four wine glasses on a small table in the Estermanns' living room yet later photographs did not show them. Accounts of the position of the bodies varied suggesting that they had been moved. An official from the Vatican Government arrived and photographed the scene with a Polaroid camera. These original photographs, like the wine glasses, also disappeared, after which a second photographer, this time a staff photographer from *L'Osservatore Romano*, appeared and took a second series of photographs. These became the ones used during the subsequent official Vatican enquiry.

The Italian authorities were not informed of what had occurred, nor asked for assistance. Although Rome has at least three world-class forensic facilities, Secretary of State Cardinal Sodano ordered that the autopsies were to be performed in the highly inappropriate Vatican mortuary that lacked many of the necessary facilities. When a Vatican ambulance arrived to transport the bodies to Rome's Gemelli polytechnic it was sent away again. The Secretary of

State saw no need to disturb the Fondo Assistenza Sanitaria – the Vatican's internal medical assistance service – or its doctors or specialist staff. The Corpo di Vigilanza, the 120-strong police force that is entirely independent of the Swiss Guard, took charge of proceedings. The three bodies were removed by members of the Swiss Guard to the Vatican mortuary at midnight. The Estermanns' apartment was then finally sealed.

Long before this, in fact within the first fifteen minutes of the discovery, the Vatican spokesman Navarro-Valls had already arrived at the complete truth. He was aided in this remarkable feat by a number of factors. Firstly, Cédric Tornay's service weapon, the Swiss-made 9mm SIG pistol, had been discovered beneath his body. Secondly, a letter that Tornay had written to his mother then handed to a friend to give to her had been taken from the Swiss Guard, opened and photocopied before the original was resealed. Within the letter Tornay refers to the *benemerenti* medal that is awarded to members of the Swiss Guards after three years' service:

'Mummy,

I hope you will forgive me because of what I have done but they were the ones who drove me on. This year I was due to receive the *benemerenti* and the Lieutenant Colonel refused it to me. After three years six months and six days spent here putting up with all the injustices. The only thing I wanted they have refused me. I must do this service for all the Guards remaining as well as for the Catholic Church. I have sworn to give my life for the Pope and this is what I am doing. I apologise for leaving you alone but duty calls. Tell Sara, Melinda and Daddy that I love you all. Big kisses to the Greatest Mother in the World.

Your son who loves you'

Thirdly, several members of the Swiss Guard when interrogated and threatened with being accomplices to the attack talked of how upset Tornay had been shortly before the deaths when he had discovered that the three-year service medal that he cherished had been denied him by Estermann. Tornay's friends also told of how Estermann had made young Cédric Tornay's life a living hell for a long time but that was an aspect that Navarro-Valls chose to suppress. The essence of the Vatican's version of events had been communicated to a number of interested parties before 9.30 p.m. It was given a more public airing at midnight with a statement to the waiting crowd of TV, radio and press reporters:

'The Captain-Commander of the Pontifical Swiss Guard, Colonel Alois Estermann, was found dead in his home together with his wife Gladys Meza Romero and Vice-Corporal Cédric Tornay. The bodies were discovered shortly after 9 p.m. by a neighbour from the apartment next door who was attracted by loud noises. From a first investigation it is possible to affirm that all three were killed by a firearm. Under the body of the Vice-Corporal his regulation weapon was found. The information which has emerged up to this point allows for the theory of a "fit of madness" by Vice-Corporal Tornay.'

The following afternoon Navarro-Valls, again without benefit of forensic evidence or an adequate investigation, elaborated on his instant verdict. "There is no mystery," he told his audience.

'The hypothesis of a fit of madness on Tornay's part yesterday evening is the same as yesterday and today I can say that it is much more than a hypothesis. The

> Vatican has the moral certainty that the facts are as I have stated.'

It developed into a vintage performance from the Vatican spokesman. Navarro-Valls often has a tenuous grasp on reality but as with any good spin doctor he has complete belief in whatever he happens to be saying. He now told the media that Tornay's first two shots had been fired at Estermann and his third at Gladys Meza Romero. Then, after placing his gun in his mouth, Tornay had committed suicide by shooting himself. The injuries that Estermann had sustained had caused 'in practical terms, in physiological terms, instant death'.

Navarro-Valls had now hit his stride. Tornay's motive was 'a long deep-seated belief that his talents and abilities were not adequately acknowledged by his superiors'. This feeling had been 'dramatically enhanced by a courteous and firm, but not harsh' reprimand from Estermann, three months earlier when Tornay had spent a night away from the Vatican barracks without permission. Following Estermann's refusal to award him the standard three-year service medal, Tornay's unstable character, 'a character that accumulates things and explodes without logic', had pushed him over the edge. This instant analysis of a situation that, by his own version, had been festering for months 'could not have been foreseen by anyone'. The Swiss Guard were exemplary; their selection process flawless. According to Navarro-Valls, 'It was a tragedy that could have happened in any branch of society.'

Pressed by a reporter to explain the seven-month delay before Estermann's promotion, a delay that had not only left the Guard without a Commander but had also become the cause of comment far beyond the Vatican Village in the international press, Navarro-Valls muttered vaguely about 'a long and complicated selection process that is hampered by historical factors', then glibly observed, 'Sometimes you don't even notice that the perfect candidate is right under your nose.'

Then he tossed the media a titbit. He revealed that Cédric Tornay had written a letter to his family and entrusted it to a friend.

'Yes, the Vatican does have a copy but I am not going to reveal its contents out of respect for Tornay's family. It is up to them to decide whether its contents should be made public. I will say however that the letter's contents support my diagnosis of "a fit of madness".'

In fact, Navarro-Valls had already secretly orchestrated the leaking of Tornay's letter to the Italian press. The original version written in French had been rather badly translated into Italian for their convenience.

In one area at least Navarro-Valls seriously over-egged the Vatican pudding. He stressed that the three bodies were all fully clothed when found. This observation excited much speculation within both Italian and international media. Had the handsome Cédric and the stunning former model, Gladys, been caught by a jealous husband? However, reports of the rampant homosexuality throughout the Vatican tilted the media enquiry simultaneously in another direction. Were Estermann and Tornay lovers?

The secrecy with which the Secretary of State surrounded the deaths; the lack of involvement of the very competent Italian police; the refusal to allow the autopsies to be performed at the Gemelli or one of the other Rome institutes; the fact that the entire Swiss Guard, the forensic experts and a number of other individuals had been forced to take an absolute vow of silence; the fact that if Tornay had determined to kill Estermann and then commit suicide then the act of killing Meza Romero had no meaning or purpose; the calm writing of the letter that contradicted Navarro's theory of an explosion of mad rage – these were just a few of the hares that were out running around in the Vatican Village.

Prelates who had never met Tornay quickly delivered a character assassination, while piling eulogy after eulogy on the departed Estermanns. Much of what was occurring had a familiar ring. In many ways it replayed certain events in September and October 1978 that followed the murder of Albino Luciani, the Smiling Pope, John Paul I. His dead body was almost certainly moved after discovery. The Secretary of State imposed a vow of silence on the Papal Household. A number of items vanished from the Papal Apartments. A tissue of lies concerning the late Pope's state of health was planted in the media. A secret autopsy or detailed examination of the dead body was carried out behind locked doors. No report of this has ever been made public. There was also a sustained character assassination of the dead Pope. The Secretary of State lied about who found the Pope's body, what time it was found and the nature of the documents that were found in the Pope's hands. It is the way that these things are dealt with in this totalitarian country. It has always been this way.

On 22 June 1983, fifteen-year-old Emanuela Orlandi, the daughter of a Vatican employee, disappeared at 7 p.m. while on her way back to her Vatican home from a music lesson. Subsequently the Italian police intercepted phone calls to the Vatican in which callers claiming to be the kidnappers of Emanuela demanded the release of the Pope's would-be assassin Mehmet Ali Agca. The mention of Agca's name catapulted a run-of-the-mill story to international news. The Pope took a continued personal interest in the case and made a number of public appeals to the kidnappers on behalf of the parents. The Italian police installed an intercept within the Vatican as the kidnappers (who by now had revealed evidence that confirmed they were indeed holding Emanuela) demanded direct access to Secretary of State Casaroli. The abductors phoned several times but the tapes, complete with the intercept, vanished from within the Vatican. Italian Judge Priore, the man responsible for investigating every ramification of the Agca affair, attacked the Vatican within his report as obstructive and uncooperative with the exception of one prelate, Cardinal Oddi, who testified that he saw the young girl getting out of a car with a priest some hours after her disappearance.

The judge subsequently discovered years later that a few days before the attempt to kill the Pope, Agca had attended a church service in Rome. Photos taken at the time showing the Pope paying a visit to the church service also showed Ali Agca sitting in the front row. An official invitation was required for this service. Agca's had been arranged by Ercole Orlandi – the father of the girl kidnapped two years later. Judge Priore's attempts to pursue this lead again met with obstruction from Vatican officials. One particular Vatican source that had repeatedly and deliberately sidetracked the Italian investigation was the second-highest-ranking officer within the Vatican Central Office of Vigilance, the same police force that was put in control of the Estermann affair. The officer, Raul Bonarelli, had his phone tapped by Italian magistrates and a taped conversation established that certain documents on the Orlandi case 'went to the Papal Secretariat of State'. The magistrates sent three requests to the Vatican asking that they be allowed to interrogate staff within the Secretariat and members of the Swiss Guards to establish what these documents contained. Every request was denied.

This is the Vatican way: whether it is papal murder, attempted papal murder, triple killings, abduction or child abuse or financial crime – cover it up. Lie, prevaricate, deny.

Emanuela was almost certainly subsequently murdered by her captors.

Thus the Vatican machine began its cover-up in spring 1998. Within days it was claimed that Estermann had been a spy for the East German secret service, the Stasi. It is certainly true, and not surprising, that many intelligence agencies ran spies within the Vatican, and still do. The major world powers have long coveted the extraordinary quality and quantity of information the Vatican acquires from its official diplomats and its global network of lay members and clergy. The allegation that Estermann was spying for the Communists in the heart of Christianity surfaced in Berlin in an anonymous letter to the newspaper the *Berliner Kurier*. It was full of detail of how Estermann had approached the East German trade mission in Berne in 1979 and had offered his services. This was prior to his May 1980 start with the Swiss Guard. A year later he was on duty in St Peter's Square when Agca shot Pope John Paul II. The Stasi story was a nine-day wonder and then faded away. It is occasionally resurrected but in truth it is a fabrication.

I talked to Peter Brinkmann, the German editor who broke the story. 'I was given a bum steer. There is nothing to the story,' he assured me. Through contacts within German intelligence I was able to establish this directly from the former Stasi section that handled such foreign agents. Not a single piece of evidence that backs the story up has come to light since the anonymous letter landed on Peter Brinkmann's desk in May 1998.

Judge Marrone placed the Vatican's judicial inquiry in the hands of the Promoter of Justice, Nicola Picardi, a strategy that showed Vatican insiders clearly that this would be a Vatican-controlled operation. If Picardi was functioning as the equivalent of an investigating prosecuting counsel where was the counsel for the defence? Who was representing Tornay's mother, Muguette Baudat? Long divorced from Cédric's father, she had, despite her own Protestant faith, honoured a promise she had made to her ex-husband and brought Cédric up in the Catholic faith.

Within a few hours of being told that 'Cédric has murdered two people and then killed himself' by her local parish priest in Valais, the chaplain of the Swiss Guard, Monsignor Alois Jehle, was attempting to persuade Muguette that she should not come to Rome for the funeral, or to view her son's body. He told her that the head had been ripped off, that the body was in a state of putrefaction, that the hotels were all full. The mother would not be dissuaded. When she arrived in Rome, she was immediately put under pressure by both Monsignor Jehle and the Secretary of State, Cardinal Sodano. It would be better, they urged Muguette, if after the funeral service Cédric's body was cremated. The shocked and grieving woman said she wanted time to consider. They told her they would draw up the necessary legal documents and get her to sign them on the following morning. By then she had enough presence of mind to reject the Vatican plan to destroy the most crucial piece of evidence.

When Muguette viewed the body of her son in the Guards chapel he had been dressed in his uniform and looked at peace with the world; only his chipped two front teeth indicated the trauma of his death. Later she was drawn to a very distressed young man sitting on a bench crying and shouting. When she attempted to comfort him, he told her that his name was Yvon Bertorello, that he was a priest, that he should have been there to stop the tragedy and that her son had been murdered. He told Muguette that he had the proof in his briefcase. Later she was told by Vatican officials that Bertorello was Cédric's 'spiritual father'. Whatever the truth, Bertorello vanished into the Vatican mists.

The following day after the funeral service she was told to stay in her hotel room and wait for a call from the Pope as he might find time to see her. She was still waiting for the call in the evening when she had to catch her return flight to Switzerland. Despite various letters written to the Pope and to Vatican officials, the papal call never came. When she had told the Vatican investigating magistrates of her conversation with her son's 'spiritual father' she was informed that they had no idea who Bertorello was.

From the outset of this affair, the Vatican, from the Pope downwards, took a very specific position towards Cédric Tornay and his mother and the rest of his family. The Vatican, without benefit of a full investigation or an inquest, determined that Tornay was guilty and by some convoluted thinking so by association were his mother and his sisters. The Estermanns were accorded the rare posthumous honour of a requiem Mass in St Peter's Basilica. Conducted by Secretary of State Cardinal Sodano and concelebrated by a further sixteen cardinals and thirty bishops, it lacked for nothing.

Tornay's funeral service was held privately in the small Santa Anna Church on the very edge of the City State. His fellow Swiss Guards were there in force with a poignant space left in their ranks where Cédric Tornay had stood. The ceremony was conducted by a Swiss bishop, Monsignor Amédée Grab, who also entertained no doubts as to the precise course of events in the Estermann apartment. 'God will forgive him for what he did because of the fragility of the human condition.'

The day after the Tornay letter to his mother had been leaked to the press by Navarro-Valls, it appeared in the Italian newspapers. Most of the Estermann eulogies contained reference to the fact of his bravery when the Pope had kept his appointment in St Peter's Square in May 1981. Many told the story of how Estermann, with no thought to his own life, leapt on the papal vehicle when the first shot was fired and shielded the body of John Paul II. It was a heroic and unimaginably brave act. It was also a fantasy. Estermann had been between 100 and 150 yards from the vehicle when the Pope was shot. The three men who held and comforted Karol Wojtyla were his long-term friend and secretary Stanislaw Dziwisz, Francesco Pasanisi, a senior Italian police officer, who had for a number of years acted as liaison between the Italian force and Vatican security, and the Pope's valet, Angelo Gugel. Estermann was nowhere near the jeep and, by the time he arrived, Agca was already disarmed and under arrest.

Estermann's fictitious role, which he eagerly accepted, was the creation of Navarro-Valls and other Opus Dei members. In yet another of the Vatican Village power struggles they were determined to place him at the head of the Swiss Guard. Though not a member, both Alois Estermann and his Venezuelan wife were 'close to Opus Dei', the classic phrase that is used to describe those who are members in all but name.

When Roland Buchs had been appointed Commander of the Swiss Guard it had taken only forty-eight hours to fill the vacancy. His successor Estermann was not appointed for seven months. It was hinted that the reason was because he was 'a commoner' and not from a titled Swiss family. That had not stopped Roland Buchs getting instant promotion. Within the Vatican Village they give two reasons for the delay: first, a long sustained power struggle between Opus Dei and the Vatican Masons and second, deep concerns over Estermann's allegedly very active homosexual life. Cédric Tornay had told his mother many months earlier that he was investigating links between Opus Dei and the Swiss Guard.

The allegations about the triple deaths both at the time and since are seemingly endless. One would have hoped that the judicial enquiry that had been set up within twenty-four hours of the deaths would have addressed each and every one of these allegations. When the secret internal investigation published its conclusions some ten months after the event, the Vatican's report, at least the scant fifteen pages that it deigned to make public, very typically left many questions unanswered. During the ten months of investigation the Promoter of Justice Nicola Picardi and a variety of experts created forensic reports, accumulated five police reports and interviewed nearly forty witnesses including a detailed interrogation of Yvon Bertorello, Tornay's spiritual father. All this was reduced to fifteen pages, which essentially confirmed the story put out by the Vatican Press Officer less than fifteen minutes after the three deaths.

The report itself was riddled with highly speculative conclusions. Witnesses said that they had seen four wine glasses on the table immediately after the neighbour Anna-Lina arrived, which suggested that a fourth person had been present in the room at the time of the deaths or was expected to arrive. The 'Promoter of Justice' discounted the possibility that there may have been four glasses on the basis that they were not there when the investigation got underway, ignoring the possibility that they may have been deliberately moved. Picardi attempted to eliminate the presence of the fourth person by saying 'the small size [of the apartment] would not have permitted the presence of a fourth person and, above all, no trace of a scuffle had been found and everything had been in order.' That ignored the fact that a number of prelates and investigators had fitted in comfortably when they had searched the room. The report seems less like a factual account based on forensic evidence and more and more a descent into supposition designed to support a previous conclusion. It would not stand up in an Italian, English or American court for five minutes.

Muguette Baudat has asked the Vatican on numerous occasions to make available to her the entire report created by Picardi along with all other evidence that the Vatican holds on this affair, particularly the report on the secret post-mortem. They have consistently refused, and the mother who buried her son has no idea why he really died. The ubiquitous Navarro-Valls said, 'We understand and respect her pain, but the truth is the truth and it has to be accepted.'

Writing a few weeks after the triple deaths in the Italian magazine *L'Espresso*, Sandro Magister, a seasoned Vatican-watcher, expressed a caustic view of Navarro-Valls's account. He was astonished, he said, that the Vatican's Press Officer's story of the murders was 'for once, close to being believed. Which for him is a rarity.' Muguette Baudat, still convinced that the 'truth has yet to be established', retained top lawyers Jacques Vergès and Luc Brossollet who in January 2005 stated that they would seek a murder inquiry under the Swiss judicial system. Over a year later, Muguette was still seeking 'the truth'.

Navarro-Valls has the power of life and death over the livelihoods of all Vatican-accredited journalists, and he does not hesitate to abuse it. When a journalist has his/her accreditation withdrawn by this man he or she can no longer function effectively for his or her employer. This happened to Domenico Del Rio of *La Repubblica* when he was stopped by Navarro-Valls from accompanying the Pope on a papal flight to Latin America. His sin was to interview and record theologians and historians who had expressed critical opinions on Cardinal Ratzinger's comments calling for a return of the values of the restoration. He was replaced on the flight by an Opus Dei journalist, Alberto Michelini.

The Italian Vaticanologist, Sandro Magister, has recounted that in September 1988 during the Pope's African tour, while the Pope and a number of the press were on a trip outside Harare, Navarro-Valls held court with the remaining members of the press at the poolside of the Sheraton Hotel. Perhaps on that day the Spaniard had a little too much sun. He was spectacularly indiscreet as he talked of Vatican initiatives in Mozambique, Angola and South Africa. The following day, newspapers around the world carried reports of what had been a highly secret Vatican agenda. Secretary of State Casaroli was furious, and suddenly the Vatican Village had come to the African continent. Recriminations, charges and counter-charges flew around like unguided missiles. The reporters who had accompanied the Pope had missed a major story; so they too were angry. In the midst of the hysteria Navarro-Valls suddenly materialised. Taken to task both by the Secretary of State and a large number of reporters, he flatly denied that he had talked about any of the subjects and the claims that he was the definitive source were all 'without any foundation. They are fantasies.' When a tape recording was played to him he denied it was him. When it was pointed out that part of his briefing had been replayed on Italian radio, he continued to deny he had ever talked to anyone by the pool.

When this débâcle was written up by Tullio Meli, the *Giornale* Vatican representative, Navarro-Valls banned him from the next papal flight. In 1989 during a trip to Bratislava the Pope worked hard to convey his thoughts on Christian Europe and his initiative to hold a Pan-European Synod. Curiously, the following day's international coverage of the Papal tour ignored the Papal initiative and focused on the scoop that Navarro had given them, that the Pope's next trip would be to meet Fidel Castro in Havana. The reality was that the Pope did not arrive in Havana until nine years later.

In September 1996 while the Pope was visiting Hungary, Navarro-Valls wiped out all mention of the Papal tour by choosing to reveal something he had denied for many years:

the Pope was suffering from Parkinson's disease. Excited with all the attention he was getting, Navarro-Valls told the media that the Pope was also suffering from a mysterious unidentified virus of the intestine. Four days later the Pope's doctor Renato Buzzonetti, who regards Navarro-Valls as his personal cross, dismissed the story of the mysterious virus. 'It does not exist outside the fevered mind of its inventor.' The Pope was suffering from appendicitis.

In many Third World villages one can still find the story-teller, a man who at the sight of a listening audience can spin fantasy and weave a myth. To find such a man in the Vatican Village is entirely to be expected. By early 2005 the Vatican Village appeared to be functioning in a curious state of suspended animation. While it was true that changes continued to occur, they were minimal. Transfers and promotions very largely occurred on the outer edges of the chessboard. The main players, the key pieces, appeared to be frozen in time and place. The papacy of Pope John Paul II had to all intents and purposes ended several years before. Cardinal Ratzinger continued to publish pro-nouncements on Catholic dogma; no matter how contro-versial or divisive they were, the faithful were reassured that they had all been approved by the Holy Father.

In fact, papal ghostwriters have been the practice for many years. As the late Pope himself observed: 'Since I became Pope, it's been much easier because other people write for me.' A few essential passages, a short outline and Wojtyla would hand the task to others. The missionary Piero Gheddo wrote *Redemptoris Missio* in 1990, the theologian Bishop Carlo Caffarra *Veritas Splendor* in 1993 and fellow theologian Bishop Rino Fisichella obliged with *Fides et Ratio* in 1998. All three encyclicals were published as infallible documents in the Pope's name.

Opus Dei member Cardinal Julian Herranz Casado con-tinued to arrange very discreet meetings either in the city or slightly further afield at a secluded villa in Grottarossa. Those who attended were invariably cardinals 'of a certain age', men still eligible to vote in conclave. The others of the cabal continued to fulfil their respective roles but above all of them was the man who was Pope in all but name: Archbishop Stanislaw Dziwisz. 'It is the Holy Father's wish,' was the constant refrain that was heard from the son who had become the father. In October 2003 when Cardinal Ratzinger talked publicly of how seriously ill the Pope was, the Cardinal, whom Karol Wojtyla had described in a rare tribute as 'a trusted friend', was reduced to tears by the verbal tongue-lashing he received from Dziwisz. An extraordinary example of the real power of the 'other Pope', the servant who had become the master.

On the evening of 2 April 2005, the earthly life of Pope John Paul II came to an end. Before the body of the man from 'a far country' was laid in its final resting place, the lobbying, the speculation, the jostling for position was in full flow.

Cardinal Ratzinger's ascent to the papal throne was not quite the serene progress that news media reports have described but with Pope Benedict XVI residing within the papal apartments, it would seem on the surface little has changed within the Vatican village. The Polish mafia have largely been replaced by a German entourage. Monsignor Georg Gänswein from the Black Forest has replaced the 'other Pope' who has returned to Poland as Archbishop of Cracow. Dziwisz was promoted to cardinal in March 2006, thus making him a candidate for the next papacy. In the village the jostling is, if anything, more frenetic. Delation – the practice of secretly denouncing a superior or a rival – is on the increase. Every village in the world has the potential to produce the malicious letter writer. Few could match the village across the Tiber.

The latest round of the endless battle for increased power among the various Vatican security forces commenced soon after Benedict's election. The Swiss Guard are seeking to establish themselves as 'the primary force'. The Vatican police, some twenty men larger, insist they are the Italian police force *numero uno*, who are frequently obliged to deal with both parties' dream of taking over complete control of Vatican security. Other turf wars involve a range of senior posts where retirement of the incumbent is well overdue. Secretary of State Cardinal Sodano heads an eminent group of leading Vatican officials who are already past the retirement age of seventy-five years. The Secretary of State is but one example. Any Vatican-watcher expecting a greater degree of veracity as a result of that particular departure should not hold their breath.

Epilogue

A T THE END of January 2005 the Pope contracted a fever; his public audiences were suspended for a day or two because of flu-like symptoms. The day or two were destined to grow, for on the night of Tuesday, 1 February, Karol Wojtyla was rushed to the Gemelli Hospital in Rome. So rapid was his departure that the Prefect of the Pontifical Household was not informed of the decision to call an ambulance until the Pope was already absent. Predictably, Vatican spokesman Navarro-Valls declared on Wednesday morning that there was 'no cause for alarm'.

Influenza is often referred to as 'the friend of the elderly' for its ability to bring life to its final conclusion. For a man approaching his eighty-fifth birthday who, for at least fifteen years, had suffered from Parkinson's disease, the odds against surviving such a plebeian illness were alarmingly high. Over that passage of time, his breathing had grown more laboured, his throat and chest had become increasingly constricted, his stooped posture inevitably constricted his diaphragm, preventing the muscles from functioning normally. Any respiratory infection that attacked such a frail body could prove fatal.

The world's news media rushed to Rome. Arrangements long-made at hotels and vantage points throughout the city

were activated. Simultaneously, the media speculation began. Was this the final chapter? If he did survive, should he
resign? If he died who would follow? Who were the leading
papabile? The various symptoms of Parkinson's were, with
one exception, publicly discussed at great length. The exception was the levels of dementia that occur because of the
ever higher dosages of specific drugs that are needed for
more advanced symptoms.

After nine days in the Gemelli Hospital the Pope's
condition had improved dramatically and he returned to
the Vatican. The media focus then shifted to a debate on
whether or not Wojtyla should resign and vacate the papal
throne. The debate quickened when Secretary of State
Cardinal Sodano responded to questions about papal
resignation with, 'That is a matter that we should leave
to the Pope's conscience.' Apart from Karol Wojtyla's own
moral sense, to assist him he had around him the men who
for some time had been in control of the Roman Catholic
Church, an inner circle which had undergone some
changes and shifts of power since 2003: Cardinals Ratzinger, Re, Ruini, and Sodano. There was also the man
who was the greatest power behind the throne: Papal
Secretary and gatekeeper of all access to the Pope, Archbishop Stanislaw Dziwisz who for some time had been
leading the fight against the pressure for the Pope to
resign.

During the ensuing days various Vatican statements
assured the public that the Pope had fully recovered. The
reality, as was usually the case with Vatican statements, was
somewhat different. The infection was still active and the
Pope's breathing very laboured. The Vatican press spokesman's confident image of a rapidly recovering Wojtyla was
demolished when on 2 February he was again rapidly
returned to the Gemelli Hospital and within the hour a
tracheotomy was performed. A tube was inserted into his

throat to assist his breathing. A few days later on Sunday the Pope, now mute and wan, was wheeled to a window of the hospital shortly after the Angelus blessing which for the first time in over twenty-six years had been conducted without the Pope. Giant screens in the Square showed a younger, vigorous Karol Wojtyla.

On 8 March it was announced that the Pope would not preside over any of the major liturgical celebrations of Holy Week and Easter. As the month progressed and Karol Wojtyla, a man clearly near death, returned again to his Vatican home, I was frequently reminded of a particular conversation with a Vatican resident. It was shortly after Karol Wojtyla's visit to Slovakia in September 2003. I had found the spectacle of the suffering Pope deeply disturbing and expressed the view that the trip should never have been made and should certainly have been abandoned.

'The show has continued,' my informant told me, 'and will do so because the Holy Father wishes it to continue. The actor within the Holy Father is dying hard. He refuses to walk off stage. He is a man terminally drugged on the adulation of the audience.'

Now throughout the month of March much of the world was watching what more than one commentator called 'his greatest performance'. It is not true that everyone fights for life, that none seek death. Some do indeed go gently, but Pope John Paul II raged against the final darkness in a manner reminiscent of the two wartime uprisings in Warsaw when men, women and children resisted the occupying enemy for week after week.

Karol Wojtyla's personal struggle reached its apogee on Easter Sunday when he struggled in great distress and anguish to utter a blessing to the crowd gathered below his window in St Peter's Square. He slapped his forehead in vexation but could not utter a single syllable. The 'great communicator' had been permanently silenced.

A few days later during the afternoon of Saturday 2 April Karol Wojtyla murmured, 'Let me go to the house of the Father.' He lapsed into coma and died six hours later at 9.37 p.m.

The very public manner of his approach to that death inspired some and appalled others. Many Catholics previously opposed to euthanasia began to reconsider their position. Commentators informed their readers that the Pope had wanted the 'faithful to draw lessons from his agony'. One thing is certain: it was markedly different from the grim, solitary death of his abandoned predecessor, Albino Luciani.

The hyperbole that followed Pope John Paul II's death was boundless. 'The greatest Pole of all time.' 'A colossus.' 'A solitary Atlas, holding up the Church and the world.' 'A golden beacon for gilded youth.' With the pilgrims in St Peter's Square chanting, 'Make him a saint! Make him a saint now!' came news of yet more miracles attributed to the power of Karol Wojtyla: the chapel at Kalwaria 'saved from a fire by an icon blessed by the Holy Father'; a defunct television set in the Ukraine suddenly 'whirring into life just as the Pope arrived in the country. It continued for his entire stay then died again.' As for his legacy, in death much was claimed for him just as it had been in life. Many of those claims fly in the face of the factual evidence contained within this book.

The end of his papacy on 2 April has been seen as the end of an era. In fact, the papacy of John Paul II had already ended for many well before that date. Exactly when depends on where one looks and what part of the Wojtyla legacy one considers.

In Austria, not only the papacy but their formal links with the Catholic Church ended for hundreds of thousands during the abuse scandal involving Cardinal Groer in 1995. For a further 50,000 Austrians, it ended when they left the Church in 2004 after the paedophile scandals in the St Pölten diocese that forced the resignation of Bishop Krenn. For many other Austrians the Wojtyla papacy had ended even earlier, with the initial appointment by the Pope of Groer in 1986 and Krenn in 1987, and George Eder as Archbishop of Salzburg in 1989. All three appointments were instances of Wojtyla's ignoring strong local resistance and insisting on appointing archconservatives. Eder, for example, blamed sex education for promoting 'a Communist take-over of our society', and considered AIDS 'a form of divine punishment'. Austria was by no means unique in having hard-line conservatives forced upon her. It was the order of the day for papal envoys who were, in the words of one Vatican source, 'basically under concealed orders to nominate conservatives. They were pushing them into Brazil, France, Germany, the US, even in the small appointments.'

The papacy of Pope John Paul II ended for many in Latin America during the early 1980s when it became obvious that Karol Wojtyla approved of the counter-insurgency tactics of the Reagan administration. Over one quarter of a million people died in just two of the countries – Guatemala and El Salvador – where the US-backed death squads operated. The 'El Salvador Option' was reactivated in 2005 and by early February was being seriously considered by the Pentagon for Iraq. The proposed target this time were the Sunni population, or that part of it that allegedly supported the insurgents.

In Chile, the papacy of Wojtyla ended for a significant section of the population in 1987 when he became only the second head of state, the other being the president of

Uruguay, to set foot in the country since General Pinochet had murdered his way to the presidency. Wojtyla's presence ensured very favourable media coverage of the Pinochet regime, not least because the Pope studiously avoided any public criticism of the military junta, and made only a passing reference to those subjected to torture and to those who had disappeared. An open-air mass was violently disrupted by security forces when, complete with tanks and armoured cars and water cannon, they attacked a minority of some 500 students demonstrating against Pinochet, causing the Pope, the Vatican retinue and the Chilean hierarchy to choke with the tear gas. Cardinal Fresno, Wojtyla's appointee in Santiago, declared that he considered the police the principal victims. He condemned 'this incredible assault on the police, Papal guards, journalists, priests and the faithful'. It would be subsequently established that during the Pinochet era over 35,000 citizens were tortured, the overwhelming majority of the 3,400 women detained had been victims of sexual violence, and between 5,000 and 10,000 Chileans had been murdered.

On this 1987 Latin American trip, Karol Wojtyla had astonished the press on the plane flying to Chile when he compared the situation in Chile favourably with the Communism of his motherland. 'In Chile, there is a system that at the present time is dictatorial but the system is by its very definition transitory.' When it was suggested that transition was already under way in Poland, the Pope disagreed. 'There are no grounds for hope on that score. In Poland, the struggle is much more difficult, much more demanding.' For a man that many claim created Solidarity, and then virtually single-handedly destroyed European Communism, his observations show a depressing lack of both faith and vision. In Poland, change was most certainly occurring: in just two more years, there would be free elections and a few months later, the Berlin Wall would come down.

In Argentina, the reign of Wojtyla ended for many of the faithful well before his April 1987 visit. Many by then were disenchanted with a man who had remained silent for nearly a decade on the tortures and murders perpetrated by the generals. The widespread complicity of the Catholic hierarchy with the military junta, without a word of criticism from the Holy Father, further alienated Argentinians. Then in 1987 with the country finally returned to democracy, the Pope chose that moment to lecture the newly elected Raul Alfonsin and the population at large on the importance of human rights.

Wojtyla compounded what many had seen as an ill-defined and offensive speech by subsequently refusing to meet the mothers of May Square, women whose relatives had vanished without trace, courtesy of the junta. He then attacked, in typical Wojtyla style, a proposed law on divorce. Throughout his entire reign he never discovered an acceptable response to democracy when the democracy in question had proposed or had enacted legislation of which he disapproved.

For Mexico, the end of the Wojtyla reign was already under way at the time of the Pope's second trip to the country in 1990. The 'radical and anti-religious movement' that Secretary of State Casaroli had predicted in secret talks with the Reagan delegation in 1987 was evident. There was within the country a growing awareness of the role of the Catholic Church in the demise of the Mexican Indian. Before the visit, 300 bishops in Mexico City had signed an open letter calling on the Church to beg for pardon for its 'complicity in the colonisation and enslavement of the native peoples'. Secular groups were now heard in the land voicing similar sentiments.

Karol Wojtyla, a man seen by many of his admirers as an individual possessing a towering intellect, demonstrated on occasion extraordinary ignorance. Preparing for a mid-

1985 trip to Africa, which included a visit to Cameroon, he asked a member of the Curia to write a speech. During the Papal briefing, the Monsignor objected, 'Your Holiness, you idealise too much. The slave trade began from there.' The Pope was stunned. Having subsequently studied the factual history, Wojtyla then wrote and delivered a powerful plea, asking the people of Cameroon for forgiveness.

For many, not only in Cameroon but throughout Africa, the late Pope's vehement opposition to the use of condoms in the fight against the spread of the HIV/AIDS virus not only ensured in the hearts and minds of many a premature end of the Wojtyla papacy, it also ensured the premature death for an unquantifiable number of Africans. In Kenya, Cardinal Maurice Otunga staged public condom-burning ceremonies. In Nairobi Archbishop Raphael Ndingi Mwana a'Nzeki warned the population that condoms actually gave those who used them AIDS, a view also held by leading Vatican spokesmen.

The Vatican's failure, from Pope John Paul II down, to acknowledge the role of the Rwandan Roman Catholic hierarchy in the country's genocide is yet another part of the Wojtyla legacy: nearly one million slaughtered and not a single proponent of liberation theology in sight.

The Pope's hostility towards liberation theology did not merely spring from his fear of Communism. It also emanated from his ignorance of the history of the American Indians. When during the 1980s, he read for the first time the writings of Bartolome de las Casas, the sixteenth-century Spanish missionary and historian, he admitted to being shaken. But in 1990 he still clung to a defence of the Church's historical role. During his speeches in Mexico, he admitted past errors, but always countered these with specific examples of the good performed by religious figures. In Vera Cruz, speaking of Mexico's history, he declared that '. . . . conquest and evangelisation occupy a

decisive place, brilliant when taken together, yet not without shades of grey'.

To describe the enslavement of an entire nation in such
a manner caused a deep and lasting anger within Mexico.
By the time of his next trip to the country in 1993, there
were frequent media attacks on the Catholic Church's
historical role in Mexico. It was widely believed that
the Pope had come on a pilgrimage of expiation towards
the Indians. He did not fulfil that expectation; he again
only admitted mistakes in the past. But even when confronted with overwhelming evidence, he continually attempted to distance the Church from the actions of the
colonising Spanish. His defence of the Church was at all
times loud and clamorous. There was no mention of the
forced conversions, the torture of the Indians, the destruction of ancient books of Mayan history, the seizure of land
by the Church, the brutal crushing of every Indian uprising under the blessing of the cross. By 1993 the papacy of
Pope John Paul II was, for the majority of Mexicans, a
thing of the past.

Just how profoundly Latin America has rejected the
Wojtyla message can be gauged by the ballot box. The late
Pope regularly condemned liberation theology and left-
wing politics. He aligned the Church alongside President
Reagan's foreign policies for the region. As of mid-2006 the
White House found itself with six left-wing anti-US leaders
in its own backyard.

In the Netherlands, it was the Wojtyla suppression of the
liberal majority of bishops that was for many of the faithful
the defining moment. Their treatment by the Pope and
senior members of the Curia during a two-week period
in 1980, details of which are recorded in an earlier chapter,
was akin to something out of the sixteenth century. When
details eventually leaked out, there was outrage among the
Catholic faithful in Holland. It was anger that five years

later, when the Pope visited, was still very much on display. For the Dutch, the Wojtyla papacy finished very early. Holland's experience was not unique. A great many episcopates that had embraced the spirit of Vatican Council II's reforms felt the papal lash. Throughout much of Europe, the United States and Latin America, papal discussion was replaced with papal directive.

In Spain, three million have left the Catholic Church in the past four years. After the election of the Socialist government in March 2004, the exodus has been accelerating. A government elected by the majority on a mandate that included relaxation of the abortion and divorce laws produced a furious response from Wojtyla and those around him within the Vatican. Spanish government plans which included altering the status of Catholic education from compulsory to optional and a draft bill to allow homosexual marriages put both the Vatican and the Spanish Church on a war footing. Cardinal Antonio Maria Rouco proclaimed from the pulpit that there is 'sinning on a large scale taking place in Madrid'. He had no doubt whom to blame for what he clearly saw as a recent phenomenon: 'Major powerful currents of thinking and influential institutions of economic and cultural and political power' – Church-speak for 'the Spanish government'.

Four hundred and seventy-one victims of the Spanish Civil War of 1936–1939 have been beatified as martyrs; not one of them came from the thousands upon thousands of Republicans slaughtered by Franco's fascists and the Third Reich. Only supporters of the late General Franco have been put forward by the Spanish Church for beatification. In this, as in much else in his life, Karol Wojtyla showed consistency. As a young man in Cracow he was an enthusiastic supporter of Spanish fascism.

For many years the recurring mantra of the Church with regard to its own growth had been to refer to South

America and Africa as the future of the Church – these regions where they could confidently predict huge growth in the numbers of the faithful. In 1985 the Church claimed Latin America contained 338 million Roman Catholics. By late 2004 the mantra was being uttered more in hope than certainty. In Brazil, the census for 2000 had revealed a twenty per cent fall in the number of Catholics during the preceding forty years. The Vatican blamed the dramatic decrease on the aggressive advance of evangelical sects, religious indifference, and the lack of effective and firm pastoral outreach. Only twenty-five per cent regularly attend mass and fifty per cent attend only on special occasions. It is a similar story throughout the continent. The Pope blamed 'the nefarious action of sects'. During his meeting with the bishops, he listed the social problems that the Church must face in the Western hemisphere. These included drug abuse, family breakdown, guerrilla warfare, international terrorism, migration and the gap between rich and poor. The current condition of the Church itself was not on the list.

Again, in late 2004, Cardinal Ratzinger, during a sweeping critique of European secularism, said: 'A society in which God is completely absent self-destructs.' Neither the Pope nor Ratzinger appeared able to comprehend the Catholic Church's role in the creation of the current secular society. The Pontifical Council for the Family lays the blame at the doorstep of the European lawmakers, who have 'been guilty of undermining the family'. They blame Catholic theologians who have given intellectual support to this sort of legislation. No one acknowledges clerical sexual abuse as a key factor. No one admits that continuous financial corruption during much of Wojtyla's papacy has played its part in the mass exodus from the Church. In May 2000, Cardinal Biffi, considered by some at the time as a leading contender to succeed Pope John Paul II, declared that all Catholics should follow Christ's example of poverty by donating all of their wealth to the Church, which would in turn be exceedingly rich. 'Christ may have been a carpenter with a frugal lifestyle, who attacked moneychangers in the temple, but that was no reason for the Church to renounce wealth,' said the Cardinal.

It is precisely this mentality that has driven Vatican Incorporated for decades. The pursuit of wealth by the Church brought about its involvement with Sindona and Calvi. Just as a decade later it was responsible for the Vatican Bank's involvement in 'the mother of all bribes'. It has also brought about the one-billion-dollar claim against the Vatican by US insurance commissioners that is currently working its way through US courts. It has also brought about the multi-million-dollar claim against the Vatican on behalf of former Yugoslavian citizens that is also being processed through US courts.

A year after Cardinal Biffi's plea for an even wealthier Church, the Vatican announced its first budget deficit for eight years. Cardinal Sergio Sebastini, President of the Vatican's Prefecture of Economic Affairs, blamed lower revenues from securities and, above all, fluctuations in the exchange-rate. No mention was made of the devastating effect that the continuing clerical sexual abuse scandals was having on the finances of many individual dioceses around the world. But then neither was any mention made of billions of dollars that poured into the Catholic Church's coffers, courtesy of the taxpayers in Italy, Germany, Spain and other countries.

One of the continuing features of the Church during the reign of John Paul II was an ability to apologise for its errors, providing that the error in question had been perpetrated hundreds of years ago, and a complete failure to acknowledge more recent sins. Wojtyla's predecessor, John Paul I, observed during his tragically brief reign, 'I have noticed two things that appear to be in very short supply in the Vatican; honesty and a good cup of coffee.' Nothing has changed in those areas over the ensuing years.

The obituaries for Pope John Paul II abound with myths, fantasies and disinformation. Just as Wojtyla's early years do not, in fact, contain a slave labour camp, heroic acts in the Cracow ghetto and a brave stand against the Third Reich, the postwar years do not, in fact, reveal a man who continually confronted the Communists but a man who was thought of so highly by the regime that they were instrumental in setting him on the path to St Peter's throne.

The files that the Polish secret police kept on Wojtyla confirm that this was a man constantly seeking quietude. The legacy that had already been claimed for this Pope – even before his burial – that of 'John Paul the Great', flies in the face of the realities. The Wojtyla Papacy has been crammed with further myths, which tell us far more about those guilty of such extravagant claims than they do of the man himself. He never claimed to have sustained Solidarity during its early months, nor did he ever claim to have single-handedly brought about the collapse of European Communism. On the contrary, he is on record on a number of occasions as believing that it was indestructible.

What is true is that Mikhail Gorbachev, the man who did play the defining role, is on record as saying,

'Everything that happened in Eastern Europe in these last few years would have been impossible without the presence of this Pope, and without the important role, including the political role, he played on the world stage.'

Certainly, the Pope's contribution was important, as was Ronald Reagan's and to a lesser extent, Margaret

Thatcher's, but the crucial role was played by Gorbachev as an earlier chapter demonstrates. Commenting on the claims of many writers including his chosen biographer, George Weigel, that the Pope was largely responsible for the fall of Communism, Karol Wojtyla described such assertions as 'ridiculous'. Karol Wojtyla had quite different aspirations.

The actual agenda of this Pope had been a grand design, not merely for Europe, but the entire world. A pilgrim determined to bring a great spiritual reawakening, Wojtyla believed that he could turn back the idea of materialism that he saw engulfing country after country. He aspired to become a global evangelist, taking the gospel to the ends of the earth, turning the cultural clock back to an earlier time by demonstrating the supremacy of Roman Catholicism not only over Communism, but also capitalism. If he had succeeded, he would indeed have deserved the appellation 'John Paul the Great'. His personal legacy contains, at least in part, the reasons for his failure.

Wojtyla, a man who prided himself on speaking many languages, listened in none of them. But then no Pope in 2,000 years has been listened to by more and heeded by fewer. As the late Vaticanologist, Peter Hebblethwaite, remarked during the early years of this reign, 'They like the singer, not the song.' The line of theologians, priests and nuns that dared to hold views and opinions contrary to Wojtyla, only to find that they had been silenced, is a long one. The kind of theologians that Pope John Paul II admired were men such as the Jesuit theologian, Avery Dulles, who became the first US theologian to be made a cardinal. A year earlier, Dulles is on record as declaring

'the laity should not be consulted on matters of doctrine, because in the modern secular world it is hard to determine who are the truly faithful and mature

Catholics deserving of consultation. . . . faith is the acceptance on the basis of authority not reason, and furthermore proposing reasons may stimulate contrary reasons leading to fruitless debate.'

Cardinal Dulles epitomises Wojtyla's legacy of conservative Catholics, who have never accepted the central messages of Vatican Council II; men who now have their hands on the levers of power within the Church, courtesy of Wojtyla; men who wholeheartedly endorse the sentiments contained in the observation the late Pope made to *Time* magazine writer, Wilton Wynn: 'It is a mistake to apply American democratic procedures to the faith and the truth. You cannot take a vote on the truth. You must not confuse the *Sensus Fidei* (sense of faith) with consensus.'

Wojtyla was much given to talking of truth. When another reporter, Marco Politi, asked on the flight to Cuba what he would say to Fidel Castro the Pope replied, 'I shall ask him what his truth is.' For Wojtyla the question was rhetorical. For the man from Poland there was only one truth, not the word of God but the words of Wojtyla. It was only with the greatest difficulty that Cardinal Ratzinger was able to persuade the Pope from declaring *Humanae Vitae* an infallible document. The fact that Pope Paul VI had shrunk from taking that very step when banning artificial contraception did not deter Wojtyla. He knew, just as he had always known, where 'the truth' lay on birth control or abortion or homosexuality, the ordination of women or one hundred other issues that have divided so many. In 1995, Ratzinger confirmed that Karol Wojtyla's Apostolic Letter *On reserving priestly ministry to men alone* was an infallible papal statement, the first time in nearly forty years that infallibility had been claimed for a papal utterance.

The Swiss theologian Hans Küng, one of the first to be silenced by the Wojtyla papacy, has observed: 'After the fall

of Soviet Communism, the Roman Catholic Church represents the only dictatorial system in the western world today
. . . one which confers a monopoly of power to one man.'
On another occasion Küng, having described the Wojtyla
papacy as 'a new phase of the Inquisition', observed, 'The
present Pope suppresses problems instead of solving them.'
Even the gentle and charming world-renowned US commentator on the Vatican, Redemptorist Father Francis X.
Murphy, was moved to describe Pope John Paul II as 'very
dictatorial'.

It was a trait that despite the charm and the charisma was
never far from the surface when the former actor was 'on
stage'. Perhaps the majority of the vast throngs that gathered to see and hear him around the world were a great deal
more 'mature' than the conservative theologians of this
world realised. Most certainly they have been able to
distinguish between the man and his message – a message
that all too frequently was delivered devoid of compassion
or humanity. The man they embraced: the message, they
have rejected. The cult of personality that Pope John Paul II
so revelled in focused very precisely on the man, at great
cost to the faith. The more powerful the cult became, the
more it successfully distracted from the fact that Karol
Wojtyla functioned like a mid-nineteenth-century Pope.
No partnership with his fellow bishops. No collegiality.
No dialogue or discussion, merely an unquestioned primacy
that inevitably atrophied.

The rejections took many forms. In January 1991, with
Ronald Reagan two years gone from the White House,
there was not even an illusion of the mythical alliance with
the Vatican. For President George Bush, the papacy was
over. In the build-up to the first Gulf War the President
ignored both the private and public appeals from the Pope
that war should be avoided, and that there should be peace
talks to negotiate Iraq's withdrawal from Kuwait.

When a groundbreaking peace conference in Madrid, which would see the first ever face-to-face negotiations between Israel and the Palestinians, was proposed, Israel vetoed the presence of the Vatican delegation. That the Holy See has vital interests in the area counted for nothing, it seemed, to the Israeli government who gave as the reason for the veto the fact that diplomatic relations did not exist between the two countries. Israel did not have diplomatic relations with a number of the Arab nations attending but that apparently did not matter. This was a direct insult to a pope, who, notwithstanding a string of *faux pas*, had worked so hard for reconciliation with the Jewish faith. In October 1991 the conference duly took place without Roman Catholic representation.

The unkindest cut of all occurred in June 1991. It was the fourth trip back to his homeland and the first since the free elections. Lech Walesa had been elected President in December 1990. The country was enjoying its first taste of real democracy. The Pope not only distrusted democracy, but his words and actions over the past three decades confirmed he actively disliked democracy as a form of government. His failure to reconcile a life that was lived under and shaped by a range of totalitarian influences with democracy offers at least part of the explanation for his ultimate failure as a global evangelist. That failure was on full public display during his eight-day visit in 1991. Exactly twelve years earlier, the Pope had come to Poland, where he was acclaimed by millions throughout the journey. The people knew that with his immense moral authority, this Pope – their Pope – had given the country a precious gift, the right to hope, the right to put their collective fears to one side. In the years ahead, the fears would return, but the hope was for many inextinguishable. Wojtyla did not create Solidarity. Its roots lay in the past, in places and dates well remembered: Poznan 1956 through to Gdansk in 1980. Neither did the Pope initially offer the

Solidarity movement any support until he was reassured in the autumn of 1980 that 'yes, it will survive'.

But in 1980 from the first day in the Gdansk shipyard, Wojtyla's moral authority was symbolically in evidence. A large photo of the Pope guarded the gates, and in the dangerous months and years that lay ahead, there was always the knowledge among the people that 'our man in Rome' was one of them, a Pole. Now in 1991 the struggle had come of age: the little electrician was President. Veteran Solidarity advisor, Tadeusz Mazowiecki, had been until the previous year Poland's first non-Communist Prime Minister. An untidy, volatile democracy with many flaws had Poland in its thrall. The country was in tumult, and at the centre, most ironically, was the issue of abortion.

As previously recorded, it was the abortion issue, above all other controversies, that exercised Karol Wojtyla. The Polish Church had already discovered that it could no longer demand the unquestioning obedience in the face of 'the common enemy of Communism', that had been the status quo since the early postwar years. The old order had changed, and with that had gone the assumptions of religious allegiance. Cardinal Glemp and his colleagues had demanded that the abortion laws introduced by the Communist regime during the 1950s, laws that had enabled the majority of women, if they so wished, to procure a legal abortion, should be repealed and replaced with a complete ban. This had provoked widespread uproar in the country. Wojtyla, during the months prior to his fourth trip home, had been kept fully informed of the debate.

For the trip to his homeland, the Pope had chosen as the theme of his visit the Ten Commandments. In the pouring rain at the Kielce Flying Club in Poland he addressed a crowd of some 200,000. Addressed is not what he actually did. He harangued them.

'There has to be a change in the way you treat a newly conceived child. While it may come unexpectedly, it is never an intruder, never an aggressor . . . You must not confuse freedom with immorality.'

Lashed by the wind and the rain, he looked for all the world like an Old Testament prophet.

'I say this because this land is my mother; this land is the mother of my brother and sisters. This land is my home and for that reason, I allow myself to speak this way.'

Constantly emphasising his words with a clenched fist, he shouted against the wind,

'All of you must understand that the way you deal with these questions is thoughtless. These things cannot but cause me pain, and they ought to pain you too. It is easier to tear down than to build up. Destruction has been going on for too long. Now, we need to rebuild. You cannot just heedlessly destroy everything.'

The spectacle of the Pope losing his temper did not impress his audience. Before his return, many within the country had been equally unimpressed with the increasing arrogance of the Polish Church towards the laity. From the hierarchy down to the local priest, many were giving the impression that they would fill the vacuum left by the Communists. The people had other ideas.

Wojtyla's attacks on this tour were not confined to the abortion debate. He attacked their adultery, their preoccupation with materialism. He blamed the media; he blamed Western Europe. If he grew angry, so did those who heard him speak or read what he said. The women of Poland were particularly incensed; they believed that they, not the Church, should choose how many children they should have. He even managed to deeply offend the small community of Jews who had not been driven out of Poland by the unceasing anti-Semitism. He achieved this by equating the Holocaust with the 'great cemeteries of the unborn, cemeteries of the defenceless, whose faces even their own mothers never knew'.

The laws on abortion after constant pressure by the Polish Catholic Church hierarchy were changed. Now it is very difficult to obtain a legal abortion. One of Poland's leading gynaecologists explained to me how the stricter regulations have affected Polish women. 'The wealthy go abroad and obtain abortions. The poor have babies.'

During 2003 and the following year, the Pope staked much on winning the argument he was having with the European Community. At every opportunity, he demanded that the constitutional treaty pay full acknowledgment to its Christian heritage. If Cardinal Casaroli had still been at the helm in the Secretariat of State, a number of Vatican insiders felt the demands would not have reached such a shrill level, that there might have been rather more 'quiet diplomacy'. The rejection caused further damage to the image of the Catholic Church. It powerfully underlined how impotent Wojtyla's papacy had become.

In mid-2003 when the Vatican lobbying of the European Union had grown frenetic, the Pope issued a new Apostolic Exhortation. The document summarises the work of the Synod of Bishops for Europe, which had concluded its meetings in Rome in October 1999. The Pope seized the chance yet again to condemn Europe. To attack the continent that you were simultaneously lobbying on a crucial issue demonstrates how badly the Pope lacked wise counsel. The Europe of the Wojtyla document is 'disoriented, uncertain, without hope'. The malaise includes 'a plummeting birth rate, the shortage of vocations to priestly and religious life, the collapse of marriages, the loss of reverence for human life, and the many signs of spiritual and psychological isolation'. Christianity 'that has sustained Europe for centuries has been replaced by a sort of practical agnosticism and religious indifference'. Wojtyla concluded that Europe is now suffering through 'a profound crisis of values'.

There is much truth within the document. It would perhaps have had greater resonance within Europe if the Pope had been equally perceptive about the total failure of his Church to address not only what ailed Europe, but also what ailed the Roman Catholic Church. He might then have arrived at the conclusion that the crisis within the Vatican was directly linked to the problems across the Tiber. That the Church by her inaction is directly responsible for the continuing clerical abuse and that the effect it is having on societies in many countries is directly responsible for the profound loss of faith that has resulted did not occur to Pope John Paul II.

The late Pope and his cardinals had known since at least the early 1980s that such sexual abuse was widespread: in truth, the Catholic hierarchy had always known. Instead of taking firm, early, decisive action they chose to perpetuate the secret system and such behaviour stripped the Pope and many of his princes of every single shred of moral authority. Now as we approach the second anniversary of Karol Wojtyla's death, still nothing in real terms has been done.

Within a great many countries, particularly the United States, Karol Wojtyla's failure to deal effectively with the continuing cancer of abuse has, from the mid-1980s onwards, caused ever-increasing numbers of Roman Catholics to conclude that the papacy of Pope John Paul II had ended long before April 2005.

As for the papal attack on Europe's 'profound crisis of values', one can only hope that Pope Benedict XVI will reflect on that denunciation in the light of Europe's response to the earthquake and tsunami that struck on 26 December 2004. The response from the British public was to donate over £372 million. There was a comparable response throughout Europe, the USA and beyond. Governments around the world pledged billions of dollars, huge amounts of material, medical and volunteer aid, a wonderful example of the true solidarity that Wojtyla so treasured. That instinctive response, 'a commitment to the common good', as the late Pope described the true moral value of Solidarity, in his 1987 encyclical *Sollicitudo Rei Socialis* – On Social Concern – that global response was a powerful illustration that neither Christianity in general nor Catholicism in particular have a monopoly on compassion.

On 13 May 1981 the attempt on the Pope's life came within a microscopic distance of succeeding. Karol Wojtyla and many of those close to him believed that the Virgin Mary intervened and gave the Pope 'a second life'. From his various comments and also his writings it is obvious that self-criticism did not play a significant role in either the Pope's 'first' or 'second' life. The perfect child became the flawless man and then the infallible Pope.

To celebrate his eighty-fourth birthday in May 2004 Wojtyla published *Wstańcie, chodźmy!* – 'Get up and Let Us Go!' – an autobiographical work on his years as a bishop in Cracow. At one point, the author considers his use of authority.

'The faculty of admonition also certainly belongs to the role of the pastor. In these terms, I have done too little. There was always a problem of equilibrium between authority and service. Perhaps I should rebuke myself, for not having tried hard enough to command.' The self-criticism is short-lived. A few lines later, Wojtyla wrote: 'In spite of the interior resistance I feel for the act of rebuking, I think I have made all the necessary decisions.'

I leave the reader to judge, within the many aspects of the papacy that this book examines, whether or not Pope John Paul II 'made all the necessary decisions', but two in particular should cause even the most devout supporter of the late Pope to give pause. Because of his continuing failure to make 'the necessary decisions', a corrupt archbishop retained control of the Vatican Bank for a further decade. Because of Wojtyla's inability to make 'the necessary decisions', rampant clerical sexual abuse had continued unchecked and had directly resulted in mass desertions from the faith in many countries. From his earliest days as a bishop in Cracow, Karol Wojtyla constantly avoided making the 'necessary decisions'. His papacy is riddled with countless examples of fatal vacillation. That failure to act has left the Church in crisis, both financially and spiritually.

On 13 May 2005, Pope Benedict XVI announced the immediate opening of a cause for the beatification of Pope John Paul II. The usual five-year waiting period that is required after the death of the candidate for beatification has been waived. As befits the pop-star Pope, his elevation is being fast-tracked. The rush to sainthood has begun.

What the Church needed after the death of Pope John Paul II was a leader that would perform the Herculean task of cleaning the Augean stables he had inherited. What it got were men who allowed the disgraced Cardinal Law, the former archbishop of Boston, to preside over the Mass marking the fourth day of the *novendiales*, the nine-day period of formal mourning. It was an official mark of approval for a man who had lied, prevaricated and applied the secret system to cover up for numerous sexually abusing priests, thus allowing them to continue, in some cases for decades, to maim and injure the innocent.

What the Church subsequently got was Cardinal Ratzinger, the late Pope's closest associate for more than 20 years. Pope Benedict XVI's election demonstrated that there is indeed a life after death. The name on the headed notepaper may have changed. The management is the same. The conservative wing, to the intense delight of Opus Dei and the other reactionary elements within the Church, easily outmanoeuvred the reforming liberals and elected a 78-year-old man more than three years past his normal retirement age with a medical history that includes at least two strokes. His personal history includes volunteering – contrary to Ratzinger's assertions, registration was not compulsory – for the Hitler youth movement. His own account of his later activities in the *Wehrmacht* also lacks clarity.

Cardinal Ratzinger as the then Head of the Congregation for the Doctrine of the Faith refused on several occasions to investigate repeated allegations including sworn affidavits that the founder of the Legionnaires of Christ, Marcial Maciel Degollado, had constantly sexually abused young members of his organisation. The Cardinal was very aware in what high regard Maciel was held by Pope John Paul II. With Wojtyla dead and Ratzinger duly elected as his successor, the evidence against Marcial Maciel, that for years had been disregarded, was finally acted upon. In 2007 the Vatican announced that after an intensive examination of the various accusations the Congregation of the Faith under the guidance of its new Prefect Cardinal William Levada decided 'taking account of the advanced age of the Reverend Maciel and his delicate health to refrain from taking action against Maciel' but instead to invite him to 'a reserved life of prayer and penance, renouncing every public ministry'. This was not, however, the signal that the much-needed reforms regarding clerical sexual abuse were about to be implemented. Ratzinger is also on record as having issued a written warning to every Roman Catholic bishop in the world of the strict penalties facing those who referred allegations of sexual abuse to the civil authorities. He thus ensured that his predecessor's desire that the Church should cover up such activities – a view that Karol Wojtyla had expressed to the Austrian bishops in 1998: 'like every house that has special rooms that are not open to guests the Church also needs rooms for talks that require privacy' – would continue to be official policy.

An indication of some of Pope Benedict XVI's priorities can be gauged from the fact that in spring 2006 he summoned the world's cardinals to Rome for 'a day of prayer and reflection', held behind closed doors. This all-day session with the cardinals was to discuss 'the four key issues facing the Church: a bid to heal the breach with Catholic traditionalists; relations between Christianity and Islam; the status of retired bishops; and preparations and use of liturgical texts'. By the end of 2006 there were also indications that a reform of the Vatican Bank and the other financial arms of Vatican finance was moving up the Papal agenda. Much further down the list are concessions on the use of condoms to fight the modern plague of AIDS. Issues such as an honest examination of the Catholic Church's role in the global collapse of Christianity are totally off the radar.

Speaking in a series of meditations on Good Friday 2005, the then Cardinal Ratzinger said, 'how much filth there is in the Church, and even among those who, in the priesthood, ought to belong entirely to Christ!' Quite so, Holy Father. Quite so.

As a direct result of Karol Wojtyla's Papacy, the power of the Church had been profoundly reduced and its glory severely tarnished.

David A. Yallop
27 January 2007

Author's Note

Vatican Incorporated (August 1978)

These notes are an extremely short summary of part of a detailed investigation originally published as part of *In God's Name* in 1984 and in subsequent years. They are for the convenience of readers who have yet to read *In God's Name*. They briefly outline the nature of the scandal which confronted Pope John Paul I and his successor.

The Church which Albino Luciani inherited had come a long way from the Church of Christ for the poor. The Vatican controlled immense secret wealth, not only in works of art and buildings, but in productive assets, in a huge portfolio of stocks and shares and real estate across the world. It operated two banks, the Vatican Bank (formally named the Institute for Religious Works) and APSA, the Extraordinary Section of the Administration of the Patrimony of the Holy See.

Built on special privileges, the Vatican's wealth was hidden from view (even by itself) by an arcane and opaque accounting system, and fiercely denied by its spokesmen. In 1970 a Swiss estimate put the total productive capital of the Vatican at $13 billion, *excluding* the vast global assets owned or controlled by the Vatican Bank.

This new wealth of the Church began with Mussolini. In 1929 with the Lateran Treaty he ended nearly sixty years of conflict between the Holy See and the Italian state. It gave the Church a regular income in cash and bonds, and more important, a series of exemptions from taxation and disclosure. In 1942 Mussolini gave the Vatican's 'ecclesiastical corporations' even more favourable treatment in tax and company law. This made them a very attractive conduit for all manner of funds and transactions, including criminal ones. The Church was equally successful in negotiating with Hitler. The 1933 Concordat with Nazi Germany gave the Church regular income from the German state – 'church tax', deducted at source from nearly all German incomes.

In 1929 Pius XI appointed a layman, Bernardino Nogara, as the Church's 'fund manager'. Nogara took the job only on condition that he had total freedom to invest, with no restraint from Church doctrines. Over the next thirty years he played the gold and futures markets with immense success, bought the Vatican interests in a collection of banks, a huge portfolio of stocks and shares and valuable real estate throughout the world.

Not surprisingly, this immense new wealth attracted attention from the Italian state. From 1962 to 1968 the Vatican had a long-running dispute with successive Italian governments over the payment of taxation on its share dividends. The Church was attacked by politicians, the media and public opinion. It was embarrassed by the scale of its holdings in Italian industry, including essential services such as water and power (where the Church had no wish to answer to consumer complaints) and prohibited articles including contraceptives. In 1968, seeking to combine higher profits with lower controversy, the Vatican decided on a major switch in its policy, away from Italian assets in favour of the United States and offshore investments.

This decision led the Church into a series of scandalous, criminal and financially disastrous relationships which cost it uncounted millions and threatened its entire moral reputation. The Church's resources and, above all, its immunities and privileges were used knowingly on a massive scale for evasion of taxes and exchange control, money laundering, racketeering and fraud. The Church collectively profited from this criminal activity, as did senior members personally. The Church's associates made systematic use of blackmail, murder and terror in their activities.

The main protagonists in these relationships were: Bishop Paul Marcinkus, Michele Sindona, Licio Gelli and Roberto Calvi.

Marcinkus rose from bodyguard to Pope Paul VI to his controller and gatekeeper to head of the Vatican Bank, without ever acquiring the necessary ability or integrity for any of his promotions. He offered respectability and concealment for the risky or criminal enterprises of Sindona and Calvi, as he sought to increase the assets of the Vatican Bank.

Sindona built a successful career as a servant and frontman for the Mafia, and then used his excellent connections, particularly with the Vatican, to build an immense fraudulent empire. He was assisted by Licio Gelli, master blackmailer, fascist, not just a double but a multiple agent, partner of escaped Nazis, drug traffickers and ultra-right military regimes in Latin America.

Gelli was master of the secretive, conspiratorial, immensely powerful P2 Masonic lodge. Its members included Sindona and Umberto Ortolani, a lawyer and businessman with highly placed friends in the Vatican. Through Ortolani, the P2 lodge built a network of contacts in the Vatican.

Roberto Calvi was paymaster to P2. He was also a banker, money launderer for the Mafia and a fraudster, once a partner of Sindona's who became his bitter rival.

By the time Albino Luciani succeeded as John Paul I, the financial empire built by Michele Sindona had collapsed leaving thousands of ruined investors. Calvi's empire was vulnerable. It was built on a house of cards known as the Banco Ambrosiano. The Vatican was heavily implicated in each empire. Both men were under criminal investigation in the US and Italy: Sindona was fighting extradition.

The only thing protecting them was their relationship with the Vatican through Marcinkus. But Albino Luciani was determined to fire Marcinkus, clean up the Vatican's finances and make them transparent. His reforms, if implemented, would have destroyed the criminal alliances that had existed between the Vatican Bank and organised crime for over a decade.

Notes

Chapter 1: God's Will

1. A full account of the investigation that led to my conclusion can be found within *In God's Name*.
2. See Author's note.
3. *Witness to Hope*.
4. *Wisdom of Solomon* 7:15.
5. Michele Sindona had organised the Vatican Bank accounts for the Gambino, Inzerillo and Spatola families.

Chapter 2: 'It Depends on Whose Liberation Theology . . .'

6. *Catholic Social Ethics*, 2 volumes, by Karol Wojtyla.
7. *John* 8:32.
8. *John* 2:19.

Chapter 7: The Market Place

9. The Virgin Mary was also an honorary colonel in the prewar Polish army.

Chapter 8: The Jewish Question

10. Marek Halter speaking to PBS TV.

Chapter 9: Beyond Belief

11. Father Doyle's career in the Vatican's diplomatic service came to an abrupt end in early 1986 after pressure from a clique within the American bishopric. He was then commissioned as a US Airforce Chaplain. Father Peterson was destined to die prematurely in April 1987.

Chapter 11: Thou Shalt Not . . .

12. Carl Bernstein and Marco Politi in 'His Holiness'.

Chapter 13: The Village

13. Father Marcial Maciel Degollado, Founder of the Legionnaires of Christ. See Chapter 'Beyond Belief'

Bibliography

BOOKS:

'Be Not Afraid!' André Frossard In Conversation With John Paul II, André Frossard, The Bodley Head, London And St Martin's Press 1984

'Hart und kompromilos durchgreifen': Die SED contra Polen 1980–1981. Geheimakten der SED-Führung über die Unterdrückung der polnischen Demokratiebewegung, Manfred Wilke and Reinhardt Gutsche, Akademie Verlag Gmbh, Berlin 1995, made available by Dr Wolfgang R. Lehner, Vienna (Stenographic Report Of The Meeting Of Leading Representatives Of The Participating States Of The Warsaw Pact On 5 December 1980 In Moscow – pp. 140–195 translated by Margaret C. Shanks, London)

A Catholic Dictionary Containing Some Account Of The Doctrine, Discipline, Rites, Ceremonies, Councils, And Religious Orders Of The Catholic Church, William E. Addis and Thomas Arnold, Virtue & Co. Ltd, London 1928

A Catholic Myth: The Behaviour And Beliefs Of American Catholics, Andrew M. Greeley, Collier Books, Macmillan, New York 1990

A Democratic Catholic Church: The Reconstruction Of Roman Catholicism, Eugene C. Bianchi and Rosemary Radford, Crossroad, New York 1992

A Documentary History Of Religion In America Since 1865, Second Edition, Edited By Edwin S. Gaustad, William B. Eerdmans Publishing Company, Grand Rapids 1993

A History Of Christianity, Paul Johnson, Weidenfeld & Nicolson, London 1976

A History Of God, Karen Armstrong, Knopf, New York 1993

A ogni morte di Papa, Giulio Andreotti, Rizzoli, Milan 1982

A Pope For All Christians? An Inquiry Into The Role Of Peter In The Modern Church, edited By Peter J. McCord, SPCK, London 1977

A Secret World: Sexuality And The Search For Celibacy, A. W. Richard Sipe, Brunner-Mazel, New York 1990

Ad Limina Addresses: The Addresses Of His Holiness Pope John Paul II To The Bishops Of The United States During Their Ad Limina Visits, March 5–December 9, 1988, Pope John Paul II, United States Catholic Conference, Washington DC, 1989

Agostíno Casaroli: Uomo del Dialogo, Alceste Santini, Edizioni San Paolo, Torino 1993

All You Who Labor: Work And The Sanctification Of Daily Life, Stefan Wyszynski, Sophia Institute Press, Manchester, NH, 1995

Amchurch Comes Out, The US Bishops, Pedophile Scandals And The Homosexual Agenda, Paul Likoudis, Roman Catholic Faithful Inc., Petersburg, Illinois 2002

American Democracy & The Vatican: Population Growth & National Security, Stephen D. Mumford, Humanist Press, Amherst, NY, 1980

American Diplomacy, George F. Kennan, University Of Chicago Press, Chicago 1984

Anatomy Of The Vatican, An Irreverent View Of The Holy See, Paul Hofmann, Robert Hale Limited, London 1985

Annuario Pontifico, per l'anno 2001, Città Del Vatican, Libreria Editrice Vaticana, Rome 2001

Archbishop Oscar Romero: A Shepherd's Diary, translated By Irene B. Hodgson, CAFOD, London 1993

Assassinati in Vaticano, 4 Maggio 1998, Jacques Vergès and Luc Brossollet (translated by Patricia Scaramuzzino), Kaos Edizioni 2002

Auf, lasst uns gehen! Johannes Paul II (translated By Ingrid Stampa) Verlagsgruppe Weltbild 2004

August 21st, The Rape Of Czechoslovakia, Colin Champman, Cassell & Company Ltd, London 1968

Betrayal, The Untold Story Of The Kurt Waldheim Investigation And Cover-Up, Eli M. Rosenbaum with William Hoffer, St Martin's Press, New York 1993

Beyond The Threshold: A Life In Opus Dei, María del Carmen Tapia, Continuum Publishing Group 1999

Beyond Tolerance: Child Pornography On The Internet, Philip Jenkins, New York University Press 2001

Bugie di sangue in Vaticano, Discepoli Di Verità, Kaos Edizioni 1999

Burning Truths, An Update On: Immoral Celibacy; John Paul I's Sudden Death, Segregations; 'Infallibility'; Vatican And Parish Finances; 'Scandal-Dread'; Sham; Squirming Assets . . . Basil Morahan, published by author, Ballina, 1993

Captive Hearts, Captive Minds, Madeleine Landau Tobias and Janja Lalich, Hunter House, Alameda, CA 1993

KGB: History of foreign political operations from Lenin to Gorbachev, Christopher Andrew and Oleg Gordievskiy, 1992

Cardinal Sin And The Miracle Of Asia, Felix B. Bautista, Vera-Reyes, Manila 1987

Cardinal Wyszyński: A Biography, Andrzej Micewski, Harcourt Brace Jovanovich, Orlando, Florida 1984

Catholic Schools In A Declining Church, Andrew M. Greeley, William C. McCready, Kathleen McCourt, Sheed & Ward, Kansas City 1976

Catholicism And History, The Opening Of The Vatican Archives, Owen Chadwick, Cambridge University Press 1978

Caveat: Realism, Reagan, And Foreign Policy, Alexander Haig, Macmillan, New York 1984

Choosing God – Chosen By God, Jean-Marie Lustiger, Ignatius Press, San Francisco 1991

Christianity In Crisis, Hank Hangraff, Harvest House Publishers, Eugene, Oregon 1993

Church: Charisma & Power, Liberation Theology And The Institutional Church, Leonardo Boff, The Crossroad Publishing Company, New York 1986

Churchgoing & Christian Ethics, Robin Gill, The Press Syndicate of the University of Cambridge, Cambridge, UK 1999

CIA, The 'Honourable' Company, Brian Freemantle, Michael Joseph Ltd, London 1983

City Of Secrets, The Truth Behind The Murders At The Vatican, John Follain, HarperCollins Publishers Inc., New York 2003

Crimes In The Jasenovac Camp, Croatian State Commission For Establishing Crimes Of Occupying Forces And Their Assistants, Baja Luka 2000.

Crossing The Threshold Of Hope, Pope John Paul II, Knopf, New York 1994

Dans le Secret des Princes, Christine Ockrent And Alexandre De Marenches, Edition Stock, Paris 1986

Deadly Secrets: My 25 Years In The CIA, Ralph W. McGhee, Sheridan Square Publications Inc., New York 1983

Der Fall Ledl: Im Auftrag des Vatikans, Leopold Ledl, Fama-Verlag, Wien 1989

Der Vatikan heiligt die Mittel, Heribert Blondiau And Udo Gümpel, Patmos Verlag, Düsseldorf 1999

Die Jugendgedichte des Papstes, Karol Wojtyla (translated by Blasius Chudoba), Verlag Styria; Burgschmiet-Verlag 2000

Disturbing The Peace: A Conversation With Karel Hvizdala, Vaclav Havel, Vintage Books, New York 1991

Ecumenism And Charismatic Renewal, Cardinal Léon Joseph Suenens, Darton, Longman And Todd, London 1978

Edward Gierek Replika, Janusz Rolicki, Polska Oficyna Wydawnicza 'BGW', Warszawa 1990

Edward Gierek: Przerwana Dekada, Janusz Rolicki, Polska Oficyna Wydawnicza 'BGW', Warszawa 1990

Entrez dans l'espérance, avec la collaboration de Vittorio Messori, Jean-Paul II, Plon/Mame, Paris 1994

Faith According To St John Of The Cross, Karol Wojtyla, Ignatius Press, San Francisco 1981

Feature Study, Anna-Teresa Tymieniecka, Phenomenology Information Bulletin (published by the World Institute For Advanced Phenomenological Research And Learning) 1979

For The Record, From Wall Street To Washington, Donald T. Regan, Hutchinson, London 1988

From A Far Country: The Story Of Karol Wojtyla Of Poland, A. Kijowski and J. J. Szczepanski, with the collaboration of Krzysztof Zanussi, Eri/Neff, Santa Monica, CA 1981

From The Shadows, Robert M. Gates, Simon & Schuster, New York 1996

Fruitful And Responsible Love, Karol Wojtyla, St Paul Publications, Slough 1978

Future Church, A Global Analysis Of The Christian Community To The Year 2010, Dr Peter W. Brierley, Monarch Books And Christian Research, London 1998

Gesù lava più bianco, Bruno Ballardini, Edizioni Minimum Fax 2000

Gift And Mystery: On The Fiftieth Anniversary Of My Priestly Ordination, Pope John Paul II, André Deutsch, London 1979

Gone But Not Forgotten, Church Leaving And Returning, Philip Richter and Leslie J. Francis, Darton Longman & Todd, London 1998

Hinter der Schwelle: Ein Leben im Opus Dei, Maria del Carmen Tapia, Benzinger Verlag 1994

His Holiness: John Paul II And The History Of Our Time, Carl Bernstein and Marco Politi, Penguin Group 1997

Holy Alliance, Carl Bernstein, *Time*, 24 February 1992

How The Pope Became Infallible, Pius IX And The Politics Of Persuasion, August Bernhard Hasler, translated By Peter Heinegg, introduction by Hans Küng, Doubleday, New York 1981

I Mercanti del Vaticano – Affari e Scandali: L'impero economico delle anime, Mario Guarino, Kaos Edizioni 1998

I Papi del XX Secolo, Giancarlo Zizola, Tascabili Economici Newton, Rome 1995

I.G. Farben, Richard Sasuly, Boni &Gaer, New York 1947

Ihr habt getötet (Orginalausgabe: *Bugie Di Sangue In Vaticano*), Discepoli Di Verità (translated by Christian Försch), Aufbau-Verlag 2003

Il Conclave, Giancarlo Zizola, Newton Compton, Rome 1993

Illustrissimi: Letters From Pope John Paul I, Alberto Luciani, Little, Brown, Boston 1978

In Banks We Trust, Penny Lernoux, Anchor Press/Doubleday, New York 1984

In God's Name, David Yallop, Jonathan Cape, London 1984

In The Vatican, Peter Hebblethwaite, Sidgwick & Jackson, London 1986

Industry And Ideology, I.G. Farben In The Nazi Era, Peter Hayes, Cambridge University Press 2001

Infallibility: The Crossroads Of Doctrine: Peter Chirico, Sheed, Andrews and McMeel, Kansas City 1977

Inside The Council: The Story Of Vatican II, Robert Kaiser, Burns & Oates, London 1963

Inside The Vatican: The Politics And Organization Of The Catholic Church, Thomas J. Reese, Harvard University Press, 1998

Instructions From The Centre, Top Secret Files On KGB Foreign Operations 1975–1985, Christopher Andrew and Oleg Gordievsky, Hodder & Stoughton, London 1991

John Paul II For Peace In The Middle East, Pope John Paul II, Libreria Editrice Vaticana, Vatican City 1991

John Paul II On Science And Religion: Reflections On The New View From Rome, George V. Coyne, SJ, Robert John Russell and William R. Stoeger, SJ, Eds, Vatican Observatory Publications, Rome 1990

John Paul II's Ostpolitik? Alexander Tomsky, Religion In Communist Lands (Summer 1980): 139–40

John XXIII Simpleton Or Saint? Giacomo Lercaro & Gabriele De Rosa, Geoffrey Chapman Ltd, London 1967

Jugement À Moscou: Un dissident dans les archives du Kremlin, Vladimir Bukovsky, Laffont, Paris 1995

Karol Wojtyla: The Thought Of The Man Who Became Pope John Paul II, Rocco Buttiglione, Eerdmans, Grand Rapids 1997

KGB: The Inside Story Of Its Foreign Operations From Lenin To Gorbachev, Christopher Andrew and Oleg Gordievsky, London: Hodder & Stoughton; New York: Harper & Row 1990

Kościól Epoki Dialogu, Andrzej Bardecki, Znak, Kraków 1966

Landslide, The Unmaking Of The President, 1984–1988, Jane Mayer and Doyle McManus, Collins, London 1988

La Restaurazione di Papa Wojtyla, Giancarlo Zizola, Bari: Laterza 1985

Le Successeur, Giancarlo Zizola, Desclée De Brouwer, Paris 1995

Le Vatican mis à nu, Groupe 'Les Millénaires' (translated By Pierre-Emmanuel Dauzat), Editions Robet Laffont Sa, Paris 1999; (Original Edition: *Via col vento in Vaticano*) Kaos Edizioni Milano 1999

Lead Us Not Into Temptation, Catholic Priests And The Sexual Abuse of Children, Jason Berry, foreword by Andrew M. Greeley, University of Illinois Press, Urbana And Chicago, USA 2000

Letters From Medjurgorje, Wayne Weible, Centre For Peace, Ilford, UK 1992

Letters From Prison And Other Essays, Adam Michnik, University of California Press, Berkeley 1987

Letters From Vatican City, Vatican Council II (First Session); Background To Debates, Xavier Rynne, Faber & Faber, London 1963

Letters To My Brother Priests: Holy Thursday (1979–1994), Pope John Paul II, Scepter Publishers/Midwest Theological Forum, Princeton/Chicago 1994

Listy Pasterskie Episkopatu Polski 1945–1974 (Pp. 829–836), Editions Du Dialogue, Paris 1975

Lives Of The Popes: The Pontiffs From St Peter To John Paul II, Richard P. McBrien, HarperSanFrancisco, San Francisco 1997

Love And Responsibility, Karol Wojtyla (translated By H. T. Willetts) Ignatius Press, San Francisco 1993

Medjugorje: Religion, Politics, And Violence In Rural Bosnia, Mart Bax, VU Uitgeverij, Amsterdam 1995

Memoirs, Mikhail Gorbachev, Doubleday, New York 1995

Memories, Andrei Gromyko (translated by Harold Shukman), Century Hutchinson Ltd, London 1989

Mistero Vaticano: la scomparsa di Emanuela Orlandi, Pino Nicotri, Kaos Edizioni 2002

Mord im Vatikan, Valeska Von Roques, Hoffmann und Campe Verlag 2003

Moscow And Beyond: 1986–1989, Andrei Sakharov, Vintage Books, New York 1992

Nazi Gold, Ian Sayer and Douglas Botting with *The Sunday Times*, Granada Publishing, London 1984

Nella Chiesa per il mondo: Omelie E Discorsi, Agostíno Casaroli, Rusconi Libri, Milano 1987

Next to God, Poland, Bogdan Szajkowski, St Martin's Press, New York 1983

Notes Rzymski, Adam Boniecki, Znak, Kraków 1988

Observer In Rome: A Protestant Report On The Vatican Council, Robert McAfee Brown, Doubleday, Garden City, New York 1964

One Nation Under God: Religion in Contemporary American Society, Barry A. Kosmin and Seymour P. Lachman, Harmony Books, New York 1993

Paul VI: The First Modern Pope, Peter Hebblethwaite, Paulist Press, New York/Mahwah, New Jersey 1993

Pedophiles And Priests, Philip Jenkins, Oxford University Press 1996

People Of God – The Struggle For World Catholicism, Penny Lernoux, Penguin Books, New York 1989

Perestroika: New Thinking For Our Country And The World, Mikhail Gorbachev, Harper And Row, New York 1987

Pilgrim To Poland, Pope John Paul II, St Paul Editions 1979

Poles Apart, Solidarity And The New Poland, Jacqueline Hayden, Irish Academic Press, Dublin 1994

Pontifikat Jana Pawla II: 1983–1988, Mieczysław Maliński, Ksiegarnia Sw. Wojciecha, Poznań, Poland 1991

Pope John Paul II: The Life Of Karol Wojtyla, Mieczyslaw Malinski, Seabury, New York 1979

Pope John XXIII, Letters To His Family, translated By Dorothy White, Geoffrey Chapman, London 1970

Power And Authority In The Catholic Church, Cardinal Cody In Chicago, Charles W. Dahm in collaboration with Robert Ghelardi, University Of Notre Dame Press, Notre Dame, Indiana 1981

Power And Principle, Zbigniew Brzezinski, Farrar, Straus and Giroux, New York 1983

Presidential Power And The Modern President: The Politics Of Leadership From Roosevelt To Reagan, Richard E. Neustadt, The Free Press, New York 1991

Puebla: A Pilgrimage of Faith, Pope John Paul II, St Paul Editions, Boston 1979

Reagan At Intermission, Carl Bernstein, New Republic, January 20, 1985

Red Runs The Vistula, Ron Jeffery, Nevron Associates, Peterborough 1989

Religion, Revolution And Reform: New Forces For Change In Latin America, William V. D'antonio, Frederick A. Praeger, New York 1964

Russia And Armed Persuasion, Stephen J. Cimbala, Rowman and Littlefield 2001

Saints and Sinners: A History Of The Popes, Eamon Duffy, Yale University Press, New Haven 1997

Santo Domingo And After: The Challenges For The Latin American Church, Gustavo Gutiérrez, Francis McDonagh, Cândido Padin, OSB, and John Sobrino, SJ, Catholic Institute For International Relations, London 1993

Selling God, American Religion In The Marketplace Of Culture, R. Laurence Moore, Oxford University Press 1994

Sign Of Contradiction, Karol Wojtyla, Seabury, New York 1979

Six Million Did Die, Arthur Suzman and Denis Diamond, South African Jewish Board Of Deputies, Johannesburg 1978

Sources of Renewal: The Implementation Of Vatican II, Karol Wojtyla, Harper and Row, San Francisco 1980

Soviet Jewish Immigration And Soviet Nationality Policy, Victor Zaslavski and Robert Brym, Macmillan, London 1983

Soviet Jewry In The Decisive Decade, 1971–1980, Victor Zaslavsky and Robert J. Brym, 1983, Edited By Robert O. Freeman, Duke University Press, Durham, North Carolina 1984

Spiritual Pilgrimage: Texts On Jews And Judaism 1979–1995, edited by Eugene J. Fisher and Leon Klenicki, Crossroad, New York 1995

Spoko! Czyli Kwadratura Koła, Jacek Kuroń, Polska Oficyna Wydawnicza 'BGW', Warszawa 1992

Strands Of Nazi Anti-Semitism, Professor Philippe Burrin, Europaeum Lecture, Delivered at the Taylorian Lecture Theatre, Oxford University, 16 May 2001

Swiss Connection: Die verborgene Seite der schweizer Wirtschaft, Gian Trepp, Wilhelm Heyne Verlag 1999

Synod Extraordinary, The Inside Story Of The Rome Synod, November/December 1985, Peter Hebblethwaite, Darton, Longman and Todd, London 1986

The 'Summa Theologica' Of St Thomas Aquinas Part 1, Literally Translated By Fathers Of The English Dominican Province, Burns Oates & Washbourne Ltd, Publishers To The Holy See, London 1941

The 1917 Pio-Benedictine Code Of Canon Law In English Translation With Extensive Scholarly Apparatus Dr Edward Peters, Ignatius Press, San Francisco, CA 2001

The Achievements Of General Jaruzelski, Abraham Brumberg, *New Leader*, 26 December 1983

The Acting Person, Karol Wojtyla, D. Reidel Publishing Company, Dordrecht 1979

The Anatomy Of The Catholic Church, Gerard Noel, Hodder and Stoughton, London 1980

The Apparitions Of Our Lady At Medjugorje, Svetozar Kraljević, Informativni Centar Mir, Medjugorje 1999

The Battle For Auschwitz, Catholic-Jewish Relations Under Strain, Emma Klein, Frank Cass & Co Ltd, London 2001

The Book of Gomorrah, Mediaeval Source-book, St Peter Damian, translated by Owen J. Blum, OFM, The Catholic University of America Press 1990

The Catholic Ethic And The Spirit Of Capitalism, Michael Novak, The Free Press, New York 1993

The Changing Face Of The Priesthood, Donald B. Cozzens, The Liturgical Press, Collegeville, Minnesota 2000

The Changing Vatican, Alberto Cavallari, Faber & Faber, London 1966

The Church And Jewish People: New Considerations, Cardinal Johannes Willebrands, Paulist Press, Mahwah, New Jersey 1992

The Church And The Left, Adam Michnik, University Of Chicago Press, Chicago 1993

The CIA, A Forgotten History, William Blum, Zed Books, London 1986

The Code Of Canon Law In English Translation, Collins Liturgical Publications, London 1983

The Collected Plays And Writings On Theater, Karol Wojtyla, Introductions By Boleslaw Taborski, Berkeley University Of California Press 1987

The Confessions, St Augustine, Collier Books, Macmillan, New York 1961

The Crime And Punishment Of I.G. Farben, The Birth, Growth And Corruption Of A Giant Corporation, Joseph Borkin, co-published by Doubleday and The Catholic Truth Society, London 1997

The Crisis In The Churches, Spiritual Malaise, Fiscal Woe, Robert Wuthnow, Oxford University Press, New York and Oxford 1997

The Culture Of Disbelief, How American Law And Politics Trivialize Religious Devotion, Stephen L. Carter, Basic Books, a division of HarperCollins Publishers, Inc., New York 1993

The Dark Heart Of Italy, Travels Through Time And Space Across Italy, Tobias Jones, Faber And Faber, London 2003

The Encyclicals Of Pope John Paul II, Pope John Paul II, Our Sunday Visitor Publishing Division, Huntington, Indiana 1996

The Fourth Session, The Debates And Decrees Of Vatican Council II, September 14 To December 8, 1965, Xavier Rynne, Farrar, Straus and Giroux, New York 1966

The Genius Of The Vatican, Robert Sencourt, Jonathan Cape, London 1935

The Hidden Pope, The Untold Story Of A Lifelong Friendship That Is Changing The Relationship Between Catholics And Jews; The Personal Journey Of John Paul II And Jerzy Kluger, Darcy O'Brien, Daybreak Books, USA 1998

The Holocaust And The Christian World, Carol Rittner, Stephen D. Smith, Irena Steinfeldt, Kuperard, London 2000

The Holocaust Revisited: A Retrospective Analysis Of The Auschwitz-Birkenau Extermination Complex, Central Intelligence Agency, Washington: 1979

The Holy See At The Service Of Peace: Pope John Paul II Addresses To The Diplomatic Corps (Various), Pope John Paul II, Pontifical Council For Justice And Peace, Vatican City 1988

The Jeweler's Shop, Karol Wojtyla, Ignatius Press, San Francisco 1980

The Macmillan Atlas Of The Holocaust, Martin Gilbert, Macmillan, New York 1982

The Making Of The Pope Of The Millennium: Kalendarium Of The Life Of Karol Wojtyla, compiled and recorded by Adam Boniecki, MIC, Marian Press – Marians Of The Immaculate Conception & Association Of Marian Helpers, Stockbridge Massachusetts 2000

The Making Of The Popes, Andrew M. Greeley, Futura Publications, London 1979

The Making Of The President 1960, Theodore H. White, Giant Cardinal Edition Published by arrangement with Atheneum House, Inc., USA 1962

The Mind Of Pius XII Edited By Robert C. Pollock, 1st Edition, W. Foulsham & Co. Ltd, London 1955

The Mitrokhin Archive, The KGB In Europe And The West, Christopher Andrew and Vasili Mitrokhin, Allen Lane/The Penguin Press, London 1999

The Money Lenders, Bankers In A Dangerous World, Anthony Sampson, Hodder and Stoughton, Sevenoaks, Kent 1981

The Nazi Persecution Of The Churches, 1933–1945, J. S. Conway, Regent College Publishing 2001

The Neocatechumenal Way According To Paul VI And John Paul II, Ezekiel Pasotti, St Paul's, Middleborough, UK, 1996

The Next Pope: An Enquiry, Peter Hebblethwaite, HarperCollins, London 1995

The Ostpolitik Of The Vatican And The Polish Pope, Religion In Communist Lands (Summer 1980): 13–21, Hansjakob Stehle

The Papacy And The Middle East: The Role Of The Holy See In The Arab-Israeli Conflict 1962–1984, George E. Irani, University Of Notre Dame Press 1986

The Papacy Today, Francis X. Murphy, Weidenfeld and Nicolson, London 1981

The Plot To Kill The Pope, Paul B. Henze, Charles Scribner's Sons, New York 1983

The Polish August, Neil Ascherson, Penguin Books Ltd, Harmondsworth, UK 1981

The Polish Church Under Martial Law, Tadeusz Walendowski, Poland Watch (Fall 1982), 54–62

The Polish Revolution: Solidarity, Timothy Garton Ash, Penguin Books, London 1999

The Pope And The New Apocalypse, The Holy War Against Family Planning, Stephen D. Mumford, Center For Research on Population and Security, Research Triangle Park, NC, 1986

The Pope Speaks To The American Church: John Paul II's Homilies, Speeches And Letters To Catholics In The United States, Pope John Paul II, HarperSanFrancisco, San Francisco 1992

The Pope Speaks: Dialogues Of Paul VI With Jean Guitton, English Translation By Anne And Christopher Fremantle, Weidenfeld and Nicolson, London 1968

The Pope's Divisions, The Roman Catholic Church Today, Peter Nichols, Penguin Books, Harmondsworth 1982

The Popes In The Twentieth Century, From Pius X To John XXII, Carlo Falconi (translated from the Italian by Muriel Grindrod) Weidenfeld and Nicolson, London 1967

The Ratzinger Report: An Exclusive Interview On The State Of The Church, Joseph Ratzinger and Vittorio Messori, Ignatius Press, San Francisco 1985

The Rise And Fall Of The Bulgarian Connection, Edward S. Herman & Frank Brodhead, Sheridan Square Publications Inc., New York 1986

The Road To The White House 1996: The Politics Of Presidential Elections, St Martin's Press, Inc., USA 1996

The Runaway Church, Peter Hebblethwaite, Collins, London 1975

The Second Session, The Debates And Decrees Of Vatican Council II, September 29 To December 4, 1963, Xavier Rynne, Farrar, Straus and Company, New York 1964

The Stripping Of The Altars: Traditional Religion In England c. 1400–c. 1580, Eamon Duffy, Yale University Press, New Haven and London 1992

The Theology Of Marriage And Celibacy, St Paul Editions, Boston 1986

The Third Session, The Debates And Decrees Of Vatican Council II, September 14 To November 21, 1964, Xavier Rynne, Farrar, Straus & Giroux, New York 1965

The Tide Is Running Out, Dr Peter Brierley, Christian Research, London 2000

The Unknown Lenin: From The Secret Archive, Richard Pipes (ed.), Yale University Press, New Haven, Connecticut 1996

The Vatican And Eastern Europe, Wilfried Daim, Frederick Ungar, New York 1970

The Vatican Empire, The Authoritative Report That Reveals The Vatican As A Nerve-Center Of High Finance – And Penetrates The Secret Of Papal Wealth, Nino Lo Bello, Simon & Schuster, New York 1968

The Vatican Papers, Nino Lo Bello, New English Library, Sevenoaks, Kent 1982

The Vatican, The Story Of The Holy City, Ann Carnahan, Odhams Press Limited, London 1950

The Way, Josemaría Escrivá, Little Hills Press, Sydney 2003

The Wisdom Of John Paul II, The Pope On Life's Most Vital Questions, Nick Bakalar and Richard Balkin, HarperSanFrancisco, USA 1995

The Year Of Armageddon: The Pope And The Bomb, Gordon Thomas, Granada 1984

The Year Of Three Popes, Peter Hebblethwaite, Collins, Glasgow, UK 1979

Their Kingdom Come, Inside The Secret World Of Opus Dei, Robert Hutchison, Transworld Publishers Ltd, London 1997

To The Ends Of The Earth, The Hunt For The Jackal, David Yallop, Jonathan Cape, London 1993

Turning Point For Europe? Cardinal Joseph Ratzinger, Ignatius Press, San Francisco 1994

UK Christian Handbook: Religious Trends 1998/99 No. 1, 2000/2001 No. 2, 2002/2003 No. 3, (ed.) Peter Brierley, Christian Research

Vatikan – Die Firma Gottes, Hanspeter Oschwald, Piper Verlag 2000

Vatikan, Die Macht der Päpste, Guido Knopp, Wilhelm Goldmann Verlag, München 1998

Veil, The Secret Wars Of The CIA 1981–1987 Bob Woodward, Simon & Schuster, London 1987

Verschwörung gegen den Papst, Valeska Von Roques, Karl Blessing Verlag 2001

Victory: The Reagan Administration's Secret Strategy That Hastened The Collapse Of The Soviet Union, Peter Schweizer, Atlantic Monthly Press 1996

When A Pope Asks For Forgiveness: The Mea Culpas Of John Paul II, Pauline Books and Media, Boston 1998

White Smoke, Andrew M. Greeley, Forge Books 1997 (Reprint)

Who Financed Hitler, The Secret Funding Of Hitler's Rise To Power 1919–1933, James And Suzanne Pool, Macdonald and Jane's Publishers, Great Britain 1979

Why Priests? Hans Küng, The Fontana Library Of Theology And Philosophy, 1972, New Edition: Fount Paperbacks, London 1977

Windswept House, Malachi Martin, Main Street Books 1998

Witness To Hope: The Biography Of Pope John Paul II, George Weigel, Harper Perennial 2005 (Updated)

Wojtyla: Un Pontificato Itinerante, Domenico Del Rio, Edizioni Dehoniane Bologna, Bologna 1994

Words From Heaven: Messages Of Our Lady From Medjugorje, A Friend Of Medjugorje, Caritas of Birmingham, Alabama, by permission of Saint James Publishing 1989

World Christian Encyclopedia: A Comparative Study Of Churches And Religions In The Modern World 1900–2000, edited by David B. Barrett, Oxford University Press, New York 1982

Wspólne Dziedzictwo: Judaizm i Chrześcianstwo w Kontekscie Dziejów Zbawienia, Hedwig Wahle, Biblos, Tarnów, Poland 1993

US GOVERNMENT DOCUMENTS:

Asian Organized Crime Hearing Before The Permanent Subcommittee On Investigations Of The Committee On Governmental Affairs United States Senate One Hundred Second Congress, First Session, October 3, November 5–6, 1991, US Government Printing Office Washington: 1992

CIA and State Department Intelligence Reports: Previously secret/confidential cable traffic covering Polish political aspects and the Papacy from October 19, 1978 to March 1, 1991

Drugs, Law Enforcement And Foreign Policy: Hearings Before The Subcommittees On Terrorism, Narcotics And International Communications And International Economic Policy, Trade, Oceans And Environment Of The Committee On Foreign Relations United States Senate, One Hundredth Congress, First Session, May 27, July 15 and October 30, 1987, Part 1 US Government Printing Office, Washington: 1988

Drugs, Law Enforcement, And Foreign Policy: Panama Hearings Before The Subcommittee On Terrorism, Narcotics And International Communications And International Economic Policy, Trade, Oceans And Environment Of The Committee On Foreign Relations United States Senate, One Hundredth Congress, Second Session, February 8, 9, 10 and 11, 1988, Part 2 US Government Printing Office, Washington: 1988

Federal Government's Response To Money Laundering, Hearings Before The Committee On Banking, Finance And Urban Affairs, House Of Representatives, One Hundred Third Congress, First Session, May 25 and 26, 1993, US Government Printing Office Washington: 1993

Hearings Before The Select Committee On Intelligence Of The United States Senate On Nomination Of Robert M Gates, To Be Director Of Central Intelligence: February 17 and February 18, 1987: US Government Printing Office Washington: 1987

Money Laundering Hearings Before The Subcommittee On Financial Institutions Supervision, Regulation And Insurance Of The Committee On Banking, Finance And Urban Affairs, House Of Representatives One Hundred And First Congress, First Session, November 14 and 15, 1989, US Government Printing Office Washington: 1990

Money Laundering Legislation Hearing Before The Subcommittee On Financial Institutions Supervision, Regulation And Insurance Of The Committee On Banking, Finance And Urban Affairs, House Of Representatives One Hundred And First Congress, Second Session, March 8, 1990, US Government Printing Office Washington: 1990

State Department/Rome Embassy cable traffic including cable traffic between Ambassador General Vernon Walters and successive Secretaries of State, 1980–1988

State Department/Rome Embassy cable traffic, 1945–1980

United States Government Anti-Narcotics Activities In The Andean Region Of South America, Report Made By The Permanent Subcommittee On Investigations Of The Committee On Governmental Affairs Of The United States Senate, US Government Printing Office Washington: 1990

PAPAL DOCUMENTS CONSULTED:

Encyclicals:
Quanta Cura,	1864
Humanae Vitae,	1968
Redemptor Hominis,	1979
Dives in Misericordia,	1980
Laborem Exercens,	1981
Slavorum Apostoli,	1985
Dominum et Vivificantem,	1986
Sollicitudo Rei Socialis,	1987
Redemptoris Mater,	1987
Redemptoris Missio,	1990
Centesimus Annus,	1991
Veritatis Splendor,	1993
Evangelium Vitae,	1995
Ut Unum Sint,	1995
Fides et Ratio,	1998
Ecclesia De Eucharistia,	2003

LETTERS OF POPE JOHN PAUL II:

On combating abortion and euthanasia, 1991
Letter to Women, 1995

APOSTOLIC EXHORTATIONS
OF POPE JOHN PAUL II:

Catechesi Tradendae	1979
Familiaris Consortio	1981
Reconciliatio et Paenitentia	1984
Christifideles Laici	1988
Pastores Dabo Vobis	1992
Ecclesia in Africa	1995
Vita Consecrata	1996
Ecclesia in Oceania	2001
Ecclesia in Europa	2003
Pastor gregis	2003

APOSTOLIC CONSTITUTIONS CONSULTED:

Sapientia Christiana	1979
Magnum Matrimonii Sacramentum	1982
Sacrae Disciplinae Leges	1983
Divinus Perfectionis Magister	1983
Spirituali militum curae	1986
Pastor Bonus	1988
Ex Corde Ecclesiae	1990
Fidei Depositum	1992
Universi Dominici Gregis	1996
Ecclesia in Urbe	1998

APOSTOLIC LETTERS CONSULTED:

Rutilans Agmen	1979
Domincae Cenae	1980
Amantissima Providentia	1980
Sanctorum Altrix	1980
Egregiae Virtutis	1980
A Concilio Constantinopolitano	1981
Salvifiic Doloris	1984
Redemptionis Anno	1984
Dilecti Amici	1985
Omnium Ecclesiarum Matri	1987
Sescentesima Anniversaria	1987
Spiritus Domini	1987
Duodecim Saeculum	1987
Iuvenum Patris	1988
Euntes in Mundum	1988
Litterae Encyclicae	1988
Ecclesia Dei	1988
Mulieris Dignitatem	1988
Vicesimus Quintus Annus	1988
On the Fiftieth Anniversary of the Beginning of the Second World War	1989
Apostolic Letter for the organization of the ecclesiastical jurisdictions in Poland	1992
Ordinatio Sacerdotalis	1994
Tertio Millennio Adveniente	1994
Orientale Lumen	1995
For the Fourth Centenary of the Union of Brest	1995
Operosam Diem	1996
Laetamur Magnopere	1997

Ad Tuendam Fidem	1998
Dies Domini	1998
Apostolos Suos	1998
Inter Munera Academiarum	1999
Novo Millennio Ineunte	2001
To the Catholic People of Hungary	2001
Misericordia Dei	2002
Rosarium Virginis Mariae	2002
Spiritus et Sponsa	2003
Mane nobiscum Domine	2004
The Rapid Development	2005

CHURCH DOCUMENTS CONSULTED:

Lumen Gentium	1964
Nostra Aetate	1965
Dignitatis Humanae	1965
Gaudium Et Spes	1965

SYNODAL AND CONGREGATIONAL DOCUMENTS CONSULTED:

Instruction On Certain Aspects Of The 'Theology Of Liberation', Congregation For The Doctrine Of The Faith, 1984

Notes On The Correct Way To Present The Jews And Judaism In Preaching And Catechesis In The Roman Catholic Church, Commission For Religious Relation With The Jews, 1995

Instruction On Christian Freedom And Liberation, Congregation For The Doctrine Of The Faith, 1986

Domum Vitae, Congregation For The Doctrine Of The Faith, 1987

Vademecum For Confessors Concerning Some Aspects Of The Morality Of Conjugal Life, Pontifical Council For The Family, 1997

We Remember: A Reflection On The Shoah, Commission For Religious Relations With The Jews, 1998

'Dominus Iesus' On The Unicity And Salvific Universality Of Jesus Christ And The Church – Declaration, Cardinal Joseph Ratzinger, Catholic Truth Society, Publishers to the Holy See, London 2000

Declaration On Procured Abortion, Congregation For The Doctrine Of The Faith, 1974

Speeches by Pope John Paul II:

Address of Pope John Paul II to the United Nations General Assembly, October 2, 1979

Address of Pope John Paul II to the United Nations General Assembly, October 5, 1995

ARCHIVES CONSULTED:

British Library, London

British Newspaper Library, London

Fachbibliothek für Geschichtswissenschaften, University of Vienna, Vienna

Polish State Archives, Cracow and Warsaw, including commercial registers covering compulsory requisition of East German Chemical Works (Solvay), newspapers and periodicals, 1930–1978

Polish State Archives, Spytkowice branch: Solvay plant plans, maps of location, railway maps, 1935–1950

Polish State Files on Karol Wojtyla, including Sluzba Bezpieczeństwa (SB – Secret Police) reports covering 1948–1978, Cracow and Warsaw Archives, including Archiwum Urzłedu ds. Wyznań – Wydzial II: Rzymskokatolicki: Nasza taktyka w stosunku do kardynalów Wojtyly i Wyszyńskiego (5 VII 1967)(Our tactics regarding Cardinals Wojtyla and Wyszyński)

Jagiellonian University, Cracow

Soviet Archives Project: posted by Vladimir Bukovsky, Russian documents of Secretariat of Politburo and Politburo Protocols on Poland 1980–1984 (English translation by Margaret C. Shanks, London)

Cold War International History Project: Woodrow Wilson Center for Scholars, Washington

DEPOSITIONS/TRANSCRIPTS/LEGAL DOCUMENTS:

Diocesan records from Lafayette, covering Glenn Gastel et al, individually and on behalf of their minor child versus the Archdiocese of New Orleans and others including Father Gilbert Gauthe

Alperin v the Vatican Bank, legal action filed in the San Francisco Federal Court, November 1999, by Serb, Jewish and Ukrainian Holocaust survivors against the Vatican Bank, the Franciscan Order and Croatia Liberation Movement seeking the return of Nazi loot stolen from wartime Yugoslavia. A large quantity of documents including: Deposition, Dallas, December 2005, from former Special Agent William Gowen covering the transportation of gold and other valuables looted from the Croatian Treasury and taken to the Vatican

The Reagan Papers: previously classified documents covering a wide range of activities 1980–1988, courtesy of The Ronald Reagan Library, Texas

Grand Jury transcripts, affidavits, indictments and trial transcripts concerning Martin Frankel and others duly charged on 24 counts of Federal corruption and the theft of USD 200 million

The Sipe Report: A. W. Richard Sipe, *Executive Summary*, 1986

Confidential Crisis Proposal, by The Rev Thomas Doyle, OP, Ray Mouton and Dr Michael Peterson, 1985

Doyle-Demarest Legal Memo, May 1996

Vatican Judicial Report, witness statements and depositions concerning the deaths on 4 May 1998 of Colonel Alois Estermann, Gladys Meza Romero and Vice-Corporal Cédric Tornay

PERIODICALS – ORIGINS:

National Catholic Documentary Service, Washington, 1978–1983

Catholic World News Agency, 2000–2005

REPORTS:

Annual Consolidated Budget of the Holy See, 1985–1989

Annual Reports of The Catholic Office For The Protection Of Children And Vulnerable Adults, published in UK 2002/2003/2004

Careful Selection And Training Of Candidates For The States Of Perfection And Sacred Orders by the Sacred Congregation of the Religious, February 1961

Crimine Sollicitationis, issued by Pope John XXIII outlining the procedure to be followed in cases of sexually abusing priests using the pretext of confession, 1962

John Jay College Of Criminal Justice Report On Clerical Sexual Abuse In The United States, 2004

Le Moyne College/Zogby International 'Contemporary Catholic Trends' Poll Report, 2002

Nolan Report, April 2001

Report on '*The Problem Of The Sexual Abuse Of African Religious In Africa And Rome*', Sister Marie MacDonald, 1998

Report on '*The Sexual Abuse Of Religious And Non-Religious Women By Priests*', Sister Maura O'Donohue, MD, February 1994 (The above two reports were made available to the author by Vatican sources.)

Roman Catholic Clericalism, Religious Duress And Clerical Sexual Abuse, The Rev Thomas Doyle, March 2001

The Catholic Priest In The United States: Psychological Investigations, Eugene Kennedy, PhD and Victor Heckler, PhD, 1972

The BCCI Affair, A Report To The Committee On Foreign Relations, United States Senate, By Senator John Kerry And Senator

Hank Brown, December 1992, US Government Printing Office, Washington: 1993

The Crisis In The Catholic Church In The United States, a report prepared by the *National Review Board for the Protection of Children and Young People*, February 2004

The Ferns Report, October 2005: Irish Government inquiry into over 100 allegations of child sexual abuse between 1962 and 2002 made against 21 priests operating under the aegis of the Diocese of Ferns

The Role Of The Church In The Causation And Treatment And Prevention Of The Crisis In The Priesthood, a report based on the records of 1,500 priests treated for mental problems, Dr Conrad W. Baars, November 1971

Through The Lens Of The Organisational Culture Perspective: A Descriptive Study Of American Catholic Bishops' Understanding Of Clergy, Sexual Molestation And Abuse By Children And Adolescents, Dr Barbara Susan Balboni: PhD dissertation (Boston North Eastern University) 1998

NEWSPAPERS, PERIODICALS AND ON-LINE SERVICES CONSULTED:

Austrian: including *Der Standard, Die kleine Zeitung, Die Presse, Format, Kirche Intern, Kronenzeitung, Kurier, profil* (made available by Dr Wolfgang R. Lehner, Vienna)

English-language: including *America, Commonweal, The Tablet, The Washington Post,*

French: *including La Croix, L'Express, Le Monde, Le Monde Diplomatique, Libération*

German: including *Berliner Kurier, Berliner Morgenpost, Der Spiegel, Die Zeit, Frankfurter Allgemeine Zeitung, Hamburger Abendblatt, Hamburger Morgenpost, Stuttgarter Zeitung, Süddeutsche Zeitung*

Italian: including *L'Osservatore Romano, Corriere della Sera, Famiglia Cristiana, Il Giornalino, Il Giorno, Il Mattino, Il Messaggero, Il Mondo, L'Espresso, La Nazione, La Repubblica, 30 Giorni*

Polish: including *Forum, Gazeta Krakovska, Tygodnik Powszechny, Tribuna Ludu*

Spanish: including *Avui, El Informador (Mexico), El Mundo, La Vanguardia, Tiempo de Hoy*

Swiss: including *Blick, Facts, L'Echo, Le Temps, Neue Zürcher Zeitung, Sonntagszeitung, Wochenzeitung*

ORIGINS: *National Catholic Documentary Service*, Washington, 1978–1983

Catholic World News Agency, 2000–2005

OTHER DOCUMENTS:

La Liberación Integral En América Latina, Monsignor Oscar A. Romero, *Opiniones Latinoamericanas*, Coral Gables, Florida 1979

Soviet Deliberations during the Polish Crisis, 1980–1981: edited, translated, annotated and introduced by Professor Mark Kramer, 22 documents and 15 transcripts of Soviet Communist Party (CPSU) Politburo meetings, Woodrow Wilson International Center for Scholars, Washington, DC. [Author's note: the Woodrow Wilson Center contains a rich source of material for any student of the Cold War. A great many additional documents, too numerous to cite, were also consulted.]

The Draft Constitutional Treaty For The European Union, Presented To Parliament By The Secretary Of State For Foreign And Commonwealth Affairs By Command Of Her Majesty, 2003, Crown Copyright 2003

The Millennial Pope, transcripts of PBS TV programmes

Index

Subheadings are arranged in ascending page number order.